Delphi™ Programming Unleashed

Charles Calvert

D1561001

SAMS

This book is dedicated to my wife Margie for her love and patience, and to the Pacific Ocean and Monterey Bay for their spiritual guidance and support.

Copyright © 1995 by Sams Publishing

International Standard Book Number: 0-672-30499-6

Library of Congress Catalog Card Number: 94-65306

98   97   96   95   4   3   2

Interpretation of the printing code: the rightmost double-digit number is the year of the book's printing; the rightmost single-digit, the number of the book's printing. For example, a printing code of 95-1 shows that the first printing of the book occurred in 1995.

Composed in AGaramond and MCPdigital by Macmillan Computer Publishing

Printed in the United States of America

Trademarks

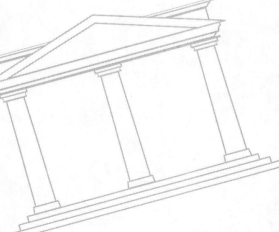

Introduction

Contents

Part II   The Elements of Language: Simple Types, Floating Point Numbers, and Branching and Looping

Part V Living in the Land of OOP: Components, Objects, and Advanced Programming Topics

Acknowledgments

Authors do not work alone. A number of people supplied help or information while I was writing this book. Without their cooperation and aid, this book could not have been finished.

When working with databases and networks, I got an almost endless stream of willing help from Dan Daley, Nimish Vora, and Marc Cousineau. I also got help on these subjects from Scott Clinton, Klaus Krull, Anders Hejlsberg, David Raccah, and Keith Bigelow.

On general programming issues, I received copious help from Xavier Pacheco, Steve Teixeira, David Intersimone, Steve Trefethen, Danny Thorpe, Zack Urlocker, and Pat Ritchie. Others who provided useful information were Dave Scofield, Allen Bauer, Gary Whizin, Dave Roehr, Bill Weber, Chuck Jazdzewski, Jason Sprenger, Ray Kaestner, Mark Edington, Richard Nelson, and Frank Frazier.

On the non-technical side, the following people provided much needed patience, understanding, and advice: Margie Calvert, David Intersimone, Zack Urlocker, Carol Martin, and Adm. James Calvert. Of this group, Margie and David both deserve special thanks for their seemingly endless supply of willing cooperation during the writing of this book.

Finally I want to thank the people at Sams who labor long hours to bring this and other technical books to market. Their jobs are not easy, and I have come to appreciate and respect their skill and dedication. In particular, Mary Inderstrodt, Angelique Brittingham, and Chris Denny were the major forces behind the editing and production of this book. Chris must have answered or processed hundreds, if not thousands, of my e-mail messages. Mary provided the understanding and sympathetic ear that most writers hope to find when working with an editor. Special thanks to Mary and Chris for going above and beyond the call of duty!

About the Author

Charles Calvert is the author of *Teach Yourself Windows Programming in 21 Days* and *Turbo Pascal Programming 101* (both also published by Sams). For the last several years, he has worked at Borland International, where he is now a manager in Developer Relations. He lives with his wife Marjorie Calvert in Santa Cruz, California.

About This Book's Subject Matter and Style

This book offers a relatively complete description of the Delphi environment, tools, and language. I start at the very beginning with a few sample programs designed to highlight the programming environment, give an exhaustive description of the entire language—followed by an extensive look at the client/server tools, and wind up with a lengthy, detailed analysis of many important advanced techniques.

Because the scope of this book is so large, I have the luxury of discussing both introductory and advanced techniques within a single volume. My promise to you as a reader is that I will shortchange neither the introductory nor the advanced sections of the book. You will find the introductory sections easy to read, thorough, and as entertaining as possible. Likewise, the advanced sections will challenge all but the most experienced programmers. They present the reader with a thorough description of how to extend Delphi so it can access the entire range of Windows programming.

As an author, I have two major objectives. The first is to be thorough, and the second is to be readable and entertaining. If I accomplish only the first goal, I will produce a reference book that is useful to advanced programmers but relatively useless as a teaching tool. To avoid this shortcoming, I always place emphasis on the act of teaching the reader how to use a particular tool, feature, or programming construct. In my experience, the best possible way to achieve this end is to provide entertaining examples that are described in lively, straightforward language. As a result, this book will strive to be both thorough and entertaining. I see it as my job to achieve both ends.

> **NOTE**
>
> When I use the word *thorough*, it is probably worth taking a moment to clarify exactly how I'm using the term. If you are going to master a language, you need to understand the entire subject, from beginning to end. You need to have a single place where you can turn whenever you need a description of the features, grammar, and structure of any aspect of the language. The entire range of the language has to be covered and explained in detail. That is the purpose of this book. However, I will not waste your time and mine by detailing information that is readily available in the online help. If you want a reference to the components used in the environment, just pop up the online help. If you want to find out how to create programs, turn to this book.

Flipping through the Table of Contents, you may have noticed that I don't always divide material into neat little chapters, one on tokens, one on types, one on operators, one on sets, and so forth. Certainly it would be simplest for me to approach things that way. However, most people are totally confused by a methodology based solely on such a logical and categorical breakdown of the subject matter. My approach is to start with simple, easy-to-understand issues, and then to move on to increasingly complex ideas when the reader is ready for them. The point here is to concentrate on the way the human mind works, rather than to force a systematic breakdown of the subject matter.

The Encyclopedia Britannica provides a very systematic analysis of most of the fundamental knowledge available to members of western civilization. Yet very few people attempt to educate themselves or their children by starting at Volume One, letter A, and reading through to the end. Instead, people try to find ways to absorb knowledge that are more natural, as well as more pleasant. In this book, I take a similar approach. I eschew a totally logical breakdown of the categories such as you might find in a reference book. Instead, I try to present material in a way that makes it easiest to absorb.

However, I am aware that readers will also want to look up information in this book. As a result, I do try to cover subjects in relatively localized areas. That way you can turn to the index or Table of Contents to find where I discuss a particular topic. In other words, I localize information about a particular topic in certain distinct areas, but I don't force an artificial or overly didactic categorization of the various parts of Delphi to dictate the order in which I present the material.

NOTE

This book makes heavy use of online tools. Take the time to explore the CD-ROM that comes with this book. It is designed to complement the book, and it contains databases that serve as an extended index into the more obscure matters covered in this book. The CD also contains many lengthy programs not mentioned in this book, as well as useful code fragments and various other materials. The CD-ROM also contains many code listings that would not fit into the book. I will also post related materials online. On CompuServe, type GO SAMS, or try the Borland BBS: 408-431-5096. My IDs: CompuServe: 76711,533 or 71601,1224. AOL: CHARLIECAL. Internet: ccalvert@wpo.borland.com.

I am very much aware that this approach is different than that used in many standard—and extremely admirable—texts on programming. However, I'm certain that the technique I use here enables you to learn the material in the shortest possible period of time and with the greatest degree of both thoroughness and enjoyment.

I have one final comment about the overall structure of this book. On several occasions, I ask you to put this book aside and run a program that appears on disk. In short, there are times when I abandon paper and ink altogether and instead use the computer as a teaching medium. I do this because it is sometimes easier to show you how to do something on screen than it is to explain it on paper. Hence, little by little, we enter the digital age.

Who Should Read This Book

Delphi comes in two different forms:

- A pricey client/server version that contains tools for writing database applications in a networked environment.

- A less-expensive desktop version that contains some database tools but does not provide access to major servers such as Oracle, Sybase, or the full-blown copy of Interbase.

This book is comprehensive enough to appeal to both sets of readers. If you are interested in mission-critical database projects, you will find that all the information you need is included here. Programmers who are primarily interested in desktop applications will find that a wide variety of programming issues are discussed in depth.

Overall, there are three different types of people whom I perceive as potential readers of this book:

- The first are members of MIS departments in large or mid-sized businesses. These people need a tool that can help them perform workday programming tasks quickly and efficiently, with a minimum of fuss. I believe many of them will find Delphi, and its built-in database tools, to be the answer to a long-felt need. Many of these people may have considerable experience with another language, such as PowerBuilder, the XBase languages, BASIC, or C. As a result, I try to explain how Delphi accomplishes familiar tasks that have parallels in other languages.

- The second group of people are casual programmers who don't have the time or inclination to fully develop their talent. Whether they are building database applications or standard Windows applications, these people need a product that is easy to use and relatively simple to understand. Delphi will appeal to these programmers because it is intuitive and clearly and wisely structured.

- The final group of people who might read this book are programmers who prefer to work alone or in small groups rather than as part of a large corporation or mid-sized business. Because they are not part of a large team, these people need a tool that enables them to perform certain tasks quickly and efficiently. Programmers in this third school are likely to be some of the biggest adherents of Delphi. This product suits itself well to talented programmers with an independent bent. The tool is easy to use and powerful enough to enable programmers to reach down to the lowest levels of computing where the real leverage can be found. A good number of these programmers may have little or no interest in databases.

All three groups of people are important to me. I like folks who work in information services for large corporations because I deal with them every day at work. I know who these individuals are, and I know what kind of tools they need.

I also have a natural affinity for people who don't want to pursue the arcane details of any programming language. For instance, I have a great love of music, but little time to develop my talents as a musician. As a result, I'm always seeking tools that make it easier for an amateur such as myself to make the music I hear in my head. I understand that someone can be quite serious about a topic without being, or wanting to be, an expert in it. Delphi will give these people a chance to step into the world of Windows programming and quickly produce the tools they desire for their hobbies or for their main line of work.

Finally, I'm especially drawn to programmers who have an independent streak. I believe that computers offer a tremendous opportunity for people to express themselves and to contribute to society through the exercise of their God-given talents, whether they be for art, business, or science. These programmers will love Delphi because it enables them to get the grunt work done quickly, while still giving them access to low-level computing features such as assembly language and the Windows API.

I welcome all three groups of readers. Delphi is riding the wave of the future, and the surf's up.

Of course, there are others who might be drawn to this book. Many scientists need to be able to do simple programming jobs as part of their day-to-day work. This book will show them how to harness the power of a visual environment to display their data in a meaningful manner.

During my working days at Borland Tech Support, I occasionally talk to professionals in the medical or legal professions who use computers to manage some portion of their work. These people need to have some programming skills in order to achieve their goals, but nothing dictates that they need to master multiple inheritance or the arcane details of an AVL tree. Delphi is the ideal tool for a professional of this sort who wants to use a programming language as an adjunct to their regular work.

Other users simply want help managing their financial affairs. Or perhaps they might be musicians who want to get better control over their synthesizers.

None of the individuals mentioned in the last few paragraphs need a complex tool such as C/C++, and certainly they don't even want to hear about assembly language. Instead, they are likely to be drawn to a language like Delphi. It has the flexibility and ease of use that quite precisely fits their needs.

This book is meant for people who have at least some previous programming experience. I have made every attempt to make sure this book covers the language from the very first steps through to some of the most complex. This means that it could theoretically be used by someone who has never written a line of code in their life. However, I think there are other Delphi books on the market that might be better suited for absolute beginners.

My main goal, therefore, is to give the professional programmer, as well as the serious hobbyist, a single-volume guide to this fascinating language. In short, I want to write a book that I personally would find useful, were I to spot it on a bookshelf.

Though writing and programming can be work at times, overall these activities are fun for me. They are playful activities that happen to serve a useful purpose. If your job as a programmer has become a bit boring for you in recent years, I ask you to kick back for a second, loosen that collar, roll up your sleeves, and see if you can rediscover how to have some serious fun. I promise you that programmers who enjoy their work are at least three times more productive than those who take their jobs too seriously.

What Can You Do with Delphi?

Any kind of Windows program that you might imagine can be created with Delphi. It is an ideal tool for creating games, utilities, custom controls, visual design tools, artist's tools, and a host of other powerful and intriguing applications. However, one of Delphi's greatest strengths is its capability for creating extremely advanced database applications.

Delphi has a set of built-in data handling tools that compete with anything found in more traditional database development tools. However, you can use Delphi not only to create your own applications but also to complement the work you do in products such as Paradox or dBASE. In particular, you will find that it is possible to design a powerful database application without writing more than a few simple lines of code. Furthermore, you can use Delphi to create DLLs that can be linked into your dBASE or Paradox applications.

Creating database forms with fields or grids where users can enter names, numbers, or other pieces of information is part of the bread-and-butter functionality of the Delphi environment. These forms can be drawn on the screen with the mouse or created automatically by a programming tool called an Expert. There is no need to write any code while designing the interface of a database application.

Connecting to Oracle, Sybase, Informix, dBASE, Paradox, or other local and networked servers is easy. Delphi doesn't care how the information is stored on disk. Thanks to Borland's BDE technology, a wide variety of formats are handled completely transparently. Easy access to ODBC technology is also available simply by installing a new driver in the IDAPICFG utility.

Delphi supports pass-through SQL, which means that you can talk directly to servers in a tongue they fully support. Delphi does not have to parse or understand the SQL commands you issue; instead, they can be passed on untouched to the server. Furthermore, the BDE provides very fast SQL access to databases that outshines anything you are likely to see from PC-based tools that don't use the BDE.

However, there is no reason why you can't use Delphi to write a simple address book meant to be used by a single machine. Delphi is very flexible when it comes to database applications. Furthermore, it is designed so you can easily upscale a single-user database to be used on a multi-user network environment.

Obviously, database applications are some of the key tools that can be developed using Delphi. However, it's important to note that Delphi itself is written in Delphi. This helps to illustrate that you can develop all kinds of tools with this compiler.

Application development is aided by the inclusion of VBXs, which are a kind of add-in tool originally created by Microsoft for Visual Basic. Version 1.0 of this format is supported by Delphi, so you will find it easy to add these tools to your applications.

VBXs are, however, limited in several ways. As a result, Borland has created its own form of VBX, called a component, that does everything a VBX does and then considerably more. Specifically, when you need to port to 32-bit applications, VBXs won't be in their native environment, whereas Borland Visual Controls will port over almost effortlessly.

Delphi also provides full access to the Windows API. Because it also produces small, fast executables, there is very little in the way of Windows programming that can't be best done using Delphi. This book spends considerable time discussing Windows programming techniques and showing how you can use Delphi to tap into the kind of advanced Windows programming techniques usually found in a book on Object Pascal or C++ programming.

When seen from a certain perspective, there are really only two kinds of programming languages. One kind provides specialized tools that enable you to quickly develop a certain kind of application, and the other kind provides a general language that gives you full access to everything on a machine. Paradox, Visual Basic, PowerBuilder, Actor, Smalltalk, and all 4GLs are examples of the first kind of language. C++, Turbo Pascal, and Delphi are examples of the second kind of language. The unique thing about Delphi is that it provides components and visual tools that make the product seem like a 4GL, while still providing full access to the all the features supplied by Windows and the Intel architecture.

What Kind of Experience Do You Need?

Some of the material covered in this book, such as OLE and object-oriented architectures, is fairly advanced. Normally books covering this kind of material must by their very nature exclude beginners, and certainly this book is slanted toward more advanced users. However, the sheer size of the book is very large, and it is intended to cover the entire product, from its simplest to its most complex reaches. This gives me the scope to start at the very beginning and build up slowly to a number of fairly advanced topics.

Delphi was designed from the bottom up to be accessible to people who are not full-time programmers, or who regard programming as only one facet of their job. As a result, even advanced subjects such as OLE or relational database programming can be approached with simple visual tools. In other words, it is easy to write databases or OLE programs using Delphi.

As computers become an ever larger part of contemporary life, I think it will become commonplace to expect at least modest programming skills to be part of the repertoire of all well-educated people. To achieve this end, it is necessary for computer languages to have a structure that is relatively straightforward. Delphi tries to achieve that goal so it can appeal both to casual programmers and to serious spelunkers of the 80x86 architecture.

> **NOTE**
>
> When computer users refer to 80x86 systems, they are talking about a series of chips that sprang from the Intel line. For instance, 8088, 80286, 80386, 80486, and Pentium computers are all part of the 80x86 family. Referring to the whole group of computers by this one name is simply an easy shorthand agreed upon by most of the industry.

You do not need to be an experienced Windows programmer to use this book. Delphi manages to reduce most Windows programming concepts to a series of steps that are so simple that anyone can grasp them in just a few minutes. As a result, subjects that would normally take days to understand are covered here in just a few sentences. Given Delphi's capability to simplify many Windows programming tasks, it would be silly to devote any more time to them.

This book is meant to appeal to Paradox, dBASE, PowerBuilder, and Visual Basic programmers. However, I don't explicitly attempt to draw parallels between techniques found in each of those languages and their Delphi equivalents.

This book is meant to appeal to a wide range of professionals and serious part-time programmers, as well as those who want to move from a position as a hobbyist into the world of professional programming.

System Requirements

The minimum hardware requirement for Delphi is a 386 computer with at least 6 MB of memory. However, the comfort zone begins with a 486 33 MHz containing at least 8 MB of memory.

If you are not sure how much memory your machine has, you can check your documentation, call your manufacturer, or, if you have DOS version 4.0 or above, you can type MEM at the DOS prompt.

On my home machine, I get the following output when I type MEM in a Windows DOS box:

```
c:\wp\delphi>mem
Memory Type        Total  =  Used  +  Free
— — — — — — — —    — — —     — — —     — — —
Conventional        640K       48K       592K
Upper               155K      155K         0K
Reserved            384K      384K         0K
Extended (XMS)    7,013K  4,187,7   13,544K
— — — — — — — —    — — —     — — —     — — —
Total memory      8,192K  4,188,3   14,136K
Total under 1 MB    795K      203K       592K
Largest executable program size      592K (606,272 bytes)
Largest free upper memory block        0K      (0 bytes)
MS-DOS is resident in the high memory area.
```

The key number to look at here is the first one in the first column on the eighth line, where it says Total memory. In my case, this number is 8192 KB, which means I have 8 million, 192 thousand bytes, or 8 megabytes (MB), of memory on my machine. If the number was 4096 KB, I would have 4 MB on my machine. If it was 2048 KB, I would have 2 MB of memory on my machine, which is probably not enough to do any serious programming.

When you are inside a Windows DOS box, the amount of free memory is sometimes larger than the amount of total memory available. Specifically, 14,136 is larger than 8,192. This is because Windows uses your hard drive to create virtual memory that can be swapped back and forth from disk. Below you will find a listing from my work machine, with the MEM command issued after Windows has been closed:

Memory Type	Total	Used	Free
Conventional	639 KB	213 KB	426 KB
Upper	0 KB	0 KB	0 KB
Reserved	129 KB	129 KB	0 KB
Extended (XMS)	23808 KB	2254 KB	21554 KB
Total memory	24576 KB	2596 KB	21980 KB
Total under 1 MB	639 KB	213 KB	426 KB

The largest executable program size is 426 KB (436,080 bytes), and the largest free upper-memory block is 0 KB (0 bytes). MS-DOS is resident in the high-memory area.

Note that in this case the free memory, 21,980, is smaller than the total memory, 24,576.

Here are three different types of machine you can use to approach Delphi:

- If you are simply eager to learn the basics of Windows programming, perhaps you can get by with the minimum configuration of a 386 and 4 MB of memory.

- If you are trying to use a machine that gives at least minimal comfort, you can perhaps shuffle along with a 486 33 MHz with 6 MB of memory.

- If you want to get the most out of your available time and resources, you should have at least a 486 66 MHz with 8 MB or more of memory.

In all cases I recommend avoiding SX machines, such as the 486SX or 386SX. If you happen to have the latter machine, you might not find it an insurmountable burden, but you have to realize that Windows and Delphi will seem slow and clumsy. That's not Windows fault, and it's not Borland's fault—it's a hardware problem. If you are currently thinking about buying a machine, you should consider only DX machines, and you should aim to get at least a 486, but preferably a Pentium.

The amount of RAM you need depends on your circumstances. If you use Windows for only a single task, you can probably get by on only 4 MB. However, if you spend a lot of time in Windows, you will want at least 8 MB, and possibly 12 or 16 MB. If you plan to keep your machine for three or four years, get at least 16 MB.

Think in terms of the number of chores you might be conducting simultaneously. For instance, when I'm writing this book, I need to keep both my word processor and Delphi open at the same time, and I usually want to supplement them with an open DOS window. This means I need plenty of RAM, at least as much as 8 MB. In fact, my home machine, which has 8 MB on it, feels cramped to me. At work I have a 24 MB machine, and that is quite comfortable.

Having a color system makes Windows considerably easier to use, and in 1995 it is almost a necessity. The whole point of the Windows environment is to make it easy for users to find their way about in complex applications. As a result, various color-coding schemes can be used to great effect. Furthermore, you will find that some advanced SuperVGA video cards can greatly improve the speed at which Windows runs. Therefore, if you possibly can, you should consult contemporary computing journals to help you track down a fast, SuperVGA-based color video system.

My final point in terms of system requirements is that Windows 3.1 users should be running on top of DOS 5.0 or higher. You need to be able to fine-tune your environment so that it runs as quickly and smoothly as possible. To do that requires the presence of tools that first showed up on DOS 5.0, and which have been at least incrementally improved in subsequent versions.

Of course, many programmers might be avoiding DOS altogether and running an advanced operating system such as NT, OS/2, or Windows 95. If you can afford it, this is certainly the preferred course to take.

If you are planning to buy a system today, and you want to use it for programming, you should get a Pentium machine with at least 16 MB of memory, a color monitor, and a SuperVGA card. Anything less would be outdated before you have a chance to work it in.

> **NOTE**
>
> I'm sure some readers might be a bit nonplused by the financial outlays suggested by this brief overview of the system requirements for a typical Windows machine. The point to keep in mind is that the speed of most hardware components has been doubling every 18 months for at least the last decade. As a result, systems that had once seemed quite adequate are now looking a bit long in the tooth. This does not mean that these machines are useless. However, they might not be the ideal platform for cutting-edge endeavors such as Windows programming.

I am aware that about six to nine months after this book is published, a 32-bit version of Delphi will ship. Some of what I have said here will not apply to that version of Delphi, but most of the contents of this book will still be useful. In other words, at the time of this writing, it does not look like programming a 32-bit Delphi under Windows 95 will radically alter the relevancy of the majority of techniques described in this book.

What Platforms Can You Target?

Delphi is a Windows-based tool. It doesn't produce DOS applications, and at the time of this writing there are no firm plans for it to produce native OS/2 applications. These facts won't please everyone, but there are good reasons why things have turned out this way.

When I worked at Borland Tech Support, one of the brightest engineers in the department sat just across from me. He's an extremely adept programmer who can handle some of the most challenging calls with extraordinary aplomb. However, on bad days, he can sometimes get a slightly strident tone to his voice, especially when he's on a call that tries his patience.

One day during the winter of 1993 or 1994, he was talking to a customer, and I noticed that his voice was getting louder and louder as the call went on. He was still being scrupulously polite, but I noticed that there was an edge to his voice. A rather long pause occurred on our end of the conversation, and then suddenly I heard the single, quite loud pronouncement, "Look, you have to understand, DOS is dead!"

It seemed to me that a silence settled over all the nearby desks for just a few heartbeats, as if everybody was taking this in, weighing its merits. Then, little by little, the busy hum of business was restored, first with just a few clicks of the keyboard, the sound of a chair squeaking, and finally with a low murmur of voices humming along at their usual rate. From nowhere, however, was there so much as a single sound of protest.

Perhaps in my own mind that was the moment when I finally understood that it was true, that for better or worse, Windows, OS/2, and UNIX had become the main environments in the world of PCs.

Of these three operating environments, Borland has decided to target this version of Delphi solely at Windows users, and specifically at Windows 3.1 users. This version of Delphi doesn't support DOS, and it doesn't support OS/2, and it won't produce 32-bit applications. The reason for this is simply that Windows 3.1 has a huge market share. Maybe five years from now everyone will look back and laugh at the days when Windows was king. Right now, however, Windows is THE environment. Specifically, it is Windows 3.1 that reigns over the rest of the PC world. At this writing, Windows NT is still a very minor player on the scene, but Borland will soon produce a version of Delphi aimed at NT and Windows 95.

The latest technologies, such as multimedia, object-oriented systems, and 32-bit microkernel architectures, are all finding a place on Windows-based systems. It's not the only hot environment by any means, but it is still the place where the largest numbers of creative, hardworking, savvy minds are combining their talents to fashion the future of computing and of the entire electronic landscape, from academia to Wall Street to Hollywood.

This doesn't mean that there aren't very good, even sometimes overpowering, reasons to use other operating systems. Nor does it mean that someone is old-fashioned or out of it if he or she prefers DOS or UNIX. That kind of talk is nonsense. Certainly Windows isn't better just because it has the largest number of adherents. The majority is often dead wrong.

My only point is that Windows is a huge mountain dominating the current computing landscape, and that is why Borland has targeted it for the first version of Delphi. I hope that in the future there will be a Delphi for OS/2, even for UNIX and DOS. For now, however, there is only a Windows environment, and it doesn't take a great deal of thought to see why it was the only reasonable choice for the premier run of this new language. Delphi will run as a 16-bit application under Windows 95 or Windows NT, but it will not run on Windows 3.0.

Language Wars?

I don't have much patience with language bigots. I don't think any one language is best; I simply think there are certain tools that are best for certain jobs. Nevertheless, it is possible to talk about the relative value of certain compilers in certain circumstances. In this section, I compare Delphi to various other languages, not to state that one is better than another, but to point out the relative position of a language such as Delphi.

There is a dream lurking in the minds of many people who become, or want to become, programmers. They all have a vision of what could be accomplished if only they could truly harness the power residing inside every computer. Anybody who takes programming seriously, and who can thus become good at it, has to have that spark in them first. There has to be a moment when you look metaphorically inside the PC and understand the worlds there to be conquered. You have to think, "If only I could harness all that latent potential." Delphi is a good tool for programmers of this stripe.

The factors that frustrate most programmers are twofold. On one hand, there are applications or computer languages that are extremely powerful and easy to use but are constructed with built-in limitations. FoxPro, PowerBuilder, OPAL, Visual Basic, and the DOS batch language are examples of these kinds of tools. They are all easy to use, but they are also very frustrating because they are so limited. They take a person so far, and then they leave the person stranded wishing that a tool had various missing features.

On the other hand, there are tools like Turbo Pascal, the C/C++ language, or the weird, labyrinthine world of assembly language programming. These compilers give dedicated souls relatively complete control over the computer. These are the true hackers' tools, which provide you with the power you need to fulfill a real programmer's dream. However, the gift tastes bitter at times, because on some occasions the tools themselves are more complex and frustrating than the original problem that needed to be overcome. (This from someone who knows C/C++ well, and who has an enormous respect and admiration for the language.)

The point here is that Delphi steers a path between these two extremes. It is based upon Borland's Object Pascal, which is a complete, powerful, and very subtle object-oriented language. The fundamental elements of Object Pascal are as easy to use as BASIC or the DOS batch language. At the same time, in recent years Object Pascal has developed to the point that it encompasses the same scope as C/C++.

Let me make it clear that I personally have two favorite languages: Delphi and C++. Both give me the power and flexibility that I need to achieve any programming task I want to pursue. Here are my perceptions of the relative merits of the two languages. I'll start with Delphi:

- Delphi is easy to use.
- Delphi helps you reach your goal quickly.
- Delphi's syntax is clean, elegant, and easy to read and write.

The great advantages of C++ follow:

- It has extraordinary flexibility.
- It provides good control over nearly every aspect of the programming environment, no matter how mundane or esoteric. In other words, the language itself has few built-in default settings, and you have control over nearly everything.
- It provides at least potential portability across platforms.

All of the core object-oriented programming techniques are fully implemented in Delphi. For instance, Delphi supports real virtual methods, real encapsulation (including the use of the `Public`, `Private`, and `Protected` keywords), real polymorphism, and real inheritance. It also adds features such as runtime type checking, the `Published` keyword, properties, and functions that return complex types. In short, Delphi is a fully implemented object-oriented language, in the most complete sense of the word.

I believe Delphi is more completely object-oriented than C++, but it is probably not quite as completely object-oriented as Smalltalk. However, Delphi shares several traits in common with Smalltalk, including the sense that everything in the language should be encapsulated inside an object. There is not, however, an insistence on this point, only a sense that this is the best approach. For instance, Delphi automatically writes some portions of a program for you, and when it does so, it produces fully object-oriented code.

> **NOTE**
>
> Some C++ programmers will be disappointed to learn that Delphi lacks multiple inheritance as well as function overloading. The Delphi developers decided to exclude these features from the compiler on the grounds that they usually cause more trouble than they save. Delphi does, however, support a limited form of operator overloading via a useful syntactical construct called a Property. This doesn't mean that you can't accomplish the same things in Delphi that you can accomplish in C++. It's just that Delphi asks you to achieve your goals by using a simpler syntax that is easier to read and write, and which is in every sense of the word fully object-oriented.

The key point to grasp is that Delphi offers both ease of use and nearly unlimited technical depth. This language is so easy to use that most people can be taught the basics in a matter of only a few short hours. Relative competence can be taught in only a few short weeks. Three months would be plenty of time to turn a complete neophyte into a productive Delphi programmer.

Becoming an expert Delphi programmer, of course, is considerably harder to achieve, and might take years. For instance, if you enter the keyword ASM, Delphi allows you to start writing a block of assembler code at any point in your program. This is an advanced feature that will take most programmers a long time to master.

Windows is an enormously complex and powerful operating environment. Its entire vista of exciting opportunities is open to Delphi programmers. There is no need to say "Darn, if only I was working in C, I could do what I want." You are working in Delphi, and that means that if it can be done on a computer, it can be done with your compiler. All you have to do is learn how.

> **NOTE**
>
> The only Windows programming project I know that can be accomplished in C but not in Object Pascal is the writing of Virtual Device Drivers (VxDs). This limitation occurs in part because Microsoft has established a standard for 16-bit Virtual Device Drivers that involves a number of peculiar oddities. Furthermore, Windows Virtual Device Drivers are usually written in assembler, not in C. This is a special case in

> which a company has intentionally used an obscure, proprietary format. It is an
> extremely rare exception that covers a rather esoteric area of programming, and it is a
> barrier that is likely to disappear with the advent of 32-bit VxDs and 32-bit Delphi
> tools. So, with this one exception, you can rest assured that Delphi will have the power
> to complete any Windows programming chore.

My point in this section is not to try to convert C++ programmers to Delphi. I have seen enough of the programming world to know that nothing can shake the faith a die-hard C++ programmer has in his or her tools. However, C++ programmers who are very interested in objects might well be attracted to Delphi.

In the final analysis, Delphi probably lies about halfway between C++ and Smalltalk. It is, in my opinion, a more truly object-oriented language than C++, but it does not take the paradigm as far as Smalltalk. On the other hand, Delphi offers the same small, fast executables that you can get from C++, but which Smalltalk fails to provide. If this sounds interesting to you, you are bound to enjoy programming in Delphi.

Where Is Delphi Headed?

Delphi beta testers who spent any time scanning through the code in the Visual Control Library (VCL) subdirectory, noticed that there are many passages that feature the words WIN32. In all of these code fragments, the compiler is instructed to compile the code one way if WIN32 is defined and another way if it is not defined. For example, the following excerpt is from the beta version of MESSAGES.PAS:

```
{$IFDEF WIN32}
  TMsgParam = Longint;
{$ELSE}
  TMsgParam = Word;
{$ENDIF}
```

This code says, in effect, that if WIN32 is not defined, TMsgParam should be a Word, and if it is defined, it should be declared as a Longint.

What this means to the average user is that the groundwork for supporting WIN32 is built into this version of the compiler. In fact, this framework was included in the very first versions of Delphi that emerged from the developers well over a year before the product's release. In other words, the designers of this product knew from the very beginning that it would eventually be ported to a 32-bit environment. They have explicitly stated that they designed it so that it will run smoothly in the 32-bit world.

NOTE

WIN32 is the API developed by Microsoft, first for Windows NT and also for Windows 95. An API is an Application Programming Interface, which means that it is a set of routines that can be called by programmers when they want to put together applications such as word processors, spreadsheets, databases, or compilers. More specifically, WIN32 is a set of over 1,000 calls that can be made inside a 32-bit Windows environment. Most of these calls can also be made inside WIN32s, which is a small 32-bit kernel that rides on top of the 16-bit Windows 3.1 environment. The two key features of NT that are missing from WIN32s are threads and true multitasking. However, WIN32s still enables programmers to write 32-bit apps that can address a full 4 gigabits of memory.

To sum up, the future of Delphi will feature three key elements:

- 32-bit computing
- The Delphi environment
- The WIN32 API as it is manifested in systems such as NT, WIN32s, and the upcoming Windows 4.0

Looking beyond that, it is possible that Borland might produce an OS/2, UNIX-, or DOS-based Delphi, but it is not at all certain. Developments on that front will become apparent only at some later date.

About the Layout of this Book

This book is designed so that it can be read from cover to cover and then later be treated as a general reference. In particular I try to start with simple material and then move on to more advanced subjects in the latter half of the book.

The book is divided into five main sections. Part I is meant to introduce you to Delphi and to answer many general questions that may be of interest to you at this time. Most of the material in this first chapter has been relatively abstract, in that it deals with general types of questions rather than with specific programming examples. Chapters 2 and 3 are designed primarily to familiarize you with the Delphi environment. Advanced programmers will probably find little that interests them in Chapter 2, but Chapter 3 has a little something for everyone.

The real work of this book begins in Part II, which describes the Delphi language in some depth. This section will be familiar ground for all those who have worked with any version of Borland or Turbo Pascal. Experienced users should still read this section, because it doubles as an introduction to the main visual controls. In fact, I introduce many Windows controls simply as asides to whatever the main topic of conversation happens to be at the time. Normally, it would take several hundred pages to adequately explain these controls. Delphi makes the task so easy, however, that you can cover these subjects in just a few moments.

Part III covers more advanced elements of the programming language.

By the time you reach Part IV, all the introductory programming issues should be behind you. This means it is time for you to start building powerful database applications that can be used to solve real problems in the day-to-day life of individuals and businesses. This section concentrates on creating and accessing databases, creating one-to-many relationships, using calculated fields, using SQL, and connecting to server data. A discussion of the Local Interbase Engine also appears in this section.

Part V explores objects and components. It gives you the tools you need to build real applications. This section takes the building blocks presented in the previous section and shows how they have been harnessed to produce the Delphi environment. In this section of the book, you will start using object-oriented techniques to build nontrivial applications. By the time you are done with this section, the basic format of the new object-oriented model should be clear to you.

Finally, don't forget that there are many additional materials on the CD-ROM. I have included many programs there that were too long to fit in the book, or which I did not have time to discuss in the available space. I also add various other Delphi- or Pascal-related materials that might be of interest to the reader.

NOTE

The programming information in this book is based on information for developing applications for Windows 95, made public by Microsoft as of 9/9/94. Since this information was made public before the final release of the product, there might be changes to some of the programming interfaces by the time the product is finally released. We encourage you to check the updated development information that should be part of your development system for resolving issues that might arise.

The end-user information in this book is based on information on Windows 95 made public by Microsoft as of 9/9/94. Since this information was made public before the release of the product, we encourage you to visit your local bookstore at that time for updated books on Windows 95.

If you have a modem or access to the Internet, you can always get up-to-the-minute information on Windows 95 direct from Microsoft on WinNews:

On CompuServe: `GO WINNEWS`

On the Internet:

```
ftp://ftp.microsoft.com/PerOpSys/Win_News/Chicago
http://www.microsoft.com
```

On AOL: keyword `WINNEWS`

On Prodigy: jumpword `WINNEWS`

On Genie: `WINNEWS` file area on Windows RTC

You also can subscribe to Microsoft's WinNews electronic newsletter by sending Internet e-mail to `news@microsoft.nwnet.com` and putting the words `SUBSCRIBE WINNEWS` in the text of the e-mail.

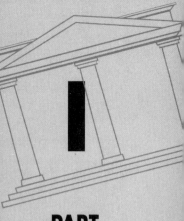

PART

Delphi Building Blocks: The Delphi Environment, Visual Programming, and Program Structure

Welcome to Delphi

1

Overview

This chapter contains the following three parts:

- The first section is a general introduction to Delphi and to the intent and purpose of this book.
- The second features two sample programs that give you an initial taste of the ease and power inherent in the Delphi programming environment.
- The final section includes a general introduction to this book's structure and specific advice on the tools and hardware you will need if you want to program in Delphi.

The main goal of this first chapter is to convey my sense of excitement and enthusiasm about Delphi, and also to prepare you for the task that lies ahead. Throughout this entire project, reader and writer will work together toward one goal: mastery of Delphi. Welcome aboard.

Introducing Delphi

Delphi is a unique new product that takes the best of Borland's compiler technology, combines it with the best of Borland's database technology, and throws in some new visual programming tools, thereby producing a hybrid product that gives programmers an unprecedented ability to quickly construct both standard applications and client/server applications. Stated slightly differently, Delphi is a product that utilizes visual tools to help make it possible to integrate Borland's compiler and database technology into one powerful tool.

Delphi exists for three reasons:

- The world needs a powerful and sophisticated client/server tool.
- Programmers need to use visual tools to help bring complex projects to completion in a relatively short period of time.
- The complexity of contemporary programming demands that programmers have access to reusable object-oriented code to help them complete robust, sophisticated programs.

Anyone who has ventured into the client/server world knows that there is a lack of good tools in that environment. Slow, interpreted languages, general protection faults, and an inability to handle large tables have become problems that have driven major corporations to their knees when they try to build client/server applications.

Part of what Delphi is all about is supplying the world with a good client/server tool that can solve even large and complex problems. Delphi is a real compiler that directly harnesses the power of a sophisticated, object-oriented language. Programmers can expect Delphi applications to run many times faster than programs made with client/server tools that use interpreted languages. Furthermore, Delphi relies on the Borland Database Engine to perform sophisticated database tasks in a short period of time. This means that the database tools around which the client/server portion of Delphi is built are part of a mature and sophisticated technology.

Delphi is much more than a client/server tool, however. It is also a solution to the growing complexity of producing any type of Windows application.

The next three sections of this chapter discuss the following topics:

- Delphi as a desktop tool
- Delphi as a visual programming tool
- Delphi as a client/server tool

I have chosen this order because it represents the layers out of which the product is built. At the core of the product is the compiler, on top of that visual tools are constructed, and then using the compiler and visual tools, you get access to client/server technology.

> **NOTE**
>
> Some people might think that this order should be reversed, and that the client/server technology should come first. However, products that take this approach tend to be slow and inflexible because they, quite simply, have put the cart before the horse. If you start out with a good object-oriented compiler, you have a language flexible enough to perform any client/server-specific task. However, if you start with only a few good ideas on how to implement a client/server tool, your tool will prove top-heavy, and it will be very difficult to provide the power and flexibility needed to resolve complex programming problems. Good tools are built on good foundations. The foundation of Delphi is its excellent object-oriented compiler.

When you are reading the next three sections, it is important to remember that Delphi is built entirely in Delphi. The compiler is built primarily in assembler, but the programming environment, the visual tools, and the object hierarchy are built in Delphi. In short, the core of the product, the pieces you will use day in and day out, are all written in Delphi. The programming environment is a testament to the product's own power. It would be ridiculous to even attempt a similar task using any other client/server tool on the market today.

The other parts of Delphi represent the triumph of object-oriented programming. For instance, the editor is part of a technology that is shared across several different Borland products, and it is written in C. Likewise, the Borland Database Engine is also shared across a number of Borland tools, so it was not written in Delphi. Nevertheless, Borland's excellent object-oriented technology makes it possible to smoothly integrate all these tools, thereby providing the most powerful infrastructure possible.

Delphi as a Desktop Tool

Users are no longer satisfied with simple text mode programs that run from the DOS prompt and give users menus that let them select from choice A, B, or C. Even the rankest neophyte computer user now expects multitasking windowed environments that fully support the mouse.

Anyone who has tried to program Windows or OS/2 from scratch in a sophisticated language such as C or Turbo Pascal knows that it is a demanding, time-consuming task. Delphi exists because programmers need to find a way to eliminate some of this complexity without losing access to low-level functions.

Delphi provides two powerful features that help resolve these problems:

- Delphi is an object-oriented language that fully supports encapsulation, inheritance, and polymorphism, as well as other important features such as runtime type checking, exceptions, and properties.
- Delphi objects can be compiled into components that can be manipulated via the mouse and the object inspector. Other languages support components, but only Delphi provides a technique for fully integrating objects and components in a natural and easy-to-use manner.

Because Delphi is a compiled language, it enables you to produce small, fast executables in a matter of seconds. In fact, Delphi is the world's fastest compiler, and it also produces very small executables. Delphi programs typically range between 200 KB and 500 KB, but if you create programs that don't contain any part of the object hierarchy, your executables can be as small as 5 KB or 6 KB.

Delphi also can produce DLLs, and it can link in DLLs that are written in C, or in any other language. You can use object-oriented code inside Delphi DLLs, and you can place Delphi forms inside DLLs. Support for both the native Pascal and "cdecl" declarations enables you to access code from a wide range of sources, including the DLLs found in the Microsoft OLE2 SDK.

Delphi is a playful language. It can help take the drudgery out of even the most mundane portions of a programmer's work. This is a tool that gives programmers a chance to take control of their Windows-based machines in a way never before possible. As befits such an important topic, I have tried to make this book as interesting, entertaining, and informative as the genre allows. From beginning to end, it is written with the sure knowledge that programming in Delphi should be above all both intriguing and fun.

Here are some of the key features of Delphi:

- Delphi is easy to use.
- Delphi is fun to use.
- Delphi has very few built-in limitations. Learn the language inside out, and it will give you the power you need to accomplish your goals.

Delphi's powerful, fast, object-oriented compiler is one of its great strengths. However, it is important to remember that the compiler is only one-third of what makes the product important. The other two key points are Delphi's visual tools and its client/server tools.

> **NOTE**
>
> Don't worry if some of the these terms, such as "object-oriented" and "event-driven," are new to you. The purpose of this book is take you through the technical aspects of the language in a thorough and easy-to-understand manner. By the time you finish reading this book, these concepts will be a familiar and simple part of your day-to-day programming repertoire.

Delphi as a Visual Programming Tool

Visual programming environments such as Delphi enable you to use the mouse and a series of specialized software tools to design applications quickly and easily. People often refer to the act of creating programs using visual tools as RAD, or Rapid Application Development.

Delphi has a series of experts and other specialized tools that help speed application development. For instance, database programmers can use an expert to automatically generate forms that show one-to-many relationships between two tables. The Delphi Query Builder includes visual tools to create complex SQL statements, and you can use the DataSet editor to gain complete control over the way users access the fields of a table. In particular, you can enforce how data is displayed to the user, and you can gain complete control over what keys the user can use when entering data. This allows means for enforcing how users enter dates, numbers, monetary values, and virtually any other type of input stored in a database.

> **NOTE**
>
> I wrote this book while Delphi was in Beta. As a result, it was not clear at the time of the writing which portions of the product would be included in the desktop version and which would be included only in the high-end, client/server version. As a result, I will usually not state whether a particular feature belongs in a particular version of the product. For instance, the Query Builder ships only with the high-end version of the tool, yet I do not stress that fact while discussing it. Borland, or other third parties, will often sell portions of the high-end product separately.

Delphi provides an easy visual means for creating programs that display database blob fields such as memos or graphics. Furthermore, you will see in later chapters of this book that it is easy to create a program that plays WAV files or movies files.

The Gallery in the Delphi Options menu provides a means for storing form and application templates. This means you can create a set of custom forms or applications that can be shared across a network, so that members of a team can create applications with a specific look and feel.

This same kind of flexibility is available from the Component Palette, which is a totally configurable and extensible tool. You will see in later chapters how you can create custom Component Palettes tailored for the needs of a particular set of developers. This way you can create and store components that have a particular look and feel, and then ensure that a particular group of programmers has easy access to these tools. All the applications coming from your company, or your department, can thereby take on a specific look and feel, without any one programmer having to do anything more than point and click with the mouse.

The single greatest advantage of visual programming is that it enables newcomers to begin writing real programs right from the start. However, the technique is also useful to experienced programmers because it enables them to accomplish complex tasks with just a few clicks of the mouse.

Experienced Windows programmers know that some tasks, such as manipulation of listboxes, scrollbars, or graphics shapes, always require you to write the same lengthy lines of code over and over again. Object-oriented programming helps shorten the task by encapsulating some of these tasks in relatively simple wrappers. Visual programming takes the whole paradigm one step further by enabling you to point and click once or twice with the mouse, thereby saying, in effect: "Do this same old task for me again, but quickly, and behind the scenes, so I don't have to bother with it for the umpteen-thousandth time."

Here is another way of looking at the same issue. Delphi has been designed to enable you to access its objects via visual tools such as components and VBXs. Other languages have already started using visual tools, but Delphi is unique in that it's easy to convert any object that you create into a visual tool that can be manipulated with the mouse. In other words, there is a seamless integration of Delphi's objects and Delphi's visual tools.

If you want, you can manipulate any Delphi component, object, or VBX entirely in code. That means you can create descendants of any object or component, and you can make full use of polymorphism, inheritance, encapsulation, virtual methods, and all the other key object-oriented features.

> **NOTE**
>
> Due to limitations in the design of Microsoft's VBX format, you can't create a real descendant of a VBX. Delphi objects and components, however, are not saddled with the limitations inherent in VBX controls. Furthermore, Delphi will automatically encapsulate a VBX inside an object wrapper, so VBXs start to take on some of the traits of objects, even if they are not fully object-oriented in the true sense of the word.

One of the great benefits of the seamless integration of objects and visual tools is that Delphi encourages good object-oriented programming habits. As you will see when you become proficient in the language, Delphi makes it easy for you to construct visual objects that can be reused. It is too early in this book to begin explaining the exact mechanisms involved, but one of the benefits of creating a visual object, otherwise known as a component, is that objects of this type are easily reused in multiple projects.

Let me state this matter another way to make sure that you understand what I mean. If you take the simple steps necessary to upgrade a Delphi object into a visual tool, what you have done is created something called a component. Components have simple visual interfaces that make it very easy for you to reuse them in multiple projects. They also can easily be shared with other programmers. Furthermore, because components are really objects, other programmers can create a descendant of the component you have created and then add or change its capabilities. This is something you can't do with VBX controls.

NOTE

Components and VBX controls have a great deal in common. To an inexperienced user, components and VBX controls will probably seem almost identical. However, the differences between them are twofold:

■ Delphi components are written in the native Delphi language. This means they can be linked directly into your program, and are therefore small and fast. VBXs exist as separate binaries and cannot ever be truly linked into an executable in the strict and most useful sense of the word.

■ Delphi components are objects, and therefore it is easy to create a descendant of any existing component. This makes Delphi components much more flexible than VBX controls.

It will take some time before most readers fully understand how visual tools are put together. You can rest assured, however, that if you read this book carefully you will understand them from top to bottom. In fact, many programmers may want to go on to produce visual tools as commercial products. If that is one of your goals, you have come to the right place. One of this book's primary goals is to explain how visual tools are engineered and how you can "roll your own" components.

Delphi as a Client/Server Tool

Many, if not most, users of the language are attracted to Delphi because of its client/server capabilities. Delphi makes it easy for you to build scaleable database applications that can be designed on a single system, and that can then be effortlessly translated into a networked environment where the Borland Database Engine gives you access to Interbase, Oracle, Sybase, and several other major servers.

If you have a background of using SQL code, you will be glad to know that Delphi can pass any SQL statement on to its native environment. In other words, you can write an SQL statement, and Delphi will pass it through unchanged to Interbase, Oracle, Sybase, and so on, so that it can be executed on the server. Furthermore, the Borland Database Engine has an intelligent caching system that makes it easy for you to continue working even if you make a query that generates a huge data set.

Of course, if you don't want to use SQL, you can usually write native Delphi code instead. Many programmers will end up using a combination of SQL statements and native Delphi code. If you learn how to combine these two techniques, you will have the ability to quickly produce mission-critical networked applications.

Delphi is a serious client/server tool. It has links to project management tools and to database design tools. It enables you to easily create one-to-many relationships, joins on multiple tables, and calculated fields. It also provides several ways to expose only certain fields from tables to your users. Delphi has support for indexing, sorting, deleting, adding, and editing records.

Above all, Delphi is fast. You can use it to build elaborate front ends and complex, multiwindowed environments that would overwhelm anything that can be produced by other visual programming tools.

Delphi is also a fully scaleable database tool. This means that you can write code on a single-user machine and then automatically switch it over to a network by making only a few very minor changes. The most useful tool for providing this functionality is the Local Interbase Engine. The full-blown Interbase product is an SQL server used by major corporations to perform mission-critical tasks. A special local version of that server ships with Delphi. You can write code that accesses this local version of the server. When you have your design thoroughly debugged, you can change a single line in your Alias and move the whole application onto the network. The Local Interbase Engine will be carefully explained in this book.

Though many users like to use Delphi primarily as a client/server tool, the product is also a fully functional stand-alone relational DBMS that uses Paradox or dBASE files. This means you have instant access to all the Paradox or dBASE files that may exist in your organization, company, or home. If you have an existing dBASE or Paradox application that needs to be upgraded or expanded to encompass complex new features, Delphi may well be the tool you need.

NOTE

I should perhaps add that Delphi is a good tool for creating simple database applications for use in your home. I have developed a number of these applications and use them regularly because they are small and fast. It can be trying to have to load Paradox or dBASE every time you want to access a list of your most commonly used addresses. Delphi enables you to almost effortlessly construct a small application that will access that information in just a few quick seconds. The people who built Delphi's client/server technology probably weren't thinking of this kind of feature when they built the product, but it is there if you need it or want it.

Before closing this section, I should perhaps add that Delphi's power exacts some price from the user. This tool is meant to be used by programmers. If you don't want to write any code, you should probably stick with a product like Paradox or dBASE. However, the client/server end of this product is much easier to use than the Borland Database Engine, the Paradox Engine, the old Pascal Database Toolbox, or any of a number of other database tools that have been traditionally used by programmers.

In fact, you can open and display a table in Delphi without having to write any code. You can even perform fairly complex one-to-many relationships without having to write any code.

In short, Delphi's visual tools make this product very easy to use. However, its capabilities cannot be fully utilized by those with little or no computer experience.

NOTE

One of the ideal uses for Delphi is to teach a child how to program. If you have a clever teenager whom you think might one day make a good programmer, I would definitely consider having Delphi be his or her first language. The playfulness of this tool should appeal to youngsters, and its breadth and depth will enable them to go on learning until they understand everything their imagination and intelligence can grasp.

By now you are probably ready to see Delphi in action. Before discussing any other general topics, I want to give you a chance to use the tool. So, without further adieu, it is time to get some hands-on experience with Delphi.

Compiling and Running an Existing Program

Delphi programs are called *projects*. Every project has a main file, which usually has the letters DPR as an extension. DPR stands for Delphi Project. The main module for a Delphi program might be called LIFE.DPR, or TWOQUERY.DPR.

NOTE

Before reading any further, you should be sure that you have the product installed, and that it is working correctly. If you are having trouble with the installation, call Borland Technical Support for assistance. Installation-related calls are free of charge.

As a rule, the source for every Delphi program should be stored in its own subdirectory. This is necessary because most Delphi programs consist of several different modules, or files. (The final executable, however, can be stored in one file with an EXE extension.) I find it difficult, if not impossible, to keep the source files for a single project sorted out if I mix several different projects in one subdirectory. See Figure 1.1 for a directory listing of a typical Delphi project.

FIGURE 1.1.

Delphi programs usually contain several different source files, which are best stored in a single directory.

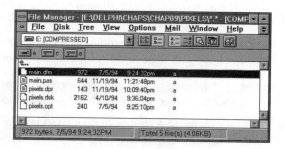

NOTE

If you are having trouble understanding terms such as "files" and "directories," you should probably set this book aside for a while and spend some time with a book on basic Windows or DOS computing. This book is meant for readers who have some former programming experience in at least one other relatively sophisticated tool. An intelligent reader who has no programming experience but a good knowledge of computers can probably also follow along, though it will be a bit tougher for such a reader. However, I can't cover both programming and computer basics in the same volume. In the long run, that kind of endeavor would be a disservice to both neophytes and experienced computer users.

The next few paragraphs explain how to compile and run a prewritten Delphi program. In particular, I will show you how to run one of the sample programs that ships with the compiler, and then one of the programs that come with this book. To get started, launch a copy of Delphi, and check to see if it looks something like the image shown in Figure 1.2.

FIGURE 1.2.

The Delphi programming environment as it appears when first launched.

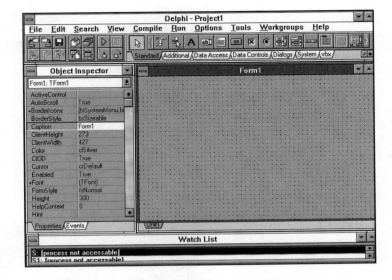

You should be sure to install the sample programs that ship with the compiler and with this book. Both sets of demos are listed and described in the Delphi documentation or on the CD that comes with this book. Demos are one of the most important learning tools for programmers. To help make them more comprehensible to you, I have created a database listing all of their main features. I'll show you how to run that database in just a moment. By the way, it is not advisable to try to compile and run the demos directly from the CD unless you are a relatively experienced Delphi user. Instead, first install them on your hard disk, and then run them.

To run a Delphi program, first open the File menu by clicking it with the mouse or by holding down the Alt key and pressing the letter F. (In the future I will refer to such key combinations with a simple abbreviation such as Alt+F.) After you open the File menu, the screen should look like Figure 1.3.

To load a project, you should click the words "Open Project" or press the letter R. (The complete key combination for loading a project is therefore Alt+F+R.) At this stage you should be looking at the Open Project dialog box, which is shown in Figure 1.4. This is a standard dialog box, of the type that you will write code to create many times while reading this book. Using this type of dialog box should be familiar to most readers. If it is not, you should refer to a book on running Windows.

FIGURE 1.3.

The File menu from the Delphi programming environment.

FIGURE 1.4.

You can use the Open Project dialog box to select a project.

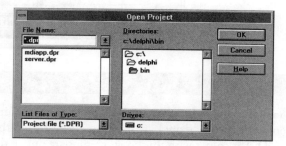

Figure 1.5 shows what the screen looks like after you have used the Open Project dialog box to select TWOQUERY.DPR from the CHAP01 subdirectory. This subdirectory was created when you originally installed the code that came with this book. Click the OK button and load the program into the Delphi environment. The screen should now look something like the image shown in Figure 1.5.

Once it is loaded, there are four ways to compile and run the TWOQUERY program:

■ Click the Run menu once and then click again on the first item in that menu, which is also labeled Run.

■ Press Alt+R+R, which first selects the Run menu and then activates the Run option, as shown in Figure 1.6.

■ Press the F9 key once. (Users of other Pascal programming environments should note that this key combination used to be Ctrl+F9.)

■ Click the green arrow on the speedbar.

FIGURE 1.5.

Delphi after you have loaded the TWOQUERY.DPR program.

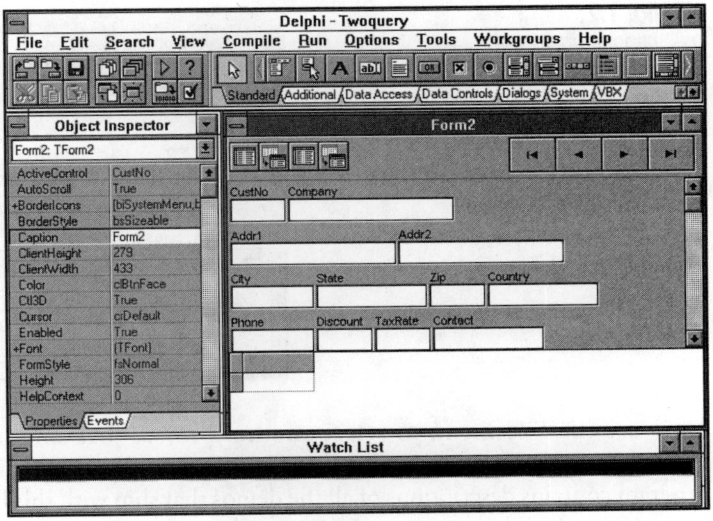

FIGURE 1.6.

The Run menu from the Delphi environment.

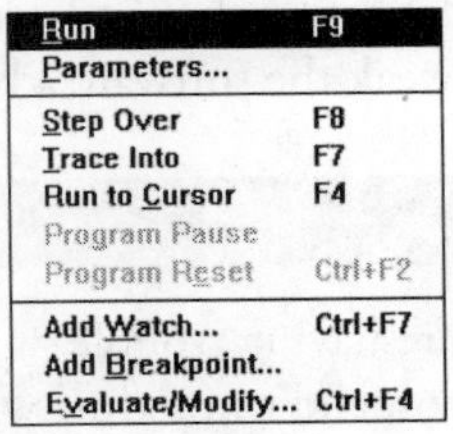

The TWOQUERY program links two databases together. The address of a customer is at the top of the screen, and the orders associated with that customer are at the bottom of the screen, as shown in Figure 1.7. The address and the orders are each kept in separate files that are native to the Borland Paradox database system. Delphi enables you to create, manipulate, and delete Paradox, dBASE, and SQL-based files.

The two files in the TWOQUERY program are linked together automatically by Delphi, using a technique called Linked Cursors. Both files contain a field called Customer Number, and Delphi knows how to find records from each file that share the same Customer Number. This is a fundamental relational database technique that will be explored in depth later in this book.

After you have had a chance to experiment with the TWOQUERY project for a while, you can close the program by double-clicking the system icon in the upper-left corner of the window. Delphi may ask you if you want to save any of the changes made to the TWOQUERY program; at this stage, I recommend that you select no, so that you leave the program exactly as you found it.

FIGURE 1.7.

The TWOQUERY.DPR program links two separate Paradox files together by keying on the Customer Number field.

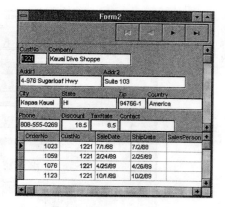

Now use the File menu to select another project that shipped with this book, called DEMOBASE.DPR. It is stored in the ..\SOURCE\UTILITIES directory. The DEMOBASE program contains descriptions of all the demos that ship with this book. Use the Open Project option from the File menu, not the Open File option. If you use the latter option, you will get only a selection of available files that end with a PAS extension, and you will not be able to see DPR files unless you tweak the software a bit.

NOTE

Once again, if you are having trouble navigating through the DOS directory structure, you should probably spend some time with a book about the basics of the DOS and Windows environments before trying to continue learning Delphi. As a writer, I naturally want to hang on to every reader who happens to pick up this book, but I would be doing you a disfavor if I encouraged you to continue in the face of insurmountable odds. If directories confuse you, spend some time studying DOS and Windows, and come back to this book later. That will be the quickest way for you to learn Delphi.

The DEMOBASE program has a number of features that are explained in depth in the Help file that accompanies the program. To access the Help file, select Help from the menu and then click the word Contents, as shown in Figure 1.8.

For now it is not important that you understand how the code for the DEMOBASE program works, or even how to use the program itself. The key point is that you know how to locate and load an existing program. You will find it easy to create programs of this type before you are through reading this book.

FIGURE 1.8.

Help for many Windows programs can be obtained by selecting Help | Contents from the menu at the top of the programming environment.

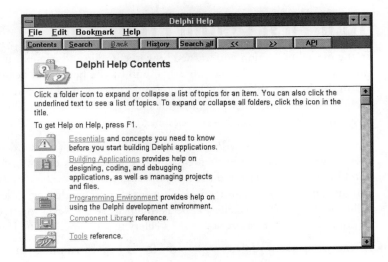

Before moving on to the next section of this chapter, it might be fun for you to run the LIFE program that appears in the GAMES subdirectory created when you installed the code from the CD. After loading the project, open up the Options | Environment selection from the main menu and make sure that the Show compiler progress option is selected, as shown in Figure 1.9. Now select Run | Build from the menus, and you will be able to see the compiler race through the job of constructing the program.

FIGURE 1.9.

The Options | Environment menu choice provides an option for turning on or off the compiler progress dialog box.

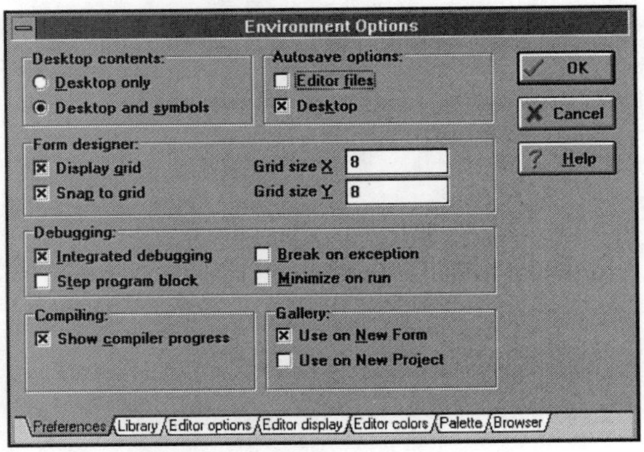

The LIFE program also comes equipped with extensive online help, and I suggest that you use it to learn about the program. Using the help files is a way of getting you to rely on the fact that this book makes extensive use of disk-based tools. For now, books are still every bit as useful as computer programs when it comes to education, but I sense that the future holds a perhaps inevitable tilt away from paper and ink and toward interactive educational tools. This is a subject that will be explored throughout this book.

Your First Delphi Program

In the preceding section you learned how to compile and run existing Delphi programs. It is now time for you to take the proverbial bull by the horns and begin writing your own programs. In the past, this meant that you would fire up an editor and start typing in code. With Delphi, however, the first programs I'll show you don't require you to write any code at all. Everything is done through visual design tools.

To get started, select New Project from the File menu. (You can do this by clicking the File menu with the mouse and then clicking the word New, or you can press the Alt+F+N key combination.) Once again, if the compiler asks you to save changes to the LIFE program, you can just answer no, because you don't want to start modifying code that you might not yet fully understand. (If the Gallery appears when you select New Project, choose the Blank Project option. You will hear more about the Gallery in Chapter 3, "The IDE.")

After starting a new project, pop up the fly-by help by running your mouse along the bottom of the Component Palette, as shown in Figure 1.10.

FIGURE 1.10.

The Component Palette features a handy fly-by help feature.

Label Control

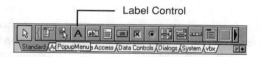

The third item from the left on the Palette is a label control, which is identified by an icon with a big A on it. Click once on this icon and then click the mouse on the window labeled Form1. A small label will appear, as shown in Figure 1.11. (If you have trouble viewing the label, try installing it by clicking once on the form and then dragging the mouse for a moment before releasing the mouse button.)

FIGURE 1.11.

A label control after it has been placed on a form.

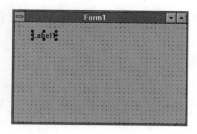

Make sure you can see little black dots at the corners of the label, as shown in Figure 1.11. These dots identify the label as being selected. If you cannot see the dots at the corners of the control, try clicking it once with the mouse.

Now you can type in a caption for the control. In this particular case you might want to type in Is there anybody home? If the AutoSize property is set to False, the words may be partially obscured, as shown in Figure 1.12. To remedy this situation, either set AutoSize to True or place your mouse on one of the black dots you see at the corners of the label. When your cursor turns into a little arrow, you can click and drag to change the shape of the label. That is, you can click the left mouse button, hold it down, and then drag to the right, left, up, or down, until all the text you typed is visible, as shown in Figure 1.13.

FIGURE 1.12.

Partially obscured text in an edit control.

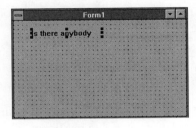

FIGURE 1.13.

Your first Delphi program, as it might appear on your screen.

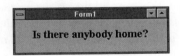

As you type text in the edit control, you will see that the same text also appears in the Object Inspector on the left of the screen. In particular, use the arrow keys to find the Caption property editor on the Object Inspector and note that it contains the same words as those that appear inside the edit component. The Object Inspector enables you to view and alter the current state of the components or forms in your program. You will learn all about the Object Inspector later in this book.

> **NOTE**
>
> When you type information in a label control, you will find that the size of the control will change as you type if you set the AutoSize property to True, which is the default value. If AutoSize is set to False, you will have to manually change the size of the control with the mouse, as described earlier. To learn more about the label control, type 10 or 15 words into the Caption property. Then turn AutoSize off and WordWrap on. (The list is sorted alphabetically, so you may have to scroll down to reach the WordWrap Property Editor.) Now try resizing the control both horizontally and vertically. Turn WordWrap off and try the same actions. If you want, you can continue experimenting with some of the other properties, such as color and font.

Now that you have the text set up on the form, you can run the program by pressing F9 or by selecting Run from the Run menu. A few moments after you have selected F9, the completed program should appear on-screen.

> **NOTE**
>
> This first program does nothing more than display Is there anybody home? on the screen. Most likely, your question will be answered by a resounding silence. However, if the computer answers back Hello world!, you should probably get up immediately and call one of the following people:
>
> A) Marvin Minsky
>
> B) Your psychiatrist

After you have taken sufficient time to admire your first program, you can close it and prepare to engage in a brief exercise in Zen mysticism. This exercise consists of the simple act of clicking once on the File menu and then selecting the New Project option. When you do this, the computer will ask if you want to save the changes to your first program. I suggest that you select No. The fact that your first program will now disappear, never to be regained, might be a bit upsetting at first, but the ancient Zen masters recommend it as a way of becoming one with your CPU.

The idea for the next program has probably already crossed your mind. The impulse being so strong, I want to give it at least semi-official status by asking that you now attempt to place every single control from the first two or three pages of the Component Palette on a single form. To do so, you need to click each of the pages of the Component Palette in turn, starting with the word Standard, moving on through Additional, and perhaps one or two more. When you select each page, run the mouse along the bottom of the visible icons, so that you can see the name of each control. Then click each icon in turn and try to find a place for it on the form. My efforts in this regard are shown in Figure 1.14, which depicts the MOBIGGER program.

FIGURE 1.14.

The MOBIGGER program is loaded down with many tools from the Component Palette.

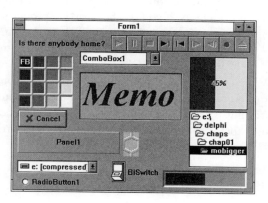

You may find that your computer will complain before you get through more than a page or two of controls. The most likely source of trouble will be that you simply run out of available memory, or resources. If this happens, don't bother to pursue the project any further. The point here is simply to acquaint you with the act of using the Component Palette, and to help you start to become familiar with some of the available options.

NOTE

The fact that I have asked you to create a program that probably pushes your system right to the edge of its capabilities is not entirely capricious or arbitrary. As a programmer, it is often my lot to test the limits of the envelope. The actual programs you design, of course, should be as small and compact as possible. It is, however, important to understand what your system can and cannot do. You should also be familiar with the symptoms that accompany the act of stressing your system beyond the limits of its capabilities. If this causes your system to crash, you should simply reboot and pick up the pieces. There is nothing wrong with crashing the system during development; only after you create a finished program do crashes become shameful!

For now, I'm not going to ask you to do any more programming. If the examples I have shown you here make you fear that there might not be enough real code in this book, I suggest you flip ahead and see if some of the projects in the body of the book look more challenging or informative. I'm sure you will find that there is no shortage of real programs in this book. This is a serious book with honest goals.

NOTE

During development, this book accidentally outgrew the binding capabilities of contemporary printing presses. As a result, most of the source code listings were removed to make room for the text. The code, of course, is available on CD; or if you don't have the CD, you can get the code from me at CIS: 76711,533, AOL: CHARLIECAL, Internet: `ccalvert@wpo.borland.com`.

The examples I have presented in this chapter are meant only to give you the flavor of what visual programming is like. I don't, however, want to mislead you by letting you think that visual programming obviates the need to write real code. That is not at all the case. The point is simply that visual tools are fun to use, and furthermore, they have reached a highly sophisticated state. They enable you to create stunning effects with very little effort on your part.

Summary

In this chapter you got a chance to become familiar with the outline of this book, the basic feature set accompanying Delphi, and some of the key factors in the Delphi programming environment. You also had an opportunity to get some hands-on experience using Delphi to create some simple, and fairly flashy, demo applications.

It is said that the ancient Chinese sage Chou Wini spoke the following words before disappearing into the mountains to lead a life of contemplation: "He who read book through from beginning accrue great advantage."

No one is sure exactly what Chou meant by these words, nor are they sure if Chou really said them. In fact, there are many who doubt that Chou ever existed. Nonetheless, many students of the great art of programming believe there is wisdom in Chou's most famous utterance. Perhaps it is best to simply end this chapter with those words, and let you make up your own mind about them.

The Programming Environment

Overview

This chapter discusses the Delphi programming environment, concentrating on the big, important tools that programmers use on a day-to-day basis. To the degree to which it is practical, I will attempt to make this an exhaustive description, but I will omit details that are either trivial or easily discovered via the online help.

In particular, this chapter introduces the main parts of the environment, including the following:

- Forms Designer
- Object Inspector
- Editor window
- Online help
- Component Palette
- Speedbar
- Menu and Menu Designer
- The Command Line Compiler

In writing this chapter, I have tried not to merely list the key parts of the environment, but to describe some of the reasons for their existence. However, this is not a particularly technical chapter, and many readers who have been programming in Windows for years will be forgiven if they tend to skim through it.

The material in this chapter should be read in conjunction with the next chapter. After reading them both, you should be able to get a fairly in-depth feel for the way the Delphi environment is set up.

The Overall Structure of the Environment

Before identifying specific portions of the Delphi programming environment, I would like to mention a few general characteristics that help give Delphi its shape and form. You will find that many of these traits define the overall structure of the work you do in Delphi.

The appearance of the Delphi environment differs from that seen in many other Windows applications. For instance, Borland Pascal for Windows 7.0, Borland C++ 4.0, Word for Windows, and the Program Manager are all MDI applications and therefore have a different look and feel than Delphi. MDI applications follow the Multiple Document Interface specification, which defines a particular way of arranging a series of smaller windows inside a single larger window.

Delphi follows a different specification, called the Single Document Interface (SDI). SDI was chosen for Delphi in part because it adheres closely to the application model being used in Windows 95. (Windows 95 is the name for the new 32-bit operating system currently being developed by Microsoft, and due for release in the second half of 1995.)

SDI provides for a more object-oriented and document-centric view of applications. Rather than confining a set of preplanned windows inside a single larger window, SDI allows windows of all shapes and sizes to be added to an application. This prepares the way for a world in which applications are easily extended either by users or by third-party programmers. In fact, you will find that Delphi is both configurable and extensible. You can literally link your own binary files into the environment.

When you use SDI applications like Delphi, you might find that it is simplest to minimize other applications before you begin your work. If you then want to switch to another application, just click the minimize button above Delphi's main menu to minimize any windows associated with the visual programming environment and to clear the deck for work on other applications. Delphi makes it easy for you to provide this same model for your own applications.

The Major Players

The five major players in the Delphi environment are listed here. Of these five players, the first two—the Forms Designer and the Editor window—are the most important.

- Forms Designer
- Editor window
- Component Palette
- Object Inspector
- Online help

There are other important players in Delphi, such as the toolbar, the menu system, the watch window, and a slew of other dialog boxes that enable you to fine-tune either your program or the environment. However, the five features listed here are the ones that stand out most strongly for regular users of the environment.

Delphi programmers spend most of their time going back and forth between the Forms Designer and the Editor window (which is sometimes called just the Editor for short). Before you get started, make sure you can recognize these two important components. The Forms Designer is shown in Figure 2.1, and the Editor window is shown in Figure 2.2. (The Editor is sometimes hidden behind the Forms Designer, and vice versa. To switch back and forth between the two, press F11 or F12.)

FIGURE 2.1.

The Forms Designer is the place where you create the visual interface for your program.

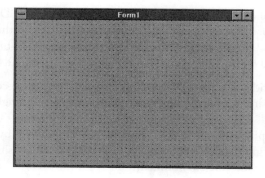

FIGURE 2.2.

The Editor window is where you create the logic that governs your program.

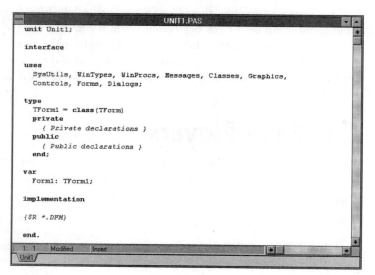

The Delphi Forms Designer is so intuitive and easy to use that creating a visual interface is child's play. The Forms Designer consists primarily of a single window made up of a blank slate that you fill in with various tools you select from the Component Palette.

Despite the importance of the Forms Designer, the place where programmers spend the majority of their time is in the Editor. Logic is the driving force behind programs, and the Editor is the place where you codify the logic of your program.

The Component Palette, shown in Figure 2.3, enables you to select the tools you want to place on the Forms Designer. To use the Component Palette, just click any of the available tools, and then click a second time on the Forms Designer. The tool you have chosen will become a visible object on the Forms Designer that you can then manipulate with the mouse.

FIGURE 2.3.

The Component Palette is where you select tools that will be placed on your form.

The Component Palette uses a paging metaphor. Across the bottom of the palette is a list of tabs such as Standard, Additional, Dialogs, and so on. If you click one of these tabs, you can then flip to the next page in the Component Palette. This type of paging metaphor is used widely in the Delphi IDE and is something that you can easily make use of in your own applications. (Look on the Additional page, and you will see that a Tabs component is available for you to use as you please.) Although it doesn't work in the Component Palette, most of the time Delphi allows you to hotkey between tabbed pages by pressing Ctrl+Tab.

If you place a TEdit component on a form, you can drag it around from place to place. You can also use the tabs on its edges to stretch it back and forth so that it becomes larger or smaller. Most of the other components can be manipulated in a similar manner. However, the non-visual components, such as the TMainMenu object and the database access components, don't change shape after being placed on the Forms Designer.

If you look to the left of the Forms Designer, you can see the Object Inspector, which is shown in Figure 2.4. Note that the information in the Object Inspector changes, depending on which component on your form is selected. The key point to remember is that each component is really an object, and that you can change the traits of that object via the Object Inspector.

FIGURE 2.4.

The Object Inspector lets you define the traits of the components you place on your form.

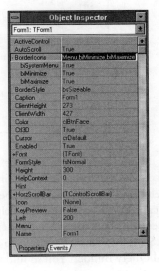

The Object Inspector contains two lists of categories, both of which can be used to define the behavior of a particular component. The first category is a list of properties, and the second is a list of events. If you want to change the traits associated with a particular component, you can often do so via the Object Inspector. For instance, you can change the name and size of a TLabel component by manipulating the Caption, Left, Top, Height, and Width properties in the Object Inspector.

You can use the tabs at the bottom of the Object Inspector to flip back and forth between the Properties page and the Events page. The Events page is associated with the Editor window. If you click the right side of the Events page, that code will be written into the Editor, and the Editor will immediately be brought to the forefront so you can add additional logic. This aspect of the Delphi environment is discussed in depth later in this chapter.

The last of the major players in Delphi is the online help. To access this nifty tool, just choose the Help menu item and select Contents. This brings up the screen shown in Figure 2.5.

FIGURE 2.5.

The online help is a magic reference book that helps you quickly find all kinds of information.

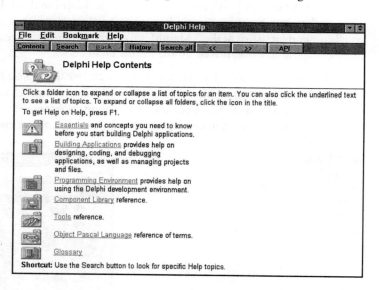

The online help is divided into several sections. The first section is the description of Delphi proper. You can access a description of the Windows API by pressing the API button in the top of the online help. By choosing the File | Open option and browsing in the .\DELPHI\BIN subdirectory, you can find other important help files. For example, the CWG.HLP file describes how to add components to the Component Palette. CWH.HLP describes how to make help files. LOCALSQL.HLP describes how to use the local SQL language, and VQB.HLP describes the Visual Query Builder. You should take the time to explore all the help files in the .\DELPHI\BIN subdirectory.

For now, the most important part of the online help is visible in the window shown in Figure 2.5. This window is divided into seven major categories, each associated with its own icon. Pop open the online help and examine the list that is displayed when you click the Programming Environment icon. This list, shown in Figure 2.6, gives you a useful reference for many of the main subjects covered in this chapter.

FIGURE 2.6.

A handy reference for the Delphi programming environment is available in the online help.

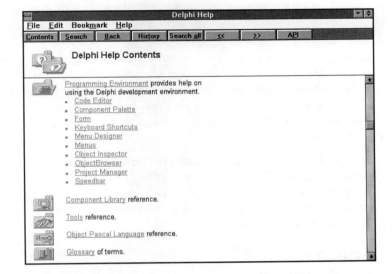

A final important feature of the online help is the Search button, located at the top of the help window. You can use this button to search for help on a particular topic. If you pop up the Help menu from the main menu in Delphi, you can choose between the following three options:

- Contents
- Topic Search
- How to Use Help

The second of these options brings up a dialog box that looks almost identical to the Search dialog box you get from inside the online help. However, this is a special search program written by Borland that enables you to search across multiple help files, including files that you personally add to the environment.

It's time to call it a wrap, and to conclude the first stage in this introduction to the Delphi environment. The main point to remember is that the Delphi environment is dominated by two major players, the Forms Designer and the Editor window, and that the other major players include the Component Palette, the Object Inspector, and online help.

The Supporting Players

This section focuses on three tools that you can think of as supporting players in the Delphi environment:

- Menu System
- Speedbar
- Image Editor

Menus provide a fast and flexible interface to the Delphi environment because they can be manipulated using a series of very short keystrokes. They are also handy because they use words or short phrases, which some users think are more precise and comprehensible than icons or pictures. You can use the menus to perform a wide range of tasks, but perhaps the most common tasks are opening and closing files, manipulating the debugger, and customizing the environment.

The speedbar appears directly beneath the menu, and to the left of the Component Palette, as shown in Figure 2.7. The speedbar does many of the same tasks that can be performed with the menus, except that it is intended specifically to be used with the mouse. If you hold the mouse over any of the icons on the speedbar, you will see that fly-by help is available to explain the functions of these icons.

FIGURE 2.7.

The speedbar appears to the left of the Component Palette and directly above the default position for the Object Inspector (FT4).

If you right-click the speedbar, a popup menu appears. Choose Configure from this menu, and you will be presented with a speedbar Editor dialog box that enables you to change the tools seen on the speedbar. In particular, you can drag the right edge of the speedbar back and forth to change its size, and you can use drag and drop properties to pull an existing bitmap off the toolbar. You can choose new tools from the speedbar Editor and place them on the speedbar. For instance, you might want to remove three existing bitmaps from the speedbar and replace them with bitmaps that enable you to cut, copy, and paste components or text with a single click of the mouse.

NOTE

Bitmap is the Windows word for a picture. More specifically, bitmaps are individual pixels arranged to create a visual image such as an arrow, a checkmark, a face, or any other image that can be shown in two dimensions. Most windows bitmaps can be saved to files that have a BMP extension.

The Image Editor, shown in Figure 2.8, is similar to the Paintbrush program that ships with Windows. You can access this module by selecting Image Editor from the Tools menu. I'm not going to describe this tool here because you are probably familiar with similar packages such as Paintbrush, but I did want to be sure you were aware of its existence.

FIGURE 2.8.

The Image Editor can be used to design backdrops, bitmap buttons, and other visual parts of your program.

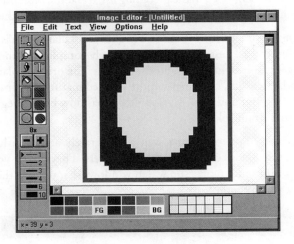

By now, you have had a look at most of the elements you will use in your day-to-day life as a Delphi programmer. I have discussed these elements in broad terms, so that you can begin to get a feeling for the overall structure and purpose of the Delphi programming environment.

The Technical Tools

Five other major tools ship with Delphi that I have not yet discussed. These are as follows:

- The integrated debugger
- The stand-alone debugger
- The command-line compiler
- WinSight
- WinSpector

I place these tools in their own category, not because they are less important than the other tools, but because they play a highly abstracted, technical role in programming. The database tools will all be discussed separately in Part IV, "Visual Database Tools: Tables, Datasets, and SQL."

NOTE

There are two different versions of Delphi: the client/server version and the desktop version. Because the desktop version does not include the stand-alone debugger, owners of that product can skip the portions of the text that refer to that tool.

Of the tools mentioned in the preceding list, by far the most important is the integrated debugger. This is a fully integrated GUI debugger that functions in the same window as the Editor.

I'm not the one to tell the story, but this particular tool has an enormously complex history behind it. It was, quite frankly, an extremely complicated and difficult tool to develop, and its genesis was somewhat long and drawn out. The original plan was to have this tool ship with Borland Pascal 7.0, but it never quite reached maturity in time to make the ship date, so it first appeared in Borland C++, version 4.0. It has now been integrated into Delphi, where it plays a very important role.

No one can hope to become even a moderately accomplished programmer without having detailed knowledge of the available debuggers. They enable you to step through your code one line at a time, and to open up watch windows that tell you the current value of the active variables in your program.

NOTE

If you have never used a debugger before, it will probably take you several hours to become proficient using the integrated debugger. My bet is that within the first week after you learn to use it, you will find that it saves you at least a full working day's worth of frustrating debugging. The simple fact is that I can't really imagine doing any serious development without firing up the debugger on a frequent basis.

The difference between the integrated debugger and the stand-alone debugger is mostly a matter of degree. The stand-alone debugger does everything the integrated debugger does and then some. As a rule, I consider the stand-alone debugger to be faster, and much more powerful, than the integrated debugger. However, it is not as convenient a tool to use, in large part because you have to entirely exit the Delphi programming environment to use it.

The basic rule of thumb I am employing at the time of this writing looks like this:

- If I have a simple problem that I believe can be easily fixed, I usually use the integrated debugger to try to solve it in a few quick steps.
- If I have a complex problem that requires the use of some heavy guns, I load up the stand-alone debugger and use it to peer deeply into memory, looking down far into the depths of the machine.

In short, I use the integrated debugger whenever I can, and turn to the stand-alone debugger only when I need to do very detailed work.

If you want to use the stand-alone debugger, you must first compile your program with Debug info turned on. To set this option, go to Options | Project and turn to the Linker page. There you will find an option to set "Debug info in EXE." This must be turned on before you compile a program to run in the stand-alone debugger. You should also make sure that all three of the Debugging options are turned on in the Compiler page of the Options | Project menu.

The command-line compiler, called DCC.EXE, is useful primarily when you want a second means to compile applications before using them with the stand-alone debugger. Many C/C++ programmers have an aversion to the IDEs that are supplied with their products. There is, however, a very intimate connection between a Delphi program and the Delphi environment. Most programmers will probably find it much simpler to work inside the IDE, rather than trying to design programs from the command line. However, there are bound to be at least a few independent souls with different ideas, and I'm sure they will be glad for the command-line compiler.

Though it is not documented, DCC can also be used to make DOS and DOS protected-mode applications. This feature is handy, but it does not allow you to port full-blown Delphi applications from Windows to DOS. Instead, it lets you create non-VCL-based programs and run them from the DOS prompt. Users of Borland and Turbo Pascal might find this tool useful because it fixes some minor bugs found in Borland Pascal 7.0. However, at the last moment before the final release, the developers severly curtailed this feature, most likely because they had no time to test it and did not want to be responsible for a product they had not tested. Nonetheless, if you can supply a copy of the SYSTEM unit, you can compile DOS apps by passing /CD to DCC, and you can compile protected-mode DOS applications by passing /CP to DCC.EXE. To create Windows applications, pass /CW to the compiler:

```
DCC /CW SIMPLE.PAS
```

The command-line compiler will be discussed further in Chapter 32, "Using DDEML and OLE with Delphi."

NOTE

The acronym IDE stands for Integrated Development Environment. This is the term Borland uses to refer to the main working platform that it ships with its products. The term derives from the fact that the development environment contains several integrated tools, such as a debugger, editor, and compiler. Throughout this book, I will consider the terms IDE and programming environment synonymous.

Neither WinSight nor WinSpector are likely to be much use to you until you become an experienced Windows programmer. This doesn't mean that you shouldn't fire them up and experiment with them as soon and as often as you like. These tools play a peripheral, and highly technical, role in my day-to-day programming work.

Of the two, WinSight is probably the most powerful and the most useful. Its main function is to enable you to spy on the Windows messaging system. Windows is an event-driven operating system. Almost all the major and minor occurrences in the Windows environment take the form of messages that are sent between the various windows on the scene in great flurries of activity, just the way gusts of wind blow in thousands of snowflakes during a blizzard. When you want to spy on these messages, you should use WinSight.

WinSpector is used to perform postmortems on ill-behaved applications. It gets called when an application fails, and it dumps a record of the current state of the machine into a text file. You can review this record in an attempt to figure out what has gone wrong. The WinSpector tool can be particularly useful when a program is already in the field, because you can have users run it in order to gain important information about the state of their machines when a crash occurs. This enables you to find out facts that your users might not otherwise have the technical skills necessary to report.

The Standard Components

Not all of the 14 components listed on the first page (the Standard page) of the Component Palette shown in Figure 2.9 are centrally important to most programming endeavors, but the vast majority of them are. Nobody can get by very long without edit controls, listboxes, pushbuttons, or most of the other components you find on the top of the Component Palette. These tools are as much a part of Windows programming as is the mouse or a traditional resizable window.

FIGURE 2.9.

The controls listed on the first page of the Component Palette.

The components listed on each page are configurable. That is, you can replace the components that ship with the product with new components, and you can change the order or number of components listed on each page. This capability is useful for a couple of reasons. First, you might find or create new controls (such as an edit or a listbox) that suit your needs better than the ones that ship with Delphi. Second, you might belong to a shop that wants to produce a custom set of controls with a particular look and feel. If that is the case, you can easily replace or modify the components that ship with the product.

The standard Delphi components are listed here, with some of the more important tools accompanied by explanatory text. As you read about these components, it would be helpful for you to have the computer running nearby, so that you can manipulate each component and get an idea about how it works.

- **The Arrow Cursor:** I am throwing you a curve here, because the arrow depicted on the far left of the Component Palette isn't really a component. The arrow cursor is included on the Component Palette pages as a handy feature you can use to cancel the selection of a component.

- **TMainMenu:** This component enables you to place a menu at the top of your program. When you first place a menu on your form, it appears as a simple icon with a picture of a menu painted on top of it. Icons of this type are referred to as nonvisual components, because they cannot be seen at runtime. As you will see later in this chapter, creating a menu is a three-step process. You place the component on a form, click the Items property in the Object Inspector, and finally define individual menu items by typing in the Caption property of the Object Inspector for the Menu Builder. When you are finished, all you need to do to make the menu visible is run your program. This subject is explained in detail in the online help and will be referenced again later in this chapter.

- **TPopupMenu:** This component lets you create popup menus such as the ones you see when you click the right mouse button on the Editor window.

- **TLabel:** This component's sole purpose is to display text on-screen. You can change the control's font and color by double-clicking the Font property in the Object Inspector. You will find that it is easy to change the text at runtime, via a single line of code.

- **TEdit:** This component is a standard Windows edit control. It can be used for displaying short fragments of text and for enabling users to enter text dynamically at runtime. All Delphi programs are automatically marked so that they will run as full-fledged Windows 3.1 applications. This means that you can use the ReadOnly property to turn a TEdit into a fancy label. This choice can be appealing when you need to exercise special traits of edit controls—for example, if you need to highlight text—but you still don't want the user to be able to edit the text that is on display.

■ **TMemo:** This component is really just another form of the TEdit control. It is meant to be used with large selections of text that require multiple lines for proper display. TMemo controls feature word wrap, cut and paste, and other basic editorial functions. Even TMemo controls have their limits, however, and you will find that they aren't suitable for editing large documents that contain more than 10–20 pages of text. (There are VBXs on the market that can be used to edit larger blocks of text, and it is likely that native Delphi components with similar capabilities will appear on the market.)

■ **TButton:** This component is used to enable users to select options or to give commands at runtime. Delphi makes it extremely easy for you to add these controls to your programs. Once you place them on the form, you can double-click them to create a response method in the Editor window. You can then fill in that space with a simple Windows command such as a call to the MessageBox function:

```
procedure TForm1.Button1Click(Sender: TObject);
begin
  MessageBox(Handle, 'Fast Code',
             'The Delphi Way', mb_Ok);
end;
```

■ **TCheckBox:** This component enables you to display a line of text with a small window situated in front of it. You can cause a checkmark or X to appear in the small window, thereby designating that something has been selected. For instance, if you select Options | Project from the main menu, you will see the Compiler Options dialog box. The entire dialog box consists of little more than a series of checkboxes that show whether you have selected particular compiler options.

■ **TRadioButton:** This component enables the user to select only one of several different options. For instance, if you go once again to Options | Project in the main menu and select the Linker Options page, you will see that the Map file and Link buffer file sections both consist of a series of radio buttons. Only one of these options can be selected at any time.

■ **TListBox:** This component is used to present the user with a list in a scrollable window. The classic example of a listbox in the Windows environment appears whenever you select File | Open from the main window of most applications. A File dialog box then appears, enabling you to scroll through a selection of files or directories in a listbox.

■ **TComboBox:** This component is a lot like a listbox, except that it also enables you to type into a small edit control that is placed at the top of the listbox. There are several different kinds of combo boxes, but one of the most popular is probably the dropdown combo box, which you see at the bottom of the dialog box that appears when you choose File | Open from the main menu.

- **TScrollbar:** This component appears automatically in edit controls, memo controls, and listboxes if a scrollbar is needed to scroll additional text into view. Scrollbars usually don't play a major role in most day-to-day programming chores, so this chapter discusses them only briefly.

- **TGroupBox:** This component is used primarily for visual purposes, and as a way of telling Windows how to tab through a series of controls. Referring once again to the Compiler Options page from the Options | Compiler menu choice, you can see that Code Generation, Runtime Errors, Syntax Options, Debugging, and Numeric Processing each appear in a TGroupBox.

- **TPanel:** This component, like the TGroupBox control, is used primarily for visual purposes. Except for the designation of tabbing groups, its main purpose is purely decorative, but it can also convey information to the user about how certain controls might be linked together conceptually. To use a TPanel, simply place it on a form and then drop other controls on top of it. TPanels are often used when constructing toolbars or status bars.

- **TScrollBox:** This component provides a place on a form that you can scroll both horizontally and vertically. Unless you explicitly turn it off, the entire form also provides this same functionality, which can be controlled via the HorzScrollBar and VertScrollBar properties. However, there are times when you might want only a particular portion of your form to scroll. In such cases, you should use the TScrollBox component.

That completes the roundup of the controls in the first page of the Component Palette. If you need additional information, Delphi comes with a handy online reference to its major components.

Other Pages in the Component Palette

This section provides a complete listing of the other components that ship with Delphi, arranged by page.

The Additional Page

BitBtn
SpeedButton
TabSet
NoteBook
TabbedNoteBook
MaskEdit
OutLine
StringGrid

DrawGrid
Image
Shape
Bevel
Header
ScrollBox

The DataAccess and DataControls Pages

The database components are addressed separately in Part III of this book.

The Dialogs Page

OpenDialog
SaveDialog
FontDialog
ColorDialog
PrintDialog
PrinterSetupDialog
FindDialog
ReplaceDialog

The System Page

Timer
PaintBox
FileListBox
DirectoryListBox
DriveComboBox
FilterComboBox
MediaPlayer
OleContainer
DDEClientConv
DDEClientItem
DDEServerConv
DDEServerItem

The VBX Page

BiSwitch
BiGauge
BiPict
TKChart

Samples

Gauge
ColorGrid
SpinButton
SpinEdit
DirectoryOutline
Calendar

Please note that you can also access all the components via the View | Component List menu choice. This option is essential if you don't have, or don't want to use, a mouse. It is also useful if you are looking for a component but can't remember which page it is on. The Component List dialog's key feature is that it enables you to search for a component by name. Incremental searches are supported, so you can type the letter R and see all the components that begin with the letter R, and then type the letter E and see all the components that begin with RE, and so on.

The Object Inspector In Depth

Earlier in this chapter, I took a brief look at the Object Inspector. Now it's time to examine this important tool in more depth. The key point to understand about the Object Inspector is that it can be used to change the traits of any component you drop onto a form. In fact, it can also be used to change the traits associated with the form itself.

The best way to understand how the Object Inspector works is with some hands-on experience. To start out, open a new project by choosing the File | New Project option from the main menu. Then drop a TMemo object, a TButton object, and a TListBox object onto the form, as shown in Figure 2.10.

FIGURE 2.10.

A simple TForm object with TMemo, TButton, and TListBox components arranged on its surface.

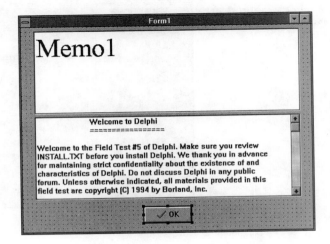

The first thing to learn about a form is that it starts with the Ctl3D style turned on by default. Go to the Object Inspector and double-click several times on the space to the right of the Ctl3D property. You should be able to see the property change back and forth from true to false each time you double-click. Notice that this action radically changes the appearance of the form. Also note that changing the Ctl3D property on the form automatically changes the Ctl3D property on each child window placed on the form.

To get a better feel for how this works, turn Ctl3D off on the form, and then turn it on in the TMemo component. To do this, first select the form itself and click the Ctl3D property so that it is turned off. Then click once on the TMemo component and select the Ctl3D property from the Object Inspector. You can see that changing the Ctl3d property on the TMemo has no effect on the other controls. This shows that the relationship between a form and its child controls is unique with respect to the Ctl3D property.

Go back to the form and reset Ctl3D so that it is turned on. Now hold down the Shift key and click once on the TMemo and once on the TListBox. Both should now have little blocks in their corners demonstrating that they are selected.

Once you have selected two or more controls at the same time, there are a number of operations you can perform on them. For instance, if you press the Ctrl key and the arrow keys, you will find that they move in tandem across the form. If you press the Shift key and the arrow keys, you can resize them as objects. Now try opening the Edit | Size menu option and setting both the Width and Height fields to Grow to Largest, as shown in Figure 2.11. Now both controls will be exactly the same size. Next, choose Edit | Align, and choose Center in Window for the Horizontal value. (See Figure 2.12.)

FIGURE 2.11.

The Edit menu gives you access to two dialog boxes that can be used to synchronize a selected set of components.

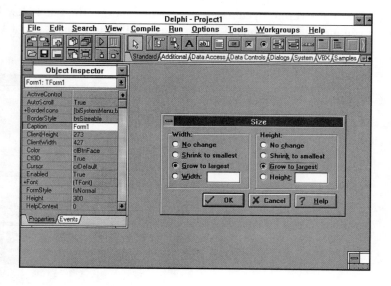

FIGURE 2.12.

The Alignment dialog box helps you arrange the components you place on your form.

Because you have selected two components at once, the Object Inspector has been changed to show only the fields that both objects have in common. This means that any changes you make to the properties in the Object Inspector will affect not one, but two separate components. For instance, you can change the color of both forms by changing the Color property at the top of the Object Inspector so that it reads clTeal.

There are three ways you can change the color of a property in the Object Inspector. One way is to simply type in the name or hex number associated with a new color. The second way is to press the little arrow on the right of the box and select the color with the mouse. The third way is to double-click the right-hand column next to the word Color. A moment later a Color dialog box appears and enables you to select the color you want.

The Font property works in a manner very similar to the Color property. To see how this works, first select the Font property for the TMemo object and double-click the entry column. A Font dialog box appears, like the one shown in Figure 2.13. Select the Times New Roman font and set its size to a very large figure, such as 72. Then change the color of the font with the combo box in the bottom-left corner of the dialog box. When you click the OK button, the default text that appears in your TMemo control has been radically altered.

FIGURE 2.13.

The Font dialog box enables you to choose from an array of fonts, sizes, and styles.

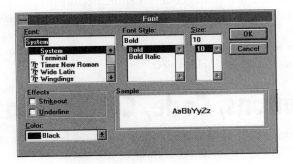

To conclude this brief tour of the Object Inspector, double-click on the Items property for the TListBox. A dialog box will appear, and you can type in lines of text that will appear in the listbox. Try this once to see how it works. First type in a few words, with each word on its own line, and then click the OK button. The text you wrote will appear in the listbox.

You can take this one step further if you like, by again double-clicking the entry column to the right of the Items property. This time choose the Open button at the bottom of the String List Editor. Go to the root directory for Delphi and select the README.TXT file, or any other text file that catches your eye. For instance, you could pop into the DEMOS subdirectory and select a Pascal source file. Now when you close the dialog boxes and return to your main form, you should find the text file you selected displayed in the TListBox component. At this time, you might want to press F9 to run your application so you can see what it looks like in action.

Saving the Program

You have put a bit of effort into the program you've been working with over the last few pages, so you might want to save it. Doing so will enable you to recall the program again at a later time if you want to review it, work on it some more, or show it to a friend.

The first step in saving the program is to create a subdirectory for it using the Microsoft File Manager, or some other tool of your choice. In this particular case, you might first want to create a subdirectory in which to place all your programs, and then under that subdirectory create another subdirectory for this specific program. For example, you could create a directory called MYCODE and then beneath it create a subdirectory called TIPS1, which would contain the program you have just been working on.

After creating a subdirectory to save your program in, choose File | Save Project from the menu. You will be prompted to save two files. The first file is the unit you have been working on, and the second file is the project file that owns your program. Save the unit as MAIN.PAS and the project as TIPS1.DPR. (Any file with a PAS extension and the word "unit" at the top of it is referred to as a *unit*. Units will be discussed in more detail in another section of this chapter.)

You will find that throughout this entire document, project files are named with a word that describes the program, and the first unit in the project is saved under the name MAIN.PAS. That is, the project has a particular name, such as TIPS1, and the file that defines the main actions of that project is called MAIN. Later in your training, you will see how to create more than one unit in a single project.

TButtons, Code, Captions, and Z Orders

After closing the application you created in the last section, you will be placed back in design mode, where you can learn a few last tricks about the Object Inspector and Forms Designer.

Drop a TButton, TMemo, and TListBox on a form. Place the TButton control so that it rests half on and half off a TMemo field, as shown in Figure 2.14. Now Choose Edit | Send to Back from the main menu. This pushes the TButton control behind the TMemo component. This is known as changing a component's Z order. The letter Z is used because mathematicians usually designate the third dimension with the letter Z. That is, X and Y are used to designate the width and height axes on a graph, and Z is used to designate depth.

FIGURE 2.14.

A TButton control resting half on and half off a TMemo field.

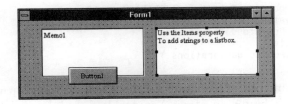

Take a few moments to experiment with sending the button to the front and back of the TMemo component. If you lose track of it altogether, you should be able to find it again in the combo box at the top of the Object Inspector.

Move the button back down to the bottom of the screen, so that it is no longer touching the TMemo object. Now expand the Object Inspector so that you can see both the button's Name property and the Caption property at the same time. Change the name of the button to Terminate. Notice that the caption has been changed at the same time. This dual change will occur only if you haven't made any previous changes to the Caption field.

The text you see on the surface of the button is actually the Caption property, and the Name property is an internal reference you will use when you write code. If you open up the Editor window, you will see the following code fragment:

```
TForm1 = class(TForm)
  ListBox1: TListBox;
  Memo1: TMemo;
  Terminate: TButton;
  private
    { Private declarations }
  public
    { Public declarations }
end;
```

In this fragment, the TButton is named Terminate because you assigned this word to its Name property. Note that the TListBox and TMemo fields still have default names associated with them.

Now double-click on the TButton object. You will be taken to the Editor window, where you'll see a fragment of code that looks like this:

```
procedure TForm1.TerminateClick(Sender: TObject);
begin

end;
```

This code was created when you clicked the button, and it will be executed every time you run your program and click the Terminate button. In addition, you will see that the class definition at the top of the file now includes a reference to the new `TerminateClick` method:

```
TForm1 = class(TForm)
  ListBox1: TListBox;
  Memo1: TMemo;
  Terminate: TButton;
```

```
    procedure TerminateClick(Sender: TObject);
  private
    { Private declarations }
  public
    { Public declarations }
  end;
```

Take a moment to consider the process described in the last paragraph. Initially, you were looking at a plain button on a form. You double-clicked that button, and then the code shown here was automatically pasted into your Editor.

It is now time for you to write a line of code. This is a very simple snippet of code that consists only of the word Close:

```
procedure TForm1.TerminateClick(Sender: TObject);
begin
  Close
end;
```

When this code is executed, it closes the main form. To test the code, run the program and click once on the Terminate button. If you have done everything correctly, the form will automatically close and you will be returned to design mode.

Before moving on to the next section, you might want to keep the Editor window open and move over to the Name field in the Object Inspector. Change the name of the button to something else, such as Ok. Press the Enter key once to set your changes in place. Look over at the Editor window, and you will see that the code you wrote has changed:

```
procedure TForm1.OkClick(Sender: TObject);
begin
  Close
end;
```

Notice that similar changes also transformed the class definition at the top of the file:

```
  TForm1 = class(TForm)
    ListBox1: TListBox;
    Memo1: TMemo;
    Ok: TButton;
    procedure OkClick(Sender: TObject);
  private
    { Private declarations }
  public
    { Public declarations }
  end;
```

Tutors

Delphi provides a number of interactive tutors, many of which are complementary to the material you will find in these training chapters. In the first version of Delphi, there are seven tutors available. If you have trouble loading the tutors, see "Configuring Delphi for Interactive Tutors" in the online help.

The first two tutors cover introductory material. The first tutor parallels much of the material discussed in this chapter. It shows you the important elements in the environment such as the Editor window and the Object Inspector. The second tutor covers the basics of creating a simple application and gives you a look at edit controls, listboxes, and buttons.

Besides these intial tutors, there are several other ones available when you click the large buttons shown on the left side of the main screen for the tutors. For instance, the bar that says "Creating a User Interface" is actually a button.

The remaining tutors are listed here:

- **EventHandlers:** A quick look at how to handle events, as well as an overview of saving a Delphi project.
- **The User Interface:** How to add components to a form, and how to arrange them. The tutor concludes with a section that gives you a set of lookup tables that describe 60 different components that ship with Delphi.
- **Setting Component Properties:** How to change a component's color either in code or via the Object Inspector. This tutor provides information on the Name and Caption properties, nested properties, and multiple component selection. It ends with a large lookup table that provides information on key properties.
- **Writing Event Handlers:** This tutor provides a more in-depth look at event handlers. Topics include the structure of a procedure header and techniques for handling default events.
- **Database Applications:** The first portion of this tutor takes a look at the TTable object, and the second portion covers TQuery objects and related SQL issues.

Workgroups

Delphi provides full support for integrated third-party version control systems. When properly installed, these systems appear on their own menu titled "Workgroup."

To get started, you need a copy of a major version control system, such as PVCS. In particular, you should copy the file called PVCSVMW.DLL into your DELPHI\BIN subdirectory. Next, open the DELPHI.INI file in a text editor and add the following lines to it:

```
[Version Control]
vcsmanager=c:\delphi\bin\stdvcs.dll
```

This line declares a new section in the INI file called Version Control. The only statement in this section specifies that the Version Control Manager (vcsmanager) is called STDVCS and is located in the DELPHI\BIN subdirectory. The file called STDVCS ships with Delphi and serves as a link between Delphi and third-party tools such as PVCSVMW.DLL. Any company that creates a file such as STDVCS can then link its own version control system into the Delphi environment. As a result, the system is completely configurable and extensible.

After you link in the Version Control system, you will be able to check files in and out. Furthermore, you can store these files in their own archives, so that you can have different archives for different projects that your team is working on.

PVCS is a separate product that does not ship with Delphi. It is, however, used widely throughout the computer industry. Because of its popularity, the developers of Delphi decided to ship an interface unit for this product with each version of Delphi. As stated earlier, you can use this unit, or you can create your own interface unit for any third-party or privately built version control system.

> **NOTE**
>
> People who want to create their own version control system interface should use something called the Tools API. This API is an advanced subject that is covered in Part V of this book, in the section called "Component Building." For now, I will say only that the actual Delphi interface unit for version control systems is called VCSINTF.DLL, and it is found with the other runtime library source code files.

Summary

This chapter gave you an overview of some of the most important aspects of the Delphi environment. You learned about forms, and about how to place components on them. You also saw how to explore those components with the Object Inspector, and how to start working with the Editor.

Remember that the Delphi environment is thoroughly documented in the online help. Nothing I can say here could possibly compete with the online help's capability to supply you with an interactive and easily accessible explanation of the IDE.

In the next chapter, you'll get a more technical discussion of certain key aspects of the IDE, and you'll see how these aspects relate to the overall topic of programming. You will also learn about ways to fine-tune the IDE. In a sense, the next chapter is really only a continuation of the things you have learned in this chapter, but you will explore them in more depth and from a more technical point of view.

The IDE

Overview

Now that you know your way around the basic features of the Delphi environment, it is time to learn how to take full control of the IDE in which you will work. The Delphi IDE is highly configurable, and you can take advantage of many options that will make the programming environment conform to your needs. In this chapter, you learn how to do the following:

- Add and remove forms and units from a project
- Manage the windows on the desktop
- Create separate executables for Intel systems that run Windows
- Familiarize yourself with important properties shown in the Object Inspector
- Fine-tune a project via the Options | Project menu choice
- Fine-tune the IDE via the Options | Environment menu choice

At the end of this chapter, I compare the new object model used in Delphi to an object model that was used in Turbo Pascal for Windows. This comparison is of interest to only a few readers, but for them it is an important general topic that deserves attention early in this book.

Overall, this chapter is slanted toward experienced programmers. There are many things that veterans need to know up front, before they try to start using the product. Therefore I discuss them here, at the cost of confusing the hardiest and most willing intermediate programmers.

In saying all this, I don't want to make the chapter sound too formidable. Much of it is simple introductory material that will help you get acquainted with the IDE.

A Delphi Project

All Delphi projects have at least five files associated with them. PROJECT1.DPR and UNIT1.PAS are source files that Delphi compiles into coded instructions. The other three files are related to project management and are usually not changed directly by the programmer. Following is a summary of the files:

- The main project file, which starts out being called PROJECT1.DPR.
- The primary unit file, which is where you start writing the code for your programs. It's called UNIT1.PAS by default, but I suggest that you change the name to MAIN.PAS.
- The options file, called PROJECT1.OPT by default, is a text file used to store the settings associated with your project. For instance, the compiler directives you select are stored in this file.
- The main form file, which is called UNIT1.DFM by default, is used to store information about the appearance of the main form.
- The desktop file, which is called PROJECT1.DSK by default, contains information about the state of the IDE.

Of the five files listed previously, you are responsible for naming and maintaining only the DPR file and the PAS file. The others will be cared for automatically by the system. In particular, you give the DPR and PAS filenames when you choose the File | Save Project menu item. As a rule, you don't edit the DPR file explicitly, although you can examine its source code by choosing View | Project Source from the main menu.

Another way to group the five files is by project and form: PROJECT1.DPR, PROJECT1.DSK, and PROJECT1.OPT control the project and the settings of the IDE. UNIT1.PAS and UNIT1.DFM define the main form and unit. Of course, all these default names are likely to change when you start working on a project. The project files take on the name you want to give to your program, and the form and unit files are often given names that help explain their contents.

The File Menu

When you want to save a project, click the File menu or press Alt+F to open it. The File menu is organized as follows:

> New Project
> Open Project
> Save Project
> Save Project As
> Close Project
> —
>
> New Form
> New Unit
> New Component
> Open File
> Save File
> Save File As
> Close File
> —
>
> Add File
> Remove File
> —
>
> Print
> —
>
> Exit
> —
>
> 1 PREV1.DPR
> 2 PREV2.DPR

As you can see, the File menu is divided into six main sections. Here is a description of those sections:

- The first section gives you control over the project as a whole.
- The second section gives you control over the forms, units, and components in a project.
- The third section lets you add files to or remove files from a project.
- The fourth section handles printing chores.
- The fifth section gives you a way of exiting the IDE.
- The sixth section, the history list, provides a handy list of recently used projects so that you can select one quickly.

As you'll see later in this chapter, most of the options in the File menu are also available in the Project Manager, which you can display from the View menu. Some of these options also appear on the speedbar. This strategy is typical of Delphi: It provides multiple ways for you to do the same tasks, so that you can decide which way is most efficient for your particular situation.

Each option in the File menu is explained in the online help. To reach this portion of the Help file, choose Help | Topic Search. When the Borland Search dialog box appears, type File menu and press Enter. Select File Menu from the topic listbox at the bottom of the dialog. You will see a help screen like the one in Figure 3.1.

FIGURE 3.1.

Delphi includes a help screen that explains how to use the File menu.

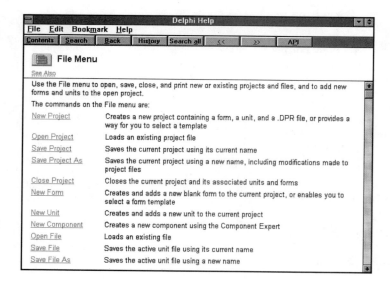

The portions of the help screen that appear in green text (for example, New Project, Open Project, and so on) are hypertext links to pages that explain these subjects in more detail. Click these links to reach a description of the option. You can return to the previous page by selecting the Back button at the top of the help window.

> **NOTE**
>
> Hypertext is a technique for jumping from one part of a document to another. For instance, you might encounter a technical term in a help document. If that word appears in bold green print, you can click it with the mouse and jump immediately to a place in the text that defines and explains it.

Most of the choices in the first section of the File menu should be fairly easy to understand. New Project starts with a new PROJECT1.DPR and a new UNIT1.PAS, Open Project opens an existing project, and so on.

From previous experience with Windows, you might expect the menu shortcut for opening a new project to be Alt+O. However, that isn't the case in Delphi. Instead, you open a new project in Delphi with the menu shortcut Alt+F+N. (In Delphi, Alt+F+O opens a new unit.) Other Delphi menu shortcuts you will want to know are Alt+F+R for opening an existing project, Alt+F+S for saving a file, and Alt+F+V for saving a project. Note that Alt+F+S saves just the current file instead of the entire project. To ensure that all your changes are saved, you should choose Save Project (Alt+F+V) regularly.

> **NOTE**
>
> There are various shortcut keystrokes that can be associated with some of the menu items. However, the particular shortcuts available to you will depend on your choices for the Options | Environment | Editor Display | KeyStroke Mapping menu choice. Note that tweaking this option will change the shortcut keystrokes displayed on the menus themselves. The Options | Environment menu item is discussed later in this chapter.

You can see that the first two choices in the second section let you create a new form or a new unit. If you choose New Form, you create a unit that contains Delphi visual controls. If you choose New Unit, you create a text file that contains nonvisual code, or code that creates visual elements by directly calling the Windows API. In short, the former creates a unit with a form associated with it, whereas the latter creates a unit with no form.

> **NOTE**
>
> When you choose New Form, the Gallery may appear. If it does, choose Blank Form. Throughout the majority of this book, if the Gallery appears when you choose New

Project, you should choose Blank Project. Whether the Gallery appears when you choose New Form or New Project depends on your setting for the Options | Environment | Preferences | Gallery menu choice. The Gallery is discussed later in this chapter.

An understanding of the differences between projects and units will help you better understand the differences between units and forms. A project file compiles to an EXE file that can be run stand-alone from the File Manager. A unit, on the other hand, compiles into a binary file with a DCU extension. A program can have only one EXE file, but it can be dependent on multiple DCU files.

If you have used C, BASIC, or assembler, you can draw a parallel between DCU files and OBJ files. The OBJ files that make up a project in C are similar to the DCU files that make up a project in Delphi. You can also draw a parallel between the TPU files associated with Pascal projects and the DCU files used in Delphi projects.

To sum up, every project has a main file with a DPR extension and possibly some supporting modules that have PAS extensions. The PAS files compile to DCU binary files. You can use the same DCU file in multiple executables. That is, you can store a set of handy routines in a unit and link that unit into multiple executables.

It is possible to imagine a Delphi program that at least appears to consist of essentially only one file. You see several such programs in this book, particularly programs that don't use objects, or that use the WINCRT unit. However, most programs aren't complete without some additional units, just as a computer isn't complete without a monitor or hard disk.

Here is what you get if you choose New Unit from the File menu:

```
unit Unit2;

interface

implementation

end.
```

Here is the code produced if you choose New Form:

```
unit Unit3;

interface

uses
  SysUtils, WinTypes, WinProcs,
  Messages, Classes, Graphics,
  Controls, Forms, Dialogs;

type
  TForm3 = class(TForm)
  private
    { Private declarations }
  public
```

```
    { Public declarations }
  end;

var
  Form3: TForm3;

implementation

{$R *.DFM}

end.
```

For now, it's important to understand the most fundamental distinctions between choosing the New Form and New Unit options. In particular, you should note that both options create a new unit, but one unit has a form associated with it. Because each form is encapsulated in an object, you'll also see a new class declaration in the unit associated with a form.

File | Open File opens any unit you want to study or reference in your program. If that unit has a form associated with it, the form will also be available after you open the unit. If the form isn't immediately visible, you can display it by selecting the upper-right member of the four navigational tools, which are shown in Figure 3.2, or by pressing F12.

FIGURE 3.2.

Use the navigational tools to select a form or unit associated with your current project.

When you create a new unit, Delphi gives it a default name. You can change that name to something more meaningful by choosing Save File As from the File menu. As I have already mentioned, I always name the first unit in a project MAIN and consider it to be an adjunct to the DPR file. I give additional units names that I find meaningful and hopefully self-explanatory.

The Save File option saves the file you are currently editing. It doesn't save the entire project. As a result, it is wise to choose Save Project on a regular basis, just to be sure that all the changes you have been making are preserved. The Close File option removes a file from the Editor window. I usually choose this option only when I want to clean up my workspace.

The File menu also contains an option called New Component. This starts an expert that helps you assemble your own components. To find out more about this feature, you should read Chapter 29, "Creating Components."

Before closing this section, I want to reiterate a key point: you should regularly choose File | Save Project! If you choose Save File exclusively during a long session, you are likely to eventually lose information.

Managing a Project

Now that you know the basics about using the File menu to create a project, the next step is to move on to the Project Manager, which enables you to get an overview of your project. The Project Manager, shown in Figure 3.3, is divided into two parts. The top part is the speedbar, which presents a list of icons. Beneath the speedbar is a list of the modules in your project. You can access the Project Manager from the View menu.

FIGURE 3.3.

Use the icons at the top of the Project Manager to add and delete the modules shown in the bottom part of the manager.

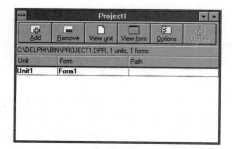

Use the plus and minus icons at the top of the Project Manager to add and remove files from a project. Making these changes affects the uses clause of your source files. In other words, if you add a file to a project, a reference to the new unit is included in your DPR file. (If you don't have experience with Pascal, don't worry about these references to the uses clause. That subject is covered in depth later in this document. For now, you need to know only that the uses clause lets you reference a routine in one unit while you are in another unit.)

Here is a brief list of the icons in the Project Manager:

- The plus and minus icons add or delete files from a project.
- The next two icons allow you to zoom in on the source or the form that is highlighted in the bottom part of the Project Manager.
- The next icon brings up the Project Options dialog box, which you can also bring up by choosing Options | Project. This dialog box will be explained in more depth later on.
- The Update button on the far right of the Project Manager is used if you manually change the source of your DPR file, and then need to force an update to your project so that it reflects your changes.

You can right-click the Project Manager to quickly access numerous features. As a rule, you should try right-clicking everything in the Delphi IDE, since there are many popup windows available that provide shortcuts for reaching various features. In particular, the Component Palette, Speedbar, and Forms Designer all support right clicks.

An Overview of Other Menu Options

You learned about the File menu earlier in this chapter. In this section, I discuss a number of other important options—from the Edit, Search, View, Compile, and Run menus—in rather general terms. After that, I narrow the focus again so you can get a good look at the Options menu, which has a number of powerful and subtle features.

The Edit Menu

The Edit menu has Undo and Redo features, which can be very useful when you make mistakes in the Editor window. Don't forget about these features. Sometimes you can mistakenly erase or change several days worth of work. In such cases, all is not lost. I have often stepped back through the last 20 or more changes that I have made in the Editor. For instance, there have been times when I have tried to improve an algorithm, only to find that I broke it entirely. With the Undo feature, it's easy to undo several hours worth of work by repeatedly pressing Alt+Backspace or Ctrl + Z, depending on your key mapping.

> **NOTE**
>
> If you have selected the default key mapping from the Options | Environment | Editor Display page, you should choose Ctrl+Z as a shortcut for undo. I am a long-term Turbo Pascal and Turbo C user, so I chose the classic key mapping, which uses Alt+Backspace as the shortcut. The actual menu items in Delphi always stay the same, but the shortcuts you use for accessing these items vary depending on your key mapping. For more information, look up File Menu in the online help and then choose "File Commands Keyboard Shortcuts" from the bottom of the Search dialog. When you are done, you should open up the Bible and read the section on the Tower of Babel!

The online help explains how you can use the Options | Environment dialog to tweak the undo feature. The ability to limit the number of possible Undo operations might be useful if you are working with very limited hardware resources, but normally you would leave this number as high as possible, because you never know when you might want to undo several hours worth of work. However, you should note that the Undo buffer is now cleared every time Delphi generates code. Shades of Joseph Heller's *Catch 22*!

The Cut, Copy, Paste, and Delete options from the Edit menu are common to nearly all Windows applications, and the Bring To Front, Send To Back, Align, and Size options have already been discussed. The latter four options help you quickly "prettify" the appearance of components placed on a form.

The Align, Size, and Tab Order options help define the way your controls appear on the screen. You can use the Lock Controls option to prevent from accidentally moving the controls you have placed on a form. The Scale and Creation Order menu items are advanced options you can read about in the online help. To find help on a menu item, select it and then press F1.

The Search Menu

The Search menu has a Find Error option that helps you track down errors that occur at runtime. For instance, if you accidentally overwrite the bounds of an array, a dialog box appears specifying the address in your program where the error occurred. You can then choose Search | Find Error and enter the address supplied by the system at runtime. If possible, the IDE takes you to the place in your code where the error occurred.

At the bottom of the Search menu is an option to browse a particular symbol from your program. Delphi comes with a very sophisticated browser that lets you see the structure of your program. It lets you see your code from several different perspectives. For instance, you can browse through a visual representation of the objects in your code, or you can view your program symbolically on a unit-by-unit basis.

The View Menu

You can also access the browser via the View menu, which is located next to the Search menu. Other important parts of the View menu include the following:

- The Project Manager.
- An option to hide or show the Object Inspector.
- An option to hide or show the Alignment Palette, which duplicates and enhances some of the options from the Align option in the Edit menu.
- The Watch, Breakpoint, and Call Stack options, which are all related to the debugger and are discussed later in this chapter.
- The browser, which is discussed later in more depth.
- The Component List, which provides an alternative to the Component Palette. You might use the Component List instead of the Component Palette if you don't want to use the mouse or if you want to search for a component by name, rather than by flipping through the pages of the Component Palette.
- The Window List, which provides a list of all the windows open in Delphi.
- The New Edit Window option, which provides a means of opening up an additional Editor window. This might be useful in several different situations, such as when you want to view two versions of the same file or two different locations in the same file.

■ The Speedbar and Component Palette options, which let you show or hide these tools. These options are useful when you are concentrating entirely on the code in an Editor window and don't want to bother with anything else that might clutter up the screen.

The Compile Menu

You use the Compile menu to compile or build a project. The old DOS, Windows C++, and Pascal IDEs had an option in the Run menu called Make, which rebuilt any units you changed since the last Make, but it didn't rebuild units that hadn't changed. This option has been incorporated into the Run and Compile menus. If you select this option, whenever you recompile your program, Delphi checks to make sure all the units in your project are up to date. The Build option, on the other hand, recompiles every unit in your program for which source code is available. A third option, called Syntax Check, ensures that you have written valid code that can be compiled, but it won't actually recompile the DCU associated with any of your files. Use Syntax Check if you want to make a quick scan of the syntax in the work you have been doing. At the very bottom of the menu is an option called Information, which you can use to check on the status of your application, the size of your Code, Data, and Stack segments, the size of the local heap, and the number of lines processed in the last compile.

The Run Menu

You can use the Run menu to compile and run your program and to specify any parameters you want passed to your program on the command line. Options for debugging your program are also listed in this menu.

The Options Menu

The Options Menu is the most complex part of the menu system. It is the control center from which you can configure the options for your project and for the entire IDE. There are seven menu items in the Options menu:

Project
Environment
Tools
Gallery

—

Open Library
Install Components
Rebuild Library

The first four menu items all lead to dialog boxes. Except for the Tools menu, each of these dialog boxes are large, multipaged dialog boxes of considerable complexity. Following is a general overview of the Options menu:

- The Project menu item lets you select options that directly affect your current project, such as compiler directives. For instance, this is where you turn on range checking or stack checking.

- The Environment menu item lets you change settings that configure the entire IDE. For instance, if you want to change the colors used in the Editor or if you want to define the way a particular keystroke works inside the IDE, you should select this option.

- The Tools menu item lets you add or delete selections from the Tools popup menu. If you have an editor or a debugging tool that you use frequently, you can use Options | Tools to add it to the Tools popup menu. In this way, the functionality of the entire IDE can be extended.

- The Gallery menu item lets you define specific options for Form Experts and templates and for Project Experts and templates. The Experts and templates provide ways to speed up or automate construction of the visual elements of a program. (This subject is discussed in the Chapter 19, "Creating Simple Database Programs.")

- The final three choices in the Options menu let you configure the Components Palette.

The Options | Project dialog box has five pages associated with it:

- The Forms page lists the forms in your project and lets you decide if Delphi should create them automatically or if you will create them yourself in one of your units.

- The Application page lets you define elements of your project such as its title, help file, and icon.

- The Compiler page includes choices about code generation, runtime error handling, syntax, numeric processing, and debugging.

- The Linker page defines map file options, buffering during the link stage, debugging for the stand-alone debugger, and the size of your stack and heap. There is also a selection on this page that enables you to optimize for size and load time. When I select this option, I generally cut about 10 percent off the size of my excutables. Code optimizers have been a source of bugs on many other compilers. However, Delphi's optimizer first appeared so late in the product's beta cycle that I don't want to venture an opinion as to its reliability; though so far I have not heard of any bugs associated with it.

■ The Directories/Conditionals page lets you specify conditional defines and paths that are specific to a particular project.

After the following paragraph of general information, each page is described in detail in its own section.

You can manually tweak everything you see in the pages mentioned here via the OPT file or by changing the actual source files in your application. In other words, the options shown on these pages are placed there for convenience, not because they are the sole means of setting the options. For instance, when you create a project called MYEXE.DPR, the compiler automatically generates an OPTions file called MYEXE.OPT. Every entry in MYEXE.OPT corresponds to one of the entries in the pages shown earlier. This idea is discussed in more detail in the section titled "Compiler Page."

FIGURE 3.4.

The Application page helps you define the main unit, title, icons, and help files for your project.

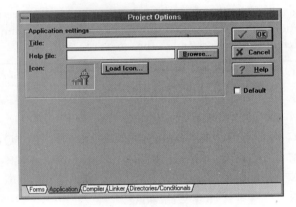

Application Page

The Application page, shown in Figure 3.4, lets you choose a title, help file, and icon for your application.

Compiler Page

I mentioned earlier that there is a correspondence between the information in the Options | Project dialog box and the information stored in the OPT file that is associated with every Delphi project. To understand this principle, take a moment to consider the directives shown on the Compiler page in Figure 3.5.

FIGURE 3.5.

The Compiler page from the Options | Project menu choice.

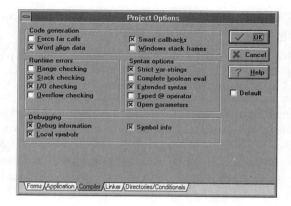

The following table shows how the various compiler directives are listed in the OPT files, the Options | Project menu, and inside the code of a program. Each row in the table shows three different ways to accomplish the same task:

OPT File	Options Page	Editor Symbol
F	Force far calls	{$F+}
A	Word align data	{$A+}
G	286 instructions	{$G+}
K	Smart callbacks	{$K+}
W	Windows (3.0) stack frames	{$W+}
R	Range checking	{$R+}
S	Stack checking	{$S+}
I	I/O checking	{$I+}
Q	Overflow checking	{$Q+}
V	Strict var-strings	{$V+}
B	Complete boolean eval	{$B+}
X	Extended syntax	{$X+}
T	Typed @ operator	{$T+}
P	Open parameters	{$P+}
D	Debug information	{$D+}
L	Local symbols	{$L+}
Y	Symbol info	{$Y+}
N	Numeric processing	{$N+}

To turn on an option in the OPT file, set its value equal to 1, as follows:

```
A=1
```

This is equivalent to checking an option in the Compiler page and to inserting {$A+} in your code. To turn an option off in the OPT file, set it equal to 0:

```
A=0
```

This is equivalent to unchecking an option in the Compiler page and to inserting {$A-} in your code.

Most programmers will probably want to control these settings from the Compiler page. However, Delphi offers the ability to take other approaches if you prefer. Remember that any options you specify in your code will take precedence over the options you specify in the OPT file or in the Compiler page.

Linker Page

The Linker page of the Options | Project menu is shown in Figure 3.6.

FIGURE 3.6.

The Linker page from the Options | Project menu choice.

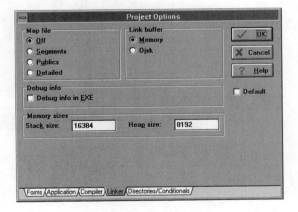

I'm going to skip the references to the map file and debug information because they belong in a discussion of the debugger. The Link buffer file option lets you choose whether the linker's buffer is in memory or on disk. If it is in memory, it will be faster, but it might, in a few isolated cases, cause a memory crunch during compilation.

The Stack size and Heap size options are much more important. Here is how they look in the OPT file:

```
[Linker]
...
StackSize= 16384
HeapSize=8192
```

As shown here, Delphi sets a program's default stack and local heap size to 8192 bytes each. You might want to change StackSize in some of your programs, but it is usually not appropriate to set it to a figure larger than 32,768. If the two figures add up to more than 65,536, an error will result and you won't be able to compile your program.

Directories/Conditionals Page

The Directories/Conditionals page, shown in Figure 3.7, lets you extend the number of directories where the compiler and linker search for DCU files.

FIGURE 3.7.

The Directories/Conditionals page from the Options | Project menu choice.

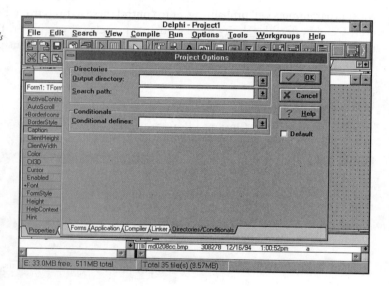

The DELPHI.INI file contains another such list of directories. Remember that the OPT file lists options specific to a particular project, but the listing in DELPHI.INI applies to any project you create.

You can add directories to the list in the Directories/Conditionals page by typing in directory names you want associated only with this project. For instance, suppose you had a special set of routines for handling the serial port. Suppose further that you stored these routines in a particular directory. In such a case, you might list its path here, because it is likely to be of use only to one or two programs and would be irrelevant to most projects you build. If you wanted all your projects to access this DCU, you should list its path in the dialog Options | Install Components displays.

The Output directory option lets you specify where you want the compiler to place the DCU and EXE files you are creating. There is no way to tell the compiler to place DCUs in one directory and EXE files in another. I should mention that most programmers leave the Output directory option blank, which means that the output from the compiler simply ends up in the current directory with your source files.

The Conditional defines option is pretty much self-explanatory to experienced programmers, and beginning programmers aren't going to be interested in this subject, so I'm going to pass over it without any further discussion. If you want more information on this subject, refer to the online help.

Forms Page

The Forms page, shown in Figure 3.8, lets you choose the main form for your project. The changes you make here are reflected in the DPR file associated with a particular project. For instance, in the following project file, Form1 is designated as the main form of the project because it is referenced first in the main block of the program:

```
program Project1;

uses
  Forms,
  Unit1 in 'UNIT1.PAS' {Form1},
  Unit2 in 'UNIT2.PAS' {Form2};

{$R *.RES}

begin
  Application.CreateForm(TForm1, Form1);
  Application.CreateForm(TForm2, Form2);
  Application.Run;
end.
```

If you changed the code so that it read

```
begin
  Application.CreateForm(TForm2, Form2);
  Application.CreateForm(TForm1, Form1);
  Application.Run;
end.
```

then Form2 would be the main form of the project. The Application page of the Options | Project menu gives you a second way to control this same piece of code.

You can also use this page to decide which forms will be auto-created at startup. You have the choice of automatically allocating memory for a form at startup, as shown earlier, or waiting to call Create until the time when you actually need the form. If you choose the latter method, you will put yourself to additional trouble, but you will use memory more efficiently. Call CreateForm in the DPR file, but call Create when you are in one of the units of your project.

FIGURE 3.8.

The Forms page from the Options | Project menu choice.

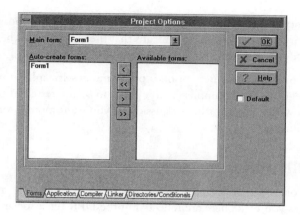

Configuring the IDE

The Options | Environment menu choice presents you with a dizzying array of pages and controls that let you tweak how the IDE appears and functions. Delphi lets you change the environment in five major ways:

- You can decide which portions of your project Delphi will save automatically.
- You can change the colors used in the IDE.
- You can turn syntax highlighting on and off.
- You can decide what appears on the Component Palette.
- You can have some fairly extensive control over the keystrokes used inside the IDE.

The first page accessed from the Options | Environment menu choice is shown in Figure 3.9.

FIGURE 3.9.

The Preferences dialog box is accessed from the Options menu.

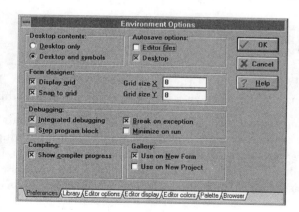

The Preferences dialog box is important primarily because it lets you specify whether you want the IDE to automatically save the changes to your code and to the environment.

Beneath that are some settings for the Form designer's grid. Most users want to have integrated debugging turned on, and many users like to have the Compiler Progress dialog box shown whenever they compile, though it does slow things down a bit.

The Editor Options, Editor Display, and Editor Colors pages let you change the default colors and keystrokes used in the IDE. The Editor Display page is shown in Figure 3.10, and the Editor Colors page is shown in Figure 3.11.

FIGURE 3.10.

The Editor Display page from the Options menu.

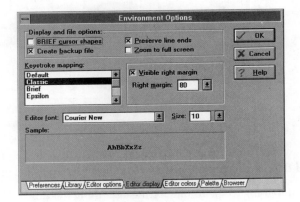

There are several ways you can customize the keymapping used by the Editor. For instance, many Borland users are accustomed to having the F5 key maximize the Editor window. The Classic keymapping supports that keystroke, but other keymappings don't. Other people might be used to pressing F3 to repeat a search for text, which the Default keymapping supports. There are four keymappings to choose from:

- The Default keymapping uses the choices that Microsoft encourages all programmers to use. If you are new to Windows, or if you are already familiar with these keymappings, the Default keymapping might be a good choice.

- The Classic keymapping is the one that should be most familiar to veteran Borland C++ and Borland Pascal users. It supports many of the old WordStar key combinations, and it steps you through the debugger in the familiar way. This is the keymapping I use, perhaps for no better reason than that I have become accustomed to it.

- The other two choices imitate the Epsilon and BRIEF editors. If you are familiar with those editors, you will probably find these options appealing.

You can find the precise definition of the keystrokes for any keymapping by searching on the words "key mapping" in Help | Topic Search.

If you want to customize the colors in the IDE, you should choose the Editor Colors page, shown in Figure 3.11.

FIGURE 3.11.

The Editor Colors page enables you to change the look of the syntax highlighting in the Editor window.

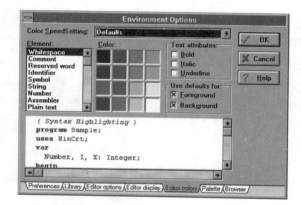

To switch from one page to another, use the mouse or press Ctrl+Tab. Most programmers find that latter keystroke handy to know about, especially near the end of a long day.

I'm not going to spend much time describing the Editor Option page, shown in Figure 3.12. However, it's worth mentioning that you can specify exactly how you want to handle tabs by tweaking the controls on this page. The online help describes all these feateures in considerable detail. To find explanations on how a particular setting in the IDE works, select the relevant page or option and press F1. The online help automatically pops up and takes you to a description of the option you selected.

FIGURE 3.12.

The Editor Options page enables you to configure some detailed aspects of the way the Editor works.

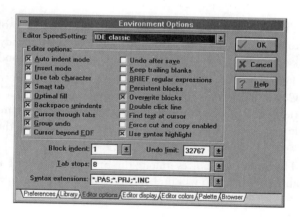

The Options | Environment dialog also contains pages for configuring the Browser and the Component Palette. Alternatively, you can configure these tools by right-clicking them while you are working in them. Notice that you can get the Browser to qualify all the variables it lists. If you want to collapse the long listing of Exceptions that you find in the Browser, simply type in the word Exception in the Collapse Nodes combo box from the Browser page of the Options | Environment dialog.

The only other point I want to make about tweaking the environment is to reiterate that all these options are recorded not only in the IDE, but also in the DELPHI.INI file in the Windows directory. You should be sure that there is only one such file on your hard disk, and it should be located in the Windows directory. If you have more than one copy on disk, changes made to DELPHI.INI might appear to have no effect, because the IDE might be reading another copy of the file instead of the one you're editing.

VCL and OWL

This section is aimed only at people who come to Delphi directly from the world of Turbo Pascal for Windows. Others will want to skip this section.

Veteran Pascal programmers are bound to be confused by the fact that there are now two different object models available to programmers. One is called the old object model, and it was the basis on which OWL was built. The other is called the new object model, and it gives the VCL its syntax.

For all intents and purposes, the old object model is a subset of the new object model. In other words, everything you could do in the old object model you can still do in the new model, but there are many things the new model can do that the old model could not.

Here is a very simple old style object:

```
PMyObject = ^TMyObject;
TMyObject = Object(TObject)
  Data: Integer;
  procedure Show;
end;
```

Here is a very simple new style object:

```
TMyClass = class(TObject)
  Data: Integer;
  procedure Show;
end;
```

I show you this code not because I want to teach you any specific syntax. That will come later. The point right now is simply to give you an example of each model so that you will recognize it when you see it.

The question, of course, is why is there a new object model? There are several different answers to that question:

- The first reason for creating a new object model was that it was time for Pascal to make the transition to 32-bit code. The future of programming, and computing in general, lies not with the old 16-bit environments such as DOS 6.*x* and Windows 3.*x*, but with Windows 95, Windows NT, OS/2, UNIX, and perhaps with one of the new operating systems aimed at the PowerPC. The old object model was tied in to a 16-bit operating system, and to prepare it for a 32-bit system meant that old OWL code was going to be broken. The developers decided that if they were going to have to break some code, they might as well do all they could to make the whole object model as powerful as possible.

- The second reason for creating a new object model was to prepare the way for a visual programming environment. In particular, the language needed to support the properties that show up in the Object Inspector, and it needed to provide a syntax that would make it possible to add and remove objects from the Component Palette.

- A third reason for the existence of the new object model is that Delphi is a fully object-oriented programming environment. In other words, even the simplest Pascal programs are now object-oriented. This meant that it was essential that the object model be readily comprehensible even to neophytes. For instance, in Chapter 5, I explore Pascal programming. The very first examples I produce are fully object-oriented. The old object model was simply too complex for beginning programmers. The new object model, when used in conjunction with the visual programming tools in the IDE, is simple enough to be used even by first-time programmers.

The old object model was heavily dependent upon pointers. The new object model also makes very heavy use of pointers, but this fact is concealed from the user. The desire to conceal pointers stems from two factors, as follows:

- First, the new object model is meant to be accessible to beginners, and pointers are a distinctly advanced programming feature.

- Also, under the old object model, nearly every object that programmers created was immediately pushed up on to the heap. In short, as far as Pascal programmers were concerned, all objects were accessed through pointers, and the few exceptions to this rule were so infrequent that they appeared as confusing anomalies. If virtually all objects needed to be created on the heap, then why not just push them all up there by default, and let the user ignore the fact by supplying a simple syntax for referencing objects? That, at any rate, is the choice the developers made, and it represents one of the key benefits of the new object model.

It might be helpful at this stage to give another concrete example. Given the declarations introduced earlier, users of old style objects would write code that looks like this:

```
var
  MyObject: PMyObject;
begin
  MyObject := New(PMyObject, Init);
  MyObject^.Show;
  Dispose(MyObject, Done);
end;
```

To push an old style object up on the heap, programmers called New, and to delete it from the heap, they called Dispose. To access one of the methods of an old style object, it was necessary to dereference the pointer with the caret symbol (^).

To do the same thing with the new object model, you would write code that looks like this:

```
var
  MyClass: TMyClass;
begin
  MyClass := TMyClass.Create;
  MyClass.Show;
  MyClass.Free;
end;
```

There are obvious parallels between the two object models, but clearly there is no need to call New or Dispose, nor is there any need to dereference an object with the caret symbol. However, the MyClass variable shown here actually is a pointer, and the object exists on the heap. In fact, it is totally legitimate to see if MyClass is equal to nil:

```
if MyClass <> nil then
  MyClass.Destroy;
```

This last example is not only legitimate but is in fact lifted nearly directly from the Free procedure in the Run Time Library (RTL).

> **NOTE**
>
> Nowhere in this section have I stated that the old object model is being replaced because it was ill-conceived. The old object model was indeed very serviceable, and it had an elegance and clarity that was lacking from many other object-oriented languages. Furthermore, the new version of Delphi fully supports the old object model, as long as you don't mix the old and new models inside a single unit, and as long as you include the VER70 conditional define at the top of any unit that includes old object model code. For the sake of clarity, I should perhaps state this a second time in a slightly different manner: Delphi enables you to include both the new and old object models in a single executable, but not inside a single unit.

Finally, I want to add that none of the changes to the syntax of the new object model affect the way you treat normal pointers. In other words, if you create a pointer to an array, or a variable of type pointer, you need to call New and Dispose, and you need to dereference it with the caret symbol. Only objects that are part of the new object model don't need to be dereferenced.

Summary

In this chapter you learned about Delphi projects and about the ways you can use the IDE to control them. Three topics in particular were emphasized:

- Starting, saving, and modifying projects using the File menu
- Tweaking the features of a project using the Options | Project menu
- Customizing the IDE using the Options | Environment menu

By now you should start to have a feel for the way Delphi works and for how you will be interacting with the IDE. Of course, it will take time before all this seems natural to you; but after reading this chapter you should find that you have developed a general understanding of the basic tools in the Delphi environment.

One final point that I want to make is that Delphi is a tool with an incredible number of complex features. No one can master the whole compiler in just a few days. You should not worry if you understand only some of its features when you first start working with it. The other options will become clear as you grow with the product.

The Structure of a Delphi Program

Overview

To fully understand and take advantage of Delphi, you need to develop a familiarity with the ObjectPascal language. The visual portion of Delphi is extremely powerful, but the real key to your success as a programmer depends on how well you understand coding techniques.

To help acquaint you with Delphi's language, this chapter discusses seven major topics:

- Creating and using procedures
- Creating and using procedures with a visual tool
- Identifying the parts and names of the code in a typical Delphi program
- Recognizing and using the basic components of an object-oriented language
- Using multiple forms within a single program
- Allocating and deallocating memory for forms at runtime
- Using the WinCRT unit to emulate simple DOS programs

As I discuss these topics, I'll be showing you four very simple example programs. As a side benefit, the code you'll be seeing demonstrates techniques for using several important Windows controls. For some readers, certain portions of this chapter will be old hat, but many portions contain information unique to the Delphi environment.

A Fundamental Building Block: Procedures

In cases like this, it's probably best to start at the beginning, which means taking a close look at *procedures*. For now, you can think of a procedure as a block of code designed to accomplish a single task. For instance, if you want to write your name to the screen, prompt the user for a number, or read some values from a file, you probably want to encapsulate that process within a single procedure or group of procedures.

Procedures serve the same function in programming that paragraphs do in writing. They break up long bodies of code into manageable chunks that can be easily grasped. Just as paragraphs are broken up into sentences, so are procedures broken up into *statements*. For now, you can think of a statement as any block of code that contains a single semicolon. The semicolon always appears at the end of a statement, just as a period ends a sentence. Furthermore, most statements are only one line long. Statements are discussed in greater depth during the first part of Chapter 8, "Branching and Integers."

Enough theory. Let's take a look at an actual procedure:

```
procedure Button1OnClick;
begin
  Edit1.Text := 'No matter, never mind!';
end;
```

This procedure, called `Button1OnClick`, displays an appealing, but nevertheless extreme philosophical position in an edit control, as shown in Figure 4.1.

FIGURE 4.1.

A simple program that displays a single line of text in an edit control.

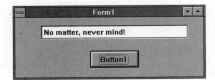

Most of the time, the basic framework of a procedure is created automatically by the compiler. It is only necessary for you to fill in a few lines of code to form the body of the procedure. Nonetheless, it is vitally important that you understand the basic structure of a procedure. If you don't understand the fundamental elements of Delphi's language, you will never be able to use it correctly.

The procedure depicted previously has two parts. The first is the *header*:

```
procedure Button1OnClick;
```

The second is the body:

```
begin
  Edit1.Text := 'No matter, never mind.';
end;
```

In turn, you can see that the header itself is broken up into three parts. The first and last parts are pure syntax. They consist of the word `procedure` and the trailing semicolon that rounds off the line of code. In between, you find the procedure's name, which should be as descriptive as possible. In this case, the name `Button1OnClick` tells you that this procedure is executed when someone clicks the mouse on button number one.

> **NOTE**
>
> It's important to give sensible names to the procedures, types, and variables in your programs. Every procedure you create should do only one thing, and the name you give it should describe that one thing as clearly as possible. Many good names for procedures contain a verb and a noun. For instance, `GetFirstName`, `LoadFile`, `OpenFile`, `PostError`, and `ExitProgram` are all good names for procedures.

The body of a procedure is always encapsulated within a `begin..end` pair. This syntax forms the bookends around a code block. From a purely technical point of view, these two symbols exist primarily to tell the compiler where a block of code begins and ends. As a result, it is very important that every `begin` statement be matched up with an `end` statement. If these symbols are not paired off in a logical fashion, the compiler races off searching for the next pair, and the certain result is an error of one kind or another. For instance, you don't want to write code that looks like this:

```
begin
begin
  Edit1.Text := 'No matter, never mind.';
end;
```

or like this:

```
begin
  Edit1.Text := 'No matter, never mind.';
end;
end;
```

It may seem unlikely that you would ever make mistakes like these, but if your procedures grow long, it is easy to make these errors.

The only line of code from the `Button1OnClick` procedure that hasn't been discussed is the simple statement that uses the assignment operator `:=` to assign a string to the edit control:

```
Edit1.Text := 'No matter, never mind.';
```

For now, all you need to know is that this line of code causes four words to be shown in an edit control. These four words are set off by single quotes, and together they form a syntactical element called a *string*. You will hear more about strings and the *assignment operator*, `:=`, in the next few chapters.

Take a few moments to review the key points discussed in this section of the chapter:

- A procedure is made up of two parts. The first part is called the header, and the second part is called the body.
- A header begins with the word `procedure`, followed by the name of the procedure, and finally the whole line is rounded off with a semicolon.
- The body of a procedure is always encapsulated within a `begin..end` pair. Furthermore, the final `end` statement has a semicolon after it. Between the `begin..end` pair, you usually find a series of statements. As a rule, statements end with a semicolon.

The last few paragraphs have plunged unremittingly into the depths of various syntactical issues. It's territory that this book will visit again in many different guises. But for now, you can breath a sigh of relief, for the next section temporarily abandons technical issues in favor of some simple visual programming techniques.

NOTE

Object Pascal is not a case-sensitive language. In other words, the compiler does not care whether you write `EDIT1.TEXT` or `Edit1.Text`. For that matter, it won't bat an eyelash if you write `eDiT1.tEXt`. The compiler just doesn't care about capitalization. People, however, do care. As a result, Borland has established a set form for capitalization, and I try to follow it with only one or two minor variations. You need not conform to this style if it doesn't please you, but it certainly won't do you any harm to follow suit.

Creating Procedures with Visual Tools

Earlier, you saw that the syntactical framework of a procedure can be created with the help of visual tools. It's now time to create CONTROL1, a program that will help you learn more about the specific techniques involved in creating this framework.

To create CONTROL1, use the mouse to place a TEdit component on a form. When you're done, your form should look like the one shown in Figure 4.2.

FIGURE 4.2.

The form for the CONTROL1 program.

Now go to the Object Inspector, select the Events page, and double-click the OnDblClick entry, as shown in Figure 4.3. In the blink of an eye, a code window is displayed, and the basic framework of a procedure is pasted inside it. The result looks something like the window shown in Figure 4.4.

FIGURE 4.3.

To create a procedure, simply double-click the space to the right of the words OnDblClick.

When creating a procedure as previously described, you can either tell Delphi to create a default name, or you can type in your own procedure name. For now, you'll probably want to have Delphi create the default name for you. To do this, double-click the property editor to the right of the title in the Events page. If you prefer to use a different name, just type in the name you want and press Enter.

FIGURE 4.4.

After you double-click an edit control, a procedure is automatically pasted into an Editor window.

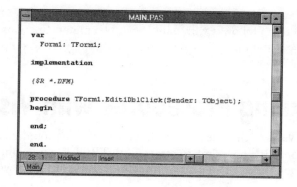

Now edit the body of the procedure so it looks like this:

```
procedure TForm1.Edit1DblClick(Sender: TObject);
begin
  Edit1.Text := 'You clicked on the edit control';
end;
```

Take a moment to save the program. You should call the project CONTROL1, and the main source file MAIN. Now, run the program. Notice that when you double-click the edit control, the text inside it changes, as shown in Figure 4.5.

FIGURE 4.5.

The edit control in program CONTROL1 changes when you double-click it.

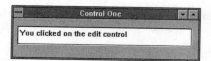

Listings 4.1 and Listing 4.2 show the complete code for the CONTROL1 program. (If you're having trouble creating this program, you can use the copy of the code that's on your program disk.) An explanation of this code is provided in the next section of this chapter.

Listing 4.1. The CONTROL1 program shows you how to create and use a Delphi procedure.

```
program Control1;

uses
  Forms,
  Main in 'MAIN.PAS' {Form1};

begin
  Application.CreateForm(TForm1, Form1);
  Application.Run;
end.
```

Listing 4.2. The unit that contains the main body of code for the CONTROL1 program.

```
unit Main;

{ Program copyright (c) 1994 by Charles Calvert }
{ Project Name: CONTROL1 }

interface

uses
  WinTypes, WinProcs,
  Classes, Graphics, Controls,
  Printers, Menus, Forms, StdCtrls;

type
  TForm1 = class(TForm)
    Edit1: TEdit;
    procedure Edit1DblClick(Sender: TObject);
  end;

var
  Form1: TForm1;

implementation

{$R *.DFM}

procedure TForm1.Edit1DblClick(Sender: TObject);
begin
  Edit1.Text := 'You clicked on the edit control';
end;

end.
```

You can see in the listings that there are two main source files used in the CONTROL1 program. The first file is called CONTROL1.DPR, and the second file is called MAIN.PAS. An in-depth explanation of both modules will be presented in the next section. However, I'll say a few words about them here, so that you can start thinking about some of the fundamental concepts they use.

When your program is loaded into memory, the two lines of code in CONTROL1.DPR are called first. These lines of code are generated automatically by the compiler and are surrounded by a begin..end pair:

```
begin
  Application.CreateForm(TForm1, Form1);
  Application.Run;
end.
```

This code's job is to first allocate memory for the main form:

```
Application.CreateForm(TForm1, Form1);
```

Then, it gets the form up on the screen and responds to events that occur inside it. It does the latter task with a single command:

```
 Application.Run;
```

This instruction tells the predeclared object called `Application` to begin processing the events that occur during the run of a program. For now, you don't need to know what class `Application` is all about, or what specific role it plays in your program. All you need to know is that the `Application` object has the intelligence needed to handle the program flow at runtime.

As a rule, the project files Delphi builds for you remain almost identical for all programs in this book. Project files usually do little more than launch the main form and quickly fade into the background. As a result, I generally won't show you the project file for a program.

You've just learned a little about the structure of a Pascal program. You also learned how to create a procedure using visual programming tools. In particular, you learned how to create a procedure that responds to a double-click on a particular control. The steps involved were simple:

- Place a control on a form.
- Select its `DblClick` method from the Events page on the Object Inspector. You can either type in the name of the procedure you want to create and press Enter, or double-click the proper entry to have Delphi create a default name. In either case, the result is a procedure listed in the Editor window.

When you've created the procedure, you can fill in its body with code of your own design. The next section, which describes MAIN.PAS, continues to unravel some of the mysteries of visual programming.

The Main Parts of the CONTROL1 Program

Even though there's a lot of code in the CONTROL1 program, it's important to remember that Delphi generated most of it automatically. The programmer had to type in only one line:

```
 Edit1.Text := 'You clicked on the edit control';
```

Despite the ease with which it was created, CONTROL1 still has a fairly complicated underlying structure. You'll be creating many programs that have the same basic composition, so it's important for you to understand how it's put together. That's why I'm going discuss the main parts of the source code before I move on to discuss the procedure you just created.

You saw in the last section that CONTROL1 is divided into two parts. The first part is a project file called CONTROL1.DPR, and the second part is a unit called MAIN.PAS.

Units never stand alone. They can't be executed by themselves, but must first be linked into an executable. In this case, unit MAIN happens to be part of a larger program called CONTROL1. CONTROL1.DPR depends on unit MAIN. It's not complete without it. You can tell which units a module depends on by checking its uses clause (the clause beginning with the word uses). Once again, here is the complete source code for CONTROL1.DPR:

```
program Control1;

uses
  Forms,
  Main in 'MAIN.PAS' {Form1};

begin
  Application.CreateForm(TForm1, Form1);
  Application.Run;
end.
```

CONTROL1.DPR lists unit MAIN in its uses clause. As a result, CONTROL1.DPR is said to *depend* on MAIN.PAS. Notice that the word Form1 appears in a comment (indicated by curly braces) after the word Main. This is a reminder from the compiler to the programmer to help him or her remember that Form1 is associated with MAIN.PAS. In other words, the code for the visual component called Form1 is kept inside MAIN.PAS. The use of the word in as part of a uses clause makes it clear to the compiler which module contains the unit called MAIN. Furthermore, it states that Main is part of the project called Control1, while Forms is merely listed in its uses clause. Units that are part of a project are listed in the Project Manager, which as you recall, is accessible from the top of the View menu.

When you create a project file, you must always put the word program at the top of it (or allow the compiler to place it there for you):

```
program Control1;
```

Likewise, when you create a unit, you must always place the word unit at the top (or allow the compiler to place it there for you):

```
unit Main;
```

There is no functional difference between a unit that Delphi generates automatically and a unit you create in a text editor: Both units function in exactly the same way. Code that's generated by the compiler doesn't have anything special or magical about it; it's just created differently (and more quickly and conveniently) than code you create in an editor.

Notice that MAIN.PAS is divided into three sections:

- Title
- Interface
- Implementation

If you stripped out all the other code and left only these main sections, the module would look like this:

```
unit Main;

interface

implementation

end.
```

This code, which represents a unit in its simplest possible form, compiles without error. It won't, however, do anything useful. To make a unit functional, you need to add more code. What you see above is just the skeleton—the bare bones—of a unit.

Here is one way to think about the difference between the interface and the implementation. An interface is the visible portion of a unit. It is the unit's *face*, as in *interface*. When any other part of the program looks at a unit, all it sees is this visible portion, the unit's face. Everything else is hidden, internal to the unit, part of the implementation. These hidden parts tend to contain the actual "brains" of a unit. That is, the implementation is where you write code that performs actions. Thus, the external interface, like the human face, is visible to others; the internal implementation, like the human brain, is hidden from others.

Therefore, a unit is divided into two sections. One is the outward appearance, or face; the other is the internal engine, or brain. The first section is called the interface, and the second the implementation. The interface is public, and can contain only declarations; the implementation is private, and can contain both declarations and code.

It is also possible to add a section beginning with the word `initialization`, which appears right before the word `end` in the previous example. `Initialization` sections can be used to initialize global variables to a particular value. In Turbo Pascal, all `initialization` sections were marked off by a simple `begin..end` pair, but that syntax has now been changed to more explicitly mark the significance of the section. As a rule, `initialization` sections should be left empty in programs written by beginning or intermediate programmers. The problem is not that `initialization` sections are complex, but that they represent an unnecessary temptation. In particular, you might be tempted to declare a large group of global variables and initialize them all at the bottom of your units. This is a dangerous practice that can lead to poor program design. As a rule, most variables should be declared as parts of an object, and global variables should only be declared in rare circumstances when there is no other possible solution to a complex problem.

Objects and the Interface of MAIN.PAS

The interface section of a Delphi program is used to declare any public sections of code that appear in a unit. In this particular case, you can see that the code for MAIN.PAS has a `uses` clause, a type section, and a variable section:

```
unit Main;

{ Program copyright (c) 1994 by Charles Calvert }
{ Project Name: CONTROL1 }

interface

uses
  WinTypes, WinProcs,
  Classes, Graphics, Controls,
  Printers, Menus, Forms, StdCtrls;

type
  TForm1 = class(TForm)
    Edit1: TEdit;
    procedure Edit1DblClick(Sender: TObject);
  end;

var
  Form1: TForm1;

implementation
```

There are various other syntactical elements that can appear in an interface, but there is no need to be exhaustive at this early stage. In fact, the only part of the interface that should concern you right now is the TForm1 object definition:

```
TForm1 = class(TForm)
  Edit1: TEdit;
  procedure Edit1DblClick(Sender: TObject);
end;
```

> **NOTE**
>
> A detailed description of classes and object-oriented programming is covered in Chapter 27, "Objects, Encapsulation, and Properties." For now, however, I'm just going to say a few introductory words about the subject.

The code shown here declares the existence and structure of an object called TForm1. The keyword used in Delphi to designate an object declaration is class. For instance, the following line of code states that TForm1 is declared to be a class that is descended from another class called TForm:

```
TForm1 = class(TForm)
```

Programmers use classes in part because they need to encapsulate a set of related data and procedures under a single aegis. Objects serve much the same purpose as a chapter in a book. Related code can be encapsulated under a single object, the same way several related topics can be encapsulated inside a single chapter in a book.

In particular, this object definition states that class TForm1 has one piece of data called Edit1 and one procedure called Edit1DblClick. Edit1 references the class that controls the physical edit control, which you see on the screen when you run the program. When you need to query the edit control or change the state of the edit control, you use the Edit1 variable. For instance, the following line of code places a string inside the edit control called Edit1:

```
Edit1.Text := 'You clicked on the edit control';
```

A procedure that is part of an object is sometimes referred to as a *method*. All methods are either procedures or functions, but not all procedures or functions are methods. It is completely acceptable to refer to a routine that is part of an object by the names procedure or function. However, a procedure that is not part of an object should never be called a method. You should note that I sometimes call the same block of code either a procedure or a method. For all practical purposes, right now you can think of the two words as synonymous, as long as you recall that methods are always parts of objects.

Take a moment to consider one more quick definition before moving on. A variable such as Edit1, which appears as part of an object, is sometimes called a field of an object. The same syntax is used when referring to the fields of a record. So, a variable that is part of a record is called a field of the record, and a variable that is part of a class definition is called a field of that object.

Frankly, the details of how to define a class can become quite complex; for now, it is best if you start out with a few very general ideas. As time goes on, you can dig deeper and try to come to an understanding of all the major aspects of object-oriented code. To get there, however, you first need to learn the basic facts about objects, and learn to at least recognize one when you see one. The brief explanation presented here should be enough to get you at least that far.

In this section, you learned about the interface of a Delphi program. The interface contains declarations, but no code. You will never see the body of a procedure in an interface section. The most important declaration in most Delphi interface sections is the declaration for the object representing the main form.

The Implementation of MAIN.PAS

After the interface section of a unit, you find the keyword implementation. The implementation portion of a unit is where procedures or methods are actually defined. The header of a procedure or method may appear in a unit's interface, but its body always appears in the implementation, along with a second version of its header.

Anything that appears in a unit's implementation that is not referenced in the interface is private to that unit. This means that a procedure or method listed in an implementation cannot be called from another unit unless its header is listed in that unit's interface.

All of the syntactical elements listed in the interface section can also be listed in the implementation. For instance, classes, types, and variables can all be declared inside a program's implementation. The only difference, of course, is that these declarations are now local to the particular unit in question. This means they cannot be called or referenced from another unit.

The key point for you to grasp right now is that the implementation is the place where procedures and methods are defined or implemented. Specifically, code fragments (such as the following one) always appear in the implementation section of a unit. They can never appear in the interface.

```
procedure TForm1.Edit1DblClick(Sender: TObject);
begin
  Edit1.Text := 'You clicked on the edit control';
end;
```

Notice that the procedure listed here contains a header and a body. If you look carefully, you see that the procedure's name is qualified by the word TForm1. This means that Edit1DblClick is a method of class TForm1. The portions of an object that do something are called methods. For instance, the Edit1DblClick method displays a string in an edit control.

I'm sure you have noticed that the header for the Edit1DblClick method has a set of parentheses at the end with the words Sender and TObject inside them:

```
procedure TForm1.Edit1DblClick(Sender: TObject);
```

This additional piece of syntax is called a parameter.

The parameter called Sender references the control that was used to call the method. If you double-click the edit control, causing the Edit1DblClick method to be called, a copy of the Edit1 object is passed to Edit1DblClick in the parameter called Sender.

Parameters take a little while to understand, so I address them separately in the next section. In this case, there is nothing in the parameter called Sender that is of interest to the CONTROL1 program, so the parameter is simply ignored.

The body of the Edit1DblClick method looks like this:

```
begin
  Edit1.Text := 'You clicked on the edit control';
end;
```

As you learned earlier, the begin..end pair surrounding the body of the code is merely a syntactical convention used to tell the compiler where the body of your code begins and ends.

For now, all you need to know about Edit1 is that it is of type TEdit. TEdit is a class used to manipulate an edit control. The actual definition of the TEdit class is found in a unit called CONTROLS.PAS.

In the last few sections, you have learned about the basic parts of a Delphi program. In particular, you learned the following:

- Every Delphi program has at least two main parts. The first is a project file such as CONTROL1.DPR, and the second is one or more units such as the module MAIN.PAS shown earlier.

- Units are divided into three main sections. The first is the title, the second is the interface, and the third is the implementation.

- The interface section of a unit is where you declare any public portions of your code. For instance, the class called Form1 is defined in MAIN.PAS, but referenced twice in PROJECT1.DPR. If Form1 was not listed in the interface of MAIN.PAS, there would be no way for PROJECT1 to even know that Form1 existed. As a result, unit MAIN and Form1 could not be linked into the program.

- The implementation section of MAIN.PAS is where the body of the procedures used in MAIN.PAS are defined. You can declare a procedure or object in an interface, but you define it in the implementation. Everything you see in the interface is merely preliminary. The actual body of the code appears in the implementation.

- After the title, interface, and implementation, the fourth optional section of a unit is called the initialization section. The initialization section gets called first, just as you must type WIN before you can start Windows. The short program called INITDATA, found on disk with the code for this chapter, shows how to use an initialization section.

- A class can be used to encapsulate a set of procedures and data that are logically bound together. For instance, the visual element called Form1, its edit control, and the Edit1DblClick method are all part of one large logical entity. It makes sense to think of them as parts of a single object, just as a steering wheel, engine, and tires may be part of a single car. One of the purposes of classes is that they help to create order out of diversity. Objects are discussed in greater depth in Part III, and in many other parts of this book.

I hope the material presented in this section has helped you grasp the major blocks of code and the major syntactical elements that are found in every Delphi program. I am aware that this material can be difficult, but it forms the basis for Delphi programs. If you are having trouble with this material, you can rely for awhile on the fact that almost all of the code explained here is generated automatically by the compiler. All I have done in this section is explain why the code exists and what functions it performs. If you have understood the broad concepts that I am referencing, you should get along fine for now.

Passing Parameters

Procedures are passed parameters to supply them with information that they can process. Suppose you have a procedure that, given the current date, calculates the number of days left in the year. In the design phase, you might decide to pass a parameter (containing the current date) to this procedure. It could then process the date that you passed to it and print the result to the screen.

The following program, called PARAMS, is designed to demonstrate how to use parameters. As a side benefit, it also shows you how to do the following:

- Create your own procedures

■ Add procedures to an object so they become methods of that object

■ Call one procedure from within another procedure

The PARAMS program enables you to type a string in an edit control. After you click a button, this string is copied to six other edit controls, so that one string is repeated seven times, as shown in Figure 4.6.

FIGURE 4.6.

Killing seven birds with one stone is the goal of the PARAMS program.

To get started, create a form like the one shown in Figure 4.7. It should contain seven edit controls, labeled Edit1 through Edit7. At the bottom of the form, place a button called Button1. Using the Object Inspector, change the caption of Button1 so that it says Call Procedure WriteAll. Figure 4.8 shows how the Object Inspector should look after you change Button1's caption.

FIGURE 4.7.

The form for the PARAMS program contains seven edit controls and a button.

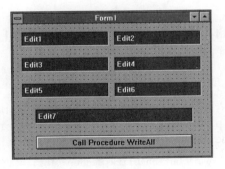

After designing the form for the PARAMS program, glance at the program's main unit. Class TForm1 should now look like this:

```
TForm1 = class(TForm)
  Edit1: TEdit;
  Edit2: TEdit;
  Edit3: TEdit;
  Edit4: TEdit;
  Edit5: TEdit;
```

```
    Edit6: TEdit;
    Edit7: TEdit;
    Button1: TButton;
  end;
```

FIGURE 4.8.

*The Object Inspector after
Button1's Caption
property has been changed.*

Notice that it contains eight fields, one for each of the visual components you created. Remember that you can use these fields to query or manipulate the controls at runtime.

The next step is to add a method that will be called when the user clicks the form's button. To do this, either select the OnClick method from the Object Inspector's Events page or double-click the button itself. When you're done, the following code should be generated:

```
procedure TForm1.Button1Click(Sender: TObject);
begin

end;
```

The currently selected control appears at the top of the Object Inspector in a dropdown combo box. In this program, the Object Inspector is used only to modify Button1. Therefore, you should use the combo box at the top of the Object Inspector to be sure that Button1 is selected, and not the main form or one of the edit controls.

The PARAMS program serves no useful function other than to show you how to write a procedure and pass a parameter to it. In particular, the program responds to a click on Button1 by grabbing the current text from Edit7 and passing it to a procedure called WriteAll:

```
procedure TForm1.Button1Click(Sender: TObject);
begin
  WriteAll(Edit7.Text);
end;
```

I'll explain the WriteAll procedure soon; for now, you need to be sure that you understand what's happening inside Button1Click. The key point to grasp here is that Edit7 is of type TEdit, and all TEdit components have a property called Text. The Text property is part of the TEdit class; it resides in the TEdit object and provides access to the text that the edit control displays onscreen. On startup, the text in Edit7 is the string Edit7. During the course of the program, you can change this string by clicking on the edit control with the mouse and typing in a new string.

The text to be displayed in the six uppermost edit controls is passed to procedure WriteAll as a parameter. To pass a parameter to a procedure, you just write the name of the procedure and enclose the parameter to be passed in parentheses:

```
WriteAll(Edit7.Text);
```

Again, let's suppose you have a procedure that calculates the number of days left in a year. If the name of that procedure is CalcDaysLeft and the current date is stored in a variable called CurrentDate, you can call the procedure by writing:

```
CalcDaysLeft(CurrentDate);
```

The actual header for the procedure might look something like this, with TDate being a user-defined type:

```
procedure CalcDays(CurrentDate: TDate);
```

To return to the case at hand, the goal of the WriteAll procedure is to copy the text in Edit7 to all six of the other edit controls. Here's what the procedure looks like:

```
procedure TForm1.WriteAll(Edit7String: String);
begin
  Edit1.Text := Edit7String;
  Edit2.Text := Edit7String;
  Edit3.Text := Edit7String;
  Edit4.Text := Edit7String;
  Edit5.Text := Edit7String;
  Edit6.Text := Edit7String;
end;
```

There's no way to automatically generate code for this kind of procedure; you must design and write the code yourself. To get started, create the procedure's header:

```
procedure TForm1.WriteAll(Edit7String: String);
```

Although they were mentioned earlier, it won't hurt to take a second, closer look at procedure headers. They consist of five parts:

- The first part is the word procedure, and the fifth part is a semicolon. Both of these elements have purely syntactical purposes: They inform the compiler that a procedure is being defined, and that its header ends at a particular point.

- The second part of the header is the word TForm1, which qualifies the procedure name so the compiler knows that this is a method of the TForm1 class.

- The third part of the header is the procedure's name; I've chosen to call it WriteAll. If you want to, you can change this name to virtually any combination of letters. You can't, however, start an identifier with a number. For instance, 1WriteAll and 2WriteAll aren't valid identifiers.

- The fourth part of the header is the parameter. Parameters are declared inside parentheses and consist of two parts. The first part is the name of the parameter, and the second part is its type. These two parts are separated by a colon. If you pass more than one parameter to a procedure, each parameter should be separated by a semicolon, like so:

```
procedure Example(Param1: string; Param2: string);
```

By this time, you've had plenty of opportunities to learn what a string is, but this is the first time you've worked explicitly with a string type. A variable declared to be of type string can hold any string that is shorter than 256 characters. If you're confused about variables and types, you should refer to an introductory book on Pascal programming. For now, all you need to know is that the parameter called Edit7String can be used to hold whatever text was in the control called Edit7.

After you've created the header for the WriteAll procedure, you need to copy it into the TForm1 class declaration:

```
TForm1 = class(TForm)
  Edit1: TEdit;
  Edit2: TEdit;
  Edit3: TEdit;
  Edit4: TEdit;
  Edit5: TEdit;
  Edit6: TEdit;
  Edit7: TEdit;
  Button1: TButton;
  procedure Button1Click(Sender: TObject);
  procedure WriteAll(Edit7String: String);
end;
```

The relevant method is the last one listed, right before the word end. As you can see, the entire WriteAll header has been copied verbatim into the class declaration, with the exception of the class name itself. There's no need to include the class name qualifier because everything in the TForm1 class declaration is automatically a member of the TForm1 class.

The actual body of the WriteAll procedure is trivial:

```
begin
  Edit1.Text := Edit7String;
  Edit2.Text := Edit7String;
  Edit3.Text := Edit7String;
  Edit4.Text := Edit7String;
  Edit5.Text := Edit7String;
  Edit6.Text := Edit7String;
end;
```

This code assigns the contents of the parameter called Edit7String to each of the remaining edit controls on the form. Other than issues of convenience and flexibility, there's no significant difference between modifying the Text property of an edit control at runtime and modifying the same property during design time using the Object Inspector.

The following listings have the full code for the PARAMS program. I even included the project file, though I won't usually be doing that during these chapters. The code looks a bit long when typed out like this, but remember that you need to type in only 10 lines of this program. The rest is generated automatically by Delphi. If you have trouble creating this program, you can find the full source code on the disk.

NOTE

This book was written while Delphi was in beta. As a result, it is possible that the following code might differ in some minor way from the final syntax used in the shipping product. If you are having trouble with this code, check to see whether there were last-minute corrections that appear only in the code on the CD-ROM that ships with this book. If that fails, write me by either electronic mail or snail (U.S. Postal) mail, and I will provide you with updated code. My addresses are listed at both the beginning and end of this book. If you send snail mail, please include a self-addressed, stamped envelope. Code updates will also appear on Borland BBS and Internet sites under the name MDCSC???.ZIP, in which the question marks represent version or part numbers.

Listing 4.3. The project file for the PARAMS program does nothing more than launch the main form.

```
program Params;

uses
  Forms,
  Main in 'MAIN.PAS' {Form1};

begin
  Application.CreateForm(TForm1, Form1);
  Application.Run;
end.
```

Listing 4.4. The source for the PARAMS program shows how to use edit controls and how to pass parameters.

```
unit Main;

{ Program copyright (c) 1994 by Charles Calvert }
{ Project Name: PARAMS }

interface

uses
  WinTypes, WinProcs, Classes,
  Graphics, Controls,
  Printers, Forms, StdCtrls;

type
  TForm1 = class(TForm)
    Edit1: TEdit;
    Edit2: TEdit;
    Edit3: TEdit;
```

continues

Listing 4.4. continued

```
    Edit4: TEdit;
    Edit5: TEdit;
    Edit6: TEdit;
    Edit7: TEdit;
    Button1: TButton;
    procedure Button1Click(Sender: TObject);
    procedure WriteAll(Edit7String: String);
  end;

var
  Form1: TForm1;

implementation

{$R *.DFM}

procedure TForm1.WriteAll(Edit7String: String);
begin
  Edit1.Text := Edit7String;
  Edit2.Text := Edit7String;
  Edit3.Text := Edit7String;
  Edit4.Text := Edit7String;
  Edit5.Text := Edit7String;
  Edit6.Text := Edit7String;
end;

procedure TForm1.Button1Click(Sender: TObject);
begin
  WriteAll(Edit7.Text);
end;

end.
```

When experimenting with the PARAMS program, you might try changing the names of the WriteAll procedure and Edit7String parameter. These are two elements of the program that you have almost complete control over. Other words such as procedure, string, begin, and end are *reserved words*, which means they can't be used for any purpose other than the ones officially designated by the language. For this reason, you can't name a procedure or variable string, end, begin, and so on. For example, the following declarations won't compile:

```
procedure Begin;
procedure Class;
program String;
```

For a complete list of reserved words, see Delphi's online help. Don't bother trying to memorize all the reserved words in the language. The compiler always tells you if you try to use one incorrectly, usually by popping up a message saying Identifier expected. Identifiers are the names assigned to variables, procedures, types, and nearly all other syntactical elements in a program. For instance, Form1, Control1, Main, WriteAll, and Button1Click are all identifiers. When you get a message such as Identifier expected, the compiler (in its own cryptic way) is usually trying to tell you that it expected an identifier, but instead found a reserved word.

In this section, you learned how to pass a parameter to a procedure and how to create your own procedures. I know that technical terms and new concepts are flying fast and thick in this chapter. However, what's really important is that you grasp the broad concepts, rather than memorize all the specifics. If you can complete each of the following tasks, you're doing fine:

- Create a procedure using visual techniques.
- Add code to your procedure. The code can perform any useful function, such as inserting text in an edit control.
- Recognize the keywords implementation and interface as being specific to units.
- Recognize the declaration of an object when you see it.
- Recognize the difference between a method and a field of an object.
- Recognize a parameter to a procedure and realize that it's a way to pass information to the procedure.

It's icing on the cake if you can write your own procedures or create your own units at this point. This chapter is meant to help you understand the basics about procedures, classes, and units. Readers with more experience may be picking up more detailed information, but it's not essential that you do so right now.

Delphi is an easy language to use. If you reach the stage at which you know it very well, you'll be able to create very powerful professional-looking programs. A less thorough knowledge still lets you get serious work done with Delphi. For instance, neither a scientist who uses Delphi to help track data, nor a home user who wants help managing financial records, needs a detailed understanding of the language.

More Procedures, More Controls

Now that you have the basics down, it's time to put your knowledge to work by using some of the major controls on the Standard Component Palette, which is shown in Figure 4.9 and described in detail in Chapter 3, "The IDE."

FIGURE 4.9.

The Standard Component Palette contains a wide array of powerful controls.

The program you're about to create is an extension of the CONTROL1 program you created at the beginning of this chapter. If you like, you can copy the code from that program into a new directory called CONTROL2. However, there's no real need to do this. You can simply continue working with the CONTROL1 program, adding more code to it where appropriate.

Starting with the code found in the CONTROL1 program, you can now proceed to build a more complex program that reveals a lot about the controls used in Delphi programs.

First, add a static control to your form and name it `Lselection`. Set its caption to Selection, as shown in Figure 4.10.

FIGURE 4.10.

The `Control1` main form after a static control has been added.

Now select the `OnDblClk` method from the Events page of the Object Inspector, and double-click it. Another procedure is created automatically, and a few small changes are made to the `Form1` object at the top of your code. The next step is to modify the `LSelectionDblClick` procedure so that it looks like this:

```
procedure TForm1.LSelectionDblClick(Sender: TObject);
begin
  Edit1.Text := 'You double-clicked on a label';
end;
```

Run the program and double-click the label. You'll see that the edit control changes to display the text you specified in the `LSelectionDblClick` method. Now close the program to return to design mode.

The previous code shows the pattern that's used throughout this program. Specifically, you'll add a control to the form, and add code so a click or double-click on that control places descriptive text in the edit control.

While you're still in design mode, add a large group box beneath the edit control and label. Then, add two radio buttons and two checkboxes to the group box, as shown in Figure 4.11. Finally, add a single button at the bottom of the form. Stretch it out so that it covers nearly the entire width of the form. Name the button `BClose` and give it the word `Close` as a caption. More specifically, the `Name` property in the Object Inspector should be `BClose`, and the `Caption` property should be `Close`. (If you assign the name `Close` to the button, you'll get an error.)

You should add the group box to the form before you add the radio buttons, checkboxes, or other controls that you want to place on the group box. If you move these controls from the surface of the form onto a group box, you may run into trouble later. (Namely, the control will still think the form is its parent, and it won't move with the group box when the group box is moved.) To avoid this problem, it's better to first place the group box on the form, and then place the radio buttons and other controls on top of the group box. You can then drag the entire collection of controls by moving the group box. However, if you forget to place a TGroupBox onto a form before adding the controls that belong on top of it, you can rectify the problem by highlighting the controls, choosing Edit | Cut from the main menu, and pasting the controls onto the surface of the group box. (Note that everything said in this paragraph about group boxes is also true for panels. The two components behave in the same way, even though they are slightly different in appearance.)

FIGURE 4.11.

The main form for the CONTROL2 application, as it appears after it has been populated with a variety of controls.

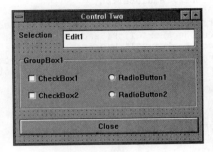

The final step in this process is to create an OnClick method for each of the new controls you've created, except the group box. Each of the methods should contain explanatory text, following the general pattern shown in this RadioButton1Click procedure:

```
procedure TForm1.RadioButton1Click(Sender: TObject);
begin
  Edit1.Text := 'Click on RadioButton1';
end;
```

When you're done, the code you've created should look like the program shown in Listing 4.5. This time, I omitted the project file because it is almost identical to the project file from the other applications shown in this chapter. If you need further direction, review the source code found on the CD-ROM.

Listing 4.5. The CONTROL2 program gives names to some of the major components used in Windows programs.

```
unit Main;

{ Program copyright (c) 1994 by Charles Calvert }
{ Project Name: CONTROL2 }

interface

uses
  WinTypes, WinProcs, Classes,
  Graphics, Controls, Printers,
  Menus, Forms, StdCtrls;

type
  TForm1 = class(TForm)
```

continues

Listing 4.5. continued

```
    LSelection: TLabel;
    Edit1: TEdit;
    BClose: TButton;
    GroupBox1: TGroupBox;
    CheckBox1: TCheckBox;
    RadioButton1: TRadioButton;
    CheckBox2: TCheckBox;
    RadioButton2: TRadioButton;
    procedure Edit1DblClick(Sender: TObject);
    procedure LSelectionDblClick(Sender: TObject);
    procedure CheckBox1Click(Sender: TObject);
    procedure CheckBox2Click(Sender: TObject);
    procedure RadioButton2Click(Sender: TObject);
    procedure RadioButton1Click(Sender: TObject);
    procedure BCloseClick(Sender: TObject);
  end;

var
  Form1: TForm1;

implementation

{$R *.DFM}

procedure TForm1.Edit1DblClick(Sender: TObject);
begin
  Edit1.Text := 'Double click on edit control';
end;

procedure TForm1.LSelectionDblClick(Sender: TObject);
begin
  Edit1.Text := 'Double click on label';
end;

procedure TForm1.CheckBox1Click(Sender: TObject);
begin
  Edit1.Text := 'Click on Checkbox1';
end;

procedure TForm1.RadioButton1Click(Sender: TObject);
begin
  Edit1.Text := 'Click on RadioButton1';
end;

procedure TForm1.BCloseClick(Sender: TObject);
begin
  Edit1.Text := 'Click on Button';
end;

procedure TForm1.CheckBox2Click(Sender: TObject);
begin
  Edit1.Text := 'Click on CheckBox2';
end;

procedure TForm1.RadioButton2Click(Sender: TObject);
begin
```

```
    Edit1.Text := 'Click on Radiobutton2';
end;

end.
```

This program serves two purposes:

- It shows how to create procedures, and how to fill out the bodies of these procedures so that they perform a useful action. In this case, the only purpose of each of these procedures is simply to write a line of text in the form's edit control. This is a simple task, but it serves to clearly illustrate what a procedure is, and what its syntax looks like in a code window.

- It illustrates the names and appearance of several important controls. As a programmer, it's important for you to understand the rudimentary facts about edit controls, labels, radio buttons, checkboxes, buttons, and group boxes. If these controls are unfamiliar to you, you should refer to an introductory book on the Windows environment.

Working with Forms

Most Delphi projects consist of a DPR file and one or more units. Most, if not all, units in a project contain a form. At runtime, the creation of a form involves two steps:

- Delphi registers the objects in the form with the system. This step occurs automatically, without any intervention on your part.

- Memory is allocated for the form via a call to CreateForm.

The following is the default syntax for a simple Delphi DPR file:

```
program Project1;

uses
  Forms,
  Unit1 in 'UNIT1.PAS' {Form1};

{$R *.RES}

begin
  Application.CreateForm(TForm1, Form1);
  Application.Run;
end.
```

The compiler inserts the call to CreateForm. If you omit the call, Application.Run returns immediately and the program is over at almost the same moment it began.

The main block of more complex programs might look something like this:

```
begin
  Application.CreateForm(TForm1, Form1);
```

```
    Application.CreateForm(TForm2, Form2);
    Application.CreateForm(TForm3, Form3);
    Application.CreateForm(TForm4, Form4);
    Application.Run;
end.
```

In this code fragment, the last three calls to `CreateForm` allocate memory for forms that aren't visible when the program is first launched. You can make them visible by writing

```
Form2.Visible := True;
```

or

```
Form2.Show;
```

In most cases, the calls to show a form come in response to a click on a button or menu item. For example, if you want a click on a button to launch a second form, you should create an `OnClick` method for the button by double-clicking it while in design mode. Then, fill in the resulting procedure so that it looks like this:

```
procedure TForm1.Button1Click(Sender: TObject);
begin
  Form2.Show;
end;
```

After you fill in the procedure, the second form becomes visible. You can switch to and from this second form with a click of the mouse. When you want to shut down the second form, you can just call the `Close` method:

```
procedure TForm2.Button1Click(Sender: TObject);
begin
  Close;
end;
```

This call causes the second form to hide itself, but not to deallocate its memory. There is no real distinction between calling `Close` on the second form and writing the following code:

```
procedure TForm2.Button1Click(Sender: TObject);
begin
  Visible := False;
end;
```

However, if you call `Close` on an application's main form, it causes the entire application to shut down and all of the memory associated with it to be deallocated.

NOTE

The code for the TWOFORM program is in the CHAP04 directory on this book's CD-ROM.

The TWOFORM program is very straightforward. It consists of two forms, each with one button. The button on the first form is called bLaunch, and the one on the second form is called bClose. Notice that you can't name the button on the second form Close, because that would conflict with the Close method.

The only other portion of the program worth mentioning is the second uses clause in the MAIN form:

```
uses
  ModTwo;
```

This statement references the program's second module, which is called MODTWO.PAS. The reference is necessary because, otherwise, the first form is unaware of the second form's existence. You need to use this syntax to explicitly clue the form in on the design of the program.

In this section, you've taken a look at one of the most commonly used programming techniques in the Delphi environment. In the next section, you can see how to create something that looks and feels like a modal dialog box, but isn't really a modal dialog box.

Creating Modal Dialogs

When a modal dialog box appears, it's the only part of an application that can get user input. None of the other buttons, menus, or windows respond until you close the modal dialog box. The File Open dialog box, accessible from the File menu of most Windows applications, is an example of this type of dialog box.

Delphi enables you to create traditional Windows dialog boxes using Resource Workshop or command-line tools such as BRC.EXE or RC.EXE. In fact, if you do a little exploring with the File Manager, you see that Delphi generates a small RES file to accompany most of the applications you build. However, resources are not the standard means for Delphi programmers to create a dialog boxlike object.

I use the phrase *dialog boxlike object* because standard Delphi dialog boxes are not "real" Windows dialog boxes. There are no resource files for these dialog boxes; instead, they're saved as DFM files. If you're not familiar with the terminology used here, there's no need for concern. The main point is simply that Windows has a set of relatively complex tools and commands that are normally used to create a dialog. Delphi takes a different approach. It provides you with a simple means of creating something that looks and feels like a standard Windows dialog, but isn't nearly so difficult to make.

To create a dialog box in Delphi, just create a standard form. If you want it to appear in a modal state, make the following call, in which Form2 is the name of the form you want to show, and Return is an integer value:

```
Return := Form2.ShowModal;
```

To close a modal dialog box, set the TForm property called ModalResult equal to one of the following values:

```
mrOk
mrCancel
mrAbort
mrRetry
mrIgnore
mrYes
mrNo
```

To close a modal dialog box in response to a button click, write code that looks like this:

```
procedure TForm2.Button1Click(Sender: TObject);
begin
  ModalResult := mrOk;
end;
```

The value you assign to `ModalResult` is what's returned from `ShowModal`. This lets you write code such as the following:

```
Return := Form2.ShowModal;
if Return = mrOk then
  MessageBox(Handle, 'Ok', 'Hi', mb_Ok);
```

The code for the FORMAL1 program is on this book's CD-ROM. You'll probably notice that the source code for the FORMAL1 program is very similar to that of the TWOFORM program in structure, even though the details are a bit different. FORMAL1 features two forms. The first form in the program launches the second form as a modal dialog. The second form, which is depicted in Figure 4.12, contains Cancel and Ok buttons. The code associated with the Cancel button sets `ModalResult` equal to `mrCancel`, and the code for the Ok button sets `ModalResult` equal to `mrOk`.

> **NOTE**
>
> The code for the FORMAL1 program is in the CHAP04 directory on this book's CD-ROM.

Figure 4.12 shows the FORMAL1 program's form.

The FORMAL1 program is interesting primarily because it shows how to return a value from a modal form, and how to handle that value when you receive it. In particular, the following method shows how to close a modal form while simultaneously signaling the parent form that the user wants to cancel any activity that might have occurred in the form:

```
procedure TForm2.Button2Click(Sender: TObject);
begin
  ModalResult := mrCancel;
end;
```

There's no reason that you can't return any integer from a form via the `ModalResult` property. You don't have to return one of the `mr` constants shown previously; you can return a literal number or some constant that you define for your own purposes:

```
ModalResult := 35;
```

FIGURE 4.12.
The modal form from the
FORMAL1 program.

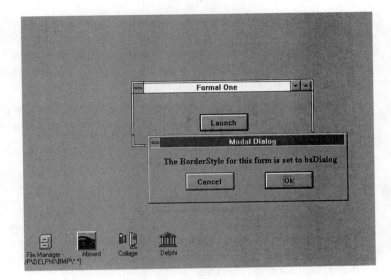

This means that there are about 32,000 possible return values, which should provide all the freedom you need to create a wide variety of forms, all returning a multitude of possible integer values.

Freeing Forms at Runtime

In large programs, and particularly in large database programs, you usually don't want to create all the forms in your program at the time of initial startup. There are often times when you would prefer not to find code that looks like the following in your program:

```
begin
  Application.CreateForm(TForm1, Form1);
  Application.CreateForm(TForm2, Form2);
  Application.CreateForm(TForm3, Form3);
  Application.CreateForm(TForm4, Form4);
  Application.CreateForm(TForm5, Form5);
  Application.CreateForm(TForm6, Form6);
  Application.CreateForm(TForm7, Form7);
  Application.Run;
end.
```

The problem with this code is that it allocates a large chunk of memory for the program's forms at startup. As I hinted earlier, programmers want to be able to dynamically allocate and dispose memory for a form at runtime. Your code should look like this:

```
begin
  Application.CreateForm(TForm1, Form1);
  Application.Run;
end.
```

Next, you want to have the option of allocating resources for the other forms only when you need them. In most programs, this ability won't be missed, but for cases in which secondary forms allocate large chunks of memory, it becomes a necessity. That's why I'll show you a way to write large programs with many forms that still contain simple startup code like the two-line example shown previously.

As it happens, you're free to move CreateForm calls out of the main project file and into other units of your program. In particular, you can write code that looks like this:

```
procedure TForm1.Button1Click(Sender: TObject);
begin
  Form2 := TForm2.Create(Application);
  Form2.ShowModal;
  Form2.Free;
end;
```

This code allocates the memory for a form, displays it, and then disposes it by calling Form2.Free. Notice that you don't call CreateForm in this situation, but instead call TForm2.Create and assign the Application object as the form's owner. This syntax is preferred unless you're working in the main block of a DPR file.

The previous code guarantees that the memory for Form2 is only used while it's being displayed. As soon as the user closes the form, the memory associated with the form is disposed by a simple call to Free. This technique helps you create large programs that leave a relatively small memory footprint.

You should be careful, however, when writing code that looks like this:

```
procedure TForm1.Button1Click(Sender: TObject);
begin
  Form2 := TForm2.Create(Application);
  Form2.Show;
end;
```

The code shown here allocates memory for a form and displays it as a *modeless dialog box*. As a result, the user can switch back to Form1 and launch a second copy of Form2 without ever disposing of the first copy. Unless you're absolutely sure you know what you're doing, this scenario can quickly lead to a memory leak. The simplest solution, of course, is to call ShowModal rather than Show, and then to call Free as soon as ShowModal returns.

If you're careful, there are ways to create logic like that shown previously in the second code fragment, but you must be sure that you know what you're doing and why you're doing it before you attempt this kind of maneuver. Specifically, you can respond to the user's request to close the second form by creating an OnClose event handler:

```
procedure TWinForm.FormClose(Sender: TObject;
                             var Action: TCloseAction);
begin
  Action := caFree;
end;
```

By setting `Action` to `caFree`, you ensure that the runtime library code in `TForm.Close` never references any of its variables, but simply calls `Free`. It is important to make sure that none of the form's variables are referenced, because they'll be invalid after the call to `Free`. If you have the runtime library, you can look in the `Forms` unit to see the actual source code for `TForm.Close`.

`TCloseAction` is an enumerated type with the following declaration:

```
TCloseAction = (caNone, caHide, caFree);
```

If you set `Action` to `caHide` instead of `caFree`, the default action occurs: The form becomes invisible, but isn't destroyed. Setting `Action` to `caNone` ensures that nothing happens inside of `TForm.Close`.

Because the technique shown here can be so useful, I've included a second version of the FORMAL program on this book's CD-ROM. This version demonstrates how you can write code that opens multiple forms of the same type in a modeless state.

> **NOTE**
>
> The code for the FORMAL2 program is in the CHAP04 directory on this book's CD-ROM.

When looking at the code to the MODFORM.PAS unit, you need to understand two separate, but related, code fragments. If the user clicks Button1, the system executes the `Close` command in the `Button1Click` method. Calling `Close` eventually generates an `OnClose` event, which is handled by the `FormClose` method. As stated earlier, `FormClose` can set `Action` to one of three recommended paths:

- `caHide`: The form is hidden.
- `caFree`: The form is destroyed.
- `caNone`: Nothing should occur.

The FORMAL2 program also uses a `TTimer` object and the `MemAvail` call to track memory usage in the program. Specifically, the current amount of available memory is displayed every tenth of a second in a label located on the first form. Timers are discussed in the next section.

Before closing this section, it's worth reminding you that when you give a form or component an owner, that owner is responsible for disposing the form. As a result, you can create six or seven forms and know that they will be deallocated when their owner is freed. In particular, at shut down, Delphi iterates through the `Components` array that belongs to each component on the screen, and it calls `free` on each of those components.

Using the WinCRT Unit

Old hands at Turbo Pascal programming are bound to be a bit surprised by some of the material that's been presented in this chapter. Visual Programming with Delphi is very different from Object Pascal as we used to know it.

These experienced souls might be glad to hear that it's possible to create a program using Delphi that is a good deal like the Pascal used by DOS programmers. I've intentionally avoided describing that technique because I want to be sure that you understand that Visual programming is every bit as simple as DOS programming. In fact, it might be a bit simpler.

I know, however, that some programmers may want to port apps over directly from DOS with a minimum of fuss. In certain very limited circumstances, this is possible due to the good graces of the WinCRT unit, which also shipped with earlier versions of Turbo and Borland Pascal for Windows. (Users of the Borland C/C++ compilers will recognize the WinCRT unit as being akin to EASYWIN programs.)

There are two ways to create a WinCRT program. The simplest is to use the Project Expert found in the Gallery. Specifically, you choose CRT Application from the Gallery. However, you won't learn much about the structure of these programs if you automate the task of creating them. As a result, I will explain the way to create a WinCRT program on your own, so that you can see the relationship between these programs and standard Delphi programs.

To create a WinCRT program by hand, first start out just as you would in a normal program. Go to the File menu and select New. Now, click once on the Project Source menu choice from the View menu.

When you look at the project file that has been created by the compiler, it should look like this:

```
program Project1;

uses
  Forms,
  Unit1 in 'UNIT1.PAS' {Form1};

{$R *.RES}

begin
  Application.CreateForm(TForm1, Form1);
  Application.Run;
end.
```

To convert this program into a WinCRT program, change the uses clause and the main body of the program:

```
program Project1;

uses
  WinCRT;
```

```
begin
  WriteLn('Look ma, no forms!');
end.
```

Before saving the project, remove UNIT1.PAS from the project by opening the Project Manager, highlighting the words Unit1, and then clicking the minus (–) symbol. Now save the project under a name of your own choosing. In this particular case, you might want to choose the name EASYWIN.

When you save your program, you see that its title automatically switches to EasyWin:

```
program EasyWin;
```

I point this out to remind you that you are still working in a Visual Programming environment in which certain portions of your code can be changed automatically by the compiler. But, other than this one small factor, you are totally on your own. By removing the reference to FORMS and UNIT1, and replacing them with the WinCRT, you have severed your main ties to the world of Visual Programming.

If you run the EasyWin program, it creates a window like the one shown in Figure 4.13.

FIGURE 4.13.

The EASYWIN program displays a single string in an otherwise barren window.

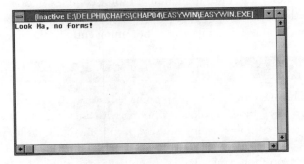

Old hands at Pascal understand that this string appeared through the good graces of the WriteLn procedure, which is still supported in Delphi under certain limited circumstances. In this case, you can use WriteLn as long as you include the WinCRT unit:

```
WriteLn('Look ma, no forms!');
```

If you omit the reference to the WinCRT unit from your program, you get a runtime error 105. (See Figure 4.14.) All but the most careful programmers see this error sooner or later, and it will save you time if you remember this very common way of generating a 105 error.

FIGURE 4.14.

The bitter fruits of running the EASYWIN program without listing WinCRT in its uses clause.

NOTE

The EASYWIN program displays the word *Inactive* in its title. This specifies that the program has finished its run, but that the main window of the app is being held open so that the user can view the results of the run. This type of message would make no sense in a true event-oriented Windows program, but it does make sense inside the limited scope of a WinCRT application.

For now, I'm not going to go into any more depth describing the WinCRT unit. I simply wanted to let you know that it exists, and that it will be referenced in many other places throughout this book. You should understand, however, that WinCRT programs do not support the full range of functions and capabilities offered by either Delphi or a standard DOS program. Even when used in conjunction with the WINDOS unit, WinCRT is still very limited in scope.

I strongly recommend that you adopt Delphi in its entirety, and use WinCRT only for very simple projects. My personal preference is to use WinCRT primarily as a convenient hacker's tool. It's helpful when you need to experiment with small fragments of code in order to grasp some new ideas, or to straighten out some complex algorithms. However, you can usually slap together a real Delphi program much faster than you can build a WinCRT program. So, perhaps, WinCRT is on its way to becoming entirely obsolete.

NOTE

The one group of people who have historically been most enamored of the WinCRT unit are students who are working with a teacher who uses a DOS- or UNIX-based Pascal compiler. Many of these people use WinCRT to imitate the types of programs their teachers have created using Turbo Pascal 6 or 7 for DOS. If you find yourself in this position, you should probably try to pick up a DOS compiler to use while you are in the course. My experience is that it's best to use the same compiler as your fellow students, because it helps to level the playing field. In this case, you will almost always be at a disadvantage if you're using a different tool from your teacher. However, students can get by using Delphi if they are willing to do some extra work. Also, if you get a chance, you might show Delphi to your teacher, so that he or she can see that there is something new, and better, in the world.

Summary

This chapter covers a great deal of material that is essential to Delphi programming. Specifically, you learned about the following:

- The major parts of a program
- The way project files and unit files interact
- How to create and use procedures
- How to pass parameters to a procedure
- How to recognize many of the important controls such as edit controls, labels, buttons, radio buttons, and group boxes

Despite the wide range of material covered in this chapter, most of the information was not particularly difficult. You've seen a lot of technical terms in this chapter, but the actual programming skills you've been asked to master have been fairly simple. For example, it's a breeze to slap a few controls onto a form and create a few methods that make them hop through some hoops.

Visual programming is fun. Just relax and play around with the compiler for awhile, taking the time to create a few methods and change the text in an edit control or two. Delphi can be a very simple tool to use. At the same time, it gives you enormous benefits in terms of programming capabilities. The more fully you understand the information in this chapter, the more fully you'll be able to exploit the capabilities of this programming environment.

What is a Graphical Environment?

Overview

In this chapter you will be introduced to graphics and the basic way it is handled inside Delphi. Everyone new to Delphi should be sure to go through most of the material in this chapter, because it covers many fundamental points about the way Delphi handles components. In short, the discussion of graphics programming will also demonstrate some basic facts about components and the relationship between components and Object Pascal.

The goals of this chapter are threefold:

- To get you up to speed on Graphical User Interfaces (GUIs) and the basic logic of drawing graphics
- To show you the TShape and TCanvas components, and to explain how Delphi uses them to draw images
- To give you additional experience working with the basic elements of procedures, event handlers, and components

This chapter starts with several pages of exposition on the topic of Graphical User Environments and graphics-mode programming. This is fundamental material that you have to understand if you are going to get serious about Windows programming. If you are an experienced Windows or graphics programmer, you may find that you can skip or skim the first two sections of this chapter.

Graphics and graphics components are part of the basic syntax of the Delphi language. As you will see in the next few chapters, no programmer is equipped to do any serious work without a knowledge of types, branching, and looping. Basic graphics programming is now just as fundamental, and all programmers should understand how it works.

What is a Graphical User Interface?

Windows runs in graphics mode, not text mode. Some people who usually work at the DOS or UNIX prompts might not be fully aware of the difference between graphics mode and text mode. Furthermore, many people are confused about graphics modes, graphics drivers, palettes, 8-bit versus 16-bit versus 24-bit graphics, and the elemental units of graphics modes, which are pixels.

As a result, it's perhaps best to start at the beginning and explain why people have moved from text mode to graphics mode, even though graphics mode is slower and demands more expensive hardware. The key point to understand is that a traditional text mode screen is divided into 2,000 individual sections or *characters*, while a traditional graphics screen is divided into at least 307,200 sections, or pixels. The figures alone help to explain why graphics mode is more powerful than text mode.

In particular, a text mode screen is usually 80 characters wide and 25 characters deep. Graphics screens, on the other hand, are usually at least 640 pixels wide by 480 pixels deep. See Figure 5.1. for an illustration of the two types of screens.

FIGURE 5.1.

Graphics screens are usually 640×480, and text screens are usually 80×25.

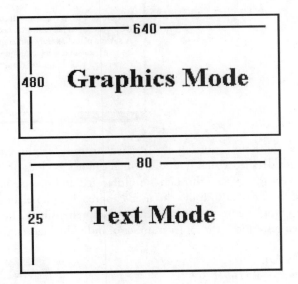

Graphics screens have a finer resolution than text screens. This makes it possible to create much more interesting and realistic effects than any that can be produced in text mode. For instance, Figure 5.2 and Figure 5.3 illustrate the differences between a sentence written in text mode, and the same sentence written in graphics mode. Overall, it seems hard to deny that graphics mode offers some obvious advantages for which users would quite naturally be willing to make some sacrifices.

FIGURE 5.2.

A portion of a poem by Samuel Taylor Coleridge, shown in text mode using the standard built-in character set.

FIGURE 5.3.

Another excerpt from the same Coleridge poem, but shown in graphics mode using a truetype font.

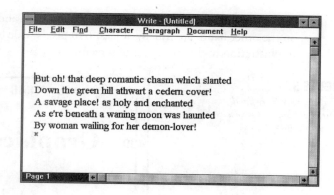

Figure 5.4 shows a portion of the speedbar from Delphi. Graphics mode makes it possible to produce detailed visual symbols, which can act as clues or guides for users who want to find easy ways to navigate through a multifaceted and diverse interface. In other words, graphics mode can help to simplify the user's approach to an elaborate tool, and can indeed help to make complex interfaces more readily comprehensible. The key point here is that it is the increased resolution, the larger number of individual facets, that makes all this possible.

FIGURE 5.4.

The speedbar from Delphi makes the program's resources more accessible.

Finally, perhaps the greatest advantage of graphics mode is that it allows art to become a common feature of the computer world. Figure 5.5 shows a type of art that mathematics produces via fractal manipulations. This image was produced by the FRACDLL program, which appears on the CD accompanying this book. That program will be discussed in depth in Chapter 33, "DLL Basics and VCL DLLs."

What all this adds up to is that graphics modes make it easier for programs to convey information. Nearly everyone in contemporary society desperately needs to be able to work with large blocks of information in the simplest way possible. This is what GUIs are all about. They make information palatable.

When personal computers first came out, it was enough that they were powerful. Users, impressed with the new technology, were willing to learn arcane interfaces, each of which tended to differ from one program to the next. Today's users and today's marketplace demand that programs be easier to use.

FIGURE 5.5.

A fractal design created with the FRACDLL program that comes with this book.

For now, the best solution to this need is a well-designed GUI such as Windows or OS/2. Well-designed GUI's shorten learning curves. Furthermore, if it's helpful to draw a graph or picture of a concept, GUIs can easily handle this task. Finally, modern operating environments such as Windows and OS/2 enable programmers to integrate sound and motion pictures into their programs. The latter technology is still in its infancy, but in this book you will write programs that show how easy it is to communicate large amounts of data via a short movie shown on a computer.

Graphics mode offers a very clear demonstration of why users are willing to work with larger and slower codebases if the advantages are obvious and significant. Everything about graphics mode is much slower than text mode, by several orders of magnitude. The hardware itself is slower, and the code that is written to manipulate the graphics is much larger, slower, and more complex. But most users prefer graphics mode to text mode, except when working on certain isolated problems. Furthermore, modern computers run graphics applications more quickly than the old technology could run text-based applications, and this is a situation that will continue to improve exponentially over the years.

Technical Aspects of Graphics Mode

There are a number of points about graphics modes that some users find confusing. The first is the idea of a pixel. A pixel is a single point of light on the screen. On most computers, a pixel is so small that users are not even aware that they exist. They are simply too tiny for the naked eye to perceive, unless they are seen as isolated colored points on a black background. If you want to see individual pixels being turned on one at a time, you can run the PIXELS program that is supplied on the disk. The code for this program will be explained in Chapter 9.

If you have a color system, the PIXELS program demonstrates that not only can each individual pixel on the screen be turned on and off individually, it can also be assigned its own color. All of the displays you see in Windows are the result of manipulating these individual points of light.

> **NOTE**
>
> Those who remember the Bush administration need to be assured that these are not political points of light, but physical points of light!

The letters VGA stand for Video Graphics Array. The 640×480 VGA mode used on many PCs was a standard developed by IBM back in 1987.

The VGA standard took the computer world by storm because it introduced relatively high-resolution graphics shown in 16 easily accessible colors. However, many computer users now want higher resolutions. As a result, SuperVGA modes with resolutions of 800×600 and 1024×768 were made popular by a wide variety of companies, not one of which was powerful enough to create a standard.

Furthermore, it has turned out that many computer users want to work with more than the 16 colors produced by 4-bit graphics cards. At the time of this writing, many programs use 256 color 8-bit graphics, and even 24-bit graphics cards that can produce millions of colors.

If you take a moment to do a little math, you can easily see the kind of calculations involved in defining a 1024×768, 8-bit color screen. For instance, 1,024 times 768 equals some three quarters of a million pixels, or more precisely 786,432 pixels. Each one of those pixels can be assigned to any one of 256 different colors. Furthermore, 786,432 times 256 equals... Well, never mind—you get the idea!

Painting a single screen that operates at this resolution is a task of fantastic complexity. In fact, some PCs can't be run effectively at that level of detail, though many can. Because the 18-month rule states that processors should double in speed every year and a half, it might not be long until everyone has graphics systems at least that powerful.

Graphics mode obviously introduces numerous complexities that make the programmer's job difficult. The *coup de grace* is delivered when one considers the mess created by the complete lack of standards in this field. For instance, one video card might implement a 1024×768 screen in a particular fashion, while the next card might have a totally different way of implementing the same resolution. The end result is that it can be extremely complicated for programmers to start working with the SuperVGA modes, which are, unfortunately, expected by many sophisticated users.

I'm explaining all of this primarily because it is important that users understand the graphics-related issues encountered when working in Windows. Any single Windows program can end up being run on a very wide variety of graphical systems. In other words, if you write a Windows program and unleash it upon a perhaps unsuspecting public, you have to understand that it could be run one day on a 640×480 black-and-white system, and the next day on a 1024×768 256-color system.

Such a prospect would be entirely too daunting for the vast majority of programmers were it not for the fact that Windows provides methods for taming all this diversity. Specifically, Windows has worked out a system whereby most programmers never write directly to a video card. Instead, they program something called a *device context*, which is in turn linked into a series of drivers written by video card manufacturers. These drivers always present a uniform interface to Windows, while at the same time implementing device-specific code to manipulate the hardware.

As a Windows programmer, you don't ever directly manipulate the video hardware. Instead, you deal with a stable API that calls functions, which manipulate an abstract entity called a device context. The device context, in turn, talks to a driver written by a hardware manufacturer, and the driver talks to the hardware. This arrangement makes it possible for you to write one set of code that will work on a very large variety of systems.

Once again, the main theme here is that people are willing to put up with bulky code bases and time delays in order to find some way to tame complexity. In this case, it's not the user, but the programmer who is willing to trade the speed of direct hardware access for the benefits to be found in a single stable API.

Of course some programmers, particularly game writers, simply can't stand to not have direct access to the hardware. By optimizing their code for a specific purpose, they feel that they can make their games more lively. However, they can't accomplish this goal unless they are proficient at writing or manipulating a large body of assembly language code, which has to be tuned, retuned, written, and rewritten for each of the 10 or 15 popular video cards that are found on the market.

Furthermore, these game programmers might find that a new video card appears on the scene, which is powerful and inexpensive enough to gain a significant market share. Once again, they have to dig down to the assembler level and start figuring out how to write for this particular card. Windows programmers, on the other hand, simply assume that every version of this card will be distributed with a free Windows video driver. This means that they don't have to change a line of their code. It's ready to run, because the video card's driver fully supports the Windows API.

> **NOTE**
>
> A few further points can be made about this issue. One is that many DOS gamers write code that is aimed at a very easy-to-use, very low-resolution video mode, which allows only 320×200 pixels per screen and 256 colors. Their skills are indeed formidable, but their problem is less complex than that presented by Windows, where many different resolutions are expected to be supported by all software.
>
> On the other side of the coin, not all video drivers written for Windows perform as well as they should. As a result, some of the very best Windows software manufacturers end up writing their own drivers, or at least portions of their own drivers. These extremely sophisticated programs are usually aimed at a narrow market, such as CAD programs or presentation software. Most Windows programmers, however, don't need to worry about the problems faced by these very sophisticated programs that typically make extensive use of very esoteric graphics calls.
>
> Finally, Microsoft has made some recent attempts to improve the speed of graphics performance under Windows. In particular, they have released the Wing library, Pascal-based translations that are readily available from CompuServe: just type GO DELPHI.

In the contemporary programming world, it seems that one is always trading speed for convenience. What makes it possible is the 18-month rule discussed in Chapter 1, "Welcome to Delphi." The end result is the need for ever larger and more powerful systems.

In this particular case, you have seen that Windows provides a single API that enables you to tame an array of video cards with a single stroke. Yes, your code would run faster if you wrote directly to video. On the other hand, the work involved in single-handedly writing even a simple non-Windows graphics program that could run on all systems would be prohibitively expensive for most developers. To overcome this problem, Windows programmers can use an API that handles all the graphics-oriented details. Fortunately, Windows provides one of the best available solutions to this need. It's not perfect, but it's very good.

Coordinates and the *TPoint* and *TRect* Structure

Delphi uses several different structures to encapsulate basic graphics-oriented programming ideas. If you are going to program in Windows, you have to get a feeling for what these structures are all about.

The TRect type is used to describe the four corners of a rectangle. It does so by assigning values to a point in the upper-left corner of the rectangle, and a second point in the bottom-right corner of the rectangle, as shown in Figure 5.6. (As you will see in a moment, this is a slight oversimplification, but is nonetheless a valid way to think about a TRect structure.)

FIGURE 5.6.

The top-left and bottom-right corners of a rectangle that is 800×600.

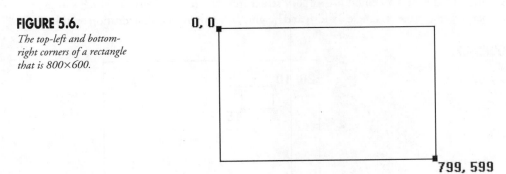

The coordinates of the forms used in a Delphi program can be described in terms of the four coordinates of a TRect structure. For now, it's simplest to think of the top-left corner of a form as residing at point (0, 0). Given that assumption, the bottom-right corner of the rectangle always contains the values associated with the width and height of the form.

This whole subject might be easiest to describe via an analogy. Suppose you own a plot of land 800 yards wide and 600 yards deep. Furthermore, suppose you want to be able to describe various locations on the land as if they were part of a grid, for which each point in the grid can be assigned an x and y value.

To get started, you might assign the upper-left (northwest) corner of the land the values Left := 0 and Top := 0. The bottom-right corner of the land would then be assigned the values Right = 799 and Bottom = 599. You could then use a TRect structure to describe the entire plot of land thusly: (0, 0, 799, 599).

Suppose you walked 20 yards to the west along the northern boundary of the land. Now you would be at location (20, 0), with 20 being the x or horizontal coordinate, and 0 being the y or vertical coordinate. Having started on your venture, you bravely move south an additional 10 yards. You are now at location (20, 10).

Having arrived at this spot, you decide that you like the quality of the soil near you, so you plant a flag there to mark the coordinates. This coordinate, at (20, 10), is equivalent to an Object Pascal TPoint record, with the x coordinate set to 20 and the y coordinate set to 10.

The next thing you do is walk an additional 15 yards east and 25 yards south, and then plant a flag at your current position, which is (35, 35). The two flags you have planted now describe a rectangle, which resides inside of the larger 800×600 rectangle that you own. (See Figure 5.7.) If you wanted, you could now set this area aside as a nice place to build a garden. When referring to the area, you could use a TRect structure (20, 10, 15, 25), in which the last two numbers represent the rectangle's width and height, rather than an actual location on the screen.

FIGURE 5.7.

Using a coordinate system to define a smaller rectangle inside a larger rectangle.

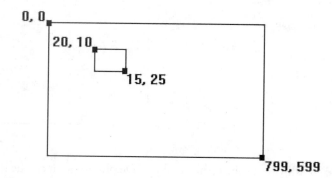

There are two different ways to look at a TRect structure. From one point of view, a TRect is four separate coordinates on a grid: (Left, Top, Right, Bottom). From another point of view, a TRect is two points, one describing the TopLeft corner and the other describing the BottomRight corner: (TopLeft: TPoint, BottomRight: TPoint). I haven't yet covered complex data types such as records, but you will have a chance to read about them later. For those who know about them from prior experience, here's what the declaration for a TPoint looks like:

```
TPoint = record
  x: Integer;
  y: Integer;
end;
```

And here's what a TRect looks like:

```
TRect = record
  case Integer of
    0: (Left, Top, Right, Bottom: Integer);
    1: (TopLeft, BottomRight: TPoint);
end;
```

> **NOTE**
>
> The TRect structure is a called a variant record. Variant records can be seen from two different perspectives, depending on your needs. For instance, the previous record can be seen as either four discrete points, or as two TPoint structures. That is, you can see it as (20, 10, 15, 25) or as ((20, 10), (15, 25)). All of this will be explained in more detail later, but the key point to grasp is that both syntaxes describe the same rectangle, each having its own advantages under certain circumstances.

If you take a moment to consider the matter, you can see that the TRect structure and the co-ordinate system described earlier can play a crucial role in Windows programming. For instance, if you place a button in a form, it can be viewed as a small rectangle inside of a larger rectangle. In other words, important coordinates in screen real estate are measured just like in the previous farming example.

At this stage, you should once again run the PIXELS.DPR program, which came on the CD accompanying this book. That program paints a series of individual pixels on the screen. That is, it turns on and off the smallest possible units of light that can be painted on a graphics screen. When I say that a typical graphics screen is 640×480 pixels in size, the units I'm referring to are the tiny dots of light you see in the PIXELS program.

> **NOTE**
>
> If you are not already an experienced programmer, don't bother trying to understand the PIXELS program. Instead, just run it and see what it does. The technical side of the program is explained in Chapter 9, which discusses loops.

Throughout this book, I'm going to make references to screen coordinate systems, and to the pixels that are used to paint a computer screen. These are basic units out of which the visual portion of the Windows environment is constructed. They are small and clumsy to use at times, and they force us all to invest in expensive hardware. Nevertheless, they are part of what Windows is all about.

Simple Graphics Code with *TShape*

The simplest graphics shape to draw to the screen is a rectangle. Delphi provides three ways to draw rectangles to the screen; I am going to show two of them in this chapter. The third method involves writing Windows API code to manipulate the current window's device context. The first method for drawing rectangles utilizes the TShape component, and the second uses the TCanvas object.

> **NOTE**
>
> I sometimes use the words object and component interchangeably. This is technically correct because all Delphi components are objects by definition. Some objects, however, are not components. That is, they cannot be automatically placed on the Component Palette. TCanvas is such an object. You will always use code to manipulate TCanvas and any other object that is not instantiated as a component. If you want to start manipulating it as a visual object, you have to make at least a few minor changes

to the way it operates so that it can become a component. As it happens, the TShape component really is little more than a thin wrapping around one facet of the TCanvas object.

The TShape component resides on the Additional page of the Component Palette. If you click its icon and drop it onto a form, you have created a rectangle. Use the mouse to resize it so that it looks like the graphic shown in Figure 5.8. Notice that to reshape the component, you must click it, and then select one of the black tabs on the edges of the component. Remember to hold the left mouse button down while you are reshaping the object.

FIGURE 5.8.

The RECT1 program shows how to use the TShape *component.*

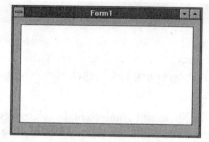

If you look at the Object Inspector, you see that a TShape object has 15 visible properties. Most of these properties are discussed in the next few pages.

The size of the TShape object is defined by designating coordinates in the Left, Top, Height, and Width properties. The coordinates are stated in terms of the form in which they are located, not in terms of the entire screen. This is like the earlier farming example. You don't describe a particular place on a farm by referring to its distance from the edges of the country in which it resides. Instead, you say that such and such a plot is X number of yards from the edges of the farm's property. In the same way, you don't normally refer to a rectangle on a form in terms of its location on the entire screen, but only in terms of its location relative to the form on which it resides.

NOTE

The distinction between viewing coordinates in terms of another window, or in terms of the entire screen, is technically referred to as the difference between client coordinates and screen coordinates. There are Windows functions such as ScreenToClient and ClientToScreen, as well as GetWindowRect and GetClientRect. These functions enable you to move back and forth between the two different coordinate systems. However, for now, we are working only with fundamental Delphi properties, so you should think primarily in terms of client coordinates, which are calculated relative to the window in which the object resides. The only Delphi object that regularly uses screen coordinates is the Form itself, which calculates its left and top coordinates in terms of the entire screen. This may sound more complicated at first, but the concepts involved are really very simple. The form's left and top coordinates describe the distance from the upper-left corner of the form to the upper-left corner of the screen. The top and left coordinates of objects dropped onto a form are described in terms of their distance from the upper-left corner of the form.

Here are the four coordinates used to define the location of the TShape object:

- **Left:** Locates the left side of the rectangle, relative to the left side of the form on which it resides.
- **Top:** Shows how far the top of the shape is from the top of the form.
- **Width:** Shows how wide the form is, that is, how far the right side of the rectangle is from the left side of the rectangle.
- **Height:** Defines the height of the rectangle. Again, this is not the distance from the top of the screen, nor from the top of the form, but the distance from the top of the rectangle!

NOTE

When making advanced calculations about the height and width of a form, you sometimes need to take the border and caption of the form into account. You will see an example of this in just a few more pages. However, the ClientWidth and ClientHeight properties also provide information that takes things such as borders and captions into account.

While in design mode, try dragging the shape with the mouse and watching the Object Inspector at the same time. You see that the Left, Top, Width, and Height properties change dynamically when you reshape or move the component.

If you want, you can directly type in the coordinates of the TShape component in the Object Inspector. If you want the component to be exactly 100 pixels in width, simply type the number 100 in the Width column.

NOTE

Advanced Windows programmers know that it is possible to change the size of the units used to measure the location of objects. That is, it's possible to change the mapping mode used to calculate screen coordinates. This topic is not germane to the current discussion, and for now these advanced programmers should always assume that the current mapping mode is mm_Text.

This section has given you a very basic overview of how to draw rectangles using the TShape component. In the next few sections, you will see more details about the best way to handle this process. At the same time, you will be learning many rules that apply to the basic manipulation of components.

Changing the Shape of a Component at Runtime

If you want to change the shape of a component at runtime, you can do so by manipulating the relevant properties. For instance, there is no practical difference between entering 100 in the Width property of the Object Inspector at design time, and executing the following code at runtime:

```
Shape1.Width := 100;
```

The RECT2 sample program on your disk shows how to enter the coordinates of a shape object into four edit controls, and then assigns those values to a shape object at runtime. To build the RECT2 project, place a TPanel and a TShape object on a form. Place four edit controls on the panel, as shown in Figure 5.9. There are a number of tricks that you can use to help arrange these controls, and I will explain them to you soon.

FIGURE 5.9.

The RECT2 program enables you to change the shape of an object at runtime.

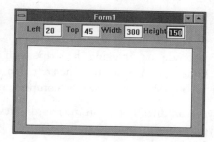

After you have placed the controls on the form, select all four of the edit components by holding down the Shift key and clicking once on each of the components. As you click each control, you should see little boxes appear at its corners, thereby signifying that it is selected. When all of the controls are selected, you can let up on the Shift key. Select the Text property from the Object Inspector and type in the number 100. The number should simultaneously appear in all four edit controls. Now select the Events page from the Object Inspector and create a method for the OnExit event of the controls. Fill in the method so that it looks like this:

```
procedure TForm1.Edit1Exit(Sender: TObject);
begin
  Shape1.Left := StrToInt(Edit1.Text);
  Shape1.Top := StrToInt(Edit2.Text);
  Shape1.Width := StrToInt(Edit3.Text);
  Shape1.Height := StrToInt(Edit4.Text);
end;
```

Some of the steps you just completed may need some explanation. The key point to grasp is that you have found a way to highlight a group of controls and perform the same action on each one. For instance, you typed in the number 100 in the Object Inspector, and all the edit controls changed at once because they were all selected. Furthermore, you found that you could easily associate one method with all four edit controls. Whenever an OnExit event is generated by any of these controls, you can now be sure that the method you have created will be called.

> **NOTE**
>
> This technique only works if all the controls you selected share the same property. For instance, if you select both a label control and an edit control, you cannot change the text associated with either one, because one uses the Caption property to control its text, and the other uses the Text property.
>
> You've seen that you can select multiple controls by holding down the Shift key and clicking each control. You can perform the same action by clicking the form next to a control, and then dragging a box around a set of controls. To test this, drop two or three label controls on the main part of this form and select them all using the mouse. To perform the same actions for a control placed on a panel, hold down the Ctrl key while you are clicking and dragging.

OnExit events are generated when the user leaves a particular control. It's not enough just to switch between one application and another application; instead, you must leave the edit control for another control on the same form. Typically this is done with a mouse click or a key stroke. For instance, if you run this program, you can generate an OnExit event by pressing the Tab key, or by holding down the Shift key and pressing the Tab key. The first method moves you to the next edit component, and the second method moves you to the previous edit component.

> **NOTE**
>
> Remember that you can change the tab order of items on a form by selecting the Edit | Tab Order menu choice. Note that if you want to change the tab order of items on a panel, you must select the panel and then open the Tab Order dialog.

The code in the method shown previously goes out to the edit controls and grabs the information stored in them, and then assigns these values to the coordinates of the TShape control. For instance, you could use this technique to assign the controls the following coordinates: (20, 50, 380, 200). Every time you move on to a new edit control, an OnExit event is generated, and the changes you have made take effect dynamically.

In this section, you have seen how to control the size of a component at runtime. In the process, you have also learned a great deal about the way components act, and how you can configure them at design time. One of the points you should be grasping by now is that visual controls are easy to use, but nonetheless, there are quite a few subtle tricks that can be mastered in order to optimize their use. In particular, you have seen that you can select multiple components, perform one action, and have it affect multiple parts of your program.

> **NOTE**
>
> To see why properties function as they do, you need to understand something about what the developers were trying to accomplish when they built the product. As you already know, every component that you manipulate inside Delphi is really just an object. When the developers of Delphi were designing the product, they decided that there should be little or no difference between objects and the things they represent. In other words, if you are working with a button object, the developers wanted you to feel that the code encapsulating and representing the button was the same thing as the button itself. Hence, they created properties.
>
> If you change the Width and Height properties of a button, the button changes its width and height immediately. There is no need for you to change the Width and then tell the object to redraw itself, although this is exactly what you have to do if you are dealing with raw data. Properties are more than a simple representation of data. Instead, they make the data come alive. Change the Width field of an object, and the object changes shape right before your eyes. Properties give you the illusion that you are dealing with a real object, and not with a code-based representation of an object.
>
> When you understand why properties exist, it becomes obvious that they are not directly connected to the Object Inspector. Rather, the Object Inspector is merely a convenient way to help you use properties at design time. There is, however, no reason

at all that you cannot change properties at runtime; in fact, this is a very common thing to do, especially if you have a complex interface that can respond to the user's needs.

The Align, Size, and Alignment Palette Dialogs

In the RECT2 program, you had to place four edit controls on a panel, and then choose their size and alignment. A simple way to expedite this matter is to select all four edit controls, and then choose the Size or Align option from the Edit menu. Note that the ellipses after the Size and Align options mean that a dialog is associated with that menu choice. The Size dialog is shown in Figure 5.10, and the Align dialog is shown in Figure 5.11.

FIGURE 5.10.

The Size dialog enables you to easily coordinate the sizes of multiple controls.

When you are working with the Size dialog, the best way to proceed is to size one of the edit controls individually. For instance, you might give the first control a height of 30 and a width of 40. Then, select all the controls, open the size dialog, and choose Grow to Largest for both the width and height. When you click the OK button, you find that all the controls are now the same size.

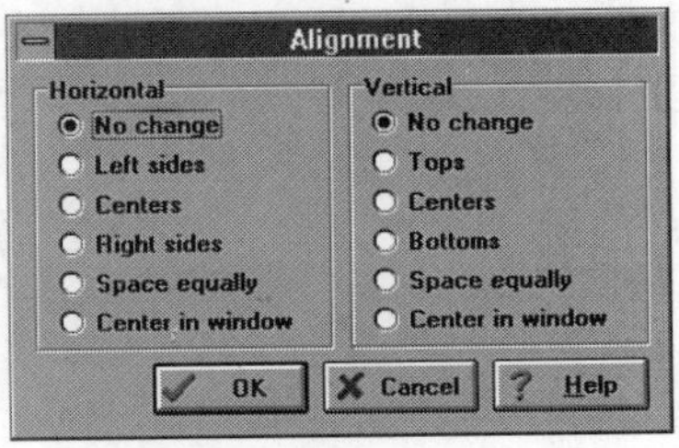

FIGURE 5.11.

The Align dialog enables you to arrange multiple components on the form in an orderly manner.

Obviously, there are a number of different permutations you can run on this sequence. I leave it to you to experiment with the controls to find the method that best suits your needs. Remember that if you have further questions about the Size dialog, you can turn to the online help.

The Align dialog works in a manner very similar to the Size dialog. To use it, select all four edit controls and then choose Space Equal from the Horizontal group box. Now open the dialog a second time, and choose Center in Window from both the Horizontal and Vertical groups. Once again, there are a number of variations you can run on this system, but I leave it up to you to experiment with the dialog, and to look up certain specific issues in the online help.

> **NOTE** .
>
> Delphi also lets you align components using the Alignment Palette from the View menu. Unlike the Alignment dialog, the Alignment Palette stays open on your desktop while you are working with a form. The Alignment Palette, however, has a number of less than purely intuitive icons on it. Most readers will probably need to spend a little time with the online help before they know how to use each of its options.

Colors, Scrollbars, and Shapes

The TShape object can do more than simply draw a white rectangle on the screen. For instance, if you pull down the list associated with the Shape property in the Object Inspector, you see that you can easily work with ellipses, circles, squares, and other assorted shapes. Furthermore, if you expand the Brush property, you can change the shape's color. The Pen property enables you to change the width and color of the outline of a TShape object.

> **NOTE**
>
> Don't forget that you can expand properties that have a plus sign (+) next to them by double-clicking on the property's name. A Color property always has a dialog associated with it. To bring up the dialog, double-click the area to the right of the Color property. Select a color from the dialog and click the OK button; the color you chose automatically takes effect.

As just described, it's trivial to change the major characteristics of a TShape object at design time. However, to make the same changes at runtime takes a little more work. The SHAPEDEM and SHAPEDEM2 programs on your disk show you how to proceed.

At its core, the SHAPEDEM program consists of nothing more than a TShape object placed on a form, along with two scrollbars and a few buttons. What's interesting about the program is the ease with which you can change the size, color, and shape of the TShape object at runtime.

Next, you find the code for the program in Listings 5.1 and 5.2. Remember that if you want to view the source for the DPR file in your projects, you can select the View | Project Source menu item.

Listing 5.1. The code for SHAPEDEM.DPR.

```
program Shapedem;

uses
  Forms,
  Main in 'MAIN.PAS' {Form1};

begin
  Application.CreateForm(TForm1, Form1);
  Application.Run;
end.
```

Listing 5.2. The code for the main unit in SHAPEDEM.DPR.

```
unit Main;

{ Program copyright (c) 1994 by Charles Calvert }
{ Project Name: SHAPEDEM }

interface

uses
  WinTypes, WinProcs, Classes,
  Graphics, Forms, Controls,
  StdCtrls, Dialogs, ExtCtrls;

type
  TForm1 = class(TForm)
    Shape1: TShape;
    ComboBox1: TComboBox;
    ShapeColor: TButton;
    ColorDialog1: TColorDialog;
    FormColor: TButton;
    ScrollBar1: TScrollBar;
    ScrollBar2: TScrollBar;
    procedure ComboBox1Click(Sender: TObject);
    procedure ShapeColorClick(Sender: TObject);
    procedure FormColorClick(Sender: TObject);
    procedure ScrollBar2Change(Sender: TObject);
    procedure ScrollBar1Change(Sender: TObject);
```

continues

Listing 5.2. continued

```delphi
  private
    { Private declarations }
  public
    { Public declarations }
  end;

var
  Form1: TForm1;

implementation

{$R *.DFM}

procedure TForm1.ComboBox1Click(Sender: TObject);
begin
  Shape1.Shape := TShapeType(ComboBox1.ItemIndex);
end;

procedure TForm1.ShapeColorClick(Sender: TObject);
begin
  if ColorDialog1.Execute then
    Shape1.Brush.Color := ColorDialog1.Color;
end;

procedure TForm1.FormColorClick(Sender: TObject);
begin
  if ColorDialog1.Execute then
    Form1.Color := ColorDialog1.Color;
end;

procedure TForm1.ScrollBar2Change(Sender: TObject);
begin
  Shape1.Height := ScrollBar2.Position * 2;
end;

procedure TForm1.ScrollBar1Change(Sender: TObject);
begin
  Shape1.Width := ScrollBar1.Position * 3;
end;

end.
```

In the next few paragraphs, you'll learn how to change the color of the form, the shape shown on the form, and the size and shape of the object itself.

When you run the SHAPEDEM program, it looks like the graphic shown in Figure 5.12. Use the program's scrollbars to change the size of the figure in the middle of the screen. Use the combo box to select a new shape for the object, and use the buttons to bring up a dialog that enables you to change the color of either the form or the shape.

FIGURE 5.12.

You can use the scrollbars and buttons to change the appearance of the SHAPEDEM program's form.

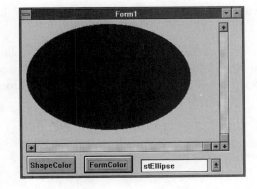

To create the program yourself, start by dropping down a button and a TColorDialog. The TColorDialog is found on the Dialogs page of the Component Palette. Now change the name on the button so that it reads *FormColor*. Double-click the button to create a method in the editor that looks like this:

```
procedure TForm1.FormColorClick(Sender: TObject);
begin
  if ColorDialog1.Execute then
    Form1.Color := ColorDialog1.Color;
end;
```

When you run the program, the code shown here pops up the ColorDialog, as shown in Figure 5.13.

FIGURE 5.13.

The ColorDialog gives the user an easy way to select a valid color at runtime.

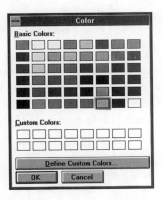

If the user clicks the OK button in the form, the following line of code is executed:

```
Form1.Color := ColorDialog1.Color;
```

This line of code sets the `Color` property for `Form1` to the color that was selected by the user inside of `ColorDialog1`.

The technique just shown can be used to change the color of the `TShape` object. All you need to do is drop down a `TShape` object from the additional page, and then drop down a button and change its name to `ShapeColor`. Double-click the button and create a method that looks like this:

```
procedure TForm1.ShapeColorClick(Sender: TObject);
begin
  if ColorDialog1.Execute then
    Shape1.Brush.Color := ColorDialog1.Color;
end;
```

What could be simpler?

Notice that the code written here is all but self-documenting. Anyone with even the slightest acquaintance with programming can just glance at this procedure and determine what it does.

You should now run the SHAPEDEM program so that you can see how easy it is to change the color of the elements on the form. Of course, you don't have to give the user the exclusive right to control all the elements of your program. Sometimes you can take the initiative. For instance, you could change the color of your form, or of an element on your form, in order to focus the user's attention on a particular part of the screen.

It makes sense that it should not be very difficult to change the color of an object found on one of the forms you create. But, using scrollbars to change its shape at least appears to be a more difficult task. In fact, experienced Windows programmers know that using scrollbars in a Windows program can be a fairly difficult task, requiring you to trap a number of messages in a complex `case` statement. Delphi, however, reduces the entire task of responding to a scrollbar with a single line of code.

To get started, first drop two scrollbars on the screen and set the `Kind` property of one of them to `sbHorizontal`, and the `Kind` property of the other to `sbVertical`. Now, turn to the Events page of the Object Inspector, and create a method for the `OnChange` property of each scrollbar. Fill in the methods with two lines of code so that they look like this:

```
procedure TForm1.ScrollBar1Change(Sender: TObject);
begin
  Shape1.Width := ScrollBar1.Position * 3;
end;

procedure TForm1.ScrollBar2Change(Sender: TObject);
begin
  Shape1.Height := ScrollBar2.Position * 2;
end;
```

The code shown here sets the width and height of the `TShape` object to the current position of the thumb on the scrollbar. For aesthetic reasons, I've opted to multiply the `Position` property by either 2 or 3, so that the shape can range over a fairly large portion of the form. The key point, however, is that it is extremely easy to write Delphi code that performs a task, which would be relatively complex to execute if you had to work directly with the Windows API. Delphi always makes you feel as though you are working directly with an object, and tries to hide the complexities that are introduced by the Windows API.

> **NOTE**
>
> The need to multiply the scrollbar position by either 2 or 3 is not entirely satisfying. As a result, I've implemented some more complex code in the second version of this program that shows a better way to handle this problem.

The final part of the SHAPEDEM program is a bit more challenging than the first two parts. It is also considerably more illuminating and shows a good deal about the power of Delphi's language.

If you create the SHAPEDEM program from scratch, you need to type in the names of the shapes that appear in the combo box. For instance, you need to manually type in the words stCircle and stSquare. These are the same names you see listed in the Object Inspector for the Shape1 object under the property called Shape. In other words, if you highlight Shape1 on the form and look at the shape property in the Object Inspector, you find a list of the possible shapes that can be associated with this object. These are the same shapes you should list in the combo box.

As I said earlier, it's not possible to get access to the Object Inspector at runtime. As a result, you need to first drop down a combo box and then manually type these names into the Items property for the combo box that is located on your form. To get started, first highlight the combo box on the form by clicking on it. Then, double-click on the right side of the Items property in the Object Inspector. This pops up a String list editor, as shown in Figure 5.14.

FIGURE 5.14.

The String list editor enables you to type in a set of default names that appear in a combo box.

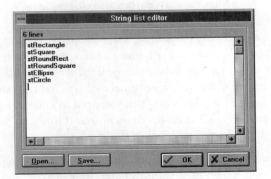

The actual items that you type into the String list editor are shown next. Be sure to type them in exactly as shown, and in the identical order.

```
stRectangle
stSquare
stRoundRect
stRoundSquare
stEllipse
stCircle
```

You can find these words listed in the online help under the listing for TShapeType. Or, if you want to go back to the original source code, you find the following enumerated type:

```
TShapeType = (stRectangle, stSquare, stRoundRect,
              stRoundSquare, stEllipse, stCircle);
```

> **NOTE**
>
> You can also access the names of the members of enumerated type by using the GetEnumName and GetEnumValue functions from the TypeInfo unit.

There is always code that stands behind the object you see in a Delphi program. Because you are a Delphi programmer, you have complete access to this code. Nothing is hidden from you. This is why you can change nearly every aspect of your program at runtime.

In this particular case, you need to write only one line of code, which should be executed in response to a click on the combo box by the user. To create the code, highlight the combo box on the form and then select the Events page in the Object Inspector. Now find the OnClick method in the Object Inspector and double-click the area to its right. Using this technique, create a method that looks like this:

```
procedure TForm1.ComboBox1Click(Sender: TObject);
begin
  Shape1.Shape := TShapeType(ComboBox1.ItemIndex);
end;
```

This line of code sets the Shape1.Shape property to the shape that the user has selected in the combo box. The code works because of the correspondence between the ordinal members of an enumerated type and the numerical value of the various items in a combo box. In other words, the first element in an enumerated type has the value zero, as does the first item shown in a combo box. For now, that's all you need to know. This topic will be taken up again, however, at the end of Chapter 8, "Branching and Integers," where you will get a chance to examine enumerated types in detail.

When you revisit this program in Chapter 8, you will see that there are several ways that it can be improved. To see these improvements immediately, you can run the SHAPDEM2 program, which is stored with the other programs from Chapter 5, "What is a Graphical Environment?," and Chapter 8. However, you should probably ignore the code for this program right now, because it involves a number of concepts most readers have not yet seen.

Using the *RGB* Function

Whenever a TShape component is painted, its interior and border are drawn in particular, pre-defined colors. By default, these colors are white and black, respectively. More specifically, the interior of the ellipse is filled with the color of the currently selected brush. You can change this color by making an assignment of the following type:

```
Shape1.Brush.Color := MyNewColor.
```

The RGBSHAPE program on your disk shows how you can get very specific control over the colors of an object that you paint to the screen. The letters RGB stand for red, green, and blue; each of the these colors makes up one of the colors passed to the RGB function itself:

```
function RGB(R: Byte; G: Byte; B: Byte): LongInt;
```

The parameters passed to this function describe an intensity to be assigned to one of these three colors. These numbers always exist within a range between 0 and 255.

If you pass the RGB function the following parameters, it will return a long integer representing the color red:

```
var
  Red: LongInt;
begin
  Red := RGB(255, 0, 0);
  Shape1.Brush.Color := Red;
end;
```

Here's how you get the colors green and blue:

```
Green := RGB(0, 255, 0);
Blue := RGB(0, 0, 255);
```

If you combine these three colors in various ways, you can produce particular shades. For instance, if you drop a button into a form and respond to a button click with the following code, you draw a bright yellow ellipse on the screen:

```
procedure TForm1.Button1Click(Sender: TObject);
begin
  Shape1.Brush.Color := RGB(255, 255, 0);
  Shape1.Shape := stEllipse;
end;
```

To achieve the color gray, pass in the following parameters:

```
Gray := RGB(127, 127, 127);
```

To get a fleshlike color, enter:

```
Skin := RGB(255, 127, 127);
```

You see how it works. Remember that the first parameter controls the amount of red in the final color, the second the amount of green, and the third the amount of blue. RGB: red, green, blue!

The RGBSHAPE program has a TShape component, three labels, three scrollbars, and three edit controls. Figure 5.15 shows what the program looks like in design mode.

FIGURE 5.15.

The RGBSHAPE program enables you to get a fine-tuned adjustment to the colors in a component.

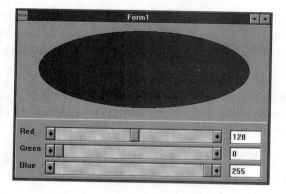

The RGBSHAPE program has only one method:

```
procedure TForm1.ScrollBar1Change(Sender: TObject);
begin
  Shape1.Brush.Color := RGB(Scrollbar1.Position,
                     Scrollbar2.Position,
                     Scrollbar3.Position);
  Edit1.Text := IntToStr(Scrollbar1.Position);
  Edit2.Text := IntToStr(Scrollbar2.Position);
  Edit3.Text := IntToStr(Scrollbar3.Position);
end;
```

This method first uses the current positions of the scrollbars to assign a color to the TShape objects brush. To make this work correctly, I set the Max property for each scrollbar to 255. When the color has been drawn on the screen, I show the actual numbers passed to the scrollbar in the edit components.

The point of the RGB program is to give you a graphical representation of the way the RGB function works. You might also find that this program helps you choose colors that you want to use in your own programs.

NOTE

When working with the RGBSHAPE program, some users may find that Windows cannot create pure tones for some colors, but instead creates a kind of patchwork that approximates the shade described by the parameters passed to the RGB function. However, you can generally get pure tones if you set each of the parameters to 0, 128, or 255. Numbers halfway between 0 and 128 also usually produce pure tones. Of course, the actual results you see depend on whether you are using a 16-color card, 256-color card, or some video card that offers many thousands of colors.

Listing 5.3. The code for the main unit in the RGBSHAPE program.

```
unit Main;

{ Program copyright (c) 1994 by Charles Calvert }
{ Project Name: RGBSHAPE }

interface

uses
  WinTypes, WinProcs, Classes,
  Graphics, Forms, Controls,
  StdCtrls, SysUtils, ExtCtrls;

type
  TForm1 = class(TForm)
    Panel1: TPanel;
    ScrollBar1: TScrollBar;
    ScrollBar2: TScrollBar;
    ScrollBar3: TScrollBar;
    Shape1: TShape;
    Red: TLabel;
    Green: TLabel;
    Blue: TLabel;
    Edit1: TEdit;
    Edit2: TEdit;
    Edit3: TEdit;
    procedure ScrollBar1Change(Sender: TObject);
  private
    { Private declarations }
  public
    { Public declarations }
  end;

var
  Form1: TForm1;

implementation

{$R *.DFM}

procedure TForm1.ScrollBar1Change(Sender: TObject);
begin
  Shape1.Brush.Color := RGB(Scrollbar1.Position,
                    Scrollbar2.Position,
                    Scrollbar3.Position);
  Edit1.Text := IntToStr(Scrollbar1.Position);
  Edit2.Text := IntToStr(Scrollbar2.Position);
  Edit3.Text := IntToStr(Scrollbar3.Position);
end;

end.
```

Using *TCanvas* to Draw Shapes

As I said earlier, the TShape object is not the only technique for drawing shapes on the screen. At times it is more convenient to simply draw them with the TCanvas object.

TCanvas provides many different ways to draw shapes, but perhaps the most important are the Ellipse and Rectangle procedures:

```
procedure Ellipse(X1, Y1, X2, Y2: LongInt);
procedure Rectangle(X1, Y1, X2, Y2: LongInt);
```

Both of these methods enable you to draw a shape to the screen by simply writing code like this:

```
Canvas.Rectangle(10, 10, 100,  100);
```

This code draws a rectangle to the screen with the left and top points set to 10 and 10. The next two numbers, 100 and 100, do not designate that the rectangle has a width and height of 100. Instead, these numbers state that the rectangle's right and bottom points are 100 pixels distant from the left and top parts of the form. As a result, it is often simplest to write code that looks like this:

```
var
  X,Y: Integer;
begin
  X := 10;
  Y := 10;
  Canvas.Rectangle(X, Y, X + 20, Y + 10);
end;
```

The preceding code designates that the rectangle should have a width of 20 and a height of 10.

You can draw ellipses the same way you draw rectangles:

```
var
  X,Y: Integer;
begin
  X := 10;
  Y := 10;
  Canvas.Ellipse(X, Y, X + 20, Y + 10);
end;
```

The code shown here draws an ellipse with a bounding rectangle exactly the same size as the rectangle shown in the previous example. The graphic shown in Figure 5.16 demonstrates how you can use a rectangle to define the shape of an ellipse.

If you want to change the color of a shape that you draw to the screen, you can do so with the Brush property of a TCanvas object:

```
Canvas.Brush.Color := clRed;
```

FIGURE 5.16.

The Ellipse *procedure draws a rounded figure that fits exactly inside a bounding rectangle.*

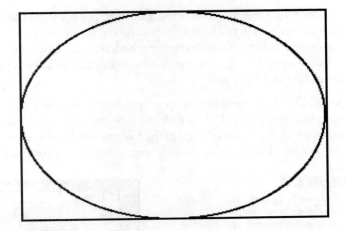

TCanvas.Brush is of type TColor. The constant clRed is one of many colors that can be taken on by the TColor type. Here are a few other available types:

clAqua	clBlack	clBlue
clDkGray	clFuchsia	clGray
clGreen	clLime	clLtGray
clMaroon	clNavy	clOlive
clPurple	clRed	clSilver
clTeal	clWhite	clYellow

All of these colors represent particular results that are returned from the RGB function. For instance, clRed is the same color you get if you pass RGB the parameters 255, 0, and 0.

The CANSHAPE program found on your disk demonstrates a few simple ideas about using the TCanvas object to draw shapes to the screen. The basic idea of the program is to enable you to click a portion of the screen and see a small circle appear to mark the location of the click.

The main function for the program occurs in response to an OnMouseDown event. To create the event, select the form and then choose the Events page from the Object Inspector. Now double-click the area to the right of the OnMouseDown event and create the following function:

```
procedure TForm1.FormMouseDown(Sender: TObject;
                       Button: TMouseButton;
                       Shift: TShiftState;
                       X, Y: Integer);
begin
  Canvas.Brush.Color := ShapeColor;
  Canvas.Ellipse(X, Y, X + 10, Y + 10);
end;
```

The `FormMouseDown` function draws a small ellipse at the coordinates logged each time a mouse click occurs. The actual coordinates that you use are automatically passed to you in the X and Y parameters of the `FormMouseDown` method. As you can see, the actual width and height of the ellipse is set to 10, which is a relatively small value on screens that are usually somewhere between 600 and 1100 pixels in width.

The CANSHAPE program uses a simple menu to enable you to choose the color of the circles you place on a screen. Delphi makes it very easy for you to create menus. To get started, select a menu from the Standard page of the Component Palette, drop it on a form, and then double-click on it to bring up the Menu Designer, which is shown in Figure 5.17.

FIGURE 5.17.

The Menu Designer enables you to create menus with just a few short moments of work.

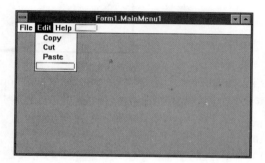

To create a menu item, simply begin typing and you see that your words appear in the menu itself, and also in the Caption property in the Object Inspector. By using either the mouse or the arrow keys, you can move down into a popup menu or further to the right. The menu for this program has the word *ShapeColor* on the menubar itself, and a popup menu beneath, with the words Red, Blue, and Green on it (as shown in Figure 5.18). When typing in the words, press Enter after each.

FIGURE 5.18.

The menu for the CANSHAPE program.

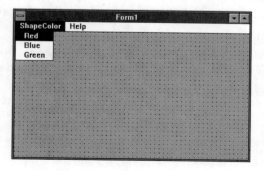

If at design time you double-click any of the menu items listed above, an associated method is created, just as a method is created when you double-click a button. Furthermore, if you turn to the Events page in the Object Inspector, you can see that the previous technique creates a method for the `OnClick` event, which is exactly the same thing that happens when you double-click the button.

The actual methods you create should look like this:

```
procedure TForm1.Red1Click(Sender: TObject);
begin
  FShapeColor := clRed;
end;

procedure TForm1.Blue1Click(Sender: TObject);
begin
  FShapeColor := clBlue;
end;

procedure TForm1.Green1Click(Sender: TObject);
begin
  FShapeColor := clGreen;
end;
```

`FShapeColor` is a global variable that you must declare yourself, which you should place in the declaration for the form object:

```
TForm1 = class(TForm)
    MainMenu1: TMainMenu;
    Shape1: TMenuItem;
    Red1: TMenuItem;
    Blue1: TMenuItem;
    Green1: TMenuItem;
    procedure FormMouseDown(Sender: TObject; Button: TMouseButton;
      Shift: TShiftState; X, Y: Integer);
    procedure Red1Click(Sender: TObject);
    procedure Blue1Click(Sender: TObject);
    procedure Green1Click(Sender: TObject);
  private
    FShapeColor: TColor;
  public
    { Public declarations }
  end;
```

For now, you should not worry about the declaration made here, because the whole subject of variables will be explained in depth over the next few chapters.

The key point to grasp about the CANSHAPE program is that it enables you to choose colors from a menu, and to then draw a small circle with that color at a particular location on the screen. The program serves as a brief introduction to the `Canvas` property, and to the basic steps involved in creating and using a menu.

Listing 5.4. The code for the main unit in the CANSHAPE program.

```
unit Main;

{ Program copyright (c) 1994 by Charles Calvert }
{ Project Name: CANSHAPE }
```

continues

Listing 5.4. continued

```
interface

uses
  WinTypes, WinProcs, Classes,
  Graphics, Forms, Controls,
  Menus;

type
  TForm1 = class(TForm)
    MainMenu1: TMainMenu;
    Shape1: TMenuItem;
    Red1: TMenuItem;
    Blue1: TMenuItem;
    Green1: TMenuItem;
    About1: TMenuItem;
    About2: TMenuItem;
    procedure FormMouseDown(Sender: TObject; Button: TMouseButton;
      Shift: TShiftState; X, Y: Integer);
    procedure Red1Click(Sender: TObject);
    procedure Blue1Click(Sender: TObject);
    procedure Green1Click(Sender: TObject);
    procedure About2Click(Sender: TObject);
  private
    FShapeColor: TColor;
  public
    { Public declarations }
  end;

var
  Form1: TForm1;

implementation

uses
  About;

{$R *.DFM}

procedure TForm1.FormMouseDown(Sender: TObject;
                               Button: TMouseButton;
                               Shift: TShiftState;
                               X, Y: Integer);
begin
  Canvas.Brush.Color := FShapeColor;
  Canvas.Ellipse(X, Y, X + 10, Y + 10);
end;


procedure TForm1.Red1Click(Sender: TObject);
begin
  FShapeColor := clRed;
end;

procedure TForm1.Blue1Click(Sender: TObject);
```

```
begin
  FShapeColor := clBlue;
end;

procedure TForm1.Green1Click(Sender: TObject);
begin
  FShapeColor := clGreen;
end;

procedure TForm1.About2Click(Sender: TObject);
begin
  AboutBox.ShowModal;
end;

end.
```

Listing 5.5. The code for the About box in the CANSHAPE program.

```
unit About;

{ Program copyright (c) 1994 by Charles Calvert }
{ Project Name: CANSHAPE }

interface

uses
  WinTypes, WinProcs, Classes,
  Graphics, Forms, Controls,
  StdCtrls,  Buttons, ExtCtrls;

type
  TAboutBox = class(TForm)
    Panel1: TPanel;
    OKButton: TBitBtn;
    ProgramIcon: TImage;
    ProductName: TLabel;
    Version: TLabel;
    Copyright: TLabel;
    Comments: TLabel;
  private
    { Private declarations }
  public
    { Public declarations }
  end;

var
  AboutBox: TAboutBox;

implementation

{$R *.DFM}

end.
```

As a final touch to round out this chapter, I have added an About box to the CANSHAPE program. The actual dialog used in shown in Figure 5.19.

FIGURE 5.19.

The About box for the CANSHAPE program is a variation on the dialog stored in the Gallery.

To create the About box, first select the Options | Environment | Preferences dialog from the menu, and then make sure that Gallery: Use on New Form has an X in its checkbox. Close the Environment dialog and select New Form from the speedbar. Select the About box from the Gallery dialog, as shown in Figure 5.20.

FIGURE 5.20.

The Gallery dialog contains some default forms, and enables you to add your own forms if you wish.

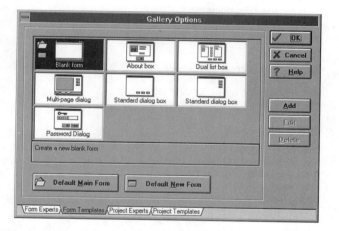

NOTE

You can add new dialogs to the Gallery by right-clicking any form and selecting the Save as template. You can also save an entire project to the Gallery by right-clicking the Project Manager. The Gallery will be discussed in more depth in Chapter 19, "Creating Simple Database Programs." However, I introduce it here briefly so that you will be aware of its existence.

After you have selected the About box dialog from the Gallery, you can modify it as you would any other dialog. In particular, you might want to add the name of the dialog, a copyright notice, and a brief comment on what the program does.

Save the dialog into the CANSHAPE directory, under the name ABOUT.PAS. Go to the top of the MAIN.PAS unit and add a uses clause that references the unit:

```
...
var
  Form1: TForm1;

implementation

uses
  About;
...
```

In this particular case, it doesn't matter whether you add the reference to unit About in the long uses clause at the top of the program, or if you add it in the implementation, as shown previously.

> **NOTE**
>
> The location of an item in a uses clause becomes important only when you are working with complicated programs, in which one unit might reference another unit, which might, in turn, reference the first unit. This is called a circular unit reference, and can usually be resolved by moving the relevant portions of the uses clause in one unit from the interface to the implementation.

After creating the uses clause, you should add a Help | About reference to the menu, and then double-click the menu item so you can add the following line of code:

```
procedure TForm1.About2Click(Sender: TObject);
begin
  AboutBox.ShowModal;
end;
```

The subject of modal dialogs will be introduced again later in the book, but for now you should simply note that the code shown here pops up the About dialog, and terminates only after the user closes the dialog. This means the user cannot use any other portion of the program while the dialog is visible. Dialogs that act this way are called modal dialogs.

Opening Forms as Text Objects

Delphi supports Two Way tools, which means that you can open a form as either a visible object, or as a text object. You might want to open a form as a text object if you need to edit it for internationalization purposes, or if you want to save it into an archive.

If you want to view the main form for the CANSHAPE program as a text object, go to the File | Open File menu choice and pop up the Open File dialog. At the bottom-left corner of the dialog, there is a combo box that enables you to select Form Files, as shown in Figure 5.21. Choose this option, and then open MAIN.DFM. If Delphi asks you whether you want to save and close the Form Designer, choose Yes. You then see the text shown in Listing 5.6. This text describes the main form as code. You can edit this text if you wish; when you close the text view of the form, the changes you have made will be visible.

FIGURE 5.21.

The Open dialog enables you to select either files with a PAS extension, or files with a DFM extension.

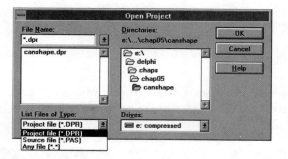

Listing 5.6. The main form for the CANSHAPE program, when viewed as text.

```
object Form1: TForm1
  Left = 154
  Top = 130
  Width = 435
  Height = 281
  Caption = 'Form1'
  Menu = MainMenu1
  PixelsPerInch = 96
  OnMouseDown = FormMouseDown
  object MainMenu1: TMainMenu
    object Shape1: TMenuItem
      Caption = 'ShapeColor'
      object Red1: TMenuItem
        Caption = 'Red'
        OnClick = Red1Click
      end
      object Blue1: TMenuItem
        Caption = 'Blue'
        OnClick = Blue1Click
      end
      object Green1: TMenuItem
        Caption = 'Green'
        OnClick = Green1Click
      end
    end
    object About1: TMenuItem
      Caption = 'Help'
      object About2: TMenuItem
```

```
        Caption = 'About'
        OnClick = About2Click
      end
    end
  end
end
```

If you want to get a sense of how to edit a form when it's in text mode, you can change one of the caption properties shown earlier, and then close the DFM file. When you bring up the dialog once again, you see that the caption now has the value you assigned to it when the form was being viewed in text mode.

You can always edit a component as text, even if you don't have the entire form open in text mode. For instance, you can drop a button on a form, highlight it, choose Cut from the Edit menu, and then paste the object into a text editor:

```
object Button1: TButton
  Left = 112
  Top = 16
  Width = 89
  Height = 33
  TabOrder = 0
  Caption = 'Button1'
end
```

It doesn't matter what text editor you use. For instance, you could use the editor built into Delphi, or you could paste the text into the NotePad program. Now edit the text by changing the Caption, and by changing the type from TButton to TRadioButton:

```
object Button1: TRadioButton
  Left = 112
  Top = 16
  Width = 89
  Height = 33
  TabOrder = 0
  Caption = 'Charlie'
end
```

Now, copy the new code into clipboard and paste the button back into the Forms Editor. You'll see that the caption has been changed, and its type has been changed from TButton to TRadioButton. Be sure to try this technique on your own computer, because it is both fun to watch and instructive regarding the way Delphi handles visual objects.

If you are interested in an advanced use of this capability, see the FRM2COMP program that ships on the CD in the PROGRAMS subdirectory. It shows how you can convert a form into a component.

Summary

In this chapter you learned how to use the TCanvas and TShape objects to draw simple geometric forms to the screen. In particular, the chapter taught you a lot about using colors, calculating coordinates, and working with rectangles and ellipses.

As a subtext running throughout most of the chapter, you learned a number of important points about how to control components both at design time and runtime. In particular, you saw how the coordinates of a component are mirrored in that component's properties, and how you can control those coordinates both at design time and runtime. You also got a brief peek at the Gallery, and at editing Forms as text.

In general, you should now know enough about components and graphics to enable you to manipulate these two features in the simple ways required during the next several chapters. These chapters will discuss the basics of programming with Object Pascal, and introduce a few more simple graphics issues (particularly in Chapter 9). Graphics programming will be visited again in the section on objects and in the last section of the book, which is about advanced Windows programming.

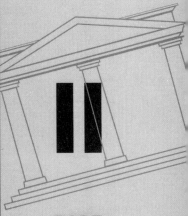

PART

II

The Elements of a Language: Simple Types, Floating Point Numbers, and Branching and Looping

Variables and Types

6

Overview

To understand Delphi, you must come to grips with the ObjectPascal language. The visual portion of the product is extremely powerful, but the real key to your success as a programmer lies with your understanding of coding techniques.

This chapter and the next 10 chapters concentrate on the basics of coding the ObjectPascal language. My goal is to present the reader with a useful introduction to the act of writing code. I start at the very beginning and work through all the major features of the language.

The next few chapters are aimed at someone who is unfamiliar with ObjectPascal. However, they also can serve as a refresher course for people who have been away from programming for a while, or have been working with another language.

However, even experienced programmers will find the next few chapters enlightening. There are three reasons for this:

■ These chapters contain a lot of simple programs that show how to accomplish daily tasks with a visual programming tool. In particular, I use these chapters to introduce the basic techniques for using edit controls, labels, listboxes, radio buttons, and checkboxes.

■ The visual paradigm has had a major impact on the language. Code is structured differently than it used to be. The new visual programming techniques have changed everything, and to get into the swim as quickly as possible you need to see exactly where the visual paradigm meets the fundamental elements of the written language.

■ Some experienced programmers may not know Windows programming very well. As a result, they will benefit from writing simple programs that utilize many of the key features of the Windows environments.

As mentioned in Chapter 1, "Welcome to Delphi," I have made the decision not to devote entire chapters to introducing the major Windows controls. Instead, I concentrate on a subject more worthy of your time: the ObjectPascal language. Delphi makes Windows controls so easy to use that there is no need to discuss their basic functionality in any depth. You can get up to speed with them in just a few minutes, and most of the details about their behavior are addressed thoroughly in the online help. After you have worked with these controls for a while, I will come back to some of them in the chapters on object-oriented programming. I will then analyze the structure of some of these controls, which is a fairly complex subject, and I will show how to access their advanced capabilities. However, the simple act of using an edit, listbox, or radio button control needs no more discussion than basic use of the WriteLn procedure in DOS. All you need is a few hints, and you will be ready to go.

In particular, this chapter introduces the concept of variables and how they are treated in Delphi. This is one of the most fundamental ideas in computer programming. In particular, you will look at two basic types of variables:

- The first is a string variable, which is designed to give you an easy way to manipulate relatively small amounts of text.

- The second type is a numeric variable or integer. It is generally used to manipulate whole numbers.

After you have had a chance to grasp the basics of this subject, the next chapter presents an exhaustive examination of all the basic Delphi types, from strings to integers to floating point numbers. This chapter is meant to give you an introduction and overview of the entire subject, and the next chapter explores it in depth.

As always, even people who are already familiar with this material will find something useful here. Specifically, this chapter presents the user with two sample programs that reveal much about the way Delphi works. Even if you are a pro who already understand variables, you should take the time to run each of the sample programs.

Variables: The Basics

In Chapter 4, "The Structure of a Delphi Program," most of the words you wrote to the screen came in the form of string literals. For instance, you wrote

```
procedure Button1OnClick;
begin
  Edit1.Text := 'No matter, never mind!';
end;
```

where the words No matter, never mind! were a string literal. String literals get their name because you are literally writing the text exactly where it is used in the code.

> **NOTE**
>
> In the computer world, any word, phrase, or sentence that is comprised of written words is called a *string*. For instance, heathen is a string. So is papacy. As you can see, Pascal programmers follow the European rule of always placing strings in single quotes. Most of the time, strings are representations of English words that you can find in the dictionary. However, there is no reason why a string could not be a series of nonsense characters, such as sdf#%34.

New programmers may see string literals as quite a natural way to represent data, but you will find that programmers usually work with variables or constants rather than string literals. This is because variables are more flexible than string literals.

Everyone has been using variables in one form or another since they learned basic math. For instance, in the formula

```
X = 1 + 1;
```

the letter X is a variable that is, coincidentally, equal to the value 2.

Variables reserve a place in the computer's memory where a particular value can be placed. In the preceding example, the letter x is reserving a place on the page where the result of the addition 1 + 1 can be placed. In the same way, variables in a computer program reserve a place inside the computer where a particular value can be placed. Many times that value will be the result of a computation, but it can just as easily be a string, or even a much more complex structure such as an array or an object.

The Rainman Comes in the Wolfman's Disguise

Before getting into the details of how variables work, it is probably a good idea for you to develop a mental image that will help make the subject more tangible. One metaphor you might find useful is what I call the *memory theater*.

The memory theater is a model for the way the memory and logic chips inside a computer actually interact. Specifically, I'm talking about dynamic memory, or RAM, which is the place where much of the action in a computer takes place. In this analogy, the memory inside a computer is like the seats inside a huge auditorium. All of these seats are lined up as if they were part of a giant amphitheater, with the performers on stage in front of the seats equivalent to the computer's CPU.

> **NOTE**
>
> Every programmer should have a general understanding of both CPUs and RAM. You don't need to know everything about your hardware, but you need to know the fundamentals.
>
> RAM is an acronym for Random Access Memory. When a program or piece of data is read off a disk or hard drive, it is being read into RAM. While code or data is on a disk or drive, it is quiescent—it is in a static state. The moment it gets read into RAM, it is in play, just as a ball in a sporting event is in play once it's on the court. As a rule, RAM functions properly only while a computer is running. The moment you turn a computer off, you lose anything stored in RAM that has not already been saved to disk.
>
> The CPU, or Central Processing Unit, is the chip that does the computation inside a computer. If you want to add 2 and 2, the part of the computer that actually does the processing is called the CPU. Most computers that will run Delphi use Intel CPUs such as the 386, 486, or Pentium.

Before the advent of Windows, most programmers working on an Intel platform had only one megabyte of RAM to work with when they wrote their programs. Of that 1 MB, only 640 KB was actually available to the programmer. The rest was claimed by the operating system or the hardware.

When thinking of the memory theater, picture a CPU being placed in front of an auditorium that holds an audience with 640,000 members. Most Windows machines, however, work with 4, 8, or even 16 MB of RAM. This means that there are between 4 and 16 million seats in the memory theater. Modern memory management techniques create something called *virtual memory,* which expands the actual number of seats in the memory theater to well above even such a huge number as 16,000,000.

It is crucial to understand that every variable used in a Delphi program will take a spot in one or more of those millions of available seats. For instance, a string consisting of the single word "hello" will take up six seats. Five of those seats will be for the letters in the word, and the sixth will be used to define its length. Small numbers such as 1 or 5 might take up only one seat in the memory theater. A larger number such as 2,000,000 might take up four seats, and decimal numbers such as 2.1 might take up four or more seats.

The memory theater is an experimental theater that invites audience participation. Specifically, the CPU requests that certain members of the audience remember a particular piece of information. Most of the time the variables in the audience are simply waiting somewhere in RAM, sitting quietly in their seats. But then suddenly the CPU may request that variables in a particular section of the audience report on the values they have been remembering.

Suppose that at a particular point in time, the CPU asks one member of the audience, the one in row 5, seat 10, to reveal the number it was assigned. Perhaps it will say 2. Suppose further that when queried, a second variable also says the number 2.

The CPU then turns to some very special members of the audience who are sitting in roped-off sections called the code segment or stack segment. The CPU always turns to these members when it needs to know what to do next. It is their job to prompt the CPU. "Do this," they say, or "Do that." In this particular case, the CPU asks the folks in the code segment what it should do next, and they tell the CPU to add the two numbers and then assign the result to another variable sitting in the audience. The CPU gladly does this and then passes the result, which is 4, to a member of the audience sitting at a particular pre-assigned seat.

You can push this metaphor to even greater extremes by imagining the CPU as something of an idiot savant. For instance, many people may recall the character played by Dustin Hoffman in the film *Rainman.* You could give him a set of numbers and he could perform incredible feats with them, such as multiplying 1,234 by 1,234 in his head in only a few seconds. But in other parts of his life, he had to be led around almost literally by the hand.

The same thing occurs in the memory theater. The CPU can perform incredible feats that awe all but the most jaded members of the audience. However, the CPU is helpless without the code segment, stack segment, and the rest of the audience. He needs the code to tell him what to do next, and he needs RAM to act as his memory. You see, the sad fact is that the CPU can remember only a very few things at a time, and once he has forgotten them, they are gone completely, as if he had never seen them. The only way he can ever get them back is if the folks in the code segment, stack segment, or data segment tell him exactly where that information is stored.

In a sense, what you have seen presented here is a metaphor for the inner workings of a computer. In this metaphor, a single actor (or perhaps a troupe of actors) called the CPU stands in front of a huge auditorium. This auditorium is filled with an audience, some of whom participate in the play by acting the part of variables. These variables store the information used during the play. Another part of the audience is called the code segment, and it remembers the events that are going to take place during the play.

As it is described here, some readers may complain that the memory theater must be the sight of some very bizarre performances. All in all, I would have to say that this is true. We are in the 1990s now. We're nearing not just the turn of the century but the turn of the millennium. Some pretty remarkable and unusual things have been happening, not the least of which has been the advent of computers and the extraordinary, and delightful, performances they put on.

The Programmer as Playwright

From the previous description, it is obvious that the performances that take place in the memory theater are scripted by someone. As it happens, that person happens to be you, the programmer. It is your job to write the code memorized by the people in the code segment; and it is your job to decide which members of the audience will be active players, or variables.

It's time now to start working with some specific coding examples. To get started, use the visual programming tools to create a form like the image you see in Figure 6.1. Specifically, you need to create a form called the THelloForm and then add a label with the words "Enter your name" in its caption field. Next, create two edit controls with the default names Edit1 and Edit2. Finally, add two buttons at the bottom of the form. Name the first button BOk and the second BConfirm, and give them the captions Ok and Confirm.

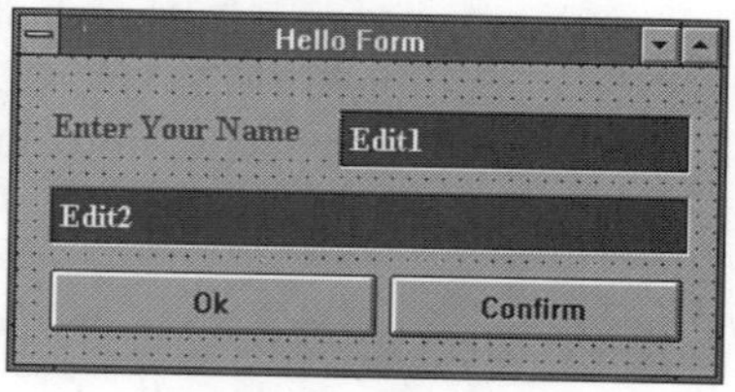

FIGURE 6.1.

The Hello form has a label, two edit controls, and two buttons.

Double-click the OK button and write the following code in response to its `OnClick` event:

```
procedure TFHelloForm.BOkClick(Sender: TObject);
begin
  Close;
end;
```

This button can now be used to close the entire form when the user wants to exit the program.

Now double-click the Confirm button and create a method that looks like this:

```
procedure THelloForm.BConfirmClick(Sender: TObject);
var
  Name: String;
begin
  Name := Edit1.Text;
  Edit2.Text := 'You entered: ' + Name;
end;
```

The code in the `BConfirmClick` method has something new in it that you have not seen before. It has a variable called `Name`, which is of type string.

The most important part of the `BConfirmClick` method is the actual declaration of the variable:

```
var
  Name: String;
```

This declaration starts out by writing the keyword var, which tells the compiler that you are about to declare one or more variables. On the next line you declare the variable itself, by writing the name of the variable followed by a colon and then its type.

After the description of the memory theater, you should be ready to understand exactly what this code does. Specifically, it tells the compiler to set aside 256 seats in the amphitheater for the express purpose of remembering a person's name or any other data that might be typed into the computer's first edit control. When the computer sees this instruction, it immediately finds 256 members of the audience who aren't doing anything else, and it tells them that they must dedicate their lives wholeheartedly and without reservation to the single purpose of remembering up to 256 characters of input.

> **NOTE**
>
> There is always the possibility that you will ask the computer for some memory, say 256 bytes worth, and there is no more memory available. Because that contingency is very remote at this stage of the game, I'm not going to explain how to deal with it quite yet. I will, however, point out that 10 or 15 years ago, many people bought computers that had only 16,000 or even 4,000 bytes of RAM available. On such small machines, programmers were always wrestling with "out of memory" errors.

Because this is such a small program, you can be fairly certain that simply declaring the variable Name will guarantee that you have 256 bytes of memory set aside in the memory theater. If the user enters a name in the first edit control and then presses the Confirm button, the following lines of code get executed:

```
Name := Edit1.Text;
Edit2.Text := 'You entered: ' + Name;
```

The first line gets the string that the user entered and stores it in the variable called Name. Suppose that the variable Name has seats 1–256 reserved in row J of the memory theater. After the assignment shown in the first line of code, the people in those seats will be remembering the name the user typed in. For instance, if the user typed in the word Margie, seat J-2 would be remembering the letter M, seat J-3 would be remembering the letter a, and so on. In the Delphi world, the first seat in the row, J-1, would remember the length of the string, which in this case happens to be 6. The people sitting in seats J-7 through J-256 are still part of the string name, but they get to sit this one out, because there is nothing for them to do. Take a look at Figure 6.2 to get a visual image of this state of affairs.

FIGURE 6.2.

The folks in row J of the memory theater are wholeheartedly dedicated to the sole purpose of remembering the contents of the variable Name.

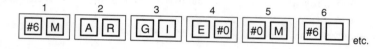

The final line of code in this procedure combines a string literal with your variable and shows the result in the second edit control. In particular, the words "You entered:" are combined with the user's name to form a string such as "You entered: Margie."

In short, the program first prompts the user to enter his or her name. After the name is entered, the user can press the Confirm button to see a copy of the string assigned to the variable called Name. Take a look at Figure 6.3 to see how this looks on-screen.

FIGURE 6.3.

The Hello program as it might appear to the user.

Of course, it is not going to do you much good just to look at this information here on the written page. Instead, you need to get in there with the lions and gladiators and actually write and run the code that makes this program tick. Specifically, Listing 6.1 shows you the complete code from the main unit of the program. If you need any further help, you can find the program on the CD that comes with this book.

Listing 6.1. The Hello program shows how to use a string variable.

```
unit Main;

{ Program copyright (c) 1994 by Charles Calvert }
{ Project Name: HELLO }

interface

uses
  WinTypes, WinProcs,
  Classes, Graphics,
  Controls, Forms, StdCtrls;

type
  THelloForm = class(TForm)
    Edit1: TEdit;
    Edit2: TEdit;
    BOk: TButton;
    LEnterName: TLabel;
    BConfirm: TButton;
    procedure BOkClick(Sender: TObject);
    procedure BConfirmClick(Sender: TObject);
  end;

var
  HelloForm: THelloForm;

implementation

{$R *.DFM}

procedure THelloForm.BOkClick(Sender: TObject);
begin
  Close;
end;

procedure THelloForm.BConfirmClick(Sender: TObject);
var
  Name: String;
begin
  Name := Edit1.Text;
  Edit2.Text := 'You entered: ' + Name;
end;

end.
```

When you look at the code shown here on the printed page, it looks a bit intimidating. But it was necessary for the programmer to type in only the six lines belonging to the BOkClick and BConfirmClick functions. This is very little effort for an enormous payoff. Don't let the chance to actually run this code pass you by. It isn't enough just to read this book. You have to get into the amphitheater itself and wrestle with some lions.

> **NOTE**
>
> Delphi puts some default text in the edit controls you create. For instance, it puts the word EDIT1 in the TEdit component of that name. For now, I am just leaving that text there, so you will not have any trouble designing the forms. In other words, the text provides a ready-made label that describes each component on the form, and for now I will consider that those labels might help the reader find their way around. However, later I will show you several different ways to remove the labels. If you are bothered by this issue, one simple way to remedy the problem is to set the Text field in the Object Inspector to an empty string. The same effect can be obtained for TLabels by setting the Caption field to a blank string, though of course this might not make much sense in many cases.

It's really amazing to me that even beginning programmers can use Delphi to create such a complex program with so little work. In the old days, such a program would take hundreds of lines to create, and beginners wouldn't be ready for it until they had several weeks of programming experience.

An Introduction to Integers

Now that you have at least a general idea of what a string variable is, the next step is to learn about numeric variables. At this stage, all the numbers you work with will be whole numbers; that is, they will not include any decimals.

In Pascal, whole numbers come in three main flavors: Bytes, Integers, and LongInts. All three types are explained in depth in the next chapter, but for now all you need to know is that LongInts can encapsulate the widest range of numbers. Specifically, numbers assigned to a LongInt variable can range in size from –2,147,483,648 to 2,147,483,647. This gives you plenty of room to work with as far as most normal calculations are concerned.

> **NOTE**
>
> All whole numbers are integer types, even though some might be called Bytes, others Integers, and yet others LongInts. In other words, there is a general class of variable called an integer, and it has three specific manifestations: Byte, Integer, and LongInt.
>
> Here is another way to look at it. Roses, pansies, and begonias are all flowers. Similarly, Byte, Integer, and LongInt are all integers. It just happens that one member of the integer class has the same name as its parent class. It's no big deal once you get the hang of it.

Creating a `LongInt` is a lot like creating a string. For instance, you might write something like this to create `LongInt` variables named x and y:

```
var
  x,y: LongInt;
```

Start out by writing the keyword var, which tells the compiler that what follows will be a series of one or more variables. Then write the name of the first variable, followed by a comma and the name of the second variable. After giving the names of both variables, enter a colon and then the type.

> **NOTE**
>
> There is no difference between writing
>
> ```
> var
>   x,y: LongInt;
> ```
>
> and writing
>
> ```
> var
>   x: LongInt;
>   y: LongInt;
> ```
>
> The two declarations have identical meanings.

Once you have declared a numeric variable, the basics of using it are relatively intuitive. For instance, you might write a statement like this:

```
x := y + 3;
```

In such a statement, x would be equal to 5 if y was equal to 2, and x would be equal to 0 if y were –3.

A Variable's Type Defines its Capabilities

Before you start working with numeric variables in a real program, it is important to understand the enormous impact a type has on the capabilities of a variable. For instance, a numeric variable can't be treated as a string, and a string can't be treated as a number:

```
var
  i: Integer;
  S: String;
begin
  i := S; { Error! }
end;
```

This code will not compile because the types are incompatible.

This does not mean that is not possible to convert a string into a number or a number into a string. Delphi provides several built-in functions that can help you perform this task.

Consider a case in which you have one integer variable and one string variable. To convert a string into an integer, you can use the built-in Delphi function called StrToInt:

```
var
  A: LongInt;
  B: String;
begin
  B := '12';        { B holds a 2-character String }
  A := StrToInt(B);{ Transform String '12' into an integer }
end;
```

As you'll see later in this book, a function is just a procedure that returns a value. For now it is not so important that you understand functions in any significant depth. You can just treat them as black boxes that perform a specific chore or function. For instance, if you pass a string to the StrToInt function, the string pops out the other end as an integer. Thus, the StrToInt function provides a simple way of converting strings to integers.

Conversely, you may need to convert an integer into a string. To do this, use the IntToStr function:

```
var
  A: LongInt;
  B: String;
begin
  A := 12;
  B := IntToStr(A);
end;
```

Once again, the IntToStr function can be treated as a black box. Pop an integer in at the far right end, and it pops out on the far left as a string.

The reason the IntToStr and StrToInt functions are so important is that most of the controls used in Delphi work only with strings. For instance, if you want to display a numeric value in an edit field, you first have to convert it into a string before it can be assigned to the edit control's text field. For instance, the following assignment won't work:

```
var
  x: LongInt;
begin
  Edit1.Text := x;
end;
```

Before you can assign x to Edit1.Text, you need to first convert it into a string:

```
  Edit1.Text := IntToStr(x);
```

If you ever do try to assign an integer value where a string is expected, or vice versa, you will get a compiler error when you try to run the program. Specifically, the compiler will come back and say you have created a type mismatch, as shown in Figure 6.4.

FIGURE 6.4.

Delphi reporting a type mismatch error.

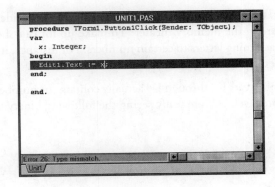

```
                    UNIT1.PAS
procedure TForm1.Button1Click(Sender: TObject);
var
   x: Integer;
begin
   Edit1.Text := x;
end;

end.



Error 26: Type mismatch.
Unit1
```

Perhaps at this stage it would be helpful to go back to the memory theater in order to get a better feeling for variables and their types. Suppose that you declared a string variable and assigned it the word CAT:

```
var
  S: String;
begin
  S := 'CAT';
end;
```

Furthermore, suppose that this string were assigned seats J-1 through J-256 in the memory theater. This means that seat J-1 would have the value 3 in it, because the string is three characters long. Seat J-2 would have the letter C in it, J-3 would have A, and J-4 would have T.

As you probably know, computers aren't innately capable of treating any area in memory as a word or letter. In fact, all computers know how to do is to recognize a series of ON/OFF switches that can be regarded as simply a series of zeroes and ones. Internally, the computer sees the value zero like this:

```
0
```

and the value one like this:

```
1
```

To get higher numbers, you need to continue this binary sequence. Therefore, the numbers zero through ten look like this:

```
0000 == 0
0001 == 1
0010 == 2
0011 == 3
0100 == 4
0101 == 5
0110 == 6
0111 == 7
1000 == 8
1001 == 9
1010 == 10
```

Clearly, these long series of zeroes and ones never provide room to directly write the letter A anywhere in the memory theater. To make up for this shortcoming, programmers devised a way of assigning letters to certain numbers. For instance, it is traditional to assign the value 65 to the letter A, 66 to the letter B, 67 to C, and so on.

Therefore, seats J-2 through J-4 actually contain the numbers 67, 65, and 84. If you look down one more level, you are really seeing the following binary values:

```
01000011
01000001
01010100
```

Conceptually, here is what all three levels look like when viewed at one time:

```
J-2 = 'C' = 67 = 01000011
J-3 = 'A' = 65 = 01000001
J-4 = 'T' = 84 = 01010100
```

As far as the hardware is concerned, the value in J-2 is just a bunch of zeroes and ones that are not particularly meaningful to most people. If you come up one further level of abstraction, the value in J-2 is the number 67. Then finally, you can look at the value from yet a third perspective and view it as the letter C.

Most of the time programmers view values in memory as either numbers or characters. They don't tend to view any value in binary terms except in certain very clearly defined circumstances. However, the computer will not normally know whether to treat a value as a character or number unless you specifically tell it which choice you want to make. This is why you need to give each of your variables a specific type. If you say a particular area in memory is part of string, you are telling the compiler: "Hey, don't treat this as a number, treat it as a character!"

Now, suppose you tell the compiler to treat one area of memory as a string and a second area of memory as a number. Then suppose you assign the first value to the second area, as per the following example:

```
var
  x: LongInt;
begin
  Edit1.Text := x;
end;
```

The compiler quite rightfully comes back at you and says, "Hey, one minute you tell me to treat the value x as an integer, and two nanoseconds later you want me to start thinking of it as a string. Forget it. You don't have your act together, so I'm flagging this as a type mismatch error!"

The material in this last section got a bit abstract at times, but it was nonetheless extremely important. To sum up, you have learned three things:

- The capabilities of any particular variable are prescribed by its type.

- Certain types are not directly compatible with one another, and as a result there are occasions when you must perform conversions between different types.

- On the lowest level, computers regard all data (and all code, for that matter) simply as a series of zeroes and ones. To graduate from that level, you need to specifically tell the compiler to regard a particular piece of data as having a certain type, such as a string or integer.

Some of this may not have jelled in your mind yet. If this is the case, you might want to reread it again a few days or weeks from now. You can get by for a time without grasping this information in its entirety, but in the long run you will never become a good programmer unless you know it deep down in your soul.

Working with Integers

Now it's time to create a simple program, called Adder, that works with integers. This project enables the user to enter two numbers and then adds them together when the user presses a button labeled Add.

To begin, create a form that looks like the image shown in Figure 6.5.

The two edit controls are labeled Enum1 and Enum2, and at startup neither has any text inside it. Notice that there is a fourth label called LResult. This is where the result of the programs calculations will be displayed. Adder uses a label control for this purpose rather than an edit control because there is no need for the user ever to change the value displayed in this field.

FIGURE 6.5.

The form for the Adder program has four labels, two edit controls, and two buttons.

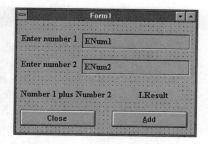

Label one of the buttons Close and have it respond to a click with the predefined Close method:

```
procedure TForm1.BCloseClick(Sender: TObject);
begin
  Close;
end;
```

Label the other button Add and have it respond with the following block of code:

```
procedure TForm1.BAddClick(Sender: TObject);
var
  FirstNum,
  SecondNum,
  Sum: LongInt;
begin
  FirstNum := StrToInt(ENum1.Text);
  SecondNum := StrToInt(ENum2.Text);
  Sum := FirstNum + SecondNum;
  LResult.Caption := IntToStr(Sum);
end;
```

This code fragment begins by declaring three variables, all of type LongInt. These integer values will be used to perform the simple math that is required of this program.

However, before any calculations can be made, it is necessary to translate the string values returned by the edit controls into numerical values. As explained earlier, the simplest way to do this is with the StrToInt function.

For instance, if the user entered the character 2 in the edit control and 2 in the second edit control, the text properties of both edit controls would return the string 2. After running those values through the StrToInt function, the end result would be two integer variables set to the numerical value 2.

The following line adds the first number and the second number together and stores the result in the integer variable Sum:

```
Sum := FirstNum + SecondNum;
```

This means that at runtime, the variable in the memory theater called FirstNum would hold the value 2 and the variable in the memory theater called SecondNum would also hold the value 2. The local idiot savant, Dustin CPU Hoffman, would then add the two numbers together and place the result in the seats of the memory theater that are labeled Sum. (See Figure 6.6.)

FIGURE 6.6.

The memory theater stores the values added together by the CPU. The result is also stored in the memory theater.

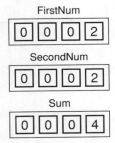

FirstNum

SecondNum

Sum

Once the two numbers are added together, the only chore left to accomplish is the simple act of converting the value held in Sum back into a string so that it can be displayed in the LResult label:

```
LResult.Caption := IntToStr(Sum);
```

Listing 6.2 presents the code from the main module of the Adder program in its entirety.

Listing 6.2. The Adder program demonstrates how to work with numerical values.

```
unit Main;

{ Program copyright (c) 1994 by Charles Calvert }
{ Project Name: ADDER }

interface

uses
  WinTypes, WinProcs,
  Classes, Graphics,
  Controls, Printers,
```

continues

Listing 6.2. continued

```
  Forms, StdCtrls;

type
  TForm1 = class(TForm)
    Label1: TLabel;
    Label2: TLabel;
    Label3: TLabel;
    ENum1: TEdit;
    ENum2: TEdit;
    LResult: TLabel;
    BAdd: TButton;
    BClose: TButton;
    procedure BCloseClick(Sender: TObject);
    procedure BAddClick(Sender: TObject);
  end;

var
  Form1: TForm1;

implementation
uses
  SysUtils;

{$R *.DFM}

procedure TForm1.BCloseClick(Sender: TObject);
begin
  Close;
end;

procedure TForm1.BAddClick(Sender: TObject);
var
  FirstNum,
  SecondNum,
  Sum: LongInt;
begin
  FirstNum := StrToInt(ENum1.Text);
  SecondNum := StrToInt(ENum2.Text);
  Sum := FirstNum + SecondNum;
  LResult.Caption := IntToStr(Sum);
end;

begin
end.
```

I Take Exception to that Error!

Some readers have probably noticed that the Adder program makes no provisions for error checking. For instance, if the user happened to type a word instead of a number in one of the edit controls, experienced programmers might expect that Adder would unceremoniously crash, or at least fail to give valid output. Remarkably enough, this is not what happens.

If the user types the word `Hallie` in one of the edit controls and then presses the Add button, the program answers back by popping up a message box with the words "Hallie is not a valid integer value." (See Figure 6.7.)

FIGURE 6.7.

The Adder program reports on invalid user input.

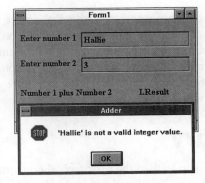

If you look at the code for the Adder program, you can see that nowhere is there a provision made to check for errors or to create a string like the one shown in Figure 6.8. The reason the program is nonetheless able to catch the user's error is because of a new Pascal coding technique called *Exceptions*.

It is still too early in the book to delve into such a complicated topic as Exceptions. Nonetheless, I want to at least introduce the subject so you are aware that an important error-checking capability has been added to Pascal, and that this capability is built into many of the native functions and objects.

Specifically, if you look in CLASSES.PAS, the `StrToInt` function looks like this:

```
function StrToInt(const S: string): Longint;
var
  E: Integer;
begin
  Val(S, Result, E);
  if E <> 0 then ConvertError(FmtLoadStr(SInvalidInteger, [S]));
end;
```

Old hands at Pascal will notice that this function relies on the `Val` procedure to do the grunt work. Indeed, for years this has been the way Pascal users converted a string to an integer, and of course they can continue to do so if they wish.

What's new in the `StrToInt` function is the code that does something called "raising an exception." At this stage, there is absolutely no need to understand exactly what is going on here. Nor is there any need to worry about whether you are going to get a chance to understand this material. Never fear, this stuff is covered in glorious, illuminating detail—just not quite yet. For now, all you need to know is that there is a new device at work in Pascal called Exceptions, and that it can help with error checking. Exceptions will be covered in Chapter 34, "Exceptions."

I said in Chapter 1, "Welcome to Delphi," that Pascal was structured so that you could reach down into the depths of the machine and perform the subtle operations that make code really sizzle. If you want, you can work with a set of robust tools that will help you quickly write intelligent, well-structured code.

This is one of the cases where you see a fork in the road. Most programmers, and especially most experienced programmers, will want to rely on Pascal's Exceptions, which easily add effective error checking to your program. Others might want to try to tighten things up a notch by circumventing this excellent new technique. Delphi makes it easy for you to take either route. Regardless of which route you take, you can be sure you are getting to your destination in the fastest, leanest way possible. There is nothing dweebish or second-rate about Delphi.

Summary

In this chapter, you learned the basic facts about variables. In particular, you were introduced to string and integer variables. You saw that LongInts are a particular kind of integer, and that they can be used to hold relatively large numbers.

This chapter also introduced you to the memory theater. The memory theater is just an analogy. It can, however, help you visualize how variables look when they are stored in RAM. Astute readers may even have noticed a parallel between the way seats are numbered in the memory theater and the way real blocks of memory are addressed. For instance, there is a certain parallel between the byte that sits in row J, seat 10, and the byte that resides at segment 52, offset 10 in memory.

Exceptions were also introduced in this chapter. Exceptions provide built-in error checking for many of the operations you perform on a daily basis in Delphi. You will learn more about Exceptions in later chapters.

Integers in Detail

Overview

In this chapter you learn about the fundamental Delphi Integer types. For instance, you will read about the following:

- The simple numerical types such as ShortInts, Bytes, Integers, Words, and LongInts.

- You will also learn about Chars, which are closely related to Bytes, but are used to hold alphanumeric values such as A, B, or C.

- Along the way you'll get experience writing procedures, creating variables, and using button controls, edit controls, memo fields and a few other visual pro gramming tools.

- This chapter also introduces you to the debugger.

To be utterly frank, I must confess that a discussion of the fundamental integer types is not the sexiest topic covered in this book. It is, however, relatively straightforward, and absolutely essential. You have to understand the basic types out of which the language is made. If you don't, you won't be able to create the kinds of programs you envision in your mind's eye.

Types: A Definition

In the last chapter you were treated to a fairly in-depth description of what types are and what their purpose is inside a Delphi program. However, it might be helpful if I recapitulate the basics in just a few short sentences.

With one or two relatively minor exceptions, every variable you declare must have a type. When you declare a variable's type you are setting up the limits inside of which it will perform. For instance, an integer variable must be a whole number. It cannot be a string, or a number with a decimal point in it.

On a more fundamental level, a type definition tells the compiler how to treat data that resides in RAM. From the computer's point of view, any single byte in memory is just a series of zeroes and ones. There is nothing inherent in those zeroes and ones that could convey to the computer whether they are part of an integer, real number, or string. Somehow, you, the programmer, have to tell both the compiler and the computer what "type" of data is residing at a particular address. You have to say: "Look, those guys right there, sitting in seats J-1 through J-256 of the memory theater—they are a string. Each individual byte is really a letter in the alphabet; not a number."

Ultimately, the technical term "type" can be defined like this:

- A *type* declaration tells the compiler how to treat the bytes found in a specific area of memory. Furthermore, that definition declares and proscribes the usefulness of the bytes residing in that area.

The preceding definition is the kind that's great once you understand the definition of a type. It helps to encapsulate it in a few neat phrases. However, it won't make much sense to a neophyte. If you are having trouble understanding types, you might want to read on for a while so you can get a few practical examples, and then come back and reread this section and the relevant portions of the last chapter.

Ordinals Part I: *ShortInt*

There are five main ordinal types for numerical values. These types are called scalar types because they are numbers that follow one another in a predictable and very precise order. For instance, the numbers 1, 2, 3, 4, and so on, are scalar because they follow each other like notes on a scale when you are taking piano lessons. Do, Re, Me, Fa, and so on.

Each type can encapsulate numbers within a certain range. In turn, each variable of a particular type takes up a certain amount of space in memory; that is, they take up *x* number of seats in the memory theater.

The list shown next gives you an overview of each of the five integer types. Take a look at the table, and then read on to get a more detailed description of the particulars involved with using any one type.

Type	Range	Format
ShortInt	–128 .. 127	Signed 8-bit
Integer	–32768 .. 32767	Signed 16-bit
LongInt	–2147483648 .. 2147483647	Signed 32-bit
Byte	0 .. 255	Unsigned 8-bit
Word	0 .. 65535	Unsigned 16-bit

The first thing you need to understand about integer values is this business about signed and unsigned numbers. To get this straight, you really need to go back down to the bit level for a few moments.

As you recall from the last chapter, a particular byte in memory really consists of a series of ones and zeroes. Specifically, a byte contains 8 binary, or bit, values, each of which is either a one or a zero.

If you have 1 bit to work with, the largest possible number you can express is 1. In fact, with a single bit, you can only express two numbers: the first is zero and the second is one. If you have two bits to work with, you can express up to four numbers, as shown here:

```
00 == 0
01 == 1
10 == 2
11 == 3
```

With three bits in your repertoire, you can handle eight numbers:

```
000 == 0
```

```
001 == 1
010 == 2
011 == 3
100 == 4
101 == 5
110 == 6
111 == 7
```

and so on.

As it turns out, the largest number you can show with 8 bits is 255:

```
11111111 = 255
```

and the largest number you can show with 7 bits is 127. If you count zero as the first number in the series, this means there are 256 possible values you can store in 8 bits and 128 possible values that can be stored in 7 bits.

Even a moment's thought shows that there is no built-in way for a binary number to express a negative value. All you have is ones and zeroes—just a series of on-off switches. There's no place in there for a minus sign.

So how are you going to express a negative number?

The solution engineers came up with was to regard the first bit in a series of bits as the "sign" that shows whether or not a number is negative. If a number is typed as a signed number and the first bit is one, the number is negative.

> **NOTE**
>
> It does not follow from this logic that the binary number 10000001 is therefore −1. In fact, a technique called *two's compliment notation* reveals −1 to be 11111111 and −2 to be 11111110, and so on, until you reach −128, which is 10000000. When using two's compliment notation, zero is considered a positive number. In other words, −1 is the first negative number and 0 is the first positive number. To write −1, set all 7 available bits to 1. From there you can start counting down to the lowest possible number, which is reached when all 7 bits are set to 0. Understanding two's compliment notation is not important for your study of Delphi. It is, however, important for you to understand that a signed number is limited in scope because it can use only 7 bits rather than 8.

All integer numbers that are smaller than zero must use the first bit to show that the number is negative. This means that there are only 7 bits left over in an 8-bit byte once you've decided the first bit is dedicated to showing whether the number is negative or positive.

You've already seen that there are only 128 possible numbers you can express with 7 bits. That means the highest possible signed 1-byte integer value is 127, and the lowest possible value is

−128. (Remember that zero is counted as a positive number, so positive numbers have one more member in their camp and therefore can't count quite as "high" as negative numbers.)

If you followed the discussion up to this point, you understand the smallest possible integer type, which is the ShortInt. It's an 8-bit number, which means it can have a total of 256 possible values. Because it uses its eighth bit to designate its sign, it can range only from −128 to 127.

Take a moment to hone in on a few specific examples. Consider the following declaration:

```
var
  i: ShortInt;
```

Given the preceding declaration, the following assignment is legal:

```
i := 127;
```

but this next one generates a "constant out of range" error from the compiler, because you can't express the number 128 in only seven bits:

```
i := 128;
```

To test this out with Delphi, just drop a button on a form and then double-click the button. You are immediately placed inside a Button1Click method, which is as good a place as any to test out some code. For instance, if you want to see the "constant out of range" error you could create a procedure that looks like this and then press F9 to compile and run:

```
procedure TForm1.Button1Click(Sender: TObject);
var
  i: ShortInt;
begin
  i := 128;
end;
```

When writing code like this, your goal is not to create a program that does anything useful. Instead you are just mucking about with frivolous syntactical conglomerations merely for the sake of seeing how the language responds to a particular situation. You are writing code for code's sake, as it were. It's precisely this kind of seemingly pointless hacking that forms the foundation on which good programmers build their careers.

NOTE

Just for the fun of it, I ran some very unofficial tests to see how long it took me to generate the template for a Button1Click method. During the tests, I started with Delphi loaded, my hands at rest on the keyboard. I considered the job done once I had a TForm1.Button1Click method in the editor. The first couple times I tried, it took me between two and three seconds to create the template for the TForm1.Button1Click method. But after several tries I could accomplish the whole task in less than a second. I found this remarkable for two reasons:

- I was able to create a Windows program in under a second.
- It shows that with almost no effort at all, you can use Delphi to begin sketching out a quick idea or programming experiment. Most programmers love finding a language that provides this kind of ease of use. It's hard to work with a language that's always asking you to work 10 minutes, 15 minutes, even a half-hour before you are set up and ready to start programming. The very easy-to-use DOS-based Pascal compiler forced you to type in the words begin and end. Here, even that relatively trivial task is circumvented, thereby allowing you to write code even faster than you can in DOS!

Ordinals Part II: *Bytes* and *Chars*

After the ShortInt, the next integer value in the series is a Byte, which is an unsigned 8-bit value. This means it uses all 8 bits to count with, and does not set aside one bit to "sign," whether it is negative or positive. It is therefore an "unsigned" integer.

After the discussion in the last section, it should come as no surprise that a variable of type Byte can have a range from 0 to 255. This means no variable that is declared to be of type Byte can ever have a negative value. The following code, for instance, generates a "constant out of range" error:

```
procedure TForm1.Button1Click(Sender: TObject);
var
  A: Byte;
begin
  A := -1;
end;
```

Closely related to a byte is the Char, which is also an unsigned 8-bit value. Chars are used not for holding numbers, but for holding characters. For instance, the letter A could be assigned to a Char:

```
var
  Ch: Char;
begin
  Ch := 'A';
end;
```

It's important to note that there is a distinction between the number 1 and the character value '1'. For instance, if a variable x is declared as an integer value, it would make sense to use the number 1 in the following statement:

```
x := 1 + 2;
```

But it would not make sense to write

```
x := '1' + 2;
```

In the same way, it would make sense to use a variable of type `Byte` in a mathematical statement, but it would not normally make sense to use a `Char`:

```
var
  Ch: Char;
  x, i: Integer;
begin
  i := 2;
  x := 2 + i;  { This makes sense }
  Ch := '2';
  x := 2 + Ch; { This is nonsense }
end;
```

In the example shown here, the compiler generates a "type mismatch" error. It's complaining because I've used a `Char` where one would normally use an integer or other numerical value.

NOTE

In this chapter's code I introduce a few comments, which appear between curly braces { and }, or between asterisks and parenthesis (* and *). Anything that appears between these symbols is ignored by the compiler. This allows programmers to leave notes to themselves or to others.

For better or worse, I don't place much stock in commenting code line-by-line, though I believe in placing general comments at the top of all significant modules and in front of any tricky routines. My aversion to detailed comments stems from the fact that they prevent me from seeing the code clearly. In fact, when I find a heavily commented code fragment that is hard to understand, I often end up deleting or hiding the comments so I can get a good look at the actual code. Despite many programmer's best efforts, their comments just end up confusing me.

Most, but by no means all, of the best programmers I've met tend to avoid comments altogether, or to use them only very sparingly. Some managers, however, insist that you comment your code in the hopes that it will then be easier for future programmers to maintain. If I had to choose between no comments and some comments, I would choose some comments. If I had to choose between no comments and line-by-line comments, I would choose no comments. In short, I occupy the middle ground in this heavily debated issue. Ultimately, the decision rests in your own hands, and you should adopt the style that you feel enables you to produce the best code.

At times, some programmers may feel that I comment my code too heavily. If you find that my comments are getting in your way, you can use the syntax highlighting to set comments to the same color as the background. This makes the comments disappear, at least temporarily. If you have succeeded in deciphering the passage and wish to edit it, you should of course make the comments visible again.

Don't worry about comments slowing down your code. They are completely ignored by the compiler and have no impact on code size.

I explained in the last chapter that alphanumeric values such as 'A' or 'B' are represented internally by a series of zeroes and ones. During that discussion I pointed out that the letter 'A' is usually associated with the number 65, which looks like this in binary: 01000001. This means that characters 0 through 64 are not assigned to letters, but to other values such as commas or periods, or perhaps to no value at all.

The character sets I'm describing here are the ones associated with the 16-bit Win31 that runs on top of DOS. NT has a totally different system for tracking characters, and most likely so will Chicago (Windows 95), though that is not entirely clear at this time. In this book I'm sticking with the system that is used by the majority of readers at the time this book comes out, though of course I assume the reader understands that I'm being forced to make a difficult decision while we are in this period of transition. One thing you can count on, however, is that the basic principles I'm outlining here will hold true for whatever particular syntax any one system might adopt. In other words, the letter A might not always be the 65th item in a character set, but for the foreseeable future there will always be a character set, and the letter A will always be the *n*th character in that set.

In the nongraphical portions of the DOS world, programmers were used to always working with the same character set, which was commonly referred to as the ASCII character set. As demonstrated by Figure 7.1, it is indeed possible to exactly imitate that character set while inside of a Windows program. But you should understand that this is only one of many character sets available to Windows programmers, and that it is most commonly associated with the rarely used Terminal font.

FIGURE 7.1.

The standard ASCII character set as shown by the CHARSET program.

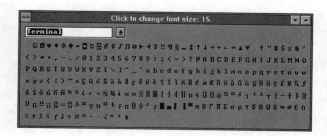

To understand Figure 7.1, you have to view each individual character as one of the 255 possible values that can be associated with type Char. The first character in the upper-left corner is associated with number zero, and it is blank. The one to its right, which looks like a smiley face, is associated with number 1, the next with number 2, and so on. As you can see, the 66th character is an A; the 67th, a B; and on through the alphabet. Note the small letter 'a' is associated with ordinal number 97.

As stated earlier, the character set associated with DOS nearly always looked exactly like the scene depicted in Figure 7.1. As a result, many DOS programmers who are new to Windows expect to be able to print the smiley face to the screen by printing a Char type with a value of 1. This line of reasoning, however, is severely flawed, because Windows uses a wide variety of character sets, most of which don't look even remotely like the one shown in Figure 7.1. For instance, the System font, which is used by default in most Windows controls, looks like the image shown in Figure 7.2. The elegant Times New Roman font, which is a TrueType font, is shown in Figure 7.3. Figure 7.4 depicts the WingDings font, which you will note contains no standard letters at all. Instead, it contains only a series of little pictures that might prove useful to a programmer or other Windows user.

FIGURE 7.2.

The System font is used by default in most Windows controls.

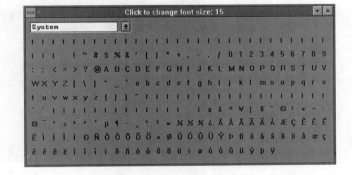

FIGURE 7.3.

The Times New Roman font is a TrueType font, and can therefore be blown up to many times its normal size without much loss of resolution.

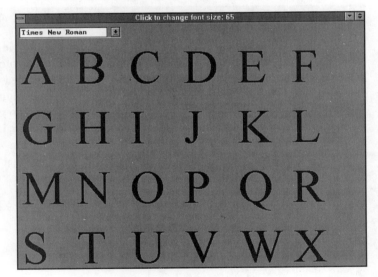

The important thing to pick up on here is that there are many different character sets available to you inside of Windows.

As a rule, each character set is associated with a particular font, but "fonts" and "character sets" are not interchangeable terms. In particular, any one font is always associated with a certain type of line or shape. For instance, the shapes and curves associated with the letter "A" in the Times New Roman font are totally missing from the "A" in the system font. It's these distinctive shapes that define a font, rather than the character set. However, in the current versions of Windows, it happens that certain character sets are reliably associated with certain fonts.

FIGURE 7.4.

The Wingdings font consists of a series of pictures.

> **NOTE**
>
> The program used to create Figures 7.1 through 7.4 is written in Delphi and appears on the accompanying disks under the title CHARSET. Unfortunately, the code uses some looping and branching techniques that won't be explained until the next chapter. As a result, you'll have to wait a bit before you get an explanation of how the program works. If you want to run the program, however, feel free to do so, because the experience will probably help you better understand the material in this chapter. When running the program, you will find that clicking the main form with the right and left mouse button makes the current font change size. Note also that the very educational CHARMAP program that ships with every copy of Windows can help you understand how characters are put together.

The *Chr* and *Ord* Functions

Suppose you are working with the Terminal font and want to assign the letter A to a variable of type Char. Here's two different ways to do it:

```
var
  Ch: Char;
begin
  Ch := 'A';
  Ch := #65;
end;
```

By now, both techniques should be readily understandable. In the first case you are assigning the letter to a variable of type Char with an intuitively obvious syntax. The second case should also make sense to you, since you already understand that the letter "A" is associated with the ordinal value 65. The pound sign (#) in front of the number 65 is just Delphi's way of specifying that the number is to be treated as an index into the character set, not as an integer.

If you are going to use the pound sign notation, you have to know what character you want to use before you compile the program. There are, however, occasions when you won't know this fact until runtime. In cases like that, you can use the Chr function, which, like IntToStr and StrToInt, comes with your compiler. Here's a tiny example showing how to use the Chr function:

```
var
  Ch: Char;
  X: Byte;
begin
  X := 65;
  Ch := Chr(X); { Ch now equals 'A' }
  X := X + 2;   { X now equals 67   }
  Ch := Chr(X); { Ch now equals 'C' }
end;
```

In this example, the byte X is assigned a value of 65. Then the Chr function is used to convert the byte into a Char. The 65th Char is the value A. When 2 is added to X, it becomes 67, and the Chr function is used to convert the integer 67 into the Char value C.

Before explaining the Chr function in any more depth, let me introduce you to the Ord function, which converts characters into integers:

```
var
  Ch: Char;
  X: Byte;
begin
  Ch := 'C';
  X := Ord(Ch);        { X = 67 }
  Ch := Chr(X + 2);    { Ch := Chr(Ord(Ch) + 2) }
  X := Ord(Ch);
end;
```

This code assigns the letter 'C' to the variable Ch, and then uses the Ord function to convert that value into the integer 67, which is assigned to X. The next step is to add two Chars to 67, yielding #69, which is the letter "E."

In cases like this, seeing is believing, so you should now get ready to fire up Delphi and prepare yourself for a little workout with the debugger. To get started, create a form like the one shown in Figure 7.5.

FIGURE 7.5.

The form for the CHAREXP program.

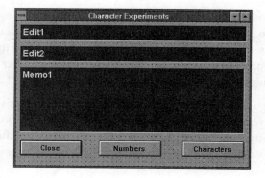

Now type in and run the following program, which encapsulates the two functions shown previously.

Listing 7.1. The CHAREXP program shows how to convert between an integer and a character.

```
unit Main;

{ Program copyright (c) 1994 by Charles Calvert }
{ Project Name: CHAREXP }

interface

uses
  WinTypes, WinProcs, Classes,
  Graphics, Controls,
  Printers, Forms, StdCtrls;

type
  TCharXForm = class(TForm)
    BNumbers: TButton;
    Edit1: TEdit;
    Edit2: TEdit;
    BChars: TButton;
    BClose: TButton;
    Memo1: TMemo;
    procedure BNumbersClick(Sender: TObject);
    procedure BCharsClick(Sender: TObject);
    procedure BCloseClick(Sender: TObject);
  end;

var
  CharXForm: TCharXForm;

implementation
uses
  SysUtils;

const
  CR = #13#10;
```

```
{$R *.DFM}

procedure TCharXForm.BNumbersClick(Sender: TObject);
var
  Ch: Char;
  X: Integer;
begin
  Ch := 'C';
  X := Ord(Ch);
  Edit1.Text := 'X starts as: ' + IntToStr(X);
  Ch := Chr(X + 2);    { Ch := Chr(Ord(Ch) + 2); }
  X := Ord(Ch);
  Edit2.Text := 'X ends as: ' + IntToStr(X);
  Memo1.Text := 'Ch := ''C'';' + CR +
                'X := Ord(Ch);' + CR +
                'Ch := Chr(X + 2);' + CR +
                'X := Ord(Ch);';
end;

procedure TCharXForm.BCharsClick(Sender: TObject);
var
  Ch: Char;
  X: Integer;
begin
  X := 65;
  Ch := Chr(X); { Ch now equals 'A' }
  Edit1.Text := 'Ch starts as: ' + Ch;
  X := X + 2;    { X now equals 67   }
  Ch := Chr(X); { Ch now equals 'C' }
  Edit2.Text := 'Ch ends as: ' + Ch;
  Memo1.Text := 'X := 65;' + CR +
                'Ch := Chr(X);' + CR +
                'X := X + 2;' + CR +
                'Ch := Chr(X);';
end;

procedure TCharXForm.BCloseClick(Sender: TObject);
begin
  Close;
end;

end.
```

Note that CHAREXP uses a memo field to display a short code fragment so the user can see exactly what is going on, as shown in Figure 7.6.

CHAREXP offers an excellent opportunity for you to start working with the debugger. I'm assuming you are using the keystrokes associated with the Classic IDE option from the Options | Environment | Summary page. If you use a different set of keymappings, just select items from the menus, rather than use the hotkeys I suggest here.

FIGURE 7.6.

The CHAREXP program helps explain the Chr *and* Ord *functions.*

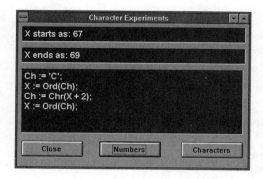

To get started, move the cursor over the first active line in the BNumbersClick procedure, which happens to be line 38:

```
Ch := 'C';
```

Now press Ctrl+F8 to set a breakpoint, or choose the Breakpoint option from the Debug menu. When you are done, your code should look like the image shown in Figure 7.7.

FIGURE 7.7.

Placing a breakpoint on a line of code in the editor.

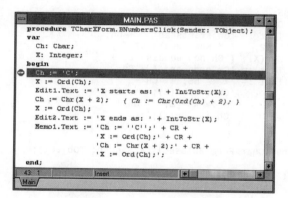

Once the breakpoint is set, run the code and select the Numbers button. When you do so, the CHAREXP program stops running and the focus shifts to the editor window. At this stage, you can use the F8 key to step through each line in the BNumbersClick procedure. When you are done, the program regains the focus.

After you have stepped through the procedure once, select the Numbers button again so that you are returned to the first line in the BNumbersClick procedure. This time you can set some watches so that you are able to see what is happening to the program's variables while the procedure is executing.

Select Ctrl+F7 to bring down the Watch Properties dialog box and type Ch as shown in Figure 7.8.

FIGURE 7.8.

The Watch Properties dialog gives you a chance to type in the name of a variable you want to view.

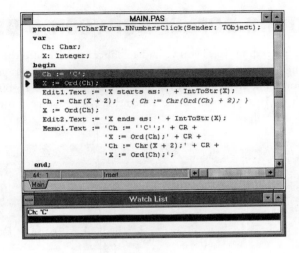

After selecting OK from the Watch Properties dialog, the Watch List window appears, with the variable you entered visible inside it. Note that next to the variable is a number. This number is the current value of your variable. When you step through the program, this value changes. In this way, you can keep track of exactly what is taking place in memory.

FIGURE 7.9.

The Watch List window after the user has selected to view both the X and Ch variables.

NOTE

A Watch window allows you to peer into memory. It's as if you had a special camera focused on various seats inside the memory theater. The moment any of the values stored with one of the members of the memory theater changed, you could see the change on your special video screen. In short, a Watch window is like a security camera trained on certain members of the audience. Anything that occurs in a particular seat or set of seats is noted in the Watch window.

You might want to take some time now to play with the CHAREXP program. Use the debugger to examine variables and to step through the code. If you want, you can change the values used in the BCharsClick and BNumbersClick methods. Programming is almost always a hands-on experience. I can tell you about certain important ideas in the pages of this book, but to make the information your own, you need to fire up Delphi, the debugger, and your imagination.

On the Border Between 8 and 16 Bits

In the preceding pages you've had a chance to delve into the inner workings of Delphi by exploring ShortInts, Bytes, and Chars. All three of these types use only 8 bits, or 1 byte, worth of memory. The next step is to explore Words, which are 16-bit unsigned values, and Integers, which are 16-bit signed values. When that's done, you can move on to LongInts, which are 32-bit signed values.

> **NOTE**
>
> The information I am specifying here applies to the 16-bit version of Delphi that was designed to run on Windows 3.1. Sometime after this is book is published, there will be a 32-bit version of Delphi, in which the rules will be somewhat different. Integers, for instance, will be 32 bits under the 32-bit version of Delphi.

I'm reviewing this material in considerable detail because I want you to understand what's going on behind the scenes. The goal here is for you to learn how to master Delphi. To do that, you need to meet everybody who's part of the grand play. Not just all the obvious players, but also the little guy behind the curtain who's pulling all the strings.

If all I did was present you with long columns of facts and figures arranged in the mind-numbing columns found in dry reference books, you would be fine—up to a point. But in every serious programming project there comes a time when you're backed into a corner. To get out, you need to know precisely what is going on inside your code. That's when you have to go behind the curtain yourself, elbow the little guy out of the way, and start pulling strings and throwing switches. That requires not just a little knowledge or a little skill—that requires mastery.

16-Bit Integers

The largest number you can count to with 8 bits is 255. But with 16 bits at your command, you can get all the way up to 65535.

```
11111111            = 255
1111111111111111    = 65535
```

If you are working with a signed 16-bit value, the range available to you is −32768 to 32767. As I'm sure you know by now, you can't count higher than 32,767 because the 16th bit is being used to designate whether the number is positive or negative.

> **NOTE**
>
> Just for the sake of clarity, let me take a moment to remind you of the definition of a *bit*, which is the smallest unit stored in memory. From the computer's point of view, everything in memory is just a bit value, which can be set to either zero or one—that is, it can be turned either on or off. Computers typically group bits into sets of 8, 16, and 32, depending on the current circumstances. This chapter is about the way those groupings are handled in Delphi.

Programmers and computers often think in terms of the powers of 2. They count like this: 2, 4, 8, 16, 32, 64. Because of their affinity for the powers of 2, many programmers refer to 65,535 by the shorthand expression 64 KB.

As you probably know, the 64 KB limit has haunted programmers for many years. This occurred because the Intel 8086 family of computers, and the DOS operating system that ran on them, are both based on a 16-bit system, which is discussed in Chapter 17, "Understanding the Windows Environment." Since you can only count up to 64,000 with a mere 16 bits, for a long time, users of Intel computers kept running up against 64 KB limits. One of the biggest of those limits is that no single pointer can address more than 64 KB of memory at any one time. This means that no matter how big the memory theater might be, no one entity inside of it can ever use more than 65,535 members of the audience at any one time. It's important to understand that this version of Delphi still has this limitation.

Of course, all these limitations are beginning to fall by the wayside. For instance, it's been a few years now since the 32-bit 386 processors appeared on the scene. And during the next few years, operating systems such as NT, Windows 95, OS/2 Warp, and Next will move us inexorably into the world of 32-bit code.

I say all this in part because I want to be sure you understand the central role 16-bit variables of type Word or Integer have played in programming. For years, these 16-bit variables have been the coin of the realm. Many programmers think of a Byte as half a Word, and as LongInt as what is called a double word. That's part of the culture of programming on Intel-based machines. But of course, all that is beginning to change.

> **NOTE**
>
> Working with Integer or Word values is very much like working with ShortInts and Bytes, except for the fact that you have a larger range available to you. The only obvious problem you need to watch out for is the fact that you should not use commas in your code. For instance you don't want to write the following:

```
var
   A: Integer;
begin
   A := 16,000;
end;
```

The compiler places the cursor right after the number 16 and says that it is "expecting a semicolon." The reason for this complaint is simply that the compiler doesn't know what to do with the comma. To remedy the situation, you can change the body of the preceding code fragment so that it looks like this:

```
A := 16000;
```

It's a little harder for people to read, but the compiler accepts it and you can get on to more important matters.

To sum up, 16-bit integers come in two flavors. The first is the common signed 16-bit value called an Integer, and the second is the slightly less common unsigned 16-bit value called a Word:

- Integers: range from –32768 to 32767
- Words: range from 0 to 65535

Here is how to declare and use variables of type Integer or Word:

```
var
  i: Integer;
  j: Word;
begin
  i := -32768;
  j := 65535;
end;
```

Of course, the numbers I assigned to the variables in the above example were chosen entirely at random, except that I made sure they fit within the legal range for Integers or Words. Given the preceding declarations, the following code would not be correct, because of range errors:

```
i := 65535;
j := -32768;
```

The following, however, would be completely legal:

```
i := 10;
j := i;
```

You will work with Integers and Words many times while writing Delphi programs. If need be, fire up the programming environment and experiment with these types until they begin to feel familiar.

32-Bit Integers

Using 32 bits, you can express a very large number that looks like this: 4,294,967,296. To comfort myself, I sometimes say this number out loud: four billion, two hundred and ninety-four million, nine hundred and sixty-seven thousand, two hundred and ninety-six. Saying it out loud like that sometimes helps me feel as though I know what such a huge number really represents. Of course, if you want, you can just call it four gigabytes. But no matter what you call it, this is a number that starts to push up against the limits of the human imagination.

In Delphi the only 32-bit integer you can use is a signed 32-bit number with the following range: –2147483648...2147483647. For most purposes this will do fine, at least while you are waiting for the first release of a 32-bit version of Delphi.

> **NOTE**
>
> A number type called a Comp lets you use integer values that are much larger than the range of a LongInt. However, Comps have some special properties that I don't want to introduce at this time, so you will have to wait to learn about them until the discussion of real numbers in Chapter 10, "Real Numbers, Functions, and Operators."

Because a LongInt has the largest possible range of all the integer values, it is the one best suited for use by beginning programmers. For instance, consider the following example, which is typical of the type of code that has tripped up beginners for many years:

```
var
   A, B, C: Byte;
begin
  A := 200;
  B := 6;
  C := A * B;
end;
```

If you ran this code in a program, you would find out that C doesn't contain the value you would expect, which is 1200. The problem is that the variable C is declared to be of type Byte. This means it can be assigned possible values from 0 to 255. Therefore, it cannot possibly contain the correct answer, which is way above 255.

After all you've read about the valid ranges of integers, even the greenest recruit is likely to claim that he or she would never make such a mistake. But lo and behold, in the heat of the moment, mistakes like this do get made. In fact, all programmers make mistakes like this on occasion.

One way to avoid this embarrassing pratfall is to declare integer variables of type LongInt:

```
var
   A, B, C: LongInt;
begin
```

```
  A := 200;
  B := 6;
  C := A * B;
end;
```

This way you will be safe under normal circumstances. However, you still need to be aware of the limitations you are facing. For instance, the following code would result in an error:

```
var
  A: LongInt;
begin
  A := 2147483647 + 1;
end;
```

The problem here is that we are adding one to the maximum value that can be placed in a LongInt. The result cannot be contained inside a variable of type LongInt, and the code will therefore produce erroneous output.

Furthermore, it's worth noting that the compiler will not normally make a peep when it sees code like this, nor will a runtime error occur when the code is executed. Of course, with a problem as potentially serious as this one, the designers of Pascal were motivated to come up with some form of solution. Pascal is meant to be easy to use, but traps like overflow errors can creep up on even experienced programmers.

The solution to the overflow problem comes in the form of overflow checking, which can be turned on at the top of your programs by simply adding the following syntax:

```
{$Q+}
```

Specifically, if you turned overflow checking on in a particular unit, the code at the top of the unit should look something like this:

```
unit Main;
{$Q+}
interface

uses
  WinTypes, WinProcs, Classes,
  Graphics, Windows, Controls,
  Printers;
```

It's also possible to turn overflow checking on by choosing Options | Project from the menu. Before the introduction of OPT files, I preferred to hardcode compiler settings into my program so that I could always see the current settings at a glance. This is important in part because options like overflow checking necessarily slow down your code. As a result, you will want to turn overflow checking off before you release your code to the public. You can do this by changing the + after the letter Q to a -:

```
{$Q-}
```

> **NOTE**
>
> The overflow checking option is a compiler directive. Compiler directives placed in your code always begin with a curly brace and a dollar sign. When you are developing your programs, you should almost always turn on overflow checking, range checking, and stack checking:
>
> ```
> {$Q+,R+,S+}
> ```
>
> When you are finished debugging your program, you should turn these options off to get the maximum speed possible:
>
> ```
> {$Q-,R-,S-}
> ```

The examples of overflow errors I've shown previously should be tested out by most people new to programming. Don't just take my word for it that you can't fit the number 1200 in a byte. Instead, start up Delphi, drop a button and edit control into a form, and run some tests so you can see for yourself. Figure 7.10 shows what the form might look like after you have slapped it together.

FIGURE 7.10.

The interface for the TYPE-OH program.

Below you will find code that can serve as a starting point for your experiments with overflow problems. Play with this code for awhile. Change the declarations for variables A, B, and C from Byte to type LongInt. Try changing the numbers so you can find the acceptable range of a 16-bit integer. For instance, try setting the value of B first to 6, and then to 60, and finally to 600, while changing the type of the variables back and forth between Integer and LongInt. Try turning overflow checking on and off, either through the Options menu, or by placing a {$Q+} or {$Q-} at the top of your program. Once you've played with overflow issues for awhile, you should find that it's an easy topic to master. Most readers, though, probably need some hands-on experience before they will get the hang of this subject. So go ahead and boot up the compiler. Get your feet wet!

Listing 7.2. The Type-Oh program gives you a chance to experiment with the valid ranges for the various scalar types.

```
unit Main;

{ Program copyright (c) 1994 by Charles Calvert }
{ Project Name: TYPE-OH }

{Q+}

interface

uses
  WinTypes, WinProcs, Classes,
  Graphics, Controls, SysUtils,
  Printers, Forms, StdCtrls;

type
  TForm1 = class(TForm)
    Edit1: TEdit;
    Button1: TButton;
    procedure Button1Click(Sender: TObject);
  end;

var
  Form1: TForm1;

implementation

{$R *.DFM}

procedure TForm1.Button1Click(Sender: TObject);
var
  A, B, C: Integer;
begin
  A := 600;
  B := 200;
  C := A * B;
  Edit1.Text := IntToStr(C);
end;

end.
```

Pred, Succ, Inc, Dec, and Computer Science

In this chapter I've thrown around the words scalar and ordinal to describe the simple integer types. I use these terms in order to convey to you some of the properties of this class of numbers.

For instance, you can use the Succ function to find the successor to all but the highest value of any of the ordinal types. Consider the following example:

```
var
  A, B: Integer;
begin
  A := 10;       { A = 10 }
  B := Succ(A); { B = 11 }
end;
```

Conversely, you can use the Pred function to find the predecessor of all but the lowest value of any of the ordinal types:

```
var
  A, B: Word;
begin
  A := 10;       { A = 10 }
  B := Pred(A); { B = 9  }
end;
```

Two other functions commonly used with simple integer values are Inc and Dec. The Inc function can increment a value, and the Dec function can decrement a value. Consider the following examples:

```
var
  A: Word;
begin
  A := 1;         { A = 1  }
  Inc(A);         { A = 2  }
  Inc(A, 10);     { A = 12 }
  Dec(A, 10);     { A = 2  }
  Dec(A);         { A = 1  }
end;
```

You can increment or decrement a number by any whole integer value. For instance, you can write Inc(A, 5) or Inc(A, 23). You can pass either one or two parameters to this function. If you pass one parameter, the variable you pass will either be decremented or incremented by one, depending on which function you call.

The functions High and Low can also be used to determine the maximum and minimum values associated with any particular type. Consider the following example:

```
var
  i, j: Integer;
begin
  i := Low(j);   {i = lowest possible integer: -32768  }
  j := High(i);  {j = highest possible integer: 32767  }
end;
```

You can apply High and Low to any of the integer types, such as Word, Byte, or ShortInt.

Of all these functions, the ones I use the most are Inc and Dec, but they all have their place. Furthermore, in concert they all work together to help you understand the key points about integer types:

- These ordinal types are always integers. That is, they are whole numbers.
- They all have a starting and stopping point. For instance, Bytes start at the value 0 and end at 255.

■ Except for the highest and lowest values of any type, you can always get the next number in the series by adding 1 to the current number, and you can get the previous number in the series by subtracting 1 from the current number. In other words, you can apply the Pred and Succ functions to these simple ordinal types.

To help you get an overview of all these ideas, I've included the ORDINALS program on the CD accompanying this book. If you want to create the program from scratch, start by designing a form that looks like the image in Figure 7.11.

FIGURE 7.11.

The form for the ORDINALS program.

Listing 7.3. The ORDINALS program shows some basic properties of ordinal numbers.

```
unit Main;

{ Program copyright (c) 1994 by Charles Calvert }
{ Project Name: TYPE-OH }

{Q+}

interface

uses
  WinTypes, WinProcs, Classes,
  Graphics, Controls, SysUtils,
  Printers, Forms, StdCtrls;

type
  TForm1 = class(TForm)
    Edit1: TEdit;
    Button1: TButton;
    procedure Button1Click(Sender: TObject);
  end;

var
  Form1: TForm1;

implementation

{$R *.DFM}

procedure TForm1.Button1Click(Sender: TObject);
var
  A, B, C: Integer;
begin
```

```
  A := 600;
  B := 200;
  C := A * B;
  Edit1.Text := IntToStr(C);
end;

end.
```

Summary

In this chapter you learned about the integer types. In particular you learned about ShortInts, Bytes, Integers, Words, and LongInts. You saw that each of these types has a particular range associated with it.

You also saw that Chars are very much like Bytes. Internally, the two types are actually identical. It's just the way the compiler treats them that makes one represent a number and the other represent a character. You can use the Ord and Chr functions to translate back and forth between Chars and Bytes, or between Chars and any other integer value that fits within the required range.

At the end of the chapter you got a chance to see some of the properties of integers. These properties all involve the way integers exist on a scale that ranges from a particular point up to another point, with each value between being separated by exactly one.

All in all, you should find integers fairly easy to work with. They are an intuitive "type" of value, and one that programmers use many times during the course of an average day.

Branching and Integers

Overview

This chapter covers the boolean, enumerated, and subrange types. As an added bonus, you will also learn a good deal about branching and operators.

As a way of introducing you to these concepts, the narration begins by presenting a simple definition of statements and expressions. These two syntactical elements form the building blocks out of which most routines are constructed.

The focus then moves on to a discussion of branching, particularly if..then..else clauses. Near the end of the chapter you are introduced to another form of branching called a case statement. Other subjects you'll get a chance to explore include simple and compound statements, as well as the complete set of Pascal operators.

The main theme of this chapter is the continued examination of simple types. To help pique your interest, throughout the entire chapter there is also an ongoing discussion about the relationship between computers and logic.

> **NOTE**
>
> This is one of the points in the book where some readers may wonder why I don't divide material up into neat little chapters, one on types, one on operators, one on sets and enumerated types, and so on. Certainly it would be simplest for me to approach things that way. However, as I said in Chapter 1, I prefer a more natural, rather than purely methodical, breakdown of the subject matter. I don't want to force you to do the programming equivalent of reading the encyclopedia through from the letter A to the letter Z. The point here is to concentrate on the way the human mind works, rather than on some entirely artificial, all too systematic, breakdown of the subject matter.

Statements and Expressions

The fundamental building block out of which all Pascal programs are made is the statement. Each statement in a program ends with a semicolon, just as a sentence ends with a period.

The following short code fragment contains five statements, each on its own separate line:

```
Inc(B, 5);
A := B;
A := A + 2
Edit1.Text := IntToStr(A);
Label2.Caption := S + ' incremented by 5 is ' + S1;
```

Some of the preceding statements have operators in them, such as

- The assignment operator, which looks like this: :=
- The addition operator, which looks like this: +
- The string concatenation operator, which looks like this: +

Note, however, that the first statement shown previously does not have any operators in it. Furthermore, the following code fragment exists as one long compound statement that encapsulates two simple statements:

```
begin                          { Begin Complex Statement }
  A := High(B);                { Simple Statement        }
  Edit1.Text := StrToInt(A);   { Simple Statement        }
end;                           { End Complex Statement   }
```

The point here is simply that any block that ends with a semicolon (or a period) is a statement. Given this definition, any `begin..end` pair constitutes a statement regardless of how long or complex it might be.

`if` statements can be equated with sentences, and `then` expressions can be thought of as roughly the equivalent of a phrase. In the following statement:

```
A := 2 + 2;
```

the portion that reads `2 + 2` is an expression.

Expressions always contain at least one operator. Consider the following examples:

```
A * B
-A
```

Both of these code fragments are expressions. The first is an expression because it contains the multiplication operator, and the second is an expression because it contains a minus sign, which is a unary operator. *Unary* operators can be used with a single operand, while *binary* operators such as plus or minus are used with two operands. In the expression `A * B`, `A` and `B` are operands, while the `*` symbol is the binary operator for multiplication.

A student in school would earn red marks on a term paper if it contained sentences that looked this:

```
Sammy ran smack.  Into the door.
```

The teacher would complain because both of the preceding sentences are incomplete. In particular, the second one is clearly only a prepositional phrase rather than an entire sentence.

In the same way, the Pascal compiler will complain if you write the following grammatical atrocity:

```
begin
  A := B
  2 + 2;
end;
```

One of the problems here is that `2 + 2` is an expression and cannot stand alone as if it were a full-fledged statement. Furthermore, `A := B` actually is a statement, so it should be followed with a semicolon, just as every sentence must be followed with a period.

> **NOTE**
>
> It is legal—in fact, many people think it proper—not to put a semicolon after the last simple statement inside a compound statement. For instance, the following code is entirely correct:
>
> ```
> begin
>   B := 1 + 2;
>   A := B
> end;
> ```
>
> You will probably catch me both omitting and inserting a semicolon after the last simple statement in a compound statement. Certainly the compiler doesn't care which technique you use, and the same machine code is generated in either case. When pressed to state my position, I would probably say that I prefer to see a semicolon after every statement, regardless of its position in the body of your code. One reason for this becomes apparent if you add a third simple statement to the preceding example:
>
> ```
> begin
>   B := 1 + 2;
>   A := B
>   Edit1.Text := Int2Str(A);
> end;
> ```
>
> By adding the third line of code, I stranded the second statement in a position where it needs a closing semicolon. Being prey to human frailty, I'm inclined to forget to add the needed syntax, and I therefore become unwilling prey to the compiler's nagging complaints about my forgetfulness. In order to avoid a somewhat haughty reprimand from the compiler, I tend to prefer to write the following:
>
> ```
> begin
>   B := 1 + 2;
>   A := B;
> end;
> ```
>
> I want to stress however, that this is purely my opinion, and certainly it's not a very deeply held belief. Either way is fine with me.

In this section you got a chance to look at statements and expressions. You learned that statements usually end with a semicolon, and that some statements can be more than one line in length and can, in fact, encapsulate other statements. Code fragments that are not complete statements, but which contain operators, are called expressions.

Let me wind things up here by saying that I don't want to put anyone off by dwelling on such a pedantic subject. I'm totally aware that someone could program for years without ever knowing the terms *expression* or *statement,* and yet I doubt he or she would be any the worse for the omission. I explain these terms solely because I am communicating to you in large part via the written word. In such circumstances it's important to have a common set of terms that have a mutually understood definition.

If Not Now, Then When?

There is a very profound connection between code and logic. At times the two terms can even become interchangeable. In such cases people often refer to a section of code as logic, as in the phrase: "That's a nice piece of logic."

Logical statements frequently have branches in them. Consider the following syllogism:

> *All philosophers are men.*
> *Socrates was a philosopher.*
> *Therefore, Socrates was a man.*

Proponents of a feminist grammar, lovers of prepositional calculus, and many college sophomores would probably be eager to disagree with this sentiment, and perhaps their objections are not without merit. Nonetheless, others have found a rather comforting logic in its soothing cadences.

If the reader is willing to grant it some conditional merit, at least for the sake of argument, it's possible to use it as the basis for the following elementary piece of logic: "If Socrates is a philosopher, then he is a man."

Here's another, less debatable (and therefore less interesting) syllogism:

> *All fish live in the water.*
> *Anchovies are fish.*
> *Therefore, anchovies live in the water.*

I'm aware that there are many who could find good reasons for disagreeing with even this simple piece of reasoning. Nevertheless, if you will grant its validity merely for the sake of argument, it will allow us to make the following simple statement: "If a sardine is a fish, then it lives in the water."

Now that you've got the hang of this, consider the following syllogism that involves a kind of logic that can be easily expressed on a computer:

> All positive numbers are larger than or equal to zero.
> Five is greater than zero.
> Therefore, five is a positive number.

In this chapter you'll see that it's possible to wrestle with such a statement using Delphi. In order to do this, you first need to have an in-depth knowledge of if..then statements, enumerated variables, and the assignment operator. In the next few sections, you learn how to proceed.

> **NOTE**
>
> While you are reading the next few sections, you might want to contemplate the following sentiment:
>
> > Only reasoning beings can understand logic.
> > Computers comprehend logic.
> > Therefore, computers are reasoning beings.
>
> I'll leave it to you to decide whether you think this syllogism has any validity.

In the paragraphs shown previously, you saw the statement: "If Socrates is a philosopher, then he is a man." In Delphi, you can capture something very much like that statement in the following piece of code:

```
if Socrates = Man then
  Socrates := Philosopher;
```

The goal of the next few sections of this book is to show you a meaningful way to start using and writing statements like this in a Delphi program.

if..then Statements

Consider the following code fragment:

```
var
  A,B: Integer;
begin
  A := 3;
  B := 7;
  if B > A then
    Edit1.Text := IntToStr(B);
end;
```

The code shown here first declares two variables, assigns values to them, and then launches into an if..then statement.

if...then statements are branches in the code of a program. For instance, in the preceding case, first the line assigning 3 to the variable A is executed. Then 7 is assigned to B. The next line is then executed. That line states that if the value of B is larger than the value of A, then B should be translated into a string and shown in an edit control.

The code branches when it comes to the if statement. if statements force an evaluation to be made, and if the evaluation turns out a certain way, the code branches in one direction. Otherwise, it goes in a different direction.

Consider the following example, where the code shown previously is slightly modified:

```
var
  A,B: Integer;
begin
  A := 3;
  B := 7;
  if B > A then begin
    Edit1.Text := IntToStr(B);
    A := B;
  end;
end;
```

In this case, a begin..begin pair extends the range of code over which an if..then statement has control:

```
if B > A then begin
  Edit1.Text := IntToStr(B);
  A := B;
end;
```

Here it's not just one line that is executed if a particular statement is true, but two. This is a fork in the river of code that is more significant than that shown in the first if statement.

Branches in a body of code can be further controlled by if..then..else statements:

```
if B > A then
  Edit1.Text := IntToStr(B)
else
  Edit1.Text := IntToStr(A);
```

Here you can see that an if statement causes the code to branch in opposed directions. If B is larger than A, then the value of B is shown in the Edit component. Otherwise, the value of A is displayed.

The next few sections of this chapter explore the various branches in your code that are created by if..then statements. As you will see as you read on, the seemingly simple logic of an if..then statement can have enormous power when combined with the speed and precision of a computer. The key point you need to grasp is that even very complex ideas can often be broken down into a series of if..then statements.

Assignment Operators, Equals Signs, and *if..then* Statements

Delphi programmers need to have a very clear vision of the role played by the assignment operator, which looks like this: :=. In particular, it's important that you don't confuse the assignment operator with the equals sign (=) used in math and in common English.

Consider the following code fragment:

```
var
  A,B: Integer;
begin
  A := 3;
  B := 7;
  if B > A then
    A := B;
end;
```

It happens that this code compiles without complaint from Delphi. Yet if it is written out the wrong way as a series of propositions in the English language, it could be interpreted to be somewhat absurd:

```
A equals 3.
B equals 7.
If B is larger than A then A equals B.
```

What's happening here is a purely semantic confusion regarding the significance of the assignment operator. The assignment operator doesn't suggest that one value is equal to another, rather it states that some variable is to be assigned a certain value. Therefore, the code written previously can be translated into logical English phrases by this method:

```
Let A be assigned the value 3.
Let B be assigned the value 7.
If B is larger than A, then let A be assigned the value of B.
```

When you read the three statements written previously, they still may not seem very practical, but at least they make sense.

The key point here is to realize that the assignment operator is not the same thing as an equals sign.

NOTE

In day-to-day usage, I find it impractical to always be saying statements like "Let X be assigned the value of Y." As a result, if I'm reading A := B out loud, I say: "A colon equals B." Other people prefer to say "A is assigned the value of B," or "A gets B," or even "B is assigned to A." All these phrases have their uses, and they are all perfectly acceptable, but still I find it simplest to actually speak the parts of the operator out loud: "colon equals."

Consider the following `if..then` statement:

```
if A = B then Edit1.Text := 'Identity';
```

In this case, there is no colon before the first equals sign. This occurs because the first expression is a boolean evaluation. That is, the code checks to see if the person sitting in `A`'s seat in the memory theater is remembering the same value as the person in `B`'s seat. If that is the case, the word `Identity` is *assigned* to `EDIT1.TEXT`. Clearly, there is a big difference between the equals operator and the assignment operator. Fortunately, the compiler prompts you whenever you start mixing them up. Therefore, all you have to do is understand the difference. You don't always have to remember it.

> **NOTE**
>
> I mentioned previously that sometimes I find the compiler's constant reminders about my mistakes to be a bit annoying. However, think of what might happen when AI and multimedia techniques become just a little more advanced. I imagine the picture of a person appearing in the upper-right corner of a screen. Then a soothing voice chimes in with: "Now Charlie, it seems you've mixed up boolean and assignment operators again. Are you sure you want to do this, or would you like me to fix it for you?" Argh!

Using *if...then* Statements and Enumerated Types

Now that you understand a few things about `if..then` statements, it's time to see how they can be used with something called an enumerated type, to considerably expand the reasoning powers of your computer. An enumerated type lets you to associate words with a small number of scalar values.

Consider the following code fragment:

```
var
  Publisher, Sierra, Maxis, Origin: Byte;
  GameName: String;
begin
  GameName := Edit1.Text;
  Sierra := 0;
  Maxis := 1;
  Origin := 2;
  if GameName = 'SimCity' then Publisher := Maxis;
end;
```

In this example, four variables of type `Byte` are declared. They are called `Publisher`, `Sierra`, `Maxis`, and `Origin`. The last three terms are the names of famous publishers of games, just as Borland is the name of a famous language, database and compiler maker, and Sams is the name of a famous publisher of computer books. The body of the code shown previously checks a value entered by the user in a text field, and then sets the value of the variable Publisher on the basis of this entry. In other words, the previous code shows a simple-minded technique that enables you to encode the name of a publisher in a single byte of data.

For reasons I will explain in a moment, it turns out that this is an operation that programmers want to perform on many occasions and for many different reasons. As a result, the designers of Pascal allow you to use the enumerated type as a shorthand method for writing the code shown previously:

```
var
  Publisher : (Sierra, Maxis, Origin);
  GameName: String;
begin
  GameName := Edit1.TextOut;
  if GameName = 'SimCity' then Publisher := Maxis;
end;
```

The two examples shown previously have virtually identical meanings, but the second takes up only seven lines, while the first takes up ten. The second code fragment is also much easier to read than the first.

In the second case, the variable Publisher is an enumerated type that can have three possible values. The first value is Maxis, the second Sierra, and the third Origin. Each value in an enumerated type is assigned a number. The value of each number assigned to an element in an enumerated type is defined by its position. In this case, the order in which the enumerated types are declared dictates that the compiler would assign Sierra the value zero, Maxis one, and Origin two. Note that this is the same thing you did explicitly in the first example shown previously.

To find out the integer value associated with an enumerated type, just use the Ord function:

```
var
  A: Integer;
  B: (Zero, One, Two);
begin
  A := Ord(Zero); { A is assigned the value 0 }
end;
```

The following program, called FASTENUM, allows you to test out the example shown previously with a just a few simple lines of code. Start by sticking a button and label control in the middle of a form, as shown in Figure 8.1.

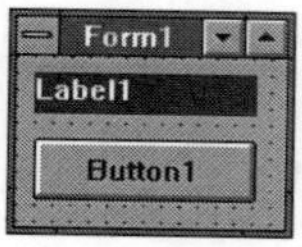

FIGURE 8.1.

*The form for the
FASTENUM program.*

While still in design mode, double-click the button and enter the following code:

```
procedure TForm1.Button1Click(Sender: TObject);
var
  A: Integer;
  B: (Zero, One, Two);
begin
  A := Ord(Two);
  Label1.Caption := IntToStr(A);
end;
```

When you run the program, click the button to see the value you have created. You can experiment with this program by changing the first line of code so that instead of finding the ordinality of Two, you pass One or Zero to the Ord function:

```
A := Ord(One);
```

If you have any trouble putting the preceding example together, you can find a copy of it on disk under the name FASTENUM.

Enumerated Types: Some Theory

Enumerated types are used fairly often in Pascal, so it might be worth spending a little time explaining why they exist and how to use them. I include sections like this because I want you to not simply memorize a set of facts, but to understand the theory behind those facts. It's my experience that I have a much better ability to recall and utilize a subject once I understand the theory behind it.

It might have occurred to some readers that in the example about game publishers, it would have been possible simply to declare the variable Publisher as a string and then write the following code:

```
begin
  Publisher := Edit1.Text;
end;
```

Indeed, in many circumstances that might be the best thing to do. On the other hand, if you encode the name of a publisher in a byte value, then you have several advantages:

- A Byte takes up 255 less seats in the memory theater than a string does. In other words, it saves memory.
- It's easy for a processor to evaluate an expression that compares Byte values:

  ```
  if Publisher = Maxis then DoSomething;
  ```

  String comparisons, on the other hand, require considerably more work on the part of the processor:

  ```
  if Publisher = 'Maxis' then DoSomething;
  ```

  In the first case, the computer needs to check the values of only two seats in the memory theater, while in a case similar to the second it's possible (but not likely) that up to 512 separate bytes might have to be compared before you'd know for sure whether identity exists. Obviously, the first method is considerably faster than the second.

■ Lastly, it's possible to use Bytes in syntactical constructions where you can't use strings. One of the most important of these constructions is the case statement. (You learn about case statements later in this chapter.) Enumerated types are also valuable in certain mathematical statements. For instance, suppose you have a list of ten game publishers, where the first five are small companies and the last five are large companies. If you encode the names of the companies in Byte values, you can make statements like the following:

```
if Publisher > 5 then Edit1.Text := 'Large Company';
```

Furthermore, if you had a list of ten games owned by a particular individual, you could add up the numbers associated with the publisher of each game, divide by ten, and find out whether that person is more interested in games from small companies or large companies. Such information might be useful to a marketing research firm.

SHAPEDEM Revisited

In Chapter 5, you saw the SHAPEDEM program, which made special use of enumerated types. Go back now and open up that program again, so you can follow the discussion as closely as possible.

When you first saw the program, I made light of the following line of code, which makes use of an enumerated type:

```
procedure TForm1.ComboBox1Click(Sender: TObject);
begin
  Shape1.Shape := TShapeType(ComboBox1.ItemIndex);
end;
```

Here is the declaration for TShapeType, as it appears in the StdCtrls unit:

```
TShapeType = (stRectangle, stSquare, stRoundRect,
              stRoundSquare, stEllipse, stCircle);
```

If you look at the declaration for the enumerated value TShapeType, you see that the first of its elements is called stRectangle. By definition, this element has the ordinal number 0 assigned to it by the compiler. That's the actual meaning of the elements of an enumerated type: They are just easily remembered words that stand for simple ordinal numbers. In this case, stRectangle represents the ordinal value 0, stSquare represents the ordinal value 1, stRoundRect is 2, and so on.

As you recall, the SHAPEDEM program has a combo box in it with the following strings typed into its Items property:

```
stRectangle
stSquare
stRoundRect
stRoundSquare
stEllipse
stCircle
```

The items in a combo box can also be referenced by ordinal numbers. The first one in SHAPEDEM's combo box is `stRectangle`, the second `stSquare`, and so on. The numbering in a `TComboBox` is zero-based, so `stRectangle` has the value `0`, which is exactly the same value it has in the enumerated type!

To compare the items in the combo box and the items in the enumerated type, all you have to do is make a simple typecast, and the compiler understands that if you select the zeroth item from the combo box, you want to work with element zero in `TShapeType`. That's why it's important for you to enter the strings into the combo box in a particular order: They need to match the order in which the shapes are declared in `TShapeType`.

More About Typecasts

A typecast is really a very simple concept, which might be intuitively obvious to you after the description shown previously. However, I remember having a little trouble with this concept when I first learned to program, so it might not hurt to examine the idea a little more closely.

Here is the declaration for the `ItemIndex` property in a `ListBox`:

```
property ItemIndex: Integer;
```

Obviously, this property is not of the same type as the `Shape` property from a `TShape` component:

```
property Shape: TShapeType;
```

However, one of the main themes of this chapter is that both `Integers` and enumerated values are really only variations on the simple integer type. That is, they are both ordinal values based on simple whole numbers such as 0, 1, 2, and 3.

As a result, under some circumstances it's safe to "assume" that an `Integer` and `TShapeType` variable are really of the same "type." It's not safe to do this under all circumstances, and so Delphi would normally flag the following assignment as a type mismatch:

```
Shape1.Shape := ComboBox1.ItemIndex;
```

Indeed, it is right that Object Pascal should flag this as an error. Delphi is a highly typed language, as it should be if it is going to help you write error-free code.

Nonetheless, after the explanation you have seen here, you and I both know for certainty that under these particular circumstances it's safe to compare `Shape1.Shape` and `ComboBox1.ItemIndex`. What is needed, however, is some way to tell the compiler that this is an okay thing to do. Delphi provides the following technique to relay this information to the compiler:

```
Shape1.Shape := TShapeType(ComboBox1.ItemIndex);
```

This syntax is called a *typecast,* and it consists of simply stating the type you want to use, and then wrapping the expression you want to convert in parentheses.

> **NOTE**
>
> Delphi's as and is operators can be used to complement typecasts in certain circumstances. They would not, however, be useful in the example shown here. To learn more about these special operators, see the discussion of them later in this chapter and look up "Is," "As," and "Run Time Type Information" in the online help.

To sum up, the key point is that the elements of TShapeType and the elements in a combo box have something in common: They can both be reduced to series of simple zero-based ordinal numbers. By using a typecast, you can tell the compiler that the values in the combo box and the values in TShapeType have something in common, and that they can be compared.

Menus and the SHAPEDEM2 Program

The SHAPEDEM program has the virtue of being easy to write and easy to understand. However, this program can be improved so that it continues to work as planned even if the user resizes the main form at runtime. In order to achieve this goal, several things have to be done:

1. The button and combo box have to be taken off the screen and replaced by menus.
2. The scrollbars have to change position when the form is resized.
3. The Position property of the scrollbars needs to change to reflect the size of the form.

If you glance at Figure 8.2, you can see how the program will look after these changes have been made. Listing 8.1. shows the code for the new program.

FIGURE 8.2.

The SHAPDEM2 program is smart enough to respond when the user resizes the form.

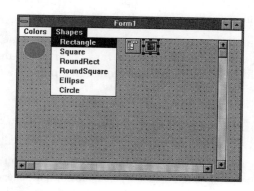

Listing 8.1. The SHAPDEM2 program includes a `FormOnResize` method. The main unit of the program is shown here.

```
unit Main;

{ Program copyright (c) 1994 by Charles Calvert }
{ Project Name: SHAPDEM2 }

interface

uses
  WinTypes, WinProcs, Classes,
  Graphics, Forms, Controls,
  StdCtrls, Menus, Dialogs, ExtCtrls;

type
  TForm1 = class(TForm)
    Shape1: TShape;
    ColorDialog1: TColorDialog;
    ScrollBar1: TScrollBar;
    ScrollBar2: TScrollBar;
    MainMenu1: TMainMenu;
    Shapes1: TMenuItem;
    ShapeColor1: TMenuItem;
    FormColor1: TMenuItem;
    Shapes2: TMenuItem;
    Rectangle1: TMenuItem;
    Square1: TMenuItem;
    RoundRect1: TMenuItem;
    RoundSquare1: TMenuItem;
    Ellipes1: TMenuItem;
    Circle1: TMenuItem;
    procedure NewShapeClick(Sender: TObject);
    procedure ShapeColorClick(Sender: TObject);
    procedure FormColorClick(Sender: TObject);
    procedure ScrollBar2Change(Sender: TObject);
    procedure ScrollBar1Change(Sender: TObject);
    procedure FormResize(Sender: TObject);
  private
    { Private declarations }
  public
    { Public declarations }
  end;

var
  Form1: TForm1;

implementation

{$R *.DFM}

procedure TForm1.NewShapeClick(Sender: TObject);
begin
  Shape1.Shape := TShapeType((Sender as TMenuItem).Tag);
end;

procedure TForm1.ShapeColorClick(Sender: TObject);
begin
```

continues

Listing 8.1. continued

```
   if ColorDialog1.Execute then
     Shape1.Brush.Color := ColorDialog1.Color;
end;

procedure TForm1.FormColorClick(Sender: TObject);
begin
  if ColorDialog1.Execute then
    Form1.Color := ColorDialog1.Color;
end;

procedure TForm1.ScrollBar2Change(Sender: TObject);
begin
  Shape1.Height := ScrollBar2.Position;
end;

procedure TForm1.ScrollBar1Change(Sender: TObject);
begin
  Shape1.Width := ScrollBar1.Position;
end;

procedure TForm1.FormResize(Sender: TObject);
var
  Menu,
  Caption,
  Frame: Integer;
begin
  Caption := GetSystemMetrics(sm_cyCaption);
  Frame := GetSystemMetrics(sm_cxFrame) * 2;
  Menu := GetSystemMetrics(sm_cyMenu);
  Scrollbar1.Max := Width;
  Scrollbar2.Max := Height;
  Scrollbar2.Left := Width - Frame - Scrollbar2.Width;
  Scrollbar2.Height := Height - Frame - Caption- Menu;
  Scrollbar1.Top := Height - ScrollBar2.Width - Frame - Caption - Menu;
  Scrollbar1.Width := Width - Scrollbar2.Width - Frame;
end;

end.
```

If you run the preceding program, you find that it continues to work properly if you resize the main form. Furthermore, you now can choose the shapes and colors from a menu, which gives the program a more streamlined look. The following paragraphs describe how to create the second version of this program.

To get started, create a new project and a TColorDialog, a TShape object, and a TMainMenu. The menu you create in this case will have two entries on the menubar—one labeled Colors, and the second labeled Shapes. Beneath these two menu items you should create two popup menus. The first has these items in it:

```
Shape Color
Form Color
```

and the second contains these items:

```
Rectangle
Square
RoundRect ·
RoundSquare
Ellipse
Circle
```

When you create the second list of items, go to the Properties page in the Object Inspector and assign the `Tag` property for each item a number. Give `Rectangle` a `0`, `Square` a `1`, `RoundRect` a `2`, and so on.

The two methods created for the menu items in the Colors menu should be completed exactly as the two related methods were in the first SHAPEDEM program:

```
procedure TForm1.ShapeColorClick(Sender: TObject);
begin
  if ColorDialog1.Execute then
    Shape1.Brush.Color := ColorDialog1.Color;
end;

procedure TForm1.FormColorClick(Sender: TObject);
begin
  if ColorDialog1.Execute then
    Form1.Color := ColorDialog1.Color;
end;
```

As you can see, nothing has changed from the first version of the program to the second, other than the methods shown previously are now called from a menu rather than from buttons. (Well, some of the procedure names also have changed slightly. You can use the `Name` property in the Object Inspector to make the same changes in your program.)

Likewise, the response to a click on an item from the second popup menu is nearly identical to the code shown in the first version of this program. The difference, of course, is that now you are responding to clicks on a menu item, rather than two clicks on a combo box:

```
procedure TForm1.NewShapeClick(Sender: TObject);
begin
  Shape1.Shape := TShapeType((Sender as TMenuItem).Tag);
end;
```

Once again, the code here works, because scrollbars have a property called `Max`, which describes the maximum number that can be returned to the `Position` property. In other words, if you pull the scrollbar thumb all the way to the end, the `Position` property returns the value you designate in the `Max` property.

NOTE

The expression "Sender as TMenuItem" uses Run Time Type Information. RTTI enables you to determine the type of an object at runtime. For instance, the following code will execute the hypothetical `DoSomething` function only if `Sender` is really of type `TMenuItem`:

```
if Sender is TMenuItem then DoSomething;
```

The as operator takes this whole concept one step further, but lets you make safe typecasts. For instance, the expression Sender as TMenuItem gets translated into the following by the Delphi compiler:

```
if Sender is TMenuItem then
  TMenuItem(Sender)
```

If you use the as operator and the types are not appropriate, Delphi will raise an exception. Exceptions are explained in Chapter 34, "Exceptions."

The is and as operators are used frequently in the code that accompanies this book. In general, RTTI is one of the more valuable syntactical features in the Delphi language, and you should be sure to take the time to practice using them until you understand them.

In the first SHAPEDEM program, I left the Max property on each ScrollBar at the default value of 100. As a result, if the thumb is pulled all the way to the end of the control, the Position property will be set to 100. If the thumb is back at the beginning of the scrollbar, the Position property will be the same as the value specified in the Min property of the scrollbar, which in SHAPEDEM stays at the default value of zero.

SHAPEDEM2 changes the Max property so that the range of the Position property in the scrollbar bar reflects the current size of the form, even if the form is resized at runtime. Here's the method that makes this work:

```
procedure TForm1.FormResize(Sender: TObject);
begin
  Scrollbar1.Max := Width;
  Scrollbar2.Max := Height;
end;
```

This function gets called every time the form is resized. The header for this method can be created by selecting the OnResize property from the Events page of the Object Inspector for Form1. The two lines of code inside the method simply set the maximum width and height of the scrollbar to the maximum width and height of the form. That way, you can always make the shape at least as large as the form itself. After making these changes, you no longer need to multiply the Position values times either 2 or 3:

```
procedure TForm1.ScrollBar2Change(Sender: TObject);
begin
  Shape1.Height := ScrollBar2.Position;
end;
```

A last twist to this program allows the two scrollbars to always follow the edges of the form when they move. Performing this action requires that you write code that is a bit more complex than the code I have shown you so far.

```
procedure TForm1.FormResize(Sender: TObject);
var
  Menu,
  Caption,
  Frame: Integer;
begin
  Caption := GetSystemMetrics(sm_cyCaption);
  Frame := GetSystemMetrics(sm_cxFrame) * 2;
  Menu := GetSystemMetrics(sm_cyMenu);
  Scrollbar1.Max := Width;
  Scrollbar2.Max := Height;
  Scrollbar2.Left := Width - Frame - Scrollbar2.Width;
  Scrollbar2.Height := Height - Frame - Caption- Menu;
  Scrollbar1.Top := Height - ScrollBar2.Width - Frame - Caption - Menu;
  Scrollbar1.Width := Width - Scrollbar2.Width - Frame;
end;
```

The code shown here occurs in response to a `FormResize` message. This event is listed in the Event page of the Object Inspector when the form itself is selected. Needless to say, `OnResize` messages are sent to the form whenever the user grabs hold of the border and makes the program either larger or smaller. The message is also sent when the form is maximized, but not when it is minimized.

The first thing the method does is query the system to find out the size of the form's caption, frame, and menu. This information is retrieved by the `GetSystemMetrics` call. `GetSystemMetrics` is a part of the Windows API, and therefore belongs to neither `ObjectPascal` nor the VCL. The entire Windows API is available to you if you need to access it. This means that any documented or undocumented call that can be made to the operating system can be accomplished from within Delphi.

> **NOTE**
>
> There is a very minor exception to this rule regarding the availability of the entire Windows API. The `wsPrintF` API function takes a variable parameter list, which is not supported by Delphi. As a result, it cannot be called from a Pascal-based language. However, the Delphi `Format` function is easier to use than `wsPrintF`, and it uses arrays of const to exactly duplicate the functionality you find in `wsPrintF`. If you have some obscure reason for wanting to call a Windows API function to obtain these kinds of services, you can call `wvsPrintF`. Except for `wsPrintF`, every other function in the Windows API is available to you. Support for CDECL declarations even allows you to call functions in OLE2 API.

More specifically, the `GetSystemMetrics` call asks you to pass in one of a series of constants that inform the operating system about the information you need. For instance, passing in `sm_cyCaption` tells the `GetSystemMetrics` function to return the height of the caption in pixels. A complete list of these constants is available in the online help, an excerpt from which is quoted here:

```
SM_CXBORDER  Width of window frame that cannot be sized.
SM_CYBORDER  Height of window frame that cannot be sized.
SM_CYCAPTION Height of window title.
SM_CXCURSOR  Width of cursor.
SM_CYCURSOR  Height of cursor.
```

The actual listings in the online help are quite extensive, and you will find that there are many facts about the system that can be retrieved using this function.

During the `OnResize` event, the program also calculates the new size of the scrollbars:

```
Scrollbar2.Left := Width - Frame - Scrollbar2.Width;
Scrollbar2.Height := Height - Frame - Caption- Menu;
Scrollbar1.Top := Height - ScrollBar2.Width -
                  Frame - Caption - Menu;
Scrollbar1.Width := Width - Scrollbar2.Width - Frame;
```

The calculation shown here involves very simple math. For instance, the left side of the vertical scrollbar needs to be set to the width of the entire form, minus the width of the frame, minus the width of the scrollbar itself. This is elementary logic, but once you have encoded it, the scrollbar moves along very neatly with the sides of the form.

> **NOTE**
>
> There is one final fact you need to know about the SHAPDEM2 program. As you've probably noticed, every form comes equipped with two scrollbars that appear automatically whenever you make a form smaller than the area taken up by the controls that are displayed on it. These scrollbars can be very useful at times, but they are not exactly what you need in the current circumstances. As a result, you want to be sure to deactivate both of these scrollbars by setting the `Visible` properties to `False`. You can locate the scrollbars themselves in the Object Inspector for the main form. The first is listed as `HorzScrollbar` and the second as `VertScrollbar`. Just make both of these puppies invisible so that they do not play any role in the SHAPEDEM2 program.

Reasoning with Computers

The following short program, called REASON, allows you to utilize the things you have learned about `if..then` statements and enumerated types. In a surprisingly thorough manner, it encapsulates the logic behind the following syllogism, which you saw earlier in the chapter:

> *All positive numbers are larger than or equal to zero.*
> *Five is greater than zero.*
> *Therefore five is a positive number.*

To get started, create a form that looks like the image shown in Figure 8.3. It features two labels, an edit control, and a button.

FIGURE 8.3.

The form for the REASON program.

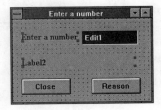

When running the REASON program, the user is prompted to enter a number, and when he or she clicks the Calc button, the code determines whether the number is negative or positive. In this fashion, you can see that it is possible to use Delphi to perform a rather crude form of reasoning.

Before discussing this issue any further, you should take a moment to get this program up and running. Here's the code:

Listing 8.2. The REASON program allows you to encapsulate the main ideas of a syllogism in a Delphi program.

```
unit Main;

{ Program copyright (c) 1994 by Charles Calvert }
{ Project Name: REASON }

interface

uses
  WinTypes, WinProcs, SysUtils,
  Classes, Graphics, StdCtrls,
  Controls, Printers, Forms;


type
  TForm1 = class(TForm)
    Label1: TLabel;
    Edit1: TEdit;
    BCalc: TButton;
    Label2: TLabel;
    BClose: TButton;
    procedure BCalcClick(Sender: TObject);
    procedure BCloseClick(Sender: TObject);
  end;

var
  Form1: TForm1;

implementation

{$R *.DFM}

procedure TForm1.BCalcClick(Sender: TObject);
var
```

continues

Listing 8.2. continued

```
  A: LongInt;
  S: String;
  Gender:(Negative, Positive);
begin
  A := StrToInt(Edit1.Text);

  if A >= 0 then
    Gender := Positive
  else
    Gender := Negative;

  if Gender = Positive then
    S := 'The number is positive'
  else
    S := 'The number is negative';
  Label2.Caption := S;
end;

procedure TForm1.BCloseClick(Sender: TObject);
begin
  Close;
end;

end.
```

In the preceding code, you can see that the TForm1 object contains five different fields. The first field is called Label1, the second Edit1, and so on. As you learn later, each field is a variable that points at any object with a structure similar to the TForm1 object. In other words, the TForm1 object actually encapsulates at least five other objects, each of which lends it support and grants it certain capabilities.

Furthermore, you should note that the TForm1 object has two methods. *Methods* are procedures that belong to an object, and they always perform an action, even if it is merely to assign a value to a variable.

The first method in the REASON program is called BCalcClick, and the second is called BCloseClick. I have given each of these methods names that start with B because each is associated with a button, and the first letter of button is B.

I give you this material on objects now simply to help you give names to the various parts of your programs. Don't worry if it doesn't all make sense to you yet; the many different facets of object-oriented programming will be gone over in considerable depth during the chapters dedicated to that subject.

Figure 8.4 shows how the REASON program appears when it's running.

FIGURE 8.4.

The REASON program as it appears when it's running.

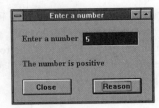

The key method in the REASON program is `BCalcClick`:

```
procedure TForm1.BCalcClick(Sender: TObject);
var
  A: LongInt;
  S: String;
  Gender:(Negative, Positive);
begin
  A := StrToInt(Edit1.Text);

  if A >= 0 then
    Gender := Positive
  else
    Gender := Negative;

  if Gender = Positive then
    S := 'Then number is positive'
  else
    S := 'The number is negative';

  Label2.Caption := S;
end;
```

This method declares an `Integer` called `A`, a `String` called `S`, and an enumerated type called `Gender`. It then uses these raw elements to perform a feat of elemental logic. Specifically, it encapsulates the concepts `Positive` and `Negative` in a enumerated variable:

```
Gender:(Negative, Positive);
```

Then it expresses the idea that positive numbers are larger than or equal to `0` in this code:

```
if A > 0 then
  Gender := Positive
else
  Gender := Negative;
```

Finally, it translates this knowledge into spoken English:

```
if Gender = Positive then
  S := 'Then number is positive'
else
  S := 'The number is negative';
```

And it displays the results to the user:

```
Label2.Caption := S;
```

Both of the `if...then` statements shown in the REASON program feature an `else` clause. This syntax is very easy to understand, because it's almost identical to the grammatical structures found in the English language. Consider the following sentence: "If it is sunny, then we shall go swimming; else we shall stay indoors and play cards." If the sentence were written as pseudo Pascal code, it might look like this:

```
if Sunny = True then
  Swim
else
  PlayCards;
```

In the same way, it's possible to translate the Pascal `if..then..else` clause from the REASON program into English: "If the number is positive, then write 'The number is positive', else write 'The number is negative'."

If you need to express more complex ideas, you can write compound `if..then..else` statements, like the one shown here:

```
if Sunny = True then
  Swim
else
  if (Sunny = False) and (Gender = Female) then
    Kiss
else
  PlayCards;
```

The code shown here will compile if you declare `Sunny` as a boolean, define `Swim`, `Kiss`, and `PlayCards` as procedures, and declare `Gender` as an enumerated type containing two elements called `male` and `female`:

```
type
  Gender = (male, female);
```

The SWIMKISS program, found on disk, demonstrates how all this works. The code for the program also demonstrates how to use the TRadioGroup object, which was added to Delphi fairly late in the beta process.

The only thing even remotely difficult about the syntax for `if..then..else` statements is the fact that you must omit the semicolon before the word `else`. There is no semicolon placed there because the compiler needs to know that the `if..then` statement of which it is a part has not yet ended. Semicolons belong at the end of the statement, not in the middle. Remember, the semicolon is omitted because the compiler needs some way of knowing that the statement isn't over, and that an `else` clause follows immediately thereafter.

Similarly, in the code example shown previously, the word `Swim` by itself is a statement. However, in this case, you must not put a semicolon after it because of its position in the compound statement of which it is a part. This is a rule that takes a little getting used to. But like it or not, it's a fact of life.

Overall, I find `if..then` statements intuitive and easy to use. The syntax is very much like spoken English, and as a result most people take to it like the proverbial duck to water.

NOTE

The method for indenting an `if..then` statement shown in this program follows the classical model:

```
if A > 0 then
   Gender := Positive
else
   Gender := Negative;
```

Code that follows this structure is extremely easy to read. However, I will at times abandon this model and write something that looks like this:

```
if A > 0 then DoSomething;
```

or even:

```
if A > 0 then DoOneThing

else DoTheOtherThing;
```

Remember that you are trying to create code that is easy to maintain. To my mind, `if..then` statements written on a single line can, under most circumstances, be crystal clear. Nor do I believe that a more dogmatic approach is correct or superior simply by definition. I am, however, hoisting up a flag here so you will know this is a subject about which some people can get a little hot under the collar. My suggestion is to follow your own preferences in this matter, so long as you are working with very short statements. (Treatment of longer statements follow.)

`if..then` statements can become a bit confusing when they encompass numerous sub-statements. Consider the following code fragment:

```
if A > 0 then begin
   DoStepOne;
   DoStepTwo;
   DoStepThree
end else begin
   DoThis;
   DoThat;
end;
```

Note that the entire block of code shown adds up to one single compound statement. The compound statement begins with the word `if` and concludes with the second use of the word `begin`. The code fragment shown here must use additional `begin..begin` pairs because the compiler needs to have some way of knowing that you are creating a lengthy compound statement.

If you take the time to contemplate it, this example shows that without properly placed `begin..begin` pairs, the compiler would never know what it was you wanted to do.

Here is the way the code would look if there were only one statement in the second half of the `if..then..else` clause:

```
if A > 0 then begin
  DoStepOne;
  DoStepTwo;
  DoStepThree
end else
  DoThat;
```

As you can see, there is no need for a `begin..begin` pair if you only want to add a single additional statement to a larger compound statement.

Needless to say, when you are writing lengthy `if..then` statements, it is absolutely essential that you establish a consistent method of indentation and that you stick with it under all circumstances. Specifically, when working with long compound statements, if you place your cursor under the i in the word `if`, you should be able to press the down arrow key *x* number of times and then find your cursor directly under the e in the word `begin`. (See Figure 8.5.) You should always strive to achieve this goal if it's at all practical. There is no need to be utterly dogmatic in your style of indentation, but it is folly to write long compound statements that do not follow a strict agenda regarding indentation.

FIGURE 8.5.

The word if *and the word* begin *should be placed in the same column.*

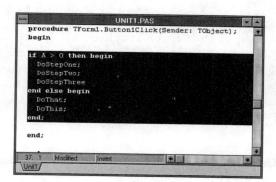

Before closing the discussion of the REASON program, it's probably best to play it safe and state explicitly that I don't think that it proves computers perform acts similar in import to those performed by human philosophers or logicians. Nor am I claiming that computers can prove or even write syllogisms, though that is probably not beyond their scope. My only point is that computers do have an affinity for logic, and that via a few lines of Pascal code they can be taught to do some very elemental reasoning.

Two hundred years ago, the only things that understood logic on this planet were human beings. Now there are two different "entities" that understand logic: humans and computers. Frankly, I'm not sure exactly what this means, but programmers should at least be aware that they tread on some fairly interesting and controversial territory.

Booleans

Once you understand enumerated types, it's easy to understand the basics about the `Boolean` type. Specifically, the following declaration of an enumerated type pretty much sums up booleans in a simple way that should by now be easily comprehensible to you:

```
Boolean = (False, True);
```

This type declaration shows that a `Boolean` variable can be set to either `True` or `False`, and that `False` is associated with the number `0` and that `True` is associated with the number `1`. For instance, if you declare the variable `A` as an integer, it would evaluate to one in the following statement:

```
A := Ord(True)
```

Conversely, in the following example `A` would evaluate to zero:

```
A := Ord(False);
```

Over the years, programmers have found that its extremely useful to be able to assign the values `True` or `False` to a variable. In fact, the idea is so valuable that booleans are now predeclared as their own type that you can use with any variable in your program. For instance:

```
var
  Big: Boolean;
```

Given a declaration like the one shown above, you can use the variable `Big` in this fashion:

```
  Big := True;
```

or

```
  Big := False;
```

So far, everything's exactly the same as it would be with an enumerated type. However, since the compiler has built-in knowledge of boolean variables, it's possible to use them in statements like this:

```
  if Big then Label1.Caption := 'The variable is big';
```

or conversely:

```
  if not Big then Label1.Caption := 'The variable is small';
```

The syntax shown here is bit more powerful than the kind you can use with standard enumerated types. For instance, an enumerated type would force you to write

```
  if Big = True then DoSomething;
```

but booleans allow you to write

```
  if Big then DoSomething;
```

The point here isn't really that it's important to save the time associated with tapping out a couple of words. Rather, the important fact is that a form of boolean logic is built right into the Pascal language. This makes the language more comprehensible to its human users.

> **NOTE**
>
> Boolean variables get their name from George Boole, a mathematician who created a kind of algebra of reason called *Boolean Logic*. It turned out that many of his ideas are extremely applicable to computers; in fact, he was something of an early pioneer of computers.

Just for the sake of clarity, you might want to take a look at two more short examples. Consider the following code fragment:

```
var
  Wide, Narrow: Boolean;
begin
  Wide := True;
  Narrow := False;
end;
```

In this code example, the variable `Wide` is declared to be of type `Boolean`. In the first active line of code, `Wide` is assigned the value `True`. Conversely, `Narrow`, which is also declared to be of type `Boolean`, is declared as `False`.

Of course, there is nothing special about the words `Wide` and `Narrow`. I could just have easily chosen other words such as `Sunny`, `Sandy`, `Fat`, `Thin`, `Wet`, `Grassy`, or what have you. Most of the time you will end up using boolean variables in `if..then` statements. The basic idea is that you are able to test whether or not a boolean variable is true. If it is true, you can take a certain course of action:

```
if Wide then DoSomething;
if not Narrow then DoSomething;
```

> **NOTE**
>
> Boolean variables are 1 byte in size. They can only assume the values 1 or 0 — that is — `True` or `False`. Programmers who want to go beyond the basics of Delphi might also use types called `ByteBool`, `WordBool`, and `LongBool`. The size of each of these types is obvious from a simple glance at their names. Less obvious is the fact that these variables can assume integer values other than zero or one. Any nonzero value associated with one of these variables evaluates to `True`.

Subrange Types

The last simple integer type to be covered in this chapter is called the *subrange type*. These types enable you to set a limit on the range of numbers that can be assigned to a certain variable.

Suppose you were writing a computerized version of the game of chess. In that situation, you might declare a variable called Players, which could only be set to the values 1 and 2. Any other values would be invalid, since all chess games assume the presence of two opponents. In such a situation the following declaration of a subrange type might be useful:

```
var
  Player: 1..2;
```

This declaration tells the computer that the variable Player can be assigned to either the value 1 or the value 2. Any other assignment would cause a compiler error.

Given the declaration of Player shown previously, the following line of code would be given a clean bill of health by the compiler:

```
  Player := 1;
```

This line, however, would produce a constant out of range error, as shown in Figure 8.6:

```
Player := 3;
```

FIGURE 8.6.

A constant out of range error generated by the misuse of a subrange type.

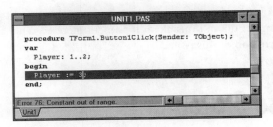

To be utterly truthful, I have to admit that I don't use subrange types in my code very often, though I'd probably be better off if I did. They can be helpful when you want to do everything you can to make sure that you don't make any careless errors while coding. For instance, suppose someone were writing a computerized card game. In it, they might want to make the following declaration to help them represent a deck of cards:

```
var
  Cards: 1..52;
```

Suppose while coding they accidentally wrote the following statement:

```
Cards := 6 * 10;
```

when what they meant to write was

```
Cards := 5 * 10;
```

Because `Cards` is declared to be of a subrange type, the compiler catches the error and you can correct the mistake immediately, rather than having it appear later on as a bug in your program.

In general, subrange types are easy to use. Declare the name of a type or variable and then write an equals sign or colon, followed by a constant, two dots, and a second constant. The values on both sides of the dots must be constants. The following example declares cards as an enumerated type and then lists several different subrange types:

```
type
  Cards = (Hearts, Diamonds, Clubs, Spades);
  TRedSuits = Hearts..Diamonds;
  TBlackSuits = Clubs..Spades;
  TGames = 1..12;

var
  Players: 1..2;
  RedSuits: TRedSuits;
  BlackSuits: TBlackSuits;
  Games: TGames;
```

> **NOTE**
>
> If you use a constant expression in the declaration of a subrange type, be sure the compiler doesn't mistake it for an enumerated type! See the online help for further discussion of this issue.

case Statements

So far, all the examples of enumerated types that I have shown involved only a few possible choices. But the next sample program, called MUSICTYP, works with an enumerated type that contains eight different members:

```
    Music: (Blues, Classical, Folk, FolkRock,
            Jazz, NewAge, Rap, Rock);
```

Working with a large number of options is a common situation in computer programming. Unfortunately, an ordinary `if` statement can be a very clumsy way to handle this situation. The following logic, for instance, is entirely legal, but is messy and difficult to read:

```
var
  S: String;
begin
  if Music = Blues then
    S := 'Blues'
  else
```

```
      if Music = Classical then
        S := 'Classical'
      else
        if Music = Jazz then
          S := 'Jazz'
        else
          if Music = Rap then
            S := 'Rap'
          else
            if Music = Soul then
  etc, etc...
```

To avoid this kind of confusion, Pascal provides you with the case statement. case statements work only with simple ordinal types such as the ones you've been reading about in the last two chapters. Here's an example from the MUSICTYP program that shows how to write a simple case statement:

```
var
  S: String;
begin
  case Music of
    Blues: S := 'Blues';
    Classical: S := 'Classical';
    NewAge: S := 'New Age';
    Folk: S := 'Folk';
    FolkRock: S := 'Folk Rock';
    Jazz: S := 'Jazz';
    Rap: S := 'Rap';
    Rock: S := 'Rock';
  end;
end;
```

It's also possible to write case statements using the Integer or Char type. Consider the following example, which assumes the declaration of a variable named A, which is of type Integer, and a variable named S, which is of type String:

```
case A of
  1: S := 'One';
  2: S := 'Two';
end;
```

case statements begin with the word case and conclude with the word begin. Each individual member of a case statement includes a colon.

It's possible to have multiple compound statements inside a single case statement. Suppose the existence of a variable Ch, which is of type Char. Furthermore, suppose the user has been able to input data into this variable as part of a multiple-choice test, where the valid answers range from 'a' to 'd':

```
case Ch of
  'a': begin
    Label1.Caption := 'Option A selected';
    Label2.Caption := 'You get two points';
  end;
```

```
'b', 'c': begin
  Label1.Caption := 'Option B or C selected';
  Label2.Caption := 'You get zero points';
end;

'd': Label3.Caption := 'Option D earns five points';

else
  Label1.Caption := 'Invalid Choice';
end;
```

This case statement allows two things to happen if the user enters the letter a, and two things to happen if the user enters either b or c. On the other hand, if the user enters the letter d, only one thing happens. A special addition to the structure of case statements lets you use an else clause to specify a specific action if the user chooses anything besides a, b, c, or d.

Now that you've had a look at the basic elements of a case statement, you're ready to take a look at the MUSICTYPE program. This example uses radio buttons to allow the user to select their favorite type of music from a wide variety of options.

The form for the MUSICTYPE program is shown in Figure 8.7. As you can see, the program contains eight radio buttons, one for each type of music listed in the included enumerated variable. Each of these radio buttons is placed on top of a single large group box. As mentioned earlier, each set of radio buttons you use in a program should be placed on its own group box. Furthermore, it's best to select the group box into the form before adding the radio buttons.

FIGURE 8.7.

*The MUSICTYPE
program, with eight radio
buttons.*

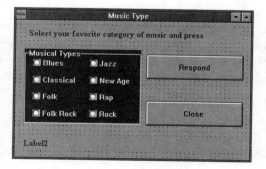

The MUSICTYPE program also includes two labels and two buttons. One of the labels is used to give instructions on how to use the program, while the other provides a place to print the program's output. One of the two buttons closes the program when the user is finished. The other can be selected by the user after he or she has specified a preferred choice of music.

Without further ado, you can now proceed to get the MUSICTYPE program up and running. Here is a copy of the source to the body of the program:

Listing 8.3. The MUSICTYPE program shows how to use a case statement.

```
unit Main;

{ Program copyright (c) 1994 by Charles Calvert }
{ Project Name: MUSICTYP }

interface

uses
  WinTypes, WinProcs,
  Classes, Graphics, Buttons,
  Controls, Printers, Forms, StdCtrls;

type
  TForm1 = class(TForm)
    BRespond: TButton;
    GroupBox1: TGroupBox;
    RJazz: TRadioButton;
    RRock: TRadioButton;
    RClassical: TRadioButton;
    RBlues: TRadioButton;
    RNewAge: TRadioButton;
    Label1: TLabel;
    Label2: TLabel;
    BClose: TButton;
    RRap: TRadioButton;
    BFolk: TRadioButton;
    BFolkRock: TRadioButton;
    procedure BRespondClick(Sender: TObject);
    procedure RClassicalClick(Sender: TObject);
    procedure RRockClick(Sender: TObject);
    procedure RJazzClick(Sender: TObject);
    procedure BCloseClick(Sender: TObject);
    procedure RBluesClick(Sender: TObject);
    procedure RRapClick(Sender: TObject);
    procedure RNewAgeClick(Sender: TObject);
    procedure BFolkClick(Sender: TObject);
    procedure BFolkRockClick(Sender: TObject);
  private
    Music: (Blues, Classical, Folk, FolkRock,
            Jazz, NewAge, Rap, Rock);
  end;

var
  Form1: TForm1;

implementation

{$R *.DFM}

procedure TForm1.BRespondClick(Sender: TObject);
var
  S: String;
begin
  case Music of
    Blues: S := 'Blues';
    Classical: S := 'Classical';
    NewAge: S := 'New Age';
```

continues

Listing 8.3. continued

```
        Folk: S := 'Folk';
        FolkRock: S := 'Folk Rock';
        Jazz: S := 'Jazz';
        Rap: S := 'Rap';
        Rock: S := 'Rock';
      else
        S := 'to be difficult';
      end;
      Label2.Caption := 'I see you like ' + S + ' music';
end;

procedure TForm1.RClassicalClick(Sender: TObject);
begin
  Music := Classical;
end;

procedure TForm1.RRockClick(Sender: TObject);
begin
  Music := Rock;
end;

procedure TForm1.RJazzClick(Sender: TObject);
begin
  Music := Jazz;
end;

procedure TForm1.BCloseClick(Sender: TObject);
begin
  Close;
end;

procedure TForm1.RBluesClick(Sender: TObject);
begin
  Music := Blues;
end;

procedure TForm1.RRapClick(Sender: TObject);
begin
  Music := Rap;
end;

procedure TForm1.RNewAgeClick(Sender: TObject);
begin
  Music := NewAge;
end;

procedure TForm1.BFolkClick(Sender: TObject);
begin
  Music := Folk;
end;

procedure TForm1.BFolkRockClick(Sender: TObject);
begin
  Music := FolkRock;
end;

end.
```

MUSICTYP is not a particularly difficult program to understand. I've provided it here primarily because it shows how to use enumerated types and `case` statements. I suppose it's also of benefit because it shows that you have learned enough about Delphi to start writing some fairly interesting and potentially useful programs. It's not, of course, a fully functional professional program, but it provides enough hints to let you see how it might be possible to get there from here.

The most important block of code in the MUSICTYPE program is the following method:

```
procedure TForm1.BRespondClick(Sender: TObject);
var
  S: String;
begin
  case Music of
    Blues: S := 'Blues';
    Classical: S := 'Classical';
    NewAge: S := 'New Age';
    Folk: S := 'Folk';
    FolkRock: S := 'Folk Rock';
    Jazz: S := 'Jazz';
    Rap: S := 'Rap';
    Rock: S := 'Rock';
  else
    S := 'to be difficult';
  end;
  Label2.Caption := 'I see you like ' + S + ' music';
end;
```

This code sets a string variable to a particular string depending on the current value of the enumerated variable `Music`. This code shows that enumerated types can help you write very compact code that is easy to read. You will also find that `case` statements of the type shown here execute slightly faster than a series of `if..then` statements that achieve the same end.

MUSICTYP and its Radio Buttons

Most of this chapter has been fairly straightforward. However, this last section contains a number of fairly complex ideas that might not be intuitively obvious to all readers. I include this material anyhow, because it explains a number of interesting tricks that you can use to make your Delphi program more powerful.

MUSICTYP uses an oversimplified method of handling radio buttons. Specifically, it responds to a click a button by setting the variable `Music` to a particular value:

```
procedure TForm1.RJazzClick(Sender: TObject);
begin
  Music := Jazz;
end;
```

The problem with this model is that you create a lot of functions, each of which handles an extremely mundane task. To learn how to avoid this situation, you need to see the MUSICTYP2 program, which uses Delphi's delegation model to good effect.

A *delegation model* enables you to easily choose the methods associated with a particular event, or series of events. In other words, you can state that every time any of the radio buttons are selected, the same method should be called. To do this, select one of the radio buttons and choose the Events page in the Object Inspector. Then drop down the list next to the OnClick method and select the RJazzClick method. Now go through each of the controls and make sure they all respond to the OnClick method by calling the RJazzClick routine.

After you have associated the OnClick method for all the radio buttons with one routine, the next step is to delete all the RadioButton methods except for the RJazzClick method. To do this, you must delete the methods both in the implementation and the declaration for the method in the interface. When you are done, change the RJazzClick method so that it looks like this:

```
procedure TForm1.RJazzClick(Sender: TObject);
begin
  if (Sender as TRadioButton).Caption = 'Blues' then
    Music := Blues
  else if (Sender as TRadioButton).Caption = 'Classical' then
    Music := Classical
  else if (Sender as TRadioButton).Caption = 'New Age' then
    Music := NewAge
  else if (Sender as TRadioButton).Caption = 'Folk' then
    Music := Folk
  else if (Sender as TRadioButton).Caption = 'Folk Rock' then
    Music := FolkRock
  else if (Sender as TRadioButton).Caption = 'Jazz' then
    Music := Jazz
  else if (Sender as TRadioButton).Caption = 'Rap' then
    Music := Rap
  else if (Sender as TRadioButton).Caption = 'Rock' then
    Music := Rock;
end;
```

This code uses an as statement to inform the compiler that the sender that has called this method is really a TRadioButton, and that it can safely treat it as such:

```
if (Sender as TRadioButton).Caption = 'Rap' then
    Music := Rap
```

The Sender parameter is of type TObject. You will learn later that all the components used in Delphi are descendants of TObject.

Whenever the RJazzClick method gets called, a copy of the component that called it is sent in the parameter called Sender. This technique allows you to determine which component actually called the function. Unfortunately, the TObject type does not have a Caption field, so you can't simply look directly at the Sender.Caption field. The problem here is that TObject is a very simple type of object that has no caption. However, TRadioButton is a descendant of TObject, and it does have a Caption. As a result, you can tell the compiler that it is safe to assume that the component that called the method has a Caption field. You do this by using the as syntax:

```
Sender as TRadioButton
```

The as statement says that it is okay to treat `Sender` "as if" it were a `TRadioButton` object. The reason for this is simply that in this case, `Sender` really is a `TRadiobutton`. All the `RJazzClick` `OnClick` events are associated with radio buttons. As a result, it is safe to assume that the `Sender` is really a `TRadioButton` and that it will have a `Caption` field.

> **NOTE**
>
> The whole concept of objects and descendants is bound to be a little fuzzy to some readers at this point, but it will become clear during the discussion of object-oriented programming that is included in Part V of this book. In the meantime, you can use the syntax shown above even if you do not fully understand why it works.

There are a few other points of interest in the MUSICTYP program, besides the ones listed previously. For instance, you might notice the syntax used when declaring the program's most important variable, called `Music`:

```
Music: (Blues, Classical, Folk, FolkRock,
        Jazz, NewAge, Rap, Rock);
```

The first thing to notice about this variable is that it does not belong to any particular procedure, but is global to the entire `Form1` object. This means that all the methods in the `TForm1` object have access to the variable and can change it whenever they so desire.

> **NOTE**
>
> Variables like `Music` have a wider scope than the other variables you have seen so far in this book. A variables scope specifies what portions of a program can access the variable. Many variables (like the string `S` in the `BRespondClick` method) have a small local scope and can be seen only inside one procedure. Other variables like `Music` can be seen only from inside a single object. It's possible—and sometimes necessary—to declare a variable that has global scope throughout an entire program. The `Form1` variable declared by the compiler is of this type. Local and global variables, and their relative scopes, are subjects that are addressed several times throughout this book.

If you look carefully at the source code, you can see that `Music` is declared as `private`:

```
private
    Music: (Blues, Classical, Folk, FolkRock,
            Jazz, NewAge, Rap, Rock);
```

Once again, it's a little too soon to begin discussing this matter in any real depth. For that, you'll have to wait until Chapter 27, "Objects, Encapsulation, and Properties," which focuses on object-oriented programming. For now, I'll simply state that variables declared as `private` can only be addressed within a certain proscribed scope. As a rule, any variable you place inside an object should be declared `private`. The reason for this will become clear when you read Chapter 27.

Summary

In this chapter you explored branching and integer types in considerable depth. In particular, you learned about the following types:

- Boolean
- Enumerated
- Subrange

and you have learned about the following branching techniques:

- `if..then` statements
- `if..then..else` statements
- `case` statements

In many ways, the material presented here represents the first examples you have seen of real Pascal programs that have the potential to be useful. So far I'm still explaining material that's somewhat like the first rosy glow of dawn that appears in the wee hours. The sun has not actually peeked over the horizon yet, but you should be getting the sense that dawn is not far away, and that already there is enough light available for you to begin to see the rough outlines of how real Delphi programs must be put together.

Looping with while, for, and repeat Statements

IN THIS CHAPTER

Overview

In the last two chapters, you examined simple integer types that represent whole numbers. This chapter concentrates on looping. Looping is closely related to the subject of branching, in that it gives programmers a way to control the flow of a program.

As you recall from the last chapter, `if..then` statements control branching. The code of a program flows along to a certain point, and then it reaches a fork in the road called an `if` statement. An `if` statement forces your program to either execute a particular statement, or branch beyond it. The same is true of `case` statements.

Sometimes, however, you want your code not to branch in one of two directions, but instead to perform some single action over and over until you ask it to stop. This latter process is called *looping,* and it is one of the most common techniques in computer programming.

You've seen that `if` statements and `case` statements form the two primary means of branching. In the same way, there are three different means of looping:

- `for` statements
- `while` statements
- `repeat` statements

Of these three techniques, the one used most often is the `for` statement. All three techniques, however, are discussed in this chapter.

Other matters covered tangentially in this chapter include

- Using listboxes
- More about drawing simple graphics figures
- Random-number generation

In other languages it might be difficult to introduce some of the topics mentioned above on such short notice. Delphi, however, makes listboxes, graphics, and random numbers almost entirely intuitive subjects.

Why Loops?

Why, some readers might ask, is looping so important? Part of the answer is simply that computers are good at it. For instance, if you had a list of ten thousand addresses arranged in random order and were asked to continuously look up various members on that list, you would be faced with a task of enormous difficulty. Even if you devised a method of indexing the list to help locate a particular entry, you would still be very frustrated by the process.

Though a computer could also create an index, it doesn't necessarily have to because it has other effective techniques it can use. For instance, it's easy for a computer to loop through a list of a "mere" ten thousand items while looking for a particular entry. Computers can do this kind of thing in the blink of an eye. In other words, computers are frequently scanning through lists, iterating through arrays, and searching through various data structures. The reason programmers ask them to do this so often is simply because computers are good at it. Of course, computers lack certain reasoning abilities that humans take for granted, but that's another subject altogether.

Working with *for* Loops

As I implied earlier, for loops represent one of the quintessential programming techniques. Here is a the basic structure of a simple for loop:

```
for i := 1 to 10 do
   SomeAction;
```

This code fragment assumes the declaration of a variable i as an Integer. The code can be read out loud like this: "For i equals 1 to 10 do SomeAction," or like this: "For i colon equals 1 to 10 do SomeAction."

In the previous example, the for loop tells the computer to execute SomeAction ten times in a row. Each time that action is executed the integer i is incremented by one. The loop stops when i is equal to 10.

Consider the following example:

```
for i := 1 to 25 do
   ListBox1.Items.Add(IntToStr(i));
```

This code fragment again assumes that a variable i has been declared as an Integer. Instead of saying "1 to 10," this time the code asks that a particular action be iterated 25 times. More specifically, it states that the value i be translated into a string and added to the contents of a listbox 25 times.

Working with Listboxes

To get started with for loops, you can examine the FORLIST program that is provided on disk. To create the FORLIST program, first produce a form like the one shown in Figure 9.1.

A listbox control provides a place to show the user a list of items such as the files in a directory or a set of names in a list. The key traits of a listbox are that the items inside it can be scrolled up and down, and that the user can highlight or select a particular item.

Delphi allows you to manipulate listboxes with—as the song goes—the greatest of ease. The key point to keep in mind is that a Delphi TListBox object is accompanied by a list of strings that represent the items shown in the listbox. You can reference this list by writing ListBox1.Items, where ListBox1 is the name of an instance of a TListBox object and Items is the name of the list of strings. In particular, an item can be added to a listbox with the following syntax:

```
ListBox1.Items.Add('A new string')
```

where `'A new string'` is used as a sample of the endless variety of strings you can pass into a listbox.

FIGURE 9.1.

The form for the FORLIST program contains a button and a listbox.

NOTE

For all intents and purposes, you can consider the list that accompanies a listbox to be identical to the list you see inside the listbox. However, this is not actually the case, because it happens that there are really two lists, one of which is owned by Windows and the other of which is owned by Pascal. But from the programmer's point of view, the two lists can be considered identical, because all the programmer needs do is maintain the simple Delphi list. The rest is taken care of for you automatically.

FIGURE 9.2.

The FORLIST program uses a listbox to illustrate the way for loops work.

The code for the FORLIST program is shown in Listing 9.1.

Listing 9.1. The FORLIST program responds to a button click by filling a listbox with a set of numbers.

```
unit Main;

{ Program copyright (c) 1994 by Charles Calvert }
{ Project Name: FORLIST }

interface

uses
  WinTypes, WinProcs, Classes,
  Graphics, Controls, StdCtrls,
  Printers, Forms, SysUtils;

type
  TForm1 = class(TForm)
    ListBox1: TListBox;
    Button1: TButton;
    procedure Button1Click(Sender: TObject);
  end;

var
  Form1: TForm1;

implementation

{$R *.DFM}


procedure TForm1.Button1Click(Sender: TObject);
var
  i: Integer;
begin
  for i := 1 to 25 do
    ListBox1.Items.Add(IntToStr(i));
end;

end.
```

Many of the techniques used in the FORLIST code should be familiar to you by now. For instance, the program uses a button that when pressed calls a method that displays output for the user:

```
procedure TForm1.Button1Click(Sender: TObject);
var
  i: Integer;
begin
  for i := 1 to 25 do
    ListBox1.Items.Add(IntToStr(i));
end;
```

The integer i used in this program is incremented by one each time the loop is executed. Needless to say, the loop in this particular incarnation of the FORLOOP program will be executed 25 times. If you want to push on beyond those limits, you can do so easily enough by editing the `Button1Click` method so that it looks like this:

```
for i := 1 to 1025 do
   ListBox1.List.Add(IntToStr(i));
```

ZZZZIIPPP! There she goes. In the blink of an eye you've got 1,025 items in one listbox. However, you should know that there are limits to the number of strings you can put in one listbox. The exact limits are not set in stone, but it's unlikely you will ever be able to fit more than 4,000 strings in one listbox. This limitation is defined by Microsoft. Delphi could go way beyond that limit, but Microsoft's tools make that impossible. To state the matter somewhat differently: All Windows programming products wrestle with this limitation, and it is not specific to Delphi.

Turning Loops Inside Out and Other Magical Tricks of the Trade

A variation on the standard `for` loop allows you to iterate backwards through the ordinal values of a control variable. For instance, instead of counting from 1 to 25, you can count from 25 down to 1. Here's how it looks:

```
for i := 25 downto 1 do
   ListBox1.Items.Add(IntToStr(i));
```

The only difference here is that you are using the word `downto` rather than `to`.

There is nothing magical about the relationship between `for` loops and the number 1. If you want, you can count from 7 to 23, or from 15 to –12. Furthermore, in the following example the `for` loop is never executed at all:

```
for i := 11 to 10 do Something;
```

This last example seems a bit nonsensical as written, but code similar to this can be useful at times. For instance, suppose you were taking away bonus points from a student each time he or she answered a question incorrectly. Furthermore, suppose the variable X in the following example represents the total number of incorrect answers a person has given you:

```
for i := X to 10 do GiveBonusPoints;
```

In the above code fragment, any student who had more than 10 incorrect answers wouldn't get any bonus points. (Sorry about this weary pedagogical example, but it was the only one that came to mind while I was writing this chapter!)

for Loops and the Powers of Two

In the previous code, you saw the very essence of a for loop by literally watching it iterate a control variable through the integer values between 1 and 25. Of course, it doesn't take a lot of imagination to see that for loops can be put to more interesting purposes.

In the following program, a for loop is used to calculate the powers of two. Specifically, the user is asked to enter a number (n), and then the program proceeds to calculate two to the *n*th power. The form for the program (Figure 9.3) and its code (Listing 9.2) both follow:

FIGURE 9.3.

The TWOPOW program includes three labels, an edit control, a listbox and a button.

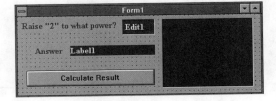

Listing 9.2. The TWOPOW program calculates the powers of two and displays them in a listbox.

```
unit Main;

{ Program copyright (c) 1994 by Charles Calvert }
{ Project Name: TWOPOW }

interface

uses
  WinTypes, WinProcs, SysUtils,
  Classes, Graphics, StdCtrls,
  Controls, Printers, Forms;

type
  TForm1 = class(TForm)
    BCalc: TButton;
    Label1: TLabel;
    Edit1: TEdit;
    Label2: TLabel;
    ListBox1: TListBox;
    Label3: TLabel;
    procedure BCalcClick(Sender: TObject);
  end;

var
  Form1: TForm1;
```

continues

Listing 9.2. continued

```
implementation

{$R *.DFM}

procedure TForm1.BCalcClick(Sender: TObject);
var
  i, j, k: LongInt;
begin
  ListBox1.Clear;
  k := 1;
  j := StrToInt(Edit1.Text);
  for i := 1 to j do begin
    k := k * 2;
    ListBox1.Items.Add(IntToStr(k));
  end;
  Label1.Caption := IntToStr(k);
end;

end.
```

To use the TWOPOW program, enter a number n in the edit control and click the button that says Calculate Result. In response, the program immediately calculates 2 to the *n*th power and displays the result, as shown in Figure 9.4. The program also uses a listbox to display the

FIGURE 9.4.

A typical run of the TWOPOW program, where 2 is calculated to the 5th power.

values it computed while performing its calculations.

The most important method in the TWOPOW program is BCalcClick:

```
procedure TForm1.BCalcClick(Sender: TObject);
var
  i, j, k: LongInt;
begin
  ListBox1.Clear;
  k := 1;
  j := StrToInt(Edit1.Text);
  for i := 1 to j do begin
    k := k * 2;
    ListBox1.Items.Add(IntToStr(k));
  end;
  Label1.Caption := IntToStr(k);
end;
```

This procedure starts off by clearing any existing entries from the listbox with the TListBox Clear method. This call serves no purpose the first time the method is called, but thereafter it ensures that the values placed in the listbox during one call to BCalcClick aren't simply appended onto an existing list.

After clearing the listbox, the next step is to set the value of k to 1. This process is called initializing a variable, and it is a step programmers often have to take. One final preliminary step is taken care of when the program snags the entry supplied by the user in the program's edit control. The input garnered from the edit control is used to control the number of iterations performed by the for loop.

Once the preliminaries described previously are concluded, the for loop itself is executed:

```
for i := 1 to j do begin
  k := k * 2;
  ListBox1.List.Add(IntToStr(k));
end;
```

As you can see, this for loop adds a begin..end pair in order to encapsulate two different substatements inside a compound statement. Each time the loop is executed, the value k is incremented by its current value times the number two. The result is the production of a list such as the one shown in Figure 9.5.

FIGURE 9.5.

The first eight powers of 2 were calculated during this run of the TWOPOW program.

It's vitally important that you understand exactly what happens to the value k each time the loop is executed. As you know, the first time through the loop k is set to the value one. This means that after substitutions are made, the code that gets executed looks like this:

```
k := 1 * 2;  { 1 is substituted for the value k }
```

Notice that I have written k := 1 * 2 rather than 1 := 1 * 2. When people new to programming first look at a statement like k := k * 2, they can easily become confused by mentally substituting the current value of k on both sides of the assignment operator. This kind of mistake is easy to make, but it's based on a misunderstanding of the import of the assignment operator.

The assignment operator signals that a particular value is going to be assigned to a variable, and that any expression on the right side of the operator will be calculated first. Specifically, in the above code 1 is multiplied by 2 and then assigned to the value k. Therefore, after the first iteration of the loop, k is assigned the value of 1 * 2, which is 2.

During the next iteration of the loop, the statement looks like this after substitutions are made:

```
k := 2 * 2;
```

Now k is equal to 4. The next step looks like this:

```
k := 4 * 2;
```

which sets k equal to 8. To help yourself visualize this process, you can do three things:

■ View the output from the program.

■ Use the debugger to watch the value of k as the loop is iterated.

■ Contemplate the following series:

```
k := 1 * 2;  { k = 2  }
k := 2 * 2;  { k = 4  }
k := 4 * 2;  { k = 8  }
k := 8 * 2;  { k = 16 }
k := 16 * 2; { k = 32 }
```

The Powers of Two, Without a Listbox

In the last two programs, I provided a listbox as an aid that in effect allows you to gaze into memory and peek at the values of a variable during each iteration of a for loop. Hopefully, this is a useful learning tool, but I don't want it to mislead you regarding the true significance of for loops.

Most of the time users never see the values that are constantly being recalculated during each iteration of a for loop. Instead, they only see the result produced after the loop has finished executing. The TWOPOW2 program, shown in Listing 9.3, illustrates this point by simply removing the listbox that was part of the original TWOPOW program. Now the user can enter a number, press a button, and wham! there's the answer. This program illustrates the speed and efficiency of for loops. The user of this program never sees what's happening behind the scenes, and as a result the program takes on the aura of magic, of expert sleight of hand, that many people associate with computers.

Listing 9.3. The TWOPOW2 program shows an easy way to calculate the powers of two.

```
unit Main;

{ Program copyright (c) 1994 by Charles Calvert }
{ Project Name: TWOPOW2 }

interface

uses
  WinTypes, WinProcs,
```

```
  Classes, Graphics,
  Controls, StdCtrls,
  Printers, Forms, SysUtils;

type
  TForm1 = class(TForm)
    BCalc: TButton;
    Label1: TLabel;
    Edit1: TEdit;
    Label2: TLabel;
    Label3: TLabel;
    procedure BCalcClick(Sender: TObject);
  end;

var
  Form1: TForm1;

implementation

{$R *.DFM}

procedure TForm1.BCalcClick(Sender: TObject);
var
  i, j, k: LongInt;
begin
  k := 1;
  j := StrToInt(Edit1.Text);
  for i := 1 to j do
    k := k * 2;
  Label1.Caption := IntToStr(k);
end;

end.
```

while Loops

If you understand for loops, it shouldn't take but a moment to catch on to while loops. When you create a while loop, the goal is to tell the processor to continue performing a certain action *while* a particular condition remains true.

In English, a while loop would look like this: "While the sun is out, you can play baseball." Or, if the sentence were structured as a pseudo Pascal statement, it would look like this:

```
while the sun is out do
  PlayBaseball;
```

And finally, here's the code as it would be expressed in a compilable Pascal statement:

```
while Sun = True do
  PlayBaseball;
```

while loops are a great deal like for loops. For instance, you can take the for loop from the TWOPOW program and translate it into a while statement:

```
procedure TForm1.BCalcClick(Sender: TObject);
var
  i, j, k: LongInt;
begin
  ListBox1.Clear;
  k := 1;
  i := 0;                              { Set i to 0  }
  j := StrToInt(Edit1.Text);
  while i < j do begin
    k := k * 2;
    ListBox1.Items.Add(IntToStr(k));
    Inc(i);                            { Increment i }
  end;
  Label1.Caption := IntToStr(k);
end;
```

The original loop was controlled by the statement for i := 1 to j. In this new version, the loop is controlled by the statement while i < j. Specifically, the control statement specifies that the loop should be executed while i is smaller than j.

Notice that this while loop requires a bit more maintenance than a for loop would. For instance, you need to initialize i to zero at the beginning of the loop, and then explicitly increment i during each iteration of the loop. As a result, a loop like the one shown could probably be best implemented as a for statement, but certainly the differences between the two methods are small enough that under most circumstances either method would be acceptable. I should point out, however, that there are occasions when while loops are more efficient or better-suited to a task than a for loop. In particular, while loops are useful if you are not able to know ahead of time exactly when a loop should end. As always, it's just a question of finding the right tool for the right job.

A Graphic Example of *while* Loops

The next three sample programs feature graphical elements that are painted to the screen during each iteration of a loop. Specifically, you will see the following:

■ How to use while loops and repeat..until loops

■ A review of ellipses and rectangles

■ How to draw lines

■ One way to share time with other processes

■ How to calculate random numbers

Perhaps the best thing to do is for you to get an example up and running right away, and then once you see how to operate a particular program, you can better understand its internals.

It's probably easiest to start off with the ELLIPSES program, which asks you how many ellipses you would like to draw and then proceeds to draw them to the screen for you. To use the program, first fill in the number of graphical figures you want to see, and then press the Start button. Sample output from the program is shown in Figure 9.6.

FIGURE 9.6.

The aptly named ELLIPSES program draws graphical shapes inside a form.

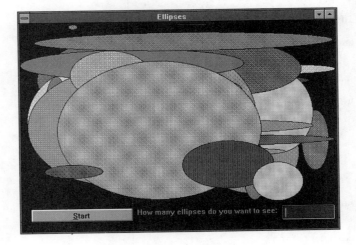

The form (Figure 9.7) and code (Listing 9.4) for the ELLIPSES program are both shown below.

FIGURE 9.7.

The form for the ELLIPSES program contains a button, a label, and an edit control.

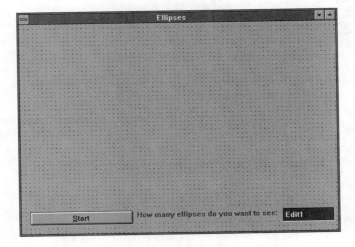

Listing 9.4. The code for the ELLIPSES program shows how to execute a simple while loop.

```pascal
unit Main;

{ Program copyright (c) 1994 by Charles Calvert }
{ Project Name: ELLIPSES }

interface

uses
  WinTypes, WinProcs, SysUtils,
  Classes, Graphics, StdCtrls,
  Controls, Printers, Forms;

type
  TForm1 = class(TForm)
    BStart: TButton;
    Label1: TLabel;
    Edit1: TEdit;
    procedure BStartClick(Sender: TObject);
    procedure FormCreate(Sender: TObject);
  end;

var
  Form1: TForm1;

implementation

{$R *.DFM}

procedure TForm1.BStartClick(Sender: TObject);
var
  i, j, x, y: Integer;
  R: TRect;
begin
  j := 0;
  R := GetClientRect;
  x := R.Right;
  y := R.Bottom - 50;
  i := StrToInt(Edit1.Text);
  while j < i do begin
    Canvas.Ellipse(Random(x), Random(y), Random(x), Random(y));
    Canvas.Brush.Color := RGB(Random(255), Random(255), Random(255));
    inc(j);
  end;
  Edit1.SetFocus;
  Edit1.Text := '';
end;

procedure TForm1.FormCreate(Sender: TObject);
begin
  Edit1.Text := '';
end;

end.
```

Notice that this program uses the OnActivate event from the Object Inspector for the program's main form. An OnActivate event is generated whenever the form is being activated, which basically means that it will be called shortly after the form is first created. The program uses this event to blank out the Edit1 component, and then to set the focus to it. I will talk more about focusing controls in the next chapter.

The key method in this program is BStartClick. The procedure begins by declaring some integer variables and a record called R, which is of type TRect. This record will be used to describe the coordinates of the program's main form. You were introduced to coordinates in Chapter 5, "What is a Graphical Environment?" To my mind, it's a complicated enough subject that some readers might want to review that material again by rereading that chapter.

The Dimensions of a Form

If you want to know the current dimensions of a form, you can assign a variable of type TRect to the GetClientRect function:

```
R := GetClientRect;
```

The result you get back will have dimensions of the following type: (0, 0, 100, 200), where 100 and 200 are sample values designating a possible width and height for a form.

For simplicity's sake, the ELLIPSES program uses the Integer x to designate the width of a form. It then assigns y to the form's height, and subtracts 50 from that value to discount the real estate that contains the form's controls:

```
x := R.Right;
y := R.Bottom - 50;
```

Take a moment to be sure you understand what this code is doing. The first step was to get the dimensions of the form by calling GetClientRect. The variable x is then assigned to the form's width, and y is assigned to its height.

It's almost time to begin the loop. The only step left is to see how many times the user wants to iterate through the loop. To get this number, just query the program's edit control:

```
i := StrToInt(Edit1.Text);
```

This simple line of code merely translates the user's input into a integer value that can be used as a control variable in a loop.

At long last, you are ready to begin the looping:

```
while j < i do begin
   Canvas.Ellipse(Random(x), Random(y), Random(x), Random(y));
   Canvas.Brush.Color :=
     RGB(Random(255), Random(255), Random(255));
   Inc(j);
end;
```

This loop draws a series of ellipses to the screen, each of which will have randomly chosen coordinates. Furthermore, the color that fills each rectangle will also be randomly chosen during each iteration of the loop.

The `while` statement shown in the code consists of calls to three different functions:

- The first is called `Ellipse`. Naturally enough, it draws an ellipse that fits inside a rectangle defined by the four coordinates passed to the function.

- The second is a call to the `Random` function that returns a random number between zero and the value specified in its parameter.

- The final call is to the `RGB` function, which blends red, green, and blue shades together to produce a specific color.

The ELLIPSES program continually changes the color of the brush that fills in the interior of the ellipse. In order to come up with a new color on virtually every iteration of the loop, the program calls on the `Random` function.

If you pass the `Random` function the number 10, it returns a randomly chosen value between 0 and 9. If you call `Random` with a parameter of 6, it returns a value between 0 and 5. The rule here is that `Random` returns a number within the range that you specify, with the range itself being zero-based. If you want to find a random number between 1 and 5, then you should pass 5 to `Random` and add 1 to the value returned by the function:

```
x := Random(5) + 1;
```

By now you should have all the facts you need to get a grasp on how the ELLIPSES program works. Take your time to study it and play with it. The program helps to illustrate the enormous power of loops and shows how computers can generate diversity even from repetition!

NOTE

Because the ELLIPSES program sets the values of x and y to the approximate width and height of the program's form, the ellipses drawn by the program will always be guaranteed to fall within the main form's dimensions:

```
R := GetClientRect;
    x := R.Right;
    y := R.Bottom - 50;
    Canvas.Ellipse(Random(x), Random(y), Random(x), Random(y));
```

For instance, if the form is 100 pixels wide, a call to `Random(100)` will always return a value that will be within the visible portion of the main form. If the `Ellipse` function were passed a width outside the dimension of the form, at least some portion of the ellipse would not be visible. Note also that the `Ellipse` function will draw a valid shape even if the last two parameters it is passed are smaller than the first two.

Open-Ended *while* Loops

The examples of while statements shown previously help to illustrate the way loops work. However, these examples let you down in one regard, because they don't show how you can use a while loop to repeat a particular action until such time as the user asks it to stop, or until some other perhaps randomly chosen trigger is set off. Rest assured, though, you can ask a while loop to simply continue a particular action until you, or the user, decide to tell it to stop.

A simplified version of the open-ended while statement from the next sample program looks like this:

```
Draw := True;
while Draw do begin
  DrawRandomLines;
  CheckUserInput;
end;
```

This code fragment asks the computer to draw lines at random coordinates on the screen until such time as the variable Draw is no longer set to the value True. At first it might seem as if this loop would never end, and indeed, all programmers need to be careful not to accidentally design a loop with no valid closing conditions.

To avoid the possibility of an endless loop, the next sample program, called LINELOOP, checks to see if the user selects a menu item labeled Stop. If the user does choose Stop, the variable Draw is set to False, and the loop ends:

```
procedure TForm1.BStopClick(Sender: TObject);
begin
  Draw := False;
end;
```

You can see the screen and sample output from the LINELOOP program in Figure 9.8.

FIGURE 9.8.

The LINELOOP program in action, busily drawing lines on the screen, waiting for the user to select Stop.

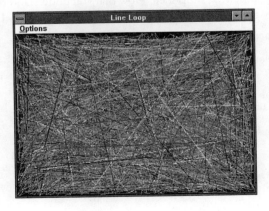

Before moving on to a description of how to draw lines, it's perhaps worth noting that the Draw variable used in the LINELOOP program must be declared as global to the entire main form. This is required because both the BStartClick and BStopClick methods need access to the variable. Here is the declaration for the TForm1 class from the LINELOOP program. Note that the Boolean variable Draw is added after the keyword private, shown here at the bottom of the declaration:

```
TForm1 = class(TForm)
  BStart: TButton;
  BStop: TButton;
  procedure BStartClick(Sender: TObject);
  procedure BStopClick(Sender: TObject);
private
  Draw: Boolean;
end;
```

Discussion of keywords such as private, public, and persistent will be postponed until Chapter 27, "Objects, Encapsulation, and Properties." For now you need only know that they designate that a particular variable or function cannot be referenced from outside of the current object and module.

The flow of the LINELOOP program is really fairly simple, but it might be worth reviewing the logic just to be sure that it is clear:

- The program declares a Boolean variable called Draw, which is global to the program's main form.

- When the user selects Start from the menu, the Draw variable is set to True.

- The program then enters a loop that continues until the Draw variable is set to False.

- The Draw variable is set to False when the user selects Stop from the menu.

When I described the BStartClick method the first time, I said that the code I was showing you was somewhat simplified. Now that you understand the flow of the program, you are ready to study the entire function, so you can see exactly how lines are created:

```
procedure TForm1.BStartClick(Sender: TObject);
var
  R: TRect;
  x, y: Integer;
begin
  Canvas.MoveTo(10, 10);
  R := GetClientRect;
  Draw := True;
  while Draw do begin
    x := Random(R.Right);
    y := Random(R.Bottom);
    Canvas.Pen.Color := RGB(Random(255), Random(255), Random(255));
    Canvas.LineTo(X, Y);
    YieldToOthers;
  end;
end;
```

The act of drawing a line is begun by moving the current drawing position to a particular x and y location with the MoveTo function:

```
Canvas.MoveTo(10, 10);
```

More specifically, this code states that the line to be drawn will begin at a point ten pixels down from the top of the form and ten pixels in from the left of the form. The line itself is drawn with the aptly named LineTo method:

```
Canvas.LineTo(X, Y);
```

After your experience with the ELLIPSES program, it should not be hard for you to understand how the x and y locations used in the LineTo function are calculated. In particular, the GetClientRect function is called to retrieve the main form's coordinates, and then the Random function is used to pick a location that's guaranteed to lie within the form's dimensions:

```
R := GetClientRect;
x := Random(R.Right);
y := Random(R.Bottom);
```

I could have combined the Random and LineTo functions:

```
Canvas.LineTo(Random(R.Right), Random(R.Bottom));
```

Of course, once the loop is started, each iteration it makes draws a new line to the screen. Furthermore, each of those iterations causes the line to be drawn in a new location and in a new color. (Well, at any rate, it most likely will be drawn in a new location and a new color. There is nothing that prevents the random happenstance of two sequentially chosen lines being drawn in the same place and in the same color; it's just unlikely. Very unlikely.)

There is, of course, one last unexplained element in this program, and that is the call to function called YieldToOthers. This function is called at the very end of each loop.

To understand exactly why it's necessary to call YieldToOthers entails grasping certain aspects about object-oriented operating systems that Delphi goes to great lengths to hide. The details of this subject are eventually broached in the last section of this book, when the subject turns to a discussion of advanced Windows programming concepts.

For now, however, I'm going to omit certain details that have no relevance to the kind of programming central to this book. This makes it possible for me to attempt to give a general explanation of what is happening.

The key point to grasp is that when a program enters a loop, it gives Windows no opportunity to poll the system to see if any other events have occurred. Specifically, it cannot check to see if anyone has clicked the Stop button shown on LINELOOP's main form.

There's a room in my house where I go sometimes to work out. When I'm in there I often turn up the music fairly loud and start doing certain repetitive exercises in a loop. If anybody happens to call on the phone or drop by the house while I'm doing that, I'm not going to know that they are trying to get my attention. I'm putting all my energy into the current task and have no room for anything else.

The same thing happens when you enter a loop in a program. The processor is furiously processing instructions as fast it can get at them, and therefore has no chance to check if a key has been pressed or if the mouse has been moved.

The following function, called `YieldToOthers`, gives the processor a chance to take a quick peek outside the room where it's working to see if anything else is going on:

```
procedure YieldToOthers;
var
  Msg : TMsg;
begin
  while PeekMessage(Msg,0,0,0,PM_REMOVE) do begin
    if (Msg.Message = WM_QUIT) then begin
      exit;
    end;
    TranslateMessage(Msg);
    DispatchMessage(Msg);
  end;
end;
```

If you take a close look at this procedure, you can see that it makes a call to function called `PeekMessage`. This function is internal to Windows, and well beyond the scope of this chapter. Nevertheless, it should be possible to make its basic purpose comprehensible. The function simply takes a quick peek outside the door of the room where Windows is working, and it checks to see if anything is going on. If there is something that needs to be done, such as updating a window, then Windows will perform the task before returning its attention to your loop. That's why they call it `PeekMessage`. It looks to see if any messages from the mouse, or keyboard, or from another program, are available for processing, and if so, it processes them. If there are no messages to process, it returns immediately to your loop. For more information on `PeekMessage`, see the API section of the online help.

> **NOTE**
>
> During the beta cycle, a function was added to the VCL that performs much the same task as my `YieldToOthers` function. The method, called `Application.ProcessMessages`, is used in other programs included with this book. `YieldToOthers` is a powerful call, however, since you have the complete source code and you can modify it for special cases. In particular, you can check to see if particular events occur; and if they do, you can set a flag causing your program to break out of the loop.

Normally you don't need to call `YieldToOthers` because the system is getting plenty of chances to poll for available messages. It's only when you enter particularly demanding code fragment, such as a loop, that the system gets completely tied up with your program.

In this particular case, the loop needs to be interrupted merely so that the BStopClick function can be called:

```
procedure TForm1.BStopClick(Sender: TObject);
begin
  Draw := False;
end;
```

Specifically, what happens is YieldToOthers gives Windows a chance to see that the user has clicked on the Stop button. In response to this action, Windows calls BStopClick, which is the function you explicitly asked Windows to call whenever the Stop button is pressed. Inside the function, the variable Draw is set to False. This is the necessary condition to end the while loop, and so the program therefore stops drawing lines to the screen when you press the Stop button.

NOTE

I'm aware that the whole idea of an operating system processing events and sending messages to an application is totally foreign to people who came from the DOS environment. Event-oriented operating systems are very efficient, but they can throw some heavy curves at programmers. As a result, I feel that this is definitely not the time to explore this subject in any depth. But don't worry, the subject will be explained in detail in Chapter 25, "Handling Messages."

Finally, you won't be able to run the LINELOOP program until you understand the basics about menus. To get started with menus, plop a TMainMenu component onto a form. Then select MainMenu1 from the Object Inspector and double-click the Items property. After the Menu Builder appears on-screen, you can simply fill in the names of the menu items you want to use, so that the menu looks like the image shown in Figure 9.9.

FIGURE 9.9.

The menu from the LINELOOP program has a popup menu called Options, with Stop and Start menu items inside it.

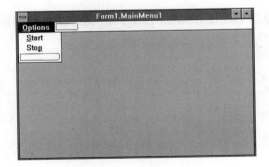

After creating the menu, it's easy to write code that responds to a particular selection. For instance, if you select the Start option in the Menu Builder, and then select the Events page from the Object Inspector, you can double-click the right side of the Object Inspector to create the framework for a method in the Editor window:

```
procedure TForm1.Start2Click(Sender: TObject);
begin

end;
```

After creating this code, the next step, of course, is to fill in the appropriate logic by writing code.

All in all, the Menu Builder is extremely easy to use. It's an intuitive tool, which you should be able to master in just a few moments.

If you haven't done so already, it's time now for you to get the LINELOOP program up and running. You can create the form for the program (Figure 9.10) by following the simple guide shown in the code for the program in Listing 9.5.

FIGURE 9.10.

The Form for the LINELOOP program contains a simple menu called Options. It has two entries: Start and Stop.

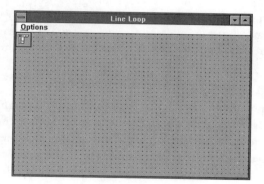

Listing 9.5. The LINELOOP program contains a while loop and a call that allows Windows to process messages.

```
unit Main;

{ Program copyright (c) 1995 by Charles Calvert }
{ Project Name: LINELOOP }

{ Note the comments above the call to YieldToOthers }

interface

uses
  WinTypes, WinProcs,
  Classes, Messages,
  Graphics, Controls, Printers,
  Forms, Menus;
```

```
type
  TForm1 = class(TForm)
    MainMenu1: TMainMenu;
    Start1: TMenuItem;
    Start2: TMenuItem;
    Stop1: TMenuItem;
    procedure BStartClick(Sender: TObject);
    procedure BStopClick(Sender: TObject);
  private
    Draw: Boolean;
  end;

var
  Form1: TForm1;

implementation

{$R *.DFM}

{ You can call either YieldToOthers, or the built
  in function: Application.ProcessMessages }
procedure YieldToOthers;
var
  Msg : TMsg;
begin
  while PeekMessage(Msg,0,0,0,PM_REMOVE) do begin
    if (Msg.Message = WM_QUIT) then begin
      exit;
    end;
    TranslateMessage(Msg);
    DispatchMessage(Msg);
  end;
end;

procedure TForm1.BStartClick(Sender: TObject);
var
  R: TRect;
  x, y: Integer;
begin
  Canvas.MoveTo(10, 10);
  R := GetClientRect;
  Draw := True;
  while Draw do begin
    x := Random(R.Right);
    y := Random(R.Bottom);
    Canvas.Pen.Color := RGB(Random(255), Random(255), Random(255));
    Canvas.LineTo(X, Y);
    YieldToOthers; { or Application.ProcessMessages }
  end;
end;

procedure TForm1.BStopClick(Sender: TObject);
begin
  Draw := False;
end;

end.
```

repeat...until Loops

Besides while loops and for loops, there is one other key looping structure frequently used in Pascal programs. These are called repeat..until loops. They differ from while loops because they will always be executed at least once. while loops, on the other hand, determine whether a condition is true; and if it is not, the body of the loop will never be executed.

The following program, called RECTLOOP, is structured exactly like the LINELOOP, except for three minor differences:

- It draws rectangles to the screen rather than lines.
- It uses a repeat..until loop, whereas the previous program used a while loop.
- It changes the color of a brush rather than the color of a pen.

Here is the repeat loop from the RECTLOOP program:

```
repeat
  Canvas.Brush.Color :=
    RGB(Random(255), Random(255), Random(255));
  Canvas.Rectangle(Random(x), Random(y), Random(x), Random(y));
  YieldToOthers;
until not Draw;
```

This loop would be nearly identical to the one in LineLoop if it were structured like this:

```
while not draw do begin
  Canvas.Brush.Color :=
    RGB(Random(255), Random(255), Random(255));
  Canvas.Rectangle(Random(x), Random(y), Random(x), Random(y));
  YieldToOthers;
end;
```

The only substantial difference between the two loops is that it is possible for the while loop never to be executed at all. The repeat loop, on the other hand, will always execute at least once, because the test condition (is Draw false?) isn't evaluated until the loop has been processed once. Therefore, the loop doesn't know whether or not to stop executing until the end has been reached.

On most occasions, however, you can use a repeat loop or a while loop as the spirit moves you. There is no particular advantage in adhering to one or the other except when you want to construct a loop that might not execute at all.

The Rectangle function referenced in the previous loop is easy to understand. The key points to grasp are simply that the upper-left corner of the square to be drawn is defined by the first two parameters passed to the rectangle function, while the second two designate the bottom-right corner of the rectangle.

Of course, in a situation such as this, where numbers are being chosen at random, there is no guarantee that the bottom-right corner of the rectangle will actually appear below and to the right of the upper-left. For instance, the following random coordinates could be chosen on any one throw of the dice:

```
Rectangle(100, 100, 1, 1);
```

In this case, the roles of the coordinates are reversed in that the first two define the bottom-right coordinates, and the last two define the upper-left. But the use of random numbers created this unusual situation, and on most occasions programmers define the upper-left first and the bottom-right second.

The inside of a rectangle is always filled in using the current brush, and the outside—or border—is filled in using the current pen. If you'd like, you can experiment further with rectangles by adding the following lines to the interior of the program's loop:

```
Canvas.Pen.Color := RGB(Random(255), Random(255), Random(255));
Canvas.Pen.Width := Random(50);
```

These two lines change the color and the width of the border drawn around each rectangle.

The form for the RECTLOOP program, shown in Figure 9.11, is no different from the form for the LINELOOP program. The code for the program is shown in Listing 9.6.

FIGURE 9.11.

The form for the RECTLOOP program, shown here, is identical to the form for the LINELOOP program.

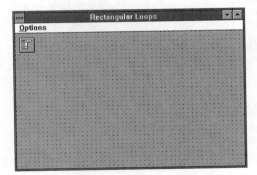

Listing 9.6. The RECTLOOP program draws a series of rectangles to the screen.

```
unit Main;

{ Program copyright (c) 1995 by Charles Calvert }
{ Project Name: RECTLOOP }

interface

uses
  WinTypes, WinProcs,
  Classes, Graphics,
  Controls, Printers, Forms,
  Messages, Menus;
```

continues

Listing 9.6. continued

```
type
  TForm1 = class(TForm)
    MainMenu1: TMainMenu;
    Options1: TMenuItem;
    Start1: TMenuItem;
    Stop1: TMenuItem;
    procedure Start1Click(Sender: TObject);
    procedure Stop1Click(Sender: TObject);
  private
    Draw: Boolean;
  end;

var
  Form1: TForm1;

implementation

{$R *.DFM}

procedure YieldToOthers;
var
  Msg : TMsg;
begin
  while PeekMessage(Msg,0,0,0,PM_REMOVE) do begin
    if (Msg.Message = WM_QUIT) then begin
      exit;
    end;
    TranslateMessage(Msg);
    DispatchMessage(Msg);
  end;
end;

procedure TForm1.Start1Click(Sender: TObject);
var
  R: TRect;
  x,y: Integer;
begin
  Draw := True;
  R := GetClientRect;
  x := R.Right;
  y := R.Bottom;
  repeat
    Canvas.Brush.Color := RGB(Random(255), Random(255), Random(255));
    Canvas.Rectangle(Random(x), Random(y), Random(x), Random(y));
    YieldToOthers;
  until not Draw;
end;

procedure TForm1.Stop1Click(Sender: TObject);
begin
  Draw := False;
end;

end.
```

Drawing Pixels to the Screen

Earlier in the book I said that I would show you how to draw pixels to the screen in this chapter. I show this program here because it includes some looping, and thus fits in with the theme of the chapter. Previously you saw how to draw rectangles, lines, and ellipses. When you add pixels to your repertoire, you will have a good grasp of the basic graphics functions in a Windows program.

The form for the PIXELS program is a very austere black, unbesmirched by controls or other obstacles. To create the form, select the Object Inspector's Color property and set it to black. The result should be something like the image shown in Figure 9.12.

FIGURE 9.12.

The austere plain black form for the PIXELS program.

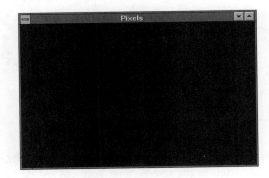

You're not quite finished with the form yet, however, because you should also set the WindowState property to wsMaximized. This forces the form to open up in its maximized state, which of course covers the entire screen.

At this stage, you should get the program up and running. To aid you in that pursuit, the code for the program's only unit is shown in Listing 9.7.

Listing 9.7. The PIXELS program paints tiny points of color on a black screen.

```
unit Main;

{ Program copyright (c) 1995 by Charles Calvert }
{ Project Name: PIXELS }

interface

uses
  WinTypes, WinProcs,
  Classes, Graphics,
  Controls, Printers, Forms;

type
  TForm1 = class(TForm)
```

continues

Listing 9.7. continued

```
    procedure FormPaint(Sender: TObject);
  end;

var
  Form1: TForm1;

implementation

{$R *.DFM}

procedure TForm1.FormPaint(Sender: TObject);
var
  R: TRect;
  i: Integer;
  Color: LongInt;
begin
  R := GetClientRect;
  for i := 1 to 10000 do begin
    Color := RGB(Random(255), Random(255), Random(255));
    Canvas.Pixels[Random(R.Right), Random(R.Bottom)] :=  Color;
  end;
end;

end.
```

As you can see, the PIXELS program is very brief. It consists primarily of a simple for loop that draws 10,000 pixels to the screen in random colors:

```
for i := 1 to 10000 do begin
  Color := RGB(Random(255), Random(255), Random(255));
  Canvas.Pixels[Random(R.Right), Random(R.Bottom)] :=  Color;
end;
```

Like all the graphics functions, you can draw pixels by accessing the form's Canvas. The Pixel function takes two parameters; the first is the column you want to place the pixel on and the second is the row. The only selection left to make is the color you want to use, which is chosen by using the assignment operator.

As it appears, the Pixel function might seem a bit confusing. If you want, you can rewrite the code so that it looks like this:

```
x := Random(R.Right);
y := Random(R.Bottom);
Canvas.Pixels[x,y] := Color;
```

In effect, you are saying that the pixel at a certain x and y coordinate should be set to a particular color. When you first start the program, all the pixels are set to black, and as the program runs, 10,000 of them are set to a randomly chosen color.

The big question about the PIXELS program is not how its loop works, but how the loop gets called in the first place. After all, the program has no controls that can be manipulated in order to call the loop.

The secret here is that the PIXELS program responds to `wm_OnPaint` events by calling a function every time the form is started up, and again every time a portion of the program is covered up by another program and then uncovered. The function in question is called `FormPaint`, and it occurs in response to `OnPaint` events. You can construct `OnPaint` events methods by turning to the Object Inspector's Event Palette.

More on Paint Methods

When Windows was created, the developers had to figure out a way to save the contents of every window on-screen, even though that window might not always be visible. Consider the Clock program that comes with Windows. This visual component of this program is naturally changing at least every second. As a result, it would not do to simply save an image of this window before it was hidden and then restore it after it was brought back to the top of the desktop.

The designers of Windows decided to send a message to each program whenever the surface of that program needs to be updated. When that message is sent, only the portions of the program that have been hidden are required to update themselves. To see how this works in practice, run the PIXELS program and then bring some other, nonmaximized program to the front by using the Alt+Tab key combination. Now bring the PIXELS program back to the front. You will see that only the portions of the program that have been hidden will be redrawn. All of this occurs only because the PIXELS program uses the `OnPaint` property.

Summary

In this chapter you learned about `for` loops, `while` loops, and `repeat` loops. In the process you got some review and further exploration of the major graphics commands. For instance, you learned that you can use

- The `Ellipse` function to draw ellipses and circles on the screen
- The `Pixel` function to draw single points of light on the screen
- The `Rectangle` function to draw squares and rectangles
- The `MoveTo` and `LineTo` function to draw lines on the screen

Other territory covered in this chapter included listboxes and the `OnPaint` property.

Real Numbers, Functions, and Operators

10

Overview

In the last three chapters you examined simple integer types, which represent whole numbers. This chapter concentrates on floating point numbers, which are often referred to as real numbers or decimal numbers.

Of particular interest to most readers of this chapter is the discussion of operators, such as +, -, and div. So far you have used operators without ever learning much about how they work. In this chapter and the next you will hear a bit more about how operators should be handled when using Delphi. In particular, you will learn a good deal about operator precedence.

Functions are one of the most important new ideas introduced in this chapter. Functions are very much like procedures, except that they return a value. You can use functions to encapsulate useful routines. For instance, there are functions that calculate the square root of a number or raise it to a particular power. The StrToInt and IntToStr routines are both functions that you have been using since the early chapters of this book. Now, however, you will learn how to write your own functions rather than simply using functions written by others.

This chapter introduces some ideas that are more complex than those you have seen before. However, none of this material should be beyond the reach of anyone who is willing to do a little work.

The Basic Floating Point Types

Integer values always represent whole numbers such as 1, 2, and 3. Numbers with decimal points in them, such as 1.2 or 5.67, are called real numbers or floating point numbers.

You have seen that there are five basic integer types used to represent whole numbers, and that each of these types has a particular range, as follows:

```
ShortInt    -128 .. 127
Byte  0  ..  255
Integer     -32768 .. 32767
Word  0  ..  65535
Longint     -2147483648 .. 2147483647
```

In the same way that integers have certain types and ranges, so do the numbers that represent decimal values, as shown in Table 10.1.

Table 10.1. The Delphi floating point types are used for working with large numbers and numbers with decimal points.

Type	Range	Significant Digits	Size in Bytes
Real	$2.9 * 10^{-39} .. 1.7 * 10^{38}$	11–12	6
Single	$1.5 * 10^{-45} .. 3.4 * 10^{38}$	7–8	4
Double	$5.0 * 10^{-324} .. 1.7 * 10^{308}$	15–16	8
Extended	$3.4 * 10^{-4932} .. 1.1 * 10^{4932}$	19–20	10
Comp	$-2^{63} + 1 .. 2^{63} - 1$	19–20	8

Of the five types listed here, 90 percent of traditional Delphi programs use the Real type. This type is native to the compiler and needs no additional support. The Single, Double, Extended, and Comp types are fully supported by Delphi, but you must first turn on numeric coprocessor support by placing {$N+} at the top of your program. You can achieve the same end by selecting Numeric Processing (8087/80287) from the Options | Project menu.

NOTE

I am actually oversimplifying matters here just a bit. The real types listed in Table 10.1 can really be broken down in to three categories. The Real type, the first one in the table, can be used without turning on coprocessor support. The next three (Single, Double, and Extended) are all decimal numbers that require coprocessor support, either in hardware or in software. Comps also require coprocessor support, but they are actually a special integer type that can be useful when you need to work with very large numbers. In particular, they are useful when you are handling money. To use Comp with money, simply translate all monetary values into pennies and use the wide range of the Comp type to handle your math. I show specific examples of how to do this in the next chapter.

When looking at the numbers listed in Table 10.1, the key point to focus on is the number of significant digits. The Real type, for instance, has 11 to 12 significant digits. This means that it can accurately express numbers such as 10,000,000,000. It cannot, however, accurately express the following number: 1,111,111,111,111. This number is thirteen digits long, and as a result the last two digits will be rounded to zeros when working with Reals.

Because real numbers are usually fractions of one kind or another, you should think not in terms of the large whole numbers shown previously, but in terms of decimal numbers. If you want to work with a number such as Pi, you will find that it can be expressed two different ways, depending on whether you are working with a Real type:

```
3.14159265360
```

or an Extended type:

```
3.141592653589793240
```

Notice that in the first case the accuracy is extended to 11 digits, whereas in the second it is extended to 18. Remember that you cannot work with numbers as large as the second type unless you have {$N+} specified at the top of your code.

It is important to understand that you can use the floating point types to work with numbers that have more than 20 digits in them, but you will lose accuracy in the last few digits of such huge numbers.

NOTE

It is possible to use Delphi to work with more than 20 significant digits. However, you cannot use the built-in types to do this. In other words, if you need to use truly huge numbers, you should turn to a third-party developer to obtain the necessary routines. (Of course, if you are clever, you could also write them yourself, though this latter approach is not recommended. For instance, you can translate numbers into strings, and then perform addition, multiplication, subtraction, and division exactly as you would with a paper and pencil, taking care to handle results that carry over from one column to the next. Because strings can accurately handle 250 digits, they can hold very large numbers with complete accuracy.

My point here can be extended to a more general theorem. With very few minor exceptions, if it can be done on a PC, you can do it in Delphi. Sometimes you may have to call on the built-in assembler that comes with the compiler, but you are still going to be able to accomplish your goal using this one compiler.

Before showing you some actual examples of working with floating point numbers, one final point needs to be made. To state the matter as simply as possible, all floating point numbers are by definition approximations. The next few paragraphs explain why computers don't naturally work with precise floating point values.

To get started, you need to remember that at their lowest level, computers are always manipulating a series of zeroes and ones. In other words, they know either off or on, with nothing in-between and nothing beyond. (This is discussed in depth in Chapter 17, "Understanding the Windows Environment.")

As everyone knows, a number like Pi has no precise definition. The example shown previously extends Pi to 18 digits, but a representation of Pi could just as easily be extended to 200 or 2000 or even 200,000 digits, without ever precisely defining the number. Obviously, there is not going to be a way to accurately express such a number using a machine that knows only zero or one, only on or off.

This same limitation holds true even for numbers such as 4.0. Computers can sometimes have a difficult time expressing a figure such as 4.0 entirely accurately as a floating point number. As a result, their internal representation of that number might really look like this: 3.99999999999999999999999999998799873. In other words, there is always the possibility of a rounding error whenever you are working with floating point numbers. This is not true of integers, or of the Comp type, but the floating point numbers are frequently approximations.

The bottom line is that there is no accurate way to express most decimal numbers using a PC. In particular, you need to be careful using any native, noninteger, Pascal type to express financial figures. The Comp type, however, is an ideal way to work with monetary values.

By saying this, I do not mean to imply that financial sums cannot be calculated accurately using Delphi on a PC. Nor do I mean to imply that there is something slipshod or cheap about the way Delphi handles real numbers. It is commonplace to make very precise calculations accurate to 10 or more decimal places using Delphi. However, there are pitfalls, many of which are discussed in depth in this chapter and the next. There is nothing here that cannot be overcome if you know what you are doing. The danger occurs if you wander in blindly with no realization that there might be hidden problems not apparent on the surface.

> **NOTE**
>
> Difficulty making absolutely accurate floating point calculations is not limited to Delphi or to any one set of languages, nor is it limited to computations made on PCs. All binary computers, and all computer languages, have to wrestle with this problem. As I said earlier, there are solutions to this problem. No one language, however, has any monopoly on these solutions. In particular, if you need to work with money on a PC, you should consider working with Binary Coded Decimal (BCD) routines from a third-party developer.

By now you should know enough about floating point numbers to get started with some hands-on examples. As usual, I begin with some very simple code and then move on to more complex examples in later portions of this chapter and in the next.

Working with Floats

To get started, pull up Delphi, select the Options | Environment menu item, and in the Preferances page make sure that Gallery | Use on New Project is checked. Now start a new project and select Crt Application from the Gallery. The code you see should look like this:

```
program Real1;

uses
  WinCrt;

begin
  WriteLn('Delphi');
end.
```

The code shown here is a WINCRT program. You can use progams like this to write the same kind of code you would have written in a DOS Pascal program. I am using it on this occasion because I want to temporarily gain access to the WriteLn procedure.

Declare a variable R, which is of type Real, assign it the value 2, and write it to the screen with WriteLn:

```
program Real1;

uses
  WinCrt;

var
  R: Real;
begin
  R := 2.0;
  WriteLn(R);
end.
```

Save this program under the name REAL1. If you compile and run your code, the result should look something like the image shown in Figure 10.1.

FIGURE 10.1.

The REAL1 program outputs data in scientific notation.

The big problem with the REAL1 program, of course, is that the output in the program's form is not very meaningful to most users, since it is displayed in scientific notation. If you want to output data in a more conventional, or readable, format, you can write the following in lieu of the WriteLn statement:

```
WriteLn(R:2:2);
```

This statement says that value R should be right justified in a field at least two characters wide, and that it should be accurate to two decimal places. In other words, the first parameter passed to WriteLn specifies the width of a column and the second specifies the number of significant digits you want to use. See Figure 10.2 for an example of how this looks on screen.

FIGURE 10.2.

Using WriteLn's two optional parameters, you can write floating point numbers in an easy-to-read format.

The program on your disk called REAL2 takes better advantage of the first parameter passed to WriteLn to arrange output into columns of data. Each column is 10 characters in width, as shown in Figure 10.3. This is another WINCRT program, only this time the code looks like this:

```
program Real2;

uses
  WinCrt;

var
  i: Integer;
  R: Extended;
begin
  R := 0.0;
  for i := 1 to 10 do begin
    WriteLn(R:10:2, R:10:2);
    R := R + (i / 10);
  end;
end.
```

FIGURE 10.3.

The REAL2 program writes data in two columns.

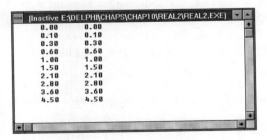

It might not be immediately obvious why the program outputs this particular set of numbers. To understand how the for loop in the REAL2 program works, you have to step through it mentally, one line at a time.

> **NOTE**
>
> This is a good time to use the debugger. You can start by putting a breakpoint on the line that reads R := 0.0. You can do so by clicking the right mouse button and then choosing Toggle Breakpoint from the resulting popup menu. Run the program until it stops on the breakpoint. Once again use the right mouse button, this time to put both R and i in the watch window. Now you are ready to go, and you can use the F8 key to step through the routine one line at a time.

The first time the loop executes, the variable R is going to be set to 0, so the output from the WriteLn statement is naturally going to be 0. After the first line of data has been painted on the screen, the following line executes:

```
R := R + i;
```

If you mentally make the appropriate substitutions, you can see that the line actually looks like this:

```
R := 0.0 + 1;
```

This sets R to the value 1, which is what gets printed out the second time the WriteLn statement is executed.

Now the calculation at the bottom of the loop looks like this:

```
R := 1.0 + 2;
```

which is 3.0. The next time the calculation is performed, it looks like this:

```
R := 3.0 + 3;
```

which is 6.0, and so on, through all 10 iterations of the loop.

All this is well and good, but there is no point in working with floating point numbers unless you start to see some nonzero values on the right side of the decimal point. To modify the REAL2 program so that it shows some more interesting numbers, you can change the formula at the bottom of the loop so that it looks like this:

```
R := R + (i / 10);
```

The output from the REAL2 program now looks like this:

```
0.00      0.00
0.10      0.10
0.30      0.30
0.60      0.60
1.00      1.00
1.50      1.50
2.10      2.10
2.80      2.80
3.60      3.60
4.50      4.50
```

If you compare this output with the output shown in Figure 10.3, you can see that it is exactly the same, except that each value is one tenth the size. This is what you would expect, because the code uses ten as a divisor.

It is important to note that in the preceding program I placed parentheses around the division operation. This forces the division operation to be performed first, before the addition. The whole subject of operator precedence and how to use parentheses is discussed in the next section.

The formula used previously still produces numbers that use only one decimal place. To see some more interesting numbers, you can try the following formula:

```
R := R + (i / 8);
```

which produces these results:

```
0.00      0.00
0.13      0.13
0.38      0.38
0.75      0.75
1.25      1.25
1.88      1.88
2.63      2.63
3.50      3.50
4.50      4.50
5.63      5.63
```

Viewing the output from this calculation, there is reason to suspect that there might not be as much detail here as needed. To check this hypothesis, you can always change the second parameter passed to WriteLn to a 4, rather than a 2. Following in the true hacker spirit, I change the second of the two columns so that it is accurate to four decimal places, while the first remains accurate to only two places:

```
WriteLn(R:10:2, R:10:4);
```

Here is the output from the most recent version of the REAL2 program:

```
0.00      0.0000
0.13      0.1250
0.38      0.3750
0.75      0.7500
1.25      1.2500
1.88      1.8750
2.63      2.6250
3.50      3.5000
4.50      4.5000
5.63      5.6250
```

The second column shows that it is indeed possible to see a bit more detail here, though none of the numbers show any complexity beyond the third decimal place. You might also notice that a comparison of the two columns reveals that Delphi rounds floating point numbers with a five in them up to the next highest digit.

> **NOTE**
>
> You should be aware that the rules Delphi uses for rounding numbers can differ depending on whether you are using the extended types such as Single, Double, or Extended. The reason for this difference is that Delphi uses internal routines to handle real numbers, but the extended types are handled by system code that resides on a math coprocessor or in a special set of routines that are part of the operating system. Windows 3.1 stores these latter routines in a file called WIN87EM.DLL. You can find this file in your WINDOWS/SYSTEM subdirectory. Note also that built-in routines such as Trunc and Round each have their own way of handling decimal places.

Another variation on this code involves dividing by an odd number and writing the answer out in three columns, each expressed to a different significant digit. Here is the new code:

```
WriteLn(R:10:2, R:10:4, R:16:10);
R := R + (i / 7);
```

Notice that the significant digit's parameter in the third number passed to WriteLn has been set to the value 10. Here is the output from the program:

```
0.00    0.0000    0.0000000000
0.14    0.1429    0.1428571429
0.43    0.4286    0.4285714286
0.86    0.8571    0.8571428571
1.43    1.4286    1.4285714286
2.14    2.1429    2.1428571429
3.00    3.0000    3.0000000000
4.00    4.0000    4.0000000000
5.14    5.1429    5.1428571429
6.43    6.4286    6.4285714286
```

Take your time studying these results. Notice, for instance, that 0.14285 is rounded up to 0.1429. Furthermore, 0.1429 is rounded down to 0.14. Notice also that calculations that yield whole numbers such as 3 or 4 are shown completely accurately up to 10 decimal places. Floating point calculations made with real numbers aren't perfect, but they are extraordinarily accurate.

As one last final experiment, add {$N+} at the top of the program, work with Extended numbers rather than Reals, and calculate the result to 18 decimal places. The output should now look like this:

```
0.00    0.0000    0.000000000000000000
0.14    0.1429    0.142857142857142857
0.43    0.4286    0.428571428571428571
0.86    0.8571    0.857142857142857143
1.43    1.4286    1.428571428571428570
2.14    2.1429    2.142857142857142860
3.00    3.0000    3.000000000000000000
4.00    4.0000    4.000000000000000000
5.14    5.1429    5.142857142857142860
6.43    6.4286    6.428571428571428570
```

To be sure that you understand how these results are obtained, I have saved this last example on disk under the name REAL3. Listing 10.1 shows the code for the REAL3 program.

Listing 10.1. The REAL3 program uses the Extended type.

```
program Real3;

uses WinCrt;

var
  i: Integer;
  R: Extended;
begin
  R := 0.0;
  for i := 1 to 10 do begin
    WriteLn(R:10:2, R:10:4, R:24:18);
    R := R + (i / 7);
  end;
end.
```

Feel free to experiment with the REAL1, REAL2, and REAL3 programs for as long as you want. This is an excellent chance to see how floating point numbers work.

In this section you learned the basic facts about floating point numbers. In particular, I have been very explicit about the fact that floating point numbers are sometimes little more than approximations and that it is not safe to attempt to use floating point numbers for directly handling monetary values. Ironically, scientists can safely make calculations that need to be accurate to five, ten, or even fifteen decimal places, whereas accountants need to be very wary of calculations that are accurate to only two decimal places. The trouble comes the moment you try to round numbers like 6.4999987999967 to either $6.49 or $6.50. If you don't keep rounding numbers to two decimal places, your margin of safety is much higher. Once again, these rounding errors are not exclusive to Delphi; they apply to all programming languages. As you will see, there are ways to handle large numbers with complete accuracy, but you must first be aware of the problems involved, and then learn how to solve them. Delphi does not always employ these safe techniques by default because there are many times when they are not needed. The developers did not want to burden you with routines that burn up a lot of clock cycles and then fail to give you access to lower-level routines that run much faster than the safer, high-level routines.

The *div* and / Operators

Earlier you worked with the REAL2 program, which went through several changes during the course of a rather lengthy introduction to real numbers. If you can pull that program up on the screen one more time, run it again with the following changes made to the main body of the program:

The Elements of a Language: Simple Types, Floating Point Numbers, and Branching and Looping

Part II

```
var
  i: Integer;
  R: Real;
begin
  R := 0.0;
  for i := 1 to 10 do begin
    WriteLn(R:10:2, R:10:2);
    R := R + (i / 8);
  end;
end.
```

Run the program once and study the output. Now change the following line in the program:

```
R := R + (i / 8);
```

so that it looks likes this:

```
R := R + (i div 8);
```

The / operator performs a division that produces a floating point result, and the div operator performs a division that produces an integer result.

Here is the output from the first version of the program:

```
     0.00        0.00
     0.13        0.13
     0.38        0.38
     0.75        0.75
     1.25        1.25
     1.88        1.88
     2.63        2.63
     3.50        3.50
     4.50        4.50
     5.63        5.63
```

Here is the output from the second version of the program:

```
     0.00        0.00
     0.00        0.00
     0.00        0.00
     0.00        0.00
     0.00        0.00
     0.00        0.00
     0.00        0.00
     0.00        0.00
     1.00        1.00
     2.00        2.00
```

As you can see, the two versions produce radically different results, even though they are identical except for the fact that one performs floating point division and the other uses integer division.

Looked at another way, the difference in output has to do with what is called a rounding error. Specifically, the first program rounds off the result of the division to somewhere around 11 or 12 significant digits, which is the number available when working with Reals. The second calculation, on the other hand, always rounds off the result of the division to a whole number.

If you substitute `div` for `/`, you will see that the resulting answers printed to the screen are always whole numbers. That is because the result of the division operation is always rounded down to the nearest whole number, which is zero. For instance, 4 divided by 8 is .5, and .5 rounded down to the nearest whole number is zero. The same occurs when you divide 7 by 8. The result is about .9, which gets rounded down to 0.

As a result of the way the numbers are rounded, the first version of the program produces a result of 5.63 in the last iteration of the loop, whereas the second produces a result of 2. Suppose this program wasn't merely an example in a computer tutorial but was part of a program used to balance people's checkbooks. If you wrote a program that used integer division where it should have used floating point division, it is easy to see how you could quickly introduce very subtle errors that produced extremely significant problems.

By now it should be fairly clear that rounding errors can end up making confetti out of even the most neatly printed computer-generated reports. In short, the whole subject of using floating point numbers is one that is fraught with potential pitfalls. It can, however, be handled properly as long as you are aware of the issues involved, and as long as you follow some of the rules outlined in this chapter and the next.

Operators and Their Precedences

So far, I have taken a fairly cavalier approach to operators. I have thrown a number of them to you, expecting you to treat them as entirely intuitive objects that need no explanation. After all, most educated people have been working with operators on a nearly daily basis since grade school, so you wouldn't think there would be a need to discuss the matter in any great depth. As it turns out, however, a number of subtle points about operators need to be discussed.

First, you need to understand that there are many different kinds of operators. In particular, the five most important classes of operators are as follows:

- Arithmetic operators, which are used to calculate mathematical operations. The arithmetic operators are `+`, `-`, `*`, `/`, `div`, and `mod`.

- Logical operators, which are typically used to manipulate numbers on the bit level, as shown in the file BINARY.PAS (that ships with this book) in the UNITS subdirectory.

- Boolean operators, which are used to test Boolean statements. The Boolean operators are `not`, `and`, `or`, and `xor`.

- Relational operators, which are used to test for relationships such as greater than, equal to, less than, and so forth. The relational operators are `=`, `<>`, `<`, `>`, `<=`, `>=`, and `in`.

- Run Time Type Information operators, of which there are two: `is` and `as`. You can use the `is` operator to check if a object belongs to a particular class or descends from a particular class. You can use the `as` operator to perform safe typecasts. For more information, see the end of Chapter 26, "Objects and Inheritance."

Don't try to memorize, or even understand, all these operators at this point. The details can come later. Right now you just need to grasp that there are several large categories of operators, and that furthermore, some operators have not yet been introduced in this book.

> **NOTE**
>
> Though the list shown earlier is fairly long, there are three more types of operators in addition to those listed. They include set operators, string operators, and the @ symbol. These latter three types of operators are not unimportant, but they tend to either be self-explanatory or linger around the edges of the language. The big four categories of operators are listed previously. The lone string operator is discussed in Chapter 14, "Strings and Text Files." The set operators are discussed in Chapter 14, and the @ symbol is discussed in Chapter 15, "Pointers and PChars."

Delphi's built-in laws of operator precedence state that some operators will force a particular calculation to be performed first, even if it is not the first operation listed in a formula. For instance, given the following formula, the result is different depending on the order in which the calculations are made:

```
N := 2 + 3 * 6;
```

I have a point I want to make, so bear with me for a moment while I go through some trivial math one step at a time.

If you examine the formula, you can see that the first two numbers can be added together to produce 5, and multiplying that by 6 yields 30:

```
2 + 3 = 5
5 * 6 = 30
```

Just to make sure the computer is really working right, I'm going to take the same formula and create a program that actually calculates its result. The EASYMATH program on your disk accomplishes this goal. To create the program, plop a label on a form and then create a FormActivate method that looks like this:

```
procedure TForm1.FormActivate(Sender: TObject; Activating: Boolean);
var
  N: Integer;
begin
  N := 2 + 3 * 6;
  Label1.Caption := IntToStr(N);
end;
```

The result of this program is shown in Figure 10.4.

FIGURE 10.4.

The EASYMATH program shows that 2 + 3 * 6 equals 20.

As you can see, there is a bit of a disagreement here. Previously, I showed clearly and indisputably that 2 + 3 * 6 equals 30. Now the computer comes along and tries to tell me that I am wrong, that I don't even know how to do simple math! Is there a bug in this compiler or what?

The explanation, of course, is that operator precedence has taken over and has forced the multiplication to be performed first:

```
3 * 6 = 18;
18 + 2 = 20;
```

When looked at this way, the computer's calculations start to make a good deal more sense. The key fact you need to know is simply that the multiplication operator always has a higher precedence than the addition operator. Therefore, the processing of an expression such as 2 + 3 * 6 always begins by multiplying 3 * 6.

Here, for your personal delectation, is a complete list of all the operators and their precedence, as they appear in the online help for Delphi:

Operators	Precedence	Category
@, not	First (high)	Unary operators
*, /, div, mod	Second	Arithmetic operators and
and, shl, shr		Bitwise operators
+, -, or, xor	Third	Arithmetic operators
=, <>, <, >, <=, >=, in	Fourth (low)	Relational operators

NOTE

Both the div operator and the / operator refer to division. Use div when you want the result to be rounded to the nearest whole number and use / when you want the result to be expressed as a floating point number. To state the matter somewhat differently, use div when you are working with integers and / when you are working with floating point types.

Something about this table has always left me a little nonplused. It has been part of the Pascal online help since the earth's crust was still cooling, so it is certainly familiar enough to many programmers, and it is certainly easy to find. Furthermore, if you stare at it long enough, it actually makes sense, so there is no hard or fast reason for my aversion to it. Nonetheless, I don't usually depend on this table to ensure that my calculations turn out as I would hope. Instead, I try to always use parentheses to show the order in which I want calculation to be performed.

For instance, if I write

```
N := (2 + 3) * 6
```

the compiler will set N equal to 30 because the parentheses tell the compiler that I want to have the addition performed first. The rules utilized here are fairly easy to understand:

- Expressions inside parentheses are always processed first.
- If there are several sets of parentheses, the expression inside the innermost parentheses is processed first. The compiler then works its way outward to the next innermost level, and so on.

Earlier, I was making a point of saying that I believe in always using these parentheses to make the code more readable. For instance, if I were working with the formula discussed here and wanted the answer to be 20, I could write

```
N := 2 + (3 * 6);
```

even though I know the parentheses are redundant. The extra set of parentheses might add a millisecond or so to the actual compilation time, but it won't affect the runtime version of my code. My golden rule, of course, is to always make my code as readable as possible.

Parentheses can be very helpful when you want to write clear, easy-to-read code. Sometimes, however, you need to use parentheses to resolve precedence issues. Suppose you have the following formula:

```
N := 122 + 33 * 46 div 5 + 4
```

This is a simple mathematical statement that should produce an obvious result.

If you plug the formula into the EASYMATH program, you will find that it yields 429. Suppose, however, that you knew the correct answer to the formula was 423, just as you knew the correct answer to the formula shown earlier was 30.

Experienced programmers might suspect that an operator precedence problem is leading to the conflicting results. Specifically, you can see that there are both a multiplication and a division statement in this program. Because both symbols have the same order of precedence, you might need to use parentheses to straighten things out and make your intentions clear to the compiler. For instance, writing

```
N := 122 + 33 * (46 div 5) + 4;
```

yields 423, which is the desired result. The key point is that the parentheses force the compiler to process the division first.

A little more work with parentheses can yield results such as 2,015 and 551. Clearly, the order in which numbers are processed, and the way parentheses are used, are big factors when working with mathematical calculations.

In these matters, a little hands-on experience is often useful. You might want to take the time to see if you can arrange the preceding formula in the EASYMATH program so that it produces 2,015 as a result. Remember, the numbers should always be listed in the same order. The point is to change the result only by adding or removing parentheses.

In this section, you learned a few basic facts about operators:

- ■ Delphi uses operators not only in arithmetic statements, but also in logical, Boolean, and other types of statements.

- ■ Operators have precedence. In particular, the multiplication and division operators have a higher precedence than addition and subtraction operators. As a result, any multiplication in a formula is by default performed before expressions involving addition.

- ■ You can use parentheses to upset the hierarchy established by the rules of operator precedence. In particular, any expression placed within parentheses is processed before any expressions placed outside the parentheses. This means that you can use parentheses to force an addition to occur before a multiplication.

- ■ If there are multiple parentheses in a single expression, the compiler starts with the innermost set of parentheses and works outward, one set of parentheses at a time.

Pascal uses operators in a very natural, well-established, and intuitive manner. Both mathematicians and other computer languages tend to treat them in a very similar manner. If the idea of operator precedence is new to you, just fire up the compiler and experiment for a while with the EASYMATH program or with some of your own creations. After a few trial runs, the subject should become clear.

Functions

Now that you know what floating point numbers are, and now that you know some of the finer points of using operators, you are ready to learn how to put floating point numbers to use in a real Delphi program. This might seem like a natural and simple step, but one or two difficulties need to be cleared up first.

As it happens, the big problem is that floating point numbers are numeric values, and the main controls, such as edits, labels, or listboxes, all require strings. What is needed, therefore, is a way to convert a floating point number into a string. It happens that this is a task best accomplished using a function.

As I said earlier, functions are just like procedures, except they are able to return a value. Consider the following procedure, which doubles a number and then prints the result to the screen:

```
procedure DoubleValue(Num: Integer);
begin
  Num := Num * 2;
  Edit1.Text := IntToStr(Num);
end;
```

This is obviously a pleasant enough little procedure that accomplishes a simple task in a relatively small number of steps.

The problem with the DoubleValue procedure, however, is that it posits the existence of an edit control called Edit1. If no such control existed, the function would not work. As a result, this function can be used only in one specific program, or at least only in a subset of all possible programs.

The solution to the problem posed earlier takes the form of something called a function. Consider the following code fragment, which is a complete and syntactically correct function:

```
function DoubleValue(Num: Integer): Integer;
begin
  Num := Num * 2;
  DoubleValue := Num;
end;
```

In the header for this routine the word procedure is now replaced by the word function. Furthermore, you can see that there is a colon at the end of the header, and that after the colon is the word Integer. This last bit of syntax tells the programmer and the compiler that this function returns an integer.

Another key piece of syntax in this function is the line that reads

```
DoubleValue := Num;
```

This syntax specifies the result of the function. That is, it states what the function should return.

NOTE

Delphi gives you two different ways to return values from a function. The first is listed previously. The second enables you to set the predeclared variable Result equal to the value you want to return from a function. For instance, using this latter method the DoubleValue function would look like this:

```
function DoubleValue(Num: Integer): Integer;
begin
  Num := Num * 2;
  Result := Num;
end;
```

There is no practical difference between the two methods. They both yield the same result.

Here is how to call the `DoubleValue` function:

```
var
  N: Integer;
begin
  N := DoubleValue(5);
  Edit1.Text := IntToStr(N);
end;
```

This example obviously yields 10 as a result. If you want to see this function in action or if you want to experiment with this code, you can run the DOUBLES program, which is included on disk. The form and the listing for this simple program are shown in Figure 10.5 and Listing 10.2.

FIGURE 10.5.

The form for the DOUBLES program contains three labels, an edit control, and a button.

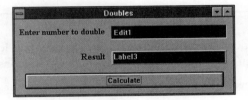

Listing 10.2. The DOUBLES program shows how to use a simple function called Double.

```
unit Main;

interface

uses
  WinTypes, WinProcs,
  Classes, Graphics,
  StdCtrls,  Controls,
  Printers, Forms, SysUtils;

type
  TForm1 = class(TForm)
    Label1: TLabel;
    Edit1: TEdit;
    Label2: TLabel;
    BCalc: TButton;
    Label3: TLabel;
    procedure BCalcClick(Sender: TObject);
  end;

var
  Form1: TForm1;

implementation

{$R *.DFM}

function Double(Num: Integer): Integer;
begin
```

continues

Listing 10.2. continued

```
  Num := Num * 2;
  Result := Num;
end;

procedure TForm1.BCalcClick(Sender: TObject);
var
  Num: LongInt;
begin
  Num := StrToInt(Edit1.Text);
  Num := Double(Num);
  Label3.Caption := IntToStr(Num);
end;

end.
```

This section introduced you to the proper technique for writing and calling a Pascal function. In particular, you learned three things about functions:

- Their headers begin with the keyword `function`.

- Their headers all end with a colon and a declaration of the type returned by the function.

- To specify the specific value to be returned by a function, write the function's name and then the value you want to return. Alternatively, you can write the word `Result`, and then the value that you want to return.

Before closing this section, I would like to make an additional point that might seem obvious at first, but which nonetheless identifies a problem that occasionally haunts even experienced programmers. The classic mistake when writing a function is to forget to return a value. I don't know how many times I have written functions that look like this:

```
function DoubleValue(Num: Integer): Integer;
begin
  Num := Num * 2;
end;
```

The specific problem is that I have neglected to add the line

```
DoubleValue := Num
```

before the word `end`.

Looking at this mistake in the light of day, you might be tempted to believe that you could never make such a silly error. And yet, I wager that most readers will make this mistake sooner or later. Furthermore, this error can cause insidious bugs that take hours to locate. Paste a little mental note in some well-lit corner of your cranium and try to remember that this simple bug can turn up in some pretty complex pieces of code.

Here is the mantra: "Don't forget to return a value from every function you write!"

> **NOTE**
>
> Experienced programmers might be interested to hear that Delphi enables you to return complex types from functions. For instance, functions can return not only strings and pointers, but also arrays, records, and objects. "Oh frabjous day! Callooh! Callay!"

Passing by Value and by Reference

Functions are not the only way to return values from a routine. A second technique involves using the keyword var.

There are two ways to pass a parameter to a procedure or function. One way is called passing the parameter by reference, and the other is called passing the parameter by value. If you pass a parameter by value, you can change it in any way you want without having to worry about the results lingering after the function ends. If you pass a parameter by reference, however, any changes made to the parameter are permanent. Consider the following procedure:

```
procedure AddTwo(Num: Integer);
begin
  Num := Num + 2;
end;
```

As listed, you could pass a number to this routine without fear that it would be changed after the procedure ended. However, if you called the following procedure:

```
procedure AddTwo(var Num: Integer);
begin
  Num := Num + 2;
end;
```

any valid number that you passed to it would be larger by 2 after the procedure was called. The difference here is that one parameter is passed by value, and the second is passed by reference. Reference parameters are declared using the keyword var.

I have always felt that the terms "by reference" and "by value" were unfortunate, because they do little to convey the difference between passing a variable parameter and a normal parameter. However, if you are at all familiar with pointers, it should make sense to hear that parameters passed by reference are actually disguised pointers. That is, the value passed is really a pointer that directly references the real variable. Passing a parameter by value, however, means that a copy of a variable is being passed, rather than a reference to the actual variable.

If you were able to understand the last paragraph, it should come as no surprise to learn that variable parameters are usually faster and less memory-intensive than parameters that are passed by value. If you are running out of stack space or if speed is important, always pass parameters by reference—that is, precede them with the word var.

If you are new to programming, make sure you don't move on to the next section until you have some feel for what is being said here. If necessary, create a small program and experiment with it until you are sure you know the difference between passing a variable by value and by reference. This is a simple idea—at least it is once you get the hang of it. However, you will not be able to get along without it. It is an essential piece of knowledge for Pascal programmers.

Using Floats and Controls Together

The DoubleValue function shown was okay as far as it went, yet I imagine that some readers may have been less than impressed with its rather limited functionality. What is needed now is a function that performs a more meaty task. To help supply that need, this section of the book provides two functions, one for converting a Real number into a string and the other for converting a string into a Real number.

Here is the function for converting a Real into a string:

```
function Real2Str(N: real; Width, Places: integer): string;
var
  TempString: string;
begin
  Str(N:Width:Places, TempString);
  Real2Str := TempString;
end;
```

To call this function, you could write code that looks like this:

```
Edit1.Text := Real2Str(5.6, 2, 2);
```

This function works very much like a cross between the IntToStr function and the WriteLn function. The last two parameters specify how you want the output to look—that is, how many decimal places you want to see and whether you want the string padded with spaces. I explain these last two parameters in more depth in a moment, but clearly there is a correspondence between these parameters and the parameters that are passed to WriteLn.

The key to understanding the Real2Str function lies in an understanding of the Str procedure, which is built into Delphi. If you want to understand one of the native Pascal functions, you usually need to do nothing more than turn to the online help. I discussed the online help in Chapter 3, but this is perhaps a good time to re-emphasize the importance of this subject by pointing you toward Figure 10.6, which shows the online help listing for the Str procedure.

Str converts a numeric expression into a string. The number should be passed in the first parameter to the function, and you can expect the result in the second parameter, which is a string. For instance, if you wrote the following code:

```
Str(2, MyString);
```

the variable MyString would contain a string with the value 2 in it.

FIGURE 10.6.

The online help entry for the Str procedure.

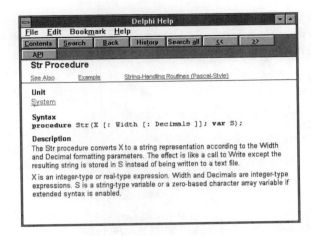

In the WriteLn examples shown, you saw how parameters can be used to specify whether the output of a real type should have a specific field width or specific number of significant digits:

```
R := 2.0;
WriteLn(R:2:2);
```

The same principle applies to the Str procedure. For instance, the preceding example from the online help includes this code fragment:

```
Str(N:Width:Places, TempString);
```

Here the variable Width specifies the width of the field to be placed in TempString, and the variable Places specifies the accuracy of the decimal translation. In particular, the following would be equivalent to the WriteLn statement shown earlier:

```
procedure TForm1.Button1Click(Sender: TObject);
var
  R: Real;
  MyString: string;
begin
  R := 2.367;
  Str(R:2:2, MyString);
  Edit1.Text := MyString;
end;
```

At this stage, you should have enough knowledge to see how the Real2Str function works. All you need to do is pass in a specific Real number, a width, and a request to have the translation accurate to a particular number of decimal places. The end result is a string of the type you desire. For instance, the preceding example would produce the following string: 2.37.

By now I'm sure you understand why the Real2Str function is so important. It provides a simple means of translating Real numbers into strings so that they can be used in Delphi controls.

A moment's thought, however, reveals that it is necessary not only to convert Reals into strings, but also strings into Reals. Here is the function that is needed:

```
function Str2Real(MyString: string): Real;
var
  ErrCode: Integer;
  Temp: Real;
begin
  If MyString[0] = #0 then Str2Real := 0
  else begin
    Val(MyString, Temp, ErrCode);
    if ErrCode = 0 then
      Str2Real := temp
    else
      Str2Real := 0;
  end;
end;
```

This function first checks to see if you have passed a string of length 0. If you have, the function automatically returns 0. The method used to check for the length of a string is simply to check the length byte, which is the first character in a string. If it is set to #0, the string must be empty. Your knowledge of the memory theater should help you understand this reasoning, but if it is unclear, don't worry, because the subject will be broached again, and in more depth, in Chapter 14, "Strings and Text Files."

The else clause after this first if statement makes use of the built-in Val procedure, which performs the opposite function from the Str procedure. Specifically, it takes a string in its first parameter and converts it into a real or integer number, which is passed in the second parameter. If an error occurs, the Integer variable ErrCode is set to a nonzero value. Errors might occur if you pass input that looks like this: 23.4M3. This string obviously cannot be translated into a Real number, so the ErrCode value would be set to 5, specifying that there was a problem in the fifth character in the string passed to Val.

It has been a bit of a march, but it is finally time to start using Reals inside a standard Delphi program. In particular, the REALSTR program, shown in Figure 10.7 and Listing 10.3, gives you both the square and the square root of a real number that the user enters into an edit control.

NOTE

When entering the form for the REALSTR program, type the following letters into the caption for the BCalc button: &Calc. Doing this produces the word Calc with the letter C underlined. As a result of this small syntactical jewel, you will be able to activate the Calc button either by clicking it with the mouse or by pressing Alt+C. If you had placed the ampersand in front of the letter A, the Alt+A combination would have activated the button. If you had placed it before the L, the Alt+L would have activated it.

You can improve the appearance of the labels used to hold the results of the program's calculations. To do this, place a panel on the form, make it the size you want the label to be, and then set its color to blue. Now put a label on top of the panel and set its color to yellow. You might also want to set the fonts to Times New Roman or to Arial. The end result is that you can write data to a label control that appears to have three dimensions.

FIGURE 10.7.

The form for the REALSTR program has five labels, an edit control, and a button.

Listing 10.3. The REALSTR program shows how to convert strings to Reals and Reals to strings.

```
unit Main;

interface

uses WinTypes, WinProcs, Classes, Graphics, Windows, Controls, Printers;

type
  TForm1 = class(TForm)
    Label1: TLabel;
    Edit1: TEdit;
    Label2: TLabel;
    LSquare: TLabel;
    Label4: TLabel;
    LSquareRoot: TLabel;
    BCalc: TButton;
    procedure BCalcClick(Sender: TObject);
    procedure FormCreate(Sender: TObject; Activating: Boolean);
  end;

var
  Form1: TForm1;

implementation

{$R *.FRM}

function Real2Str(N: real; Width, Places: integer): string;
var
  TempString: string;
begin
  Str(N:Width:Places, TempString);
```

continues

Listing 10.3. continued

```pascal
  Real2Str := TempString;
end;

function Str2Real(MyString: string): Real;
var
  ErrCode: Integer;
  Temp: Real;
begin
  If MyString[0] = #0 then Str2Real := 0
  else begin
    Val(MyString, Temp, ErrCode);
    if ErrCode = 0 then
      Str2Real := temp
    else
      Str2Real := 0;
  end;
end;

procedure TForm1.BCalcClick(Sender: TObject);
var
  R: Real;
begin
  R := Str2Real(Edit1.Text);
  LSquare.Caption := Real2Str(Sqr(R),2,2);
  LSquareRoot.Caption := Real2Str(Sqrt(R),2,2);
  Edit1.SelectAll;
  Edit1.SetFocus;
end;

procedure TForm1.FormCreate(Sender: TObject; Activating: Boolean);
begin
  Edit1.SelectAll;
  Edit1.SetFocus;
end;

begin
  RegisterClasses([TForm1, TControl, TWinControl,
                   TWindow, TIcon, TPicture,
                   TForm, TLabel, TEdit, TButton]);
  Form1 := TForm1.Create(Application);
end.
```

To use the REALSTR program, simply type a number and press the Calc button. On the form you will see the square and the square root of the number you entered. Figure 10.8 shows typical output from the program.

The REALSTR program begins by responding to the OnCreate message by focusing the Edit1 control and highlighting any characters in the control. This enables the user to immediately type a number and then press Calc or Alt+C to see a result.

FIGURE 10.8.

The REALSTR program in action, showing the square and square root of 25,000,000.

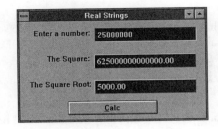

The response to a selection of the Calc button looks like this:

```
procedure TForm1.BCalcClick(Sender: TObject);
var
  R: Real;
begin
  R := Str2Real(Edit1.Text);
  LSquare.Caption := Real2Str(Sqr(R),2,2);
  LSquareRoot.Caption := Real2Str(Sqrt(R),2,2);
  Edit1.SelectAll;
  Edit1.SetFocus;
end;
```

The BCalcClick procedure declares a real variable named R and starts by initializing it with the number entered by the user in the edit control. The program then runs this string through the Str2Real function, which has already been described in depth.

The next step is to call two functions that are built into the Delphi Libraries. These functions are called Sqr and Sqrt, and they obtain the square and the square root, respectively, of any given real number. The results obtained from these functions can be passed to the Real2Str function and then displayed inside a label control.

In the code shown earlier, I perform this operation in two steps. It could, however, be broken down further in an attempt to make the code somewhat more readable:

```
var
  R: Real;
  OutCome: Real;
begin
  ...
  OutCome := Sqr(R);
  LSquare.Caption := Real2Str(OutCome,2,2);
  OutCome := Sqrt(R);
  LSquareRoot.Caption := Real2Str(OutCome,2,2);
  ...
end;
```

NOTE

Sometimes I designate the field width passed to WriteLn or Real2Str as the value 2, even though the field is clearly going to have a larger value. I do this because I want to say, in effect, "I don't care about the width of the field." I choose the number 2 here more or less at random, but I generally tend to set it to the same value as the number of decimal points that I am requesting. Hence I could also write `Real2Str(OutCome, 3, 3)`. The whole point is to find an easy way to use the function that is as intuitive as possible.

I wind up the `BCalcClick` function the same way I began the entire program. That is, I set the focus back on the edit control and select any text that might appear in the control.

The reason I select the text might not be immediately obvious to all readers. The key point is that selected text disappears the moment the user strikes a key and is then replaced by the value of the key that was hit. This system has two virtues:

- It enables the user to simultaneously view the results and the number they were derived from.

- If the user then wants to enter a new number, the old number will automatically disappear and make room for the new entry.

There is nothing standard or particularly significant about the technique used here. I show it to you simply because I want to make sure you are starting to think about how to design a useful interface to your programs, and also to show you how flexible the Windows interface can be.

Coprocessors

The 8086, 286, and 386 Intel chips did not offer much support for mathematics, and particularly not for floating point math. As a result, Intel offered a special up-sell in the form of an 8087, 287, or 387 chip. These chips fit into a special socket on the motherboard of a computer and gave PCs considerable power to handle floating point numbers. With the introduction of the 486, Intel started including floating point support as part of the main chip, thereby eliminating the need for a coprocessor.

The Extended types such as Single, Double, and Comp are all meant to be used with a coprocessor. In other words, to use them on a 286 or 386, you originally needed to buy a 287 or 387 coprocessor. Back in the wild and woolly days before Windows, Borland offered software emulation for extended types. In other words, it included code that would perform advanced floating point calculations in software. This code did not complete calculations as fast a coprocessor would, but still it fulfilled a need. When Windows came along, Microsoft included a module called WIN87EM.DLL, which can be found in the WINDOWS/SYSTEM subdirectory on your hard drive. This module will automatically emulate floating point calculations if a coprocessor cannot be found. Of course, if you are running on a 486 or better, a coprocessor will always be available.

You need to consider whether it is safe to turn on support for Extended types with the {$N+} switch. Any computer your program runs on will be able to handle these types, whether it does it by calling WIN87EM.DLL, or whether it performs the same calculations on a speedy coprocessor. To sum up, you should feel free to take advantage of the greater power of Extended types whenever you want. All you need to do to access them is turn on {$N+} or turn on Coprocessor support from the menu by choosing Options | Project | Numeric Processing.

Summary

In this chapter you learned about three important new ideas:

- Floating point numbers
- Operator precedence
- Functions

In particular, you learned that the Real floating point type is used by the majority of Delphi programmers, but that its accuracy is limited to only 11 or 12 decimal places. If you want to have greater accuracy, you should use one of the Extended types, such as Single or Double.

You also learned about the Comp type, which can be used to give Pascal programmers access to methods for making sophisticated financial manipulations. This subject is important enough to be introduced again in the next chapter, where it is discussed in depth.

Functions are one of the most important syntactical constructs in the Object Pascal language. You will see many functions in this book. In fact, the next chapter picks up where this one leaves off and gives you a chance to learn much more about functions and their uses.

Units, Real Numbers, and Functions

11

Overview

This chapter continues the discussion of real numbers, operators, and functions begun in the last chapter. In particular it shows how you can store functions in units, so that you can keep them in a single, reusable file. The practice of dividing programs into separate units forms the basis for creating large, multimodule programs.

One of the main themes of this chapter is the importance of creating friendly, easily comprehensible programs. In short, it is time to start paying more attention to the niceties of program design such as tab order, focus, and data entry.

The overriding theme of the chapter, however, is Real numbers. In particular, you will see how to create a special unit that can be used to store routines used to manipulate real numbers.

> **NOTE**
>
> This chapter is the first that will not contain full listings for all the source code. These listing were omitted because of space considerations. We (the editors and myself) had a choice between cutting chapters from the book or cutting the listings, and we decided that it would be best to cut the listings. The VIEWDOC program, found on disk, will allow you to quickly and easily find the source for any particular program. You also can use VIEWDOC to print the source for these programs.

Placing Functions in Units

In the REALSTR program from the last chapter, the code for the `Real2Str` and `Str2Real` functions is very much in evidence, but the code for the `Sqr` and `Sqrt` functions is completely hidden from the user. The reason for this is that the `Sqr` and `Sqrt` procedures are part of the System unit, which is automatically linked into every program. The `Real2Str` and `Str2Real` procedures, however, are not kept in a separate unit, so they must be explicitly defined inside unit `Main`.

You can accrue an obvious advantage by storing routines in a unit. In particular, there is no need to define such functions and procedures every time you need them. Instead, you can simply list their unit in your `uses` clause and then call them whenever the need arises.

To show you how this works, I have created a program called REALSTR2, which includes a unit that encapsulates the `Real2Str` and `Str2Real` functions. To create your own version of this program, follow these steps:

1. Create a new subdirectory.
2. Copy all the files from the REALSTR program into it.

3. Use the DOS REName command to rename the files called REALSTR.* to REALSTR2.*:

```
n realstr.* realstr2.*
```

4. Enter the REALSTR2.DPR program and change the title of the program from REALSTR to REALSTR2.

5. If it exists, delete the REALSTR2.DSK. This file might still reference the files in the REALSTR program. (In fact, the REALSTR2.OPT might also reference these files, so you might want to delete it or open it in a text editor and check its contents.)

These simple steps enable you to create a new version of the REALSTR program called REALSTR2. Compile the program and run it so you can be sure it is functioning properly.

The following code, which is part of the REALSTR2 program, shows how to encapsulate functions inside a unit and then how to call them from a second unit. There is no new code here. The point is simply that the following unit encapsulates Real2Str and Str2Real in a unit:

```
unit Mathbox;

interface

function Real2Str(N: real; Width, Places: integer): String;
function Str2Real(MyString: string): Real;

implementation

{-----------------------------------------------------
       Name: Real2Str function
Declaration: Real2Str(N: real; Width, Places: integer)
       Unit: MathBox
       Code:
       Date:
Description: Converts a Real number into a String
-----------------------------------------------------}
function Real2Str(N: real; Width, Places: integer): String;
var
  TempString: String;
begin
  Str(N:Width:Places, TempString);
  Real2Str := TempString;
end;


{-----------------------------------------------------
       Name: Str2Real function
Declaration: Str2Real(MyString: string)
       Unit: Real
       Code:
       Date:
Description: Converts a String to a Real number
-----------------------------------------------------}
function Str2Real(MyString: string): Real;
var
  ErrCode: Integer;
  Temp: Real;
```

```
begin
  If Mystring[0] = #0 then Str2Real := 0
  else begin
    Val(Mystring, Temp, ErrCode);
    if ErrCode = 0 then
      Str2Real := temp
    else
      Str2Real := 0;
  end;
end;

end.
```

To create the unit shown here, go to the Files menu and choose New Unit. Instantly, the following block of code appears in the editor:

```
unit Unit1;

interface

implementation

end.
```

You learned earlier that there are three main parts to a unit:

- The first is the title, which appears at the top. The name of the unit and the filename under which the unit is saved must always be identical.
- The second section is the interface, where you can declare the public parts of a unit.
- The third section is the implementation, where the actual functions, procedures, or methods used in a unit are defined in full.

Because all three major sections of a unit are defined for you automatically by the compiler, the actual act of creating a unit is greatly simplified. In this particular case, the first step is to bring up the Main unit from the REALSTR program, and then copy the Real2Str and Str2Real functions from it into the new unit you have started. Now save that unit under the name MATHBOX:

```
unit Mathbox;

interface

implementation

function Real2Str(N: real; Width, Places: integer): String;
var
  TempString: String;
begin
  Str(N:Width:Places, TempString);
  Real2Str := TempString;
end;

function Str2Real(MyString: string): Real;
var
```

```
    ErrCode: Integer;
    Temp: Real;
begin
    If Mystring[0] = #0 then Str2Real := 0
    else begin
        Val(Mystring, Temp, ErrCode);
        if ErrCode = 0 then
            Str2Real := temp
        else
            Str2Real := 0;
    end;
end;

end.
```

The next step is to copy the headers from the two functions to the top of the unit, where you find the interface section:

```
unit Mathbox;

interface

function Real2Str(N: real; Width, Places: integer): String;
function Str2Real(MyString: string): Real;

implementation
```

As you may recall, the interface section of a unit is public. That is, anything you declare here can be seen from within any other module that lists the MATHBOX unit in its uses clause. Specifically, if you place the following lines of code in the interface section of unit Main, you will be able to call the Str2Real and Real2Str functions from that unit:

```
unit Main;

interface

uses
    MathBox,
    WinTypes, WinProcs,
    Classes, Graphics,
    Windows, Controls,
    Printers;
```

After you have done this, you can call the Real2Str and Str2Real functions at any time from inside unit Main:

```
procedure TForm1.BCalcClick(Sender: TObject);
var
    R: Real;
begin
    R := Str2Real(Edit1.Text);
    LSquare.Caption := Real2Str(Sqr(R),2,2);
    LSquareRoot.Caption := Real2Str(Sqrt(R),2,2);
    Edit1.SelectAll;
    Edit1.SetFocus;
end;
```

You don't have to place the reference to another unit at the very top of your program. If you prefer, you can add it just after the keyword `implementation`:

```
implementation

uses
  MathBox;

{$R *.FRM}

procedure TForm1.BCalcClick(Sender: TObject);
var
  R: Real;
begin
  R := Str2Real(Edit1.Text);
  ...
```

This particular technique can be useful when you want to avoid circular unit reference errors. These occur when you need to reference a second unit from inside a first unit, while at the same time referencing the first unit from inside the second.

> **NOTE**
>
> I often consider restructuring my programs when I discover circular unit references. It can be a sign of poor program design. However, I do use circular unit references on occasion when I find that there is no other good way to resolve a problem.

Now that you know the basics about units, I want to go back to the MATHBOX module for a moment and look at the comments I place before each function. Here, for instance, are the comments that lie in front of the Real2Str function:

```
{----------------------------------------------------
       Name: Real2Str function
Declaration: Real2Str(N: real; Width, Places: integer)
       Unit: String
       Code:
       Date:
Description: Converts a Real number into a String
----------------------------------------------------}
```

As you can see, the comments run on almost as long as the code itself. Long comments like this can be confusing in languages like ObjectPascal, which are almost self-documenting. However, when you are creating a library of routines that more than one person might use, having some detailed comments can prove to be useful. In particular, I find it useful to put comments before a procedure; although I generally dislike mixing comments in with the actual body of a procedure.

I have come up with the particular arrangement you see here because it is possible to parse comments of this kind into fields that can be added to a database. Specifically, you can take a file commented like this and run it through a program that can convert it into a standard Paradox or dBase file. The resulting database can be very useful when you are trying to present a large API to a second programmer. It acts as an automated reference.

You might notice that I have also added Date and Code fields. These can be used to help with version control and to enable you to sort through the database looking for all the routines of a particular type. In particular, you can use the Code field to add any sort of indexing system you might desire. In short, it acts a little like the user-defined Tag property that is part of most Delphi objects.

The whole subject of how to convert a source file into a database file is brought up again later in this book and on the CD, where you find examples of parsing text files. If you follow through on the system presented here, you will have a built-in method of creating a reference for all your code, as well as a Delphi program that you can use to scan through this database.

The MATHBOX unit shown previously is small and seemingly rather inconsequential. However, as you begin dealing with complex subjects such as floating point numbers, you will find an ever-increasing need to maintain large libraries full of routines that can be called upon in special occasions. Right now, the MATHBOX unit is still in germinal form. As the book progresses, however, you will watch it grow, until it becomes a force that can be useful in a wide range of circumstances.

> **NOTE**
>
> One final word about units before moving on to another subject: When you create general purpose units like Mathbox, it is best to put them in a subdirectory where they can be accessed by all your programs. As you already know, most of the major units used in Delphi are kept in a subdirectory called UNITS, which is off the main Delphi directory in your hard drive. In a different part of your hard drive, you can create a second subdirectory called UNITS or MYUNITS where you can store modules such as MATHBOX. It is important to create a single unique subdirectory for all these files, because you want to keep your library path as short as possible. It is not a good idea to store these files in the DELPHI\UNITS subdirectory. A time may come when you want to delete an entire Delphi subdirectory structure and install a new version of the compiler. In such circumstances, it is best if none of your own code is stored beneath the root Delphi directory. See the README file on the CD to see exactly how I have handled this issue for the code accompanying this book.

Floating Point Numbers in the ADDALL Program

To highlight some of the key points of working with floating point numbers, I am going to show you a program that puts them to good use. In particular, the ADDALL program enables you to enter a long column of numbers and then proceeds to calculate the sum of these numbers.

The code you see here makes use of several concepts with which you are already familiar. For instance, for loops, if statements, listboxes, and the MATHBOX unit are all included in this program. Go ahead and do the best you can with it, but don't get too frustrated if it doesn't all make sense to you yet. Exposure to real code is an important part of any education, and it is okay if it takes you two or three passes to fully absorb some of this material.

To get started, you should create a form like the one shown in Figure 11.1. You can see that this form contains three labels, one edit control, one listbox, and four buttons. (The answer window is just a TLabel.) Form1 has the Ctl3D option in its Object Inspector set to true. Using the Ctl3D effect is a purely cosmetic issue, but this is not unimportant, because visually attractive programs are appealing to users.

FIGURE 11.1.

The form for the ADDALL program.

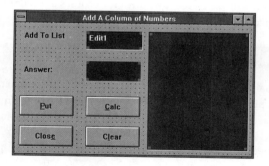

This time, I think it is simplest for you to look at the code for the program first and then come back to the text so you can get an understanding of how it works. The code to the program's main unit is on this book's CD-ROM. The project file assumes all the default values.

NOTE

The code for the ADDALL program is in the CHAP11 directory on this book's CD-ROM.

To use the ADDALL program, enter numeric data into the edit control at the top of the program and then click the Put button, or select Alt+P. When you do this, information is added to the listbox on the right side of the program. The current contents of the edit control are blanked out, and the focus returns to it. Once you have added a few numbers to the listbox, choose the Calc button and the program will add the list of numbers and display the result, as shown in Figure 11.2. If you ever add a number to the list that you want to remove, simply double-click the offending item.

> **NOTE**
>
> The captions for the buttons in the ADDALL program all use an ampersand to designate a hot key. For instance, if you write &Put in the Object Inspector, the letter P in the word Put will be underlined when you see it on the form. Now the user can simply press Alt+P to select this button.
>
> Notice also that I have set the Default property of the Put button to True. This allows you to enter a number and just press Enter to send it automatically into the listbox. If you set the Default property for a button to True, every time the user presses Enter, that button's OnClick method will get called. Look up the Default property in the online help for additional information.

FIGURE 11.2.

To use the ADDALL program, simply enter a list of numbers and press the Calc button to see their sum.

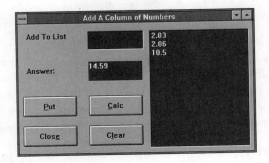

The first thing to notice about the ADDALL program is that it performs some initialization in the FormCreate method. To build a FormCreate method, select the Form1 object in the Object Inspector and then select the Events page. Now double-click the space to the right of the OnCreate property.

If you don't want to use the double-click method, don't forget that you can simply type the name of a function and press Enter. The key point is that you assign a method to the OnCreate event. In this case, it's simplest if you call the method FormCreate.

When you assign a method to an event, what you are really doing is assigning a method to a method pointer. All methods are located at some address in memory, and the events in the Object Inspector are really just pointers to methods that have a particular signature—that is, that take certain predefined parameters. You will learn more about this subject in Chapter 27, "Objects and Inheritance."

After you have created the framework for the FormCreate method, you can fill it in so that it looks like this:

```
procedure TForm1.FormCreate(Sender: TObject);
begin
  Edit1.Text := '';
end;
```

This method will be called every time the main form is created, which means specifically that it will be called on program startup. All this function does is set Edit1.Text to a blank string.

> **NOTE**
>
> The OnCreate event should not be confused with the OnActivate event, though both routines are usually called when a form is first created. However, OnActivate is also called after the user has switched back to your application after working with another program. In other words, OnActivate can be called multiple times during the life of a form, but OnCreate is called only once.

When you start the ADDALL program, the Edit1 control should have the focus. To ensure that this is the case, enter design mode, select the main form for the program, and go to the Edit | TabOrder menu item. Use the Edit Tab Order dialog box to arrange the controls so the user can tab through them in a logical manner. For instance, you will probably want to arrange the controls as shown in Figure 11.3. Please note that you will not be able to find the TabOrder menu item unless you first focus the form you want to edit.

FIGURE 11.3.

Use the Edit Tab Order dialog box to pick the order in which the controls in your program will receive focus.

The concept of focus is centrally important to Windows programming. The most obvious use of the term refers to the fact that a particular program can have the focus. For instance, at startup time the Program Manager or other shell has the focus. Then, when a user launches an executable such as Delphi, the focus switches from the shell program to the program newly launched.

Inside a particular program, different windows can have the focus. For instance, if you are writing code in Delphi, the focus is on the Editor window. If you click the Object Inspector, the focus shifts to that tool. Pressing Alt+F moves the focus to the File portion of the main menu. The key point to remember is that when a particular component has the focus, your keystrokes or mouse movements will be directed toward that component.

After the program is started and the initialization stage is complete, the next step is to respond to clicks on the Put button. You can generate the code of the BPutClick method simply by double-clicking the Put button while still in design mode. After the framework is established, you can fill it in like this:

```
procedure TForm1.BPutClick(Sender: TObject);
begin
  ListBox1.List.Add(Edit1.Text);
  Edit1.Text := '';
  Edit1.SetFocus;
end;
```

This code first takes the string from the edit control and adds it to the listbox. The code for performing this action could just as easily be written this way:

```
var
  S: String;
begin
  S := Edit1.Text;
  ListBox1.List.Add(S);
  ...
```

Frankly, there is no significant difference in taking one approach or the other. If you find the syntax in the first example confusing, you should feel free to use the second method. The key point is to understand that the code first snags a string from the edit control, then adds it to the listbox.

There is no error checking performed here, so there is nothing to prevent the user from adding a string, rather than a number, to the listbox. Furthermore, there is nothing to prevent the user from adding up a number larger than a Real can handle reliably. Checking for these kinds of errors is important, but I avoid doing so here because my main purpose is not to create a foolproof program, but to create easy-to-understand programs that show how to code in Delphi.

After the user has added a number to the listbox, the BPutClick method blanks the contents of the edit control. This enables the users to continue entering numbers without having to erase the previous number. Note that this routine is not finished until the focus has been explicitly set back on the Edit1 control. This last step is necessary because the act of clicking the Put button removed the focus from the edit control. The best way to restore the focus to the proper place is to do so explicitly by calling Edit1.SetFocus. You will find that most controls that come with the system have a SetFocus method.

Avoiding Floating Point Errors

In the last few sections, you looked at creating units and at some of the techniques used to aid in interface design. It is time now to bring the focus back more explicitly to the subject of Real numbers. In particular, the rest of the chapter works toward the creation of several useful new floating point routines that can be stored in the MATHBOX unit.

One of the best methods for avoiding errors with floating point numbers is to use something called a Binary Coded Decimal unit (BCD). BCD units work with floating point numbers in ways that are absolutely reliable. In other words, you will not have to be concerned with rounding errors when you work with a BCD unit. These units can generally be purchased from third-party vendors such as Turbo Power Software.

Besides BCD units, another safe way to work with floating point numbers that represent money is to translate dollar amounts into pennies. For instance, if you encounter a sum like four dollars and twelve cents, you can easily translate that into pennies:

$4.12 = 412 pennies

Now you can safely perform integer arithmetic with the sum 412, without having to worry about floating point rounding errors. When you are through with your calculations, you can translate the number back into dollars and cents before showing it to the user. Compared with most BCD units, this technique is extremely fast in terms of total clock cycles expended.

The following program, called MONEYINT, shows how to perform integer math when using monetary values. Notice that in it I use the Comp extended type, because it enables programmers to work with very large integers. This program uses two routines that can be added to the MATHBOX unit. The first routine translates a string containing dollar and cent values into an integer representing a certain number of pennies. The second routine converts pennies into dollar and cent amounts. Note that you won't be able to compile and run this program until you have added the necessary routines to the MATHBOX unit, as described next.

To get started with the MONEYINT program, create a form that looks like the image shown in Figure 11.4.

FIGURE 11.4.

The form for the MONEYINT program contains an edit control, a panel, a label, and two buttons.

To use the MONEYINT program, enter a dollar and cent amount in the edit control. If you then press the Calc button, MONEYINT will add $1.20 to the amount you enter and display the result in a label. Notice that the label is placed on top of a panel control. This is done so that the result displayed by the program will be more readily comprehensible to the user, as well as more aesthetically pleasing. A typical run of the program is shown in Figure 11.5.

FIGURE 11.5.

The MONEYINT program shows how to treat monetary values as integers.

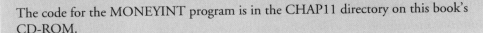

The program begins by clearing the edit control and the caption in the `FormCreate` method. The program also uses the Tab Order dialog box to ensure that the focus is first set to the edit control so the user can begin typing in numbers immediately after startup, without having to select an option or a particular control:

```
procedure TForm1.FormCreate(Sender: TObject);
begin
  Edit1.Text := '';
  Label1.Caption := '';
end;
```

> **NOTE**
>
> On most occasions, I am leaving the name of the control in the Caption or Text property of edits or labels. I do this because it enables you to detect the name of a control at a single glance. The effort required to zero these controls out in the `FormCreate` method is trivial. When shipping versions of your own products, you might not want to handle things this way, but it works out well under the current circumstances.

Besides the trivial close method, there is only one other important procedure in this program:

```
procedure TForm1.BCalcClick(Sender: TObject);
var
  C: Comp;
begin
```

```
      C := Str2Pennies(Edit1.Text);
      C := C + 120;
      Label1.Caption := Pennies2Dollars(C);
end;
```

The BCalcClick method gets called whenever the user clicks the Calc button. It translates the user's string into pennies, adds $1.20 to it, and finally translates the pennies back into a string and shows it to the user. The Str2Pennies and Pennies2Dollars functions are both stored in the Mathbox unit, as explained in the next section.

Before discussing the technical details of the Str2Pennies and Pennies2Dollars functions, I'll talk a little bit about various ways to structure a program. In this case, you can see that I do all the real grunt work in the MATHBOX unit. It was, of course, possible for me to have written a single long procedure that encapsulated all the code for translating from strings to pennies and back inside of BCalcClick. The resulting code might look something like the following example. Don't waste time studying this example, or trying to parse it; just glance at it quickly so you can see how it sits on the printed page:

```
procedure TForm1.BCalcClick(Sender: TObject);
var
  Temp, C: Comp;
  S: String;
  ErrCode, i: Integer;

begin
  S := Edit1.Text;

  { Create a valid string representing pennies not dollars}
  if S[1] = '$' then Delete(S, 1, 1);
  i := Pos('.', S);

    if i = Length(S) then begin     { Is last character a period? }
      Delete(S, i, 1);
      S := S + '00';
    end else
      if i <> 0 then begin          { Some pennies?                }
        Delete(S, i, 1);
        if i = (Length(S)) then     { Only one char after decimal?}
          S := S + '0'
        end else
          S := S + '00';            { No decimal, no pennies      }
  { Translate string into number }
  If S[0] = #0 then
    C := 0
  else begin
    Val(S, Temp, ErrCode);
    if ErrCode = 0 then
      C := temp
    else
      C := 0;
  end;

  C := C + 120;                           { Add $1.20 to total sum      }
```

```
   Str(C:0:0, S);                 { Pennies back into a string }
   Insert('.', S, Length(S) - 1); { Put in the decimal place   }

   Label1.Caption := '$' + S;
end;
```

Let me be utterly frank here and say that there are many good programmers who would prefer code like that shown above to the type of code I write. In other words, many programmers feel that the upper limit for a procedure or function should typically be about 60 lines. I, however, belong to a school of thought that tends to put the upper limit at about 25 lines, and I definitely prefer procedures that are under 10 lines in length.

More specifically, I like code that is self-documenting and easy to debug. Anyone who understands the basics about programming can tell at a glance what the following lines of code do:

```
   C := Str2Pennies(Edit1.Text);
   C := C + 120;
   Label1.Caption := Pennies2Dollars(C);
```

Clearly the first step is to convert the string value stored in Edit1 into a number. The second is to add 120 to that number, and the third is to convert the pennies back into a string that can be shown in a label control. To get the same information from the longer example, you have to scan through the code and read all the comments. Unfortunately, you don't know which comments to read in order to get a general overview. Also, the comments distract you from the functionality of the code, so that your mind is forced to move in two directions at once. In short, one half of your mind is reading code, and the other half is reading English. The end result is less than perfect for this particular programmer.

Other advantages of shorter procedures are that they are easily tested and reused. All too often, I hear programmers say, "This program is five thousand lines long! I can't break it up so that I can test one algorithm! It just can't be done." Programmers who make that kind of statement are all but admitting upfront that they have created a poorly designed program.

A function like Str2Pennies or Pennies2Dollars can be isolated and tested. If you like, you can even create a program that generates random strings and passes them to these procedures. The program could run through thousands of random strings, seeing whether any one of them could cause a crash.

The system I use will not work unless you make up useful names for procedures. For instance, if I had used abstract words like "number" or "convert" rather than specific words, my code would not be self-documenting. For instance, a name like Str2Number is too general. It doesn't tell you enough about what the procedure does. Even worse would be a version of the BCalcClick method that looked like this:

```
   C := ConvertOneWay(Edit1.Text);
   C := C + 120;
   Label1.Caption := ConvertTheOtherWay(C);
```

Names like Convert, ConvertOneWay, and ConvertIt are fatal.

If you use a lot of short methods, you will incur some overhead for each function call you make. In other words, it takes more time to call a procedure than to execute another line of code in a long procedure. However, you have to realize that on today's processors the amount of time involved is extremely small.

In general, when you are trying to decide which school of thought you belong to, you might want to study code written by experts in the programming field. For instance, the code for OWL, OWL2, the Microsoft Foundation Library, and parts of the VCL are all available. Study that code and see how the experts do it.

What you will find is that some people prefer my style of coding, and some people prefer the other. Almost everyone mixes the two styles to some degree, and there are certain basic principles, such as good naming conventions, that everyone agrees on. In the long run, you may decide to go with my style or with another style. Either way is fine. What I want you to do is be aware of the issues involved, and to consciously decide to go with one system or the other. Whatever you do, don't violate the fundamental rule of programming. That is, don't ever find yourself in a position where you have to say, "But I can't test that one algorithm! I've got a 5000-line program here. I can't break it up into little chunks!" Once you write code like that, you are doomed. If by some miracle you can bring that program to completion, you will never be able to maintain or upgrade it. Structure and design are everything in the programming world.

Upgrading the *MATHBOX* Unit

To create the MONEYINT program, it was necessary to upgrade the MATHBOX unit.

> **NOTE**
>
> The code for the newest version of the MATHBOX unit is in the CHAP11 directory on this book's CD-ROM.

The MATHBOX unit is a fairly sizable piece of code. It is not, however, nearly as large as it will be. Nor are all the routines you find in it necessarily complete. Some of them are improved in later chapters.

If you are handed code like this, the first thing you should do is read the comments at the top, and then glance through the interface. Here are the comments:

```
{
  This unit contains routines that are useful when
  you need to work with numbers. The routines you
  find here are of one basic type:
```

```
    + Conversions which translate numbers
      into strings.
}
```

The goal in this section is to give someone browsing the code a general idea of what it contains. It is easy to imagine including much more detailed comments. However, you should never create a unit that does not contain at least this much information.

Here is the interface to the MATHBOX unit:

```
function Comp2Str(N: Comp): String;
function Pennies2Dollars(C: Comp): String;
function Real2Str(N: Real; Width, Places: integer): String;
function Str2Comp(MyString: string): Comp;
function Str2Pennies(S: String): Comp;
function Str2Real(MyString: string): Real;
```

These functions are listed here primarily because they need to be declared publicly, so that they can be seen by other units. However, if you give your functions reasonable names, the interface can also provide a minimum of documentation.

Most of the functions that have been added to this unit are extremely easy to understand. For instance, the Comp2Str and Str2Comp functions are almost identical to the Str2Real and Real2Str functions, except that they work with Comps rather than Reals:

```
function Str2Comp(MyString: string): Comp;
var
  ErrCode: Integer;
  Temp: Comp;
begin
  If Mystring[0] = #0 then Str2Comp := 0
  else begin
    Val(Mystring, Temp, ErrCode);
    if ErrCode = 0 then
      Str2Comp := temp
    else
      Str2Comp := 0;
  end;
end;
```

> **NOTE**
>
> The fact that the Str2Comp and Str2Real functions are so similar is not something you should worry about. The Pascal compiler has something called a *smart linker*, which automatically filters out any code you are not going to be using in any one particular program. In other words, when you link in the MATHBOX unit, your program will include code only from the procedures that you actually call. Unused functions will not be linked into your program and therefore will not take up space in your executable. As a result, there is no downside to declaring as many functions as you might possibly need.

The `Pennies2Str` function that has been added to the MATHBOX unit looks like this:

```
function Pennies2Dollars(C: Comp): String;
var
  S: String;
begin
  S := Comp2Str(C);
  Insert('.', S, Length(S) - 1);
  Pennies2Dollars := '$' + S;
end;
```

As you can see, this function begins by calling `Comp2Str` to do most of its dirty work. Once again, you could save a nanosecond or two by encapsulating the functionality of the `Comp2Str` method inside `Pennies2Dollars`. That way you would avoid the overhead of a function call. I opt to call the `Comp2Str` function because it encourges the following programming practices:

- Writing short, easy-to-read, self-documenting functions and procedures
- Placing each step of an algorithm in a separate routine that can be isolated and debugged
- Reusing the `Comp2Str` method in other functions, thereby avoiding needless repetition of similar blocks of code

For now, I am going to say just a few words about the `Str2Pennies` function, because it involves a good deal of string manipulation, which is a subject that won't be covered until Chapter 14, "Strings and Text Files":

```
function Str2Pennies(S: String): Comp;
var
  C: Comp;
  i: Integer;
  begin
    if S[1] = '$' then Delete(S, 1, 1);
    i := Pos('.', S);
    if i = Length(S) then begin    { Is last character a period? }
      Delete(S, i, 1);
      S := S + '00';
    end else
      if i <> 0 then begin         { Some pennies?                }
        Delete(S, i, 1);
        if i = (Length(S)) then    { Only one char after decimal?}
          S := S + '0'
      end else
        S := S + '00';             { No decimal, no pennies       }
    C := Str2Comp(S);
    Str2Pennies := C;
end;
```

The key point to grasp is that this function is going to take a string such as $1.20 and translate it into pennies: 120¢. To do this, the algorithm takes three separate steps:

1. Checks to see if there is a dollar sign in front of the string, and if there is, deletes it.
2. Checks to see if the user has placed a decimal at the end of the string, and if they have, removes it and adds two zeros. This would change 23. to 2300.

3. Checks to see if the user has included any pennies, and if so, removes the decimal point and adds either one or two zeros. For instance, this would change 23.30 to 2330, and it would also change 23.3 to 2330.

In the last two sections you saw how to translate monetary values into integers. At the same time, you learned a good deal about creating units, and about methods for dividing code up into reusable modules. There has also been a rather lengthy discussion of various techniques for creating well-designed routines that can be easily comprehended and reused. I have come out in favor of writing short routines, but I have also made it clear that there are many programming styles, each of which has its own merits.

Some Trig Functions

Before closing this chapter, I am going to add five more functions to the MATHBOX unit. These functions help to complement the basic set of math routines that ship with every copy of Delphi. The built-in routines, as listed in the online help, look like this:

Abs	Returns the absolute value of the argument
ArcTan	Returns the arc tangent of the argument
Cos	Returns the cosine of the argument (x is an angle in radians)
Exp	Returns the exponential of the argument
Frac	Returns the fractional part of the argument
Int	Returns the Integer part of the argument
Ln	Returns the natural logarithm of the argument
Pi	Returns the value of Pi
Sin	Returns the sine of the argument
Sqr	Returns the square of the argument
Sqrt	Returns the square root of the argument

The six new functions added to the MATHBOX unit perform the following actions:

■ Return the log of a number
■ Raise a number to a particular power (two versions)
■ Test if two floating point numbers are equal
■ Provide the ArcSin and ArcCos of a number

Here is the function that tests to see if two floating point numbers are equal:

```
{-----------------------------------------------------
     Name: IsEqual function
Declaration: IsEqual(R1, R2: Double): Boolean;
     Unit: MathBox
     Code: N
```

```
      Date: 07/04/94
Description: Tests to see if two doubles are effectively
             equal. Floating point numbers are never
             exact, so we need an approximation.
-------------------------------------------------}
function IsEqual(R1, R2: Double): Boolean;
var
  R : Double;
begin
  R := Abs(R1 - R2);
  if R > 0.0001 then
    IsEqual := False
  else
    IsEqual := True;
end;
```

This function needs to exist because floating point numbers are approximations. As a result, you may find that two numbers that should be equal are, in fact, slightly different. The `IsEqual` function detects if the difference between any two numbers is less than .0001; and if so, it considers them equal. This enables you to safely compare two floating point numbers that might differ ever so slightly due to rounding errors, but which are, for all practical purposes, identical.

NOTE

Reading this text over, I find that I might be putting too much emphasis on the fact that floating point numbers are approximations. Most of the time you will never notice that floating point numbers are anything other than extraordinarily accurate.

However, some introductory programming writers review this entire topic without ever mentioning the possible pitfalls. As a result, some programmers release programs to the public that contain serious flaws that were not at all evident until the program comes under the extreme stresses encountered in the field. As a result, I have tried to clear up any confusion before problems begin to emerge.

One point to remember is that almost all calculators are also subject to rounding errors that are at least as serious as those discussed here, and yet many people use them all their lives without ever thinking they are anything less than completely precise.

One final point: These chapters were written before the fuss about the Intel "floating point" bug emerged. I might have taken a slightly different approach to this material had I known the entire public was about to get a course in how computers handle floating point arithmetic!

The following two functions both raise a number to a particular power:

```
{------------------------------------------------
      Name: XToTheY function
Declaration: XToTheY(x, y: Real): Real;
      Unit: MathBox
      Code: N
```

```
        Date: 02/20/94
Description: Raise X to the Y Power
------------------------------------------------------}
function XToTheY(x, y: Real): Real;
begin
  XToTheY := Exp(y * Ln(x));
end;


{----------------------------------------------------
        Name: Power function
Declaration: Power(X: Integer; Y: Integer): Real;
        Unit: MathBox
        Code: N
        Date: 02/20/94
Description: Raise X to the Y power
------------------------------------------------------}
function Power(X: Integer; Y: Integer): Real;
var
  Count: Integer;
  OutCome: Real;
begin
  OutCome := 1;
  for Count := 1 to Y do
    OutCome := OutCome * X;
  Power := OutCome;
end;
```

The first of the two examples accepts floating point numbers as parameters; the second works only with integers. The first example is powerful because it enables you to work with decimal values as input, but the second enables you to work with larger numbers. You can pick and choose between the functions, choosing the one you prefer in a particular case.

The function shown here finds the log of two real numbers:

```
{----------------------------------------------------
        Name: LogXY function
Declaration: function LogXY(x: Real): Real;
        Unit: MathBox
        Code: N
        Date: 02/20/94
Description: Log of X Y
------------------------------------------------------}
function LogXY(x, y: Real): Real;
begin
  LogXY := Ln(x) / Ln(y);
end;
```

The next two functions find the ArcSin and ArcCos of a number:

```
{----------------------------------------------------
        Name: ArcCos function
Declaration: function ArcCos(x: Real): Real;
        Unit: MathBox
        Code: N
        Date: 02/20/94
Description: Find the ArcCos of a Real
------------------------------------------------------}
function ArcCos(x: Real): Real;
```

```
begin
  ArcCos := ArcTan(Sqrt(1 - Sqr(x)) / x);
end;


{-----------------------------------------------------
        Name: ArcSin function
 Declaration: function ArcSin(x: Real): Real;
        Unit: MathBox
        Code: N
        Date: 02/20/94
 Description: Find the ArcSin of a Real
 ----------------------------------------------------}
function ArcSin(x: Real): Real;
begin
  ArcSin := ArcTan(x / Sqrt(1 - Sqr(x)));
end;
```

To test these functions, first add them all to the Mathbox unit, making sure that you take the time to expand the interface section so that it reflects the new routines you have created:

```
unit Mathbox;

{$N+}

interface

function ArcCos(x: Real): Real;
function ArcSin(x: Real): Real;
function Comp2Str(N: Comp): String;
function Int2Str(N: LongInt): String;
function IsEqual(R1, R2: Double): Boolean;
function LogXY(x, y: Real): Real;
function Pennies2Dollars(C: Comp): String;
function Power(X: Integer; Y: Integer): Real;
function Real2Str(N: Real; Width, Places: integer): String;
function Str2Comp(MyString: string): Comp;
function Str2Pennies(S: String): Comp;
function Str2Real(MyString: string): Real;
function XToTheY(x, y: Real): Real;

implementation

...
```

I do not re-create the entire unit here, but you will find it on the CD if you want to view it.

To test the new routines, you will find a program called MOREFUNC stored on the CD that comes with this book. The form for the MOREFUNC program is shown in Figure 11.6, and the code for the Main unit is on the CD. Note that the label and the four radio buttons are placed on top of panel components. When creating this program, be sure to use the Object Inspector to assign the Tag property for the radio buttons to the values 0, 1, 2, and 3. In particular, assign the following values:

- 0 to the Tag property of the radio button labeled XToTheY
- 1 to ArcSin
- 2 to ArcCos
- 3 to LogXY

As you may recall, the Tag property is a LongInt meant entirely for the user to treat in any way they wish. You could leave this field blank, store a pointer to a structure here, a pointer to an object, or you can just place simple ordinal numbers in this field. Experienced Windows programmers can draw a parallel between this field and the cbClsExtra and cbWndExtra fields that belong to a TWndClass (WNDCLASS) structure.

FIGURE 11.6.

The MOREFUNC program contains two edits, two buttons, two panels, three labels, and four radio buttons.

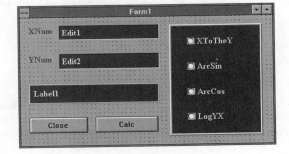

NOTE

The code for the MOREFUNC program is in the CHAP11 directory on this book's CD-ROM.

When you run this program, you can select the type of operation you want to perform by clicking a radio button. After making your selection, you can enter values in the edit controls, and then press the Calc button to see the results of the computation. Note that the ArcSin and ArcCos functions use only the value in the first edit control, and they insist that this value be in a range from −1.0 to 1.0.

To limit the range of the entries used by the ArcSin and ArcCos procedures, the BCalcClick procedure first assumes that an error will take place, and then simply tests the value of the actual input:

```
x := Str2Real(Edit1.Text);
Edit1.Text := 'Invalid Input';
if (x < 1.0) and (x > -1.0) then
  r := ArcSin(x)
else
  Exit;
Label1.Caption := Real2Str(r, 2 ,2);
```

This code attempts to calculate an answer only if the value in the first edit control is smaller than 1.0 and larger than –1.0. If this condition is not true, the program's label displays the string `Invalid Input`. This is a crude but effective means of performing runtime input control. Later in the book you will see fancier methods of performing the same ends, but for now this is a simple and useful technique that can be applied in many different situations. This code fragment uses the built-in `Exit` command. When executed, `Exit` will cause the code to immediately jump out of the current block. The most common use for this command is to force an immediate exit from a procedure. Look up "Exit Procedure" in the online help for additional information.

> **NOTE**
>
> The `if` statement shown earlier has two parts:
>
> `(x < 1.0)`
>
> and
>
> `(x > -1.0)`
>
> The two expressions are bound together by the logical operator and, so that they are both evaluated as part of a single Boolean statement. Notice that each of the two expressions is encapsulated inside parentheses. For even more clarity, another set of parentheses could be added:
>
> ```
> if ((x < 1.0) and (x > -1.0)) then
>   r := ArcSin(x)
> else
>   Exit;
> ```
>
> In this case, the outer set of parentheses emphasizes the full extent of the Boolean expression that needs to be evaluated.

One other part of the MOREFUNC program could cause confusion. If you look at the top of the code, you can see that the following type is declared:

```
type
  TCalcType = (TXToTheY, TArcSin, TArcCos, TLogXY);
```

This type is used in the main form object:

```
TForm1 = class(TForm)
  ...
private
  CalcType: TCalcType;
  ...
end;
```

The `CalcType` variable is used to track which type of calculation the user wants to perform. For instance, if the user selects the radio button called ArcSin, `CalcType` is set to the value `TArcSin`. You have probably noticed, however, that there is no point in the program where this assignment is made explicit. In short, there is no point in the code that looks like this:

```
CalcType := TArcSin;
```

Instead of writing code that features explicit assignments, the MOREFUNC program uses the following procedure:

```
procedure TForm1.RBClick(Sender: TObject);
begin
  CalcType := TCalcType((Sender as TRadioButton).Tag);
end;
```

This code works because the Tag properties for the four radio buttons have been set to the values 0, 1, 2, and 3, as shown previously. Recall that the values associated with an enumerated type are also ordinal numbers, which in this case range from 0 to 3:

```
type
  TCalcType = (TXToTheY, TArcSin, TArcCos, TLogXY);
```

Because both the Tag properties and the values of the `CalcType` variable have a one-to-one correspondence, it is possible to compare them through the means of a simple typecast, as shown in the RBClick method. In short, if `CalcType` is set to `TXToTheY`, it will have the ordinal value 0, which is equivalent to the value associated with the Tag property of the first radio button. If `CalcType` is set to `TArcSin`, it will have the value 1, which is equivalent to the value associated with the Tag property of the radio button labeled ArcSin.

That is the end of this chapter, and of this section. In future chapters more routines will be added to the MATHBOX unit, though often with less fanfare than you saw here. That is, I will sometimes need to create a routine to finish a program, and if it is related to math and it appears to be a general purpose function, I will ask you to add it to the MATHBOX unit. Other units, such as the STRBOX unit, are also developed in later chapters.

Summary

In this chapter you learned about units and floating point numbers. At the same time you picked up several hints about how to construct easy-to-use, robust applications that are simple to read and debug.

This chapter introduced the MATHBOX unit, which has grown by leaps and bounds over the space of just a few pages. The most important routines in the MATHBOX unit enable you to translate real numbers into strings and monetary values into integers. The latter functionality is valuable when you want to be sure that you do not face rounding errors when working with dollars and cents.

Throughout this chapter and the last, various sections addressed the subject of finding safe ways to work with floating point numbers. Many users are able to proceed for years without ever encountering cases where the rounding of floating point numbers becomes a problem. However, there are cases when it can surface to cause you considerable trouble, so I have worked hard to show you ways to avoid stumbling accidentally into tricky floating point rounding bugs. Remember, if you are working with money, you cannot afford to be off by even one penny. As a result, you have to pay very precise attention to rounding errors and should probably use either a BCD unit or the `Str2Pennies` and `Pennies2Dollars` functions shown here.

PART

Handling Complex Data Types: Data Structures, Pointers, and File I/O

Working with Arrays

Overview

So far, nearly all of the data types you have been working with have been simple data types. That is, they consist of one instance of a single type of variable, such as an integer, real, or boolean. Pascal provides several ways of grouping variables of one or more types together into a single structure, or type. Of these various methods, two of the most fundamental are arrays and records:

- The most common type of array enables you to group a series of variables of one type together under a single variable name. For instance, if you were going to try to represent a baseball game, one data type you might want to work with would be an array of integers from 1 to 9, where each member of the array represents an inning.

- Records enable you to easily bind together a wide variety of types under a single aegis. For instance, you could use a record to represent a single entry in a database, where each entry would contain strings representing first name, last name, address, and so on. Integers or enumerated types could be used to represent the sex or marital status of the person whose address is being listed.

Don't worry if you don't yet grasp exactly how records and arrays work. Mastering the subject is the fruit of reading this chapter and the next. The only point you need to understand at this stage is that records and arrays can be used to encapsulate multiple variables.

Both arrays and records are absolutely fundamental to your understanding of Delphi. Fortunately, neither subject is particularly difficult, once you get over a few initial hurdles. In fact, though you may not be aware of it, plain old string variables are actually a form of array. As you have seen, strings are not necessarily difficult to use, at least in most cases. The details of how strings are handled appear in Chapter 14, "Strings and Text Files."

Simple Arrays

Here is the declaration for a very simple array:

```
type
  TMyArray = array[1..10] of Integer;

var
  MyArray: TMyArray;
```

The code shown here begins by declaring a new type of data structure. In the past you have worked with integers, reals, and strings. These types were predeclared for you by the creators of Delphi. This time, however, you are the one who is declaring the data type. Specifically, you are saying that you want to declare an array of ten items, each of which is of type integer.

The next step is to create a variable of this type. Specifically, the code says that MyArray is a variable of type TMyArray. That is, MyArray represents a group of 10 integers. Remember that the type statement doesn't actually change anything in the memory theater. It is the var section, where you declare a variable of type TMyArray, that actually causes the compiler to generate instructions that will change memory inside the computer.

To help you understand exactly what is happening here, you can return again to the memory theater that was discussed back in Chapters 6 and 7. To help refresh your memory, I have included a picture of the memory theater in Figure 12.1. The metaphor I am playing on here is that RAM can be thought of as a huge audience of individual bytes arranged in seats before a stage that represents the CPU.

FIGURE 12.1.

The memory theater is a metaphor for the RAM that resides inside every PC.

When the type statement appears in the preceding code, it is as if someone with a vaguely military cast of mind stood up in front of the memory theater and said, "Twenty of you are about to be chosen to represent integer values. You are going to have to pay special attention on this job, because you are going to have to act in concert. For instance, two of you will be assigned the fifth member of this array of numbers. If I ask for the fifth number back, you have to hop to and give it to me. If I ask for the fifth number, it won't do to give me the fourth, or the sixth. When I ask for the fifth number in the array, I don't want the number five, I want the fifth number I asked you to remember. You are all members of a team. Work together like you are a hand of cards in a poker game. Two of you are the first card, the next two are the second card, and so on."

After this little speech, the frustrated military sergeant sits back down and waits for the next instruction to come down the pike. When he sees the command

```
var
   MyArray: TMyArray;
```

he runs out and selects twenty members from the appropriate section of the audience, which is probably either somewhere in the data segment or somewhere in the stack segment. "OK, you guys are it," he says. "Jones, you and Smith are array member number 1, Privates McGillicutty and McDonald, sitting next to you, are number 2, and Pointdexter, you and Schultz will be number 3."

> **NOTE**
>
> If this had been an array of Byte, it would have taken only 10 members of the audience to represent the entire array—one for each item in the array. Integers, however, are 2 bytes in size. As a result, it requires 20 members of the audience to represent an array of 10 integers.

> **NOTE**
>
> *Byte* is a generic term describing any collection of eight contiguous bits. It is also a Delphi type designating an unsigned 8-bit value. When I say an integer is 2 bytes in size, I mean that it contains 16 bits; I don't necessarily mean that it consists of two variables of type Byte, (although sometimes you can think of an integer that way). Throughout this book, I capitalize the Delphi type representing an unsigned 8-bit value. The generic term *byte* will not be capitalized unless it is the first word of a sentence. The key point to remember is that both a byte and Byte contain 8 bits. Given this common trait, it's usually not too serious an error if you think of the terms as being virtually synonomous.

When the sergeant is done, there will be 20 members of the audience in the memory theater, all sitting right next to each other, all working in concert. See Figure 12.2.

FIGURE 12.2.

A portion of the memory theater where 20 unsuspecting rubes form the members of an array of integers.

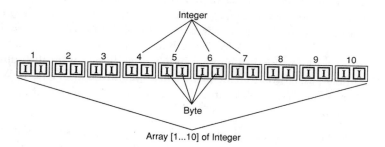

To get started working with arrays, you can take a look at the PATRIOT1 program, which is located on disk. The PATRIOT1 program uses the array declaration shown earlier to keep track of 10 important dates in American history.

You are going to see three different versions of the PATRIOT program. In the form for the first version, there is only a button and a listbox, as shown in Figure 12.3. Later versions of the program have more features and greater ease of use. In general, you may find an impulse to add features or to change the method of operation seen in the first two versions of the program. If you want, go ahead and make the changes yourself, if for no other reason than simply to get the practice. However, you should be aware that the program goes through several phases and through several improvements before reaching its final form in the PATRIOT3 program.

FIGURE 12.3.

The form for the PATRIOT1 program includes a button and a listbox.

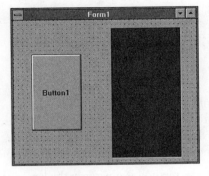

NOTE

The code for the PATRIOT program is in the CHAP12 directory on this book's CD-ROM.

The PATRIOT1 program displays a list of dates in a listbox, as shown in Figure 12.4. When the program starts, the listbox is empty; you can fill it by clicking the program's sole button. Each date shown in the program represents an important moment in American history. I have made no attempt to pick the 10 most important dates, but merely selected events that I thought were significant. For instance, I'm a big fan of Walt Whitman, so I note when *Leaves of Grass* was published. Likewise, computers play a big part in my life, so I note the date that Noyce and Kilby invented the silicon computer chip.

FIGURE 12.4.

The PATRIOT1 program displays a list of dates to the user.

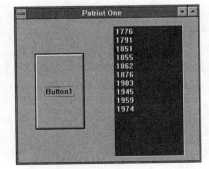

The first thing to notice about the code for the PATRIOT1 program is that an array of integers is declared in the following interface:

```
type
  TMyArray = array[1..10] of Integer;

  TForm1 = class(TForm)
    ListBox1: TListBox;
    Button1: TButton;
    procedure Button1Click(Sender: TObject);
  end;
```

In fact, it would not have mattered if this array were declared here or in the implementation. I placed it at the top of the program simply because it is easy to spot there, and because it is traditional to declare types at the top of a program. If for some reason you wanted to be sure the type was not visible outside of unit Main, you should place it in the implementation.

The Button1Click method is obviously the key to this whole program:

```
procedure TForm1.Button1Click(Sender: TObject);
var
  DateArray: TMyArray;
  i: Integer;
begin
  DateArray[1] := 1776; { Declaration of Independence          }
  DateArray[2] := 1791; { Bill of Rights                       }
  DateArray[3] := 1851; { Melville publishes Moby Dick         }
  DateArray[4] := 1855; { Whitman publishes Leaves of Grass    }
  DateArray[5] := 1862; { Emancipation Proclamation            }
  DateArray[6] := 1876; { Bell invents telephone               }
  DateArray[7] := 1903; { Wright Brothers fly plane            }
  DateArray[8] := 1945; { Atom bomb is dropped                 }
  DateArray[9] := 1959; { Noyce & Kilby invent integrated circuits }
  DateArray[10] := 1974;{ Watergate                            }
  for i := 1 to 10 do
    ListBox1.List.Add(IntToStr(DateArray[i]));
end;
```

The Button1Click method starts out by declaring a variable called DateArray of type TMyArray. As you saw earlier, this array will occupy 20 adjacent bytes in the memory theater, with each single member of the array occupying 2 bytes.

To address the first member of the array, you should enter an opening square bracket ([), then the number 1, and finally a closing square bracket (]).

```
DateArray[1]
```

When spoken out loud, this expression could be pronounced "DateArray sub 1." If you wanted to be a bit clearer, you could also say, "The first member of the DateArray."

To assign a value to that member of the array, you can write

```
DateArray[1] := 1776;
```

This places the number 1776 in the first two bytes of memory allocated for the array. Take a look at Figure 12.5 to see one way of thinking about how this actually affects the RAM inside your computer.

FIGURE 12.5.

The memory inside a computer changes when you assign a value to a member of an array.

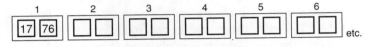

Conceptual view of an Integer

The program goes on to declare values for all 10 members of the array. It then displays them in the listbox with the following statement:

```
for i := 1 to 10 do
   ListBox1.List.Add(IntToStr(DateArray[i]));
```

If you find all these nested calls a bit confusing, you can break them out like this:

```
var
  DateArray: TMyArray;
  i, j: Integer;
  S: String;
begin
  ...  { Omitting code that doesn't change }
  for i := 1 to 10 do begin
    j := DateArray[i];
    S := IntToStr(DateArray[i]);
    ListBox1.List.Add(S);
  end;
end;
```

In this version of the method I add a variable j of type Integer, and a variable S of type String. In this excerpt, I omit showing the code that initializes the array, because it is the same as in the initial version of this method. When iterating through the loop, follow these steps:

1. Get a date from the array.

2. Translate it into a string.

3. Show the string in the listbox.

Both versions of the for loop shown earlier perform the same tasks in the same order. Over time, I have found it simplest to write the code as I do in the first example. However, if you prefer the clarity of the second method, you should use it. It would be foolish to write code that doesn't yet make sense to you just because you think it might look fancy. Programming can be a complicated job, and you should do everything possible to make it as easy on you as possible. If you want to show off, write programs that work. That is all that's necessary to win plenty of kudos.

In a moment, I will show you the second version of the PATRIOT program. Before moving on, it is worth pointing out that there is no need to assign the first member of an array an index of 1. For instance, instead of writing

```
TMyArray = array[1..10] of Integer;
```

I could just as easily have written

```
TMyArray = array[0..9] of Integer;
```

Both declarations define a type with 10 integer members. Both arrays look absolutely identical in RAM. The only difference is the way you reference the members of the array. For instance, if you used the second declaration of the array, you would write

```
DateArray[0] := 1776; { Declaration of Independence           }
DateArray[1] := 1791; { Bill of Rights                        }
DateArray[2] := 1851; { Melville publishes Moby Dick          }
DateArray[3] := 1855; { Whitman publishes Leaves of Grass     }
DateArray[4] := 1862; { Emancipation Proclamation             }
DateArray[5] := 1876; { Bell invents telephone                }
DateArray[6] := 1903; { Wright Brothers fly plane             }
DateArray[7] := 1945; { Atom bomb is dropped                  }
DateArray[8] := 1959; { Noyce & Kilby invent integrated circuit }
DateArray[9] := 1974; { Watergate                             }
```

In this set of assignments, the first member of the array is referenced with index 0. The tenth member of the array is referenced by index 9. Arrays of this type are called zero-based arrays.

It so happens that Pascal enables you to declare arrays with a wide range of indexes. For instance, both of the following arrays are legal and might prove useful under certain circumstances:

```
TMyArray = array[-25..10] of Integer;
TMyArray = array[9..239] of Integer;
```

The following array, however, is not legal:

```
TMyArray = array[0..100000] of Integer;
```

If you try to declare an array like this, you will get a "Structure Too Large" or "Ordinal Type Expected" error from the compiler. The problem is that you have declared an array that is larger than 64 KB. As you learned back in Chapter 2, it is not possible to create a single structure larger than 64 KB with a 16-bit compiler. In the future, there will be a 32-bit version of Delphi. At that time, the limitation shown here will go away.

NOTE

Even if you declare an array that the compiler accepts, you still might find that you have exceeded the memory limits designated for your program. Specifically, your data and stack segments can not exceed more than 64 KB total, when both are combined. In other words, the following set of declarations will cause trouble because together they equal more than 64 KB:

```
TMyArray = array[1..25000] of Byte;    { 25,000 bytes }
TMyArray = array[1..12000] of Integer; { 24,000 bytes }
```

```
TMyArray = array[1..8000] of LongInt;   { 32,000 bytes }
                                         { 81 KB total }
```

As I said earlier, the days when you have to wrestle with this limitation will soon disappear (in fact, they may be gone by the time you read this). For now, however, you need to be aware of the 64KB limit, especially when dealing with arrays.

Arrays of Strings

Just as you can have arrays of integers, you can also have arrays of strings. Grouping strings together in an array can be an extremely useful way to keep track of sequential pieces of information, such as the errors reported during the life of a program or text to be displayed in a control.

The PATRIOT2 program, shown later, has two parallel sets of arrays. The first array is borrowed unchanged from the first version of the program. A second array provides descriptions of the events that take place on each of the dates stored in the first array. Under this system, the first member of the first array corresponds to the first string in the second array, the second date in the first array corresponds to the second event in the array of strings, and so on. This is a concept that can perhaps be shown most clearly in a simple table:

11776	Declaration of Independence
21791	Bill of Rights
31851	Melville publishes *Moby Dick*

Here are the type definitions for both arrays:

```
TMyArray = array[1..10] of Integer;
TDescArray = array[1..10] of string;
```

As you can see, both arrays look nearly identical, except that the base type of one array is an integer, whereas the base type of the other is a string.

You would access the members of both arrays in very similar fashions:

```
var
  MyArray: TMyArray;
 DescArray: TDescArray;
  i: Integer;
  S: String;
begin
  MyArray[1] := 1;
  DescArray[1] := 'One';
  i := MyArray[1];
  S := DescArray[1];
end;
```

Despite the outward similarity between the two arrays, it is important to understand that they look very different in the memory theater. For instance, the first array takes up a total of 20 seats, whereas the second array takes up a total of 2,560 seats. Specifically, each string in the TDescArray array takes up 256 bytes. Because there are 10 strings in the array, the math is not too complex:

```
2560 := 256 * 10;
```

There are times, however, when it is a bit more difficult to calculate the exact size of a data structure. In such cases, you might want to use the SizeOf function, as shown here:

```
Size := SizeOf(DescArray);
Memo1.Text := IntToStr(Size);
```

In this example, Size is a variable of type Integer, and the text that would appear in the memo control would read 2560.

The SizeOf function returns the size of a variable or type. For instance, the following code places the value 2 in the Integer variable Size:

```
Size := SizeOf(Integer);
```

This next example would put 20 in the Size variable:

```
Size := SizeOf(MyArray);
```

If you prefer, you can simply use the Watch List to query the compiler about the size of variables you have created. This technique is shown in Figure 12.6, where you can see that I have placed a breakpoint in the FormActivate method and then added a simple SizeOf statements to the Watch List.

FIGURE 12.6.

To see the size of a variable, just call the SizeOf method, either in your code or in the Watch List.

It is very important that you eventually learn to become conscious of the size of the variables that you are going to utilize in your programs. As you know, the combined data and stack segments for your program cannot take up more than 65,000 seats in the memory theater. In fact, they have to share their cramped 64KB segment with something called the *local heap*, so they really only have access to an area that usually ranges between 50,000 and 60,000 bytes, depending on the circumstances.

Given the circumstances described in the preceding paragraph, you need to be conscious of the fact that the 2,560 seats used up by variables of type TDescArray represent a substantial stake in the memory theater. I know that it is ridiculous to be sitting in a room of 4, 6, or even 16 million seats only to be restricted to a mere 65,000 of them. Unfortunately, until the 32-bit world is finally ascendant, that is the situation, and the sooner you can come to terms with it the better.

> **NOTE**
>
> Beginning programmers rarely have to wrestle with the 64KB limit. When you write small programs, the problem doesn't come up. It will, however, almost certainly raise its head the first time you try to write a substantial program of a certain type. Specifically, the moment you need to declare a few large arrays, the 64KB segment lowers the boom, and then you will be glad for the information found in this chapter.

More About Arrays: The PATRIOT2 Program

Now that you have been introduced to the idea of using arrays of strings, you are ready to take a look at the code for the PATRIOT2 program. When looking at the form for this program, shown in Figure 12.7, you can see that it makes use of two buttons. These buttons are called *bitbtns*, or bitmap buttons, because they each consist of a button with the picture from a single bitmap in its center.

FIGURE 12.7.

The form for the PATRIOT2 program features a combo box, memo control, and two bitbtns.

> **NOTE**
>
> Bitmaps, as you recall from Chapter 4, are graphical files that have .BMP for an extension. This is the native graphics format for the Windows environment, and programs such as the Paintbrush utility that ships with Windows and the Bitmap editor that comes with Delphi, enable you to create and edit them.

When you are working with a bitbtn, you can select the Glyph property from the Object Inspector in order to choose a bitmap that will be displayed inside a button. All you need to do is select the bitmap from an Open File dialog box, and the compiler will properly display the bitmap for you. People who are familiar with Windows will probably be pleased to see how easy these buttons are to use. Certainly in the old days before the visual paradigm gained ascendancy, it was not quite so easy to create visually pleasing buttons.

The other new control in the PATRIOT2 program is the combo box shown at the top of the window. Combo boxes are a good deal like listboxes, except that they have a little edit control along the top. The edit control can help you search for information, or it can be used simply to display a selection from the combo box.

NOTE

The code for the PATRIOT2 program is in the CHAP12 directory on this book's CD-ROM.

The two buttons at the bottom of the PATRIOT2 program contain a picture of the Liberty Bell and the American flag. If you select a date from the combo box and then click the American flag, the memo box will automatically display a description of an event that occurred on that date. For instance, if you select 1959 and then click the flag, you will learn that Noyce and Kilby invented the silicon chip in that year. Needless to say, this is a date that all serious computer users should have etched firmly in their consciousness. The other button, the one that sports a picture of the Liberty Bell, can be used to exit the program.

The code that is used to fill the combo box with dates should be familiar to you from the last version of the PATRIOT program:

```
DateArray[1] := 1776; { Declaration of Independence }
DateArray[2] := 1791; { Bill of Rights }
DateArray[3] := 1851; { Melville publishes Moby Dick }
DateArray[4] := 1855; { Whitman publishes Leaves of Grass }
DateArray[5] := 1862; { Emancipation Proclamation }
DateArray[6] := 1876; { Bell invents telephone }
DateArray[7] := 1903; { Wright Brothers fly plane }
DateArray[8] := 1945; { Atom bomb is dropped }
DateArray[9] := 1959; { Noyce & Kilby invent integrated circuits }
DateArray[10] := 1974;{ Watergate }

for i := 1 to 10 do
  ComboBox1.List.Add(IntToStr(DateArray[i]));

ComboBox1.ListIndex := 0;
```

The only difference here is that I take the time to set the ListIndex property to 0. This ensures that the first date in the combo box is shown in the edit control at the top of the display. Remember that 0 selects the first item, because the list in the combo box is zero-based, just like the array shown near the end of the previous section.

NOTE

If I had accidentally set the `ListIndex` variable to 1, I would end up displaying the second date in the array rather than first. Assuming that I had indented to display the first date, the error I made would be called an "off by one" error. In the case shown previously, there is no serious damage caused by the error, but "off by one" errors can often lead to serious system crashes.

Filling out the `String` array is no more difficult than filling out the `Integer` array:

```
DescArray[1] := 'Declaration of Independence';
DescArray[2] := 'Bill of Rights';
DescArray[3] := 'Melville's Moby Dick published';
DescArray[4] := 'Whitman publishes Leaves of Grass';
DescArray[5] := 'Emancipation Proclamation';
DescArray[6] := 'Bell invents telephone';
DescArray[7] := 'Wright Brothers fly plane';
DescArray[8] := 'Atom bomb is dropped';
DescArray[9] := 'Noyce and Kilby invent integrated circuits';
DescArray[10] := 'Watergate';
```

Once the task is finished, you can see that there is a one-to-one correspondence between the two arrays. For instance, the first member of the first array is the date 1776, and the first member of the second array is a string used to inform the user of what happened in that year.

The only slightly tricky code in the PATRIOT2 program is executed in response to clicking the American flag button:

```
procedure TForm1.BitBtn1Click(Sender: TObject);
begin
  Memo1.Text := DescArray[ComboBox1.ListIndex + 1];
end;
```

If you broke out this code so that each step was clearly illustrated, it would look like this:

```
procedure TForm1.BitBtn1Click(Sender: TObject);
var
  Index: Integer;
begin
  Index := ComboBox1.ListIndex;
  Index := Index + 1
  Memo1.Text := DescArray[Index];
end;
```

Once again, there is no significant difference between these two versions of the `BitBtn1Click` method. They are simply two different ways of saying the same thing. I prefer the first example, not because it saves any significant amount of memory, nor because I hope it might somehow execute faster than the second example, but only because I find it easier to write and read. If you prefer the second method, use it.

The code shown here first retrieves the index of the currently selected item from the combo box. For instance, if the date 1776 were displayed in the edit control at the top of the combo box, the number retrieved would be 0.

The next step is to add 1 to this number. This is done in order to avoid an "off by one" error. If you didn't take the possibility of this error into account, you could end up trying to reference the zeroth member of the DescArray. Because that member does not exist, an attempt to reference it would lead to an exception.

> **NOTE**
>
> When you are doing serious work with arrays, you should always make sure that both range and stack checking are turned on. These two compiler directives can be activated by selecting the appropriate buttons from the Options menu or by writing {$R+,S+} at the top of your program.
>
> Whenever I am developing or debugging an application, I always switch those two compiler directives on and don't turn them off until I am ready to use or release the product. At that time I change the compiler directive so that it looks like this: {$R-,S-}. It is important to turn these checks off in the final release, because they will generate error-checking code that slows your program down. They should probably be left on during Beta, however.

After you have carefully retrieved the index from the combo box and you have taken the "off by one" error into account, the only thing left to do is retrieve the correct string from the DescArray and show it to the user, as follows:

```
Memo1.Text := DescArray[Index];
```

The PATRIOT2 program is useful primarily because it shows you how to work with arrays. In particular, it serves as a little meditation on the relationship between an array you might declare and the data structure that Windows uses when it stores a list of strings in a listbox or combo box.

You should probably also take a moment to think some about the general appearance of the PATRIOT2 program. Do you prefer to work with combo boxes or listboxes? Are there certain times when you might want to use one or the other? What about bitbtns? Is it fun or useful to place colorful graphics on the screen? Have the right graphics been chosen? Do you think some users might find the program more appealing or easier to use because the buttons exist? Is it possible to use colored buttons like this without displaying any text next to them? If you want to dig even deeper, what about those civilizations that were left behind because they never made the transition from picture-based alphabets to alphanumeric systems? Are icons really easier to use than text?

I'm not sure I have any specific answers to these questions, but they are still worthy of a little thought. The interface for a program is extremely important.

Constant Arrays

So far all the arrays you have seen have been initialized at runtime. However, it is possible to declare what is called a typed constant, which is initialized before compilation.

Because the subject of constants comes up here, it is important to make a distinction between typed constants and normal constants. An average constant looks like this:

```
const
   MyConstant = 25;
```

When you think about it, it is obvious that a constant would not normally be a variable. Just compare the two names: constant and variable. The two are obviously different. Specifically, the value of MyConstant cannot ever change. It is permanently fixed in place from the moment you compile the program.

The value of a typed constant, however, can be changed. When you declare a typed constant, you always includes its type in the declaration:

```
const
   MyConstant: Integer = 25;
```

This value is really more of a variable than it is a constant, but it is still arguably appropriate to declare in the constant section because it is a pre-initialized value.

The syntax for declaring a constant array looks like this:

```
type
   TMyArray = array[1..10] of Integer;

const
   DateArray: TMyArray = (1776, 1791, 1851, 1855, 1862,
                          1876, 1903, 1945, 1959, 1974);
```

This is a very clean syntax, the meaning of which should be intuitively obvious to most programmers. Specifically, you can see that an identifier, DateArray, is declared to be of type TMyArray. TMyArray, of course, is still an array of 10 integers that has been declared in the type section.

The key value of the syntax for typed constants is that it enables you to declare the values for each member of the array before compilation. Specifically, the code states that the first member of the array is the integer 1776, the second is 1791, and so on. You will find that the compiler is a bit fussy when you are making declarations of this type. It will insist that you declare all the possible values of the array and will complain if you attempt to short-change it.

The syntax for declaring an array of strings is identical to the syntax for declaring an array of integers, except that you need to obey the rules associated with strings. Specifically, you need to enclose each item in the array in quotation marks:

```
DescArray: array[1..10] of String = (
         'Declaration of Independence',
         'Bill of Rights',
         'Melville''s Moby Dick published',
         'Whitman publishes Leaves of Grass',
         'Emancipation Proclamation',
         'Bell invents telephone',
         'Wright Brothers fly plane',
         'Atom bomb is dropped',
         'Noyce and Kilby invent integrated circuits',
         'Watergate');
```

Notice that I have included the type declaration for the array in the preceding statement. In the integer array shown earlier, I made the type declaration for TMyArray first and then used that type in the declaration for the DateArray:

```
const
  DateArray: TMyArray = (1776, 1791, 1851, 1855, 1862,
                         1876, 1903, 1945, 1959, 1974 );
```

Which technique you choose to use at any one time is pretty much optional. However, it would make sense to declare the type for an array separately if you planned to have more than one variable of that type in a program. If you were going to use that type only once, you could go ahead and declare a typed constant and its array type at the same time. The following code shows an example of when you might want to declare a type ahead of time so that it can be used with two separate variables:

```
type
  TMyArray = array[1..2] of Byte;

const
  MyArrayOne: TMyArray = (1, 2);

var
  MyArrayTwo: TMyArray;
```

Now that you understand the basic idea of how to use a typed constant, the code shown in the PATRIOT3 program should be fairly easy to understand. The interface for the program is identical to the form used in the PATRIOT2 program. The code itself, on this book's CD-ROM, has a number of changes from the previous version of the program.

NOTE

The code for the PATRIOT3 program is in the CHAP12 directory on this book's CD-ROM.

The FormCreate method in PATRIOT3 is much smaller than FormCreate method in PATRIOT2:

```
procedure TForm1.FormCreate(Sender: TObject);
var
  i: Integer;
```

```
begin
  for i := 1 to 10 do
    ComboBox1.Items.Add(IntToStr(DataArray[i]));
  ComboBox1.ItemIndex := 0;
  Memo1.Text := DescArray[ComboBox1.ItemIndex + 1];
end;
```

Because the program uses predeclared typed constant arrays, there is no need to fill out the arrays at runtime. This may or may not save a few nanoseconds of time in terms of execution speed, but it certainly yields code that is much easier to read, and much more manageable.

The PATRIOT3 program changes not only the way the PATRIOT2 program is launched, but also the way it closes. Specifically, a dialog box appears when you decide to close the main form, as shown in Figure 12.8.

FIGURE 12.8.

The program queries the user before allowing the program to close.

Any user who has experience with Windows is used to seeing these kinds of windows popping up at various times to ensure that no one is making a careless error. The appropriate code from the PATRIOT3 program is shown here:

```
procedure TForm1.FormCloseQuery(Sender: TObject;
                                var CanClose: Boolean);
var
  Result: Word;
begin
  CanClose := False;
  Result := MessageBox(Handle,
                    'Are you sure you want to quit?',
                    'Patriot2', mb_YesNo);
  if Result = id_Yes then
    CanClose := True;
end;
```

As stated earlier, the code shown here is called when you try to close the main form of the program. More specifically, it is called in response to an OnCloseQuery event. These events are generated to give you a chance to check with the user before a form is closed. This can be particularly useful if you want to make sure the user has saved some data before exiting a form or program.

If you want to create a FormCloseQuery method, you should select the OnCloseQuery property from the Events page of the Object Inspector for the Form1 object. After creating the method, you will see that it takes two parameters. The first is a TObject and the second is a boolean variable called CanClose. Because CanClose is passed as a var parameter, the system will remember any changes you make to the variable. Specifically, after the call to FormCloseQuery is completed, one of two things will happen:

- If CanClose is set to True, the application will close.
- If CanClose is set to False, the application will remain open.

As a result of frequently encountering situations like this, I have learned to take measures to ensure that I return the proper boolean value. One fairly safe way to proceed is to set the variable in question to False at the beginning of the routine, and then to set it to True at the end, as long as everything has gone as planned.

Here is a short patch of pseudocode depicting a simplified version of the logic you want to use:

```
function RunATest: Boolean;
begin
  RunATest := False;
  If TheTestSucceeds then
    RunATest := True;
end;
```

In this case, I want to be sure not to return a false positive. That is, I want to be sure not to return True when the test has actually failed. To avoid this contingency, I start by setting the function's return value to False. This simple step goes a long way toward ensuring that RunATest will not return a false positive. Given this design, the function should return True only if the test in question succeeds.

This may seem like a trivial point now, but when you enter into more complex coding situations, it is a valuable aid to keep in mind. Remember: Always set important boolean values to either True or False at the beginning of a procedure or function. This will help you avoid carelessly returning a meaningless value.

Returning now to the heart of the FormCloseQuery procedure, you can see that the whole routine revolves around a call to the MessageBox function:

```
Result := MessageBox(Handle,
                     'Are you sure you want to quit?',
                     'Patriot2', mb_YesNo);
```

MessageBox is part of the standard Windows API. That is, it is not part of Pascal—it is part of the operating environment.

MessageBox takes four parameters:

- The first is a handle to the window that is going to launch the message box. For now, there is no need to have a deep understanding of what this handle actually represents. Instead, simply rely on the fact that Delphi knows you might need this handle, so it keeps it handy in a variable with the appropriate name of Handle. The whole subject of window handles and the Windows API is discussed in some depth in the last section of this book.

- The second parameter to MessageBox is the string you want to see inside the window you are about to create. For now, always be sure to pass a literal value in this parameter. Don't try to place a variable of type string in this parameter, because Windows is expecting you to pass something called a PChar. Delphi knows how to automatically translate strings that appear in quotes into PChars. If you want to pass in strings rather than PChars, use the MessageDlg procedure.

- The third parameter is the title of the window you are about to create. It will be displayed in the caption bar at the top of the window. If you set this parameter to nil, Windows will automatically place the word Error in the caption bar. This does not mean that you committed an error in your code, but only that Windows assumes you want to inform the user that an error has occurred.

- The fourth parameter passed to MessageBox is a constant that designates what sort of buttons you want to appear in the window you are creating. In the example shown previously, you need Yes and No buttons, so that the user can give an appropriate answer to the question, "Are you sure you want to quit?"

There are several different values you can pass in the fourth parameter to MessageBox. Following are some of the most important.

mb_AbortRetryIgnore	A message box containing Abort, Retry, and Ignore buttons
mb_Ok	A message box containing an OK button
mb_OkCancel	A message box containing OK and Cancel buttons
mb_RetryCancel	A message box containing Retry and Cancel buttons
mb_YesNo	A message box containing Yes and No buttons
mb_YesNoCancel	A message box containing Yes, No, and Cancel buttons

If you want a complete list of possible values, pop up the online help for Delphi. You can also ask Windows to display special icons in your message box, as shown in Figure 12.9.

FIGURE 12.9.

MessageBoxes that use the mb_IconQuestion, mb_Iconinformation, mb_Iconhand, *and* mb_Iconexclamation, *flags.*

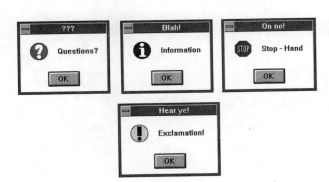

Here is a list of the constants you can pass if you want to show an icon in your message box:

mb_IconAsterisk	Same as mb_IconInformation
mb_IconExclamation	Shows an exclamation-point icon
mb_IconHand	Same as mb_IconStop
mb_IconInformation	Shows an icon depicting an i in a circle
mb_IconQuestion	Shows an icon featuring a question mark
mb_IconStop	Shows an icon featuring a stop sign

When you are using any of the constants shown here, you should or them with the button flag, like this:

```
mb_Ok or mb_IconStop;
mb_YesNo or mb_IconQuestion;
```

The or operator is a logical operator like the and operator that you saw earlier. Here is how the complete call might look:

```
Result := MessageBox(Handle,
                     'Are you sure you want to quit?',
                     'Patriot2', mb_YesNo or mb_IconQuestion);
```

The resulting message box is shown in Figure 12.10.

FIGURE 12.10.

A spruced-up version of the MessageBox *from the* PATRIOT3 *program.*

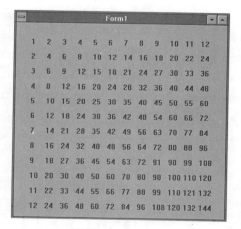

Besides the FormCloseQuery method, another important part of the PATRIOT3 program is the ComboBox1Click method:

```
procedure TForm1.ComboBox1Click(Sender: TObject);
begin
  Memo1.Text := DescArray[ComboBox1.ItemIndex + 1];
end;
```

This function is called every time the user selects a new item in the combo box. Note that the proper method to call in this case is OnClick, rather than OnChange.

The functionality for the ComboBox1Click method has already been described, because it used to be attached to the BitBtn1Click method. The key point is that now the user will immediately see the event that is associated with any date they select, whereas in the last version of the program this information could be obtained only by selecting a button.

The BitBtn1Click method now automatically increments the date being displayed. In other words, if you click the American flag button, the next date in the array is displayed, along with its associated text:

```
procedure TForm1.BitBtn1Click(Sender: TObject);
var
  Cur: Integer;
begin
  Cur := ComboBox1.ItemIndex;
  if Cur = 9 then Cur := -1;
  ComboBox1.ItemIndex := Cur + 1;
  Memo1.Text := DescArray[ComboBox1.ItemIndex + 1];
end;
```

The mechanism driving this method is revealed in the third line of the routine:

```
ComboBox1.ItemIndex := Cur + 1;
```

This code adds 1 to the number of the currently selected item from the listbox, thereby forcing the program to choose the next date.

The line shown here gets at the heart of this method, but it might be worthwhile to review the whole procedure in some detail. It begins by finding out the currently selected item in the listbox:

```
Cur := ComboBox1.ItemIndex;
```

The next line of the program tests to see if the currently selected item is the last one in the list, in which case it wraps the number around to one beneath its lowest possible value:

```
if Cur = 9 then Cur := -1;
```

This line of code is a bit confusing in part because the value of Cur, as you may recall, is zero-based. This means that the tenth item in the listbox is assigned the number 9, and therefore Cur is maxed out when it reaches not 10 but 9. To understand why Cur is then set to −1, rather than to zero, you have to recall that the next line of code automatically adds 1 to the current value of Cur. Because the first item in the list is 0, the code for BitBtnClick must set Cur to −1 in order to see it be incremented to 0 by the next line of code.

The final line of code in the BitBtnClick method selects the appropriate value from the array of strings and displays it in the program's memo control:

```
Memo1.Text := DescArray[ComboBox1.ItemIndex + 1];
```

Note that in this case it is necessary to add 1 to `ComboBox1.ItemIndex` because the `DescArray` variable is one-based, rather than zero-based.

The last few paragraphs have highlighted the need to be aware of working with a zero-based array of numbers. No one can deny that zero-based numbering can be confusing at times. However, it has the distinct advantage of directly referencing the computer's own way of viewing the world. In other words, computers usually see the first element in any series as having the number 0. This is their most natural and intuitive way of viewing the world, and if you want to work with them directly, it is best that you too begin working with zero-based arrays. However, you may also prefer to create code that is more people-centric rather than machine-centric. If so, you might want to create arrays that are usually based on the number 1. The choice is yours.

Two-Dimensional Arrays

One of the most common uses of arrays is to extend their functionality so that they have two or more dimensions. In other words, a simple array is drawn on a graph as a vector, but a two-dimensional array can best be represented by a matrix.

Here is a common declaration for a two-dimensional array:

```
type
    TMyTwoArray = array[1..4, 1..4] of Integer;
```

This array has 16 elements. The grid shows you a pictorial representation of these elements. The numbers across the top and bottom are labels for the columns and rows of the matrix, and the asterisks represent the actual members of the array:

```
      1   2   3   4
  1   *   *   *   *
  2   *   *   *   *
  3   *   *   *   *
  4   *   *   *   *
```

If you declare a variable of type `TMyTwoArray`:

```
var
    MyTwoArray: TMyTwoArray;
```

you can address the first member of the array like this:

```
MyTwoArray[1, 1] := 1;
```

After this assignment, the array would look like this:

```
      1   2   3   4
  1   1   *   *   *
  2   *   *   *   *
  3   *   *   *   *
  4   *   *   *   *
```

You can see that the first element of the two-dimensional array is now equal to 1. There is no way to predict what numbers reside in these places, so I have marked them with asterisks, which in this case means unknown. After the execution of the single line shown earlier, a programmer can be sure of only the first element, because it was explicitly set to 1.

> **NOTE**
>
> There are cases in which Delphi will automatically zero out all the elements of an array that you declare. However, if you want to be sure the elements are set to 0, you can use the FillChar procedure:
>
> ```
> FillChar(MyArray, SizeOf(MyArray), #0);
> ```
>
> This is a powerful function that you should use with care. The key point is that the second parameter passed to the function designates the size of the area that you want to zero out. If you put the number 2 in this place, only the first 2 bytes of your array would be set to 0. The third parameter passed to this function is the value you want to place in the bytes occupied by your variable. In this case I just want the bytes zeroed out, so I place #0 in this location. If I wanted them all set to the letter A, I could have put #65 here. This function is discussed in more depth in Chapter 14, "Strings and Text Files."

Here is how to address the second element in the first row of the array:

```
MyTwoArray[2, 1] := 1;
```

After this and the previous assignment statement are executed, the array looks like this:

```
    1   2   3   4
1   1   1   *   *
2   *   *   *   *
3   *   *   *   *
4   *   *   *   *
```

To fill in the entire first row of the array, you can write the following code:

```
for i := 1 to 4 do
  MyTwoArray[i, 1] := 1;
```

After this loop executes, the array looks like this:

```
    1   2   3   4
1   1   1   1   1
2   *   *   *   *
3   *   *   *   *
4   *   *   *   *
```

If you wanted to fill in the first column of the array, you would write the following code:

```
for i := 1 to 4 do
  MyTwoArray[1, i] := 1;
```

After this line of code executes, the array would look like this:

```
        1   2   3   4
   1    1   *   *   *
   2    1   *   *   *
   3    1   *   *   *
   4    1   *   *   *
```

By this time, you can begin to see how someone might go about writing code that would automatically initialize all the elements of an array to zero:

```
var
  i, j: Integer;
begin
  for i := 1 to 4 do
    for j := 1 to 4 do
      MyTwoArray[i, j] := 0;
```

If you have never seen code like this, you should be sure to study it carefully, because this kind of two-dimensional loop plays an important role in many programming projects. The key fact to grasp, of course, is that after the preceding lines of code have executed, MyTwoArray will look like this:

```
        1   2   3   4
   1    0   0   0   0
   2    0   0   0   0
   3    0   0   0   0
   4    0   0   0   0
```

Creating a Multiplication Table

Now that you understand the basics of how two-dimensional arrays are put together, you are ready to see one in action in a real program. The TWODEM1 application that accompanies this book shows how to create a simple two-dimensional array that prints out a multiplication table, as shown in Figure 12.11.

NOTE

The code for the main unit of the TWODEM1 program is in the CHAP12 directory on this book's CD-ROM.

FIGURE 12.11.

A simple multiplication table, as displayed by the TWODEM1 program.

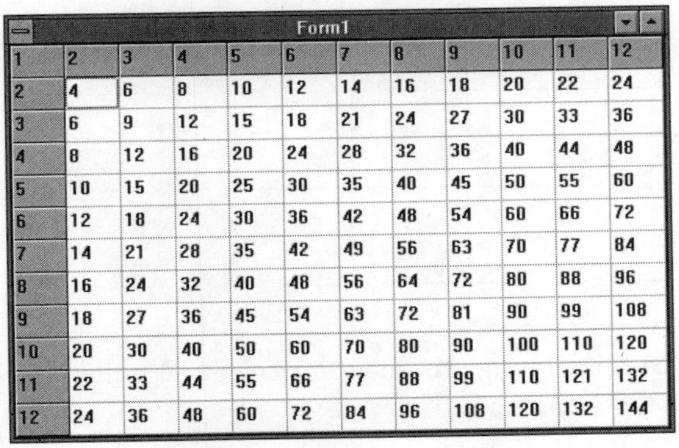

Form1											
1	2	3	4	5	6	7	8	9	10	11	12
2	4	6	8	10	12	14	16	18	20	22	24
3	6	9	12	15	18	21	24	27	30	33	36
4	8	12	16	20	24	28	32	36	40	44	48
5	10	15	20	25	30	35	40	45	50	55	60
6	12	18	24	30	36	42	48	54	60	66	72
7	14	21	28	35	42	49	56	63	70	77	84
8	16	24	32	40	48	56	64	72	80	88	96
9	18	27	36	45	54	63	72	81	90	99	108
10	20	30	40	50	60	70	80	90	100	110	120
11	22	33	44	55	66	77	88	99	110	121	132
12	24	36	48	60	72	84	96	108	120	132	144

This program uses the FormPaint event when it needs to draw on the screen. As you learned earlier, an OnPaint event gets sent whenever the surface of the form might need to be repainted. As a result, the table displayed by the program will always be complete, even if it is temporarily hidden by another window. Specifically, if the main form is hidden by another form and is then revealed, the FormPaint method will be called again. The appropriate parts of the screen will be repainted, thereby making it appear that the screen has a never-changing display of data on its surface.

The FormPaint method for the TWODEM1 program includes the following declaration:

```
MyArray: array[1..12, 1..12] of Integer;
```

This code declares a two-dimensional array with 12 items in each dimension. Notice that I do not bother to declare a type, because this program has only this one need to instantiate an array of this type. Had there been more than one place in the program where this array needed to be declared, I would have created a type called TMyArray.

The core part of the TWODEM1 program is the following code fragment:

```
for x := 1 to 12 do
  for y := 1 to 12 do
    MyArray[x, y] := x * y;
```

Here you can see that the two dimensions of the array are being filled out with the elements of a simple arithmetic matrix called a multiplication table. (See Figure 12.11.) More explicitly, the first time the loop executes, x gets set to 1, and y is incremented from 1 to 12, creating the following output:

1										
2										
3										
4										
5										

6									
7									
8									
9									
10									
11									
12									

The next time through the loop, x gets set to 2, and y is walked once again from 1 to 12, yielding the following results:

1	2								
2	4								
3	6								
4	8								
5	10								
6	12								
7	14								
8	16								
9	18								
10	20								
11	22								
12	24								

The beginnings of a multiplication table are becoming clear now. You can look up the number 2 in the column section and 10 in the row section and see that the intersection of these two points contains the number 20, which is 2 multiplied by 10. If you are not exactly sure how these numbers are derived by the loop shown earlier, you should put the x and y variables in the Watch List and step through the loop with the debugger. (Really. If what I have said doesn't make sense, use the debugger.)

Once the array is filled out, it is displayed on-screen through the following bit of code:

```
for x := 1 to 12 do
   for y := 1 to 12 do
      Canvas.TextOut(x * Space, y * Space, IntToStr(MyArray[x, y]));
```

The `Canvas.TextOut` procedure, as you recall, displays a string on the screen at a location specified by the x and y values passed in its first two parameters. The third parameter passed to the function is the string that you want to display. In other words, the following code would display the word `Simple` at the upper-left corner of a window:

```
Canvas.TextOut(1, 1, Simple);
```

You could rewrite the loop shown previously so that it performs the same action but is somewhat easier for some people to read:

```
var
  Value: Integer;
  S: String;
begin
  ...
  for x := 1 to 12 do
    for y := 1 to 12 do begin
      Value := MyArray[x, y];
      S := IntToStr(Value);
    Canvas.TextOut(x * Space, y * Space, S);
    end;
  ...
end;
```

This code first retrieves the value of a particular x and y coordinate from MyArray:

```
Value := MyArray[x, y];
```

and then translates that number into a string:

```
S := IntToStr(Value);
```

and finally displays it to the screen:

```
Canvas.TextOut(x * Space, y * Space, S);
```

Both examples of the loop displayed here accomplish the same thing. For now, you should choose the method that is easiest for you to read.

The final unexplained portion of the TWODEM1 program is the variable Space, which is retrieved from the following handwritten function:

```
function TForm1.GetSpace: Integer;
var
  TextMetrics: TTextMetric;
begin
  GetTextMetrics(Canvas.Handle, TextMetrics);
  Result := TextMetrics.tmMaxCharWidth * 2;
  Width := Result * 14;
  Height := Result * 14;
end;
```

When I say handwritten, I mean that you must write out this entire function, including its header, and you must be sure to copy the header into the private section of the Form1 object declaration:

```
  TForm1 = class(TForm)
    procedure FormPaint(Sender: TObject);
  private
    function GetSpace: Integer;
  end;
```

The function needed to be created because TWODEM1 needs to know how far apart it should space the values it writes to the screen. To obtain that distance, the program first calls `GetTextMetrics`, which returns a structure containing information about the current font. If you want, you can look up the `TTextMetric` structure in the online help, but for now I will not explain it in depth. It is covered later when fonts are discussed from the perspective of a native Windows API programmer.

For now, you need to know only that `TTextMetric` structures contain a field called `tmMaxCharWidth`, which defines the width of the largest possible character that can be printed to the screen with the current font. I double this value to find an appropriate size for space between each entry in the matrix created by the TWODEM1 program:

```
Result := TextMetrics.tmMaxCharWidth * 2;
```

Remember that `Result` is a predeclared variable supplied by the compiler whenever you want to return a value from a function.

Finally, the code sets the width and height of the entire form to the following values:

```
Width := Result * 14;
Height := Result * 14;
```

To understand this code, you need to remember `Width` and `Height` are properties of the Form that is currently being displayed on the screen. By assigning them values at runtime, you can ensure that the entire matrix is visible without the user having to resize the form.

Using the StringGrid

Delphi ships with a TStringGrid component that can be very useful when you are writing code like that shown in the TWODEM1 program. The TStringGrid is really a fancy, fully visible matrix that can be displayed on your form, inside of which you can display strings. In particular, the TWODEM2 program demonstrates how you can use a grid to display a matrix such as the multiplication table you created earlier. The key reason to use a TStringGrid is that it avoids the complications shown earlier when I found it necessary to calculate how far apart the elements in my array were to be displayed. If you use a TStringGrid object, all those calculations become superfluous, and you can work directly with an object that represents in a natural and intuitive fashion the kind of display you want to create.

NOTE

The code for the TWODEM2 program is in the CHAP12 directory on this book's CD-ROM.

The form for the TWODEM2 program consists of nothing more than a TStringGrid component placed in the center of a form. After dropping in the TStringGrid component, you should set its `Align` property to `alClient`. You also need to set the `ColCount` and `RowCount` properties for the `StringGrid1` object to 12, because you are going to be displaying a 12 by 12 matrix. You can also adjust the `DefaultColWidth` property to a comfortable value, which on my system turned out to be 55.

> **NOTE**
>
> I don't bother explaining the `ColCount`, `RowCount`, and `DefaultColWidth` properties in depth anywhere in this book. The reasons for this are twofold:
>
> ■ I find the names self-explanatory, and I don't want to burden you with an explanation of the obvious.
>
> ■ If you are having trouble grasping the properties, you can turn to online help, where they are fully referenced.
>
> The lesson, here, I suppose, is that if you give your methods and properties clear, well-thought-out names, there is very little need for further documentation.

As you can see, the code for this program is extremely brief. In fact, the entire program consists of a little window dressing stretched around the following method:

```
procedure TForm1.FormCreate(Sender: TObject);
var
  X, Y: Integer;
begin
  for x := 1 to 12 do
    for y := 1 to 12 do
      StringGrid1.Cells[X-1, Y-1] := IntToStr(X * Y);
end;
```

A quick glance at this method shows that the individual members of a TStringGrid array can be accessed through the `Cells` property, which is really a predefined array. In other words, when you are working with a TStringGrid, there is no need for you to declare a separate variable for holding your array. If you need to write code that can't afford the cycles spent on translating a numerical value into a string, and vice versa, you should create an array, as shown in the following code fragment:

```
procedure TForm1.FormCreate(Sender: TObject);
var
  MyArray: array[1..12, 1..12] of Integer;
  X, Y: Integer;
begin
  for x := 1 to 12 do
    for y := 1 to 12 do
      MyArray[x, y] := x * y;

  for x := 1 to 12 do
    for y := 1 to 12 do
      StringGrid1.Cells[X-1, Y-1] := IntToStr(MyArray[x, y]);
end;
```

The code in this second version of the FormCreate method takes the time to create a variable called MyArray, which is a simple two-dimensional matrix. When it comes time to fill in the TStringGrid, this is put to work supplying the values that will be shown on screen:

```
StringGrid1.Cells[X-1, Y-1] := IntToStr(MyArray[x, y]);
```

I show you this variation on the TWODEM2 program because it makes explicit a simple way to work with an actual array of integers, while at the same displaying them on screen in a TStringGrid.

Summary

In this chapter you were introduced to arrays and saw how to manipulate them and how to display them on screen. The examples found in this chapter include both one-and two-dimensional arrays.

Other concepts covered in this chapter include numerous tricks for creating simple, easy-to-use interfaces for your program. In particular, you have seen how to use bitbtns and how to show a matrix inside a TStringGrid.

The next chapter covers records, which are another very important means of working with large, complex data structures.

Working with Records

13

IN THIS CHAPTER

Overview

In this chapter you learn about constructing and manipulating records. You also encounter a variant called `MessageDlg` on the `MessageBox` function that enables you to use strings in place of PChars.

Simple Records

A *record* is really just a class without any procedures or functions inside it. Conversely, you can think of an object as a record that can contain not only data but also procedures and functions. In short, there is a link between records and objects. When you are learning about records, you are laying some of the basis for learning about object-oriented programming.

Records enable you to encapsulate one or more Pascal types inside a single data structure. For instance, the following record contains a string and an integer:

```
type
  TMyRecord = record
    MyString: string;
    MyNumber: Integer;
  end;
```

Records are always defined in a type section, and they begin by declaring the name of the record type, an equal sign, and then the keyword `record`:

```
type
  TMyRecord = record
```

The following examples are also valid record headers:

```
TAddress = record
TFoobar = record
TMoneyData = record
```

After you have declared the type name for a record, you can go on to add one or more fields. There is a strong parallel between the fields of a record and the var section inside a procedure:

```
var
  MyString: string;
  MyNumber: Integer;

type
  TMyRecord = Record
    MyString: string;
    MyNumber: Integer;
  end;
```

The syntax you use when you declare local variables for a procedure is virtually identical to the syntax you use when you declare the fields of a record.

The final step in declaring a record type is to add the word end, followed by a semicolon. To make your code more readable, you should be able to draw a straight line between the E in the word end, and the T in the identifier for your record type:

```
TMyRecord = Record
  MyString: Integer;
  MyNumber: Integer;
end;
```

It isn't mandatory to start your identifiers for records or other types with the letter T, but it is standard practice, and a good one at that.

After defining the type of record, the next step is to declare a variable of that record type:

```
var
  MyRecord : TMyRecord;
```

The following are also valid record declarations, based on the partially defined types listed previously:

```
var
  Address: TAddress;
  Foobar: TFooBar;
  MoneyData: TMoneyData;
```

Remember that a type declaration merely informs the compiler about a particular type. It's a definition. A variable declaration tells the compiler that a particular number of seats needs to be set aside in the memory theater.

In the case of TMyRecord, there will be 258 seats set aside in the memory theater. The first 256 seats will be for the variable called MyString, and the last 2 seats will be for the integer variable called MyNumber. Naturally there are no seats set aside for the record's header, or for the word end. When I declared TMyRecord, all I was really doing was saying that I needed 258 seats in the memory theater, and that the first 256 would be for a string and the last 2 for an integer value.

The individual bytes in memory that contain the record are just normal bytes. They are just collections of 8 bits with no particular attributes or capabilities. In other words, the 258 folks in the memory theater are just normal people who aren't necessarily associated with strings or integers. All any one of them knows how to do is remember a number between 0 and 255. When a type is declared, however, the compiler tells the computer to treat those numbers in a particular way. Specifically, it says to treat the first 256 members of the audience as a string and the last 2 as a number. The difference between a record and other declarations is that the computer is told to treat a set of variables as a unit. After learning about TMyRecord, the computer knows to treat the variable MyRecord as one unit with two parts. The first part is a string, and the second part is a number.

Now that you understand what a record is and how to declare one, the next step is to understand how to reference the fields of a record. Because of your experience with objects, this syntax should seem reasonable; but for clarity's sake, I'll spell it out in detail.

To reference the fields of an object in your code, write the record variable name followed by a period:

```
MyRecord.MyString := 'Sam';
```

This code assigns the string Sam to the field of MyRecord that is called MyString. Here is another example:

```
Edit1.Text := MyRecord.MyString;
```

The code shown here sets the text in Edit1 to the string stored in the first field of MyRecord. Notice that you use the same syntax for referencing a field of an object as you do for referencing a field of a record.

A with statement enables you to reference the fields of a record in a very convenient shorthand:

```
with MyRecord do begin
  MyString := 'Some string data';
  MyNumber := 23;
end;
```

Your program will not run any faster or slower if you use a with statement. The only reason for its existence is that it makes it easy to write very clear, easy-to-read code.

Records: A Simple Example

A simple way to think about records is to compare them to entries in a database. A typical address book has a series of addresses in it, and each address represents a single record. The addresses are all tied together because they have a series of common fields, such as First Name, Last Name, and Phone. Records don't necessarily have to have anything to do with addresses, but a single entry in an address book is a classic real-world example of a record.

The AGES1 program uses a simple record that contains fields for a first name, last name, and age:

```
TAge = Record
  FName: String;
  LName: String;
  Age: Integer;
end;
```

The form for the AGES1 program, shown in Figure 13.1, contains three labels and three edit controls, one pair for each of the fields. For aesthetic reasons, these controls are all placed on a panel. At the bottom of the control are a Close button and a View button. When the user clicks the View button, a dialog box pops up that displays the current contents of the three edit controls. The code for the AGES1 program is shown in Listing 13.1.

FIGURE 13.1.

The form for the AGES1 program contains a panel, three edit controls, three labels, and two buttons.

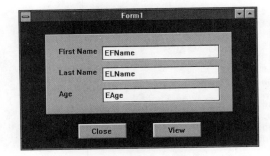

NOTE

The code for the AGES1 program is in the CHAP13 directory on this book's CD-ROM.

When the AGES1 program first appears on screen, the user has a chance to fill in all three edit controls with information, as shown in Figure 13.2. Notice that the third field must be an integer. The next step is to select the View button, at which time a message dialog box appears on screen. Message dialog boxes are similar to message boxes, but they enable you to use strings rather than arrays of Char.

FIGURE 13.2.

The AGES1 program after the user has entered some data.

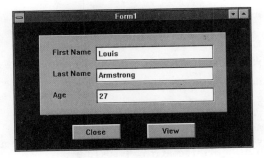

The type declaration for the TAge record is shown at the top of module Main. Immediately thereafter, you can see that a variable of type TAge is declared as a field of the Form1 class:

```
type
  TAge = Record
    FName: String;
    LName: String;
    Age: Integer;
  end;
```

354

```
TForm1 = class(TForm)
    Panel1: TPanel;
    Label1: TLabel;
    Label2: TLabel;
    Label3: TLabel;
    EFName: TEdit;
    ELName: TEdit;
    EAge: TEdit;
    BClose: TButton;
    BView: TButton;
    procedure BCloseClick(Sender: TObject);
    procedure BViewClick(Sender: TObject);
  private
    AgeRec: TAge;
  end;
```

NOTE

You should not, and in fact cannot, list variables as part of the first section of TForm descendant declaration. Instead, you should create a new section with the private or public directive and place your variables there.

Furthermore, the fact that AgeRec is listed as a field of a class helps to illustrate the way you can nest a second record or an array inside of a record or class. In other words, records can contain records or arrays.

All of the excitement in the AGES1 program is centered around the BViewClick method:

```
procedure TForm1.BViewClick(Sender: TObject);
const
  CR = #13#10;
var
  S: String;
begin
  AgeRec.FName := EFName.Text;
  AgeRec.LName := ELName.Text;
  AgeRec.Age := StrToInt(EAge.Text);
  S := AgeRec.FName + CR + AgeRec.LName + CR + IntToStr(AgeRec.Age);
  MessageDlg(S, mtInformation, [mbOk], 0);
end;
```

This method first declares a constant called CR, which contains the characters that define a carriage return. A carriage return contains the thirteenth and tenth members of the current character set. It is used to automatically move the cursor down to the beginning of the next line, as if you had pressed the Enter key on a computer. Using the thirteenth and tenth characters to do this is just a convention, but it is one that is shared throughout the PC industry.

The opening three lines of the BViewClick method fill out the various fields of the AgeRec structure:

```
  AgeRec.FName := EFName.Text;
  AgeRec.LName := ELName.Text;
  AgeRec.Age := StrToInt(EAge.Text);
```

You can see that it is first necessary to convert the string stored in an edit control into an integer before it can be stored in the Age field. If you didn't make this conversion, you would get a type mismatch error at compile time. This conversion is what forces you to enter an integer rather than a string for this field of the record.

The next line of code combines all the fields of AgeRec into a single string:

```
S := AgeRec.FName + CR + AgeRec.LName + CR + IntToStr(AgeRec.Age);
```

Because a carriage return separates the three portions of this string, each field of the record will be shown on a separate line, as shown in Figure 13.3.

FIGURE 13.3.

A message dialog box displaying each field of the AgeRec structure on a separate line.

If you did not separate the fields with carriage returns, the individual portions of the string would appear on one line like this:

```
SamJones123
```

As an alternative to carriage returns, you can place spaces between the fields to make them more readable:

```
Sam Jones 123
```

The last line of the BViewClick method pops up a dialog box with the MessageDlg command:

```
MessageDlg(S, mtInformation, [mbOk], 0);
```

Message dialog boxes are very much like message boxes, except that they have been tamed and customized for use with Delphi.

Calls to MessageDlg take four parameters:

- The first is the string you want to display.
- The second defines the title and icon displayed in the dialog box.
- The third defines the buttons you want to display.
- The fourth defines a help context. Refer to the online help for information on help contexts.

The second and third parameters need some further definition before you will understand how to use them.

The second parameter is of type TMsgDlgType:

```
TMsgDlgType = (mtWarning, mtError, mtInformation, mtConfirmation);
```

This enumerated type enables you to create four different types of dialog boxes, as shown in Figures 13.4A through 134D.

FIGURE 13.4A.

The Error dialog box.

FIGURE 13.4B.

The Confirm dialog box.

FIGURE 13.4C.

The Warning dialog box

FIGURE 13.4D.

The Information dialog box.

You can also create various arrangements of buttons in your MsgDialogs by using members of the following predeclared enumerated type:

```
TMsgDlgBtn = (mbYes, mbNo, mbOK, mbCancel, mbHelp);
```

When working with these types, you should prepare something called a *set*, which is essentially a list of numbers, variables, or constants placed inside square brackets. For instance, the following two sets are predeclared for you in the MsgDlg unit:

```
const
  mbYesNoCancel = [mbYes, mbNo, mbCancel];
  mbOKCancel = [mbOK, mbCancel];
```

If you want Yes, No, and Cancel buttons to appear in your dialog, place mbYesNoCancel in the third parameter to MessageDlg:

```
MessageDlg(S, mtInformation, mbYesNoCancel, 0);
```

The result is shown in Figure 13.5.

FIGURE 13.5.

If you use the
`mbYesNoCancel` *constant*
in a call to `MessageDlg`,
you create a dialog box
with three buttons in it.

As shown in the AGES1 example, there is no need to use a predeclared constant. If you want, you can simply type the set directly into the code:

```
MessageDlg(S, mtInformation, [mbYes, mbNo, mbCancel], 0);
```

The sample code shown here would also produce the results shown in Figure 13.5.

Working with Arrays of Records

On many occasions programmers want to work with multiple records of a particular type. For instance, if you have an address book with 10 addresses in it, you could store it in a computer by using 10 records of the same type. Many different structures can be used to manage multiple records of the same type, but one of the most convenient is an array.

Here is how to declare an array of records:

```
type
  TAge = record
    FName: string;
    LName: string;
    Age: Integer;
  end;

  TAgeArray = array[1..5] of TAge;
```

Everything in this declaration should be readily comprehensible. A variable of type `TAgeArray` can hold five records, each of type `TAge`.

Here is how you can fill in the first two records in an array of type `TAgeArray`:

```
var
  AgeArray: TAgeArray;

begin
  AgeArray[1].FName := 'J.E.B.';
  AgeArray[1].LName := 'Stuart';
  AgeArray[1].Age := 30;
  AgeArray[2].FName := 'James';
  AgeArray[2].LName := 'Longstreet';
  AgeArray[2].Age := 42;
  etc...
```

The syntax `AgeArray[1]` refers to the first record in the array. If you then add `FName` to this code, you can reference the first field of the first record.

If you want to predeclare a record as a constant, you can use the following syntax:

```
Age1: TAge = (FName: 'J.E.B.'; LName: 'Stuart'; Age: 30);
```

In my opinion, this particular construct does not represent Object Pascal's shining hour, because it appears a bit cluttered and wordy. However, its intent is clear enough. Declare a variable of type `record`, write an opening parenthesis and the name of the first field, and then follow it with a colon and the value of that field. Next move on to the second field, being careful to declare the field name first and then its value. This process is continued until you reach the end of the record.

Here is how to declare an array of five records, given the declarations for `TAge` and `TAgeArray` shown earlier:

```
AgeArray: TAgeArray = (
    (FName: 'J.E.B.'; LName: 'Stuart'; Age: 30),
    (FName: 'James'; LName: 'Longstreet'; Age: 42),
    (FName: 'George'; LName: 'Pickett'; Age: 38),
    (FName: 'Richard'; LName: 'Ewell'; Age: 46),
    (FName: 'Lewis'; LName: 'Armistead'; Age: 46));
```

Each member of `AgeArray` is set off from its fellows by a comma and a set of parentheses. The beginning and end of the entire array are also marked by a set of parentheses.

The AGES2 program replaces the View button in the AGES1 program with two new buttons called Next and Previous. If you select the Next button, you will see the next member of the `AgeArray`; if you press the Previous button, you will see the previous member of the array. The form for this project is shown in Figure 13.6.

FIGURE 13.6.

The AGES2 form has three buttons, a panel, and three sets of label and edit controls.

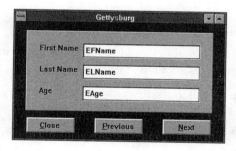

NOTE

The code for the AGES2 program is in the CHAP13 directory on this book's CD-ROM.

I want to give you a chance to fill in a few records of your own, so the AGES2 program declares an array of seven members, with the last two records left blank:

```
type
  TAge = Record
    FName: String;
    LName: String;
    Age: Integer;
  end;

  TAgeArray = array[1..Max] of TAge;

const
  AgeArray: TAgeArray = (
      (FName: 'J.E.B.'; LName: 'Stuart'; Age: 30),
      (FName: 'James'; LName: 'Longstreet'; Age: 42),
      (FName: 'George'; LName: 'Pickett'; Age: 38),
      (FName: 'Richard'; LName: 'Ewell'; Age: 46),
      (FName: 'Lewis'; LName: 'Armistead'; Age: 46),
      (FName: ''; LName: ''; Age: 0),
      (FName: ''; LName: ''; Age: 0));
```

You can fill these last two blank records in at runtime with any of the following four names, or others of your own choosing:

> Ambrose Hill, 37
> Richard Garnett, 44
> Jubal Early, 46
> Robert Lee, 57

NOTE

Some readers will recognize these men as the Confederate generals who fought at Gettysburg. They are listed along with their ages at the time of that dreadful battle. If you want to read all about the glory and horror of that terrifying event, you can check out Michael Shaara's excellent book, *The Killer Angels*. Clearly, I was under Mr. Shaara's powerful spell at the time I wrote this section of the book.

There are four key functions in the AGES2 program:

```
type
  TForm1 = class(TForm)
    ...
    procedure GetData;
    procedure SetData;
    procedure BPreviousClick(Sender: TObject);
    procedure BNextClick(Sender: TObject);
  private
    CurRec: Integer;
  end;
```

The first two read and write data from the edit controls. These functions are called `GetData` and `SetData`. The other two key functions respond to clicks on the Previous and Next buttons.

Here is the `SetData` function:

```
procedure TForm1.SetData;
begin
  with AgeArray[CurRec] do begin
    EFName.Text := FName;
    ELName.Text := LName;
    EAge.Text := IntToStr(Age);
  end;
  Form1.Caption := 'Gettysburg: ' + IntToStr(CurRec);
end;
```

To understand this function, you need to know that there is an integer type variable called `CurRec` declared as a field of `TForm1`. When the program is first activated, this variable is initialized to 1, is incremented when the Next button is pressed, and is decremented when the Previous button is pressed. `CurRec` will therefore always designate the current record the user wants to view.

If `CurRec` has a value of 1, the `SetData` function copies J.E.B. Stuart's name and age into the program's edit controls. If `CurRec` is set to 2, it is James Longstreet's turn to be center stage.

At the very bottom of the `SetData` data function is a line that changes the caption at the top of the program's form. This caption will always display the number of the current record. For instance, if `CurRec` is set to 3, the caption will look like this:

Gettysburg: 3

If `CurRec` is equal to 5, the caption will look like this:

Gettysburg: 5

The `GetData` function looks a good deal like the `SetData` function:

```
procedure TForm1.GetData;
begin
  with AgeArray[CurRec] do begin
    FName := EFName.Text;
    LName := ELName.Text;
    Age := StrToInt(EAge.Text);
  end;
end;
```

This function is used to record any changes the user might make to the data that the program displays. In particular, it records the new names entered into array members 6 and 7.

Because the user might accidentally change one of the fields, you could use a set of temporary variables to retrieve the new contents of the fields and compare them with the old contents:

```
if (NewRec.FName <> AgeArray[CurRec].FName) then
  QueryReader;
```

QueryReader might contain a MessageDlg asking the user if he or she really wanted to make changes to the current record.

The responses to the Previous and Next buttons are trivial once you have set up the GetData and SetData methods:

```
procedure TForm1.BPreviousClick(Sender: TObject);
begin
  GetData;
  if CurRec > 1 then Dec(CurRec);
  SetData;
end;

procedure TForm1.BNextClick(Sender: TObject);
begin
  GetData;
  if CurRec < 7 then Inc(CurRec);
  SetData;
end;
```

The only sections of the code worth commenting on are the places where CurRec is incremented or decremented:

```
  if CurRec < 7 then Inc(CurRec);
  if CurRec > 1 then Dec(CurRec);
```

You can see that both lines of code check to make sure that CurRec is never allowed to slip out of the bounds of the AgeArray. For instance, it would be a mistake to try to reference the zeroth element of the AgeArray, because there is no such thing defined. The same holds true for the eighth element of the array.

Because it is so very important, I discuss range checking in more detail in its own section. Just hold on a moment if you would like a more detailed explanation of what happens when you try to access members of an array for which you have not allocated any memory.

Before closing out this section, I want to say a word about the importance of the AGES2 program. If you are a newcomer to programming, this code gives you one of your first views of how to display a relatively large body of data to the user. Storing and displaying information is one of the key roles that computers play in contemporary life. Make sure you understand the techniques used in the AGES2 program. The ideas presented in its code form the basis for many vitally important programming tasks.

More on Range Checking

After reading the last section, you should have a minimal basis for understanding range checking and its importance when working with arrays. The next few paragraphs explore the subject in depth, touching on a number of issues you need to be sure you understand.

In the `AgeArray` program, there is nothing innate in the compiler or in the hardware to prevent you from trying to reference a nonexistent eighth member of `TAgeArray`. You can set `CurArray` to 8 and then call `SetData`, and the computer will do its best to satisfy your request. However, when you do so, you will start to write data into an undefined portion of memory.

The `AgeArray` takes up 3,598 seats in the memory theater. However, if you try to write to an eighth record in memory, you will be writing 514 bytes to a place that does not belong to the `AgeArray`. It is quite possible that the members of the memory theater sitting in those seats will be remembering other important pieces of information that will be overwritten when you try to access the eighth member of the array. You might even write to a portion of memory that your program does not own, or that the operating system does not give you a right to change. If that happens, a General Protection Fault will occur, for the reasons explained in Chapter 17, "Understanding the Windows Environment." However, it is very possible that you might write to this area of memory without causing any obvious ill effects. In other words, the next 514 bytes of memory might just happen to belong to your program, and they might just happen not to contain any important data or code. As a result, you might think your program is functioning properly, only to have users come back to you months later complaining of a strange bug that they access under some peculiar sets of circumstances. Those peculiar circumstances, of course, would be those in which some other part of your program tries to access those 514 bytes occupied by the eighth member of your array.

Making sure that you do not attempt to read or write beyond the beginning or end of an array is an absolutely key portion of any debugging cycle. To help you keep track of what you are doing, don't forget to turn range checking on during product development (`{$R+}`), and to turn it off (`{$R-}`) after you release your code to the public. Range checking will catch any attempt to read or write beyond the end of an array, even if those attempts would not otherwise cause any immediate damage to your program. Range checking will slow down the execution of your program very slightly, so you should turn it off when you are done.

Variant Records

On the whole, I have never found records to be a particularly complicated topic. There is, however, one peculiar twist you can run on this subject that causes confusion to many newcomers. More explicitly, the twist in question is called a variant record, and unfortunately these peculiar little structures can prove to be quite useful at times. I say unfortunately because variant records are rather odd and esoteric constructs that can be difficult to grasp.

Perhaps the best way to get started with variant records is to bring up a particular case in point that you have already encountered on several occasions. As I mentioned earlier, the `TRect` structure that Delphi uses to track the dimensions of rectangular objects is a variant record. Here is the exact definition for a `TRect`, copied verbatim from WINTYPES.PAS:

```
type
  PRect = ^TRect;
  TRect = record
    case Integer of
      0: (Left, Top, Right, Bottom: Integer);
      1: (TopLeft, BottomRight: TPoint);
  end;
```

Suppose the TRect structure looked like this:

```
TRect = record
  Left, Top, Right, Bottom: Integer;
end;
```

Or like this:

```
TRect = record
  Left: Integer;
  Top: Integer;
  Right: Integer;
  Bottom: Integer;
end;
```

Both of these declarations are identical in meaning, and they both should be readily comprehensible. In short, they state that a TRect is a record containing four integers. These integer values are used to describe the upper-left and lower-right corners of a rectangle, as described back in Chapter 5, "What Is a Graphical Environment?"

In Chapter 5, you were also introduced to the TPoint record, which looks like this:

```
TPoint = record
  X: Integer;
  Y: Integer;
end;
```

If you spend a moment contemplating the TPoint structure, you can see that it represents one half of a TRect structure:

```
TRect = record
  Left: Integer;
  Top: Integer;
  Right: Integer;
  Bottom: Integer;
end;
```

In fact, it is sometimes convenient to regard a TRect structure not as four integers, but as two TPoints:

```
TRect = record
  TopLeft, BottomRight: TPoint;
end;
```

Or, if you prefer:

```
TRect = record
  TopLeft: TPoint;
```

```
    BottomRight: TPoint;
  end;
```

The "point" here is that there are times when it might be most convenient to think of a TRect structure as looking like this:

```
TRect = record
  Left: Integer;
  Top: Integer;
  Right: Integer;
  Bottom: Integer;
end;
```

At other times you might prefer to think of it as looking like this:

```
TRect = record
  TopLeft: TPoint;
  BottomRight: TPoint;
end;
```

One of the virtues of variant records is that they enable you to address the same structure in two different ways:

```
TRect = record
  case Integer of
    0: (Left, Top, Right, Bottom: Integer);
    1: (TopLeft, BottomRight: TPoint);
end;
```

The case statement encapsulated inside this record informs the compiler that there are two different ways to treat this same record.

Consider the following code fragment, which compiles smoothly under Delphi:

```
var
  R1, R2 : TRect;

begin
  R1.Left := 10;
  R1.Top := 10;
  R1.Right := 100;
  R1.Bottom := 100;
  R2.TopLeft.X := 20;
  R2.TopLeft.Y := 20;
  R2.BottomRight.X := 120;
  R2.BottomRight.Y := 120;
end;
```

As you can see, it is possible to treat two variables of the same type in two quite distinct manners. In one case, you regard its fields as integers called Left, Top, Right, and Bottom. In the second case, you treat the same type as having fields called TopLeft and TopRight.

To see how this works, you can run the VARIANT1 program, which, as always, is located on your disks. The form for the VARIANT1 program is left unchanged. There are no buttons or other controls added. The code for the program is shown in Listing 13.1.

Listing 13.1. The VARIANT1 program shows how to use variant records.

```pascal
unit Main;

interface

uses
  WinTypes, WinProcs, Classes,
  Graphics, StdCtrls,  Controls,
  Forms;

type
  TForm1 = class(TForm)
    procedure FormPaint(Sender: TObject);
  end;

var
  Form1: TForm1;

implementation

{$R *.DFM}

procedure TForm1.FormPaint(Sender: TObject);
var
  R1, R2 : TRect;
begin
  R1.Left := 10;
  R1.Top := 10;
  R1.Right := 100;
  R1.Bottom := 100;
  R2.TopLeft.X := 20;
  R2.TopLeft.Y := 20;
  R2.BottomRight.X := 110;
  R2.BottomRight.Y := 110;
  Canvas.Brush.Color := RGB(255, 255, 0);
  Canvas.Rectangle(R1.Left, R1.Top, R1.Right, R1.Bottom);
  Canvas.Brush.Color := RGB(0, 255, 255);
  Canvas.Rectangle(R2.TopLeft.X, R2.TopLeft.Y,
                  R2.BottomRight.X, R2.BottomRight.y);
end;

end.
```

The VARIANT1 program paints two overlapping rectangles on the screen, as shown in Figure 13.7. The first rectangle is located at coordinates 10, 10, 100, 100, and the second rectangle is located at coordinates 20, 20, 110, 110.

FIGURE 13.7.

The form for the VARIANT1 program depicts two rectangles laid one on top of the other.

The key function in the VARIANT1 program is the FormPaint method. This method is really divided into two sections. The first declares the coordinates of the two rectangles:

```
procedure TForm1.FormPaint(Sender: TObject);
var
  R1, R2 : TRect;
begin
  R1.Left := 10;
  R1.Top := 10;
  R1.Right := 100;
  R1.Bottom := 100;
  R2.TopLeft.X := 20;
  R2.TopLeft.Y := 20;
  R2.BottomRight.X := 110;
  R2.BottomRight.Y := 110;
  ...
```

This portion of the code was explained earlier in this chapter.

The following code is used to actually paint the rectangles to the screen:

```
  ...
  Canvas.Brush.Color := RGB(255, 255, 0);
  Canvas.Rectangle(R1.Left, R1.Top, R1.Right, R1.Bottom);
  Canvas.Brush.Color := RGB(0, 255, 255);
  Canvas.Rectangle(R2.TopLeft.X, R2.TopLeft.Y,
                   R2.BottomRight.X, R2.BottomRight.Y);
end;
```

The code shown here sets the form's brush to a bright yellow and then paints the first rectangle to the screen. The next step is to change the brush's color to a light blue and paint a second rectangle to the screen.

If you are starting to understand how variant records work, it should come as no surprise that it makes no difference to the compiler if you draw the second rectangle to the screen with the following calls:

```
  Canvas.Brush.Color := RGB(255, 255, 0);
  Canvas.Rectangle(R1.Left, R1.Top, R1.Right, R1.Bottom);
  Canvas.Brush.Color := RGB(0, 255, 255);
  Canvas.Rectangle(R2.Left, R2.Top, R2.Right, R2.Bottom);
```

In short, it is possible to declare a TRect using one form of a variant record, and then to write it to the screen using a second form:

```
  R2.TopLeft.X := 20;
  R2.TopLeft.Y := 20;
  R2.BottomRight.X := 110;
  R2.BottomRight.Y := 110;
  Canvas.Rectangle(R2.Left, R2.Top, R2.Right, R2.Bottom);
```

In fact, there is no reason why you can't mix up the two forms as shamelessly as your heart desires:

```
  R2.TopLeft.X := 20;
  R2.TopLeft.Y := 20;
  R2.Right := 110;
```

```
    R2.Bottom := 110;
    Canvas.Rectangle(R2.TopLeft.Y, R2.Top,
                     R2.BottomRight.X, R2.Bottom);
```

All of these examples are using variable R2 to draw a rectangle with coordinates 20, 20, 110, and 110. The compiler doesn't care which syntax you use; it regards them all in the exact same way. Other programmers, however, might find the last two examples to be a bit confusing, so you should probably avoid that kind of syntax unless you have some obvious reason for wanting to work that way.

More on Variant Records

People who are familiar with the C/C++ extravaganza have probably recognized a parallel between variant records and what the good folks from AT&T called a *union*. Unions enable you to bring records of various sizes together under a single aegis. Variant records, of course, enable you to do the same thing.

Suppose an entirely hypothetical veterinarian named Dr. Gladys Day needed to keep track of several different kinds of animals. Suppose further that Gladys had a rather peculiar specialty in caring for animal's legs. In such a circumstance, Gladys might decide that she needed some data structures that looked like this:

```
type
  TLegType = (Healthy, Damaged);

  TLegs = Record
    Right,
    Left: TLegType;
  end;

  TAnimal = Record
    FrontLeg: TLegs;
    BackLeg: TLegs
  end;

var
  Animal: TAnimal;
```

These structures would enable Gladys to write code that looks like this:

```
Animal.FrontLeg.Right := Healthy;
```

All in all, a syntax of this type is pretty much the Holy Grail of programmers who aim to write clear, maintainable code. Even a nonprogrammer would probably understand what this code means at a single glance. Besides being readily comprehensible, this code is also compact and very fast.

The only problem with Gladys' fine work is that it doesn't adequately capture the situation she encounters when she works with her feathered friends from the aviary. Birds, of course, have only two legs. As a result, the TAnimal structure doesn't quite suit the case as adequately as possible.

In situations such as this, it might be time to introduce a variant record:

```
type
  TLegType = (Healthy, Damaged);

  TAnimalEnum = (Mammal, Bird, Reptile, Insect);

  TLegs = Record
    Right,
    Left: TLegType;
  end;

  TAnimal = Record
    AnimalType: TAnimalEnum;
    case TAnimalEnum of
      Mammal:(MFrontLeg: TLegs;
              MBackLeg: TLegs);
      Bird:(BLegs: TLegs);
      Reptile: (RFrontLeg: TLegs;
                RBackLeg: TLegs);
      Insect: (Foreleg: TLegs;
               MidLeg: TLegs;
               BackLeg: TLegs);
  end;
```

This code uses an enumerated type to divide the animal kingdom up into mammals, birds, reptiles, and insects. A variant record is then used to cope with the varying number of legs that might belong to a particular animal.

For instance, if the animal was a mammal, it would have four legs:

```
TAnimal = Record
  MFrontLeg: TLegs;
  MBackLeg: TLegs;
end;
```

If Gladys' thriving insect business was involved, the animal would have six legs:

```
TAnimal = Record
  Foreleg: TLegs;
  MidLeg: TLegs;
  BackLeg: TLegs);
end;
```

The initial field of the record, called AnimalType, is used to help programmers differentiate the types of records. For instance, if Gladys decides to write a procedure that takes a TAnimal variable as a parameter, she would need some way of knowing whether the record being passed in was for a mammal, bird, reptile, or insect. The field called AnimalType resolves this problem. Gladys can set the field to Mammal when she is working with a four-legged creature and to Bird when she is working with a two-legged creature.

There is, however, no need to include a field of this type. If Gladys had wanted, she could have defined the record like this:

```
TFooAnimal = Record
  case TAnimalEnum of
```

```
     Mammal:(MFrontLeg: TLegs;
             MBackLeg: TLegs);
     Bird:(BLegs: TLegs);
     Reptile: (RFrontLeg: TLegs;
               RBackLeg: TLegs);
     Insect: (Foreleg: TLegs;
              MidLeg: TLegs;
              BackLeg: TLegs);
  end;
```

The only problem with this system is that it would make it difficult to distinguish one type of record from another. There would be no way of checking whether the record described a bird or a mammal, for example.

One final point needs to be made about variant records. Obviously a record that keeps track of insects is going to need to be larger than a record that keeps track of birds. Here is the record for tracking birds:

```
TAnimal = Record
   Leg: TLegs;
end;
```

Here is the record for tracking insects:

```
TAnimal = Record
   Foreleg: TLegs;
   MidLeg: TLegs;
   BackLeg: TLegs;
end;
```

The first record will take up 4 bytes of space, and the second will take up 16.

Delphi deals with this situation by always allocating enough space for the largest possible record. In this case, that would be 7 bytes, 6 to hold an insect, and 1 more to handle the enumerated variable designating the type of animal being described.

Using TNotebook: Gladys' Animal Program

I have spent almost as much time in this chapter discussing variant records as I have discussing normal records. That ratio does not reflect real-world usage of the two types of records. About 95 percent of the time, you will be working with regular records instead of variant records. However, variant records are useful, and some of the them, such as TRect, play a big part in Delphi programming.

Here you see an example that embodies some of the solutions to Gladys' problems with her animal program. The form for this application uses a TNoteBook, which can be useful under certain circumstances.

TNoteBooks work well with variant records because they enable you to open up a window in a form that can have different controls in it depending on the circumstances. For instance, Figures 13.8 through 13.11 show different views of the form for Gladys' animal program. Each view features a different screen from the program's notebook.

FIGURE 13.8.

The notebook in the middle of the form is useful for working with insects.

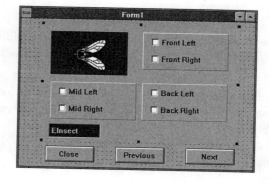

FIGURE 13.9.

The notebook in the middle of the form is useful for working with birds.

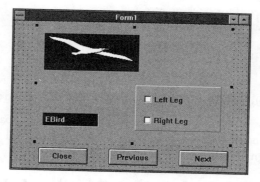

FIGURE 13.10.

The notebook in the middle of the form is useful for working with reptiles.

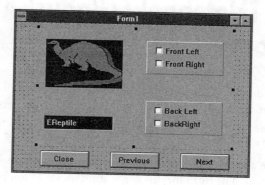

FIGURE 13.11.

The notebook in the middle of the form is useful for working with mammals.

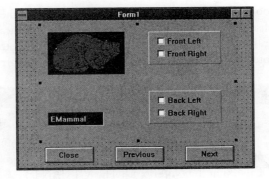

A notebook has two properties that you need to understand. One of the properties is called Pages, and the second is called ActivePage. Use the Pages property to define the number and names of the pages you want your TNoteBook to handle. As shown in Figure 13.12, the notebook for the VARIANT2 program has four pages in it, called `Bird`, `Insect`, `Mammal`, and `Reptile`.

FIGURE 13.12.

Selecting the Pages property from a notebook enables you to designate the number and names of the pages you want to use.

After you have used the Pages property to define the pages in your control, you can use the ActivePage option to select any one particular page. For instance, the page Gladys needs to work with birds has two radio buttons in it, one for the left leg and the other for the right leg. The page also has an edit control for displaying the animal's name, and it has a TImage control from the Additional palette on the toolbar.

Notebooks are easy to work with once you get over an initial conceptual hurdle. I like to think of notebooks as being similar to a stack of those little 3×5-inch cards that teachers used to encourage students to use when preparing lectures or papers. Only the top card in the stack can be seen at any one time. If you want to see the next card, slide off the top card of the stack, which reveals the one beneath it. The card you just finished using goes back on the stack so you can get it later if you need it.

A notebook is just like those little cards. Only one of them is visible at a time, and it completely obscures its fellows, which are, at least metaphorically, hidden beneath it. The Object Inspector, Editor, Compiler Options dialog, and several other parts of the Delphi environment all use notebooks, or some variation on notebooks, as part of their interface.

> **NOTE**
>
> It is not at all uncommon to combine notebooks with TTabSet controls. The VARIANT2 program, however, doesn't use them. In the same subdirectory as the other programs from this chapter, I have also created a program called VARIANT3, which uses TTabSets and TNoteBooks. The VARIANT3 program is not discussed in this book, but the code is commented. Other examples using TTabSet controls are the EASYSQL2 program and the LIFE program, both of which are found on the CD.

> **NOTE**
>
> The code for the VARIANT2 program is in the CHAP13 directory on this book's CD-ROM.

At this stage, you should be sure to go to the computer and run the VARIANT2 program. This program is not a complete answer to the problem of how to track injuries in animals' legs, but it does point the way toward some kind of acceptable solution. The key to the program, of course, is the notebook, which presents a slightly different interface for each of the four major classes of animals that Gladys encounters. The use of a TImage control containing a small picture helps to make the interface more—dare I say it—user-friendly. In particular, it helps sort out the various pages shown to the user, any one of which could easily be confused with another were it not for the visual clue provided by the bitmap.

It takes only a brief glance at the code for the VARIANT2 program to understand why I said that notebooks have only a very limited scope. The problem, of course, is that the controls placed on the separate screens of a notebook soon take up an unreasonably large amount of space inside the TForm1 object declaration. The LIFE program, included on the CD, but not discussed in this book, shows a workaround for this problem.

In the particular example shown here, the number of controls shown is probably just barely within the manageable range. In particular, you see that I use various different popular schemes to help tame the diversity:

■ If I choose not to accept the default name assigned to a control, I generally begin my identifier with an abbreviation that specifies the control's type. For instance, I place the letters CB before a checkbox, and E before an edit control.

■ I generally append a letter to the end of an identifier that specifies which page it appears on. For instance, I append an R to checkboxes on the Reptile page, and I append an M to checkboxes on the Mammal page.

■ Finally, I make the names themselves as meaningful as possible. For instance, I use names such as FrontRight and BackLeft for the front-right leg and back-left leg, respectively. Also, I try to remain consistent in my naming convention, so that the front legs of all animals are called FrontLeft and FrontRight.

These types of naming conventions are widely used throughout the industry. In particular, the whole idea of specifying a variable's type by adding a prefix was popularized by a famous Microsoft programmer named Charles Simonyi. Though this technique can sometimes make code look unnecessarily cluttered or opaque, it can, under some circumstances, help to bring some order to a confusing landscape.

VARIANT2 lists about 30 controls that are placed on the notebook. In my opinion, if you exceed this number by any considerable amount, you should consider combining several separate forms in a way that makes them appear to be part of a single entity such as a notebook. In that way you can limit the number of controls listed as fields for any particular object. This technique is used in the LIFE program, included on the CD.

The only other point that needs to be made about the VARIANT2 program is the method used to fill out the checkboxes on any one page:

```
procedure TForm1.SetData;
begin
  case Animals[CurRec].AnimalType of
    Mammal: ...;
    Reptile: ...;
    Insect: ...;
    Bird: ...;
  end; { Case }
end;
```

The code shown here is a stripped-down version of the case statement that governs the SetData procedure. It ensures that note is taken of the type of animal whose condition is displayed in the notebook.

Here is the way one portion of the case statement is actually handled:

```
    Bird: begin
      NoteBook1.CurrentPage := 'Bird';
      with Animals[CurRec] do begin
        EBird.Text := Name;
        CBLeftLegB.Check := TCheckBoxCheck(BLegs.Left);
        CBRightLegB.Check := TCheckBoxCheck(BLegs.Right);
      end;
        Form1.Caption := 'Bird: ' + IntToStr(CurRec);
    end;
```

This code is called if the current record describes the state of a bird's legs.

The first step in the preceding statement is to select the screen from the notebook that has a picture of a bird on it. The next four lines fill in the controls on the Bird page with the name of the current animal and the state of its legs.

The following line contains another typecast:

```
CBLeftLegB.Check := TCheckBoxCheck(BLegs.Left);
```

To understand what this code says, you have to note that checkboxes can be set to one of three states, which are defined in CONTROLS.PAS:

```
TCheckBoxCheck = (cbUnchecked, cbChecked, cbGrayed);
```

If you compare this enumerated type with the type declared at the top of MAIN.PAS, you can see that they are quite similar:

```
TLegType = (Healthy, Damaged);
```

The key point here is that the Healthy state has a value of 0 and the Damaged state has a value of 1. Running parallel to this arrangement are cbUnchecked and cbChecked, which have values of 0 and 1, respectively. This means that there is a direct correspondence between the identifiers Healthy and cbUnchecked, as well as between Damaged and cbChecked.

If BLegs.Left equals Healthy, the checkbox for the left leg should remain unchecked; that is, it should be assigned a value of cbUnchecked. Because Healthy and cbUnchecked both have a value of 0, it is possible to write

```
CBLeftLegB.Check := TCheckBoxCheck(BLegs.Left);
```

The typecast tells the compiler, in effect: "Yes, I know that CBLeftLegB.Check is of type TCheckBoxCheck, and I know that BLegs.Left is of type TLegType. But trust me, for now it will work out okay if you pretend they are of the same type."

ObjectPascal's great strength is that it forms an unsurpassed bridge between the human mind and the inner workings of a computer. Some languages hone closer to the computer's way of thinking, and others more artfully encompass the way people think. Delphi, however, lays claim to both worlds. Its syntax is natural and accessible to the human mind, while at the same time closely mirroring the actual processes that drive a computer. Those who have mastered the language find that it forms a powerful bridge that spans the gap between your intentions and the computer's capabilities.

Storing Records in a File

If you want to store a record in a file, Delphi provides a special means of achieving this end called a *file of record*. When using a product such as Delphi, there will be many times when you will prefer to use Paradox files, dBASE files, or a server, rather than a file of record. However, using a professional database can add two- or three-hundred kilobytes to your executable, plus the cost of distributing more than a megabyte worth of BDE DLLs. It can also slow down the program's performance, particularly when it is first being loaded into memory. As a result, at times it is considerably simpler to use a file of record, which is very fast and has virtually no overhead.

Consider the record introduced in the following code:

```
TAge = Record
  FName: String;
  LName: String;
  Age: Integer;
end;
```

If you wanted to store this record in a file, you would first declare a file variable that looked like this:

```
var
  AgeFile: File of TAge;
```

This declaration tells the compiler that you plan to work with a file that is tailor-made to hold records of type TAge. Furthermore, when you actually open the file and start reading from it or writing to it, you can use the variable AgeFile as a way of referencing it.

Here is how to open and read the first record from an existing file of record:

```
var
  AgeFile: File of TAge;
  AgeRec: TAge;

begin
  Assign(AgeFile, 'MYFILE.DTA');
  Reset(AgeFile);
  Read(AgeFile, AgeRec);
  Close(AgeFile);
end;
```

This code first uses the Assign procedure to associate the variable AgeFile with a disk file called MYFILE.DTA. The next step is to use Reset to open the file. If a file called MYFILE.DTA does not exist in the current subdirectory, the code shown here would cause an error when Reset is called. Finally, the Read procedure can be used to read the first record from the file. The first parameter passed to Read is the file variable from which the record is to be read, and the second variable is the structure into which the record will be placed. A second call to Read would cause the second record in the file to be read, and so on, until there are no more records left:

```
while not EOF(AgeFile) do
  Read(AgeFile, AgeRec);
```

In this example, the EOF function is used to detect when you have reached the end of a file.

Here is the proper way to create a file of record, and to begin writing to it:

```
var
  AgeFile: File of TAge;
```

```
  AgeRec: TAge;

begin
  AgeRec.FName := 'Eric';
  AgeRec.LName := 'Rohmer';
  AgeRec.Age := 42;
  Assign(AgeFile, 'MYFILE.DTA');
  ReWrite(AgeFile);
  Write(AgeFile, AgeRec);
  Close(AgeFile);
end;
```

Notice that the code shown here called ReWrite instead of Reset. ReWrite will always create a new file, even if an existing file of the same name already exists. This means that you have to be careful with the ReWrite statement, because it can completely erase a perfectly valid file if you accidentally use it when you meant to call Reset.

> **NOTE**
>
> There is no way to insert a record into the middle of a file of record. Instead, you need to read the entire file into memory, insert a new record into your array, and finally rewrite the entire array to disk. You can, however, overwrite any record in a file of record simply by using the Seek command to move to a particular location, and then calling Write.

The AGES3 program on the CD gives you a brief example of how to read and write from a file of record. The program uses the AGES2 program as a starting point.

> **NOTE**
>
> The code for the AGES3 program is in the CHAP13 directory on this book's CD-ROM.

The AGES3 program uses something called a *conditional define*. This enables you to write one program that can be compiled in two different ways, depending on how you want to use it. At the top of the program you see a statement that looks like this:

```
{.$Define InitValues}
```

If you remove the period from the front of this statement, it defines a value called InitValues:

```
{$Define InitValues}
```

InitValues is just an arbitrarily chosen identifier. I could have used Foo, SetValues, or virtually any other word in its place.

Conditional defines enable you to tell the compiler to record a particular piece of code when a value is defined, and to ignore that section of code if the value is not defined:

```
{$IfDef InitValues}
const
  AgeArray: TAgeArray = (
      (FName: 'J.E.B.'; LName: 'Stuart'; Age: 30),
      (FName: 'James'; LName: 'Longstreet'; Age: 42),
      (FName: 'George'; LName: 'Pickett'; Age: 38),
      (FName: 'Richard'; LName: 'Ewell'; Age: 46),
      (FName: 'Lewis'; LName: 'Armistead'; Age: 46),
      (FName: 'Frank'; LName: 'Borland'; Age: 45),
      (FName: 'Lewis'; LName: 'Carrol'; Age: 29));
{$EndIf}
```

The {$IfDef} statement at the beginning of this declaration tells the compiler that it should be included in the compilation only if the identifier InitValues is defined. The end of the section designated for special treatment is marked by the {$EndIf} statement.

> **NOTE**
>
> Code that exists within a conditional block that is not defined will not be seen at all by the compiler. It does not add to the size of the final executable, and it makes only a minimal impact on compilation time.

If you remove the period from before the conditional symbol

```
{$Define InitValues}
```

the program will compile in a mode that enables it to see the constant array of data declared at the top of module Main. In this mode, you can then choose the Write button, and the data will be written to disk. Now close the program and restore the period before the InitValues conditional define:

```
{.$Define InitValues}
```

Placing the period in this position ensures that InitValues is never defined. When you then recompile the program, you can read the data from disk, modify it, and rewrite it.

The key methods in the AGES3 program are ReadClick and WriteClick:

```
procedure TForm1.ReadClick(Sender: TObject);
var
  AgeFile: File of TAge;
  i: Integer;

begin
  System.Assign(AgeFile, 'MYFILE.DTA');
  Reset(AgeFile);
  i := 1;
```

```
  while not EOF(AgeFile) do begin
    System.Read(AgeFile, AgeArray[i]);
    Inc(I);
  end;
  System.Close(AgeFile);
  SetData;
end;
```

The `ReadClick` method first assigns `AgeFile` to the file on disk called MYFILE.DTA. It then opens the file by calling `Reset`, and proceeds to iterate over all the records in the file, reading each in turn into `AgeArray`. After it has read all the records, the next step is to close the file and display the first record to the user.

`WriteClick` returns the data to disk, preserving any changes you might have made while the program was running:

```
procedure TForm1.WriteClick(Sender: TObject);
var
  AgeFile: File of TAge;
  AgeRec: TAge;
  i: Integer;

begin
  System.Assign(AgeFile, 'MYFILE.DTA');
  ReWrite(AgeFile);
  for i := 1 to Max do
    System.Write(AgeFile, AgeArray[i]);
  System.Close(AgeFile);
end;
```

Remember that the call to `ReWrite` ensures that any existing copy of MYFILE.DTA will be erased, and that a new copy can then be written in its place. After writing the records to the file, it is essential that you call `System.Close`. If you omit the call to `Close`, you might experience a loss of data that will become apparent the next time you try to read the records back into memory.

Clearly, this program shows the beginnings of a real database. However, an array of record is not a good way to store databases that might have varying numbers of records in them. Instead, you should use a linked list, as described in Chapter 16, "Pointers, Linked Lists, and Memory." This is not to say that it's impossible to work out a scheme for storing variable numbers of records in an array of records, but only that it's not the best structure to use for this purpose.

Summary

In this chapter you learned how to work with records. Grasping this topic leaves an open path between you and the broad subject of objects, which is covered two chapters hence.

In this chapter you also learned how to work with the `MessageDlg` function and the various types associated with it. The last portion of the chapter dealt briefly with the `TNoteBook` component, as well as basic file I/O.

In general, this was not a particularly difficult chapter, though some aspects of variant records might be confusing to newcomers. As usual, the key point is to be sure you were able to follow the majority of the discussion in the chapter.

Strings and Text Files

14

Overview

This chapter takes an in-depth look at strings. You have worked with them many times already, but there are a number of features associated with them that I haven't yet had a chance to explore. This chapter also explores text files, which provide a simple mechanism for storing strings in a file.

The first part of the chapter demonstrates that strings are really only a form of array. However, a number of interesting rules specific to strings do not apply to arrays, and my goal is to explore the most important of them in very explicit detail. In particular, you will see how to search for a substring in a string and how to parse a lengthy string.

Once you understand how strings work, the next subject to approach is how to store them in text files, and how to retrieve them again from those text files. While pursuing this subject, you get a chance to see how one goes about storing numbers in a text file.

The final section of the chapter explores ways of parsing the contents of a text file and of converting the information found there into fundamental Delphi types.

A String Is Just a Form of an Array

A string is very similar, but not identical, to an array of characters. Consider the following declarations:

```
type
  TNearString = array[0..255] of Char;

var
  NearString: TNearString;
  MyString: string;
```

In this code fragment, `MyString` has all the traits of `TNearString`, plus a few special qualities. In other words, a string is a superset of an array of `char` that is 256 characters long. The first section of this chapter delineates exactly what special qualities belong to a string that do not belong to an array of `char`.

All characters in an array of `char` are equal. No one character has any special properties. In a string, however, the first character is called a *length byte*. The length byte designates how many significant characters exist inside the string. Because the first character has this special task, the first meaningful letter is always at offset one in the string.

> **NOTE**
>
> In the paragraphs that follow, you need to remember that most `chars` can be represented in two different ways. For instance, the letter A can be printed verbatim or it can be represented by the 65th member in certain character sets. If you want to refer to

the letter A by its place in a character set, you can write #65. The # in this example designates that the item in question is a char, not a simple numerical value. Therefore, the number 5 is represented as 5, but the fifth character in a character set is represented by #5. If you are having trouble grasping these concepts, you might want to refer to Chapter 7, "Integers in Detail."

Consider, for a moment, a string containing the word Hello. This string is five characters long, so the first byte in a string containing this word would be set to the fifth character in a table of characters:

```
NearString[0] := #5;
```

The next character in the array would be an H:

```
NearString[1] := 'H';   { H = #72 }
```

The rest of the letters would follow immediately after:

```
NearString[2] := 'e';
NearString[3] := 'l';
NearString[4] := 'l';
NearString[5] := 'o';
```

The end result is an array of six characters that look like this:

```
#5,'H','e','l','l','o'
```

If you took the whole process to the memory theater, what you would see is six seats lined up in a row. The guy in the first seat would be told to remember the total number of letters in the word, or words that are part of the string. The woman in the second seat would remember the first letter of the string, which in this case is H. The person in the next seat would remember the letter E, and so on.

So far so good. But what about the remaining 250 characters in the string? The answer is that it does not matter what information is stored in those bytes. They can be zeroed out, or they can hold nothing but garbage. It doesn't matter, as long as the first byte is correctly set to the total number of valid characters in the string.

If the length byte in the preceding example was accidentally set to #6 instead of to #5, then whatever letter happened to be on the mind of the person in seat seven would automatically become part of the string, usually with disastrous results. For instance, the string Hello might suddenly become any of the following:

```
Hello1
Hellob
Hello#
Hello+
```

In short, the behavior you can expect to see is entirely undefined in such situations.

The code shown here will compile and run without error:

```
var
  S: string;
begin
  S[0] := #5;
  S[1] := 'H';
  S[2] := 'e';
  S[3] := 'l';
  S[4] := 'l';
  S[5] := 'o';
  Edit1.Text := S;
end;
```

This code prints the word Hello inside an edit control. You can view this code fragment as the anatomy of a string. It shows explicitly the various parts that go into making a string.

The following code behaves in a manner identical to the code shown earlier:

```
var
  S: string;
begin
  S := 'Hello';
  Edit1.Text := S;
end;
```

This fragment is easier to write than the code shown previously. However, the fact that you can write code like this is really a special feature of the compiler. What it actually does is shown in the first example. However, it would be too much trouble to have you go through that lengthy process every time you wanted to assign a value to a string. Therefore, the compiler lets you write code like the second example.

The following short sample program, called EASYSTR, demonstrates the ideas presented in this section. Specifically, EASYSTR shows what happens if you don't treat the length byte in a string with care.

The form for the EASYSTR program includes two buttons and an edit control, as shown in Figure 14.1.

FIGURE 14.1.

To create the form for the EASYSTR program, simply drop two buttons, a panel, and a label onto a form.

NOTE

The code for the EASYSTR program is in the CHAP14 directory on this book's CD-ROM.

The EASYSTR program enables you to print a valid string and an invalid string inside an edit control. The invalid string is flawed because it has an incorrect length byte. In particular, it sets the length byte to 150, although the string you want to print is only five characters long.

This simple mistake would cause trouble in your program. However, I want to make sure you get a sense of what is going wrong, so I have added another procedure to the function that ensures that all the characters in a string get set to random values:

```
procedure ScrambleString(var S: String);
var
  i: Integer;
begin
  for i := 0 to 255 do
    S[i] := Chr(Random(255));
end;
```

This function sets all the characters in a string to random values between 0 and 255. It does this by using the Random function, which returns a random number between zero and the value passed in its sole parameter. In this case, however, the goal is not to produce a random number, but a random character. To achieve this end, the Chr function is used. As you recall, Chr is used to convert a numerical value into a character.

> **NOTE**
>
> There is no significant difference between using the Chr function and just typecasting the value returned from the random function:
>
> ```
> S[i] := Char(Random(255));
> ```
>
> This code produces the same result as when the Chr function is used.

Figure 14.2 depicts what can happen when you try to write a string to an edit control with the length byte set to an arbitrarily large value. Clearly the result is less than optimal. Random characters are scattered across the component like some kind of hieroglyphic, and the word "Hello" is discernible only after you study the output in some depth.

FIGURE 14.2.

If the length byte of string is set to the wrong value, the results can be fairly chaotic.

You can compare the general fiasco shown in Figure 14.2 with the orderly results shown in Figure 14.3. In this second case, the compiler is passed a valid length byte and the results are precisely defined and readily understandable.

FIGURE 14.3.

No matter how you scramble the extra characters in a string, the result shown to the screen will be fine as long as the length byte is assigned a valid value.

Zero-Terminated Strings

Before going on to discuss strings in more depth, I'll spend a moment talking about PChars, zero-terminated strings, and the correct way to use an array of char as a string.

A zero-terminated string has no length byte. Instead, the processor searches for a #0 character and assumes that this marks the end of a string. Specifically, if you go back to the examples shown in the last section, you can easily modify the functions so that they will print out a properly formatted zero-terminated string:

```
procedure TForm1.BCharsClick(Sender: TObject);
var
  S: array[0..25] of Char;
begin
  S[0] := 'H';
  S[1] := 'e';
  S[2] := 'l';
  S[3] := 'l';
  S[4] := 'o';
  S[5] := #0;
  Edit1.Text := S;
end;
```

This code prints the word Hello in a neat and orderly fashion. To do this, it sets the first character of a zero-terminated string to the letter H and sets the sixth character to the value of the first member of the currently selected character set. It is important to remember that you don't end zero-terminated strings with the number zero—you end them with #0. As you saw back in Chapter 7, "Integers in Detail," the number zero is usually the 48th member of a standard character set. It is entirely distinct from the first member of that character set.

Frequently, when you work with zero-terminated strings, you refer to them as a special type called a PChar. PChars are pointers to arrays of char, and as a result you must allocate memory for them before you try to use them. For instance, in the following code I explicitly allocate 26 bytes of memory for a PChar before filling it in with characters and displaying it on the screen. When I am finished, I then deallocate that memory.

```
procedure TForm1.BCharsClick(Sender: TObject);
var
  S: PChar;
begin
  GetMem(S, 26);
  StrCopy(S, 'Hello');
  Edit1.Text := StrPas(S);
```

```
  FreeMem(S, 26);
end;
```

When you allocate memory for a pointer, it is as if someone goes out into the memory theater and specifically tells a certain number of people that they are now part of a particular allocation. In this example, for instance, 26 members of the audience are grouped together under the aegis of a single PChar.

Devotees of the C/C++ language will notice that Delphi has a function called StrCopy that mirrors the job performed by strcpy in the land that AT&T made. That is, it copies one string into another. There are also functions called StrCat, StrPos, StrCmp, and so on, if you have occasion to need them. The StrPas function converts a PChar into a string.

If you want to learn a little more about PChars, you can take a look at the EASYSTR2 program, which is on this book's CD. It enables you to use the two functions shown previously.

For now, however, I'm going to back away from the subject of zero-terminated strings, content to have done little more than introduce the subject. My goal here is not yet to explain this second type of string in any detail, but only to introduce the topic so that no one is taken by surprise when they come across these types of strings in their day-to-day work.

As I hinted earlier, PChars become very important when you start working directly with the Windows API functions. That means that sooner or later you will encounter them. Because of their importance, I discuss them in depth in the next chapter, "Pointers and PChars."

Working with Strings

It is time now to explore some real-world examples of the kind of challenges you might face when working with strings. One classic problem that comes up fairly frequently is that you might need to strip blanks off the end of a string. Consider the following code fragment:

```
uses
  MathBox;

procedure TForm1.Button1Click(Sender: TObject);
var
  S: String;
  R: Real;
begin
  S := '2.03      ';
  R := Str2Real(S);
  WriteLn(R:2:2);
end;
```

At first glance you might expect this code to print the number 2.03 to the screen. However, it will not because Str2Real is unable to handle the extra spaces appended after the characters 2.03.

It is quite likely that a problem similar to this could occur in a real-world program. For instance, a programmer might ask the user to enter a string, and the user might accidentally append a series of blanks to it, or perhaps the extra characters were added by some other means.

To be sure that your program will run correctly, you have to strip those extra blank characters off the end of your string.

The following function, called `StripBlanks`, can be used to remove space characters from the end of a string:

```
function StripBlanks(S: string): string;
var
  i: Integer;
begin
  i := Length(S);
  while S[i] = ' ' do begin
    Delete(S,i,1);
    Dec(i);
  end;
  StripBlanks := S;
end;
```

This function will not change the string that you pass into it, but creates a second string that it passes back to you as the function result. This means you must use this function in the following manner:

```
S2 := StripBlanks(S1);
```

where S1 and S2 are both strings. You also can write code that looks like this:

```
S1 := StripBlanks(S1);
```

StripBlanks has one local variable, i, which is an integer:

```
var
  i: Integer;
```

This variable is set to the length of the string passed to the function:

```
  i := Length(S);
```

The length function is one of the simplest and fastest executing routines in the ObjectPascal language. In effect, it does nothing more than this:

```
function Length(S: String): Integer;
begin
  Length := Ord(S[0]);
end;
```

In short, it returns the value of the length byte that is the first character of a string.

The next line in the function checks the value of the last character in the string under investigation:

```
  while S[i] = ' ' do begin
```

More explicitly, it checks to see whether it is a blank. If it is a blank, the following code is executed:

```
Delete(S,i,1);
Dec(i);
```

The built-in `Delete` function takes three parameters. The first is a string, the second is an offset into the string, and the third is the number of characters you want to delete from the first parameter. In this case, if you passed in the string `Sam   `, which is the word Sam followed by three spaces, the last space would be lopped off so that the string would become `Sam  `, where Sam is followed by two spaces.

The function decrements the value of `i` and then returns to the top of the loop to see if the next character is a space:

```
while S[i] = ' ' do begin
```

If it is, that character is also deleted from the end of the string.

The entire process is repeated until the last character in the string is no longer a space. At that point, the function ends, and a string is returned that is guaranteed not to have any spaces appended on the end of it.

Becoming familiar with functions such as `StripBlanks` is essential for all serious programmers. It isn't really that this one particular function is so important, although I do end up using it fairly often. What is crucial here is that `StripBlanks` is the kind of function that solves a common problem likely to be encountered by programmers, and furthermore, it does so by bearing down and manipulating a chunk of data on a byte-by-byte basis.

Date-Based Filenames

This section presents another function for manipulating strings. This function is not likely to be used every day by most programmers, but when you need it, it comes in very handy indeed. The primary reason for showing it, however, is just to give an example of working with strings.

Programmers often end up making reports or gathering data on a daily basis. For instance, I sign onto an online service nearly every day, and frequently I want to store the information I glean from cyberspace inside a file that contains the current date. In other words, if I sign onto CompuServe and download the current messages from the Delphi forum, I don't want to store that information in a file called DELPHI.CIS. I want a filename that includes the current date, so that I can easily tell what files were downloaded on a particular day. In short, I want to automatically generate filenames that look like this: DE022595.TXT, PA022695.TXT, DE022795.TXT, and so on, where 022795 is a date of the type MMDDYY.

Here is a function that fits the bill:

```
{- - - - - - - - - - - - - - - - - - - - - - - - - - - - - - - - - - - - -
       Name: GetTodayName function
Declaration: GetTodayName(Pre, Ext: String): String;
       Unit: StrBox
       Code: S
       Date: 03/01/94
```

```
Description: Return a filename of type PRE0101.EXT,
             where PRE and EXT are user supplied strings,
             and 0101 is today's date. PRE must not be
             longer than 2 letters.
-----------------------------------------------------}
function GetTodayName(Pre, Ext: String): String;
var
  y, m, d, dow : Word;
begin
  GetDate(y,m,d,dow);
  Year := Int2StrPad0(y, 4);
  Delete(Year, 1, 2);
  GetTodayName := Pre + Int2StrPad0(m, 2) +
                  Int2StrPad0(d, 2) +
                  Year + '.' + Ext;
end;
```

This function, demonstrated online in EASYFILE.DPR, takes a two-letter prefix and a three-letter extension, and creates a filename of the type shown previously. The function begins by calling the built-in Pascal function GetDate, which returns the current year, month, day, and day of week as Word values. If the date were Tuesday, March 25, 1994, the function would return the following:

```
Year         := 1994
Month        := 3
Day          := 25
Day-of-Week  := 2      { 0 = Sunday }
```

Assuming that the user of this function passed in DE in the PRE parameter, and TXT in the EXT parameter, it would be fairly easy to use the IntToStr function to create something like this:

DE3251994.TXT

There are several problems with this result, the biggest being that it is 12 characters in length, which is too long for a legal filename. To resolve the problem, it would be nice to be able to change the month to a number such as 03, to keep the day as 25, and to strip the 19 from the year:

DE032594.TXT

To achieve that end, GetTodayName needs a special function that will not only convert a number to a string, but also pad it with an appropriate quantity of zeros. The following function fits the bill:

```
{-----------------------------------------------------
        Name: Int2StrPad0 function
 Declaration: Int2StrPad0(N: LongInt; Len: Integer): String;
        Unit: MathBox
        Code: N
        Date: 03/01/94
 Description: Converts a number into a string and pads
             the string with zeros if it is less than
             Len characters long.
-----------------------------------------------------}
```

```
function Int2StrPad0(N: LongInt; Len: Integer): String;
var
  S : String;
begin
  Str(N:0,S);
  while Length(S) < Len do
    S := '0' + S;
  Int2StrPad0 := S;
end;;
```

This very useful function first uses the built-in Pascal routine called Str to convert a LongInt into a string. If the string that results is longer than Len bytes in length, the function simply exits and returns the string. However, if the string is less than Len bytes, the function appends zeros in front of it until it is Len characters long. Here is the transformation caused by each successive iteration of the while loop if N equals 2 and Len equals 4:

```
2       { First iteration }
02      { Second iteration }
002     { Third iteration }
0002    { Fourth iteration }
```

The point here is that the function checks to see if the string is four characters long. If it isn't, the function prepends a zero to the string with the following code:

```
    S := '0' + S;
```

In the case of the GetTodayName function, the value passed in the Len parameter is 2, because the need is to translate a number such as 3 or 7 into a number such as 03 or 07.

The final trick in the GetTodayName function is to convert a year such as 1994 into a two-digit number such as 94. Clearly, this can be easily achieved by merely subtracting 1900 from the date. However, that sound of hoofbeats in the distance is the rapid approach of the year 2000. Subtracting 1900 from 2001 would not achieve the desired result. The code therefore first converts the year into a string, and then simply lops off the first two characters with the Delete function:

```
  Year := Int2StrPad0(y, 4);
  Delete(Year, 1, 2);
```

In this case, a 4 is passed to Int2StrPad0, because the year is originally a four-digit number.

As mentioned earlier, the Delete function is built into the Delphi language. It deletes characters from a string, starting at the offset specified in the second paramater. The number of characters to be deleted is specified in the third parameter. See the online help for more details.

Using the *Move* and *FillChar* Functions

The two built-in Delphi methods examined in this section are both very fast and very powerful. Speed of this sort is a luxury, but it comes replete with some dangers that you need to be sure to sidestep. In particular, neither the FillChar nor the Move function has much in the way of built-in error checking.

As you saw in Chapter 12, "Working with Arrays," the usual reason for using FillChar is to zero out an array, record, or string. It will, however, fill a structure not only with zeros but with whatever character you specify.

FillChar takes three parameters. The first is the variable you want to copy bytes into, the second is the number of bytes you want to fill, and the third is the character you want placed in those bytes:

```
procedure FillChar(var X; Count: Word; value);
```

Consider the following array:

```
var
    MyArray: array[0..10] of Char;
```

Given this array, the following command will set all the members of this array to #0:

```
FillChar(MyArray, SizeOf(MyArray), #0);
```

If you want to fill the array with spaces, you could use the following syntax:

```
FillChar(MyArray, SizeOf(MyArray), #32);
```

This code would fill the array with the letter A:

```
FillChar(MyArray, SizeOf(MyArray), 'A');
```

The key thing to remember when using FillChar is that the SizeOf function can help you be sure that you are writing the correct number of bytes to the array. The big mistake you can make is to write too many bytes to the array. That is much worse than writing too few. If you think of the memory theater again, you can imagine 10 members of the audience sitting together, all considering themselves part of MyArray. Right next to them are two people who make up an integer. They are busy remembering the number 25. Now you issue the following command:

```
FillChar(MyArray, 12, #0);
```

All the people who are part of the array will start remembering #0, which is fine. But the command will keep right on going past the members of MyArray and tell the two folks remembering the number 25 that they should both now remember #0. In other words, the integer value will also be zeroed out, and a bug will be introduced into your program. The result described here, you should understand, is a best-case scenario. Worst-case is that the extra two bytes belong to another program, which means that your program will generate a General Protection Fault. The moral is that you should always use the FillChar procedure with care.

A function similar to FillChar is called Move. Its purpose is to move a block of data from one place to another. A typical use of this function might be to move one portion of a string to a second string, or to move part of an array into a string. The Copy function can also be used for a similar purpose. The advantage of the Copy function is that it is relatively safe. The disadvantages are that it is less flexible and can be somewhat slower under some circumstances.

`Move` takes three parameters. The first is the variable you want to copy data from, the second is the variable you want to move data to, and the third is the number of bytes you want to move:

```
procedure Move(var  Source, Dest; Count: Word);
```

Next you will find an example of a typical way to use the function. If you enjoy puzzles, you might want to take a moment to see if you can figure out what it does:

```
procedure TForm1.Button1Click(Sender: TObject);
var
  S1,S2: String;
begin
  S1 := 'Heebee Gee Bees';
  Move(S1[12], S2[1], 4);
  S2[0] := #4;

  Edit1.Text := S2;
end;
```

The code shown here first sets `S1` to a string value. It then indexes 12 bytes into that string and moves the next 4 bytes into a second string. (Don't forget to count the spaces when you are adding up the characters in a string!) Finally, it sets the length byte of the second string to `#4`, which is the number of bytes that were moved into it. After executing this code, the final `assignment` statement will write out the word `Bees` in `Edit1.Text`. Here is how to accomplish the same task using the `Copy` function:

```
S1 := 'Heebee Gee Bees';
  S2 := Copy(S1, 12, 4);
  WriteLn(S2);
```

The first parameter to `Copy` is the string you want to get data from, the second is an offset into that string, and the third is the number of bytes you want to use. The function returns a substring taken from the string in the first parameter.

The `Copy` function is easier to use and safer than the `Move` function, but it is not as powerful. If at all possible, you should use the `Copy` function. However, there are times when you can't use the `Copy` function, particularly if you need to move data in or out of at least one variable that is not a string. Also, it is worth remembering that `Move` is very fast. If you have to perform an action over and over again in a loop, you should consider using `Move` instead of `Copy`.

As easy as it is to write data to the wrong place using the `FillChar` statement, you will find that the `Move` statement can lead you even further astray in considerably less time. It will, however, get you out of all manner of difficult corners—as long as you know how to use it.

The following function puts the `Move` procedure to practical use. As its name implies, the `StripFirstWord` function is used to remove the first word from a string. For instance, it would change the following string

```
'One Two Three'
```

into this string

```
'Two Three'
```

Here is the `StripFirstWord` function:

```
{ - - - - - - - - - - - - - - - - - - - - - - - - - - - - - - - - - - - - - - - - - - - - -
        Name: StripFirstWord function
 Declaration: StripFirstWord(S : string) : string;
        Unit: StrBox
        Code: S
        Date: 03/02/94
 Description: Strip the first word from a sentence,
              return the shortened sentence. Return original
              string if there is no first word.
- - - - - - - - - - - - - - - - - - - - - - - - - - - - - - - - - - - - - - -}
function StripFirstWord(S : string) : string;
var
  i, Size: Integer;
  S1: String;
begin
  i := Pos(#32, S);
  if i = 0 then begin
    StripFirstWord := S;
    Exit;
  end;
  Size := (Length(S) - i);
  Move(S[i + 1], S[1], Size);
  S[0] := Chr(Size);
  StripFirstWord := S;
end;
```

The first line in this function introduces you to the built-in `Pos` function, which locates a substring in a longer string. For instance, in this case the `Pos` function is used to find the first instance of the space character in the string passed to the `StripFirstWord` function. The function returns the offset of the character it is looking for.

More specifically, the `Pos` function takes two parameters. The first is the string to search for, and the second is the string you want to search. Therefore, the statement `Pos(#32, S)` looks for the space character inside a string called `S`.

If you passed in the following line of poetry: "The pure products of America go crazy," the `Pos` function would return the number 4, which is the offset of the first space character in the preceding sentence. However, if you passed in a simpler string such as `Williams`, `Pos` would return `0` because there is no space character in the string. If the function does not find a space character in the string, it returns an empty string:

```
if i = 0 then begin
  StripFirstWord := '';
  Exit;
end;
```

The built-in `Exit` procedure shown here simply exits the function without executing another line of code. This is the `StripFirstWord` function's sole, and rather limited, exercise in error-checking.

If the offset of a space character is returned by the Pos function, the Move function transfers "offset" number of characters from the string that is passed in to a local string named S1:

```
i := Pos(#32, S);
...
Move(S[1], S1[1], i);
S1[0] := Chr(i-1);
```

The next line of code sets the length byte for the newly created string, which contains the first word in the sentence.

The next three lines of code excise the first word from the original sentence:

```
Size := (Length(S) - i);
Move(S[i + 1], S[1], Size);
S[0] := Chr(Size);
```

The first step is to determine the number of characters in the sentence after the first word is removed. This is found by subtracting the number returned by Pos from the total length of the sentence. StripFirstWord then moves the remaining portion of the string from a position "offset" characters deep in the following string

```
She was a child and I was a child, In a kingdom by the sea
```

to the very first spot in the string

```
was a child and I was a child, In a kingdom by the sea sea
```

The extra characters, represented in this case by the second occurrence of sea, are then lopped off by setting the length byte to the appropriate number of characters:

```
was a child and I was a child, In a kingdom by the sea
```

The function then returns the first word of the sentence, and also the shortened sentence.

The StripFirstWord function is not perfect. For instance, some readers may have noticed that the function would not perform as advertised if the first characters of the string passed to it were spaces. However, overall, it does the job required of it. Of course, you could write a function that stripped spaces from the beginning of a string. Then you could pass a string first to the new function you have created, and then pass it on to the StripFirstWord function. In fact, you will find that I implement such a function later in this chapter.

If you have been working with a computer language for a few years, a function such as StripFirstWord is probably not very hard for you to grasp. However, newcomers are likely to find it rather challenging. This brings up two major points:

■ First, you need to become as familiar with the available debuggers as possible. Without a debugger, I would find a function such as StripFirstWord so difficult to write that I would probably throw up my hands in disgust and start looking around to see if a third-party tool vendor has already written it. As it is, I just spend a few minutes with the debugger and I have something I can use in my own programs. If you are having trouble understanding this procedure, do what I did when I created it: look at it in the debugger.

■ Second, anyone who sees the code I have written in the last few sections of this chapter must realize that Delphi does not necessarily remove all the possible challenges from a programming job. Visual programming makes life much easier for most programmers, but it does not eliminate the need to write real code. If the act of writing code bores you or frustrates you, you should probably move along to one of the many walks of life that offers more excitement for someone like you. If you are determined to persevere despite a growing sense of mordant depression, you should get to know the people who produce programmers' libraries. A good knowledge of TurboPowers' tools, for instance, can do much to help alleviate your sense of frustration. (TurboPower is located in Colorado Springs, CO. Reach them by typing GO TURBOPOWER on CompuServe.)

Most of the routines you have seen in this chapter are useful enough for you to want to save for future use. With this thought in mind, I have placed them in the STRBOX unit, which is a companion unit to the MATHBOX unit you saw in Chapter 11, "Units, Real Numbers, and Functions."

The following program, called TESTSTR, gives you a chance to work with the StripFirstWord function. This program takes any sentence you enter and separates it into a series of individual words that are displayed in a list box.

To avoid any problems that might arise from accidentally prepending spaces before a string, the TESTSTR program makes use of the following function:

```
{ - - - - - - - - - - - - - - - - - - - - - - - - - - - - - - - - - - - - - - - -
        Name: StripFrontChars function
 Declaration: StripFrontChars(S: string; Ch: Char) : String;
        Unit: StrBox
        Code: S
        Date: 03/02/94
 Description: Strips any occurances of charact Ch that
             might precede a string.
- - - - - - - - - - - - - - - - - - - - - - - - - - - - - - - - - - - - - - }
function StripFrontChars(S: string; Ch: Char): string;
var
  S1: string;
begin
  while (S[1] = Ch) and (Length(S) > 0) do
    S := Copy(S,2,Length(S) - 1);
  StripFrontChars := S;
end;
```

This routine is quite similar in functionality to StripBlanks, except that it starts at the opposite end of the string and lets you specify the particular character you want to cut. If you pass it a string and #32, it will make sure there are no spaces preceding the string.

`StripFrontChars` works its magic by first checking to see if the initial character in the string has the same value as `Ch`. If it does, it finds the second character in the string and copies it and the remainder of the string back over the first character of the string, thereby accomplishing a task similar to that undertaken by the second `Move` statement in `StripFirstWord`.

NOTE

Several places in this chapter I have shown you two different ways of accomplishing the same task. Experienced programmers know that writing code is a bit like writing prose because there are always several different ways to say the same thing. Some people believe that there are quantifiable ways of finding the best way to accomplish a particular task. To my mind, there is no objective way to determine the best course of action in many programming dilemmas. For instance, it is often true that one method is faster than another, but it might also be more difficult to maintain. Which is better, the faster code or the more maintainable code? It depends.

It is also worth pointing out that though there are few objective means of determining the best way to write a block of code, there are certain programmers who consistently write excellent code. Programming is one field in which there is little substitute for raw talent. However, average programmers can accomplish a lot if they have good toolboxes and good compilers.

The TESTSTR program uses an edit control, a button labeled Parse, and a listbox. The form for the program is shown in Figure 14.4.

FIGURE 14.4.
The form for the TESTSTR program.

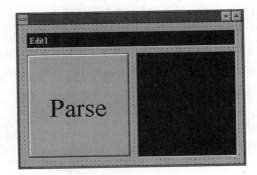

NOTE

The code for the TESTSTR program is in the CHAP14 directory on this book's CD-ROM.

The TESTSTR program uses the `OnCreate` event to specify a string and to pass it to the `BParseClick` function. This function uses `StripFirstWord` to break the sentence into individual words and to display each word in a listbox. One of the interesting aspects of the program is that it shows how you can place routines in a unit such as `STRBOX` and then call them in a neat and easily readable fashion.

There are hundreds of different functions you could write to help you perform certain string-oriented tasks. The ones in this chapter should help you get started creating a library of your own that you can turn to when you need a quick solution for a problem involving a string. The final version of the STRBOX program that ships with this book contains a number of additional string manipulation routines that I have built up over the years.

Limiting the Length of Strings

At times it seems foolish to allocate an entire 250-byte block to deal with a very short string. For instance, you might have a string that held the first name of the current user of your program. Furthermore, your input routines may limit the length of the name the user can enter. For instance, many programs give you only 30 characters in which to enter a name. If by some strange chance your name is longer than that, you are out of luck. The key point, however, is that the string that holds the user's name need never be longer than 30 bytes. Any more bytes would be wasted every time the string is used.

In situations like this, you can limit the length of the string you declare:

```
Name: string[30];
```

This syntax tells the compiler that it needs to set aside only 31 seats for this particular string. Thirty will hold the string itself, and the thirty-first holds the length byte. By declaring a string this way, you save 256 – 31, or 225 bytes.

Delphi enables you to declare strings of any length between 0 and 256—that is, the valid values range from 1 to 255. For instance, all of the following are valid string declarations:

```
S: string[1];
S1: string[255];
S2: string[100];
S3: string[25];
```

Strings of certain lengths are declared so often that you might want to create special types for them:

```
type
   TStr20: string[20];
   TStr25: string[25];
   TStr30: string[30];
   TStr10: string[10];
   TStr80: string[80];
```

Given these declarations, you can write code that looks like this:

```
var
  S1: TStr20;
  S2: TStr30;
```

The syntax shown here can help you save memory without having to perform much extra work. In fact, the types shown here are so useful that I have added them to the STRBOX unit so that you can access them easily at any time. I have also added a few other string declarations that can prove useful when you are working with files:

```
DirStr = string[67];
PathStr = string[79];
NameStr = string[8];
ExtStr = string[4];
```

The only problem with limiting the length of strings through the technique shown here is that it still requires you to know the length of a string at design time. Working with PChars and the GetMem function, it is possible to set the length of a string at runtime, which means you can make strings that are exactly long enough to hold the characters stored in them. You learn more about pointers and the GetMem function in Chapter 15, "Pointers and PChars." You also can declare a pointer to a standard string, predeclared by Delphi as a PString, and then allocate just the amount of memory you need for it.

Working with Text Files

A text file provides a place for you to store strings. The PAS and DPR source files for your programs are text files. So are the OPT and DSK files that accompany them, as well as the WIN.INI and SYSTEM.INI files that you use to configure Windows 3.1. Even the lowly AUTOEXEC.BAT and CONFIG.SYS files, which may have been the very first thing you ever learned about a computer, are nothing more than text files.

Delphi provides an extremely simple method for reading and writing these text files. To get started, you need only declare a variable of type text:

```
var
  F: System.Text;
```

Variable F now represents a text file, and it can be used to specify where you want data to be read or written.

> **NOTE**
>
> You need to qualify the type text with the name of the unit where it is declared. This is necessary because Form1 already has a variable with this name inside it, thereby causing a name conflict, because you can't use a variable as a type. To remedy the situation, you need only specify which instance of the identifier Text you want to reference. Specifically, you are saying that you want to reference the Text variable that is declared in the System unit. The same problem occurs with the identifiers Assign and Close.

Needless to say, the name conflict shown here never should have occurred, and its presence in the shipping version of Delphi is a testament to the fact that even the developers of Delphi are fallible.

After declaring the file variable, the next step is to associate it with a particular filename:

```
var
  F: System.Text;
begin
  System.Assign(F, 'MYFILE.TXT');
  ...
```

It is traditional to assign the extension TXT to a text file. Of course, many files don't follow this convention. For instance, INI files don't use the TXT extension, and neither do files labeled READ.ME. However, most text files do have a TXT extension, and this is the accepted and traditional way to treat them.

After the assignment statement, the next step is to open the file with the Reset, Rewrite, or Append routine. The Reset procedure opens an existing file:

```
var
  F: System.Text;
begin
  System.Assign(F, 'MYFILE.TXT');
  Reset(F);
  ...
end;
```

The Rewrite procedure creates a file or overwrites an existing file. The Append routine opens an existing file. It does not overwrite its current contents, but it enables you to append new strings to the end of a file:

```
var
  F: System.Text;
begin
  System.Assign(F, 'MYFILE.TXT');
  Append(F);
  ...
end;
```

NOTE

There is no simple way to open a text file and insert a string into it at a particular location. You can create a new file, overwrite an existing file, or append a string onto an existing file. You can't easily add a new string in the fourth line of a twenty-line text file. I say you can't do this easily, but there are ways to do this. They usually involve opening the file in either binary or text mode, reading its entire contents into an array or other complex data structure, inserting a string, and finally writing the file back out to disk.

Once you have opened a text file, you can write a string to it with the `Write` or `WriteLn` procedure:

```
var
  F: System.Text;
begin
  System.Assign(F, 'MYFILE.TXT');
  ReWrite(F);
  WriteLn(F, 'Call me Ishmael.');
  System.Close(F);
end;
```

Notice that the `WriteLn` statement begins by referencing the file variable as its first parameter.

The method shown here ends with a `Close` statement, which must be referenced with a qualifier representing SYSTEM.PAS. Bugs can be introduced into your program if you forget to call `Close`. More specifically, there is an internal buffer associated with each text file that cannot be flushed if you fail to call `Close`. If the buffer isn't flushed, a portion of the file will remain in memory rather than being written to disk. As a result, it appears that your program is not writing properly to the file, and programmers can spend a long time looking for a memory corruption problem when the source of the trouble is simply failing to call `Close`.

> **NOTE**
>
> The SYSTEM file is buried deep in the Delphi runtime library. Every Delphi program you create will automatically have the system file linked into it, even if you don't explicitly reference it in your uses clause. Most of the SYSTEM unit contains assembly language code for elemental routines such as `WriteLn`, `Assign`, `ReWrite`, `Reset`, and a few other functions that have survived since the earliest versions of the Turbo Pascal compiler. If you want to know more about this unit, you can look it up in the online help or look for the source code on disk. The availability of the source code depends on which version of Delphi you bought. That is, it comes with the client/server version, but not the desktop version. If it exists on your system, it would be stored somewhere beneath the source subdirectory. You can purchase the RTL separately from Borland.

If you want to read a string from a text file, you can use the `Read` or `ReadLn` statement:

```
var
  F: System.Text;
  S: String;
begin
  System.Assign(F, 'MYFILE.TXT');
  Reset(F);
  ReadLn(F, S);
  WriteLn(S);
  System.Close(F);
end;
```

Notice that this code uses the `Reset` procedure to open an existing file, and then uses `ReadLn` to retrieve the first string from this file.

You can also read and write numbers from a text file. For instance, the following code is entirely legal:

```
var
  F: System.Text;
  S: String;
  i: Integer;
begin
  System.Assign(F, 'MYFILE.TXT');
  ReWrite(F);
  S := 'The secret of the universe: ';
  i := 42;
  WriteLn(F, S, i);
  System.Close(F);
end;
```

This code writes the following line into a text file:

```
The secret of the universe: 42
```

If you had a text file with the following contents:

```
10 101 1001
20 202 2002
```

you could read the first line from this file with the following code:

```
var
  F: System.Text;
  i, j, k: Integer;
begin
  System.Assign(F, 'MYFILE.TXT');
  Reset(F);
  ReadLn(F, i, j, k);
  System.Close(F);
end;
```

The code shown here would read the numbers 10, 101, and 1001 from the file. If you wanted to read both lines from the file, you could write

```
var
  F: System.Text;
  i, j, k, a, b, c: Integer;
begin
  System.Assign(F, 'MYFILE.TXT');
  Reset(F);
  ReadLn(F, i, j, k);
  ReadLn(F, a, b, c);
  System.Close(F);
end;
```

You can use a function called EOF to determine if you are at the end of a text file. For instance, if you had a file that contained several hundred lines of numbers like those shown in the small file listed earlier, you could read the entire file in the following manner:

```
var
  F: System.Text;
  i, j, k, Sum: Integer;
begin
```

```
  System.Assign(F, 'MYFILE.TXT');
  Reset(F);
  whole not EOF(F) do begin
    ReadLn(F, i, j, k);
    Sum := I + j + k;
    WriteLn(F, 'i + j + k := ', Sum);
  end;
  System.Close(F);
end;
```

NOTE

The EASYFILE program, supplied on disk, demonstrates how to use the TTEXTREC structure to determine a file's name, and if a file is open for input, open for output, or closed. Specifically, you can typecast a variable of type text so that you can test its state, as shown here:

```
var
  F: Text;
begin
  if TTextRec(F).Mode := fmClosed then OpenTheFile;
end;
```

TTextRec is in the online help. The Mode constants are declared in SYSUTILS.PAS as follows:

```
fmClosed = $D7B0;
fmInput  = $D7B1;
fmOutput = $D7B2;
fmInOut  = $D7B3;
```

In this section, you learned the basics about text files. One of the most important points to remember is that you can open a file one of three ways:

- ReWrite opens a new file or overwrites an existing file.
- Reset opens an existing file for reading.
- Append opens an existing file and enables you to append text to the end of it. If the file does not exist, an error condition results.

Summary

In this chapter you explored strings and text files. You saw that strings are really just a special form of array, and that you can manipulate them in myriad ways by treating them as vectors filled with chars. You also saw that there are many functions used to manipulate strings. In particular, you were exposed to the Move, FillChar, Delete, Copy, and Pos routines.

The last part of the chapter presented a basic introduction to text files. You saw how to open and close these files, how to read and write to them, and how to detect if you are at the end of a text file. Look on the CD for programs showing how to parse text files.

Pointers and PChars

15

Overview

Manipulation of pointers is probably the single most powerful skill in the repertoire of experienced programmers. If you really understand pointers, little in computer programming is likely to be beyond you.

I don't mean to imply that understanding pointers makes computer programming easy. That is not at all the case. Pointers tend to be a relatively difficult subject, even in their easiest and most comprehensible forms.

Pointers are worth the struggle, however, because they enable you to directly manipulate memory. When you are dealing with pointers, there is no longer anything between you and the raw bytes of memory that exist in RAM, or in other portions of the computer's memory. With pointers, you are right there, manipulating the raw material that forms the life blood of every computer.

This chapter covers the following:

- The theory behind manipulating memory with pointers
- Using `New` and `Dispose` to allocate memory
- Using `GetMem` and `FreeMem` to allocate memory
- Debugging pointer problems with the `HeapLimit` variable
- Using pointers to open up space in the data segment
- Creating pointers to arrays
- Working with PChars

In general, this is probably one of the most important chapters in the book, particularly for people who want to explore advanced programming techniques.

Pointers and the Memory Theater

When you first start to think about pointers, you should probably try to keep the memory theater in mind. Pointers simply refer to seats in the memory theater. In fact, pointers are blocks of four seats in the memory theater that remember the location of other seats.

Suppose you have a list of 100 sentences, each of which is between 100 and 150 characters in length. Furthermore, suppose this list of sentences is not part of the body of a text, but is instead the list of error messages displayed by your program. In other words, you don't necessarily want to show this entire list to the user at once, but might want to grab the 12th string, or 23rd string, or some other particular string, and show it to the user.

Given this scenario, it might be helpful to keep a set of references to these strings, rather than wandering through the seats of the memory theater trying to find a particular string at a particular time. As it happens, there are a number of different ways you can keep these references; but one convenient way to do it would be by keeping pointers to these strings.

On the 16-bit Intel architecture, pointers occupy 4 bytes. That is, they take up four seats in the memory theater. These 4 bytes contain the address of a particular location in the memory theater. In other words, the four seats occupied by a pointer contain the reference number, or address, of other seats in the memory theater.

Suppose the first of the 100 strings you want to reference is located in Section 25, Seat 5A. One simple way to reference this number would be to create the following simple piece of syntax:

```
25:5A
```

Though this syntax might not make much sense to a total stranger, it is easily understood by someone who recognizes its purpose. Specifically, the number before the colon refers to a section number, and the number after the colon refers to a seat number. Besides its simple syntax, another advantage of this construction is that it can easily be stored in a small area. For instance, you could ask two members of the audience to remember the first half of the number, and the next two members of the audience to remember the second half of the number. The result would be that the entire number could be memorized by four members of the audience.

> **NOTE**
>
> To understand exactly what is going on here, you need to recall that while one member of the audience can remember a number between 0 and 255, two members of the audience working together can remember numbers between 0 and 65360. Some of the section and seat numbers in the memory theater are larger than 255. It therefore takes two people to remember these numbers. In other words, if a particular seat in the memory theater lies in Section 518 and has the number 2563 assigned to it, no one person in the memory theater could remember either the Section or the Seat number. Instead, two of them would have to work together to remember each number. If you are having trouble remembering how this portion of the memory theater works, go back and reread the relevant portions of Chapters 6 and 7.

Using a system where four members of the audience remember the seat number of another group of people in the audience, it is possible to have a relatively manageable block of 100 sets of pointers, where each pointer is really just four seats in the memory theater.

100×4 is equal to 400, which is a fairly large number of seats. However, if each of the strings being referenced averages 125 characters in length, the approximate number of bytes in the group is 100×125, or 12,500 seats. 12,500 is a large number of seats to have to sort through, even for a computer. Obviously, it would be helpful to be able to refer to a smaller lookup table, consisting of 400 seats, that can be broken down into groups of 4 seats each. This is what pointers do for you.

Suppose you want to find the 20th string in the group of strings. One way to find it would be to start wandering through the section where the strings are stored, looking for the beginning and end of each string, and keep looking until you finally find the string you want. A second method would be to go to the 20th pointer to see which seat number is stored there. Then you could go directly from the pointer to the string itself. In effect, the people who sit in the four seats of the 20th pointer can stand up and point directly at the seat that represents the beginning of the string you want to find, as shown in Figure 15.1.

FIGURE 15.1.

Four members of the memory theater save the seat number where a string is stored.

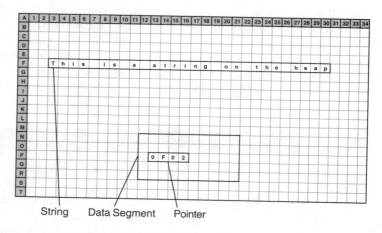

It doesn't take much imagination to see that pointers can help speed up operations inside a computer. By using pointers, you can avoid lengthy searches through hundreds of thousands of bytes, and instead be directed quickly and efficiently to the seat you want to find.

Furthermore, if you want to change the order of the strings you are referencing, you don't actually have to move a 150-character string from one place to another. Instead, you can simply change the addresses stored in the pointers. For instance, if one pointer references a string starting in seat 1A:2B and the next pointer references a string in seat 5A:6B, reversing the order of these strings is a simple matter of swapping two 4-byte pointers. This is obviously much faster than trying to move hundreds of bytes around.

Some readers might be inclined at this point to take this whole matter back one step further and ask what it is that points at the pointer. In other words, it is easy enough to imagine how the pointers described here can help you reference a particular place in memory, but how does one get to the pointer in the first place?

The short answer is that the locations of certain pointers are stored in the code segment. In other words, when you write a program, code is generated that says, in effect, go to this spot, find a pointer, and then do something with the memory referenced by the pointer. The code usually points to a place in the data segment or stack segment where the pointers you declare are stored. However, you also can have a pointer in your data segment that points to a pointer on your heap that points to yet another pointer on the heap, and so on.

You can trace this answer back even further, to the moment when a computer is first switched on. At that moment, pointers are loaded into memory that reference instructions for booting up a computer and loading the operating system. These instructions and data in turn use pointers to reference other places inside the computer, and so on. What really ends up happening is that a computer follows an endless stream of pointers, each of which keep referencing some other place in memory where data or instructions are stored.

> **NOTE**
>
> Pointers are sometimes referred to as addresses, because that is really all that a pointer represents. For instance, you might hear someone say, "Pass the address of variable J to the FooBar function." What this means is that you should pass a pointer to the variable J to the FooBar function. Pointers are really nothing more than addresses. Furthermore, you can obtain the address of any variable by appending the @ symbol before it:
>
> ```
> var
>   A: Integer;
> begin
>   WriteLn(@A);
> end;
> ```
>
> The code shown here would write the address of the variable A to the screen. In other words, it would write out the decimal number associated with the address of A. This number won't do you much good, however, because addresses are normally written in hex notation. One way to see a meaningful version of the address of variable A is to type @A in the Watch window.

Once again, I want to stress that you don't have to understand all this in order to write code. If you can begin to see what I am driving at, or if this material is already old hat to you, you are sitting in the catbird seat, with all the vast realms of the computer spread out before you. Pointers are the keys to the kingdom, and with them you can unlock virtually any door.

Allocating Memory with *New* and *Dispose*

The simplest way to allocate memory is by using New or Dispose. These functions automatically allocate the amount of memory needed to hold a particular variable. In this section you are going to learn about what it means to allocate and deallocate memory, and how these acts can be performed by using New and Dispose.

There is a parallel between the act of allocating memory in a computer and the act of reserving seats in the memory theater. When you allocate memory in a computer, all you are really doing is telling the operating system that you want to reserve a certain section of RAM until further notice. It is as if you go to the ticket office in the memory theater and say, "I want to reserve 256 seats so that I can put a string into them. Don't use those seats for anything else. They are reserved." If your needs are somewhat different, you might tell the ticket office, "I need room for an integer. Please reserve two seats for me." Once you make this request, the owners of the memory theater are honor-bound to reserve those seats until you tell them you want to dispose of them.

It is very important that whenever you allocate memory, you eventually come along and deallocate it. The problem is that there are only a certain number of seats in the memory theater. If you allocate memory and then forget to deallocate it, eventually there will come a time when you will go to the ticket office and ask for more seats and you will be told that the house is all booked.

> **NOTE**
>
> One of the problems that has haunted the world of DOS and Windows has been that there is very little to keep an ill-behaved program from taking up more seats than it reserved. Some programs simply write over the seats reserved by another program. That is, they start acting as if they owned those seats, when they were clearly reserved for someone else. If Windows is able to detect that this is happening, it generates a General Protection Fault, which says that some program is trying to write to memory that it does not own, and that the operating system is going to try to protect those violated seats by shutting down the program that is out of line. This is not the place to do much more than hint at this subject, but the move toward Windows NT, Windows 95, and OS/2 is fueled in large part by the desire to use protected-mode operating systems that are good at protecting the memory that belongs to a program.

If you call New to allocate memory, the operating system literally sets up a table that keeps track of your request, and it will not give the memory you have reserved to anyone else until you come back and say, "Okay, I'm through with this memory. You can deallocate." (The table in question is call a Descriptor table, and it can be thought of as an internal database or spreadsheet. Code that explores these tables is included on the CD.

If a programmer comes to the operating system and requests memory that is not available, the request fails and the user usually sees a sign that says "Out of Memory." In these cases, the operating system absolutely will not give up any reserved seats no matter how important the need. The issue, of course, is that information vital to the user, or to the integrity of the operating system, might be stored in any particular allocation. As a result, it is not possible to give it up until the module that allocated the memory gives the sign okaying the deallocation.

> **NOTE**
>
> Memory allocation and maintenance inside Windows are actually considerably more complex than the model I am putting forth here. For instance, it is possible for Windows to swap memory to disk. In terms of the memory theater, this is a bit like telling a group of people in one set of seats that they will have to step out into the lobby for a time, so that other people can come in and participate for a bit. When the first set of people is needed again, they can be swapped back into the memory theater and the second set of people is sent out into the lobby. These kinds of trades can and do continue indefinitely until the seats in question are deallocated. Furthermore, it is possible for the programmer to specify that certain seats can't be swapped in and out of memory in this manner.
>
> However, this is not the time to get into all these esoteric issues. For now it is simplest to imagine the audience in the memory theater as being entirely static. There will be time enough later to get into all the tricks people have created to expand the capabilities of the memory theater. The facts of the matter, however, are very simple: There are X number of seats in the memory theater. You can reserve these seats by allocating memory. If you reserve many seats and do not ever deallocate them, you will run out of seats and get an "Out of Memory" error.

Declaring Pointers: A Practical Example

It is time now to start getting down to cases. Consider the example discussed previously, where you want to declare pointers to strings. If you want to work with a pointer to a string, what you really need is a new type of pointer different from any of the ones discussed so far in this book.

Here is the simplest possible program that shows how to declare a pointer to string, allocate memory for it, and dispose of it:

```
program SimpMem;

uses
  WinCrt;

type
  PString = ^String;

var
  MyString: PString;
```

```
begin
  New(MyString);          { Allocate 256 bytes for the string }
  MyString^ := 'Hello'; { Assign a value to string            }
  WriteLn(MyString^);   { Write the value to the screen       }
  Dispose(MyString);    { Deallocate the memory               }
end.
```

To run the WINCRT program shown here, you should start a new project, open the Project Manager, and press the red minus sign to delete UNIT1.PAS from the project. The Project Manager will probably ask if you want to save UNIT1, as shown in Figure 15.2. You should answer no. Now bring up PROJECT1.DPR, save it as SIMPMEM, and edit it so that it looks exactly like the source code shown here.

FIGURE 15.2.

The Project Manager asking if the user wants to save the file deleted from a project.

I spend several paragraphs discussing this program, so if it doesn't make complete sense to you yet, don't worry. I want to start by describing the program once at a fairly high speed, go through the whole program again very slowly, and finally come back and summarize what has been said.

The program starts by declaring a new type, which is a pointer to a string:

```
type
  PString = ^String;
```

It then declares a variable of this type:

```
var
  MyString: PString;
```

In the body of the code, memory is allocated for the variable, and the variable is assigned a value and is written to the screen:

```
New(MyString);          { Allocate 256 bytes for the string }
MyString^ := 'Hello'; { Assign a value to string            }
WriteLn(MyString^);   { Write the value to the screen       }
```

Finally, the memory that was allocated is disposed; that is, it is given back to the operating system:

```
Dispose(MyString);      { Deallocate the memory               }
```

In the preceding paragraph, I gave you a quick overview of the program, but many readers probably need the action to be slowed down much further so that they can get a careful look at exactly what happened. As I said earlier, pointers are a complicated subject, so it is very appropriate that they be covered in the clearest possible terms. I therefore slow the camera way down and consider each frame of the film in detail.

In earlier chapters you worked with variables of type Integer, type Word, or type String. You can declare these types of variables with syntax that might look something like this:

```
var
  A: Word;
  B: Integer;
  C: String;
```

If you wanted to change the third variable from a string to a pointer to a string, you would write

```
var
   C: ^String;
```

In this code fragment, the caret symbol (^) identifies the variable as a pointer.

If you wanted to read the line aloud, you would say, "C is a pointer to a string," or, if you prefer, "C colon up-caret string." Of the two options, I prefer the former. The syntax itself is merely a convention. In other words, the colon and the caret were symbols that were picked more or less at random. They don't have any particular significance. What is significant is the actual meaning of the syntax, which is best expressed by the sentence "C is a pointer to a string." Here are a few more examples of bits of syntax, and a reasonable method for speaking them aloud:

```
A: ^Word;
"A is a pointer to a word."
B: ^Char;
"B is a pointer to a character."
```

Of course, if you would rather say "B colon up-caret Char," there is no harm in it. I simply happen to prefer a more literal translation of the syntax. Experienced programmers will readily comprehend either manner of speaking.

Now it is possible to go back and take a second look at the declarations at the top of the SIMPMEM program:

```
type
  PString = ^String;

var
  MyString: PString;
```

The type declaration shown here states that a PString is a pointer to a string. The var statement then declares a variable called MyString that is of type PString.

The classic mistake that can be made in cases such as this would be to write the following:

```
type
  PString = ^String;

var
  MyString: PString;

begin
  MyString := 'Hello';
  WriteLn(MyString);
end;
```

The are two problems with this code. The first is that no allocation is made for the `MyString` variable, and the second is that the variable is not dereferenced when it is used.

"Dereferencing a variable" is a fancy way of talking about using the caret syntax. This is a dereferenced variable:

```
MyString^
```

This variable is not dereferenced:

```
MyString
```

Often, the compiler will catch up with you if you forget to dereference a variable. You will get a compiler error telling you that you have a type mismatch or some other problem. The way to fix the problem is to dereference the variable involved.

Consider this statement:

```
MyString := 'Hello';
```

Given the declarations shown here, you know that `MyString` is a pointer and the string literal `Hello` is a string. You can't assign a string to a pointer. It is a type mismatch. You can, however, write the following:

```
MyString^ := 'Hello';
```

This statement says that the variable that `MyString` points to is going to be assigned a certain value. Because `MyString` points to a string, it's okay to assign a string to it.

NOTE

Many programmers like to append `Ptr` to pointer variables so that they can easily be recognized. For instance, these programmers might write

```
MyStringPtr: PString;
```

Other programmers prefer to prepend letters designating the type of variable being declared and the fact that it is a pointer:

```
lpstrMyString: PString;
```

This syntax states that `MyString` is a long pointer—that is, a 32-bit pointer—to a string. I usually don't use syntax of this type, primarily because I think it makes my code harder to read. However, there are very good arguments on the other side of this issue, and you should take the path that you find most comfortable. (You will, however, find that I sometimes distinguish one type of component from another type by using syntax closely akin to this Hungarian notation.)

As I said previously, the compiler will usually warn you if you forget to dereference a variable. There are exceptions, such as when you are using the `Move` command, or when you are using the `BlockRead` or `FillChar` commands. These functions enable you to use a pointer without dereferencing it, which can lead you down the primrose path to some fairly serious crashes. The point here is not that `BlockRead`, `FillChar`, and `Move` are poorly designed functions, but merely that they are flexible enough to enable you to make some fairly serious mistakes. As a result, you should always use these powerful functions with care.

At any rate, the key point is that the compiler will never murmur a peep if you write code like this:

```
type
  PString = ^String;

var
  MyString: PString;

begin
  MyString^ := 'Hello';
  WriteLn(MyString^);
end.
```

In fact, there are occasions when you will be able to run code like this without ever receiving an error message. However, the fact that the preceding code does not allocate any memory for `MyString` is a very serious bug, and it will eventually catch up with a programmer and cause real trouble.

The following short program will help you get a feeling for how serious it is to forget to allocate memory for a pointer:

```
program Buggy1;

{$R+,S+}

uses
  WinCrt;

type
  PString = ^String;

var
  MyString: PString;
```

```
begin
  HeapLimit := 0;
  MyString^ := 'Hello';
  WriteLn(MyString^);
end.
```

To run this program, you need to remove UNIT1 from the Project Manager, as described earlier. If you are having trouble getting this program set up correctly, you might also want to take this opportunity to reread Chapter 4, "The Structure of a Delphi Program," which has a section on WINCRT code.

The first line of this program sets `HeapLimit` to `0`, which is something you should consider doing whenever you are developing programs that use pointers. The exact meaning of this line is explained in the section on the heap manager. For now, all you need to know about the `HeapLimit` variable is that it can be used to help you find pointer errors at the very spot in your program where they occur.

> **NOTE**
>
> As mentioned earlier, one of the insidious things about pointer errors is that the line of code that causes them will often compile and run just fine. On occasion, a detectable problem will not surface until much later in your program. As a result, it appears that the error occurs in a portion of your code that is actually error free. Tracking down pointer errors can be a task strewn with red herrings. However, if you set `HeapLimit` equal to `0` in the first line of your program, you have a better chance of finding the error in the location where it occurred. When you are through debugging your program, you should remove this line.
>
> There are no panaceas when it comes to pointer problems. Many of them are by definition insidious and hard to track down. One of the ways that good programmers earn their reputation is by finding pointer errors in record time.

Another thing you should notice about the BUGGY1 program is that it includes the following compiler directives:

```
{$R+,S+}
```

This code turns on stack checking and range checking, both of which can help you detect pointer errors at the place where they occur.

The key point about the BUGGY1 program is that it does not include any code to allocate memory for a pointer. It may seem as if I am spending a long time on this point, but you will find that even the most experienced programmers frequently forget to allocate memory for pointers. It is a simple mistake to fix once you have found the error, but tracking down pointer errors is not always easy.

Here is a second version of the body of the BUGGY1 program:

```
begin
  HeapLimit := 0;
  New(MyString);
  MyString^ := 'Hello';
  WriteLn(MyString^);
end.
```

This version of the program will compile and run just fine. However, it also contains a very common, and very serious, error.

Many alert readers are probably aware that this code is missing a statement to deallocate the memory assigned to MyString. When you are thinking about this kind of thing, it is simple enough to see what is wrong. The problem, however, is that in a program that contains tens of thousands of lines of code, it is easy to forget to deallocate memory in one place or another. Once you make this mistake, it can be very difficult to track it down and eradicate it.

Here is how the body of BUGGY1 should look:

```
begin
  HeapLimit := 0;New(MyString);
MyString^ := 'Hello';
  WriteLn(MyString^);
  Dispose(MyString);
end.
```

If you accidentally leave off the last line and fail to deallocate memory, the program will still run fine. However, omitting the last line of this program is the type of error that can slowly drain the system of all its available memory.

The following program, which is available on disc, helps to illustrate what happens if you forget to deallocate memory:

```
program Drain;

uses
  WinCrt;

type
  PString = ^String;

var
  S: PString;
  i: Integer;
  Start: LongInt;
begin
  Start := MemAvail;
  for i := 1 to 10 do begin
    New(S);
    WriteLn(i, ' => ', MemAvail);
  end;
  WriteLn('========================');
  WriteLn(' Memory at Start: ', Start, ' bytes');
  WriteLn('Memory Available: ', MemAvail, ' bytes');
```

```
    WriteLn('       Memory Lost: ', Start - MemAvail, ' bytes');
end.
```

On my system, the output from a short run of this program looks like this:

```
1 => 16277056
2 => 16276800
3 => 16276544
4 => 16276288
5 => 16276032
6 => 16275776
7 => 16275520
8 => 16275264
9 => 16275008
10 => 16274752
========================
 Memory at Start: 16277312 bytes
Memory Available: 16274752 bytes
    Memory Lost: 2560 bytes
```

Because of anomalies in the Windows memory system, it is unlikely that you will end up losing exactly 10×256, or 2560, bytes when you run this program. Nevertheless, this code should help demonstrate the insidious nature of memory leaks.

In particular, suppose I have written a small utility that runs constantly on my system. Suppose further that inside that utility there happens to be a loop like the one shown earlier. The first time the utility runs, I lose about 2,560 bytes, which on most systems happens to be no major problem. However, if that loop keeps executing every 20 minutes or so, after a few hours or days, my system will crash with an "Out of Memory" error.

The error, of course, could occur while I am running some other program, which means that it would be very difficult to figure out where the error was coming from. Even if I did track the error back to its home program, it might still be difficult for me to sift through a few thousand lines of code looking for the one place where I forgot to call Dispose.

Once again, I am belaboring this point because I want to make it absolutely clear that you have to remember to call New and Dispose nearly every time you use a pointer. Furthermore, it is very natural for the soggy little computer residing between our ears to occasionally forget to call New or Dispose even if it thoroughly understands the importance of the calls. As a result, there are times when you have to track this error down at great expense in terms of time and sanity. In such cases, the first thing you should do is turn on stack checking and range checking and set HeapLimit to 0.

NOTE

The GetMem and FreeMem routines are closely related to New and Dispose. In fact, in their implementation, New and Dispose call GetMem and FreeMem. The difference between the two sets of routines is that one set automatically calculates the size of the variables for which you want to allocate memory, whereas the other asks you to specifically state how much memory you need.

```
var
   S: Pstring;
begin
  New(S);
  GetMem(S, 256);
  Dispose(S);
  FreeMem(S, 256);
end;
```

In the code shown here, the calls to GetMem and the calls to New perform exactly the same function; that is, they each allocate 256 bytes on the heap.

In this section you have learned some of the basic facts about pointers. The next section goes on to show you one very practical use for the new tool you have been studying.

Moving Variables Out of the Data Segment

In the last section you saw how to declare a pointer to a string, how to reference that string, and how to allocate and deallocate memory for the string. You can use similar techniques to allocate memory for integers, arrays, and records, and for any other type of variable you declare.

The purpose of this section is to explain the hows and whys of using pointers to move variables of all types out of the data segment and onto the heap. This is probably one of the most important sections in the entire book, and in the long run it will prove vitally important for you to understand what is being explained in these pages.

Here is code that allocates memory for a simple Integer:

```
program SimpInt;
uses
  WinCrt;

type
  PInteger = ^Integer;

var
  MyInteger: PInteger;

begin
  New(MyInteger);        { Allocate 2 bytes for the Integer }
  MyInteger^ := 25;      { Assign a value to the Integer     }
  WriteLn(MyInteger^);   { Write the value to the screen     }
  Dispose(MyInteger);    { Deallocate the memory             }
end.
```

As you can see, there is nothing significantly different about allocating memory for an Integer rather than a string. Both functions are at heart identical.

The preceding program is syntactically correct. However, it is flawed in that it doesn't really serve a useful purpose. The problem is that an Integer takes up only 2 bytes of memory, whereas a pointer takes up 4. Usually, there is no advantage in moving a value from a smaller memory space into a larger memory space. As a result, it is usually best to leave an Integer value in an Integer variable, rather than trying to move it into a pointer.

> **NOTE**
>
> By now you should be able to understand why pointers take up 4 bytes, and why Integers take up only 2. If you are having trouble with these concepts, you should review earlier sections of this chapter as well as Chapters 6 and 7, "Introduction to Variables and Types," and "Integer Types in Detail." Much of what I have written in the last 10 chapters has been building to this moment, when it becomes absolutely necessary that you begin to grasp how computers handle memory.
>
> It is also important to keep in mind that memory is treated differently in 16- and 32-bit operating systems. This book describes the 16-bit version of Delphi, which was the only one available when it was written. When the 32-bit version is released, it will have much in common with the 16-bit version, but some of the details will change. If you happen to be using the 32-bit version of Delphi, don't worry, because 98 percent of the things I say in this book apply to both versions of the product. My discussion of pointers, however, is very much centered around the 16-bit version of Delphi.

Pointers have several uses. The two most important from a typical programmer's perspective are that they are fast and can be used to conserve memory. In particular, pointers can help move variables out of the crowded data and stack segments into the wide open spaces of the heap. As a result, there is not much point in making a pointer to an integer, because a pointer takes up more space in the data segment than an integer does.

Under Windows 3.1, neither the data segment nor the stack segment can exceed 64 KB in size. In fact, the data segment usually shares the same 64KB space as the stack segment and the local heap. This means that you can't afford to waste space in either the data segment or the stack segment.

It usually doesn't take long for a serious program to use up all the available space in the data or stack segment. For instance, the following declaration uses up the entire data segment in one swoop:

```
var
  MyArray: Array[0..65535] of Byte;
```

If you made this declaration, there would be no room left for the rest of your program. As a result, it is imperative that there is a system that enables you to get around this limitation.

Consider the following program:

```
Program SimpAry;

{$ifDef Windows}
uses
  WinCrt;
{$EndIf}

const
  Max = 65000;

type
  PBigArray = ^TBigArray;
  TBigArray = Array[0..Max] of Char;

var
  BigArray: PBigArray;
  i: Word;

begin
  New(BigArray);

  for i := 0 To Max do
    BigArray^[i] := 'a';

  for i := Max DownTo Max - 10 do
    WriteLn(i, ' => ', BigArray^[i]);

  Dispose(BigArray);
end.
```

This code uses a variable called BigArray that references 65,000 bytes of memory. The code itself is fairly simple. It first allocates 65,000 bytes by calling New. It then uses a loop to put the letter *a* in every single one of the those bytes. Notice that inside the loop it is necessary to dereference the BigArray variable with the caret symbol. This is done because BigArray is a pointer to an array, not the array itself. The last lines of the preceding program write out a portion of the array to the screen and then dispose of the memory after it is no longer needed.

The variable called BigArray takes up only 4 bytes of memory in the data segment. The trick, of course, is that the variable is a pointer to an array, rather than the actually array itself.

When you declare a pointer and call New, the operating system allocates memory from the heap and returns an address to you that points to that memory. In other words, it finds a place in the vast reaches of the memory theater where there are 65,000 free seats, all lined up in a row. It then gives the seat number of the first of those 65,000 seats to four of the people sitting in your program's data segment. That way, your program can own a block of memory 65,000 bytes in size but use up only 4 bytes of memory in the data segment, as shown in Figure 15.3. Your program needs to remember only the address of the array, not the array itself.

Clearly, inside a 16-bit operating system pointers are the keys to the kingdom. Learning about pointers is a little like the moment when you first got your driver's license and access to a car. Before that day, you had the means to easily reach only the area around your house. After that day, you could travel all over your home state and take full advantage of its resources. Without pointers, you are hedged into a very small area of the memory theater. Once you learn about pointers, you essentially move from a world that is 64,000 bytes in size to one that is 4 million, 16 million, or maybe even 64 million bytes in size, depending on the scale of your system.

FIGURE 15.3.

A 4-byte pointer in your data segment can reference a 64KB block residing on the heap.

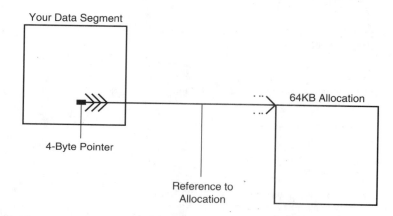

NOTE

As I write this, Windows 95, which is a true 32-bit operating system, is already in Beta. It seems likely that Windows 95 will soon be an accepted operating system, and programmers will no longer be hedged in by tiny 64KB spaces. Even after Windows 95 appears, many people will continue to use 16-bit compilers or work with 16-bit programs. As a result, 64 KB is still going to be the watchword for the next several years, and pointers are the solution.

It is probably worthwhile to point out that there are many occasions when programmers need to do something like this:

```
const
  Max = 65000;

type
  PBigArray = ^TBigArray;
  TBigArray = Array[0..Max] of Char;

var
  BigArray1, BigArray2, BigArray3: PBigArray;

begin
  New(BigArray1);
```

```
New(BigArray2);
New(BigArray3);
...
```

This code fragment allocates 195,000 bytes of memory but takes up only 12 bytes of memory in the data segment. To take this example even further, you could declare a data structure that looks like this:

```
const
  Max = 65000;

type
  PBigArray = ^TBigArray;
  TBigArray = array[0..Max] of Char;

  THugeSpaces = array[1..1000] of PBigArray;
```

This code declares an array of 1,000 pointers to 64KB chunks of memory. 1000 × 65000 is 65 million bytes of memory. Most machines don't have enough RAM to allocate that much memory; but nonetheless, the syntax of a 16-bit compiler enables you to easily declare that much memory and to manipulate it with totally legal statements. For instance, given the preceding declarations you could write code that looks like this:

```
var
  HugeSpace: THugeSpaces;

for I := 1 to 1000 do
  New(HugeSpaces[i]);
```

This is obviously very powerful code, but it unfortunately outstrips the capabilities of most hardware.

Once again, I want to emphasize the extraordinary importance of the last few paragraphs. Most significant programs contain at least five arrays, each of which are several thousand bytes in size. As a rule, you simply cannot afford to leave those arrays in the data segment. There just isn't enough room for them. You have to declare pointers to them and move them up on the heap or accept severe limitations on the size and functionality of your project. In the 16-bit world, you simply can't write many serious programs without learning about pointers. To not know about them is to limit yourself to the small-time world of simple utilities.

PChars and Arrays of Char

Both C and ObjectPascal are very powerful languages that give you full access to all the features of a computer. However, there are certain places where one language branched in one direction and the second branched in a different direction. In particular, C has a radically different way of handling strings than ObjectPascal.

Both C and Pascal are old languages that have been around since the late sixties or early seventies. During much of that time, it didn't matter that they had such radically different philosophies regarding the best way to treat strings. However, once C was chosen as a key building block for Windows, it became necessary to extend ObjectPascal's syntax to include the methods C employs when working with strings. In short, Delphi gives you the option to use PChars and arrays of Char to represent strings because that is the native way that Windows handles strings.

The developers of Delphi go out of their way to ensure that you can write complex, full-featured programs without ever having to use a PChar. That is, they intentionally make sure that you can use Delphi strings to access most of the basic functionality of a computer. The reasoning behind this decision is simply that strings are much easier to use than PChars. However, whenever you decide to step outside the native Delphi calls and start accessing the Windows API directly, you are running the risk of needing to use a PChar.

> **NOTE**
>
> The PChar type is a special kind of pointer. You need to allocate memory for it, but you usually do not need to dereference it. This can cause some confusion at first; but the key thing to remember about PChars is that they are pointers, so you have to be sure that memory is allocated for them.

There are two different ways to create a PChar. The first is simply to declare a variable as a PChar:

```
var
  S: PChar;
```

The other method is to declare it as a zero-based array of Char:

```
var
  S: array[0..100] of Char;
```

The most fundamental difference between the two declarations shown here is that the second has memory allocated for it and the first does not. In other words, the character array shown here has 101 bytes allocated for it, whereas the PChar has no bytes allocated for it. Otherwise, the two declarations are nearly identical. This identity comes about because the compiler has a special set of rules for handling PChars and arrays of Char. In other words, the array of Char shown earlier has special properties associated with it, just as a standard Delphi string is really just an array of Char with special properties.

In Chapter 14, "Strings and Text Files," you were introduced to some of the basic facts about PChars. In that chapter you learned that both strings and PChars are really just arrays of Char. Strings, however, track their length in the first byte of their data structure, whereas PChars place a null character (#0) at their end to signal their length. Because Delphi strings use a length byte, they are limited by definition to only 255 characters. PChars, on the other hand, can be up to 64 KB in length in Windows 3.1 and will have no inherent limitations under the 32-bit version of Delphi.

When working with strings, you can use the Length function to determine their size. With PChars, however, you must use the StrLen function, which is stored in the SysUtils unit:

```
uses
  SysUtils;

procedure TForm1.Button2Click(Sender: TObject);
var
  MyString: array[0..100] of Char;
begin
  StrCopy(MyString, 'Null terminated strings');
  Edit1.Text := IntToStr(StrLen(MyString));
end;
```

The code first calls StrCopy to assign a string to the PChar called MyString. It then calls StrLen to find out the length of the string. StrLen returns a word, so that value must be translated into a string before it can be shown in an edit control.

Here is a complete list of the string functions found in the Strings unit:

StrAlloc	Allocates a buffer for a null-terminated string with a maximum length of Size −1
StrBufSize	Returns the maximum number of characters that may be stored in a string buffer allocated by StrAlloc
StrCat	Appends a copy of one string to the end of another and returns the concatenated string
StrComp	Compares two strings
StrCopy	Copies one string to another
StrDispose	Disposes a string on a heap
StrECopy	Copies one string to another and returns a pointer to the end of the resulting string
StrEnd	Returns a pointer to the end of a string
StrFmt	Formats a series of arguments
StrLFmt	Formats a series of arguments; the result contains a pointer to the destination buffer
StrLCat	Appends characters from one string to the end of another and returns the concatenated string
StrIComp	Compares two strings without case sensitivity
StrLComp	Compares two strings, up to a maximum length
StrLCopy	Copies characters from one string to another
StrLen	Returns the number of characters in Str
StrLIComp	Compares two strings, up to a maximum length, without case sensitivity

StrLower	Converts a string to lowercase
StrMove	Copies characters from one string to another
StrNew	Allocates a string on a heap
StrPas	Converts a null-terminated string to a Pascal-style string
StrPCopy	Copies a Pascal-style string to a null-terminated string
StrPLCopy	Copies a maximum of MaxLen characters from the Pascal-style string Source into the null-terminated string Dest
StrPos	Returns a pointer to the first occurrence of a string in another string
StrScan	Returns a pointer to the first occurrence of a character in a string
StrRScan	Returns a pointer to the last occurrence of a character in a string
StrUpper	Converts a string to uppercase

A list very similar to this can be found in the online help, and you should refer to it whenever you have questions about the best way to handle PChars. The next few paragraphs comment on the routines in the Strings unit and offer some simple examples on how to use them.

It is easy to confuse the functionality of StrCopy and StrCat. StrCopy copies one string to another, thereby obliterating the contents of the first string. StrCat, on the other hand, appends one string onto the end of another string. The classic error to make in this regard is to attempt to use StrCat on a string that is currently set to a random value:

```
var
  S1, S2: array[0..100] of Char;

begin
  StrCat(S1, 'Hello');
  StrCat(S2, ', gentle reader');
  StrCat(S1, S2);
end;
```

The code shown here might not perform as expected, because there may be random characters in S1, and as a result the word Hello will be appended onto the end of these random characters rather than being copied into the first six letters of string S1. The correct way to handle the situation shown earlier is this:

```
var
  S1, S2: array[0..100] of Char;

begin
  StrCopy(S1, 'Hello');
  StrCopy(S2, ', gentle reader');
  StrCat(S1, S2);
  Edit1.Text := S1;
end;
```

This code always ends up with the string Hello, gentle reader in string S1. The first example might end up with this string in S1, but it is not guaranteed.

The StrNew and StrDispose functions are very useful ways of allocating memory for a string:

```
var
  S1: PChar;
begin
  S1 := StrNew('Hello');
  Edit1.Text := StrPas(S1) + ' Length: ' + IntToStr(StrLen(S1));
  StrDispose(S1);
end;
```

When using StrNew, you never have to specify exactly how many bytes you want to allocate for string S1. Instead, the compiler makes the calculation for you. This technique can be very useful when you want to make sure you are not wasting memory by preallocating arbitrarily large blocks of memory at design time. The StrDispose function provides a simple way to dispose of memory that was allocated with StrNew. Notice that you don't have to tell the compiler how many bytes to deallocate. You should also look at the StrAlloc function, which is clearly explained in the online help.

The code shown previously uses the StrPas function, which converts a null-terminated string into a Delphi string. To use StrPas, simply pass it the PChar you want to convert, and the string equivalent will be returned by the function. Nothing could be simpler.

The opposite of the StrPas function is StrPCopy, which converts a Delphi string into a null-terminated string:

```
var
  S1: String;
  S2: array[0..100] of Char;
begin
  S1 := 'Confront the difficult while it is still easy';
  StrPCopy(S2, S1);
  Edit1.Text := S2;
end;
```

Notice that the code shown here first allocates memory for S2. It would be a mistake to write code like this:

```
var
  S1: String;
  S2: PChar;
begin
  S1 := 'Confront the difficult while it is still easy';
  StrPCopy(S2, S1);
  Edit1.Text := StrPas(S2);
end;
```

When I ran the preceding function on my system, it resulted in a fatal program fault and immediate termination of my program. The problem, of course, was that no memory was ever allocated for variable S2.

All of the code you have seen in the last few pages can be found on disk in a program called PCHAR1. I don't bother to reproduce that program here, because it is nothing more than a series of buttons, each one of which is associated with one of the examples shown previously. The form for the PCHAR1 program is shown in Figure 15.4.

FIGURE 15.4.

The PCHAR1 program demonstrates some of the basic traits of null-terminated strings.

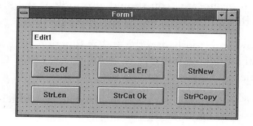

Before closing this chapter, there is one final point I want to make about PChars. If you create a procedure that returns a PChar, you should always make the routine that calls the procedure to allocate the memory for the PChar. For instance, suppose you wanted to return a string from a procedure that supplies the current date. In a case like that, the following implementation would be incorrect:

```
procedure GetDate(var Date: PChar);
begin
  GetMem(Date, 100);
  StrCopy(Date '11/01/94');
end;
```

The problem with this code fragment is that it allocates memory inside a function and then returns the string to a place that lies outside the scope of the current function. As a result, there is no guaranteed way to ensure clean up of the memory. The correct way to handle a situation like this is to insist that the calling routine allocate memory:

```
procedure GetDate(var Date: PChar);
begin
  StrCopy(Date, '11/01/94');
end;
```

A simple way to call this routine would be to write a procedure that looks like this:

```
procedure CallDate;
var
  S: array[0..100] of char;
begin
  GetDate(S);
  Edit1.Text := S;
end;
```

or like this:

```
procedure CallDate;
var
  S: PChar;
begin
  S := StrAlloc(100);
  GetDate(S);
  Edit1.Text := S;
  StrDispose(S);
end;
```

In this case, the CallDate procedure handles memory allocation for the string that will hold a date. This is always the correct way to handle this type of situation. The golden rule in this case is that a procedure that returns a modified PChar should never be responsible for allocating its memory. The calling procedure should always handle this task.

> **NOTE**
>
> In the procedure called GetDate, the Date variable is declared as a var parameter. In other words, the code looks like this:
>
> ```
> procedure GetDate(var Date: PChar);
> ```
>
> not like this:
>
> ```
> procedure GetDate(Date: PChar);
> ```
>
> This ensures that the value passed to the procedure can be modified, and that the modifications will be preserved.

The var statement is needed even though Date is already a pointer, and therefore its address is passed to the procedure automatically. In other words, what the var syntax normally does is ask the compiler to pass the address of a variable, rather than a copy of the variable.

There is a program on disk called PCHARFUN that illustrates the ideas discussed in the preceding paragraphs. The key point to remember is that any function that returns a PChar should have the calling function perform any necessary memory allocation. It is always a mistake for the called function to return a PChar that it has allocated. If you make this mistake, one of two things will happen.

■ The returned value will no longer be valid because it was a pointer that was allocated on the function's stack.

■ The returned value will probably never be properly deallocated, because there is no one who owns it and who therefore has responsibility for its deallocation.

Summary

In this chapter you learned the basics about pointers and PChars. Pointers are one of the most fundamental and important types supported by a computer. Delphi enables you to write a good deal of code without ever forcing you to think about pointers. However, the 64KB size limit on the stack and data segments can force you to work with pointers even in fairly simple programs.

PChars were also explored in this chapter. PChars can be very confusing to newcomers, in part because they are a special kind of pointer that rarely needs to be dereferenced. As a result, it is easy to make a mistake when using this type.

The next chapter takes a more in-depth look at pointers. In particular, you will get a look at linked lists and the way addresses look when you explore them with the debugger.

Pointers, Linked Lists, and Memory

16

Overview

In the last chapter you learned the basic facts about pointers. In this chapter you get a chance to explore the subject in considerably more depth. In particular, you will look at linked lists and ways to use the debugger to explore pointers.

Linked Lists

Conceptually, linked lists are fairly simple data structures. The basic idea behind linked lists is that they are used for stringing a series of records together out on the heap. The main advantages of the system are twofold:

- Linked lists are a very quick and convenient way to store many records in a single data structure.
- Linked lists move all the records onto the heap, thereby enabling you to keep track of large volumes of data that exceed by many times the 64KB limitation of the data segment.

> **NOTE**
>
> Delphi has a number of built-in objects such as TStrings, TStringList, and TList, all of which are really just object-oriented variations of linked lists. Obviously, it usually makes more sense to use these built-in structures than to create tools of your own.
>
> However, customized linked lists of various kinds are so useful, and have played such a crucial role in computing over the years, that I can't really imagine finishing this book without covering them in at least some detail. If you are a good programmer, you can use linked lists to provide small, flexible solutions to a large number of problems.

> **NOTE**
>
> The code for the LINKLIST1 program is in the CHAP16 directory on this book's CD-ROM.

LINKLST1 is another WINCRT program, so you need to remove UNIT1 from a project and modify the DPR file so that it looks like the example shown previously. I have chosen to make this a WINCRT program, not because this code couldn't be incorporated into a standard VCL project, but simply because I wanted to remove all the possible impediments to your vision of this program. In short, I wanted to make the code as simple as possible.

LINKLST1 begins by displaying the current amount of available memory, and it ends by doing the same thing. Under normal circumstances, these two figures do not match. The reason for this discrepancy is explained later.

After showing the currently available memory, LINKLST1 displays a simple list of strings that look something like this:

```
Sam1
Sam2
Sam3
Sam4
etc...
```

The list is comprised of strings that were parts of a very simple record:

```
PMyRecord = ^TMyRecord;
TMyRecord = Record
Name: String;
Next: PMyRecord;
end;
```

This record has two fields. The first is a string, and the second is a pointer to a record of type TMyRecord. I explain this latter field in one moment.

In this program, the Name field of the records used in the program gets set to values such as Sam1, Sam2, and Sam3. The code that creates these strings is very simple and should be familiar to you by now:

```
procedure GetData(var Item: PMyRecord);
begin
  Item^.Name := 'Sam' + Int2Str(Total);
end;
```

All that is happening here is that a variable called Total is being incremented inside a loop, and each time it is incremented, the function GetData is called. GetData sets the Name field of the record to the word Sam plus the value of the variable total after it has been translated into a string.

As I have said, the Name variable of TMyRecord is easy enough to understand. The tricky part is the second field, the one that's called Next. The Next field is declared to be of type PMyRecord. In other words, it is a pointer to a record of the same type as the record to which it belongs.

If you are new to linked lists, you might mistakenly be tempted to think of them as a series of Chinese boxes, each of which contains another box of its same type, only slightly smaller. A better image for a linked list might be a series of helium-filled balloons each attached to the next by a string, with the very first member tied down to a stake fixed firmly in the ground, as shown in Figure 16.1.

FIGURE 16.1.

Linked lists are like a series of balloons tied together, with the first balloon tied to a stake in the data or stack segment.

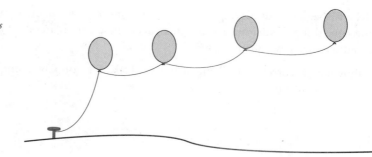

Picture a metal stake with a ring on the top of it fixed into an area of ground called the data segment. This stake has a string tied to it, and on the end of the string is a balloon. At the very bottom of the balloon, right next to the place where the string is attached, there is a second string, which in turn leads off to a second balloon. Tied to the bottom of this balloon is a third string, which leads to a third balloon, which in turn leads to a fourth string, and so on, for 10, 20, 1,000, or more balloons.

At the very bottom of each linked list is a pointer, which is fixed firmly in the solid earth of either the data or the stack segment. This pointer points off like a long string that leads to a record that is floating out on the heap. Inside this record another pointer exists, which in turn leads off like a long string to the next member in the list. This process continues until you have strung together all the records you want to work with at any one time. The key image I want you to grasp here is that the pointer field, which in this case is called Next, acts exactly like a string that leads you to the next record in the list of records that comprise what is called a linked list.

Suppose you had 20 of these records linked together. If you wanted to find the tenth record, you could start at the pointer in the data segment, feel your way along to the first record, find the pointer field in that record, feel your way along to the second record, and so on, until you had iterated through 10 records. Then you would be standing smack dab in the middle of the record you wanted to find.

Furthermore, if you had a list of this type, you could count the total members in the list by starting at the first record and proceeding until you came to a point where there was no string to lead you to another record. The question, of course, is how can you tell that you are out of records? How do you know that the next pointer you look at is the end of the road and doesn't point at another record?

The answer to this question is actually fairly simple. Every pointer can be set to one of three states. It can contain a valid address, it can contain a nonsense address, or it can contain an address that is set to zero. It is very difficult to tell the difference between a valid address and a nonsense address, because they both simply contain a set of numbers. However, pointers that are set to zero are clearly defined as invalid pointers. Therefore, you can mark the end of a linked list by setting the Next field of record to zero, which is called setting a pointer to nil.

You can set a pointer to nil by writing the following::

```
MyRecord^.Next := nil;
```

> **NOTE**
>
> I stated earlier that it is hard to tell from just looking at it whether a pointer contains a valid address or just some randomly chosen set of numbers that happened to be in a particular section of memory. The inability to make this distinction is in fact a very serious problem that can cause no end of mischief.
>
> In particular, if a program is feeling its way along the length of a linked list and it suddenly stumbles across a Next pointer that points off at a random place in memory, the computer will try to feel its way along that string to the imaginary or nonsensical location. Because there is no valid memory at this new location, the computer becomes effectively lost the moment it arrives at the end of its string. Once a computer gets lost, it is very difficult for it ever to get back on track again. Jumping to an invalid address is an excellent way to crash a computer, or at least to cause a process running under a multitasking system to be frozen and ultimately terminated by the system.
>
> As a result of the problem outlined here, it is absolutely essential that you construct all linked lists entirely out of valid addresses, and that you mark the end of each linked list with the value nil. Assigning nil to the last Next field in a linked list clearly marks that node as being the end of the road.

Here is one way to create a node in a linked list:

```
procedure CreateNew(var Item: PMyRecord);
begin
  New(Item);
  Item^.Next := nil;
  Item^.Name := '';
end;
```

This procedure starts by allocating memory for the node with the New procedure. The code then sets the Next pointer to nil and sets the Name field to an empty string. After this procedure is through, the node passed to it is fully initialized.

As stated earlier, the very first node in a linked list is attached to the data segment or stack segment. As a result, it is an exception and needs to be treated differently than all the other nodes in a list. Here is one way to create the first node in a linked list:

```
procedure DoFirst(var First, Current: PMyRecord);
begin
  CreateNew(Current);
  GetData(Current);
  First := Current;
end;
```

DoFirst calls CreateNew, then GetData, and then it sets the variable First equal to Current. You have already heard about both CreateNew and GetData, but it will take a moment to explain the last line in the DoFirst procedure.

In addition to the Total variable, the LINKLST1 program lists the following global variables:

```
var
  First,
  Current: PMyRecord;
```

These two variables are used to keep track of the members of the linked list. The First variable always points to the member of the list that is staked into the data or stack segment. The Current variable always points to the currently selected member of the linked list, which in this particular program will always be the last member of the linked list. In more complex linked list programs, a variable like Current might address a node that is in the middle of the list.

The DoFirst procedure first creates a valid node, fills it with valid data, and finally it sets First equal to this node. In other words the following line of code

```
First := Current;
```

is equivalent to the act of driving the stake attached to the first balloon into the ground. After this, the linked list is attached to the data segment by means of the variable called First.

After getting the list started, all other nodes are added onto the list by means of the Add procedure:

```
procedure Add(var Current: PMyRecord);
var
  Prev: PMyRecord;
begin
  Prev := Current;
  CreateNew(Current);
  GetData(Current);
  Prev^.Next := Current;
end;
```

Add gets passed a copy of the currently selected member of the linked list. Remember that in this linked list, Current could just as easily have been called Last.

The Add procedure declares a second pointer to PMyRecord, called Prev. Prev is set equal to Current, and then CreateNew is called. In other words, Prev remembers what Current was pointing at, and then Current is used to hold a newly created node, which is then immediately filled with data by the GetData procedure. Finally, the new Current variable is tied on to the end of the linked list with the following piece of code:

```
Prev^.Next := Current;
```

There are many, many different ways to implement a linked list. The following routine represents a second take on the Add procedure:

```
procedure Add2(var Current: PMyRecord);
var
```

```
  Temp: PMyRecord;
begin
  CreateNew(Temp);
  GetData(Temp);
  Current^.Next := Temp;
  Current := Temp;
end;
```

In this example, a variable called `Temp` is used when a new node is created. The `Next` field of `Current` is set equal to `Temp`, and finally the `Current` variable is set equal to the newly created node. Both examples take the same amount of time to execute, and both accomplish the same goal. However, looking at a second version of the `Add` procedure helps to illustrate exactly how linked lists work and exactly what needs to be accomplished to add a new node to the end of a list.

The main body of the LINKLST1 program uses the following code to create 21 nodes:

```
repeat
  Inc(Total);
  Add(Current);
until Total > 20;
```

NOTE

The main body of a Delphi program is always encapsulated in a `begin..end` pair that is terminated with a period. Most Delphi programs use this main block simply to initialize one or more forms and then call `Application.Run`. The LINKLST1 program uses this main block far more extensively than VCL programs, but there is no difference in the way the compiler handles this section of the program. In other words, it simply executes the code between the `begin..end` pair, regardless of whether that code reads

`Application.Run,`

or whether it reads

`CreateNew(Current, First);`

After the list has been created, the following procedure shows it to the user:

```
procedure Show(Head: PMyRecord);
begin
  while Head^.Next <> nil do begin
    WriteLn(Head^.Name);
    Head := Head^.Next;
  end;
  WriteLn(Head^.Name);
end;
```

This procedure is passed the variable called `First`:

```
Show(First);
```

`First` is passed to `Show` because the procedure simply displays each record in the list, starting with the first and traveling through to the end. As you will see in a moment, it is not possible to iterate backward through this particular linked list. Instead, you must always iterate through the list by starting at the beginning and moving one link at a time.

Here is how to move from the currently selected item to the next item in the list:

```
Head := Head^.Next;
```

If you pass `First` to the `Show` procedure, calling this line once will move you from the first item in the list to the second item. Calling it a second time will move you from the second item to the third item, and so forth.

The trick in the `Show` procedure is to know when you are at the end of the list. This is accomplished by the `while` statement, which enables the line shown previously to be called until the moment when the current record has a `Next` field that is set equal to `nil`. The significance of the nil `Next` pointer was described earlier:

```
while Head^.Next <> nil do begin
```

There are two other important points about the `Show` procedure. The first is that after the `while` loop ends, one more item still must be displayed to the user, so the code does that in its last line. Furthermore, you should note that `First` is passed to the `Show` procedure not as a `var` parameter:

```
procedure Show(var Head: PMyRecord);
```

but as a simple parameter:

```
procedure Show(Head: PMyRecord);
```

That is, it is passed by value, not by reference. This is done because you don't want to change the node addressed by `First`.

Because this is an important point, let's look at the same issue again from a second angle. You want to be able to pass `Show` the first member of the list:

```
Show(First);
```

If `Show` uses the following code:

```
Head := Head^.Next;
```

to iterate from the first member of the list to the second member, you don't want the variable called `First` to be affected. As a result, the correct thing to do is pass `First` by value, rather than by reference. This means a copy of the pointer will be passed to the function and not the `First` pointer itself, as explained in Chapter 10, "Real Numbers, Functions, and Operators."

One last function in the LINKLST1 program still needs to be explained:

```
procedure FreeAll(var Head: PMyRecord);
var
```

```
  Temp: PMyRecord;
begin
  while Head^.Next <> nil do begin
    Temp := Head^.Next;
    Dispose(Head);
    Head := Temp;
  end;
  Dispose(Head);
end;
```

The purpose of this procedure is to dispose of all the nodes in the linked list. In other words, it deallocates all the memory allocated by the CreateNew procedure.

Just like the Show procedure, FreeAll is passed First, and it iterates through the linked list in exactly the same manner as Show. However, as each node is reached, the FreeAll procedure disposes of it. In order to do this correctly, it must first keep a copy of the next member of the list, so that it has something to hang onto after it has deleted the current member. Then the current member, called Head in this procedure, is set equal to what was the second member of the list. In this way, the procedure iterates through the whole list, deleting the member behind it as it goes. See the sequence of pictures shown in Figure 16.2. Note that it is safe to pass First to free all as a var parameter.

FIGURE 16.2.

A linked list can be disposed of by iterating from the first item to the last, while destroying the currently selected item.

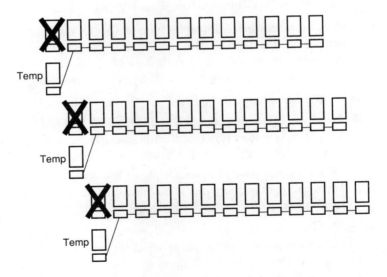

The LINKLST1 program uses Delphis built-in MemAvail procedure to list the currently available memory both at the beginning and at the end of a run. As I mentioned earlier, when run under Windows 3.1, there is usually a discrepancy between the amount of available memory listed at the beginning of this program and the amount listed at the end.

If you took the LINKLST1 program and changed the uses clause so that it referenced Crt instead of WinCrt, you could run this program from the DOS prompt. To do so, you can compile it with an old version of Turbo Pascal, or with the DCC compiler that comes with Delphi.

When running DCC, you should pass the following command line at the DOS prompt:

```
DCC /CD LINKLST1.DPR
```

The LINKLST1.EXE program created by this code will report the same amount of memory available at startup as at the end.

> **NOTE**
>
> Right before shipping Delphi, the developers removed the TURBO.TPL file that DCC.EXE uses when combiling DOS programs. However, if you have the source for Delphi, you should be able to recompile SYSTEM.PAS and begin compiling DOS and DOS protected-mode programs. You can compile SYSTEM.PAS with DCC itself, and the various related assembler files can be compiled with TASM. Borland's assembler, TASM.EXE, is available separately as an add-on product.

How can there sometimes be a discrepancy between the amount of memory shown by the program when it runs from DOS and the amount shown when it runs under Windows? Is Windows broken? Is Delphi broken? What is going on here?

This is not the time to give a full explanation of what has occurred here, but what usually causes the discrepancy is that both Delphis and Windows memory managers tend to allocate memory from the system in large chunks and then pass little bits and pieces of those large chunks to your program when you request them. As a result, the following may happen:

- Your program requests 50 bytes.
- Delphi or Windows may not have that memory available to give you. As a result, Delphi or Windows may first allocate several thousands bytes of memory, and then give you a pointer to a small, 50-byte chunk of that memory.
- When you free your 50 bytes, Delphi or Windows may not be ready to free up the larger chunk of memory that it allocated. Instead, it just takes your 50 bytes back, but doesn't free that larger block to which it belongs.

When the steps shown above occur, it will appear that memory is not being freed. However, all that's really happening is that Delphi or Windows has not deallocated a large chunk of memory from which it is giving you small chunks. A key point to grasp in this process is that your program's requests for memory pass through two memory managers. The first memory manager belongs to Windows, the second to Delphi.

If you want, you can tell Delphi not to grab memory in big chunks but to get only the exact amount you need. The mechanism for doing this has been shown to you before:

```
HeapLimit := 0;
```

This code tells Delphi's memory manager to always explicitly allocate memory directly from the operating system whenever you request it. This subject is addressed again at the end of the chapter.

If `HeapLimit` is set to 0, the LINKLST1 program should say that the same amount of memory is available when you start the program as when you end it. If the number differs, there is a chance that the Windows memory manager has not released a block of memory it allocated in order to accomadate your request. However, it is also possible that you have incorrectly entered the code for the program. You should compare the code with the listings found here or with the listings for the on-disk version of LINKLST1.

A Second Link List Example

The LINKLST1 program introduces you to linked lists and to the mechanisms that drive them. It is, however, such a stripped-down and simple example that you might not be able to see quite how useful linked lists can be. As a result I have created a second linked list program, called LINKLST2, which has three new features:

- It is integrated into the Delphi VCL environment.
- It enables you to enter new records manually.
- It enables you to delete records.

The LINKLST2 program is also unusual in that it is broken into three parts. The main form for the program, shown in Figure 16.3, enables you to iterate through the records in the linked list, to search for them by name, and to delete them. The second form in the program, shown in Figure 16.4, is used when you want to add a new entry to the linked list. The third unit has no form attached to it and is used only to declare variables common to both units, as well as one short routine that creates some dummy records to be displayed in the linked list.

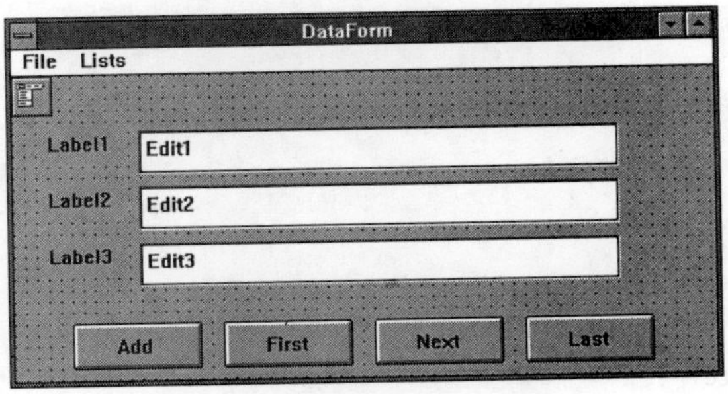

FIGURE 16.3.

The main form for the LINKLST2 program enables you to browse the list and delete records.

FIGURE 16.4.

*The second form in the
LINKLST2 program is
used for entering new data
into the list.*

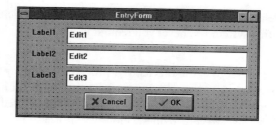

With the capability to add, delete, browse, and search for records, the LINKLST2 program
gives you most of the functionality you want in a simple linked list. The one thing that is missing is the capability to move both backward and forward through the list. This capability is
granted by a data structure called a double-linked list. An example of a double-linked list is
available on the CD in the file DBLIST.PAS. DBLIST, stored in the UNITS subdirectory.

NOTE

The code for the three parts (the unit MAIN, MAKEDATA.PAS, and ENTRY.PAS) of
the LINKLST2 program is in the CHAP16 directory on this book's CD-ROM.

The LINKLST2 program reads and writes data from both a binary and a text file. The binary
file is the main storage for the program. The text file exists because you might want to manually enter data into a text file when you are starting the program. You can then automatically
read the text file into the program's linked list. In other words, the text file is just part of a
utility, and the binary file is the main data storage.

The File menu item in the LINKLST2 program has the following entries:

```
Read Data
Create New List
Save
Exit
```

The capability to create a new list is granted to the CreateData function in the MakeData unit:

```
procedure CreateData;
var
  F: Text;
  i: Integer;

begin
  Assign(F, 'data.txt');
  ReWrite(F);
  for i := 1 to Max do begin
    WriteLn(F, 'Sam' + Int2Str(i));
    WriteLn(F, i);
    WriteLn(F, Days[i Mod 7]);
  end;
  Close(F);
end;
```

This function creates a simple text file that looks like this:

```
Sam1
1
Monday
Sam2
2
Tuesday
Sam3
...
```

The file goes through as many iterations as you specify in the Integer constant called Max.

The following rather plodding function reads the text file into a linked list:

```
procedure TDataForm.ReadTextFile(var FirstNode, Current: PMyNode);
var
  F: System.Text;
  Prev: PMyNode;
  i: Integer;
begin
  Assign (F, 'data.txt');
  {$I-} Reset(F); {$I+}
  if (IOResult <> 0) then begin
    MessageBox(Handle, 'error Reading File', nil, mb_Ok);
    Halt;
  end;
  NewNode(Current);
  ReadLn(F, Current^.Name);
  ReadLn(F, Current^.Flight);
  ReadLn(F, Current^.Day);
  FirstNode := Current;
  i := 0;
  while not Eof(F) do begin
    Prev := Current;
    NewNode(Current);
    ReadLn(F, Current^.Name);
    ReadLn(F, Current^.Flight);
    ReadLn(F, Current^.Day);
    Prev^.Next := Current;
    Inc(i);
  end;
  System.Close(F);
  CreateNewFile;
end;
```

After having read this list the first time from a text file, LINKLST2 stores its data in a binary file of the type first seen at the end of Chapter 13, "Working with Records." The CreateNewFile procedure is used to actually write the binary data to disk:

```
procedure TDataForm.CreateNewFile;
var
  F: File of TMyNode;
  Head: PMyNode;
begin
  Head := FirstNode;
  Assign(F, FileName);
  ReWrite(F);
```

```
  while Head^.Next <> nil do begin
    Write(F, Head^);
    Head := Head^.Next;
  end;
  Write(F, Head^);
  System.Close(F);
end;
```

This procedure iterates over all the nodes in the linked list and writes each one to disk. Like all the procedures in the LINKLST2 program, it would not matter if there were 5 or 5,000 records in the list. The procedures would work exactly the same under either condition. The only limit to the size of the list is the amount of available memory on your system.

The LINKLST2 program knows how to count all the nodes in the linked list:

```
procedure TDataForm.Count1Click(Sender: TObject);
var
  i: Integer;
  Head: PMyNode;
begin
  i := 1;
  Head := FirstNode;
  while Head^.Next <> nil do begin
    Head := Head^.Next;
    Inc(i);
  end;
  MessageDlg('Total = ' + IntToStr(i), mtInformation, [mbOk], 0);
end;
```

The procedure begins by moving to the first node in the list:

```
Head := FirstNode;
```

It then proceeds to iterate over all the nodes:

```
while Head^.Next <> nil do begin
  Head := Head^.Next;
  Inc(i);
end;
```

while doing nothing more than incrementing the variable i after visiting each node. At the end, i will be equal to the total number of records in the list, and the MessageDlg procedure is then called on to display that number to the user.

The Find procedure searches through all the records in the list until it finds one that has a Name field equal to a string entered by the user:

```
function TDataForm.Find(S: String): PMyNode;
var
  Head,
  Temp: PMyNode;
begin
  Head := FirstNode;
  Temp := nil;
  while Head^.Next <> nil do begin
    if Head^.Name = S then begin
      Temp := Head;
```

```
     Break;
   end;  ·
   Head := Head^.Next;
  end;
  if Head^.Name = S then Temp := Head;
  Find := Temp;
end;
```

Notice that when the sought-after record is found, the routine exits the `while` loop by calling `Break`. Delphi provides two commonly used ways for getting out of a loop:

■ A call to the `Exit` procedure breaks you out of loop and also out of the current procedure. If the current procedure is the main body of a program, a call to `Exit` ends the entire program.

■ A call to `Break` causes the code to exit the current loop, but not the entire procedure. For instance, in the preceding example, `Break` exits the `while` loop, but the following two lines are still executed:

```
if Head^.Name = S then Temp := Head;
Find := Temp;
```

Perhaps the most important procedure from the LINKLST2 program is the `DeleteNode` procedure:

```
procedure TDataForm.DeleteNode(var Node: PMyNode);
var
  Temp: PMyNode;
begin
  Temp := FirstNode;

  if Temp = Node then begin          { First Node? }
    Temp := Temp^.Next;
    FirstNode := Temp;
  end else
    while Temp^.Next <> Node do
      Temp := Temp^.Next;

  Current := Temp;

  if Temp^.Next^.Next <> nil then    { A Middle Node? }
    Temp^.Next := Temp^.Next^.Next
  else
    Temp^.Next := nil;               { Last Node? }
  Dispose(Node);
end;
```

There are three different sections in this routine. The first section checks to see if the node to be deleted is the first node in the list. If so, the code iterates down to the second node of the list, sets `FirstNode` equal to it, and then deletes the node that was at the head of the list.

The second section in the `DeleteNode` procedure checks to see if the node to be deleted is somewhere in the middle of the list. If it is, the `Next` field in the node before the one to be deleted is set equal to the node after the one to be deleted. The node between these two locations is disposed of.

The third section of the DeleteNode method checks to see if the last node in the list is the one that needs to be deleted. If it is, the Next field in the next to last node is set to nil, and the final node is disposed of.

The logic in the DeleteNode procedure is interesting primarily because it shows how you can use if statements to track down special cases. If the first or last nodes in the list need to be deleted, each one needs to be handled as a special case; otherwise, a default method is used for deleting any of the nodes in the middle of the list.

I have also included a third program, called LINKLST3, that shows the LINKLST2 transformed into a WINCRT or DOS program. This third example is provided as an afterthought, and I do not mention it again, other than to say that it is available on disk. After you start the program, choose Create New List from the menu before trying to iterate through any of the records.

Examining Pointers in the Debugger

This is one of the sections of this book that will probably glaze the eyes of beginners. If that happens to you, don't worry about it. Even after my first two years of steady programming, I'm not sure I could have made much sense of this material. Certainly it took a good five years of hard work before I felt ready to write about material like this with any confidence. In other words, this subject is by definition of interest primarily to advanced programmers. If you are an intermediate programmer who wants to make the jump to the advanced level, this is one of the areas where you will want to concentrate. I should perhaps add, however, that understanding this material does not make you, ipso facto, a great programmer. That is a gift that can be given only by God (or, if you prefer, by Fate). However, if you do master this stuff, nobody is going to call you a neophyte. That part of your career is well behind you once you are comfortable with this discussion of pointers.

Consider the program shown in Listing 16.1.

Listing 16.1. The POINTER5 program explores the strange world of pointers and Intel addressing.

```
program Pointer5;
uses
  WinCrt;

var
  A: Pointer;
  B: PChar;
begin
  HeapLimit := 0;          { Turn off sub-allocator    }
  A := Ptr(DSeg, 0);       { A "fake" pointer          }
  B := Ptr($45FF, $10);    { No memory allocation!     }
  A := nil;                { Set pointer to nil        }
  B := nil;                { Set pointer to nil        }
  New(A);                  { Pointer STILL equal nil!  }
```

```
  Dispose(A);                { Does nothing             }
  GetMem(A, 100);            { Allocate a hundred bytes }
  GetMem(B, 100);            { Allocate a hundred bytes }
  StrCopy(B, 'Test data');   { Use the allocation       }
  FreeMem(A, 100);           { Deallocate 100 bytes     }
  A := nil;                  { Set pointer to nil       }
  FreeMem(B, 100);           { Deallocate 100 bytes     }
  asm                        { Set pointer to nil: B:=nil }
    mov word ptr B, 0;       { Zero out offset          }
    mov word ptr B + 2, 0;   { Zero out segment         }
  end;                       { Close ASM block          }
end.                         { Close program            }
```

You can see that POINTER5 contains an unusually large number of comments. I have done this because I want to give you something concrete to hang onto while I discuss some pretty abstract concepts. There is, however, a second version (POINTER5A) of the program available on disk that does not have any comments. If you find the comments confusing, switch to the other version.

A quick look at this program reveals that it doesn't do anything useful. In fact, it does strange things such as create pointers that don't point at valid data. When it finally does allocate some memory, it never uses it in any conventional sense, but quickly proceeds to dispose of it.

I wrote this program primarily to give you a chance to watch pointers in the stand-alone debugger. You will probably be able to follow the first part of this discussion if all you have is the integrated debugger, but the real meat of the discussion requires the stand-alone tool.

NOTE

When you compile for the stand-alone debugger, you must make sure that the "Include TDW Debug Info" switch is turned on. To set this switch, choose the Options | Project menu selection and turn to the Linker Options page. The switch is near the bottom of the window, and it is turned on when there is an X in front of it. You should also be sure that Debug Information, Local Symbols, and Symbol Info are all turned on in the Compiler Options page from the same menu choice.

For safety's sake, it is probably a good idea to choose Build from the Run menu now. Once the settings are correctly identified, the next step is to pop up the stand-alone debugger by choosing the Tools | Turbo Debugger menu option.

Turbo Debugger does not ship with Delphi. You can, however, purchase it from Borland as a stand-alone product. It usually comes bundled with TASM, which is Borland's assembler. If you have Borland C++ 4.5 or later, you may already have a copy of a Delphi-compatible, stand-alone debugger, which is called TDW.EXE.

The first time you step through the program, you should set the following watches in the Watch window of either the integrated or the stand-alone debugger. Use the stand-alone debugger if possible, because it is designed from the bottom up for this kind of analysis of a program or code fragment.

```
A
B
@A
@B
A^
B^
DS { With integrated debugger, use "DSeg", not "DS" }
```

The @ symbol tells the debugger to return the address of a variable. You can use the @ symbol inside the code of your own programs if you want to reference, not the contents of a variable, but its address.

Step one line into the program with the F8 key so that you can set the cursor on the line that says HeapLimit = 0. The purpose of this line is simply to effectively turn off the Pascal compiler's integrated heap manager. The heap manager helps save time and system resources, but it does so by fussing around with the normal allocation of pointers. Because the goal of this exercise is to see how pointers actually work, it is best to leave the heap manager out of the picture for now.

After pressing F8 for the first time, the Watch window at the bottom of the screen should look something like this:

```
A          nil : POINTER
B          nil : PCHAR
A^         @0000:0000 : UNTYPED
B^         #0 : CHAR
@A         4057:00AA [POINTER5.A] : POINTER
@B         4057:00AE [POINTER5.B] : POINTER
```

Of course the actual addresses you see in the Watch window probably won't be identical to those you see here, but the general layout should be similar.

> **NOTE**
>
> Some curious readers may wonder how I copied the information from the Watch window in the debugger. Actually, it isn't difficult—you just need to know your way around. The key to this feat is the Log window, which can be accessed from the View menu in the stand-alone debugger. Simply follow these steps:
>
> 1. After opening the Log window, click it once with the right mouse button.
> 2. Choose "Open Log File" and click the OK button to accept the default name given to you by the debugger.
> 3. Select the window whose contents you want to save.

4. Pull down the Edit menu and choose "Dump Pane to Log."

5. Click the right mouse button again on the Log window and close the file.

When you return to DOS, you will find a file saved under the default name containing the contents of the window that was focused when you chose "Dump Pane to Log."

You probably won't have to do this kind of thing very often, but when the time finally comes around, the need is usually fairly urgent.

The last two addresses in the Watch window are important to use during this initial stage of the program analysis:

```
@A              4057:00AA [POINTER5.A] : POINTER
@B              4057:00AE [POINTER5.B] : POINTER
```

Notice that on my machine during one particular run of the program, the segment portion of the address for A and B is $4057. At the same time, when I open the Registers Pane from the View menu, I find the following listing:

```
ax 1CDA
bx 0000
cx 0000
dx 4057
si 0000
di 4056
bp 20DE
sp 20DE
ds 4057
es 0000
ss 4057
cs 3F07
ip 0016
```

(Remember, only the general format of these listings will be the same on your machine. The actual specific hex numbers listed will most likely differ.) In the example shown here, you can see that the program's data segment (ds) is also set to $4057, just like the segment value for variables A and B. This is no coincidence, because, as I said earlier, global variables in a program are always stored in the data segment. In this particular case, variable A is stored $AA or 170 bytes into the data segment. Four bytes further on you can find B, which resides at $AE, or the 174th byte of the data segment. Once again, this should not surprise anyone, because the variables were declared right next to each other in the code, and they are each 4 bytes in size. In other words, B is found 4 bytes further into the data segment than A because the intervening space is taken up by pointer A, which is 4 bytes in size.

> **NOTE**
>
> Two quick points might be helpful for some readers. First, if you ever forget how large a variable is, you can run the SizeOf function on it. Generally you don't have to recompile your code but can simply type SizeOf(A) in the Watch window, and the debugger will tell you the size of the object, which in this case is 4.
>
> Second, don't forget that Windows ships with a calculator that can help you translate hex numbers into decimal numbers. The calculator is kept in the Accessories group, and you can start it the way you would any other Windows program. Once it's running, choose the View | Scientific menu item. Type 170 into the calculator and click the button labeled Hex to see its hex value, which is AA. Conversely, you can first click the Hex button and then type AE, and the calculator will translate the number into its decimal value if you click the Dec button.
>
> Once again, you don't need to know any of these things to program in Delphi. However, if you want to get really serious about programming, you should know this material, or at least aspire to know it one day.

The key point that has been established so far is that the pointers A and B both reside in the data segment. However, it should now be obvious that there is a big difference between the address at which A and B reside and the items they point at. In fact, at this time, A and B aren't pointing at anything. Their value is currently nil.

> **NOTE**
>
> Delphi initializes all global variables to nil, or 0, on startup. If you are following along on a DOS version of Pascal which doesn't do this, you should add two lines of code to the program, which will initialize these values to nil.

Here comes the important part. A and B point at nil. That much is clear. But what exactly does this mean? What specifically does it mean to say that a pointer is equal to nil? To find out, you need to open the Dump Pane from the Watch window. Click it once with the right mouse button and select the option that says Goto. (See Figure 16.5.) A dialog box will appear and you can type the letter A into it and press Enter. This takes you to a pictorial representation of the place in the data segment where A actually resides:

```
ds:00AA 00 00 00 00 00 00 00 00
ds:00B2 00 00 00 00 00 00 00 00
ds:00BA 00 00 00 00 00 00 11 05
ds:00C2 DF 30 00 00 00 00 00 00
```

As you can see, the 4 bytes shown immediately after ds:00AA are all zeros. This is what it means to say that A is equal to nil. Just so you're sure to understand what I mean, let me show you the line again, with the relevant 4 bytes in brackets:

```
ds:00AA [00 00 00 00] 00 00 00 00
```

The last 4 bytes in the preceding line also happen to be set to zero, which once again should not come as a surprise, because they belong to B. As you saw earlier, B is also set to nil, so of course the 4 bytes in its portion of the data segment are set to zero.

FIGURE 16.5.

Searching for an address in the Dump Pane.

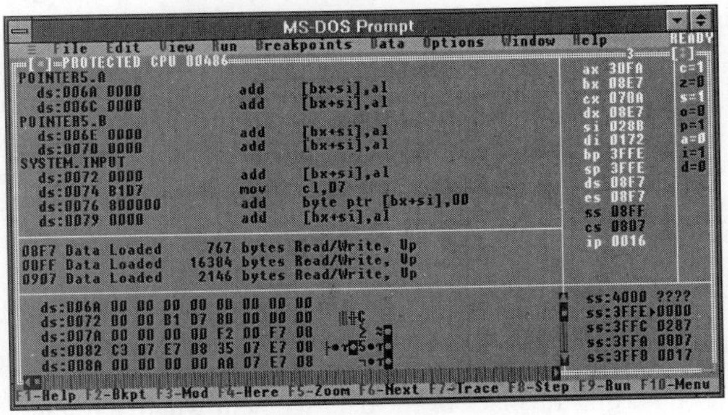

To verify the value of B, you can click once on the right mouse button, select Goto, and enter B. The Dump Pane you see will look something like this:

```
ds:00AE 00 00 00 00 00 00 00 00
ds:00B6 00 00 00 00 00 00 00 00
ds:00BE 00 00 11 05 DF 30 00 00
ds:00C6 00 00 00 00 00 00 00 00
```

Once again, it is the first 4 bytes after AE that are important. As you can see, they are set to zero, and that means that B has the value of nil.

After spending all this time getting set up, and after carefully examining the initial state of the program, it is at last time to step through the first real lines in the program:

```
A := Ptr(DSeg, 0);     { A "fake" pointer to nothing        }
B := Ptr($45FF, $10);  { No memory allocation!              }
```

The Ptr function creates a pointer that addresses a particular place in memory. Specifically, the preceding code sets the first 2 bytes at the address DS:00AA to the address of the data segment and sets the next 2 bytes to zero:

```
ds:00AA 00 00 57 40 00 00 00 00
ds:00B2 00 00 00 00 00 00 00 00
ds:00BA 00 00 00 00 00 00 11 05
ds:00C2 DF 30 00 00 00 00 00 00
```

Here is the significant line again, with the segment portion of the address in parentheses and the offset in brackets:

```
ds:00AA [00 00] (57 40) 00 00 00 00
```

The two most obvious facts about the preceding line are that the offset appears before the segment, and the numbers in the segment portion of the address are reversed. Specifically, the high byte is where you would expect the low byte to be, and vice-versa. If this strikes you as peculiar, you are a considerably calmer and more controlled person than me. Even after years of working with the Intel architecture, I am still completely floored by the fact that such a topsy-turvy memory scheme managed to win out over more logical alternatives. The simple moral of this story is that it is not reason, but the free market, that dictates the major decisions made in the computer industry. All in all, the free market is probably a respectably admirable arbiter in matters like this, yet it does yield some surprising results at times. (Given the flap over the floating point Pentium errors, I should perhaps add that I think Intel is a fine company, although I don't understand why they had to leave us with such a topsy-turvy method for storing addresses in memory.)

At any rate, the second line of code shown previously looks like this:

```
B := Ptr($45FF, $10); { No memory allocation!        }
```

After it is run, the place in the data segment where B resides looks like this:

```
ds:00AE 10 00 FF 45 00 00 00 00
ds:00B6 00 00 00 00 00 00 00 00
ds:00BE 00 00 11 05 DF 30 00 00
ds:00C6 00 00 00 00 00 00 00 00
```

Once again, here are the relevant portions marked with parentheses around the segment and brackets around the offset:

```
ds:00AE [10 00] (FF 45) 00 00 00 00
```

As you can see, the low byte at offset $AE is equal to hex 10, which is the same as the decimal value 16. The segment portion of the address is obviously set to $45FF, with the bytes reversed, as dictated by the whims of the good folks at Intel.

To sum up what has been said here, you can look down at the Watch window, which now shows A and B equal to the following:

```
A        4057:0000 : POINTER
B        45FF:0010 '' : PCHAR
```

This representation of the address is much more readable than what is seen in the Dump Pane. However, the view in the Dump Pane is perhaps more important, because it shows exactly what is happening in the memory that belongs to the data segment. Specifically, it shows that the values that had been set to nil are now pointing at particular addresses.

Notice that I say particular addresses, not valid addresses. The reason for this is that there is not anything necessarily valid about the two addresses shown earlier. To verify this, you can go to the List Pane in the CPU window. To get there, pull down the View menu and then choose CPU. The window you are interested in is the middle one on the left, as shown in Figure 16.6.

FIGURE 16.6.

The List Pane in the CPU window.

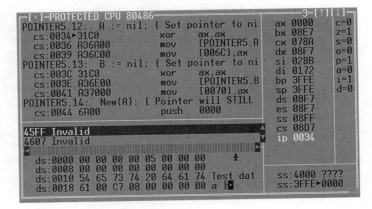

If you click the right mouse button on the Selector List Pane, you can pull up the menu with the choices Selector and Examine on it. Choose Selector, and type `$45FF` in it. You will probably end up with a List Pane that looks something like this:

```
CPU 80486
45FF Invalid
4607 Invalid
```

Here you can see that the List Pane is telling you that the selector `$45FF` is invalid. This selector is invalid because it was simply put together with the `Ptr` function without my ever having taking the time to allocate memory for it. In other words, I just put together a bogus address out of whole cloth, and the clever protected-mode operating system was able to catch me in my little ploy. (There is some chance that `$45FF` points at a valid address on your system, though it would be an unlikely coincidence. If it does say valid, try a few more random selectors such as `$65FF`, `$34CA`, or `$76FA`.)

The Selector List Pane is obviously one of the most important parts of the debugger. You can use it whenever you suspect that one of your pointers might contain garbage values.

> **NOTE**
>
> One of the key points being revealed here is that a pointer can be completely invalid even though it is not set to `nil`. At times this can be very frustrating because you are stepping through code without having any good way of telling whether a pointer is valid just by looking at it. However, the exercise shown previously reveals that you can use the Selector List Pane to examine pointers that you suspect might not have any memory allocated for them.

Remember also that the Selector List Pane works only if you are in protected mode. If by some strange twist of fate you happen to be using a DOS real-mode debugger while following along in this discussion, the comments about the Selector List Pane do not apply. However, a protected-mode DOS debugger works the same as the Windows stand-alone debugger.

There is yet a further twist to this matter. If you examine the segment for the variable A in the List Pane, you will find that it is listed as being completely valid. (4057 may not be the value you want to use on your machine. Instead, use the value of DS, which is visible in the Registers Pane.)

Here is what the List Pane shows on my machine at the time of this writing:

```
CPU 80486
4057 Data Loaded    16640 bytes Read/Write, Up
4065 Data Loaded       96 bytes Read/Write, Up
```

What is going on here? The address for A was created using the Ptr function. There was never any attempt to allocate memory for it. So why does the debugger tell you that the selector is valid?

The answer is simply that $4057 is the address of the data segment of the program:

```
A := Ptr(DSeg, 0);
```

In other words, in this case I intentionally chose a valid selector from which to create an address. As a result, the List Pane states that the selector for A is valid. This shows that it is possible to create a valid address using the Ptr function—you just have to be absolutely sure you know what you are doing. Just picking selectors out of thin air will result in invalid selectors on all but the most fortuitous of occasions.

The next couple lines of code in the program set A and B back to nil:

```
A := nil;          { Set pointer to nil          }
B := nil;          { Set pointer to nil          }
```

When you step through these lines, you should set up the Dump Pane so that it gives you a view of the place in the data segment where A and B reside. If you do this, you will see them both being set back to zero.

NOTE

Under normal circumstances, you should never set the value of a valid pointer to nil without first deallocating the memory associated with it. However, this time it is okay to do this with variable A, because it was simply set equal to memory that had already been allocated by the system. In other words, A was not the owner of the memory it addressed, it was simply borrowing it for a time. As a result, there is no need to deallocate the memory that A addresses, and there is no harm in setting its value back to zero.

There is still considerably more to be said about the POINTER5 program, but it might be worthwhile to take a moment to consider what has been said so far:

- The pointers A and B were both part of the data segment of the POINTER5 program. A resided 170 ($AA) bytes inside the data segment, and pointer B resided 174 ($AE) bytes inside the data segment.

- I haven't yet stressed this point, but the addresses of pointers A and B do not necessarily have anything to do with the value at which they point. One way to find out about the values A and B point at is to bring up the Dump Pane and go to the appropriate place in the data segment.

- When A and B are set to nil, the 4 bytes at $AA and $AE are set to zero. You can use the Ptr function to put an actual address in these bytes, and you can use the Dump Pane to watch these addresses change during the assignment.

- Merely placing an address in the bytes at $AA and $AE does not necessarily mean that these pointers are going to address valid data. For instance, you can use the Selector List Pane to examine the selector (or the entire address) of pointer B. Performing this exercise reveals that B almost certainly references completely invalid data.

- Finally, you learned that it is possible to use the Ptr function to create a pointer that addresses valid data. However, you must be very careful when you attempt to do something like this, and you must remember that the memory you are addressing probably does not belong to your pointer but to some other object in the system.

Before continuing on, let me remind you that this material is not for everybody. Peering deep into the bowels of the Intel architecture is not necessarily what programming is all about. However, if you can master this material, you will find that it can save you hours or even days of work when you stumble across certain kinds of bugs that are usually related to pointers. Furthermore, pointers are the keys to the kingdom of programming. Master them, and everything else about computer programming lies open before you—yours for the taking.

Another Type of Invalid Pointer

Someone new to pointers might write code that looks like this:

```
var
  A: Pointer;
begin
  New(A);
  ...
```

This seems like a reasonable thing to do, because you know that the New function allocates memory for pointers, and A is indubitably declared as a pointer.

The problem with this code is that the New function simply allocates enough memory to cover the area addressed by a pointer. Because an ordinary pointer variable by default does not address any memory, a call to New in this case will not result in a change to the status of A. That is, it will still equal nil. If you want to allocate memory for a variable of type Pointer, you need to call the GetMem function.

Before looking at the GetMem function, pop up the CPU window again and step through the assembler code that gets executed as a result of a New(A) statement:

```
POINTER5.14:   New(A);  { Pointer STILL equals nil! }
   cs:0044 6A00            push    0000
   cs:0046 9A5F019F3E      call    3E9F:015F
   cs:004B A3AA00          mov     [POINTER5.A],ax
   cs:004E 8916AC00        mov     [00AC],dx
```

As you can see, the compiler generates code that pushes the value $0000 on the stack and then calls a function that allocates memory from the operating system. When this call returns, ax and dx hold the offset and selector allocated by the function call, and they are moved into offset $AA and offset $AC in the data segment. However, because $0000 was pushed on the stack, the values returned in ax and dx are both zero, so the value that A addresses is still nil.

Compare the preceding example with the following code:

```
POINTER5.16:   GetMem(A, 100);  { Allocate a hundred bytes }
   cs:0061 6A64            push    0064
   cs:0063 9A5F019F3E      call    3E9F:015F
   cs:0068 A3AA00          mov     [POINTER5.A],ax
   cs:006B 8916AC00        mov     [00AC],dx
```

If you remember that decimal 100 and hex 64 are equivalent, you can see that the following code pushes the value 100 onto the stack and then calls the function that allocates memory. When it returns, ax and dx no longer contain zero, so this time A is not set to nil.

The address that is listed at offset $AA in the data segment now references real memory on the heap that belongs to variable A. To prove this to yourself, put the address shown in the Watch window next to variable A into the List Pane. You will see that the debugger lists it as belonging to a valid selector that has nothing to do with your data segment. (See Figure 16.7.) This address is to be found somewhere out on the heap, but it is now a portion of the heap that temporarily belongs to your program.

FIGURE 16.7.

Take the address ($XXXX) shown in the Watch window and enter it in the List Pane to see if you have a valid selector.

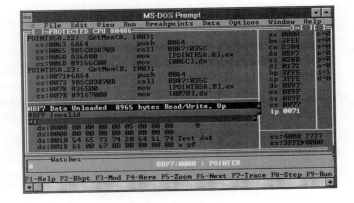

One final portion of the POINTER5 program should be mentioned:

```
FreeMem(A, 100);        { Deallocate 100 bytes        }
A := nil;               { Set pointer to nil          }
FreeMem(B, 100);        { Deallocate 100 bytes        }
asm                     { Set pointer to nil: B:=nil  }
  mov word ptr B, 0;    { Zero out offset             }
  mov word ptr B + 2, 0; { Zero out segment           }
end;                    { Close ASM block             }
```

The code shown here deallocates the memory associated with A and B. After these pointers are deallocated, you can put them in the List Pane to see that they are no longer considered valid pointers. Furthermore, this shows two different ways of setting a variable to nil. The first method simply makes an assignment:

```
A := nil;               { Set pointer to nil          }
```

The second method uses Delphi's built-in assembler to move zero into the offset and segment of the address where variable B resides.

This discussion has been fairly involved, but it should help you begin to grasp exactly how pointers are constructed, and how you can use the stand-alone debugger to spy on their inner workings.

Most of the time, built-in Delphi objects or tools such as TStringLists, TLists, and real tables will provide the simplest possible means for tracking long lists of data. However, linked lists can still be convenient if you need to create a custom list with particular properties, or if you want to write portable code that can be used both in Delphi and at the DOS prompt. The biggest advantage linked lists can bring you, however, is that they have almost no overhead. As a result, if memory usage has become a big problem in your program, you can use linked lists. However, under normal circumstances you will probably use a database table, TStringList, or TList. In particular, serious Delphi programmers should take the time to explore the TList object. On the CD, you will find the OBJECT4 program from Chapter 28 and the EXPLORER program, both of which use the TList object.

Summary

This chapter presented you with several full-length linked lists, and it showed you how you can manipulate these lists and how you can use them to store large amounts of data. In particular, you learned how to iterate through a linked list, how to count the nodes in a list, how to add and delete data from a list, and how to search for a record stored in a linked list. You also got a good look at some code that read a linked list from disk, and that enabled you to modify and then restore the list to its original location on disk.

The text of this lengthy chapter also discussed the particulars of the Intel addressing scheme, and it showed you how you can use the debugger to learn about the pointers in your programs.

Understanding the Windows Environment

17

Overview

To help orient the reader properly in the world of Windows, I'm going to spend a few pages discussing the operating environment that hosts the Delphi compiler.

In particular, I'm going to concentrate on three issues:

- What do Contemporary Operating Environments look like?
- What is *protected mode,* and why is it so important?
- What is multitasking, and how does Windows handle it?

This chapter describes the environment in which Delphi runs. As a result, it covers a great deal of material that will prove to be important to you on a day-to-day basis.

The appeal of this chapter is theoretical rather than practical. However, there are times when knowing a little theory can have very practical results.

The purpose of this chapter is to wind up the long discussion of the Delphi language that has stretched out over the last 12 chapters. It's crucial that you know the language, but that knowledge can be greatly enhanced by an understanding of the operating system that hosts the language. This chapter explores some of the features of that operating system in the hopes that it will whet your appetite for reading other books dedicated to Windows, DOS, and the 8086 architecture.

None of the information in this chapter is essential to Delphi programmers; however, it is all useful. If you are in a rush, you can skip this chapter and come back when you have time for more theoretical issues.

I think it is vitally important that programmers don't make the mistake of thinking that a subject is not important simply because it is abstract. Some subjects can be approached solely from a technical, nuts-and-bolts point of view. Programming is not one of them. You need to master the technical side of the subject, of course, but you also need to have the mental agility necessary to grasp certain theoretical issues.

Most of this book is about the technical aspects of the Delphi language; this chapter, however, is about the environment in which it lives.

Understanding Protected Mode

Windows 3.1 runs in something called *protected mode.* Protected mode was made possible by the invention of the 80286 processor in 1982. That's not a misprint. The 286 has been around since 1982. Why it didn't become popular until the last half of the eighties is a tragic story that has cost America billions of dollars and years of wasted technological effort. In fact, the maladies caused by that error still linger on like a persistent fever. Nevertheless, that particular tale lies outside the scope of this book.

To understand why protected mode was invented, you have to understand that DOS was originally written to run in only 1048 KB, or one megabyte, of memory. Furthermore, Intel came up with a rather peculiar architecture that divided all addresses in memory up into two portions: a segment and an offset. To use this system, programmers must first write the segment, a colon, and then the offset. For instance, here's an address written using this style:

```
1234:1234
```

> **NOTE**
>
> Computers are binary machines, so everything you do on them ends up being a multiple of two. For instance the precise number of bytes in one megabyte is not 1,000,000, but 1,048,576. It's merely a convention that programmers refer to this mark as if it were exactly one million bytes. In the same way, it is a convention to refer to the number 65,536 as 64 KB. Furthermore, when addresses are written out in the segmented style shown, convention demands that they be written using hexadecimal notation, rather than decimal notation. However, this is not the time to begin discussing a new numbering system, so experienced programmers will have to bear with me while I simply side-step the entire subject of hexadecimal numbers throughout most of this discussion.

The issue here is that the Intel 8086 is a 16-bit processor. Using 16 bits, the largest number you can write is 65,536. The makers of the PC didn't want their machine to be limited to such a small amount of memory, so they came up with the idea of using two 16-bit numbers to designate an address. The first 16-bit number would address a particular segment of memory, and the second 16-bit number would address an offset into that segment. When these two numbers are combined, they can refer to addresses higher than 64 KB. If this scheme of segments and offsets had not been invented, the memory theater would have an audience of only 65,536.

If you want to translate a segment and offset into a normal number, you multiply the segment times 16 and add the offset to it:

```
NormalAddress := (Segment * 16) + Offset;
```

Here's how the system works. Suppose you want to address the first byte in memory using a segmented architecture. Because a computer's memory works with zero-based numbers, the first byte would appear at segment 0, offset 0:

```
0000:0000
```

The second byte would appear at segment 0, offset 1:

```
0000:0001
```

And if you wanted to address the sixteenth byte, you would express it as follows:

```
0000:0015
```

So far so good. The catch comes when you want to address the 17th byte. Using a segmented architecture, there are two ways to write this number. The first way looks like this:

```
0000:0016
```

and the second way looks like this:

```
0001:0000
```

(Remember, I'm using decimal numbers, not hex numbers.) Using the formula I showed you previously, it's easy to see that the two numbers are really identical:

```
NormalAddress       := (Segment * 16)    +    Offset
16                  := (1 * 16)          +    0
16                  := (0 * 16)          +    16
```

Once you get the hang of this system, it becomes obvious that segments appear on 16-byte boundaries, called *pages*:

```
0001:0000 = 16
0002:0000 = 32
0003:0000 = 48
```

Just to be sure you see how each number is derived, it might be best if I explicitly perform the conversion:

```
(1 * 16) + 0 = 16
(2 * 16) + 0 = 32
(3 * 16) + 0 = 48
```

At the beginning of this discussion, I said that segments and offsets are each made up of 16-bit numbers, and that the largest decimal number you can write with 16 bits is 65,536. So, if you write the following segmented number:

```
65536:0000
```

and run it through the magic formula:

```
(65536 *16) + 0
```

you end up with the number 1,048,576. This number is the same as 1048 KB, or one megabyte.

The last paragraph shows exactly why the original IBM PC could not address more than one megabyte of memory. The problem was simply that the segmented architecture could not be used to express a number larger than 1048 KB. That was all there was to it. In a sense, what happened was that IBM, Microsoft, and Intel dropped Humpty-Dumpty onto the ground right at the beginning. After that, all the kings horses and all the kings men couldn't put Humpty together again. Though lord knows they tried!

NOTE

Observant readers might be wondering about the 65,536 bytes that form the offset of any number beginning with segment 65536. For instance, what about the following address:

65536:0001

Isn't that number larger than one megabyte, and can't it be legally expressed with the notation shown?

The answer, of course, is that yes, the address is larger than one megabyte. In fact, if you have made a study of the PC architecture, you know that the 64 KB starting at one meg plays a special role in contemporary PC memory management. However, there are enough plates up in the air right now, and there is no need to launch yet another. The point is that the original DOS-based PCs can really address 1 meg plus an additional 64 KB. That additional 64 KB is put to use in various ways on different systems. PCs, however, cannot go beyond that without special help.

In the last few pages, you saw why PCs were originally limited to one megabyte of memory. Initially, this problem was not a great concern to most computer manufacturers. However, as time went on, it began to become a very serious problem. As a result, programmers and manufacturers became very interested in something called protected mode, which became available after the 80286 appeared on the market in 1982. Protected mode is important in part because it makes it possible for PCs to break the one-megabyte boundary. This whole subject is addressed in the next section, which is about protected-mode programming and computing.

NOTE

Throughout the previous discussion, I ignored the fact that computers don't work on the base 10, or decimal system. Instead, they work on the hexadecimal system, which is base 16. The following example shows a set of real hexadecimal addresses, followed by their decimal equivalent. Just to help emphasize the points made in this section, I show that each of the following addresses is one page, or 16 bytes from the last:

Decimal, non-Hex Address	Segmented Equivalent	Difference
11AE:0000	72416	
11AF:0000	72432	16 bytes
11B0:0000	72448	16 bytes
11B1:0000	72464	16 bytes
11B2:0000	72480	16 bytes
11B3:0000	72496	16 bytes

Decimal, non-Hex Address	Segmented Equivalent	Difference
11B4:0000	72512	16 bytes
11B5:0000	72528	16 bytes
11B6:0000	72544	16 bytes
11B7:0000	72560	16 bytes
11B8:0000	72576	16 bytes
11B9:0000	72592	16 bytes
11BA:0000	72608	16 bytes
11BB:0000	72624	16 bytes
11BC:0000	72640	16 bytes

What is Protected Mode?

Reduced to its simplest concepts, protected mode is a means of ensuring the integrity of the memory used by a program. It helps to ensure that careless programs don't write to the wrong places in memory, and it will sometimes even shut them down if they do so. Protected-mode programs also address more than one meg of memory.

There are several important features of protected mode, but one of the most important is the way it handles Intel's segmented architecture. It turns out that a protected-mode address is a radically different animal from a real-mode address. The two simply cannot be equated.

In the last section you saw how segments are handled in what is called *real mode*. In protected mode, the segment part of an address is treated entirely differently. In fact, the first part of an address in protected mode is not even called a segment. Instead, it is referred to as a *selector*.

Selectors are as different from segments as a spaceship is from a horse and buggy. The two are radically different entities and cannot be assumed to have anything to do with one another. For instance, in the last section you saw that this address

0001:0000

refers to the 17th byte in memory. In protected mode, there is no guarantee that this address is equal to its real-mode equivalent. In fact, it is highly unlikely that they would refer to the same place in memory.

Here's the way things work in protected mode. The first part of a segmented address is referred to as a selector, and selectors are not a reference to a place in memory, but merely offsets into a *look-up table*. For instance, the following address

0001:0000

refers to the first entry in something called a *descriptor table*.

NOTE

Actually, the previous example of a selector has a certain hypothetical aspect, because selectors usually tend to start at values above 7. This is because the first 3 bits of a selector are used to designate its status, and can be set even though the selector actually occupies the first slot in a descriptor table. For now, however, it's probably simplest to see a one-to-one correspondence between the selector 0001, and the first slot in the descriptor table.

It's not important that you understand everything about descriptor tables. In fact, all you need to know about them is that they have two parts. One is where selectors are kept, and the second is where real memory addresses are kept. To find out where a selector points to in memory, the operating system merely looks up the entry in the descriptor table and returns with a value called a descriptor, which contains the actual real-mode address, or a logical equivalent.

Figure 17.1 uses the APPMEM program from this book's CD to show a visual representation of a few descriptors from a descriptor table.

FIGURE 17.1.

Entries from a descriptor table, as displayed by the APPMEM program.

When looking at this figure, experienced DOS users might notice that some of the addresses are familiar. For instance, the addresses B0000, B8000, and A0000 all point to video memory. These addresses regularly appear in descriptor tables since both Microsoft and Borland go to some lengths to make sure that you can find handles to important places in real memory. Of course, there is very, very little likelihood that a Windows programmer would ever want to write directly to video memory, but still these addresses are made available to you on general principles. There are two points to understand:

- The APPMEM program clearly shows that Delphi can be used to do what used to be called real "systems" programming. The programming environment gives you all the power you need to get way down into the depths of any part of the machine.

- The second point references the main theme of this chapter, which is that good contemporary programmers are, for better or worse, willing to sacrifice speed for other benefits. Specifically, the protected-mode memory addressing scheme has an extra layer of indirection built into it, and yet it is used every time a far call is made in Windows. In other words, you don't reference addresses directly; you first look them up in a table, and then you go to the appropriate location. (Just so no one gets confused, let me emphasize that it is Windows that sets up memory this way, not Delphi.)

Take a moment to consider the second point listed. In real mode, when you want to reference a specific address in memory, you simply go directly to the referenced segment and offset. But in protected mode, the operating system takes the segment, looks up the value associated with it in the descriptor table, and then jumps to the address referenced in that table.

Furthermore, besides an actual address, there is additional information stored both in the first three bits of a selector and in the descriptor that it references.

The reason this information is included is because Windows literally checks the credentials of every selector before it allows you to use it. In particular, Windows checks to be sure that selectors reference memory that is actually owned by your program. Furthermore, if you try to write to a particular place in memory, Windows makes sure that the memory in question has been marked as read/write memory. Some memory is marked as read-only, and your program will be shut down if it tries to write to it.

It might be helpful to step back and approach this problem from a different angle. The early days of PC programming were a bit like the early days in the wild west. In those times, there was a great deal of freedom, but very little law and order. The same thing could be said of the early days of programming on microcomputers. Essentially, DOS allowed you to do anything you wanted with the 640 KB of memory in which your program was free to roam. It was a very free, but lawless, world.

As the years have gone by, programmers and users have had to give up certain of the more romantic aspects of the wild and woolly early days of personal computing. Specifically, you used to be free to write directly to memory as often as you wanted. A problem arose, however, because programmers were continually writing to places that were vital to the computer's integrity. As a result, one single programming error was capable of bringing down the entire system, forcing the user to reboot.

The new system *protects* the user and the programmer from these kinds of errors. It does this by forcing the programmer to reference memory through a level of indirection. In other words, all addresses are stored inside a table, and that table contains information about the memory referenced by that address. As a result, if a programmer tries to write 500 bytes to an area in memory that's only 300 bytes in size, the operating system creates a General Protection Fault, and possibly even shuts down the offending program.

> **NOTE**
>
> The key word, of course, is protection. Protected mode gets its name from the fact that it protects the user from untamed programs that threaten to violate system integrity.

What you've got here is a classic Pat Garret and Billy the Kid story. Some people want to have the freedom to write to any address in memory. Other people want to protect the integrity of the operating system by shutting down carelessly written programs. The romance and the glamour belong to Billy the Kid, but history is on the side of Pat Garrett. Users need systems that are safe, and the first step along that path is protected mode.

Doubters might be convinced by the fact that protected mode enables programs to address memory beyond the one-megabyte limit known to the DOS world. As you saw in the last section, it's impossible to create an address more than 64 KB above one megabyte using standard real-mode segments and offsets. However, a selector isn't a real address. Instead, it's just a reference to a table where descriptors are stored. This makes it possible for protected-mode systems to reference an address above the one-megabyte line.

By definition, Intel segments are only 2 bytes in size. But descriptors are 6 bytes in size, which means there is plenty of room for storing numbers larger than 65,536. Specifically, descriptors on 286 systems set aside room for storing addresses as large as 16,777,216, which is 16 megs. Furthermore, 32-bit systems such as 486s use descriptors that reference numbers as high as 4,294,967,296, otherwise know as 4 gigabytes.

Take a look at the three numbers shown in close juxtaposition:

```
1,048,576       { The limit under DOS                  }
16,777,216      { The limit on a 286 in protected mode }
4,294,967,296   { The limit on a 386 in protected mode }
```

Protected mode clearly gives 16-bit operating systems an advantage they could not possibly have utilized under the standard restraints known to users of DOS.

The main point, however, is that the entire Intel-based computer industry is choosing protected mode over real mode even though they know it is innately slower and requires larger, bulkier code bases. Of course, once this decision is made, programmers do everything they can to write tight, fast code within the given restraints. When it comes down to a choice between speed and dependability, dependability seems to be winning out.

What is Multitasking?

After the discussion of protected mode, it's possible to give a brief and extremely general description of how Windows handles certain aspects of its multitasking chores. This is an extremely technical subject, and I have neither the qualifications nor the desire to go into any detail here. However, this is an appropriate place to make a few general comments that will help you to understand how Windows performs its magic.

> **NOTE**
>
> If you're interested in an in-depth treatment of this subject, one of the best references is *Unauthorized Windows 95*, by Andrew Schulman (published by IDG Books). Other important books on how Windows handles multitasking include *Windows Internals* by Matt Pietrek, as well as *Undocumented Windows* by Schulman, Pietrek, and David Maxey (both published by Addison Weseley). Somewhat less interesting, but still very informative, are *Inside Windows NT* by Helen Custer and *Inside Windows 95* by Adrian King (both published by Microsoft Press).

The key point to grasp is that none of the addresses used in a Windows program refer to actual, real-mode memory. Instead, they are always references to a series of tables, called descriptor tables, which are where the actual addresses for the program are stored.

Suppose you are multitasking two programs called A and B, and there is a programming error in the code of program A. Suppose the error causes program A to attempt to address code owned by program B. When it attempts to write to program B's address space, it must first pass through the descriptor table. When it does so, the operating system gets a chance to check to see if program A really owns the memory it is about to write to. When Windows sees that program A is about to address memory belonging to another program, a protection fault is generated and program A is paused, or perhaps shut down.

The two levels of indirection found in protected mode is what makes this possible. In real mode, there would be nothing to stop program A from writing wherever it wanted to write. As a result, any attempt to multitask programs in real mode would soon lead to disaster, since one ill-behaved program could quickly bring down the whole system.

Another important point about protected mode and multitasking systems becomes evident when you think of the inevitable results of crowding several programs into a limited address space.

Suppose that program A is short on room and needs to take over a block of memory owned by program B. In this case, there is nothing ill-behaved about program A; it's simply running out of room and is eyeing its neighbor's address space. In real mode, this situation would be a disaster, and a system crash would surely be imminent. Windows, however, can easily handle this situation.

Here's how it works. As you saw in the last section, a Windows program does not directly address real memory. Instead, it has selectors that reference descriptors, which are kept in a table.

If program A needs to reference a place in memory currently being referenced by program B, Windows can simply change the actual addresses stored in the descriptor table of program B. In other words, without program B ever knowing what's happening, Windows can simply move the offending block of memory out of the way. It does this by changing the information in the descriptor table. The selectors owned by program B do not change at all.

The big benefit here is that programmers do not have to take such situations into account. They can always be sure that their selectors are valid. The nitty gritty details of multitasking are handled not by the individual programmer, but by Windows. This is possible because programmers work with selectors, while the real addresses are stored in the descriptor table.

Virtual DOS Machines

If you push the concept described previously to its farthest logical extremity, you can see that it's possible to "virtualize" an entire machine inside protected-mode memory. Suppose you have a machine that contains 16 megs of memory. You can take a portion of those 16 megs and treat it as if it were a stand-alone DOS machine. That is, you can treat it as if it were a separate PC, with its own private 640KB block of memory. In fact, Intel went to considerable lengths to automate this entire process. As a result, even real-mode DOS programs multitasked under Windows no longer write to actual memory addresses. Instead, their calls are "virtualized" and therefore redirected through a table. They think they are running on a standard, real-mode DOS PC, but in fact they are running in a virtualized PC inside a block of memory that belongs to a larger, protected-mode machine.

Suppose that a particular DOS program writes directly to video memory. You would think that under Windows this would cause an immediate crash, since the program would actually be writing to addresses that were nothing more than references to places in the descriptor table. Indeed, under normal circumstances if you attempt to write directly to video memory while in protected mode, you will crash the system. Given the fact that most of the best DOS programs write directly to memory, it would seem to be impossible to multitask them under Windows. This section of the chapter is an explanation of how Windows overcomes this seeming limitation.

> **NOTE**
>
> It's important to remember that in this section I'm talking about a very special case, where Windows virtualizes a DOS program. That is, it assigns the program a block of memory and then sets things up so that the program thinks that it is running on a stand-alone machine. In other words, the operating system creates an artificial, or virtual, machine in which the DOS program runs. Inside of that virtual machine, the program finds something that looks and feels exactly like an 8086-based computer. The reality, however, is that they are merely floating inside a virtual machine created out of whole cloth from the available RAM on a machine that is probably equipped with 2, 4, 8, or even 16 megs of memory. Normal Windows programs don't use this system. This is something that happens only in DOS boxes run under Windows, on 386 and above systems.

Experienced DOS programmers know that video memory for color systems is generally stored at segment B800 in real memory. If a DOS program wants to display something on the screen, it can address the video memory stored at that address and manipulate it directly.

Now suppose that this program is being multitasked on the Windows desktop. This means that it is running under a protected-mode system. In particular, it's being run inside something called a virtual DOS machine. As a result, the address at segment B800 no longer points at real video memory. Instead it points into a table that is controlled by the protected-mode environment. This makes it possible for the system to intercept the write to real-mode memory and redirect it into a special windowed portion of the desktop.

> **NOTE**
>
> You can have several DOS windows open, each of them a "virtual" single PC running under Windows.

If a program is in a virtual DOS box and attempts to write to address B800, Windows says: "Ho, ho, ho! I see what you're up to! Well, we don't let programs do that around here! It's considered ill-behaved. But because I'm a nice guy, I'm going to redirect your video writes into a little window I've set aside for you on the desktop." The result is that direct video writes are tamed and displayed in the proper, windowed area on the desktop.

This is perhaps an occasion where it might be helpful to work with a real-world example. Over the next few paragraphs, I explore a program called DIRECT that illustrates some key points about multitasking DOS programs under Windows. The program described in this section is on the CD, so you can follow along on your computer if you have a 386 or better. In Figure 17.2, the DIRECT program is shown as it looks when run from the DOS prompt.

FIGURE 17.2.

The DIRECT program as it appears when being run from the DOS prompt.

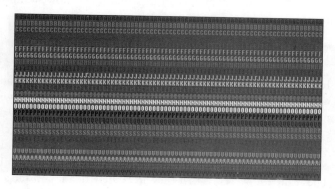

The DIRECT program draws a pattern on the screen by writing directly to the type of video memory found on a color system. Here is the code for the DIRECT program, which must be compiled using a DOS version of the Pascal compiler. Because a DOS compiler does not come with Delphi, I have included a copy of the executable on the CD:

```
program Direct;
var
  {Address Screen}
  Video: array[0..3999] of Byte absolute $B800:$0000;
  A: Byte;    { Character and attribute to write to the screen   }
  i: Integer;{ Counter                                           }

begin                                        { Init character to 'A'  }
  A := 65;                                    { Iterate video memory   }
  for i := 0 to 3999 do begin                { Write to video memory  }
    Move(A, Video[i], 1);                    { Increment character    }
    if ((i + 1) mod 160 = 0) then Inc(A);    { end loop               }
  end;                                        { Pause to view result   }
  ReadLn;
end.
```

Experienced programmers can see that this code writes directly to video memory. However, if you don't understand this code, that's not particularly important. This is DOS-specific code that is not particularly relevant to Delphi programmers, except for the fact that it reveals something about the way Windows works.

Windows, when run in enhanced mode, is able to multitask the DIRECT program inside a DOS window. Figure 17.3 shows how this looks on a typical version of Windows.

FIGURE 17.3.

*Multitasking the DIRECT
program under Windows.*

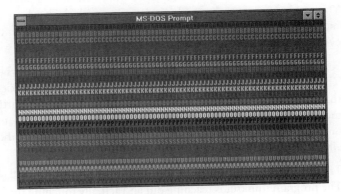

NOTE

Enhanced mode is the default mode for Windows on a 386 or better system. If you open up the About box on the File Manager or Program Manager, you will be able to see if your Windows session is running in enhanced mode. If it says that your version of Windows is running in standard mode, you will not be able to multitask this program in the same way described here.

If you are running in enhanced mode, your computer will be able to take full advantage of the 386 architecture that emerged in the 1980s. In particular, it will be able to create virtual machines, such as virtual DOS boxes, and to run individual or multiple programs inside them. Enhanced mode also enables your computer to use special tricks such as paging unused memory out of RAM and onto a hard disk, and then back into RAM when it is needed. This capability to page memory to disk enables a computer with only 8 megs of memory appear to have 12, 16, or even 24 megs of memory; a computer that has 24 megs of memory might appear to have 30 or more megs of memory, and so on.

In order to multitask a program like DIRECT, the system has to intercept every single attempt to write to video memory and redirect each call to a specific location on the screen. Because the DIRECT program writes to video memory 4,000 times, the operating system has to redirect 4,000 video writes.

The discussion here has become a bit complex, so perhaps it's time to introduce an analogy. In the old days, if you wanted to control your stereo, you did so by twisting actual physical knobs on the amplifier. In the last few years, this system has been abandoned, and now many stereo owners control their systems via a remote-control device, just like those used with TV sets.

Writing directly to video memory is a bit like turning the physical knobs on a stereo amplifier. You are, in a sense, in direct physical contact with the hardware. When you work in protected mode, however, you should no longer be in direct contact with the hardware. Instead, you run everything by remote control, as it were.

Running things by remote control adds a layer of indirection between you and the hardware. This means that everything is a little slower, and a little bulkier. At the same time, it means that you have advantages you could never get in real mode. Furthermore, advanced protected-mode technology makes it possible to create a virtual 8086 machine inside a larger environment. Windows then completely controls the behavior of the program running inside this virtual machine.

The DIRECT program running under Windows is a little like an exercise in virtual reality. The program thinks it is reaching out and actually touching the hardware, but in fact, it is only simulating such an experience. It's like putting on a pair of goggles and gloves and having a computer aid you in simulating the experience of turning up the volume on your stereo. You are actually just moving your hands about in thin air, but it looks and feels as though you are touching physical objects. The same thing happens to a program like DIRECT when run under Windows. It thinks it's talking directly to video memory, but it's actually only working with a simulation. All of this is made possible by protected mode!

If you have followed the discussion so far, it has probably occurred to you that there is no longer any point in writing directly to video memory. Doing so only forces Windows to go through a number of strange contortions in order to intercept those calls, and to redirect them to a controlled portion of the video screen; that is, it redirects them inside the boundaries of a particular window.

In protected mode, direct video writes are either going to be intercepted by the operating environment as they are in a DOS box, or they are going to crash the system (which is what can happen if you try them in a standard Windows program). As a result, direct memory access no longer makes sense under Windows. Instead you should always access memory by first going through the operating system. This allows Windows to control all the output. That means that if you move one window on top of another one, or if you minimize or maximize a window, the operating system takes care of the changes to the appearance of your window. It's no longer your responsibility to direct the output of your program to a specific location on screen.

You have to give up something in terms of speed and freedom in order to use Windows. What you get back in return is added protection, and the ability to multitask.

> **NOTE**
>
> It might be worth pointing out that the memory-management techniques described here are only the tip of the iceberg. If you dig a little deeper into this topic, you will find that you can define the attributes for a program segment. For instance, some memory can be tagged as FIXED, so that it can't be moved around using the techniques described previously. Other memory can be marked as DISCARDABLE, which means that Windows cannot only move it, but can simply throw it away for a bit, if need be. Then, if the memory is referenced, Windows is smart enough to read the memory back off disk and to move it into place. Other segment attributes include MOVEABLE, PRELOAD, and LOADONCALL. See the topic "Segment Module Definition Statement" in the Windows API online help for additional information. In Delphi, you use the $C directive to specify these attributes. For instance, the following is lifted from SYSTEM.PAS, which is included in the RTL and is built into all Delphi programs:
>
> ```
> {$C MOVEABLE PRELOAD PERMANENT}
> ```

Suppose there are three big programs running in memory. Furthermore, suppose there is no longer enough room in RAM for the current program and the other two. In such a case, Windows can literally write an entire program to a place called virtual memory, which is really located on disk. When the user wants to start using this program again, Windows just picks up the whole program, heap, data segment, and all, and then reads it back into memory. All of this can be done without the programmer having to take any specific actions. As far as the program is concerned, it is still manipulating the exact same set of selectors. It's just that the actual addresses referenced by those selectors have changed.

In other words, the program might always be addressing, say, the second selector in the descriptor table. Therefore, the address used by the program would always be 0002:0000. The address kept in the second slot of the descriptor table, however, might change many times during the life of that executable. The program doesn't need to worry about those changes. All it needs to do is remember `0002:0000`. What is actually kept in the descriptor table is irrelevant to the program. In fact, the program doesn't even have to know that the descriptor table exists!

If some of the points I've been making in the last few pages aren't entirely clear to you, do not worry. As I said earlier, you don't have to understand protected mode to run Delphi. You literally could know nothing about the subject and still be able to build relatively sophisticated programs. Delphi is designed to protect you from this kind of complexity.

I explain all this for three reasons:

- I want to show why large code bases and complex systems have been adopted in the computer industry during the last few years. If you can understand the fruits of these systems, you will be able to grasp why they have been adopted, even if you don't necessarily like the fact.

- Even if you don't understand all the details explained previously, you will still be better off if some of the facts have seeped through. The more you know about the Windows environment, the better chance you have of writing good programs. Furthermore, advanced programmers have to know this material. If you are going to get really good, you need to know how protected mode works.

- Finally, I address this material simply because it is interesting. Programmers are in the business because they want to make a living or produce a useful program. However, no one gets very far in this industry unless they also find the technology innately fascinating. To me, one of the rewards of being a programmer is that you get a good chance to learn how all this technology works.

So You Think You've Found a Bug!

Every piece of software powerful enough to do anything useful is going to contain at least some bugs. People who say otherwise usually need to spend some time with their psychiatrist. Nevertheless, it is a difficult task to effectively track down and report a real bug in a product. I for one, have often thought I found a bug in Delphi only to realize that I was making some mistake in my own code.

Let me be frank here. The odds that you have found a real bug in one of the basic Delphi functions is so small as to be nearly nonexistent. The basic syntax for the language, such as `for` loops, `case` statements, the pairing of `begin..end` statements, and variable scoping is almost certainly completely clean. The same basic code for these features has been in use for some 10 years, and you aren't likely to find a problem with it. This is particularly true of beginners, who are working with the basic elements of the language.

Sometimes you might wish that the Delphi syntax had a different structure, but this is not the same thing as a bug, and it is extremely unlikely that Borland will value your opinion so highly that it will restructure its product just to suit your needs. Everyone at Borland, however, is always willing to consider a well-thought-out suggestion. That's a totally different matter, and the company takes pride in the fact that it keeps its ear to the ground and is always sufficiently flexible to improve the product when the opportunity presents itself.

It is also extremely unlikely that anyone will find bugs in basic Delphi functions such as the string functions Length, Delete, or Copy, or in any of the routines for manipulating files. The VCL itself, of course, is brand new with the first version of Delphi, and so there is probably a measurable chance that someone will find a real bug in it. Of course, the odds are still extremely low, well below a thousandth of a percent; but it is not utterly absurd to suppose someone might find a bug in this area of the product.

If someone thinks they have found a bug in the VCL, and they want to see it fixed, they are going to have to be able to reproduce it in a very small program. No one will pay a programmer much mind if he or she calls up and says that they have a five-thousand-line program that isn't working because a VCL call doesn't work. In such a case, the problem is almost certainly in the five thousand lines the programmer wrote, not in the VCL. To prove otherwise, Borland needs to see an extremely short program that illustrates the problem, and that isolates it in such a manner that the fault cannot possibly lie elsewhere.

In general, I have found that the act of writing a small program that illustrates a problem helps me to find the errors in my own work. In short, when I am working on a big project and I stumble across a bug, I usually do two things:

- First, I recognize that the bug is almost certainly my own, and not the compilers.
- Second, I try to write a small program that exercises the relevant portions of my code.

Big programs are very hard to debug. One of the points I am going to make over and over again in this book is that it is essential that serious programmers write code that can be broken down into small components, such as objects or modules.

> **NOTE**
>
> There is, of course, one case where you might need a large amount of source code in order to demonstrate the existence of a bug. These problems involve compiling and linking issues. If you are simply unable to compile a project or if you have a project that causes the IDE to crash when it is being compiled, you should be prepared to send Borland the entire project in order to demonstrate the bug. Such problems, of course, are extremely rare, and trouble of this kind usually has to do with the setup on a particular programmer's machine. That is, you need to remove *everything* from your CONFIG.SYS and AUTOEXEC.BAT, and you need to clean up your WIN.INI and SYSTEM.INI files, as well as the Startup group in the Program Manager. If you usually work on a network, you have to boot up without the network loaded in order to test for a bug. Networks are very sophisticated, but very fragile, and they can be the source of many "bugs." After taking these steps, nearly all problems with the IDE or

compiler and linker disappear immediately. The problem, of course, was that there was some other ill-behaved TSR, driver, or program loaded into memory that was interfering with Delphi.

Many programs contain a fairly complex object hierarchy, but it should still be possible to remove layers of the hierarchy and test the underlying structure. If there is one particularly complex subset of your program that performs specialized tasks, it is essential that it be designed in such a way that it can be removed from the rest of the project and taken through its paces rigorously in a custom-made test bed.

The reason for putting so much emphasis on these matters is that they are the rules by which good programmers live. One of the single biggest trends in contemporary programming is the attempt to make it easy for programmers to construct their executables out of discreet objects that can be tested separately.

The UI, that is, the user interface, and the documentation are two areas where there is at least a significant chance that someone other than an expert programmer is likely to find a bug. Certainly there is usually little room for debate about whether or not you have found a bug in the UI or in the docs. Something in the UI either works the way it's supposed to work, or it doesn't. The docs either describe things accurately or they don't. However, Borland is not likely to recompile their product, or publish another set of books, just to fix a minor glitch. Unless something very unusual has happened, problems with the UI or with the docs are fixed when the program is reved, that is, when the next version is released.

It is considerably more serious to find a bug in the compiler than a bug in the UI. In other words, if you try to use the Print option from Delphi's menu and it doesn't print correctly on your machine, the people at Borland will try to fix the problem; but they won't loose any sleep over the issue. However, if you could prove that the virtual directive wasn't working properly in one of your object hierarchies, it would be a very serious matter, and Borland would try to fix it as quickly as possible.

If your copy of Delphi contains the VCL source code, that source code is definitive. It defines the way the product works. The docs are not definitive. In 99.9 percent of the cases the docs are right, but they don't have the authority that is visited upon the actual source code.

NOTE

The advice given in the last paragraph also applies to this book. Always consider the code on disk to be more up-to-date than the code shown in this book!

To sum up:

- Most of the so called "bugs" that get reported to Borland result from programmer error, or from machines that have not been set up properly.

- Generally, it is considered extremely amateurish to blame the compiler for a problem in a program.

- If you think you have a bug, remove all but the essential calls from your AUTOEXEC.BAT and CONFIG.SYS, clean up your Windows environment, and then write a very small program that tests the calls you are questioning. If it still appears to you that you have found a bug, give Borland a call and report it. Borland always wants to know about real bugs—it's in the company's interest to learn about them.

Finally, let me wrap all this up by saying that the Tech Support staff at Borland, and the company's representatives on various cyberspace nodes, are always willing and even eager to help out programmers who are stuck, who need advice, or who can't resolve a bug in their own code. If you want to learn about a particular tool or if you want to just chat about a technical issue with other Delphi programmers, the online services and Borland Tech Support are available.

The point of this section is not to discourage you from calling support, or to discourage you from asking for help online. The point is to make clear some of the basic facts about Delphi and bugs. In other words, call up and ask for advice any time, but think twice before calling up to report a bug, unless you are *sure* you know what you are doing. Hopefully in reading this section you have picked up on some tips that will help you save development time, and help you eliminate problems in your own code.

Summary

In the last few sections you were treated to a very generalized overview of protected-mode programming. You saw that Windows takes advantage of protected mode to make multitasking possible. Specifically, Windows uses protected mode to ensure two things:

- That no one program steps on memory owned by Windows itself or by some other program active in the current environment.

- That limited resources can be fully utilized by moving blocks of memory around, by literally discarding certain blocks of memory, or by writing the current state of an entire program to disk.

In many circles, this is quite controversial material because it forces users to abandon speed in favor of power and flexibility. Clearly I believe that the advantages protected mode gives you are well worth the price of admission.

Remember that serious bugs are those that belong to the compiler itself, and not to Delphi's UI. However, it's much easier to find a bug in the UI than it is to find a bug in the compiler.

PART

IV

Visual Database Tools: Tables, Datasets, and SQL

Creating Tables and Aliases

18

Overview

In this chapter, you learn how to create tables, how to create and manage aliases, and how to configure ODBC drivers.

The emphasis throughout this chapter is on two tools that ship with Delphi as separate executables:

- The Database Desktop (DBD.EXE)
- The Database Engine Configuration utility (BDECFG.EXE)

Both of these utilities should be familiar to Paradox users. However, those who are new to these utilities won't find them particularly difficult to use.

Delphi is a front-end tool that provides access to a wide variety of servers. The actual details of working with any one particular server differs from case to case, so in a few places this chapter refers you to the documentation that shipped with your server for specific details.

This chapter provides background knowledge that you need in order to write database applications. It does not, however, cover the actual writing of database programs. In some ways, this background knowledge is more complex and confusing than the actual act of writing database applications. Certainly this portion of the product has not been as thoroughly integrated into Delphi as it will be in future releases.

If you have never written a database program and plan to use database tools only as a peripheral part of your Delphi programming experience, you can probably skim all but the "Aliases" section of this chapter and then move on. However, if you plan to work heavily with the database tools, you should be familiar with the entire contents of this chapter.

Whatever you do, don't let the information in this chapter intimidate you. Database programming in Delphi is easy. The basics of it are much simpler than the material you have been learning about in the last few chapters.

Understanding the BDE

Delphi's database prowess stems primarily from its use of the Borland Database Engine (BDE), which is also known as the Integrated Database Application Programming Interface, or IDAPI. As you will see later in this chapter, you are free to use Microsoft's ODBC to access data, but most programmers will probably use the BDE.

> **NOTE**
>
> ODBC is a Microsoft-based specification for creating drivers that access a wide range of database formats. If you are working with standardized data that has obtained any degree of success, there is probably an ODBC driver that will let you get at it. As a rule, you should use a native BDE when you can, since it is faster. However, if there is no BDE driver for your database, you should look for an ODBC driver. ODBC drivers are run through a special "ODBC socket" that enables you to plug these drivers into the BDE.

The key point to grasp about the BDE is that all Borland database tools use it. If there is some feature of Paradox or dBASE that you wish Delphi had, there is nothing inherent in Delphi that prevents you from adding that feature. In other words, whatever database capabilities exist in dBASE or Paradox exist because they use the BDE. Because Delphi also uses the BDE, it too can have the feature.

Before closing this section, I want to say a word about the names IDAPI and BDE. Several years ago, Borland proposed a standard called the Integrated Database Application Programming Interface (IDAPI). It was created to enable applications to access a wide range of data types. For instance, with IDAPI one program can access dBASE and Paradox files.

For various reasons, the IDAPI standard was late to market. Partly out of embarrassment with its lateness and partly due to a change in tastes, Borland decided to change the name from IDAPI to the Borland Database Engine. As Delphi ships, you will find that the same technology is referred to by both names, simply because there hasn't been time to codify the change. The thing to keep in mind is that the terms IDAPI and BDE are synonymous.

Using the Database Desktop to Create Tables

There are two ways to create tables with Delphi:

- The simplest way is to use the Database Desktop (DBD).
- If you want more control over your table creation, you should use the TQuery object and SQL statements.

This chapter includes information about both techniques, but the major emphasis is on the DBD.

After starting the DBD, choose File | New | Table to create a table. The Table Type dialog box appears, as shown in Figure 18.1.

FIGURE 18.1.

A dropdown combo box in the Table Type dialog box enables you to select the type of table you want to create.

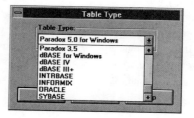

You can use the Table Type dialog box to specify the type (Paradox, dBASE, Oracle, Interbase, Sybase, and so on) and version of table you want to create. In this example, I create a Paradox 5.0 for Windows table. As a result, much of the following discussion is specific to Paradox tables.

After you specify the type of table you want to create, the DBD presents you with a dialog box that lets you specify the name and type of the fields you want to define, as shown in Figure 18.2.

FIGURE 18.2.

The DBD provides a dialog box for specifying the name and type of fields in a table.

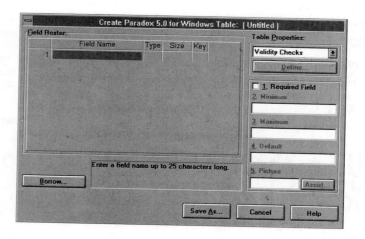

To specify the name of a Paradox field, you can type in any valid string, as specified by the following rules:

■ Names should be shorter than 25 characters.

■ Names should not begin with a blank, but they can contain blanks. However, if you think you might one day port this application to another format, it might be best to avoid spaces. The safest course in terms of portability is to choose names that are shorter than nine letters and contain no spaces.

- Don't include the bracket or parentheses characters [ ], { }, or ( ); don't use a dash combined with a greater than symbol (->); and don't try to use a lone pound symbol (#) as a name. Periods and caret symbols are considered legal characters, but it is best to avoid them because they have a special significance inside Delphi.

If you had decided to create a dBASE table instead of a Paradox table, there would have been only two rules for you to follow:

- No name can have more than 10 characters in it.
- Spaces are not allowed.

Clearly there are many names that dBASE considers legal that Paradox would reject, and vice-versa. The lesson here is not that one system is better than the other, but that you should be fairly conservative in your naming conventions if you think you might ever need to port your tables to another system.

After choosing the name of the field, you choose the field type. To get a list of available types, first select the Type field and then either press the spacebar or click the right mouse button. You can specify that a field is to be part of the primary index by placing an asterisk in the Key field. Paradox tables can have compound keys (made up of more than one field), but the first field in a primary key must also be the first field in a record.

After you have created a Paradox table, there are certain properties you might want to associate with it. For instance, you might want to add a secondary index, validity checks, or referential integrity. These features can be added by choosing Utility | Restructure from the DBD main menu, after the DB is defined, or by defining table properties during DB definition. If you add these features to a Paradox table, they will be respected by Delphi at runtime. For instance, if you add referential integrity to a pair of tables and then try to enter invalid data into the appropriate field of the child table, Delphi will raise an exception.

The list of Table properties available in dBASE files is much smaller than the list included in Paradox files. For this reason, users of local tables will find that there is probably some advantage to using Paradox tables in Delphi applications instead of dBASE files. However, many other outside factors might sway you to choose dBASE or another format instead.

After you have created a table, you can restructure it by choosing Table | Table Restructure. However, the DBD will complain if you try to restructure a table while it is being held open by another application. In other words, you should be sure that you have exclusive access to a table before you try to restructure it.

Creating Tables with SQL

If you don't want to use the DBD, Delphi enables you to create tables by using SQL statements. The actual details of the syntax for creating a table differ depending on the server you are using, but certain basic statements are accepted by almost any server.

To get started creating a table with SQL, you should first drop a TQuery object on a form. Set the DatabaseName property to a valid alias and enter the following string in the SQL property:

```
create table Address ( FirstName char(20), LastName char(20));
```

Run the program and execute the SQL statement by calling Query1.Open. The server will then create a table called Address in the current database. The table will have two character fields called FirstName and LastName, each 20 characters in length. (There is some possibility that a particular server might reject the statement shown here, but it has a very generic syntax and should be acceptable under most circumstances.)

There is virtually an endless number of possible SQL statements you can use to create a table, but the Interbase example on this book's CD-ROM might have enough variety in it to provide you with some hints on how to proceed. The code was written by Joe Fitzhenry, a talented Borland-based expert on the Interbase server. This example contains code that is likely to be specific to Interbase. If you are using a different server, your mileage may differ.

> **NOTE**
>
> A sample script (SAMPLE1.GDB) for creating an entire Interbase database is in the CHAP18 directory on this book's CD-ROM.

Remember that this sample code is Interbase-specific, and your server might not support the exact syntax. For information on the syntax supported by your server, you should refer to its documentation. Other good sources of information include basic SQL primers that can be picked up in a bookstore or library.

The Database Engine Configuration Utility

The Database Engine Configuration utility (BDECFG.EXE) has two primary purposes:

- To enable you to set up drivers for accessing tables
- To enable you to interactively create Aliases

However, it also permits specification of system settings, as well as time, date, number format, and similar types of information.

BDECFG uses a notebook tab metaphor to enable you to access each of its major sets of functionality. For instance, all the information on setting drivers is on one page, all the information for setting aliases is on a second page, all the information about system settings is on a third, and so on.

The information shown here explains some of the options you can tweak on various pages of the BDECFG.EXE program. This information is specific to Paradox files. There are similar materials for use with dBASE files, but they aren't described here; see the online help for details.

- **System:** Specifies memory and technical settings for Paradox tables. If you run into memory problems, they can often be fixed by changing the minimum or maximum buffer size, as well as the maximum amount of memory the BDE will attempt to access. The default language driver can also be specified on this page. If you want to ensure that you always use pass-through SQL on SQL databases, you can change the SQLQRYMODE setting. Finally, there is a LOCAL SHARE setting that can be used to specify whether you want to access the BDE exclusively or access BDE tables and other tables simultaneously.

- **Time:** Specifies whether the system should use a clock based on 12 hours or on 24 hours, whether the strings am and pm should be appended to times, and whether time listings should be accurate to minutes, seconds, or milliseconds.

- **Date:** Specifies what symbol should be used as a separator, whether leading zeros should be placed before single-digit months and days (for example, 01/01/56 or 1/1/56), and whether four digits should be used for years. If you want only two digits for years, you can specify whether the system should assume that you can make a real date by adding 1900 to the two digits already specified.

- **Number:** Specifies how the BDE should treat numbers. In particular, it specifies what symbol should be used to make a decimal point, what should be used as a thousands' separator, how many decimal digits should be used when converting a number into a string, and whether a leading zero should be appended onto numbers between −1 and 1.

The Database Engine Configuration utility stores information in a file called IDAPI.CFG. You must have one of these files on your system if you want to use that utility. As a rule, you shouldn't create an IDAPI.CFG file from scratch but instead should work with one that was already created by the installation program. If there is no IDAPI.CFG file on your hard drive, you should run the installation program again. After successful completion of the installation program, it would probably be a good idea for you to make a backup copy of IDAPI.CFG and save it in case of emergency.

Using ODBC, Oracle, Interbase, and Other Drivers

Delphi provides access to Microsoft's 2.0 ODBC Driver Manager. If you have a different version of the ODBC Driver Manager, follow these steps:

1. Back up your existing ODBC.DLL and ODBCINST.DLL files.

2. Copy the ODBC.NEW and ODBCINST.NEW files from your IDAPI directory into your existing ODBC directory. (By default this is WINDOWS\SYSTEM.)

3. Rename the files to ODBC.DLL and ODBCINST.DLL.

In its simplest useful state, the Database Engine Configuration utility gives you access to only dBASE files, Paradox files, and the Local Interbase Server. These drivers are listed on the first of the six pages found in the BDECFG program.

If you have the Client/Server version of Delphi, you will also have Borland SQL Links, which provides access to Informix, Interbase, Oracle, and Sybase files. If you have the Delphi Client/Server version and you see only dBASE and Paradox drivers listed, you should run the SQL links installation process again. If you have the Delphi Desktop version, you will not have built-in access to server data, except through ODBC drivers, which you can acquire and add on when and if you need them. At the time of this writing, SQL links are available from Borland as an add-on product. In some cases, it may be cheaper for you to buy the Desktop version of Delphi, and then get SQL links separately.

After you install SQL Links, there are other DLLs that must be placed on your system before you can connect to most servers. For instance, both the local and server versions of Interbase require the presence of GDS.DLL and REMOTE.DLL. SQL Links provides the intermediary between BDE and a server, but there is another layer that ships with your server that must also be present before you can connect. The files necessary for connecting to Paradox and dBASE tables are included with Delphi and should be readily available to you as long as the IDAPI directory is listed on your path.

Some users will want to use other databases, such as FoxPro or Access. To use these databases, you must have ODBC drivers installed on your system. A configuration utility for these drivers should be available as a separate applet in the Windows Control Panel, as shown in Figure 18.3. If you open up the Control Panel and don't see the ODBC applet, you need to contact Microsoft or some other vendor that provides ODBC drivers. These drivers are provided for the price of standard connect charges on CompuServe in the Microsoft SQL forum. If you don't have ODBC version 2.0 or later installed on your system, or if a file called IDODBC??.DLL is not present in your IDAPI directory, you won't be able to install ODBC drivers.

FIGURE 18.3.

The ODBC applet is visible on the third row, far right.

If you click the New Driver button on the Drivers page in the Database Engine Configuration utility, you will see the dialog box shown in Figure 18.4. The specific driver that you want to use should begin with the letters "ODBC_." A dropdown list of default ODBC drivers appears in the second field of the dialog box, and the Default Data Source Name is usually provided for you automatically.

FIGURE 18.4.

The Add ODBC Driver dialog box enables you to install drivers for Access, FoxPro, and other types of databases.

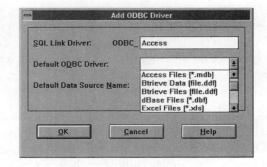

After you have installed an ODBC driver, you will be able to create an alias for a specific database.

Aliases

Aliases enable you to connect to a database. They tell the BDE where a table is stored and what tools should be used to access it. In short, an alias specifies the location and type of a database. If you store tables on a server, or if you store a set of tables in a subdirectory on your computer, it is handy to be able to reference either of these sets of files through a single word or a short phrase.

Suppose that you have an Interbase database called SALES94 placed in a subdirectory called C:\DATA and stored on a server called NELLIE. Suppose further that to access the database you need to sign on as USER1 under a particular password. Every time you want to access that server, you are going to need to reference all the information listed here. That is, you have to specify the following:

```
The server name: Nellie
The type of server: Interbase
The directory name: C:\DATA
The database name: SALES94
The user name: USER1
```

This is a lot of information to convey every time you want to connect to a particular database. One solution to this problem is to create an alias that references this information.

> **NOTE**
>
> Tables are stored in databases. Some databases consist of a single file that is divided internally into multiple tables, whereas other databases exist as a series of separate files on a disk. For instance, dBASE and Paradox tables are always stored in separate files, whereas Interbase tables are stored inside a single file with a GDB extension. Therefore, one GDB file is a single database, whereas a directory with Paradox DB files or dBASE DBF files is considered to be one database. In short, any directory that contains Paradox or dBASE files is treated by Delphi as a single database. To switch to another database, simply change the directory referenced in your alias. The subject of databases is treated in more depth at the end of the next chapter.

As a rule, you should always access database tables via aliases. However, Delphi enables you to access a local Paradox or dBASE database simply by specifying the directory where it is stored in the DatabaseName property of a TTable, TQuery, or other TDataSet descendant. Aliases are more useful than simple pathnames, however, particularly if you think the program you are creating might exist on multiple machines that aren't identically configured.

When you install Delphi, it automatically sets up an alias called DBDEMOS. This alias enables you to access tables in the \DELPHI\DEMOS\DATABASE subdirectory. Because many of the sample programs used in this book reference tables in that subdirectory, you might be able to get on for a while using only that single alias. However, over time, you will need to learn to create your own alias.

To create an alias, turn to the Aliases page in BDECFG.EXE and choose New Alias. A dialog box such as that shown in Figure 18.5 enables you to enter the name and type of alias you want to use in your program. The type of alias will be dBASE, Paradox, Interbase, Sybase, or the name of some other server.

FIGURE 18.5.

The Database Engine Configuration utility provides a dialog box where you can specify the name and type of a new alias.

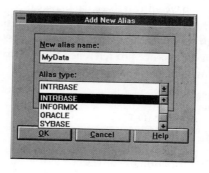

After you have created an alias, it appears in the list of Alias Names shown on the Aliases page of the Database Engine Configuration utility. It is not enough, however, to simply create the alias. You must also specify additional information, the exact nature of which differs depending on your current server. For instance, dBASE and Paradox files specify that you must fill in the path that leads to the database.

Parameters:

TYPE	STANDARD
PATH	c:\data

An Interbase server, however, asks that you specify 11 pieces of information. Fortunately, you can usually leave default or blank values in all but the Server Name or User Name parameters:

SERVER NAME	nellie:c:\data\hotline.gdb
USER NAME	user1

In this example, a database called HOTLINE.GDB is located in a directory called DATA, which is stored on the C drive of an NT server called NELLIE. The user name for the server is USER1. All the other fields in an Interbase alias can be left with default values. If you need more information about this subject, you should refer to the Interbase documentation.

As stated previously, the way you declare an alias differs depending on your server. The specifics of the information required for a particular server can be found either in the documentation for your server or for the Borland SQL Links software.

Summary

In this chapter you learned about two utilities:

- The Database Desktop, or DBD
- The Database Engine Configuration utility, or BDECFG

DBD is useful for creating and viewing tables; BDECFG enables you to configure a database, and in particular, to create an alias. You saw that the Database Engine Configuration utility enables you to install new ODBC drivers.

Alias is a technical term for a word or short phrase that refers to a particular set of tables stored in something called a database. The specifics of creating an alias differ depending on the type of server involved; but the general technique is to use BDECFG to specify the name of the server, the path to the database, and the name of the database itself.

You also got a brief look at the syntax used to create tables. The specifics of this syntax can differ depending on the particular server involved.

Database programming with Delphi is not as complex as it might seem from reading this chapter. If some of what you have read seems a bit overwhelming, just go on to the next chapter, and you may be surprised at how easy it is to create a Delphi database program.

Creating Simple Database Programs

Overview

This chapter gives you a 5,000-foot overview of working with Delphi databases. After reading it, you will be able to open tables and display them. You will learn the basic facts needed to begin manipulating TTable and TQuery objects, and you will learn how to show them in simple visual controls such as TDBGrids. The last two sections of the chapter give a broad overview of database basics. This overview might be particularly useful to someone who comes from the world of C++ or Pascal, and who is new to databases.

One of the main themes of this chapter is that TTable objects provide a simple and direct way to access tables, whereas TQuery objects enable you to access tables by writing SQL commands. Both approaches have validity, and you will choose one approach or the other depending on the circumstances governing your work.

Many programmers will learn much of what they need to know about databases simply by reading the very easy-to-understand material in this chapter. However, if you plan to spend most of your time creating database applications, this is only the beginning of your exploration of this powerful and complex topic.

TTable, TDataSource, and TDBGrid

To create a simple database application, start by placing a TTable, a TDataSource, and a TDBGrid component on a form, as shown in Figure 19.1.

FIGURE 19.1.

TTable, TDataSource, and TDBGrid arranged on a form.

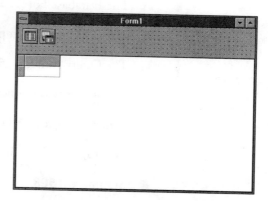

Wire these three controls together by completing the following simple steps:

1. Connect the DataSource property of the TDBGrid to DataSource1.
2. Connect the DataSet property of the TDataSource control to Table1.

After completing these steps, the three components are hooked together and can communicate with one another.

Connecting the TTable object to a table that resides on disk is a three-step process:

1. Set the DatabaseName property either to a valid alias or to the subdirectory where your data resides. For instance, if you wanted to access the demo tables that ship with Delphi, you should choose the DBDEMOS alias supplied by the install program or type c:\delphi\demos\data into the DatabaseName Property Editor, where you might need to replace c:\ with the appropriate drive on your system.

2. Set the TableName property to the name of the table you want to view; for instance, you might choose the CUSTOMER.DB table. The Property Editor drops down a list of available tables, so there is no need for you to type anything by hand.

3. Set the Active property to True, as shown in Figure 19.2.

FIGURE 19.2.

The Object Inspector after connecting to a table called Customer, using an alias called DBDEMOS.

If you have completed all these steps properly, you should now be looking at the data from the table you chose, as shown in Figure 19.3. To take this process one step further, you can compile and run the program and then begin browsing and editing your data.

FIGURE 19.3.

Simple form displaying the contents of CUSTOMER.DB.

If you want to simplify the task of browsing through the data in your application, you can go back into design mode and add the TDBNavigator control to the program described earlier. To hook this control into the loop, all you need to do is set its DataSource property to DataSource1.

Now you can run the program and begin iterating through the records with the navigator, as shown in Figure 19.4. In Figure 19.4, most of the functionality of the dbNavigator has been turned off by manipulating the `VisibleButtons` property. For instance, a navigator can automatically enable you to edit, insert, delete, post, cancel, and refresh. All of those capabilities have been disabled and hidden in the form shown here.

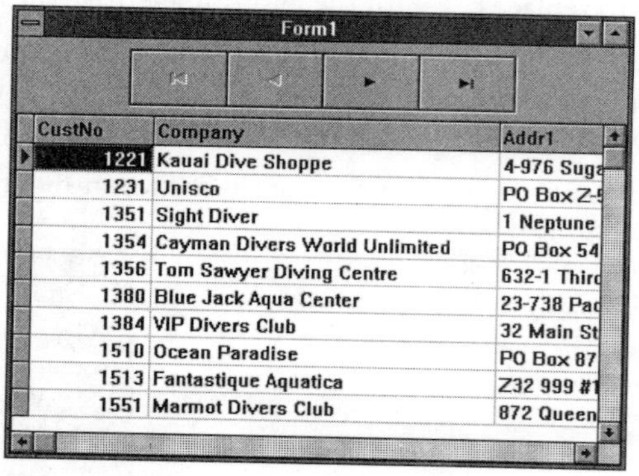

FIGURE 19.4.

A simple database program with a TDBNavigator control.

To see some additional features, you should now go back into design mode, set the `Active` property to `False`, the `TableName` property to the BIOLIFE table, and the `Active` property to `True`. The BIOLIFE.DB file, which ships with Delphi, has a BLOB field in it called Graphic. BLOB fields are used for storing binary images such as BMP files. If you drop a dbImage component on the form, you can show the contents of the Graphic BLOB field to the user, as shown in Figure 19.5. To hook up the dbImage control, set its `DataSource` property to `DataSource1` and its `DataField` property to `Graphic`. Both Property Editors have dropdown lists, so you perform the whole operation with the mouse.

You also can add a TDBMemo field to the project, and set its datasource to `DataSource1` and its `DataField` to `Notes`. The Notes field is another blob image, one that contains only text. Delphi will automatically suck the text blob out of the database and display it in the TDBMemo component, where you can edit it or delete it. Any changes you make to the text of a database will be saved automatically when you iterate on to the next record.

This program is available on disk as SIMPFORM.DPR. I don't show you the code here because the program was created entirely by manipulating properties in the Object Inspector. In short, you don't need to write a single line of code when creating SIMPFORM.DPR.

FIGURE 19.5.

Adding a TDBImage component to the SIMPFORM.

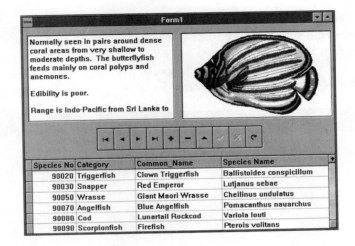

The TQuery Component

In its simplest manifestation, the TQuery component is very similar to the TTable component, except that you select the file you want to use with an SQL statement rather than a `TableName` property. To get started, drop down a TQuery, a TDataSource, and a TDBGrid component. Connect them as described in the previous section.

When it is time to connect the TQuery component to a table, set up the `DatabaseName` property as described in the previous section. Then open the SQL Property Editor and type in the following string, as shown in Figure 19.6:

```
select * from biolife
```

FIGURE 19.6.

Typing a string in the SQL Property Editor.

You are now ready to set the `Active` property to `True` and run your program.

The SQL property is the key to the TQuery component. You can use this property to enter any valid SQL statement that can be processed by your network-based server or by a local SQL server. You will see in later chapters that there are many tricks you can use to change the SQL property at runtime. For now, you need to know only that the statements you type in can be passed directly to your server, thereby ensuring that you can tap into its full power.

> **NOTE**
>
> The SQL language is described in the online help. To get started, look up "Overview of using SQL." A useful SQL reference is provided in the help for the WISQL utility that ships with Delphi.
>
> The question of whether you are using pass-through SQL is something that can be controlled from inside IDAPICFG. If you turn to the System page of that utility, you will find the SQLQRYMODE setting. It can be left blank, which is the default setting, or it can be set to Local or Server, as follows:
>
> - **Blank:** The query goes first to the server; if the server can't handle it, the BDE takes it up.
> - **Server:** The query always goes to the server; if the server can't handle it, the call fails.
> - **Local:** The call is always handled on the desktop.
>
> The code explained here is demonstrated on disk in the program SIMPQRY.DPR. In that example, you can see that dbNavigator and dbImage components have been added to the form. These components work the same way with TQuerys as they do with TTables.

The Database Form Expert

In the last few pages, you saw how to create database programs manually. There was no need for you to write any code while producing these applications, except for one short line of SQL. However, you still needed to connect the various controls and to arrange them on disk. In many cases, you can use the Database Form Expert to expedite these tasks.

One path to the Database Form Expert is located on the Help menu under "Database Form Expert." After selecting it, you can opt to create a simple form or a master/detail form. Furthermore, you can choose whether you want to work with a TTable or with TQuery objects, as shown in Figure 19.7.

FIGURE 19.7.

The opening screen of the Database Form Expert.

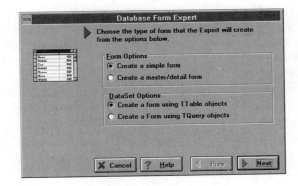

Here is a simple procedure showing how to use the database expert:

1. From the first screen, choose "Create a simple form" and "Create a form using TTable objects."
2. From the second screen, choose "DBDemos as an Alias," and select CUSTOMER.DB as a table.
3. From the third screen, select the button with the double arrow on it (>>), and move all the fields into the "Ordered Selected Fields" listbox.
4. From the next screen, choose "Horizontal."
5. On the last screen, choose "Generate a Main Form" and then select the Create button.

Congratulations! You've created a fully functional, professional-looking database application.

If you are working with a master/detail form, you will also need to designate the fields that link the two tables. To perform the latter operation, simply select the fields you want to use and then select the Add button. For instance, if you have selected the Customer and Orders table from the DELPHI\DEMOS\DATA subdirectory, you should select the CustNo fields from both tables when the expert asks you to select the "pairs of fields...that will join the two queries."

NOTE

Master/detail forms enable you to designate a particular, but very common, relationship between two tables. The classic case of a master/detail relationship occurs in the instance where you have a list of customers and a list of orders associated with that customer. When you select a particular customer in one table, you want to be able to simultaneously view all the related orders in the second table. The trick is to view only one record in the first table and then a selected subset of records from the second table.

It is no coincidence that Delphi ships with a set of tables called CUSTOMER.DB and ORDERS.DB. The key point about these tables is that for each record in the

Customer table there is one or more associated records in the Orders table. These two tables are linked by the CustNo field. That is, each Customer record has a number associated with it, and every record in the Orders table also has a field designating the number of the customer who made that order. Master/detail relationships enable you to view one customer record at a time, while simultaneously viewing all the orders made by that customer. This subject is explored in depth several times in the next three chapters.

The last screen in the Database Expert asks if you want to "Generate a Main Form." If you select this option, the form you create will be the main form in your application.

If you do not choose "Generate a Main Form," then before running your application, you need to make sure that your program has some method of launching the form you have just created. The application you are working on now has at least two forms: the form created when you chose New Project from the menu and the form built by the Database Form Expert. If all you want to do is view the form you have created, you can select Options | Project and then turn to the Forms page and set the Main Form equal to the form that displays your new form, as shown in Figure 19.8. For more information, see the material on Forms at the end of Chapter 4, "The Structure of a Delphi Program." Also, see "Calling Forms from Forms," "Sharing Forms with other Projects," and "Instantiating Forms at RunTime" in the online help.

FIGURE 19.8.

The Forms page from the Options | Project menu choice can be used to designate the main form of an application.

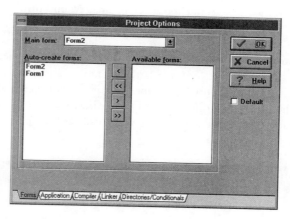

After answering the simple questions posed by the Database Form Expert, you are presented with a ready-to-run form that meets your specifications. All the controls on this form will be hooked up and arranged in a reasonably attractive manner. If you want, you can make further changes to this form while you are in design mode.

Like all the parts of Delphi, it is possible for third-party developers to extend or entirely replace the functionality of the Database Form Expert. This means that further additions to the functionality shown here are likely to appear in the near future.

The Gallery and Templates

Sometimes you might create a complex form that you would want to use over and over again in several different projects. Delphi provides a special Gallery where you can save these forms for reuse at a later time. The Gallery can also be used to save entire projects. Delphi's collection of customized forms and projects is accessible to you from the Options | Gallery menu choice. The page from the Gallery tools is shown in Figure 19.9.

FIGURE 19.9.

A set of sample templates from the Gallery.

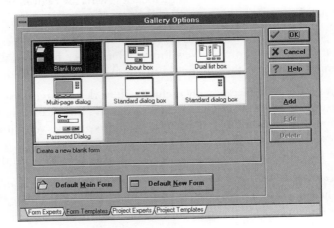

The forms and projects in the Gallery can be made accessible to you whenever you choose New Project or New Form from the File menu. To activate these features, choose Options | Environment from the menu and select "Use New Form" and "Use New Template" from the Preferences page, as shown in Figure 19.10. After you have made these selections, you can automatically choose from a suite of new forms or new projects whenever you are in design mode.

FIGURE 19.10.

The Gallery options are located on the bottom-right corner of the Preferences page.

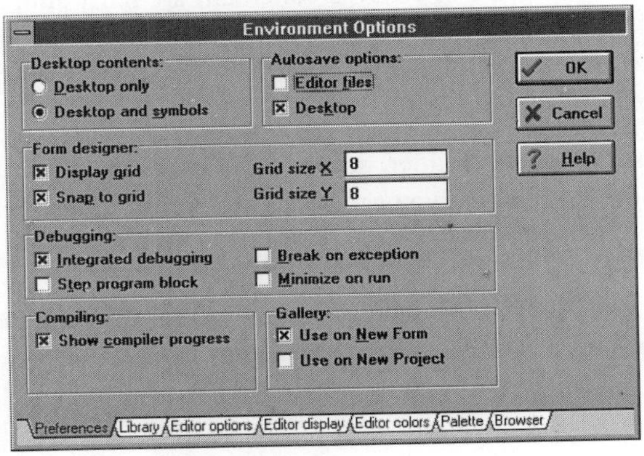

By default, the Gallery comes equipped with several standard application and form templates. You can see these templates by selecting Options | Gallery and then choosing either the Form Templates or Project Templates page. You can contribute new additions to these collections of templates and forms at any time simply by clicking the right mouse button. For instance, if you have a form that you want to save as a template, you can click it with the right mouse button to bring up a popup menu. From the menu, you should choose the option "Save as Template." To save an entire project as a template, you should first bring up the Project Manager from the View menu and then click it with the right mouse button to bring up a popup menu. From the menu, you should choose "Save as Template."

If you have added new forms or projects to the Gallery, you can select from them whenever you choose New Form or New Project. Remember, however, that you must have first set the proper controls in the Options | Environment dialog box, as described previously.

This feature can be especially useful if you work in a large department and want to make sure that every project your team creates has certain identical forms that look and feel exactly the same in all applications. For instance, Windows provides you with the Common Dialogs, which are available from the Dialogs page of the Component Palette. The Gallery enables you to create your own sets of Common Dialogs that can be used by all the members of your team.

However, even programmers who are working alone will find many good uses for the Gallery. When you store a form in the Gallery, all the code associated with the form is also stored. This means you could build up sets of customized forms and projects that have all the bare bones of a particular type of form or project stored inside them. Once again, this can help you build a set of applications with the same look or feel, or it can simply speed up the process of development and help you avoid needless repetition.

The Query Builder

Most of the elements of an SQL statement are fairly simple. However, there are times when you will need to create long SQL statements with several discreet parts. To aid in this task, the client/server version of Delphi has a Query Builder that enables you to use visual tools to create complex SQL statements.

To access the Query Builder, drop a TQuery component on a form and right-click it. A menu will appear from which you can select the option Query Builder.

The Query Builder then asks you to specify an alias, as shown in Figure 19.11.

After identifying the database you want to use, the next step is to choose a file or list of files that you want to query, as shown in Figure 19.12.

FIGURE 19.11.

The Query Builder first asks for an alias that designates the database you want to use.

FIGURE 19.12.

Selecting files from the Query Builder to use in an SQL statement.

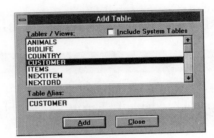

The final step is to choose the fields you want to work with, and to use the Query Builder to create a join, group, or similar construct, as shown in Figure 19.13. If you want to create a one-to-many relationship with each table shown in a separate grid, you should use the Database Form Expert.

FIGURE 19.13.

Choosing fields and their functions from the Query Builder's main window.

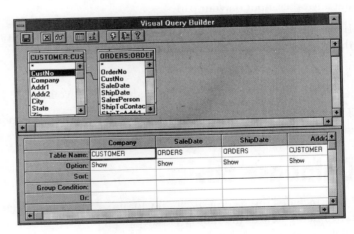

The Report Component

Delphi Enterprise ships with a copy of ReportSmith. This is a full application in its own right, and I explain at least a portion of it in Chapter 23, "Real-World Databases."

In this brief introduction to ReportSmith, I do not attempt to explain how to actually design reports. This chapter shows you how to run ReportSmith from Delphi—that is, how to print a report from Delphi—but it does not explain how to develop the report.

To get started, drop a TReport object on a form. TReport components are stored on the Data Access page of the Component Palette. Set the ReportName field to the name of a valid report, such as MYREPORT.RPT. Set the ReportDir field to the directory where your report is stored.

> **NOTE**
>
> If you use the browse icon in the ReportName Property Editor, you will be able to automatically fill in both the ReportName and ReportDir.

After setting up the TReport object, place a button on the form and associate an `OnClick` method with it. Fill the method in with a single line of code:

```
Report1.Run;
```

Now run your program and click the button. Your report will automatically be printed without any other input on your part.

If you have Delphi Enterprise and receive an error while performing the steps outlined here, there are two likely possibilities for what went wrong:

- You haven't properly installed ReportSmith.
- You don't have the RS_RUN subdirectory on your path.

The RS_RUN subdirectory contains the runtime version of ReportSmith. This is the distributable portion of the application that you can ship royalty-free with your own projects.

Database Basics

I have included this section specifically for programmers who have used C or Pascal for a long time but are new to the subject of databases. However, it contains general information that might be useful to any reader.

Many long-term programmers have never spent much time thinking about databases. Pascal and C programmers, for instance, can usually store data in linked lists and files of record and can access the structures in these files without ever once starting up dBASE, Paradox, or any of a number of other standard database tools. This means of accessing data is usually very fast and relatively simple to use.

However, when a programmer wants to deal with more than 1,000 or 2,000 records, they can suddenly come up against the limitations of linked lists, or of many of the simpler binary tree algorithms. Further problems occur when a programmer wants to change the structure of a table on-the-fly. For instance, trouble often arises when a programmer wants to add a field to a record in an established database. Complications also arise when a programmer tries to join two tables together at runtime, allow the user to edit the result, and then store both edited records in separate files.

The point I am trying to make here is simply that large and complex databases lead to large and complex programming problems. Simply defining a record, filling it with data, and blasting it onto a disk is not a solution if you want to track large, complex sets of data that are stored in many files, and that may change in subtle ways over the years. For tasks like that, you need a real database tool.

Borland has a powerful database engine called the Borland Database Engine, or IDAPI, which is short for the Integrated Database Application Programming Interface. This engine knows how to handle tables that contain millions of records. It knows how to perform joins on multiple tables. It knows how to parse SQL statements, how to create primary and secondary indices, and how to sort, search, retrieve, and store large quantities of data in a reliable and efficient manner.

Of course, the word *efficient* is one that can be interpreted many different ways, depending on the circumstances. For a real, industrial-strength database, the goal is not to be able to access small tables in short periods of time. Instead, the goal is to access any table, regardless of size, in a reasonable period of time.

If a Pascal or C/C++ programmer stores a few hundred records in a file of record, he can usually access any one of those records in the blink of an eye. If he has loaded the entire file into memory and stored it in a linked list or binary tree, he can access any of the records in a period of time that appears instantaneous to the human eye. However, if the programmer tried to use the same technique on 10,000, or 100,000 records, he or she is bound to experience a severe degradation of performance, if not an entire failure of his or her system. Furthermore, it is usually relatively difficult to perform joins, sorts, restructurings, and deletions.

A real database engine such as IDAPI might seem at least a bit slow to a C or Pascal programmer when it is working with small tables of 200 or 300 records. One of the main reasons for this is that IDAPI comes in the form of a dozen different DLLs that are stored on disk. Every time you want to use IDAPI, at least some of these files have to be read into memory, a task that takes several seconds, even on a Pentium with a fast hard drive.

> **NOTE**
>
> If you haven't done so already, you should take a moment to examine the IDAPI subdirectory that is stored on your disk. This subdirectory is created whenever you install Delphi, dBASE for Windows, the Borland Database Engine, or Paradox 5.0 or later. A number of standard files are kept in this directory. To see the main ones, type the following command at the DOS prompt:
>
> ```
> dir id*.dll
> ```
>
> The resulting output might look like this:
>
> ```
> Volume in drive C is CHASDISK        Serial number is 1200:3020
>  Directory of  c:\idapi\id*.dll
>
> idapi01.dll     394016    7-30-94    1:00
> idasci01.dll     79648    7-30-94    1:00
> idbat01.dll     105120    7-30-94    1:00
> iddbas01.dll    305040    7-30-94    1:00
> idodbc01.dll    353808    7-26-94    1:00
> idpdx01.dll     258032    7-30-94    1:00
> idqry01.dll     385216    7-30-94    1:00
> idr10009.dll     20688    7-30-94    1:00
>    1,901,568 bytes in 8 file(s)          1,941,504 bytes allocated
>   33,185,792 bytes free
> ```
>
> These are some of the key files used to drive the IDAPI database engine, or the Borland Database Engine (BDE), as it is often called. Other key files include DBCOEDIT.DLL and ILDO1.DLL. It is unlikely that all of these files would ever be loaded into memory at any one time, but just two or three of them can still add up to a significant hit on system resources.

The point here is not that the BDE is unusually slow or ponderous. In fact, it is an extremely fast and flexible engine that is considerably more powerful than many of its competitors.

The key point about IDAPI is that it enables you to scale small databases into large local or server databases with little effort and a linear, easy-to-predict, hit in terms of performance. In other words, the Borland Database Engine can handle 10,000 or even 100,000 records nearly as easily as it can handle 300 records. Of course, it takes longer for IDAPI to sort through 100,000 records than it does to sort through 1,000 records, but when it is graphed, the degradation in performance looks like a straight line. A poorly designed database, on the other hand, creates a graph that looks like a curve that quickly spirals up toward infinity. For instance, a linked list might handle 100 records in 2 seconds, 1,000 records in 20 seconds, 10,000 records in 20 hours, and 100,000 records in an infinite period of time; that is, it would crash when presented with a file containing 100,000 records.

> **NOTE**
>
> Many of the figures I'm quoting here are meant to be taken as generalizations. For instance, it is possible to create a record that is only 1 or 2 bytes. In such cases, it might be fairly easy to create linked lists that work at least reasonably well even with 100,000 elements. However, if the records were each 5,000 bytes in size, a linked list of 100,000 items would become very ponderous on even the most powerful systems. Therefore I have to ask the reader to look behind the surface level of my argument and try to see not a series of superficial facts, but the overall theme that I am trying to convey.

A real database tool does more than just enable you to work with large data sets. It must also enable you to quickly construct a table, quickly alter the fields inside it, quickly perform joins between two or more tables, and quickly sort or index the data. The capability to do these jobs on huge datasets with relative dispatch is one of the key selling points of the various databases seen on the market. For instance, when a magazine compares Borland's dBASE for Windows and Microsoft's FoxPro, it is part of their job to see how quickly each tool can perform these tasks on huge datasets. That is what the database game is all about.

By now you should be getting a good feeling for what jobs the Borland Database Engine is designed to perform. Furthermore, you should begin to understand what is expected of a first-rate networked server such as Interbase, Oracle, or Sybase. Sophisticated systems of this sort tend to be large and fairly clunky when compared to the simpler solutions used by C and Pascal programmers when they are handling relatively small sets of data. However, the initial hit you experience when using systems such as IDAPI or ODBC is quickly offset by the many benefits it gives in terms of flexibility and scalability.

What is a Table?

Pascal or C programmers can think of a table as nothing more than a simple binary file that contains a series of records or structs arranged in some specific and clearly defined fashion. That's all a table is, on the simplest and broadest level. It is just a binary file that contains multiple copies of a single record.

However, all database engines have formats that are specific to their particular brand of table. For instance, dBASE tables have one particular format, Paradox tables have another, and large sophisticated servers such as Interbase actually store all their tables as part of one larger file that frequently reaches huge sizes of 1, 10, or 20 megabytes.

All database engines, however, have a binary structure called a table; and that table contains one or more copies of what Pascal programmers would call a record, and what C programmers would call a struct. However, people new to the database world have to understand that there is a huge difference between a simple binary file of record and what is commonly called a table. Both formats store data in records that look pretty much the same to the casual user, but underneath there is a great deal of difference in terms of complexity.

Summary

This short chapter has given you the information you need to get started using the TTable and TQuery objects. These objects provide very simple means for you to access and edit data residing on a server or in a local table.

Later chapters show you how to use these tools to manually perform joins and transactions, link cursors, and accomplish other advanced database techniques. This chapter showed you two shortcuts to this end. One shortcut is the Database Form Expert, which enables you to create forms containing one or more tables quickly and easily. The other shortcut is the Query Builder, which you can use if you need to describe more complex relationships.

Also in this chapter, you were treated to a description of the Gallery. This tool can obviously be used not only with database applications but with any general VCL program you might create.

Using TTable and TDataSet

Overview

In this chapter you learn some of the basics about accessing database tables. In the examples given here, you will be explicitly working with local Paradox tables, but nearly everything explained here applies equally to dBASE files or to files located on a server.

Looking a little more deeply at the content of this chapter, you can expect to find information on the following:

- The TTable object, which provides the fastest and simplest access to tables.
- The TQuery object, which is the gateway to the flexible and powerful world of SQL.
- The TDataSet object, an ancestor of TTable and TQuery, which provides the core functionality for accessing tables and the records that lie within them.
- The TField object, which gives you access to the fields in a table or dataset. This object has powerful descendants such as TStringField and TIntegerField, all of which can be created automatically by a visual tool called the Fields Editor.
- The TDataSource object, which serves as an intermediary between data-aware controls and TTable and TQuery objects.
- The TdbGrid object, which provides a simple way to display the contents of tables to the user. TdbGrid objects support editing, deletion and insertion.
- The TdbEdit component, which allows you to display a single field from a single record, and to edit or insert the contents of that field.

Here is a second way to categorize the objects listed:

- Nonvisual: TTable, TQuery, TDataSet, TField
- Visual: TdbGrid, TdbEdit
- Link (also nonvisual): TDataSource

This latter view of the major database components breaks them down into two major categories. The nonvisual components enable you to open, close, edit, and otherwise manipulate tables, records, and fields. The visual components display the tables to use, and allows the user to edit them. The powerful TDataSource object forms a link between the visual and nonvisual database controls.

The overriding purpose of this chapter is to give you a good overview of the basic facts about using a Delphi database component called TDataSet. TDataSet is the driving force behind both the TTable and TQuery objects.

Specific information about other database issues will be presented in subsequent chapters. For instance, the TQuery object will be treated in depth in the next chapter, and a more detailed explanation of TdbGrid, TField, TStringField, and TIntegerField is found in Chapter 22, "Fields and Database Tools."

TDataSet

TTable and TQuery inherit most of their functionality from TDataSet. As a result, the TDataSet class is one of the most important database objects. To get started working with it, you need to concentrate on the following hierarchy:

```
TDataSet
    |
  TdbDataSet
    |
   / \
TTable  TQuery
```

TDataSet contains the abstractions needed to directly manipulate a table. TdbDataSet knows how to handle passwords and other tasks directly associated with linking to a specific table. TTable knows how to handle indices and the specific chores associated with linking two tables in a one-to-many relationship. As you will see in the next chapter, TQuery has specific knowledge of how to process SQL statements.

TDataSet is the tool you will use to open and navigate through a table. Of course, you will never directly instantiate an object of type TDataSet. Instead, you will usually be working with TTable, TQuery, or some other descendant of TDataSet. The exact way this system works, and the precise significance of TDataSet, will become clear as you read through this chapter.

On the most fundamental level, a dataset is nothing more than a set of records, as depicted in Figure 20.1.

FIGURE 20.1.

A dataset consists of series of records, each containing X number of fields and a pointer to the current record.

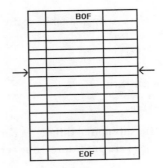

On many occasions, a dataset has a direct, one-to-one correspondence with a physical table that exists on disk. However, at other times you may perform a query or other action that returns a dataset that contains either a subset of one table, or else a join between multiple tables. The text that follows, will, however, sometimes use the terms dataset and table interchangeably if it helps to simplify the explanation of a particular concept.

You will normally instantiate an object of type TTable or TQuery in order to access the functionality of TDataSet. Because of this relationship, the code in the next few sections will always assume the existence of an instance of class TTable called Table1. Remember, however, that the functions under discussion are part of TDataSet, unless the text specifically states otherwise.

It's now time for you to begin a direct exploration of TDataSet. As you become familiar with its capabilities, you will begin to understand exactly how Delphi accesses the raw data saved to disk as a database. The key point to remember is that nearly every time a Delphi programmer opens a table, he or she will be using a class such as TTable or TQuery, which are merely thin wrappers around TDataSet.

Opening and Closing Datasets

The simplest thing you can do with a TDataSet is open or close it. This is therefore an appropriate starting point for an exploration of datasets. In the sections that follow, you will drill down deeper and learn more about the thorough access to databases provided by Delphi.

There are two ways to open or close a dataset. You can write the following line of code:

```
Table1.Open;
```

Or, if you prefer, you can set the Active property equal to True:

```
Table1.Active := True;
```

There is no difference between the effect produced by these two statements. Open, however, ends up setting Active to True, so it may be ever so slightly more efficient to use the Active property directly.

Just as there are two ways to open a table, so are there two ways to close a table. The simplest way is to call Close:

```
Table1.Close;
```

Or, if you wish, you can write

```
Table1.Active := False;
```

Once again, there is no substantial difference between these two calls. You should note, however, that Close and Open are procedures, but Active is a property.

You should also know about the TDatabase object, which exists primarily to give you a means of staying connected to a database even if you are continually opening and closing a series of tables. If you use TDatabase, you can be connected to Oracle, Interbase, or other servers without ever opening any tables. You can then begin opening and closing tables over and over without having to incur the overhead of connecting to the database each time you call Open.

The TDatabase object also enables you to start server-based applications without specifying a password; and it gives you access to transactions. For further information on TDataBase, see the TRANSACTS program, which is discussed at the end of Chapter 24.

In this section you have learned about two methods:

```
procedure Open;
procedure Close;
```

and one property:

```
property Active;
```

You also learned about the TDatabase object, which can be used to optimize code that is continually connecting and disconnecting from tables that belong to one database.

Navigational Routines

After opening a dataset, the next step is to learn how to move about inside it. The following rich set of methods and properties from TDataSet provide all the tools you need to access any particular record inside a dataset:

```
procedure First;
procedure Last;
procedure Next;
procedure Prior;
property BOF: Boolean read FBOF;
property EOF: Boolean read FEOF;
procedure MoveBy(Distance: Integer);
```

Experienced programmers will find these procedures very easy to use. Here is a quick overview of their functionality:

- Calling `Table1.First` moves you to the first record in a table.
- `Table1.Last` moves you to the last record.
- `Table1.Next` moves you one record forward, unless you are at the end of a table.
- `Table1.Prior` moves you one record back, unless you are at the beginning of the table.
- You can check the `BOF` or `EOF` properties in order to see if you are at the beginning or the end of a table.
- The `MoveBy` procedure moves you *x* number of records forward or backward in a table. There is no functional difference between calling `Table1.Next` and calling `Table1.MoveBy(1)`. Furthermore, calling `Table1.Prior` has the same effect as calling `Table1.MoveBy(-1)`. In fact, `Next` and `Prior` are one-line procedures that call `MoveBy`, exactly as shown here.

Most of these properties and methods are demonstrated in the sample program found on disk as NAVY.DPR. You can open this example directly, or construct it piece-by-piece by following the description that follows.

To get started using these navigational routines, you should:

1. Place a `TTable`, `TDataSource`, and `TdbGrid` on a form.

2. Hook the grid to the datasource, and the datasource to the table.

3. Set the DatabaseName property of the table to the DBDEMOS alias, or type in the path to the demos subdirectory (..\delphi\demos\data).

4. Set the TableName property to the CUSTOMER table.

If you are having trouble completing these steps refer to NAVY.DPR, which comes on your disks.

If you run a program that contains a TdbGrid control, you will find that you can iterate through the records in a dataset by manipulating the scrollbars on the edges of the grid. You can gain the same functionality by using the TDBNavigator component. However, there are times when you want to move through a table programmatically, without the use of the built-in visual tools. The next few paragraphs explain how this process works.

Place two buttons on a form and label them Next and Prior, as shown in Figure 20.2.

FIGURE 20.2.

The Prior and Next buttons in NAVY.DPR enable you to maneuver through a database.

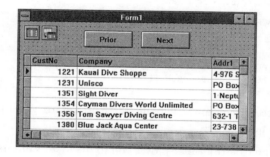

Double-click once on the Next button to create an OnClick method, and fill it in like this:

```
procedure TForm1.bNextClick(Sender: TObject);
begin
  Table1.Next;
end;
```

Perform the same action with the Prior button, so that the function associated with it looks like this:

```
procedure TForm1.bPriorClick(Sender: TObject);
begin
  Table1.Prior;
end;
```

Now run the program and click the two buttons. You will find that they easily let you iterate through the records in a dataset.

Now drop down two more buttons and label them First and Last, as shown in Figure 20.3.

FIGURE 20.3.

The Navy program with all four buttons inserted.

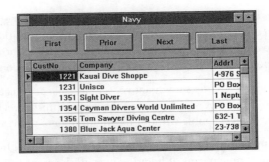

Proceed to do the same thing for the calls to `Table1.First` and `Table1.Last` as you did with `Next` and `Prior`:

```
procedure TForm1.bFirstClick(Sender: TObject);
begin
  Table1.First;
end;

procedure TForm1.bLastClick(Sender: TObject);
begin
  Table1.Last;
end;
```

Nothing could be more straightforward than these navigational functions. `First` takes you to the beginning of a dataset, `Last` takes you to the end, and the `Next` and `Prior` functions move you one record forward or backward.

`TDataSet.BOF` is a read-only Boolean property used to check whether you are at the beginning of a dataset. The BOF property returns true on three occasions:

- After you first open a file
- After you call `TDataSet.First`
- After a call to `Prior` fails

The first two items listed should be obvious to most readers. Specifically, when you open a dateset, Delphi places you on the first record, and when you call `First`, Delphi again moves you to the beginning of the dataset. The third item, however, requires a little more explanation: after you have called `Prior` enough times to get to the beginning of a file, and have then tried one more time and found that the call failed, `BOF` will return `True`.

The following code shows a very common method for using `Prior` to get to the beginning of a file:

```
while not Table.BOF do begin
  DoSomething;
  Table1.Prior;
end;
```

In the code shown here, the hypothetical function DoSomething is called on the current record and then on every other record between the current location and the beginning of the dataset. The loop continues until a call to Table1.Prior fails to move you back any further in the table. At that point, BOF returns True and the program breaks out of the loop.

To optimize the code shown above, set DataSource1.Enabled to False before beginning the loop, and then reset it to True after the loop is finished. These two lines of code allow you to iterate through the table without having to update the visual tools at the same time.

Everything said previously about BOF also applies to EOF. In other words, the code that follows provides a simple means of iterating over all the records in a dataset:

```
Table1.First;
while not Table1.EOF do begin
  DoSomething;
  Table1.Next;
end;
```

The classic error in cases like this is to enter into a while or repeat loop but to forget to call Table1.Next:

```
Table1.First;
repeat
  DoSomething;
until Table1.EOF;
```

If you accidentally wrote code like this, your machine would appear to lock up, and you could only break out of the loop by hitting Ctrl+Alt+Del and asking Windows to kill the current process. Also, this code could cause problems if you opened an empty table. Because the code uses a repeat loop, DoSomething would still be called once, even though there was nothing to process. As a result, it's better to use while loops rather than repeat loops in situations like this.

EOF returns True in the following three cases:

- If you open an empty dataset
- If you call Table1.Last
- If a call to Table1.Next fails

The last navigational routine that I want to cover is called MoveBy. MoveBy enables you to move *x* number of records forward or backward in a dataset. If you want to move two records forward, you would write

```
MoveBy(2);
```

and if you wanted to move two records backward, you would write

```
MoveBy(-2)
```

When using this function, you should always remember that when you are working on a network, datasets are fluid entities, and the record that was five records back a moment ago may now be back four records, or six records, or who knows how many records. In other words, when you are on a network, someone on another machine may delete or add records to your database at any time. If that happens, MoveBy might not work exactly as you expect. One solution to this "fluidity" problem is to use the Bookmark functions mentioned later in this chapter.

NOTE

Prior and Next are simple one-line functions that call MoveBy.

After reading this section, you should have a good feeling for how to move around in a dataset. The navigational commands you have been learning about are very easy to use, but it is essential that you understand them, because they are likely to be part of your day-to-day Delphi programming experience.

Fields

On most occasions when you want to programmatically access the individual fields of a record, you can use one of the following properties or methods, all of which belong to TDataSet:

```
property Fields[Index: Integer];
function FieldByName(const FieldName: string): TField;
property FieldCount;
```

The Fields object also has a number of useful descendant classes with names such as TStringField and TIntegerField. These child objects are discussed in Chapter 22.

The FieldCount property returns an integer that specifies the number of fields in the current record structure. If you wanted a programmatic way to read the names of these fields, you could use the Fields property:

```
var
  S: String;
begin
  S := Table1.Fields[0].FieldName;
end;
```

If you were working with a record with a first field called CustNo, the code shown would put the string "CustNo" in the variable S. If you wanted to access the name of the second field in the example, you could write

```
S := Table1.Fields[1].FieldName;
```

In short, the index passed to Fields is zero-based, and it specifies the number of the field you want to access, where the first field is number zero, the second is referenced by the number one, and so on.

If you want to find out the current contents of a particular field from a particular record, you can use the `Fields` or `FieldByName` property. To find the value of the first field of a record, index into the first element of the `Fields` array:

```
S := Table1.Fields[0].AsString;
```

Assuming that the first field in a record contains a customer number, the code shown would return a string such as `'1021'`, `'1031'`, or `'2058'`. If you wanted to access this variable as an integer value, you could use `AsInteger` in place of `AsString`. Similar properties of `Fields` include `AsBoolean`, `AsFloat`, and `AsDate`.

If you want, you can use the `FieldByName` function instead of the `Fields` property:

```
S := Table1.FieldByName('CustNo').AsString;
```

As used in the examples shown, both `FieldByName` and `Fields` return the same data. The two syntaxes are used solely to provide programmers with a flexible and convenient set of tools for programmatically accessing the contents of a dataset. When in doubt, use `FieldByName`, since it won't be affected if you change the order of the fields in your table.

The FIELDER program that ships with this book demonstrates some simple ways to use the `Fields` property of `TDataSet`. If you want to construct the program dynamically, place a `TTable`, two buttons, and two listboxes on a form, as shown in Figure 20.4. Hook up the `TTable` object to the CUSTOMER table that ships with Delphi.

FIGURE 20.4.

*The Fielder program shows
how to use the Fields
property.*

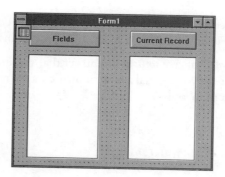

Double-click the Fields button and create a method that looks like this:

```
procedure TForm1.bFieldsClick(Sender: TObject);
var
  i: Integer;
begin
  ListBox1.Clear;
  for i := 0 to Table1.FieldCount - 1 do
    ListBox1.Items.Add(Table1.Fields[i].FieldName);
end;
```

This method starts by clearing the current contents of the first listbox, and then it iterates through each of the fields, adding their names one-by-one to the listbox. Notice that the `for` loop shown here counts from `0` to `FieldCount - 1`. If you don't remember to subtract one from `FieldCount`, you will get a "List Index Out of Bounds" error, because you will be attempting to read the name of a field that does not exist.

Assuming you enter the code shown previously correctly, you will fill the listbox with the names of all the fields in the current record structure. Delphi provides other means that enable you to get at the same information, but this is a simple, programmatic way for you to access these names at runtime.

In the FIELDER example, you can associate the following code with the second button you placed on the program's form:

```
procedure TForm1.bCurRecordClick(Sender: TObject);
var
  i: Integer;
begin
ListBox2.Clear
  for i := 0 to Table1.FieldCount - 1 do
    ListBox2.Items.Add(Table1.Fields[i].AsString);
end;
```

This code adds the contents of each of the fields to the second listbox. Notice that once again it is necessary to iterate from `0` to `FieldCount - 1`. The key point here is that the indices to `Fields` are zero-based.

> **NOTE**
>
> Much of the functionality of TField can be achieved with visual tools. In particular, you can manipulate fields with the Fields Editor, which you can access by clicking once with the right mouse button on the top of a TTable or TQuery object. This subject is explored in more depth in Chapter 22. However, good programmers know how to use both the methods of TDataSet and the Fields Editor. Furthermore, the Fields Editor can be best used to your advantage if you understand how to enhance its functionality with some of the code you are learning about in this chapter.

In this section you learned how to access the fields of a record. In the next section you will see how to use this knowledge when you want to `Append`, `Insert`, or `Edit` records in a dataset.

Changing Data

The following methods allow you to change the data associated with a table:

```
procedure Append;
procedure Insert;
procedure Cancel;
```

```
procedure Delete;
procedure Edit;
procedure Post;
```

All these routines are part of TDataSet, and they are inherited and used frequently by TTable and TQuery.

Whenever you want to change the data associated with a record, you must first put the dataset you are using into edit mode. As you will see, most of the visual controls do this automatically. However, if you want to change a table programmatically, you need to use the functions listed above.

Here is a typical sequence you might use to change a field of a given record:

```
Table1.Edit;
Table1.FieldByName('CustNo').AsString := '1234';
Table1.Post;
```

The first line shown places the database in edit mode. The next line assigns the string '1234' to the field labeled 'CustNo'. Finally, the data is written to disk when you call Post.

The very act of moving onto the next record automatically posts your data to disk. For instance, the following code has the same effect as the code shown previously, plus it moves you onto the next record:

```
Table1.Edit;
Table1.FieldByName('CustNo').AsInteger := '1234';
Table1.Next;
```

Calls to First, Next, Prior and Last all perform Posts, as long as you are in edit mode. If you are working with server data and transactions, the rules explained here do not apply. However, transactions are a separate matter with their own special rules, as explained in the next section.

Even if you are not working with transactions, you can still undo your work at any time, as long as you have not yet either directly or indirectly called Post. For instance, if you have put a table into edit mode and have changed the data in one or more fields, you can always change the record back to its original state by calling Cancel. For instance, you can edit every field of a record, and then call the following line to return to the state you were in before you began editing:

```
Table1.Cancel;
```

There are two methods, called Append and Insert, that you can use whenever you want to add another record to a dataset. It obviously makes more sense to use Append on datasets that are not indexed, but Delphi won't throw an exception if you use it on an indexed dataset. In fact, it is always safe to use either Append or Insert when you are working with a valid dataset.

On your disk you will find a simple program called INSERTS, which shows how to use the Insert and Delete commands. To create the program by hand, first use a TTable, TDataSource, and TdbGrid to open the COUNTRY table from the demos subdirectory. Then place two buttons on the program's form and call them Insert and Delete. When you are done, you should have a program like the one shown in Figure 20.5.

FIGURE 20.5.

The INSERTS program knows how to insert and delete a record from the COUNTRY table.

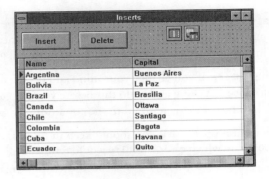

The next step is to associate code with the Insert button:

```
procedure TForm1.InsertClick(Sender: TObject);
begin
  Table1.Insert;
  Table1.FieldByName('Name').AsString := 'Erehwon';
  Table1.FieldByName('Capital').AsString := 'None';
  Table1.FieldByName('Continent').AsString := 'Imagination';
  Table1.FieldByName('Area').AsString := '0';
  Table1.FieldByName('Population').AsString := '1';
  Table1.Post;
end;
```

The procedure shown here first puts the table into insert mode, which means that a new record filled with blank fields is automatically inserted into the current position of the dataset.

After inserting the record, the next job is to assign strings to one or more of its fields. There are, of course, several ways to enter this data. Using the current program, you could simply type the information into the current record in the grid. Or, if you wanted, you could place standard edit controls on the form and then set each field equal to the value the user has typed in to the edit control:

```
Table1.FieldByName('Name').AsString := Edit1.Text;
```

If you place a table in edit mode, or if its TDataSource object has AutoEdit set to True, you can use data-aware controls to insert information directly into a record.

The intent of this chapter, however, is to show you how to enter data programmatically. Therefore, you are presented with an example where information is hardwired into the code segment of the program:

```
Table1.FieldByName('Name').AsString := 'Erehwon';
```

One of the interesting by-products of this technique is that pressing the Insert button twice in a row automatically triggers a `Key Violation` exception. To remedy this situation you must either delete the current record or manually change the Name and Capital fields of the newly created record.

Looking at the code shown previously, you will see that the mere act of inserting a record, and of filling out its fields, is not enough to change the physical data that resides on disk. If you want the information to be written to disk, you must call `Post`.

After calling `Insert`, if you change your mind and decide to abandon the current record, you should call `Cancel`. As long as you do this before you call `Post`, everything you have entered is discarded and the dataset is restored to the condition it was in before you called `Insert`.

One last related property that you should keep in mind is called `CanModify`. A table might be set to `ReadOnly`, in which case `CanModify` would return `False`. Otherwise `CanModify` returns `True` and you can enter `Edit` or `Insert` mode at will. `CanModify` is itself a read-only property. If you want to set a dataset to read-only, you should use the `ReadOnly` property, not `CanModify`.

In this section you learned how to use the `Insert`, `Delete`, `Edit`, `Post`, `Cancel` and `Append` commands. Most of the actions associated with these commands are fairly intuitive, though it can take a little thought to see how they interact with the `Fields` property.

Using *SetKey* to Search Through a File

When you want to search for a value in a dataset, you can call on three procedures, called `SetKey`, `GotoNearest`, and `GotoKey`. These procedures assume that the field you are searching on is indexed. This book ships with a demonstration program called SEARCH that shows how to use these calls.

To create the SEARCH program, place TTable, TDataSource, TdbGrid, TButton, TLabel, and TEdit controls on a form, and arrange them so the result looks like the image shown in Figure 20.6. Be sure to name the button Search, and to then wire the database controls so you can view the Customer table in the grid control.

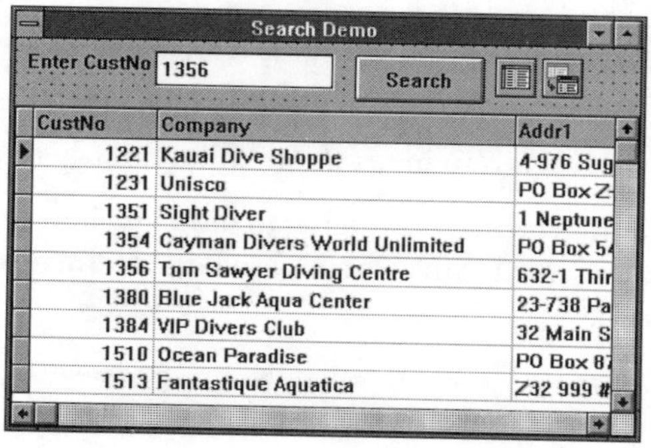

FIGURE 20.6.

The SEARCH program enables you to enter a customer number and then search for it by pressing a button.

The functionality for the SEARCH program is encapsulated in a single method that is attached to the Search button. This function retrieves the string entered in the edit control, searches the CustNo column until it finds the value, and finally switches the focus to the record it found. In its simplest form, here's how the code attached to the Search button looks:

```
procedure TSearchDemo.SearchClick(Sender: TObject);
begin
  Table1.SetKey;
  Table1.Fields[0].AsString := Edit1.Text;
  Table1.GotoKey;
end;
```

The first call in this procedure sets `Table1` into search mode. Delphi needs to be told to switch into search mode simply because you use the `Fields` property in a special way when Delphi is in search mode. Specifically, you can index into the `Fields` property, and assign it to the value you want to find.

In the example shown, the CustNo field is the first column in the database, so you set the `Fields` index to zero. To actually carry out the search, simply call `Table1.GotoKey`. If you are not sure of the value you are looking for, call `Table1.GotoNearest`. `GotoNearest` will take you to the numerical or string value closest to the one you specify.

If you are not searching on the primary index of a file, you must use a secondary index and specify the name of the index you are using in the `IndexName` property for the current table. For instance, the `Customer` table has a secondary index called `ByCompany` on the field labeled `Company`. You would have to set the `IndexName` property to the name of that index if you wanted to search on that field. You could then use the following code when you searched on the `Company` field:

```
Table1.IndexName := 'ByCompany';
Table1.Active := True;
Table1.SetKey;
Table1.FieldByName('Company').AsString := Edit1.Text;
Table1.GotoKey;
```

In this case you set the `Fields` index to 3, since `City` is the fourth field in the Customer database. Remember: This search will fail unless you first assign the correct value to the `IndexName` property. Furthermore, you should note that `IndexName` is a property of TTable, and would therefore not automatically be included in any direct descendant of TDataSet or TdbDataSet that you might create yourself.

When you are searching for a value in a database, there is always a strong possibility that the search might fail. You can raise an exception in such a case and handle the error by writing the code like this. Delphi automatically throws an exception in such a case, but if you want to handle the error yourself, you might write code that looks like this:

```
procedure TSearchDemo.SearchClick(Sender: TObject);
begin
  Table1.SetKey;
  try
```

```
     Table1.Fields[0].AsString := Edit1.Text; If not Table.GoToKey then raise
        DatabaseError.create(');
     Table1.GotoKey;
  except
    on EDataBaseError do
      MessageDlg('Value not found', mtError, [mbOk], 0);
  end;
end;
```

In the code shown, either an illegal assignment to the fields property or a failure to find the value on which you are searching, would automatically force the code to pop up an error message stating "Value not found." For more information on exceptions, see Chapter 34, "Exceptions."

Filtering the Records in a *DataSet*

The ApplyRange procedure lets you set a filter that limits the range of the records you view. For instance, in the Customers database, the CustNo field ranges from just over 1,000 to a little under 10,000. If you wanted to see only those records that had a customer number between 2,000 and 3,000, you would use the ApplyRange procedure and two related routines. When using this procedure, you must work with a field that is indexed. (As explained in the next chapter, you can perform this same type of operation on a non-indexed field by using a TQuery object rather than TTable object.)

Here are the three procedures that make up the suite of routines you will use when setting up filters:

```
procedure ApplyRange;
procedure SetRangeEnd;
procedure SetRangeStart;
```

To use these procedures

1. Call SetRangeStart and then use the Fields property to designate the start of the range.

2. Call SetRangeEnd and use the Fields property a second time to designate the end of the range you are specifying.

3. The first two actions prepare the filter; now all you need do is call ApplyRange, and the new filter you have specified will take effect.

The RANGER program, which is located on disk, shows you explicitly how to use these procedures. To create the program, drop a TTable, TDataSource, and TdbGrid onto a form. Wire them up so that you can view the CUSTOMERS table from the demos subdirectory. You need to set Ttable.Active to True. Next drop two labels on the form and set their captions to Start Range and End Range. Place two edit controls next to the labels. Finally, add a single button with the caption ApplyRange. When you are done, you should have a form like the one shown in Figure 20.7.

FIGURE 20.7.

The RANGER program shows how to limit the number of records from a table that are visible at any one time.

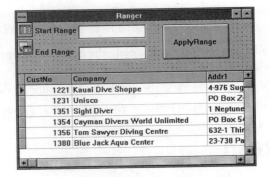

The `SetRangeStart` and `SetRangeEnd` procedures enable you to declare the first and last members in the range of records you want to see. To get started using the procedures, double-click on the button labeled ApplyRange and then create a procedure that looks like this:

```
procedure TForm1.bApplyRangeClick(Sender: TObject);
begin
  Table1.SetRangeStart;
  Table1.Fields[0].AsString := Edit1.Text;
  Table1.SetRangeEnd;
  Table1.Fields[0].AsString := Edit2.Text;
  Table1.ApplyRange;
end;
```

The `BApplyRangeClick` procedure first calls `SetRangeStart`, which puts the table into range mode and blanks out the records seen in the `dbGrid` control. Once in range mode, the program expects you to specify the beginning range, which in this case you grab from out of the first edit control. Setting the end range for the program involves following a very similar pattern. First you call `SetRangeEnd`, and then you snag an appropriate value from the second `Edit` control.

Note that you can use the `Fields` property to specify the actual range you want to use:

```
Table1.Fields[0].AsString := Edit2.Text;
```

This use of the `Fields` property is obviously a special case, since the syntax shown here is usually used to set the value of a field, not to define a range. This special case comes into effect only after you have put `Table1` into range mode by calling `SetRangeStart`.

The final step in the procedure shown above is the call to `ApplyRange`. This is the routine that actually puts your request into effect. When the call to `ApplyRange` ends, the table is no longer in range mode and the `Fields` property returns to its normal functionality.

A typical run of the program might involve the user typing in the number 4000 in the first edit control and the number 5000 in the next edit control. After entering the data, a click on the ApplyRange button would then put the request into effect.

In this section you learned how to filter the functions from a table or dataset so that you view only a particular range of records. The steps involved are three fold:

1. Call SetRangeStart and specify the beginning value in the range of records you want to see.

2. Call SetRangeEnd and specify the ending value in the range of records you want to see.

3. Call ApplyRange in order to view the results of your request.

Refresh

As you already know, any table that you open is always subject to change. In short, you should regard a table as a fluid, rather than as a static, entity. Even if you are the only person using a particular table, and even if you are not working in a networked environment, there is always the possibility that the program you are running may have two different ways of changing a piece of data. As a result, you should always be aware of the need to update, or Refresh, your current view of a table.

The Refresh function is related to the Open function, in that it retrieves the data or some portion of the data associated with a given table. For instance, when you open a table, Delphi retrieves data directly from a database file. Similarly, when you refresh a table, Delphi goes out and retrieves data directly from a table. You can therefore use this function to update a table if you think it might have changed. It is faster, and much more efficient, to call Refresh than to call Close and then Open.

CAUTION

In a networked environment, refreshing a table can sometimes lead to unexpected results. For instance, if a user is viewing a record that has been deleted, it will seem to disappear out from under the user the moment the program calls Refresh. Similarly, if another user has edited data, a call to Refresh can result in data dynamically changing while a user is viewing it. Of course it is unlikely that one user will change or delete a record while another is viewing it, but it is possible. As a result, you should use calls to Refresh with caution.

Bookmarks

It is often useful to mark a particular location in a table so that you can quickly return to it when desired. Delphi provides this functionality through three methods that use the metaphor of a bookmark. When you use these functions, it is as if you have left a bookmark in the dataset, and you can therefore turn back to it quickly whenever you want:

```
procedure FreeBookmark(Bookmark: TBookmark);
function GetBookmark: TBookmark;
procedure GotoBookmark(Bookmark: TBookmark);
```

As you can see, the GetBookmark call returns a variable of type TBookmark. A TBookmark contains enough information to enable Delphi to find the location to which it refers. Therefore, you can simply pass this bookmark to the GotoBookmark function, and you will immediately be returned to the location with which the bookmark is associated.

It's important to note that a call to GetBookmark allocates memory for the bookmark, and so you must remember to call FreeBookmark before you exit your program, and before every attempt to reuse a bookmark. For instance, here is a typical set of calls for freeing, setting, and moving to a bookmark:

```
procedure TForm1.MarkClick(Sender: TObject);
begin
if Bookmark = nil then
  BookMark := Table1.GetBookmark;
end;

procedure TForm1.Button2Click(Sender: TObject);
begin
if Bookmark <> nil then begin
  Table1.GotoBookmark (Bookmark);
  Table1.FreeBookmark(Bookmark);
Bokkmark := nil; end;
end;
```

The code shown here is excerpted from a program called BOOKMARK.DPR, which comes with this book. In the declaration for TForm1, a variable called BookMark is declared in the private section. Every time the MarkClick procedure is called, the first step is to be sure the BookMark is freed. It is never a mistake to call FreeBookmark, because the procedure checks to make sure BookMark is not set to nil. After deallocating any existing copies of the Bookmark, a new one is allocated. You can then call GotoBookmark and repeat the cycle.

Bookmarks are powerful features that can be of great benefit under certain circumstances. The developers of Delphi, for instance, used bookmarks frequently in order to develop the database components. They often have several different bookmarks open at the same time.

NOTE

Most of the features surfaced in TDataSet are built into the BDE. For instance, filters, searching for keys, and bookmarks are easily available to anyone who uses the BDE. What the developers of Delphi have done is surface these features so that they can be easily accessed using object-oriented programming techniques.

TTable

TTable adds several frequently used properties to TDataSet:

```
property DetailFields
property Exclusive
property MasterFields
property MasterSource
property ReadOnly
property TableName
```

Of the properties shown here, the most common ones are probably `TableName` and `ReadOnly`. You can use the `TableName` property to specify the table you want to open, and you can set the `ReadOnly` property to `True` or `False` depending on whether you want to allow the user to change the data in a dataset. Neither of these properties can be used when a table is active.

The `Exclusive` property lets you open a table in a mode that guarantees that no other user will be able to access it at the same time. You will not be able to set `Exclusive` to `True` if another user is currently accessing the table.

The `MasterSource` property is used to specify a TDataSource from which the current table needs to obtain information. For instance, if you linked two tables in a master/detail relationship, the detail table can track the events occurring in the first table by specifying the first table's datasource in this property. This technique is demonstrated in the following section on linked cursors.

Creating Linked Cursors

Linked cursors enable programmers to easily define a one-to-many relationship. For instance, it is sometimes useful to link the CUSTOMER and ORDERS tables so that each time the user views a particular customer's name he or she can also see a list of the orders related to that customer. In short, the user can view one customer's record, and then see only the orders related to that customer.

To understand linked cursors, you first need to see that the CUSTOMER table and the ORDERS table are related to one another through the `CustNo` field. This relationship exists specifically because there needs to be a way to find out which orders are associated with which customer.

The LINKS program on disk demonstrates how to create a program that uses linked cursors. To create the program on your own, place two tables, two datasources, and two grids on a form. Wire the first set of controls to the CUSTOMER table, and second set to the ORDERS table. If you run the program at this stage, you should be able to scroll through all the records in either table, as shown in Figure 20.8.

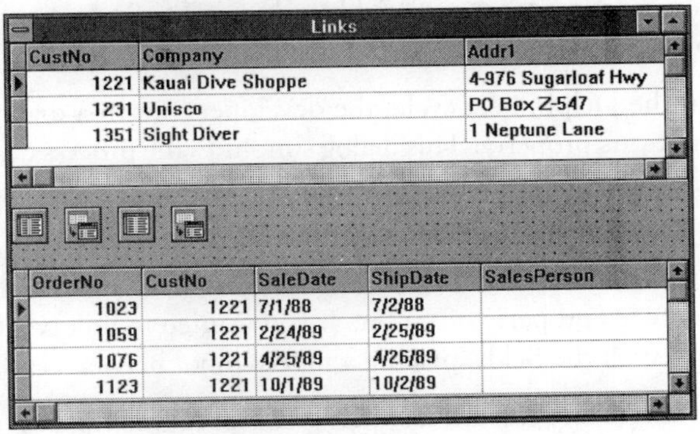

FIGURE 20.8.

The LINKS program shows how to define a relationship between two tables.

The next step is to link the ORDERS table to the CUSTOMER table so that you view only those orders associated with the current customer record. To do this, you must take three steps, each of which requires some explanation:

1. Set the `MasterSource` property of `Table2` to `DataSource1`.
2. Set the `MasterField` property in `Table2` to `CustNo`
3. Set the `IndexName` property of `Table2` to the `ByCustNo`.

If you now run the program, you will see that both tables are linked together, and that every time you move to a new record in the CUSTOMER table, you can see only those records in the ORDERS table that belong to that particular customer.

The `MasterSource` property in `Table2` specifies the `DataSource` from which `Table2` can draw information. Specifically, it allows the ORDERS table to know which record currently has the focus in the CUSTOMERS table.

The question then becomes this: What other information does `Table2` need in order to properly filter the contents of the ORDERS table? The answer to this question is two-fold:

1. It needs the name of the field that links the two tables.
2. It needs the index of the field in the ORDERS table that is going to be linked to the CUSTOMER table.

In order to correctly supply the information described here, you must first ensure that both the CUSTOMER table and the ORDERS table have the correct indices. Specifically, you must ensure that there are indices on both the `CustNo` field and the `CustNo` field in the ORDERS table. If the index in question is a primary index, there is no need to specifically name that index, and therefore you can leave the `IndexName` field blank in both tables. However, if either of the tables is linked to the other through a secondary index, you must explicitly designate that index in the `IndexName` field of the table that has a secondary index.

In the example shown here, the CUSTOMER table has a primary index on the `CustNo` field, so there is no need to specify the index name. However, the ORDERS table does not have a primary index on the CustNo field, and so you must explicitly declare it in the IndexName property by typing in or selecting the word CustNo.

Late in the Delphi beta cycle, the developers put in a dialog that appears when you click the MasterFields property. This dialog simplifies the process described here and helps to automate the task of setting up a link between two tables.

Some indices can contain multiple fields, so you must explicitly state the name of the field you want to use to link the two tables. In this case, you should enter the name CustNo in the MasterFields property of Table2. If you wanted to link two tables on more than one field, you should list all the fields, placing a pipe symbol between each one:

```
Table1.MasterFields := 'CustNo ¦ SaleData ¦ ShipDate';
```

In this particular case, however, the statement shown here makes no sense, since the SaleData and ShipDate fields are neither indexed, nor duplicated in the CUSTOMER table. Therefore, you should only enter the field called CustNo in the MasterFields property. You can specify this syntax directly in a property editor, or write code that performs the same chore.

It's important to note that this section covered only one of several ways you can create linked cursors using Delphi. Chapter 21, "SQL and the TQuery Object," describes a second method that will appeal to people who are familiar with SQL. The Database Expert provides a third means of achieving this end. As you have seen, the Database Expert is an easy-to-use visual tool. The Query Builder is yet a fourth way of creating a one-to-many relationship between two tables. Like the Database Expert, the Query Builder is a visual tool that can save you much time. However, it's best not to rely entirely on the visual tools, since there are times when you might feel limited by their functionality.

TDataSource Basics

Class TDataSource is used as a conduit between TTable or TQuery and the data-aware controls such as TdbGrid, TdbEdit, and TdbComboBox. Under most circumstances, the only thing you will do with a TDataSource object is to set its DataSet property to an appropriate TTable or TQuery object. Then, on the other end, you will also want to set a data-aware control's DataSource property to the TDataSource object you are currently using.

> **NOTE**
>
> Visual tools such as TdbEdit or TdbGrid all have a DataSource property that connects to a TDataSource object. When reading this chapter, you need to distinguish between a visual control's DataSource property and the TDataSource object to which it is attached. In other words, the word DataSource can refer to either a property or a class, depending on the context. I will tend to refer to the class as a TDataSource and the property as a DataSource; but you should watch the context in which these words are used.

A TDataSource can also have an `Enabled` property, which can be useful whenever you want to temporarily disconnect a table or query from its visual controls. This functionality might be desirable if you need to programmatically iterate through all the records in a table. For instance, if a TTable is connected to a data-aware control, each time you call `TTable.Next`, the visual control needs to be updated. If you are quickly going through two or three thousand records, it can take a considerable amount of time to perform the updates to the visual controls. In cases like this, the best thing to do is set the TDataSource object's `Enabled` field to `False`, which will allow you to iterate through the records without having to worry about screen updates. This single change can improve the speed of some routines by several thousand percent.

The `AutoEdit` property of TDataSource enables you to decide whether or not the data-aware controls attached to it will automatically enter edit mode when you start typing inside them. Many users prefer to keep `AutoEdit` set to `True`, but if you want to give a user more precise control over when the database can be edited, this is the property you need. In short, if you set `AutoEdit` to `False`, you have essentially made the table read-only.

Using TDataSource to Check the State of a Database

TDataSource has three key events associated with it:

```
OnDataChange
OnStateChange
OnUpdateData
```

`OnDataChange` occurs whenever you move onto a new record. In other words, if you call `Next`, `Previous`, `Insert`, or any other call that is likely to lead to a change in the data associated with the current record, an `OnDataChange` event will get fired. If someone begins editing the data in a data-aware control, an `OnResync` event occurs.

A TDataSource `OnStateChange` event occurs whenever the current state of the dataset changes. A dataset always knows what state it's in. If you call `Edit`, `Append`, or `Insert`, the table knows that it is now in edit mode. Similarly, after you post a record, the database knows that it is no longer editing data, and it switches back into browse mode. If you want more control, the next section in this chapter explains that a dataset also sends out messages just before and just after you change states.

The dataset has five different possible states, each of which are captured in the following enumerated type:

```
TDataSetState = (dsInactive, dsBrowse, dsEdit,
                 dsInsert,  dsSetKey, dsCalcFields);
```

During the course of a normal session, the database will frequently move back and forth between `Browse`, `Edit`, `Insert`, or the other modes. If you want to track these changes, you can respond to them by writing code that looks like this:

```
procedure TForm1.DataSource1StateChange(Sender: TObject);
var
  S: String;
begin
  case Table1.State of
    dsInactive: S := 'Inactive';
    dsBrowse: S := 'Browse';
    dsEdit: S := 'Edit';
    dsInsert: S := 'Insert';
    dsSetKey: S := 'SetKey';
    dsCalcFields: S := 'CalcFields';
  end;
  Label1.Caption := S;
end;
```

An `OnUpdateData` event occurs whenever the data in the current record is about to be updated. For instance, an `OnUpdateEvent` will occur between the time `Post` is called and the time information is actually posted.

The events belonging to `TDataSource` can be extremely useful. To help illustrate them, you will find a program on your disk called DSEVENTS that responds to all three `TDataSource` events. This program shows an easy way to set up a "poor man's" data-aware edit control that automatically shows and posts data to and from a database at the appropriate time.

This example works with the COUNTRY database and has a TTable, TDataSource, five edits, six labels, eight buttons, and a panel on it. The actual layout for the program is shown in Figure 20.9. Note that the sixth label appears on the panel located at the bottom of the main form.

FIGURE 20.9.

The DSEVENTS program shows how to track the current state of a table.

DSEVENTS has one small conceit that you need to understand if you want to learn how the program works. Because there are five separate edit controls on the main form, you need to have some way to refer to them quickly and easily. One simple method is to declare an array of edit controls:

```
Edits: array[1..5] of TEdit;
```

To fill out the array you can respond to the forms OnCreate event:

```
procedure TForm1.FormCreate(Sender: TObject);
var
  i: Integer;
begin
  for i := 1 to 5 do
    Edits[i] := TEdit(FindComponent('Edit' + IntToStr(i)));
end;
```

The code shown here assumes that the first edit control you want to use is called Edit1, the second is called Edit2, and so on.

Given the existence of this array of controls, it is very simple to use the OnDataChange event to keep them in sync with the contents of the current record in a dataset:

```
procedure TForm1.DataSource1DataChange(Sender: TObject;
                                       Field: TField);
var
  i: Integer;
begin
  for i := 1 to 5 do
    Edits[i].Text := Table1.Fields[i - 1].AsString;
end;
```

This code iterates through each of the fields of the current record and puts its contents in the appropriate edit control. Whenever Table1.Next is called or whenever any of the other navigational methods are called, the procedure shown previously is called. This assures that the edit controls always contain the data from the current record.

Whenever Post gets called, you will want to perform the opposite action. That is, you will want to get the information from the edit controls and place it inside the current record. To perform that action, simply respond to TDataSource.OnUpdateData events, which are generated automatically whenever Post is called:

```
procedure TForm1.DataSource1UpdateData(Sender: TObject);
var
  i: Integer;
begin
  for i := 1 to 5 do
    Table1.Fields[i - 1].AsString := Edits[i].Text;
end;
```

The DSEVENTS program automatically switches into edit mode whenever you type anything in one of the edit controls. It does this by responding to OnKeyDown events:

```
procedure TForm1.Edit1KeyDown(Sender: TObject;
                              var Key: Word;
                              Shift: TShiftState);
begin
  if DataSource1.State <> dsEdit then
    Table1.Edit;
end;
```

This code shows how you can use the State variable of a TDataSource object to find out the current mode of the dataset.

Tracking the State of a Dataset

In the last section, you learned how to use TDataSource to keep tabs on the current state of a TDataSet, and also to respond just before certain events are about to take place.

Using a TDataSource object is the simplest way to perform all these functions. However, if you would like to track these events without using TDataSource, you can respond to the following events from TDataSet, all which are naturally inherited by TTable or TQuery:

```
property OnOpen
property OnClose
property BeforeInsert
property AfterInsert
property BeforeEdit
property AfterEdit
property BeforePost
property AfterPost
property OnCancel
property OnDelete
property OnNewRecord
```

Most of these properties are self-explanatory. The `BeforePost` event, for instance, is functionally similar to the `TDataSource.OnUpdateData` event that is explained and demonstrated previously. In other words, the DSEVENTS program would work the same if you responded to `DataSource1.OnUpdateData` or to `Table1.BeforePost`. Of course in one case you would not need to have a TDataSource on the form, while the other requires it.

Summary

In this chapter you learned how to use the TDataSet, TField, TdbDataSet, TTable, and TDataSource classes. Through the simple techniques of exposition, example, and repetition, all the major ideas associated with objects of these types should now be clear to you.

The key points to remember are as follows:

■ TDataSet encapsulates the basic functions you will perform on a table.

■ TField is a property of TDataSet that allows you to access the contents or name of each field in a record.

■ TdbDataSet gives you the ability to associate a dataset with a given table.

■ TTable encapsulates all the functionality of a dataset, but it also gives you access to table-specific chores such as setting indices or creating linked cursors.

■ TDataSource forms a link between TTable or TQuery and any of the data-aware components such as TdbEdit or TdbGrid. TDataSource also contains three useful events that keep you informed about the current state of the database.

In the next chapter, you will learn about the TQuery object and SQL. SQL is especially useful when you want to access the advanced cababilities associated with servers and server data.

SQL and the
TQuery Object

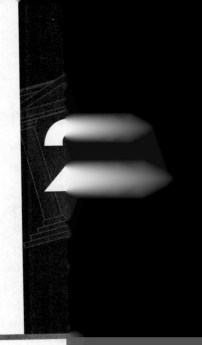

Overview

This chapter is about queries. It's a subject that lies at the heart of client/server programming, so this is one of the most important chapters in the book.

The material is broken down into the following main sections:

- The TQuery object
- Using SQL with local and remote servers to select, update, delete, and insert records
- Using SQL statements to create joins, linked cursors, and programs that search for individual records

SQL stands for Structured Query Language and is usually pronounced "Sequel," or by saying each letter ("Ess Que El"). However you choose to pronounce it, SQL is a powerful database language that is easily accessible from inside any copy of Delphi, but is distinct from Delphi's native language. Delphi can use SQL statements to view tables, perform joins between tables, create one to many relationships, or perform almost any action that your underlying database tools can perform.

Delphi ships with two local SQL engines: one built into the BDE and the other built into Interbase. As a result, you can perform SQL queries even if you're working on a stand-alone machine and don't have access to a server.

Delphi provides support for passthrough SQL, which means that you can compose SQL statements and then have them sent directly to an Oracle, Sybase, Interbase, or another server. Passthrough SQL is a powerful feature for two reasons:

- Most servers can process SQL statements very quickly, which means that you can use SQL on remote data to get extremely fast response to your requests.
- You can compose SQL statements that ask a server to perform specialized tasks unavailable through Delphi's native language.

In the last chapter, you learned a lot about how Delphi works internally, and about how to utilize its native capabilities. Now it's time to see how Delphi interacts with the database tools that exist either on your current machine or on a network.

TQuery Basics

You can create a Delphi SQL statement by using a TQuery component in the following manner:

1. Assign an alias to the `DatabaseName` property.
2. Use the `SQL` property to enter a SQL statement such as `Select * from Country`.
3. Set the `Active` property to `True`.

If you're working with local data, you can substitute a fully qualified subdirectory path for an alias. When using the latter method, it's best if you don't include the actual name of a table, but only the subdirectory in which one or more tables exist.

There are two general points that you need to understand before you proceed further:

- This chapter isn't intended to be a SQL primer, but rather a description of the TQuery object and the basic tasks you can perform with it. Even if you don't know anything about SQL, this chapter will still be helpful to you and you'll end up learning a number of basic facts about how to compose a SQL statement. However, for a detailed analysis of the language, you should turn to one of the many books and public documents available on this subject. You also can refer to the handy online reference in the help for the WISQL utility. Additional information is available in the form of a LOCALSQL.HLP file that ships with Delphi. (Open help, press ALT+F+O, and then choose LOCALSQL.HLP.)

- Because Delphi uses passthrough SQL, you'll find that you can access the unique features of the servers to which you connect. For instance, the Borland Database Engine, which ships with Delphi, provides a special, if somewhat limited, local SQL engine. To learn about the specific capabilities of that engine, you should read not only this chapter, but also the LOCALSQL.HLT file that is included with Delphi.

Overall, you'll find that the TQuery object is one of the most useful and flexible features available inside the Delphi environment. With it, you can tap into the power inherent in some of today's premier servers such as Interbase, Oracle, and Sybase.

The *SQL* Property

The SQL property is probably the single most important part of TQuery. You can access this property from the Object Inspector during design time, or programmatically at runtime. You've already seen how to access the SQL property at design time, so the next few sections concentrate on ways to manipulate it programmatically.

Most people want to access the SQL property at runtime in order to dynamically change the statement associated with a query. For instance, if you want to issue three SQL statements while your program is running, there's no need for you to place three TQuery components on your form. Instead, you can just place one on the form, and simply change its SQL property three times. The most efficient, most powerful, and simplest means of doing this is through parameterized queries, which are explained in the next section. However, this chapter first examines the basic features of the SQL property, and then covers more advanced topics such as parameterized queries.

The SQL property is of type TStrings, which means that it is a series of strings kept in a list. The list acts very much as if it were an array, but it's actually a special class with its own unique capabilities. If you want to find out everything you can about the SQL property, you should study the class TStrings or TStringList. However, the next few paragraphs review its most commonly used features.

When using TQuery programmatically, you should first close the current query and clear out any strings that might already be residing in the SQL property:

```
Query1.Close;
Query1.SQL.Clear;
```

It's always safe to call Close. If the query is already closed, the call will not cause an error.

The next step is to add the new strings that you want to execute:

```
Query1.SQL.Add('Select * form Country');
Query1.SQL.Add('where Name = ''Argentina''');
```

You can use the Add property to append from one to *X* number of strings to a SQL query, where *X* is limited only by the amount of memory on your machine.

To ask Delphi to process the statement and return a cursor containing the results of your query, you can issue the following statement:

```
Query1.Open;
```

Whenever you want to change the SQL statement, you can simple alter the strings you pass to the Add property:

```
Query1.Close;
Query1.SQL.Clear;
Query1.SQL.Add('Select * form Country');
Query1.Open;
```

The sample program called EASYSQL demonstrates this process. EASYSQL is shown in Figure 21.1.

FIGURE 21.1.

The EASYSQL program shows how to issue multiple queries from a single TQuery object.

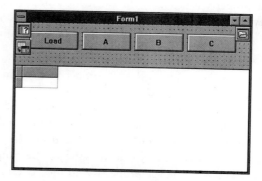

The EASYSQL program uses a feature of local SQL that lets you use case-insensitive wild cards. For instance, the SQL statement:

```
Select * form Country where Name like 'C%'
```

returns a dataset containing all the records in which the Name field begins with the letter C. The following syntax enables you to see all the countries that have the letter C embedded somewhere in their name:

```
Select * from Country where Name like '%C%';
```

Here's a statement that finds all the countries whose name ends in the letters ia:

```
Select * from Country where Name like '%ia';
```

If you want to compose a series of statements like the preceding one, you can expedite matters by using either parameterized queries or the Format function. Both of these techniques are explained in this chapter.

One of the most powerful features of the SQL property is its capability to read files directly from disk. This feature is also demonstrated in the EASYSQL program.

Here's how it works. In the EASYSQL subdirectory, there are several files with the extension SQL. These files contain SQL statements such as the ones shown previously. The EASYSQL program has a Load button that lets you select one of these text files, and then run the SQL statement stored in that file.

The Load button has the following response method for its OnClick event:

```
procedure Form1.LoadClick(Sender: TObject);
begin
  if OpenDialog1.Execute then begin
    Query1.Close;
    Query1.SQL.LoadFromFile(OpenDialog1.FileName);
    Query1.Open;
  end;
end;
```

The LoadClick method loads the OpenDialog component and enables the user to select a file with an SQL extension. The code checks to see whether the user has selected a file. If a file has been selected, the current query is closed, and the selected file is loaded from disk and displayed to the user.

OpenDialog1 has its Filter property set to the following value:

```
OpenDialog1.Filter := 'SQL(*.SQL)|*.SQL'
```

As a result, it lists only files that have an SQL extension, as shown in Figure 21.2.

FIGURE 21.2.

The Open dialog from the EASYSQL program enables you to select a prepared SQL statement from an ASCII file stored on disk.

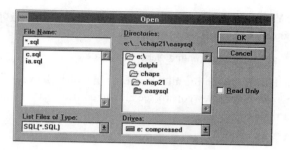

The `LoadFromFile` procedure enables you to load an entire text file at runtime by issuing a single command. The trick, then, is to store SQL statements in text files, and to load them at runtime. Because the `SQL` property can contain an essentially unlimited number of strings, there is no practical limit to the size of the SQL statement that you could load in this fashion. You can use this technique to quickly execute a series of very complex SQL statements.

In this section, you saw two methods of changing the `SQL` property at runtime. The first technique lets you add strings to the `SQL` property, run a query, change the strings, and run the query again. The second technique enables you to load one or more statements from a file. The `LoadFromFile` technique is obviously quite elegant. The first technique can be very powerful at times, but it can be a bit awkward if all you want to do is change one word in a SQL statement. In the next section, you'll learn about how you can eliminate this awkwardness by using parameterized queries.

TQuery and Parameters

Delphi enables you to compose a flexible form of query statement called a parameterized query. A parameterized query enables you to substitute variables for single words in the `where` or `insert` clause of a SQL statement. These variables can then be changed at any time throughout the life of the query. (If you're using local SQL, you'll be able to make substitutions on almost any word in a SQL statement, but this same capability is not included on most servers.)

To get started using parameterized queries, consider again one of the simple SQL statements listed earlier:

```
Select * form Country where Name like 'C%'
```

To turn this statement into a parameterized query, just replace the right side of the `like` clause with a variable called `NameStr`:

```
select * from County where Name like :NameStr
```

In this SQL statement, `NameStr` is no longer a predefined constant, but instead can change at either design time or runtime. The SQL parser knows that it is dealing with a parameter instead of a constant because a colon is prepended to the word `NameStr`. That colon tells Delphi that it should substitute the `NameStr` variable with a value that will be supplied at some future point.

It's important to note that the word `NameStr` was chosen entirely at random. You can use any valid variable name in this case, just as you can choose a wide range of identifiers when you declare a string variable in one of your programs.

There are two ways to supply variables to a parameterized SQL statement. One method is to use the `Params` property to supply the value at runtime. The second is to use the `DataSource` property to supply information from another dataset at either runtime or design time. Here are the key properties used to accomplish these goals:

```
property Params[Index: Word];
function ParamByName(const Value: string);

procedure Prepare
```

When you substitute bind variables in a parameterized query via the `Params` property, you usually take four steps:

1. Make sure the table is closed.
2. Ready the `Query` object by issuing the `Prepare` command (optional, but highly recommended).
3. Assign the correct values to the `Params` property.
4. Open the table.

Here's a sample code fragment showing how this might be done in practice:

```
Query1.Close;
Query1.Prepare;
Query1.Params[0].AsString := 'Argentina';
Query1.Open;
```

If you're not familiar with parameterized queries, the preceding code might appear a bit mysterious. To understand it thoroughly, you'll need to do a careful, line-by-line analysis. The simplest way to begin is with the third line, because it is the `Params` property that lies at the heart of this process.

`Params` is an indexed property that uses a syntax similar to the `Fields` property from `TDataSet`. For instance, you can access the first bind variable in a SQL statement by referring to element `0` in the `Params` array:

```
Params[0].AsString := 'Argentina';
```

If you combine a simple parameterized SQL statement such as

```
select * from Country where Name like :NameStr
```

with the `Params` statements shown previously, the end result is the following SQL statement:

```
select * from Country where Name like Argentina
```

What's happened here is that the variable :FileName has been assigned the value Argentina via the Params property, thereby enabling you to complete a simple SQL statement.

If you have more than one variable in a statement, you can access these other variables by changing the index of the Params property:

```
Params[1].AsString :=  'SomeValue';
```

So far, you've seen that a parameterized query uses bind variables, which always begin with a colon, to designate the places where parameters will be passed. With this concept in mind, you can move on to the other lines in the previous code fragment.

Before you use the Params variable, you must first call Prepare. A call to Prepare causes Delphi to parse your SQL statement and ready the Params property so that it's prepared to accept the appropriate number of variables. If you try to assign a value to the Params variable without first calling Prepare, Delphi raises an exception.

After you've called Prepare and assigned the correct values to the Params variable, you should call Open to complete the binding of the variables and produce the dataset that you hope to find. In this particular case, given the input shown previously, the dataset includes the contents of the record where the name field is set to Argentina.

In the EXAMPLES subdirectory, you'll find a program called EASYSQL2 that demonstrates how to use parameterized queries. The EASYSQL2 program performs a function very similar to the one shown earlier in the first EASYSQL program. However, this new version shows how parameterized queries can be used to increase the flexibility of a SQL statement.

To create the program, place TQuery, TDataSource, TdbGrid, and TTabSet components on a form. Hook up the data controls and set the query's DatabaseName property to the DEMOS subdirectory in which the COUNTRY table is found. Fill in the tabset so that it lists the alphabet from *A* to *Z*, as shown in Figure 21.3.

FIGURE 21.3.

The EASYSQL2 program shows how to use parameterized queries.

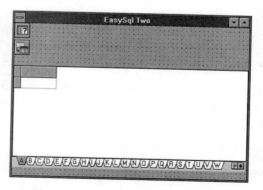

Enter the following string in the SQL property for the query component:

```
select * from Country where Name like :NameStr
```

Now all that's left to create is a response method for the OnChange property of the tabset:

```
procedure TForm1.TabSet1Change(Sender: TObject;
                               NewTab: Integer;
                               var AllowChange: Boolean);
var
  S: String;
begin
  S := TabSet1.Tabs.Strings[NewTab] + '%';
  Query1.Close;
  Query1.Prepare;
  Query1.Params[0].AsString := S;
  Query1.Open;
end;
```

The code shown here follows the four simple steps outlined previously. This is what the code does:

1. Closes the query.
2. Prepares the Params property.
3. Assigns a string to the Params property.
4. Executes the resultant SQL statement by calling Query1.Open.

The actual string assigned to the Params property consists of one of the letters of the alphabet plus the % symbol. A typical query produced by this method might look like this:

```
Select * form Country where Name like 'C%'
```

The end result, then, is that the EASYSQL2 program lets you view the contents of the table in alphabetical sequence. Press the tab labeled A, and you see only those records in the database for which the first letter of the Name field begins with an A. Press the B tab, and you see only those items with a first letter of B.

The important point, of course, is that you were able to produce the previous program by writing only five lines of code:

```
S := TabSet1.Tabs.Strings[NewTab] + '%';
Query1.Close;
Query1.Prepare;
Query1.Params[0].AsString := S;
Query1.Open;
```

plus one line of SQL:

```
Select * form Country where Name like :NameStr
```

This combination of SQL and Delphi's native language provides maximum power and flexibility when you want to produce your own applications.

Further examples of parameterized queries are found on disk as PARAMS2 and PARAMS3. The PARAMS2 program is particularly interesting because it shows how to work with two parameterized variables at once.

To create the PARAMS2 program, drop a query, datasource, and grid on a form, and place two listboxes and a TDbImage above the grid, as shown in Figure 21.4. Use TLabel objects to put the word Size above the first listbox, and the word Weight above the second listbox. Set the DataSource property of the TDBImage control to DataSource1, and type BMP in the editor for its DataField property.

FIGURE 21.4.

The form for the PARAMS2 program, as it appears at design time.

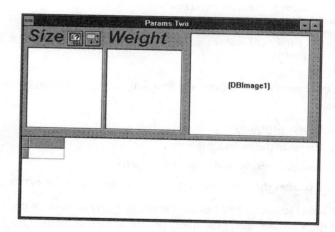

The SQL statement used in the PARAMS2 program looks like this:

```
select * from Animals
  where
    Animals."Size" > :Size and
    Animals."Weight" > :Weight
```

To satisfy the two parameters specified in this SQL statement, you should create the following method:

```
procedure TForm1.ListBox1Click(Sender: TObject);
begin
  Query1.Close;
  Query1.Prepare;
  Query1.Params[0].AsInteger :=
    strtoInt(ListBox1.Items.Strings[ListBox1.ItemIndex]);
  Query1.Params[1].AsInteger :=
    strtoInt(ListBox2.Items.Strings[ListBox2.ItemIndex]);
  Query1.Open;
end;
```

The OnClick events for both listboxes should be set to the previous routine.

When you run the PARAMS2 program, both listboxes are automatically filled with numbers that range from 0 to 42. By selecting a value from the first listbox, you specify the size of the animal you want to find; and by selecting one from the second listbox, you select its weight. Using both values together, you are able to resolve both parameterized variables, thereby effectively selecting a range of animals to view.

As a final touch, the PARAMS2 program displays a picture of the animals in question in the TDBImage control. The blob field of the table that contains the picture is called BMP. As you learned in Chapter 19, "Creating DLLs," the TDBImage control asks only that you set its `DataSource` property to a valid datasource, and its `DataField` property to the name of the blob field you want to display. In this case, the `DataSource` is `DataSource1` and the blob field is called BMP.

> **NOTE**
>
> The source code for the main unit of the PARAMS2 program is in the CHAP21 directory on this book's CD-ROM.

The *SQL* Property and the *Format* Function

I stated earlier that normally you can only use parameterized variables in cases in which there is a `where` clause or an `insert` clause. There are times, however, when these guidelines can be a bit limiting. If you find that you need more flexibility, you can use Delphi's `Format` function to create your own special version of parameterized variables.

Consider the following SQL statement:

```
Select * from Country
```

There are definitely times when you might want to parameterize the last word in this statement so that it could vary over the life of a program:

```
Select * from :FileName
```

Unfortunately, most SQL servers won't support this syntax, so you're forced to find another solution.

At times like these, the `Format` function can come to the rescue. The `Format` function works a lot like the `Printf` function found in the C language. A detailed explanation of this function is available in the online help; for now, all you really need to know about it is that it enables you to substitute variables of almost any type for certain words in a string. More specifically, you can compose a string that looks like this:

```
S := 'Select * from %s'
```

In this string, the syntax `%s` performs the same role that the `:FileName` syntax does in a parameterized query. The one difference, of course, is that you should only use `%s` when you're working with a string. If you're working with an Integer, use `%d`. Once again, you should refer to the online documentation if you want more details on how this function works.

The second parameter passed to `Format` is an array of values separated by commas. To start an array, use an open bracket. Then, include a series of values and mark the end of the array with a closed bracket:

```
Format(S, [value1, value2]);
```

When you've declared a string like this:

```
S := 'Select * from %s'
```

you can plug it into a `Format` statement:

```
Format(S, [Args]);
```

Given the preceding code, if `Args` were a string set to the value `Country`, after the `Format` function was executed you would end up with the following string in the variable `S`:

```
'Select * from Country'
```

Needless to say, this was exactly what you hoped to achieve, and the `Format` function enables you to reach your goal without any of the restrictions placed on parameterized variables.

Of course, this example was fairly simplistic, but if you wanted, you could create a string that looks like this:

```
S = 'Select * from %s where %s = %d';
```

This string contains three variables that can be changed at runtime, and it should give you some hints as to the kind of flexibility you can achieve using this system. For instance, you could write code that looks like this:

```
var
  Results,  S1, S2: string;
  Value: Integer;
begin
  S1 := 'Customer';
  S2 := 'CustNo'
  Value := 42;
  Result := Format(S, [S1, S2, Value]);
end;
```

After substitutions are made, this produces a variable that reads like this:

```
select * from Customer where CustNo = 42.
```

To see this entire process in action, refer to the PARAMS1.DPR file in the EXAMPLES subdirectory. This program lets you pick from a list of tables and display the contents of each table in a data grid.

To create the PARAMS1 program, place a query on the form and set its DatabaseName property to DBDEMOS. To create the list of tables, place a TListBox object on the form and create the following FormCreate method:

```
procedure TForm1.FormCreate(Sender: TObject);
begin
  Session.GetTableNames(Query1.DatabaseName, '',
                    False, False, ListBox1.Items);
end;
```

The call to Delphi's built-in GetTableNames routine returns a complete list of valid table names from the database specified in the first parameter. The second parameter is a string that can contain a file mask, if you so desire. For instance, you can enter 'c*.*' to get a list of all tables beginning with the letter C. The fourth parameter is a boolean value that specifies whether you want to work with system tables; and the final parameter is a value of type TStrings that holds the output from the function.

To enable the user to view the contents of the tables listed in the FormCreate method, you should add a TDataSource and TdbGrid to the form, and then wire them up.

At the very top of the unit that holds your main form, you should declare a string constant:

```
const
  BaseStr = 'Select * from %s';
```

Next, create a response method for the ListBox1.OnClick event:

```
procedure TForm1.ListBox1Click(Sender: TObject);
var
  S: String;
begin
  S := ListBox1.Items.Strings[ListBox1.ItemIndex];
  Query1.Close;
  Query1.SQL.Clear;
  Query1.SQL.Add(Format(BaseStr, [S]));
  Query1.Open;
end;
```

The first line of the code shown here assigns a string the value from the currently selected item in a listbox.

The next two lines of code check to make sure that the query is closed:

```
Query1.Close
```

and then clear out any strings currently sitting in the SQL property:

```
Query1.SQL.Clear;
```

The next line in the program adds a new SQL statement to the query. To do this, it calls on the Format function, the BaseStr constant, and the string selected from the listbox. The result is a new SQL statement that requests a dataset containing the contents of a table. For example, the string might look like this:

```
select * from Orders
```

The PARAMS1 program demonstrates how to use the Format function in lieu of parameterized queries. The Format function is useful because it is more flexible than parameterized queries.

Later in this chapter, you'll revisit this program a third time to see how you can automatically list all the tables in a particular database or subdirectory.

Passing Parameters via TDataSource

In the last chapter, you learned about a technique for creating a one-to-many relationship between two tables. Now, you'll learn about a second technique for performing the same action—this time using a TQuery object. You'll find that this second system is quite flexible because it doesn't insist that you work with indexed fields. However, indices can help speed up commands of this type.

The TQuery object has a DataSource property that can be used to create a link between itself and another dataset. It doesn't matter whether the other dataset is a TTable object, TQuery object, or some other descendant of TDataSet that you or another programmer might create. All you have to do is ensure that the dataset is connected to a datasource, and then you're free to make the link.

In the following explanation, assume that you want to create a link between the ORDERS table and the CUSTOMERS table, so that whenever you view a particular customer record, only the orders associated with that customer will be visible.

Consider the following parameterized query:

```
select * from Orders where CustNo = :CustNo
```

In this statement, :CustNo is a bind variable that needs to be supplied a value from some source. Delphi enables you to use the TQuery.DataSource field to point at another dataset, which can supply that information to you automatically. In other words, instead of being forced to use the Params property to manually supply a variable, the appropriate variable can simply be plucked from another table. Furthermore, Delphi always first tries to satisfy a parameterized query by using the DataSource property, and only if that fails, does it expect to get the variable from the Params property.

Take a moment to consider exactly what happens in these situations. As you saw in the last chapter, the CustNo field forms a link between the ORDERS table and the CUSTOMER table. Therefore, if both tables are visible on a form, the appropriate CustNo value is always available in the current record of the CUSTOMERS table. All you need to do is point the query object in the appropriate direction.

To obtain the bind value, just set the DataSource for the Query object to the TDataSource object that's associated with the CUSTOMER table. That's all there is to it! Just enter a short SQL statement, link up the DataSource property, and Bingo! You've established a one-to-many relationship like the linked cursors example from the last chapter!

On disk, you'll find an example called QLINKS that demonstrates how this technique works. To create the QLINKS program, place two TQuery, two TDataSource, and two TdbGrids on a form, as shown in Figure 21.5.

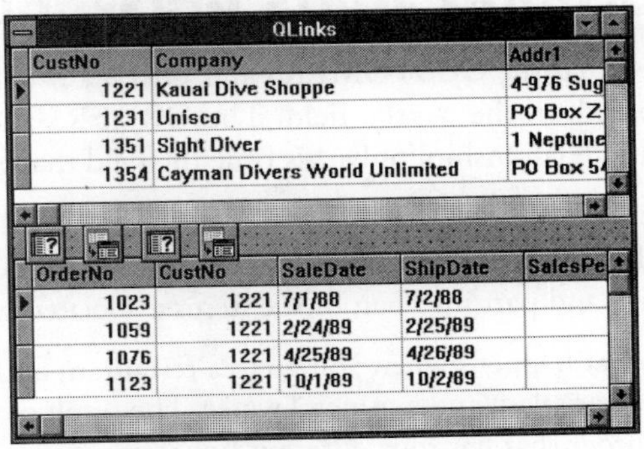

FIGURE 21.5.

The QLINKS program shows how to create a one-to-many relationship using the TQuery object.

In the SQL property for the first TQuery component, enter the following:

```
select * from Customer
```

In the second TQuery component, enter the following:

```
select * from Orders where CustNo = :CustNo
```

To complete the program, all you have to do is wire up the controls by attaching dbGrid1 to DataSource1, and DataSource1 to Query1. Perform the same action for the second set of controls, and then set the Query2.DataSource property to DataSource1. This last step is the main action that forms the link between the two tables. If you now run the program, you'll see that the two tables work together in the desired manner.

If you want to create a link between two tables using multiple fields, you can simply specify the relevant fields in your query:

```
select * from Orders
    where CustNo = :CustNo and
    CustCountry = :CustCountry
```

The important point to understand is that this one-to-many example works simply because Delphi supports parameterized variables. There is no other hand-waving going on in the background. All that's happening is that you're using a basic SQL statement to view the members of the ORDERS table that happen to have a particular customer number. The customer number in question was passed to you via the DataSource property and the bind variable you created.

The examples you've seen so far in this chapter should give you some feeling for the extreme power and flexibility inherent in the TQuery object. If you're looking for a lever powerful enough to move the roadblocks in your client/server programming world, TQuery is likely to be the tool you require.

In the next section, you'll learn more about the TQuery object when you see how to join two tables together so that you can view them both in a single dataset.

Performing Joins Between Multiple Tables

You've seen that the CUSTOMERS and ORDERS tables are related in a one-to-many relationship based on the CustNo field. The ORDERS and ITEMS tables are also bound in a one-to-many relationship, only this time the field that connects them is called OrderNo.

More specifically, each order that exists in the ORDERS table will have several records from the ITEMS table associated with it. The records from the ITEMS table specify characteristics, such as price and part number, of the items associated with a particular sale.

Consider what happens when you go to a restaurant and order steamed shrimp, a steamed artichoke, Caesar salad, and a mineral water. The result of this pleasurable exercise is that you've made one order that has four different line items associated with it:

```
Suzie Customer (Oct 1, 1994):
  ITEMS1: Shrimp         $12.95
  ITEMS2: Artichoke       $6.25
  ITEMS3: Caesar salad    $3.25
  ITEMS4: Mineral water   $2.50
```

In a situation like this, it's sometimes simplest to join the data from the ORDERS table and the ITEMS table, so that the resulting dataset contains information from both tables:

```
Suzie      Oct 1, 1994    Shrimp        $12.95
Suzie      Oct 1, 1994    Artichoke      $6.25
etc...
```

The act of merging these two tables is called a join, and it is one of the fundamental operations you can perform on a set of two or more tables.

Given the ORDERS and ITEMS tables from the DEMOS subdirectory, you can join them in such a way that the CustNo, OrderNo, and SaleDate fields from the ORDERS table are merged with the StockNo, Price, and Qty fields from the ITEMS table to form a new dataset containing all six fields. A grid containing the resulting dataset is shown in Figure 21.6.

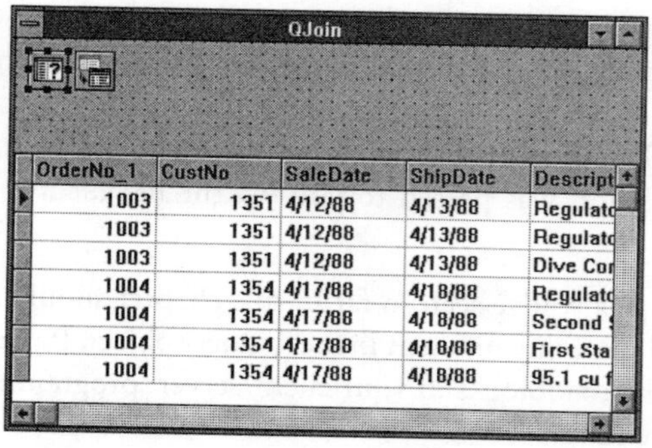

FIGURE 21.6.

The QJOIN program joins the ORDERS and ITEMS table producing a dataset with fields from each table.

There's a substantial difference between linking cursors and joining tables. However, they both have two things in common:

- They both involve two or more tables.
- Each table is linked to the other by one or more shared fields.

The act of joining the ORDERS and ITEMS tables can be accomplished by a single SQL statement that looks like this:

```
select
  O."OrderNo" , O."CustNo" ,
  O."SaleDate" , O."ShipDate" ,
  I."PartNo " , I."Qty" ,  I."Discount "
from
  Orders O, Items I
where
  O.OrderNo = I.OrderNo
```

This statement consists of four different parts:

- The select statement specifies that you expect a cursor to be returned containing some form of dataset.
- Next, there is a list of the fields that you want included in the dataset you are requesting. This list includes the OrderNo, CustNo, SaleDate, ShipDate, PartNo, Qty, and Discount fields. The first four fields originate in the ORDERS table, and the second three fields originate in the ITEMS table.
- The from clause states that you're working with two tables, one called ORDERS and the other called ITEMS. For the sake of brevity, the statement uses an optional SQL feature that lets you specify the ORDERS table with the letter O, and the ITEMS table with the letter I.
- The where clause is vitally important, because it specifies which field will link the two tables. Some servers are capable of returning valid datasets even if you don't include a where clause in your join, but the resulting set of records will almost surely not be what you want. To get the results you're looking for, be sure to include a where clause.

When you've created the SQL statement that you want to use, there is nothing at all difficult about performing a join. The QJOIN example that ships with Delphi demonstrates exactly how to proceed. All you need do is drop a TQuery, TDataSource, and TdbGrid onto a form, and then wire them up in the standard way. When you're hooked up, you can paste the query statement in the SQL property of the query, fill in the DatabaseName property, and then set Active to True. Now, compile and run the program, and take a moment to scroll through the new dataset you've created from the raw materials in the ORDERS and ITEMS tables.

There is not much point to showing you the actual source code for the QJOIN program, because all the magic occurs in the SQL statement quoted previously.

Parameterized Queries and *join* Statements

You can mix parameterized queries and join statements. This is useful if you want to show the CUSTOMERS table at the top of a form, and then beneath it, show another dataset that contains records with information from both the ORDERS and ITEMS table. The end result is a program that enables you to iterate through a list of customers in the top half of a form, while the bottom half of the form shows only the purchases associated with any particular customer, including a list of the line items that were bought. This is the type of form you'd produce if you wanted to create an electronic invoice.

The QJOIN2 program on your system shows how a program of this type looks in practice. The main form for the QJOIN2 program is shown in Figure 21.7.

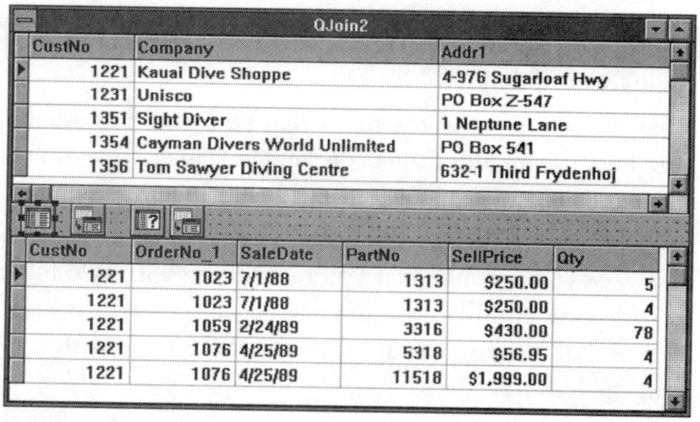

FIGURE 21.7.

The QJOIN2 program shows three tables linked together in a logical and coherent fashion.

To create this program, drop down a TTable, a TQuery, two datasources, and two data grids. Hook up the TTable, the first datasource, and the first grid to the CUSTOMERS table. Wire up the remaining controls, and specify DataSource1 in the Query1.DataSource property. Now, add the following SQL statement in the Query1.SQL property:

```
select
  O.CustNo, O.OrderNo, O.SaleDate,
  L.PartNo, L.Discount, L.Qty
from
  Orders O, Items L
where
  O.CustNo = :CustNo and
  O.OrderNo = L.OrderNo
```

The statement pictured here is very much like the one you saw in the last section, except that the where clause has been expanded to include a bind variable:

```
where
  O.CustNo = :CustNo and
  O.OrderNo = L.OrderNo
```

This clause now specifies two different relationships: one between the CUSTOMERS table and the ORDERS table, and the second between the ORDERS table and the ITEMS table. More specifically, the value for the CustNo variable will be supplied by the current record of the CUSTOMERS table via the link on the Query1.DataSource property. The link between the ORDERS table and ITEMS table will be the OrderNo field.

Conceptually, the QJOIN2 program forces you to wrestle with some fairly complex ideas. This complexity is inherent in the task being performed. Delphi, however, enables you to encapsulate these complex ideas in a few very simple mechanical steps. In short, once you understand the goal you want to achieve, Delphi enables you to perform even complex data operations with just a few minutes of work.

Open Versus ExecSQL

After you've composed a SQL statement, there are two different ways to process it. If you need to get a cursor back from the query, you should always call Open. If you don't need to return a cursor, you should call ExecSQL. For instance, if you're inserting, deleting, or updating data, you should call ExecSQL. To state the same matter in slightly different terms, you should use Open whenever you compose a Select statement, and you should use ExecSQL whenever you write any other kind of statement.

Here's a typical SQL statement that you might use to delete a record from a table:

```
delete from Country where Name = 'Argentina';
```

This statement deletes any record from the COUNTRY database that has Argentina in the Name field.

It doesn't take long to see that this is a case in which you might want to use a parameterized query. For instance, it would be nice to be able to vary the name of the country you want to delete:

```
delete from Country where Name = :CountryName
```

In this case, CountryName is a variable that can be changed at runtime by writing code that looks like this:

```
Query2.Prepare;
Query2.Params[0] := 'Argentina';
Query2.ExecSQL;
Query1.Refresh;
```

The code shown here first calls Prepare to inform Delphi that it should parse the SQL statement you gave it and ready the Params property. The next step is to insert a value into the Params property, and then to execute the newly prepared SQL statement. Note that you execute the statement not by calling Open, but by calling ExecSQL. Call ExecSQL when you don't need to return a dataset! Finally, you display the results of your actions to the user by asking the first query to refresh itself.

The INSERT2 program from the EXAMPLES subdirectory demonstrates this technique. That program uses three different TQuery objects. The first TQuery object works with a TDataSource and TdbGrid object to display the COUNTRY database on screen. In Figure 21.8, you can see that the program has two buttons: one for deleting records and the other for inserting records.

FIGURE 21.8.

The INSERT2 program uses three TQuery components and one TDataSource component.

The second TQuery object in the INSERT2 program is used to insert a record into the COUNTRY table, as explained next. The third TQuery object is used for deleting records. It has the following statement in its SQL property:

```
delete from Country where Name = :Name;
```

The code associated with the Delete button looks like this:

```
Query3.Prepare;
Query3.Params[0].AsString := Query1.Fields[0].AsString;
Query3.ExecSQL;
Query1.Refresh;
```

Query3 snags the name of the record to delete from the currently selected record in the first query. This enables the user to scroll through the list of records using the TdbGrid tool, and then delete whatever record is current. After the deletion, Query1.Refresh is called. A call to Refresh forces the query to go and obtain the most recent data from the disk, thereby allowing the program to reflect the deletion at almost the same moment it is made. (Note that a real-world program meant to be used with a typical set of users would query the user before performing a deletion of this sort.)

Here is a typical SQL statement for inserting data into a table:

```
insert into
  Country
  (Name, Capital, Continent, Area, Population)
values
  ('Argentina', 'Buenos Ares',
   'South America', 2777815, 32300003)
```

This is a convenient system, but it has the disadvantage of forcing you to hard-code values into the statement. To avoid this problem, the Query2 object has the following code in its SQL property:

```
insert
  into Country (Name, Capital, Continent, Area,  Population)
  values (:Name, :Capital, :Continent, :Area, :Population)
```

Note that in this code, all the actual values intended for insertion are specified by bind variables. These bind variables are convenient because they enable you to write code that looks like this:

```
procedure TForm1.InsertClick(Sender: TObject);
begin
  Query2.Prepare;
  Query2.Params[0].AsString := 'Erewhen';
  Query2.Params[1].AsString := 'None';
  Query2.Params[2].AsString := 'Imagination';
  Query2.Params[3].AsFloat : =  0.0;
  Query2.Params[4].AsFloat : =  1.0;
  Query2.ExecSQL;
  Query1.Refresh;
end;
```

In the code shown here, you can use edit controls to dynamically specify the values that you want to insert at runtime. Notice that once again, the program calls ExecSQL rather than Open. This is because there's no need to return a cursor from an SQL Insert statement. The procedure ends with a call to Refresh, which assures that Query1 goes out to the disk and gets the most recent data.

In this section, you've learned about the differences between ExecSQL and Open. The major point to remember is that Select statements return a cursor, and therefore require a call to Open. Delete, Insert, and UpDate don't return a cursor, and should therefore be accompanied by calls to ExecSQL. All of this is demonstrated on disk in the INSERT2 program. The call to Refresh ensures that the data displayed to the user reflects the changes made by the Delete statement.

Specialized TQuery Properties

By this time, you should have a good feeling for how to use Delphi to create and execute SQL statements. There are, however, a few properties belonging to TQuery that have not yet been mentioned:

```
property UniDirectional: Boolean;
property Handle: HDBICur;
property StmtHandle: HDBIStmt;
property DBHandle: HDBIDB;
```

The UniDirectional property is used to optimize your access to a table. If you set UniDirectional to True, you can iterate through a table more quickly, but you'll only be able to move in a forward direction.

The `StmtHandle` property is related to the `Handle` property from TDataSet; it's included solely so you can make your own calls directly to the Borland Database Engine. Under normal circumstances, there would be no need for you to use this property, because Delphi's components can handle the needs of most programmers. However, if you're familiar with the Borland Database Engine, and if you know that it has some particular capability that isn't encapsulated in the VCL, you can use the `TQuery.StmtHandle` or `TQuery.Handle` to make calls directly to the engine.

The following short code fragment shows two calls being made directly to the BDE:

```
var
  Name: array[0..100] of Char;
  Records: Integer;
begin
  dbiGetNetUserName(Name);
  dbiGetRecordCount(Query1.Handle, Records);
end;
```

Summary

In this chapter, you learned about the main features of the TQuery component. You saw that you can use this component to create SQL statements that enable you to manipulate tables in a wide variety of useful ways.

One of the keys to understanding TQuery's `SQL` property is the ability to manipulate it at runtime. In this chapter, you saw three different methods of manipulating this property. The first, and conceptually simplest, is to merely use the `SQL.Add` function whenever you needed to change a query at runtime. Parameterized queries are less wasteful than using the `Add` property, but there are some limits on what you can do with parameterized queries. To get beyond these limits, you can use the `Format` function, which enables you to create almost any kind of SQL statement you could want at runtime.

Regardless of how you treat the `SQL` property, there is no doubt that it is one of the power centers in the Delphi environment. Programmers who want to write powerful SQL applications need to know almost everything they can about the `SQL` property.

In the next chapter, you will learn how to use the DataSet Designer and the Query Builder to automate some of the database tasks you have been performing in the last two chapters.

Fields and
Database Tools

22

Overview

This chapter covers a set of visual tools you can use to simplify database development. The major areas of concentration are as follows:

- The Fields Editor
- TField descendant objects
- Calculated Fields

All three of these subjects are closely related and can be thought of as a single set of related topics.

Through the use of the Fields Editor you can influence the manner and types of data that appear in TdbEdit and TdbGrid controls. For instance, you can format data so that it appears as currency or as a floating point number with a defined precision. You also can use the Fields Editor to change the appearance of a grid so that its columns are arranged in a new order or are hidden.

At the end of the chapter is a short section on the Query Builder. In that section you will learn how to create various types of queries and how to edit the SQL statements you create.

The lessons you learn in this chapter will demonstrate a key part of the way most programmers present database tables to their users. Much of the material involves manipulating visual tools, but the basic subject matter is fairly technical and assumes a basic understanding of the Delphi environment and language.

The Fields Editor

The Fields Editor enables you to associate custom objects with some or all of the fields from a table. By associating a custom object with a field, you can control the way a field displays, formats, validates, and inputs data. The Fields Editor also lets you add new fields to a table at runtime and to then calculate the values that will be shown in the new fields. This latter procedure is referred to as *Calculated Fields*.

In this section and the next, you will be building a program called MASS, which illustrates both the Fields Editor and Calculated Fields. This is an important program, so you should try to use your copy of Delphi to follow the steps described.

The Fields Editor can be accessed from either a TTable or TQuery object. To get started, drop a TQuery object on a form, set up the DBDEMOS alias, enter the SQL statement "select * from animals", and make the table active.

Drop down the Object Selector at the top of the Object Inspector. Notice that you currently have two components in use on the form: TForm and TQuery.

Click the right mouse button once on the TQuery object and select the Fields Editor. Choose the Add button and pop up the Add Fields dialog, as shown in Figure 22.1.

FIGURE 22.1.

The Add Fields dialog box from the Fields Editor.

By default, all of the fields in the dialog box are selected. Click the OK button to select all five fields and then close the Fields Editor.

Open the Object Selector a second time; notice that there are now five new objects on your form, as shown in Figure 22.2.

FIGURE 22.2.

The Object Selector lists the objects created in the Fields Editor. You also can find this list in the TForm1 class definition.

These objects are the keys to your visual presentation of the Animals table to the user.

Here's a complete list of the objects you just created:

```
Query1NAME: TStringField;
Query1SIZE: TSmallintField;
Query1WEIGHT: TSmallintField;
Query1AREA: TStringField;
Query1BMP: TBlobField;
```

I cut and pasted this list from the TForm1 class definition found in the Editor Window. The origins of the names shown here should be fairly obvious. The Query1 part comes from the default name for the TQuery object, and the second half of the name comes from the fields in the Animals table. If I had renamed the Query1 object to Animal, I would have produced names that looked like this:

```
AnimalNAME
AnimalSIZE
AnimalWEIGHT
```

This kind of convention can be very useful if you are working with several tables and want to know at a glance which table and field are being referenced by a particular variable.

> **NOTE**
>
> The names of the fields in the example shown here are capitalized only because the table in question is a dBASE table. dBASE tables automatically capitalize all letters in field names. If I had chosen to work with some other type of table, the capitalization of the letters in the field name would have followed the rules defined by the current database.

Each of the objects created in the Fields Editor is a descendent of TField. The exact type of descendant depends on the type of data in a particular field. For instance, the Query1WEIGHT field is of type TIntegerField, whereas the Query1NAME field is of type TStringField. These are the two field types you will see most often. Other common types include TDateField and TCurrencyField, neither of which are used in this particular table. Remember that these types were selected to correspond with the field types in the table itself.

TStringField, TIntegerField, and the other objects shown here are all descendants of TField and share its traits. You can treat these objects exactly as you did the TField objects that you learned about in Chapter 20, "Using TTable and TDataSet." For instance, you can write this:

```
S := TIntegerField.AsString;
```

and

```
S := TIntegerField.Name.
```

However, these descendants of TField are very smart objects and have several traits that go beyond the functionality of their common ancestor.

To start getting a feel for what you can do with TField descendants, you should open up the Browser, turn off the option to view Private and Protected fields, and then scroll through the Public and Published properties and methods.

The most important property you will see is called Value. You can access it like this:

```
procedure TForm1.Button1Click(Sender: TObject);
var
  i: Integer;
  S: string;
begin
  i := Query1SIZE.Value;
  S := Query1NAME.Value;
```

```
  Inc(i);
  S := 'Foo';
  Query1SIZE.Value := i;
  Query1NAME.Value := S;
end;
```

The code shown here first assigns values to the variables `i` and `s`. The next two lines change these values, and the last two lines reassign the new values to the objects. It usually wouldn't make much sense to write code exactly like this in a program, but it serves to illustrate the syntax used by TField descendants.

The `Value` property always conforms to the type of field you have instantiated. For instance TStringFields are strings, whereas TCurrencyFields always return floating point double values. However, if you show a TCurrencyField in a data-aware control, it will return a string that looks like this: `'$5.00'`. The dollar sign and the rounding to decimal places are simply part and parcel of what a TCurrencyField is all about.

The preceding example might make you think that Delphi has suddenly dropped its strong typing. Nothing could be further from the case. The point here is that `TCurrencyField.Value` is declared as a `Double`. If you tried to assign a string to it, you would get a type mismatch. Likewise, `TIntegerField.Value` is declared as an integer, and so on. The preceding code is an example of polymorphism; it is not an example of relaxed type-checking.

If you want the names of each field in the current dataset, you should reference the `FieldName` property through one of the following two methods:

```
S := Query1.Fields[0].FieldName;
S := Query1NAME.FieldName;
```

If you want the name of an object associated with a field, you should use the `Name` property:

```
S := Query1.Fields[0].Name;
S := Query1NAME.Name;
```

When using the ANIMALS table, the first two examples shown above yield the string `'Name'`, while the second two lines yield `'Query1NAME'`.

Special properties are associated with most of the major field types. For instance, TIntegerFields have `DisplayFormat` and `DisplayEdit` properties, as well as `MinValue` and `MaxValue` properties. TStringFields, on the other hand, have none of these properties, but they do have an `EditMask` property, which works just like the TEditMask component found on the Additional Page of the Component Palette. All these properties are used to control the way data is displayed to the user, or the way that input from the user should be handled.

You should be aware of one more thing about the Fields Editor. You can use this tool not only to build objects that encapsulate existing fields, but also to build objects that represent new fields. For instance, suppose you wanted to create a sixth field, MASS, which contains the product of the SIZE and WEIGHT fields, in the Animals table.

To create the MASS field, open the Field Editor again and select the Define button. In the top part of the Define Field dialog, enter the word MASS. Now set its type to TIntegerField, as shown in Figure 22.3.

FIGURE 22.3.

Creating the MASS field in the Field Editor.

If you close the Field Editor and add a TDataSource and TdbGrid to your project, you will see that the Animals table now appears to have six fields, the last of which is called MASS.

Of course, it's one thing to create a field, and another to fill it in at runtime with an appropriate value. The act of placing a value in the new field you have created involves Calculated Fields, which is addressed in the next section.

Calculated Fields

Calculated Fields are one of the most valuable fruits of the Fields Editor. You can use these fields for several different purposes, but two stand out:

- If you need to perform calculations on two or more of the fields in a dataset and want to show the results of the calculations in a third field, you can use Calculated Fields. A scenario describing this type of situation was set up in the last section and will be explained further in this section.

- If you are viewing one dataset and want to perform calculations or display data that involve lookups in at least one additional dataset, you can use the Field Editor and Calculate Fields to show the results of these calculations in a new field of the first dataset.

The MASS program illustrates one example of the first of the two uses for calculated fields described previously. You got this program started in the last section when you created the field called MASS and displayed it in a grid.

To continue working with the MASS program, highlight the Query1 object and set the Object Inspector to the events page. Now create an `OnCalcFields` event that looks like this:

```
procedure TForm1.Query1CalcFields(DataSet: TDataset);
begin
  Query1MASS.Value := Query1SIZE.Value * Query1WEIGHT.Value;
end;
```

The code shown here assigns the value of the Query1MASS object to the product of the Query1SIZE and Query1WEIGHT fields. This kind of multiplication is legal to do since all of the fields are of the same type.

`OnCalcField` methods get called each time a record is first displayed to the user. As a result, all of the MASS fields displayed in the grid are properly filled in, as shown in Figure 22.4.

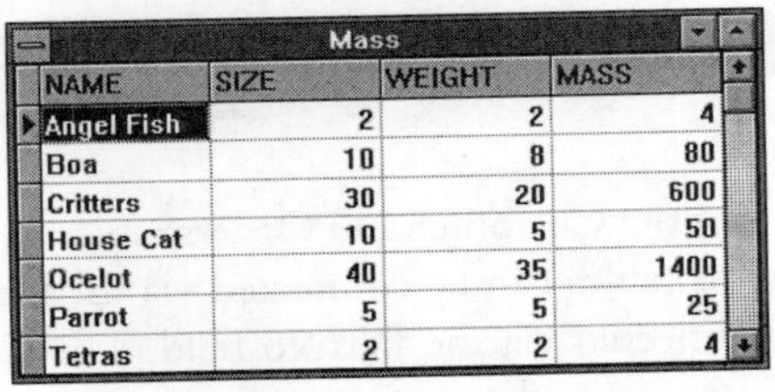

FIGURE 22.4.

The MASS field contains the product of the WEIGHT and SIZE fields.

NAME	SIZE	WEIGHT	MASS
Angel Fish	2	2	4
Boa	10	8	80
Critters	30	20	600
House Cat	10	5	50
Ocelot	40	35	1400
Parrot	5	5	25
Tetras	2	2	4

To get the image shown in Figure 22.4, I reopened the Field Editor a third time and deleted the AREA and BMP fields by selecting the Remove button. When I closed the Field Editor, the grid no longer showed those two fields, and a user of the program could thereby get a clear and simplified version of the effect of the `OnCalcFields` event.

If you choose to never instantiate a particular field in the Field Editor, the current dataset you are working with no longer contains that field. It can't be accessed programatically or visually at runtime. Usually, this is exactly the effect you want to achieve, and so this trait will generally be perceived as a strong benefit. However, there are times when it might not serve your purposes, and in those cases you should either create an object for all the fields in a table or stay away from the Field Editor altogether.

More on Calculated Fields

The program called CALCEM.DPR, shown in Figure 22.5, illustrates the second of the two ways to use Calculated Fields. This program links four tables in a fairly complex manner that strains the system's capabilities to its limits.

FIGURE 22.5.

The form for the CALCEM program as it appears at runtime.

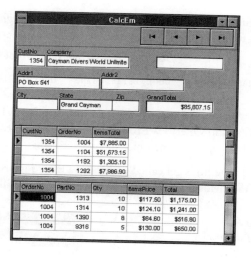

You will find that the Customer and Orders tables can be connected via the CustNo field, the Orders and Items tables can be connected via the OrderNo field, and the Items and PARTS fields can be connected via the PartNo field. The CALCEM program enables you to move through the Customer table and see the first order associated with a customer, and then all the ITEMS associated with each order. It also calculates the totals of these orders and displays the results to the user. The CALCEM program is fairly complex, but it clearly illustrates the power of Calculated Fields.

NOTE

The code for the CALCEM program is in the CHAP22 directory on this book's CD-ROM.

Here's how to get started building the CALCEM project:

1. Choose the Database expert from the Help menu.

2. On the first screen, select "Create a master/detail form" and "Create a form using TQuery Objects."

3. Choose the Next button, set the Alias to DBDEMOS, and pick the CUSTOMER.DB table from the \DELPHI\DEMOS\DATA subdirectory.

4. Choose Next and select all of the fields from the CUSTOMER tables.

5. Choose Next and select Horizontal from the arrangement of the dbEdit controls on your form.

6. Choose Next and select the ORDERS.DB table.

7. In the next two screens, select all of the fields from the table and arrange them in a grid.

8. Choose Next and select the CustNo field from both the master and detail listboxes, and then select the Add button.

9. Choose Next and generate the form.

It takes a few words to describe the preceding process, but actually issuing the commands in Delphi is easy and intuitive. When you are done, you have created a one-to-many relationship between the Customer and Orders table such that you can view a single customer, and then see all the orders associated with that customer.

Highlight the first of the two TQuery objects and set its `Active` property to `True`. Click once on Query2, press the right mouse button, and select the Fields Editor. Bring up the Add Fields dialog and add the OrderNo, CustNo, and ItemsTotal fields.

It's time to bring the Items table into the picture. The Items table shows each of the items associated with a particular order. Add a new grid called DBGrid2 and place it beneath the first grid. (To make this work, you may need to play the `Align` property of both grids, setting `DBGrid1` to `alNone` and `DBGrid2` to `alBottom`.) Add another TQuery object to the table and set the `DatabaseName` property to `DBDEMOS`. Place the following string in the Query3 component's SQL property:

```
select * from items where
  OrderNo = :OrderNo
```

In the Field Editor for Query3, use the Add Field dialog to select the Qty and SellPrice fields. Select Define and create two calculated fields called ItemsPrice and Total. Set both to be of type TCurrencyField. Set the DataSource field of Query3 equal to DataSource2.

Add a fourth query to the form and set its SQL property to the following string:

```
select * from parts
  where PartNo = :PartNo
```

and the DataSource to DataSource3.

Now if you run the program, you will see that you have a three-way join between the CUSTOMER, ORDERS, and ITEMS tables. If you look carefully at the output, you can see that the ItemsPrice and Total fields in DBGrid2 are still blank.

Here's how to perform the necessary calculations that fill in the Query3Total field:

```
procedure TCalcFrm.Query3CalcFields(DataSet: TDataSet);
begin
  Query4.Close;
  Query4.Prepare;
  Query4.ParamByName('PartNo').AsFloat := Query3.FieldByName('PartNo').AsFloat;
  Query4.Open;
  Query3ItemsPrice.Value := Query4.FieldByName('Cost').AsFloat;
  Query3Total.Value := Query3Qty.Value * Query3ItemsPrice.Value;
end;
```

This method occurs in response to an `OnCalcFields` event in the Query3 object. To create the framework for this method, turn to the Events page for Query3 and click once on the `OnCalcField` event.

The `Query3CalcFields` method shown here starts by opening up the Query4 object so that the program now has a four-way join between the Customer, Orders, Items, and Parts tables. It then grabs the ItemsPrice from the Cost field of the Parts table and multiplies this value times the Qty field of the Items table. The result is the total dollars spent on any one particular item inside the order.

At this point, the ItemsTotal field in the Orders table should equal the sum of the Total fields in DBGrid2. However, in at least the first versions of Delphi that were shipped, the ItemsTotal fields were not brought correctly in line. This is not a bug in Delphi, but just a failure on someone's part to successfully update the table. This is perhaps understandable, since the fields and data in the Customer, Orders, Items, and Parts fields were changing on a weekly, and sometimes daily, basis during the last few months before the product shipped. (One of the outcomes of those changes was that the CALCEM example became considerably more complex than I originally intended. However, I have preserved it on the grounds that it will indeed give you a significant workout on using Calculated Fields!)

The code in `Query1CalcFields` iterates the Query2 object and performs calculations on the latter's ItemsTotal field. This illustrates how you can use the `OnCalcField` event of one table to look up or calculate a value found in a second table.

The code for the `Query1CalcFields` method begins by turning off the visual representation of the Orders table and by zeroing out a variable:

```
procedure TCalcFrm.Query1CalcFields(DataSet: TDataset);
var
  R: Real;
begin
  DataSource2.Enabled := False;
  R := 0;
```

It's worthwhile to disable `DataSource2` because the code will iterate through all its records, but there is no need to waste time showing this activity to the user.

After getting preliminary setup chores out of the way, bring the Orders table into sync:

```
Query2.Close;
Query2.Prepare;
Query2.Params[0].AsString := Query1.FieldByName('CustNo').AsString;
Query2.Open;
```

The actual act of performing the calculation is simple enough:

```
while not Query2.Eof do begin
  R := Query2.FieldByName('ItemsTotal').AsFloat + R;
  Query2.Next;
end;
Query1GrandTotal.Value := R;
```

The final step is simply to have the procedure clean up after itself:

```
  Query2.First;
  DataSource2.Enabled := True;
end;
```

Taken as a whole, the `Query1CalcFields` method is fairly straightforward. The key point to grasp when studying it is simply that the `OnCalcFields` event for the Query1 table performed a search through a second table. In this particular case, an actual calculation occurred; but on other occasions you might need do no more than look up a simple value in a second table.

In this section, you gained some detailed knowledge about calculated fields. You first saw how to perform a useful calculation by multiplying two fields in a record together to produce a product that can be displayed in a calculated field. The final example in this section showed how to perform a query and then iterate through all the records in a table in order to produce the value displayed in a calculated field.

TdbGrid at Runtime

DBGrids can be completely reconfigured at runtime. You can hide and show columns, change the order of columns, and change the width of columns.

The MOVEGRID program shows how to take a DBGrid through its paces at runtime. The program is fairly straightforward except for two brief passages. The first passage involves creating checkbox controls on-the-fly, whereas the second shows how to change the order of items in a listbox on-the-fly.

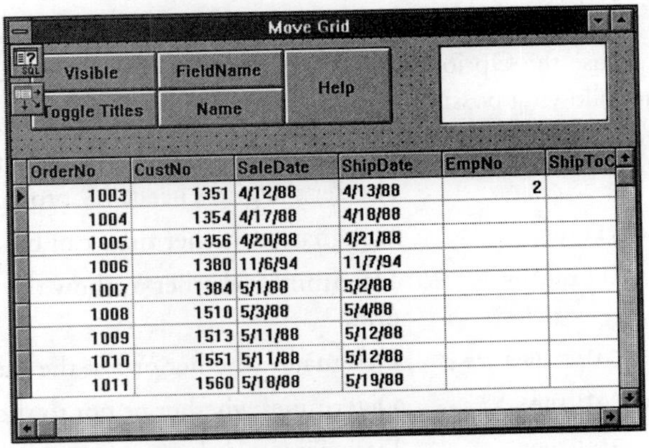

FIGURE 22.6.

The main MOVEGRID program enables you to change the appearance of a grid a runtime.

When the user wants to decide which fields are visible, MOVEGRID pops up a second form and displays the names of all the fields from the ORDERS table in a series of checkboxes. The user can then select the fields that he or she wants to make visible. The selected checkboxes designate fields that are visible, whereas the nonselected ones represent invisible fields. The program also lets you set the order and width of fields, as well as hide and show the titles at the top of the grid.

NOTE

The code for the MOVEGRID program is in the CHAP22 directory on this book's CD-ROM.

NOTE

The VisiForm unit, available in the CHAP22 directory on this book's CD-ROM, displays a set of checkboxes, where the user designates which fields are to be made visible.

In the next few paragraphs you will find descriptions of the key parts of the MOVEGRID program. Understanding its constituent parts will help you to take control over the grids you display in your programs.

Most of the code in the MOVEGRID program is fairly simple. However, the program performs a number of separate tasks. To grasp the program, it's necessary to divide and conquer. That is, take the tasks performed by the program one at a time. Find out how each one works and then move on to the next one. If you proceed in this fashion, you will find the program easy to understand.

You can use the Options field of a DBGrid to change its appearance. The Options property has the following possible values:

dgEditing	Set to True by default, it enables the user to edit a grid. You can also set the grid's ReadOnly property to True or False.
dgTitles	Designates whether titles can be seen.
dgIndicator	Determines whether to show the small icons on the left of the grid.
dgColumnResize	Designates whether or not the user can resize columns.
dgColLines	Determines whether or not to show the lines between columns.
dgRowLines	Designates whether or not to show the lines between rows.
dgTabs	Lets the user tab and shift-tab between columns.

Here is the declaration for the enumerated type where these values are declared:

```
TDBGridOption = (dgEditing, dgAlwaysShowEditor, dgTitles,
                 dgIndicator, dgColumnResize, dgColLines,
                 dgRowLines, dgTabs);
```

For instance, you can set the options at runtime by writing code that looks like this:

```
DBGrid1.Options := [dgTitles, dgIndicator];
```

If you want to toggle an option on and off, you can do so with a logical operator. For instance, the following code will add a set of titles to DBGrid1:

```
DBGrid1.Options := DBGrid1.Options + [dgTitles];
```

Given the presence of a Boolean variable called ShowTitles, the following code enables you to toggle an option back and forth at the press of a single button:

```
procedure TForm1.Button3Click(Sender: TObject);
begin
  if ShowTitles then
    DBGrid1.Options := DBGrid1.Options + [dgTitles]
  else
    DBGrid1.Options := DBGrid1.Options - [dgTitles];
  ShowTitles := not ShowTitles;
end;
```

To move the location of a column at runtime, you can simply change its index, which is a zero-based number:

```
Query1.FieldByName('CustNo').Index := 1;
Query1CustNo.Index := 2;
```

By default, the CustNo field in the Customer table is at the top of the record, in the zeroth position. The code in the first example above moves it to the second position, whereas the code that reads Query1CustNo.Index := 2; moves it to the third position. Remember, the Index field is zero-based, so moving a field to Index 1 moves it to the second field in a record. The first field is at Index 0.

When you change the index of a field, you do not need to worry about the indexes of the other fields in a record. They will be changed automatically at runtime.

The MOVEGRID program contains a listbox that displays the current order of the fields in a dataset. The code shown below responds to a double-click in a listbox by querying the user if he or she wants to change the position of the currently selected item in the listbox. The user can then enter the number to which he wants to move the currently selected field. For instance, if the user clicked the CustNo string in the listbox and entered the number 2, CustNo would move from the first to the third position in the listbox. The code shown here also moves the index of the real field from 0 to 2, thereby changing the actual position of the field in the grid. These changes are being made only to the visual representation of a dataset. The actual data on a disk is not changed by this procedure.

The following code is activitated whenever the user double-clicks the listbox:

```
procedure TForm1.ListBox1DblClick(Sender: TObject);
var
  Input, Temp, CurPos: string;
  StartPos: Integer;
```

```
begin
  Input := '';
  Temp := ListBox1.Items.Strings[ListBox1.ItemIndex];
  StartPos := ListBox1.ItemIndex;
  CurPos := 'Current Position: ' + IntToStr(StartPos);
  InputQuery(CurPos, 'New Position', Input);
  ListBox1.Items.Delete(ListBox1.ItemIndex);
  ListBox1.Items.Insert(StrToInt(Input), Temp);
  Query1.Fields[StartPos].Index := StrToInt(Input);
end;
```

The last line in the preceding example is what actually changes the index of the column the user wants to move. The two lines directly before it delete the currently selected string in the listbox and then insert it into a new position.

If you want to change the width of a column at runtime, just change the `DisplayWidth` property of the appropriate TField object:

```
Query1.FieldByName('CustNo').DisplayWidth := 12;
Query1CustNo.DisplayWidth := 12;
```

The value `12` refers to the number of characters that can be displayed in the control.

If you want to hide a field at runtime, you can set its visible property to `False`:

```
Query1.FieldByName('CustNo').Visible := False;
Query1CustNo.Visible := False;
```

Both lines of code perform identical tasks. To show the fields again, simply set `Visible` to `True`:

```
Query1.FieldByName('CustNo').Visible := True;
Query1CustNo.Visible := True;
```

In order to allow the user to decide which fields are visible, MOVEGRID pops up a second form with a series of checkboxes on it. (See VISFORM.PAS.) The program actually creates each of these checkboxes at runtime. In other words, it doesn't just pop up a form with the correct number of checkboxes on it, but instead iterates through the Query1 object, finds out how many checkboxes are needed, and then creates them dynamically at runtime.

To perform these tasks, MOVEGRID passes a copy of the Query1 object through to the form that displays the checkboxes:

```
procedure TForm1.VisibleClick(Sender: TObject);
begin
  VisiForm.ShowMe(Query1);
end;
```

The `ShowMe` method of the `VisiForm` first calls a routine called `CreateRad`, which creates the checkboxes, displays the form, and finally sets the state of the checkboxes:

```
procedure TVisiForm.ShowMe(Query1: TQuery);
var
  i: Integer;
begin
  for i := 0 to Query1.FieldCount - 1 do
    CreateRad(i, Query1.Fields[i].Name, Query1.Fields[i].Visible);
```

```
  Height := i * (RadSize + 5);
  ShowModal;
  for i := 0 to Query1.FieldCount - 1 do
    Query1.Fields[i].Visible := R[i].Checked;
end;
```

The `ShowMe` method iterates through the Query1 object and assigns one checkbox to each field. It also asks TQuery for the names of the fields, and asks whether each field is currently hidden or visible. Here is the code that creates a checkbox on-the-fly:

```
procedure TVisiForm.CreateRad(Index: Integer;
                              Name: String;
                              Visible: Boolean);
begin
  R[Index] := TCheckBox.Create(Self);
  R[Index].Parent := VisiForm;
  R[Index].Caption := Name;
  R[Index].Left := 10;
  R[Index].Top := Index * RadSize;
  R[Index].Width := 200;
  R[Index].Checked := Visible;
end;
```

Most of the code in this example is performing relatively mundane tasks, such as assigning names and locations to the checkboxes. These are the two key lines:

```
  R[Index] := TCheckBox.Create(Self);
  R[Index].Parent := VisiForm;
```

The first line actually creates the checkbox and gives it an owner. The second line assigns a parent to the checkbox.

NOTE

The difference between a parent and an owner can be confusing at times. A form is always the owner of the components that reside inside it. As such, it is responsible for allocating and deallocating memory for these components. A form might also be the parent of a particular component, which means that the component will be displayed directly on the form. However, one component might also find that another component is its parent, even though both components are owned by the form. For instance, if you place a TPanel on a form and then two TButtons on the TPanel, all three components will be owned by the form; however, the buttons will have the panel as a parent, whereas the TPanel will have the form as a parent. Ownership has to do with memory allocation. Parenthood usually describes what surface a component will be displayed on. If you get confused about this while in the midst of a lengthy programming session, you can look it up in the online help by searching on the topic Parent.

The grids supplied with the first version of Delphi are reasonably flexible objects that perform most of the tasks required of them. If you feel you need some additional functionality, check with third-party tool makers such as TurboPower software. A number of third-party grids with extended capabilities are available on the market, and some of them are well worth the purchase price.

Summary

In this chapter, you learned some fairly sophisticated methods for displaying the data from a table to the user. Some complex cases were covered, but the chapter merely touched the surface of this large subject. Good database programmers will find that there is a considerable amount of hidden power in the TField object and in the Fields Editor. This is a very strong aspect of Delphi and is bound to be expanded even further by the word of third-party developers who produce Delphi add-ons.

Real-World Databases

23

IN THIS CHAPTER

Overview

In this chapter you will get a look at a simple address book program called ADDRESS2. This program is designed to represent the simplest possible database program that is still usable in a real-world situation.

In particular, you will be getting a look at the following:

- Sorting data
- Filtering data
- Searching for data
- Printing data
- Dynamically moving a table in and out of a read-only state.
- Forcing the user to select a field's value from a list of valid responses
- Allowing the user to choose the colors of a form at runtime
- Saving information to an INI file

After finishing the chapter, you will have learned something about the kind of problems experienced when writing even a very basic database program. The final product, though not quite up to professional standards, provides solutions to many of the major problems faced by programmers who want to create tools that can be used by the typical user.

You will find that the final program is relatively long when compared to most of the programs you have seen so far in this book. The reason is that this program is meant to not just show you how to perform a particular action, but to show you how to accomplish some of the basic effects expected in real-world settings, as well as provide a minimum degree of robustness.

Defining the Data

When considering an address program, it's easy to come up with a preliminary list of needed fields:

First Name
Last Name
Address
City
State
Zip
Phone

After writing this list down and contemplating it for a moment, you might ask the following questions:

- What about complex addresses that can't be written on one line?

■ Is one phone number enough? What about times when you need a home phone and a work phone?

■ Speaking of work, what about specifying the name of the company that employs someone on the list?

■ What about faxes?

■ This is the 1990s, so what about an e-mail address?

■ What about generic information that doesn't fit into any of the these categories?

This list of questions emerges only after a period of gestation. In a real-world situation, you might come up with a list of questions like this only after you talk with potential users of your program, after viewing similar programs that are on the market, after experimenting with a prototype of the proposed program. However you come up with questions, the key point is that you spend the time to really think about the kind of data you need.

After considering the preceding questions, you might come up with a revised list of fields for your program:

> First Name
> Last Name
> Company
> Address1
> Address2
> City
> State
> Zip
> Home Phone
> Work Phone
> Fax
> EMail1
> EMail2
> Comment

This list might actually stand up to the needs of a real-world user. Certainly it doesn't cover all possible situations, but it does represent a reasonable compromise between the desire to make the program easy to use and the desire to handle a wide variety of potential user demands.

At this stage, you might start thinking about some of the basic functionality you want to associate with the program. For instance, you might decide that a user of the program should be able to search, sort, filter, and print the data. After stating these needs, you'll find that there is going to be a need to break the data up into various categories so that it can be filtered. The question, of course, is how these categories can be defined.

After considering the matter for some time, you might decide that one more field should be added to the list shown above. This field can be called Category, and it will hold a name that describes the type of record currently being viewed. For instance, some entries in an address book might consist of family members, whereas other entries might reference friends, associates from work, companies where you shop, or other types of data. Here is the revised list, with one additional field called Category, which is used to help the user filter the data he or she might be viewing:

> First Name
> Last Name
> Company
> Address1
> Address2
> City
> State
> Zip
> Home Phone
> Work Phone
> Fax
> EMail1
> EMail2
> Comment
> Category

After carefully considering the fields that might be used in the ADDRESS2 program, the next step is to decide how large and what type the fields should be.

Table 23.1. The length and type of fields used by the ADDRESS2 program.

Name	Type	Size
FName	Character	40
LName	Character	40
Company	Character	40
Address1	Character	40
Address2	Character	40
City	Character	40
State	Character	5
Zip	Character	15
HPhone	Character	15
WPhone	Character	15
Fax	Character	15

Name	Type	Size
EMail1	Character	45
EMail2	Character	45
Comment	Character	254
Category	Character	15

As you can see, I prefer to give myself plenty of room in all of the fields I declare. In particular, notice that I have opted for wide EMail fields to hold long Internet addresses, and I have decided to make the Comment field a character field rather than a memo field. The names of some of the fields have also been altered so that they don't contain any spaces. This might prove useful if the data is ever ported to another database.

Now that you have decided upon the basic structure of the table, the next thing is to work out some of the major design issues. In particular:

- The program should run off local tables, because this is the kind of tool likely to be used on individual PCs, rather than on a network. It's a toss-up about whether to use Paradox or dBASE tables, but I'll opt to use Paradox tables since they provide a bit more flexibility.
- The user should be able to sort the table on the FName, LName, and Company fields.
- It should be possible to search on the FName, LName, and Company fields.
- The user should be able to set up filters based on the Category field.
- It should be absolutely clear whether or not the table is editable, and the user should be able to easily move in and out of read-only mode.
- It should be possible to print the contents of the table based on the filters set up by the Category field.
- It's very difficult to choose a set of colors that will satisfy all tastes, so the user should be able to set the colors of the main features in the program.

A brief consideration of the design decisions make it clear that the table should have a primary index on the first three fields and secondary indices on the FName, LName, Company, and Category fields. The primary index can be used in place of a secondary index on the FName field, but the intent of the program's code will be clearer if a secondary index is used for this purpose. In other words, the code will be easier to read if it explicitly sets the IndexName to something called FNameIndex rather than simply defaulting to the primary index. Table 23.2 shows the final structure of the table. The three stars in the fourth column of the table show the fields that are part of the primary index.

Table 23.2. The fields used by the ADDRESS2 program.

Name	Type	Size	PIdx	Index
FName	Character	40	*	FNameIndex
LName	Character	40	*	LNameIndex
Company	Character	40	*	CompanyIndex
Address1	Character	40		
Address2	Character	40		
City	Character	40		
State	Character	5		
Zip	Character	15		
HPhone	Character	15		
WPhone	Character	15		
Fax	Character	15		
EMail1	Character	45		
EMail2	Character	45		
Comment	Character	254		
Category	Character	15		CategoryIndex

Now that there is a clear picture of the type of table that needs to be created, you can open up the Database Desktop and create the table, its primary index, and its four secondary indices. When you are done, the structure of the table should look like that in Figure 23.1. You can save the table under the name ADDRESS.DB.

FIGURE 23.1.

Designing the main table for the ADDRESS2 program.

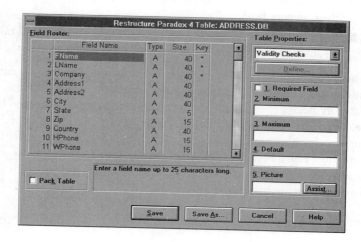

Defining the Program's Appearance

Before beginning the real programming chores, you need to create a main form and at least one of the several utility forms that will be used by the program. You can allow the Database Expert to perform at least part of this task for you, but I prefer to do the chore myself in order to give my program some individuality.

The main form of the ADDRESS2 program, shown in 23.2, contains two panels. On the top panel are all the labels and data-aware controls necessary to handle basic input and output chores. All of the main fields in the program can be encapsulated in TdbEdit controls, except for the Comment field, which needs a TdbMemo, and the Category field, which needs a TdbComboBox. The names of the data-aware controls should match the field with which they are associated so that the first TdbEdit control is called eFName, the second eLName, and so on. The TdbComboBox would therefore be called cbCategory, and the memo field mComment.

FIGURE 23.2.

The main form for the ADDRESS2 program.

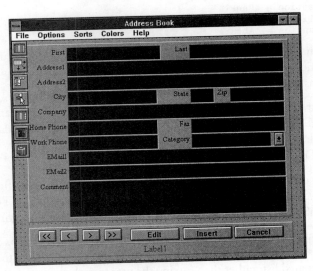

The bottom panel should contain four buttons for navigating through the table's records, as well as Edit, Insert, and Cancel buttons. The bottom half of the second panel contains one or more labels for optionally reporting on the current status of the program. You might want to divide the two portions of the second panel into separate areas by running a TBevel control horizontally across the center of the control.

The top of the program contains a menu with the following format:

```
Caption = 'File'
  Caption = 'Print'
  Caption = '-'
  Caption = 'Exit'
Caption = 'Options'
  Caption = 'Delete'
  Caption = 'Search'
  Caption = 'Filter'
  Caption = 'Set Category'
Caption = 'Sorts'
  Caption = 'First Name'
  Caption = 'Last Name'
  Caption = 'Company'
Caption = 'Colors'
  Caption = 'Form'
  Caption = 'Edits'
  Caption = 'Edit Text'
  Caption = 'Labels'
  Caption = 'Panels'
Caption = 'Help'
  Caption = 'About'
```

Each line represents the caption for one entry in the program's main menu. The indented portions are the contents of the dropdown menus that appear when you select one of the menu items visible in Figure 23.2.

After creating the program's interface, drop down a TTable and TDataSource, wire them up to ADDRESS.DB, and hook up the fields to the appropriate data-aware control. To make this work correctly, you should create an alias, called Address, that points at the location of ADDRESS.DB.

The only tricky part of this process involves the Category field, which is connected to the TdbComboBox. You make the basic connection to the TdbComboBox by settings its DataSource field to DataSource1 and its DataField to Category.

If you run the program, you will find that the TdbComboBox for the Category field does not contain any entries. The purpose of this control is to enable the user to select categories from a prepared list, rather than forcing the user to make up categories on-the-fly. The list is needed to prevent users from accidentally creating a whole series of different names for the same general purpose. For instance, if you want to be able to set a filter for the program, which presents you with a list of friends, you should create a category called Friend and assign it to all the members of the list that fit that description. If you always chose this category from a drop-down list, it will presumably always be spelled the same. However, if you rely on users to type this word, you might get a series of related entries that look like this:

Friend
Friends
Frends
Acquaintances

Buddies
Buds
Homies
HomeBoys
Amigos
Chums
Cronies
Companions

This mishmash of spellings and synonyms won't do you any good when you want to search for the group of records that fits into the category called Friend.

The simplest way to make the TdbComboBox perform its required function is to simply pop open the Property Editor for the Items property and type in a list of categories such as the following:

Home
Work
Family
Local Business
Friend

Now when you run the program and drop down the Category combo box, you will find that it contains the preceding list.

The only problem with typing names directly into the Items property for the TdbComboBox is that it is impossible to change this list at runtime. To do away with this difficulty, the program stores the list in a separate table, called CATS.DB. This table has a single character field that is 20 characters wide. After creating the table in the Database Desktop, you can enter the following five strings into five separate records:

Home
Work
Family
Local Business
Friend

The program loads these records into the TdbComboBox during the OnCreate method for the main form:

```
Table2.Open;
while not Table2.EOF do begin
  cbCategory.Items.Add(Table2.Fields[0].AsString);
  Table2.Next;
end;
Table2.Close;
```

The code shown here makes use of a second TTable object dropped onto the form. This object has its `DatabaseName` set to the address alias and its `TableName` property set to the CATS table.

To enable the user to change the contents of the CATS table, you can create a form like that shown in Figure 23.3. This form needs only contain minimal functionality, since it's best to discourage the user from changing the list except when absolutely necessary. Note that you need to add the CATS unit to the uses clause in order for this code to run.

FIGURE 23.3.

The Category Form enables the user to alter the contents of CATS.DB.

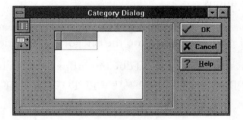

There is no need for the Category dialog, and the memory associated with it, to be created and allocated at program startup. As a result, you should open the Options | Project menu, select the Forms page, and move the Category dialog into the Available Forms column. In response to a selection of the Set Category menu item from the main form of the ADDRESS2 program, you can write the following code:

```
procedure TfrAddress.Category1Click(Sender: TObject);
begin
  CatsDlg := TCatsDlg.Create(Self);
  CatsDlg.ShowModal;
  CatsDlg.Free;
end;
```

This code creates the Category dialog, shows it to the user, and finally deallocates its memory after the user is done. This approach is taken because it assures that the Category dialog and CATS.DB are only in memory when absolutely necessary.

The skeletal structure of the ADDRESS2 program is starting to come together. However, there is one remaining task that must be completed before the core of the program is complete. There are a number of basic commands issued by the program, and these can be defined in a single enumerated type:

```
TCommandType = (btClose, btInsert, btPrior,
                btEdit, btNext, btCancel,
                btPrint, btFirst, btLast);
```

This type lets you associate each of the program's commands with the Tag field of the appropriate button or menu item, and to then associate all of these buttons or menu items with a single method that looks like this:

```
procedure TfrAddress.CommandClick(Sender: TObject);
begin
  case TCommandType((Sender as TComponent).Tag) of
    btClose: Close;
    btInsert: Table1.Insert;
    btPrior: Table1.Prior;
    btEdit: HandleEditMode;
    btNext: Table1.Next;
    btCancel: Table1.Cancel;
    btPrint: PrintData;
    btFirst: Table1.First;
    btLast: Table1.Last;
  end;
end;
```

All of the code in this program will compile at this stage except for the references to HandleEditMode and PrintData. For now, you can simply create dummy HandleEditMode and PrintData private methods and leave their contents blank.

There is no reason why you can't have a different method associated with each of the buttons and menu items in the program. However, its neater and simpler to handle things this way, and the code you create is much easier to read. The key point here is to be sure the Tag property of the appropriate control gets the correct value and that all of the controls listed here have the OnClick method manually set to the CommandClick method.

Here is a brief summary of the commands passed to the CommandClick method:

Command	Type	Name	Tag
Exit	TMenuItem	btClose	0
Insert	TButton	btInsert	1
Prior	TButton	btPrior	2
Edit	TButton	btEdit	3
Next	TButton	btNext	4
Cancel	TButton	btCancel	5
Print	TMenuItem	btPrint	6
First	TButton	btFirst	7
Last	TButton	btLast	8

At this stage, you are ready to run the ADDRESS2 program. You can now insert new data, iterate through the records you create, cancel accidental changes, and shut down the program from the menu. This is the bare functionality needed to run the program.

With the exception of the dropdown combo box for the Category field, there is nothing really new in the information presented so far for this chapter. However, the remaining portions of this chapter will tackle the issues that improve this program to the point that it might be useful in a real-world situation. All but the most obvious or irrelevant portions of the code for the ADDRESS2 program will be explained in detail in the remainder of this chapter.

It's important to note that a lot of the code ends up being considerably less formidable than it might appear at first glance. For instance, the code for the About dialog or the Category dialog is primarily created visually with very little effort on your part. Even the Search dialog, which is perhaps the most complicated of the utility dialogs, consists of nothing more than a dozen fairly straightforward lines of code. The code for the main form is bit more meaty, but most of it will become fairly transparent if you study the logic one step at a time.

Moving In and Out of Read-Only Mode

Perhaps the most important single function of the ADDRESS2 program is its capability to move in and out of read-only mode. This is valuable because it lets you open the program and browse through data without ever having to worry about accidentally altering a record. In fact, when you first open the program, it is impossible to type into any of the data-aware controls, which insures that there is no possible way to accidentally alter a record. The only way for the program to get into edit mode is for the user to press the Edit button, which then automatically makes the data live.

When the program is in read-only mode, the Insert and Cancel buttons are grayed out, and the Delete menu item is also dimmed. When you switch into edit mode, all of these controls become live and the text in the Edit button switches to read-only. All these visual clues help make the current mode of the program obvious to the user.

The functionality described is quite simple to implement. The key methods to trace are the `HandleEditMode` and `SetReadOnly` methods.

The `HandleEditMode` routine is called from the `CommandClick` method described in the last section:

```
procedure TfrAddress.HandleEditMode;
begin
  Insert.Enabled := not DataSource1.AutoEdit;
  Cancel.Enabled := not DataSource1.AutoEdit;
  Delete1.Enabled := not DataSource1.AutoEdit;
  if not DataSource1.AutoEdit then begin
    SetReadOnly(True);
    EEdit.Caption := 'ReadOnly'
  end else begin
    if Table1.State <> dsBrowse then Table1.Post;
    SetReadOnly(False);
    EEdit.Caption := 'Edit';
  end;
end;
```

The primary purpose of this code is to ensure that the proper components are enabled or disabled, depending on the current state of the program. After altering the appearance of the program, the code calls SetReadOnly:

```
procedure TfrAddress.SetReadOnly(NewState: Boolean);
begin
  DataSource1.AutoEdit := NewState;
end;
```

The center around which both of these routines revolve is the DataSource1.AutoEdit property. When this property is set to False, all the data-aware controls on the form are disabled and the user won't be able to type in them. When the property is set to True, the data becomes live and the user can edit or insert records.

Figure 23.4 shows ADDRESS2 in read-only mode.

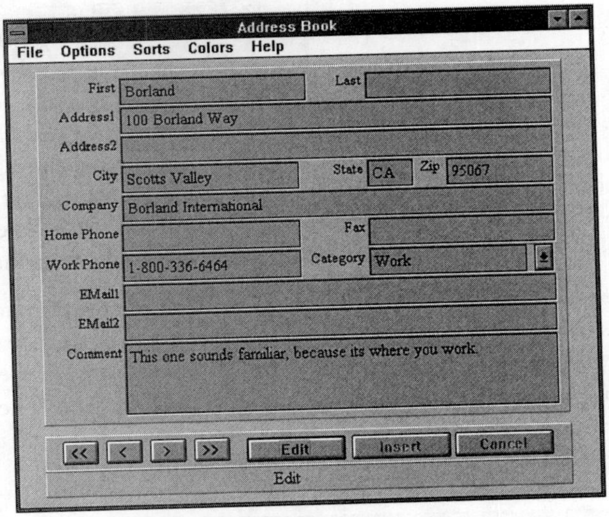

FIGURE 23.4.

ADDRESS2 as it appears in read-only mode.

The purpose of the AutoEdit property is to determine whether or not a keystroke from the user can put a table directly into edit mode. When AutoEdit is set to False, the user can't type information into a data-aware control. When AutoEdit is set to True, the user can switch the table into edit mode simply by typing a letter in a control. It's important to note that even when AutoEdit is set to False, you can set a table into edit mode by calling Table1.Edit or Table1.Insert. As a result, the technique shown here won't work unless you gray out the controls that give the user the power to set the table into edit mode. (See Figure 23.5.)

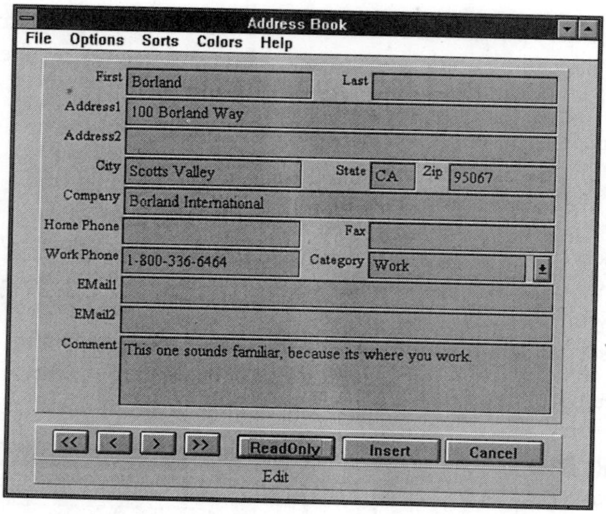

FIGURE 23.5.

The ADDRESS2 program as it appears in Edit mode.

The code in the HandleEditMode method is concerned entirely with interface issues. It enables or disables the Insert, Cancel, and Delete controls, depending on whether the table is about to go in or out of read-only mode. The code also ensures that the caption for the Edit button provides the user with a clue about the button's current function. In other words, the button doesn't report on the state of the program, but on the functionality associated with the button.

The HandleEditMode method is written so that the program is always moved into the opposite of its current state. At startup time, the table should be set to read-only mode (AutoEdit = False), and the appropriate controls should be disabled. Some of the code in the FormCreate method ensures that this is, in fact, the state of affairs at startup. Thereafter, every time you press the Edit button, the program will switch from its current state to the opposite state, from read-only mode to Edit mode, and then back again.

NOTE

Besides the TDataSource AutoEdit property, there is a second way to take a table in and out of read-only mode. This second method is really more powerful than the first, because it makes the table itself completely resistant to change. However, this second method is a bit more costly in terms of time and system resources. The trick, naturally enough, is to change the ReadOnly property of a TTable component. Here is how the SetReadOnly procedure would look if you employed this second technique:

```
procedure TfrAddress.SetReadOnly(NewState: Boolean);
var
  Bookmark: TBookmark;
begin
  Bookmark := Table1.GetBookMark;
  Table1.Close;
```

```
    Table1.ReadOnly := NewState;
    Table1.Open;
    Table1.GotoBookMark(Bookmark);
    Table1.FreeBookmark(Bookmark);
end;
```

It turns out that you cannot set a table in or out of read-only mode while it is open. Therefore, you have to close the table every time you change the ReadOnly property. Unfortunately, every time you close and open a table, you are moved back to the first record. As a result, it is necessary to set a bookmark identifying your current location in the table, close the table, and then move the table in or out of Read-Only mode. When you are done, you can open the table and jet back to the bookmark. This sounds like quite a bit of activity, but in fact it can usually be accomplished without the user being aware that anything untoward has occurred. The entire functionality described in this paragraph is encapsulated in the second version of the SetReadOnly method, shown previously. This is a classic method that you might have reason to reuse in many programs.

If you choose this second method, you would have to set the Table1.ReadOnly property to True at program startup and rewrite the HandleEditMode method so that it looks like this:

```
procedure TfrAddress.HandleEditMode;
begin
  Insert.Enabled := Table1.ReadOnly;
  Cancel.Enabled := Table1.ReadOnly;
  Delete1.Enabled := Table1.ReadOnly;
  if Table1.ReadOnly then begin
    SetReadOnly(False);
    EEdit.Caption := 'ReadOnly'
  end else begin
    if Table1.State <> dsBrowse then Table1.Post;
    SetReadOnly(True);
    EEdit.Caption := 'Edit';
  end;
end;
```

With the ADDRESS2 program, it is clear that the first technique for moving a program in and out of read-only mode is best. In other words, it's much faster and much easier to switch DataSource1 in and out of auto-edit mode than it is to switch Table1 in and out of read-only mode. However, I have shown you the second technique because there may be a time when you have to quickly open and close a table, and it is useful to have a routine to use in such cases.

On the whole, the act of moving ADDRESS2 in and out of read-only mode is fairly trivial. The key point to grasp is the power of the TDataSource AutoEdit method. Understand how it works, and you can provide this same functionality in all your programs.

Sorting Data

At various times, you might want the records stored in the program to be sorted by first name, last name, or company. These three possible options are encapsulated in the programs menu, as depicted in Figure 23.6, and also in an enumerated type declared in SEARCH.PAS:

```
TSortType = (stFirst, stLast, stCompany);
```

FIGURE 23.6.

The Sorts menu has three different options.

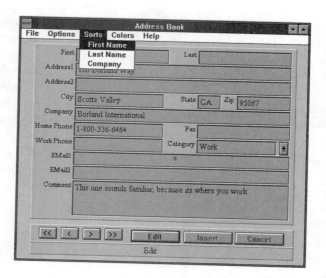

Once again, it is the Tag field from the Sorts dropdown menu that makes it possible to detect which option the user wants to select:

```
procedure TfrAddress.SortMenu(Sender: TObject);
begin
  FSortType := TSortType((Sender as TComponent).Tag);
  DoSort;
  DoSearch('A');
end;
```

FSortType is a field of TfrAddress that is declared to be of TSortType.

By now, this is an old trick that you have seen many times. The key point is to be sure to associate a different value between 0 and 2 for the Tag property of each menu item, and to then associate the SortMenu method with the OnClick event for each menuitem. If the Tag property for a menu item is zero, it gets translated into stFirst, and so on.

After finding out whether the user wants to sort by first name, last name, or company, you must perform the actual sort, which is done by simply changing indices:

```
procedure TFrAddress.DoSort;
begin
  case FSortType of
    stFirst: Table1.IndexName := 'FNameIndex';
    stLast: Table1.IndexName := 'LNameIndex';
    stCompany: Table1.IndexName := 'CompanyIndex';
  end;
end;
```

This is about as straightforward a method as you'll encounter. Changing an index involves nothing more than changing the index name property, and I have isolated this trivial chore in its own method so it can be called from multiple, and unrelated, locations in the source.

After sorting, there may be a group of blank records at the beginning of the table. For instance, if you choose to sort by the Company field, it is likely that many of the records in the AD-DRESS table will not have anything in the Company field. As a result, there could be several hundred, or even several thousand, records at the beginning of the table (which have no interest to someone who wants to view only companies). The solution, of course, is to search for the first record that has a non-blank value in the Company field. You can do this by searching for the record that has a company field that is nearest to matching the string 'A'. The actual details of searching for a record are covered in the next section.

That's all there is to sorting the records in the ADDRESS2 program. Clearly, this is not a difficult subject. The key points to grasp are that you must create secondary indices for all the fields you want to sort on, and then performing the sort becomes as simple as swapping indices, one to another.

Searching for Data

Searching for data in a table would seem like an extremely simple subject; and indeed it is quite straightforward, except for one minor catch. The problem, of course, is that when working with local tables, you can only use the GotoKey or GotoNearest methods on fields that are currently keyed. In other words, if you want to search on the Company field, it's not enough to simply declare a secondary index called CompanyIndex. To perform an actual search, you must make the CompanyIndex the active index and then perform the search. As a result, before you can make a search, you must do three things:

1. Ask the user for the string he or she wants to find.
2. Ask the user for the field where the string resides.
3. Set the index to the proper field.

Only after jumping through each of these hoops are you free to perform the actual search.

> **NOTE**
>
> It's important to note that some databases don't force you to search only on actively keyed fields. Some networked servers, for instance, don't have this limitation. But local Paradox and dBASE tables are restricted in this manner, so you must use the techniques described here when searching for fields in these databases.

To find out what string and field interests the user, the ADDRESS2 program pops up the dialog shown in Figure 23.7. This dialog contains three radio buttons and an edit control, along with a few buttons.

FIGURE 23.7.

The Search Dialog from the ADDRESS2 program.

The code to call the Search Dialog is simple enough:

```
procedure TfrAddress.Search1Click(Sender: TObject);
var
  S: string;
begin
  if not SearchDlg.GetSearchStr(FSortType, S) then Exit;
  DoSort;
  DoSearch(S);
end;
```

This code retrieves the relevant string and search field, calls the DoSort method, and finally calls a method that performs the actual search. Here is the code for the GetSearchStr method:

```
function TSearchDlg.GetSearchStr(var ST: TSortType; var S: string):
  Boolean;
begin
  Result := False;

  if ShowModal = mrCancel then Exit;

  S := Edit1.Text;

  if FirstName.Checked then
    ST := stFirst
  else if LastName.Checked then
    ST := stLast
  else
    ST := stCompany;
```

```
    Result := True;
  end;
```

This code first pops up the Search Dialog in Modal mode. If the user selects the OK button, the selected string is retrieved and the selected radio button is translated into a variable of type TSortType. In other words, the user must select a string to search on and also press a radio button in order to indicate the field he or she believes contains the string.

If the GetSearchStr method returns True, the Search1Click method calls DoSort, which sets the current index to the field that interests the user. Since the program now knows the string that needs to be found and since the index has been set to the appropriate field, it is now safe to perform a search:

```
procedure TfrAddress.DoSearch(S: string);
begin
  Table1.SetKey;
  case FSortType of
    stFirst: Table1.FieldByName('FName').AsString := S;
    stLast:Table1.FieldByName('LName').AsString := S;
    stCompany:Table1.FieldByName('Company').AsString := S;
  end;
  Table1.GotoNearest;
end;
```

The DoSearch method sets the table into SetKey mode and then tells the table to look for a particular string in the field that is currently indexed. Finally, Table1.GotoNearest is called and the table is brought as close to the sought-after record as possible.

This sounds a bit complex, but it has some hidden virtues. Since the table has already been indexed on the appropriate field, you will find that you can perform partial searches that take you near to the record you seek, even if you can't remember its exact spelling. For instance, if you know someone's name begins with Gab, but can't recall if the rest is Gabfest, Gabfald, or Gabheld, you can search on the string Gab and iterate forward from that point in search of the record in question. This is the technique used by the SortMenu method when it calls DoSearch with A as its parameter.

Once again, it turns out that the actual code for searching for data in a Paradox table is fairly straightforward. There is a curve thrown at you here because you are forced to set the table to a particular index before you can search for a value, but even this seeming inconvenience can turn out to have some fairly important hidden benefits. However, you should remember that many networked servers enable you to search on fields that are not currently part of the active index.

Filtering Data

It turns out that setting up a filter and performing a search are very similar tasks. The first step is to find out the string the user wants to use as a filter. To do this, you can call the Filter dialog, passing it the contents of the cbCategory combo box as a parameter:

```
function TFilterDlg.GetFilter(SList: TStrings): string;
begin
  ListBox1.Items := SList;
  if ShowModal = mrCancel then
    Result := ''
  else
    Result := ListBox1.Items.Strings[ListBox1.ItemIndex];
end;
```

This code accepts the list from the combo box as a parameter, displays it inside a listbox, and shows the Filter form as a modal dialog. If the user presses OK, the GetFilter function returns the selected string. If Cancel is pressed, an empty string is returned.

After retrieving the string, the ADDRESS2 program sets up the CategoryIndex and then performs a normal filter operation:

```
procedure TfrAddress.Filter1Click(Sender: TObject);
var
  S: string;
begin
  S := FilterDlg.GetFilter(cbCategory.Items);
  if S = '' then Exit;
  Table1.IndexName := 'CategoryIndex';
  Table1.SetRangeStart;
  Table1.FieldByName('Category').AsString := S;
  Table1.SetRangeEnd;
  Table1.FieldByName('Category').AsString := S;
  Table1.ApplyRange;
end;
```

This is a simple process that lets you narrow the number of records displayed at any one time. The key point to remember is that this whole process works only because the user enters data in the Category field by selecting strings from a dropdown combo box. Without the TdbComboBox, the number of options in the Category field would likely become unmanageable.

In actual practice, the act of filtering a set of records may prove to be only minimally useful at runtime. However, when you need to print a set of records, these filters can prove to be very helpful.

Printing Records

This book is not meant to be a commentary on ReportSmith. However, I will touch on this subject briefly, just to give you a few clues about how to proceed. If you want in-depth knowledge of ReportSmith, you should turn to a book on that subject or read the fairly straightforward manuals that ship with that product. Having said this, I have to add that ReportSmith is extremely easy to use, and after three or four sessions with the product you will probably know your way around without having to refer to the manual more than once or twice.

To start creating a report, bring up ReportSmith using Tools | ReportSmith and select the type of report you want to make, which is probably a label-based report. Go to the Tables page in the Report Query dialog, choose Add Table, and select ADDRESS.DB.

Next, go to the Report Variables page and create a new variable called Filter. Set its type to String, its Title to Filter List, and the prompt to "What filter do you want to use?" Set the Entry to Type-in, as shown in Figure 23.8. When you are done, choose Add.

> **NOTE**
>
> You do not have to choose Type-in as the Entry method. In fact, the ADDRESS2 program is ideally suited for using the "Choose from a Table" method. After you select this method, a space will appear in the bottom-right corner of the Report Variables page that lets you choose a table and field that contain a list of available entries. In this case, you can choose the CATS.DB table and the Category field. Now when the user wants to run the report, he or she will be prompted with a list of valid categories and can choose the appropriate one, without the likelihood of an error being introduced.

FIGURE 23.8.

Creating Report Variables in ReportSmith.

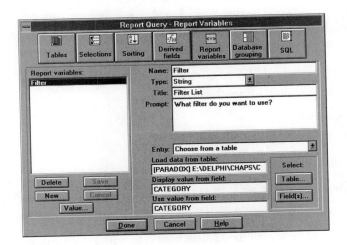

Turn to the Selections page, click the yellow number "1" in the center of the page, and choose "Select SQL selection criteria" from the dropdown list. Select the Category field from the DataFields listbox on the left, and choose "x=y" from the Comparison Operators in the middle listbox. Go back to the left-hand listbox and change the combo box at the top so it reads "Report Variables" rather than "Data Fields." Choose Filter, and then set this variable in quotes:

```
'ADDRESSxDB'.'CATEGORY' = '<<Filter>>'
```

When you are done, the dialog should like that in Figure 23.9. Now click the OK button at the bottom of the dialog.

FIGURE 23.9.

Creating SQL Selection Criteria in ReportSmith.

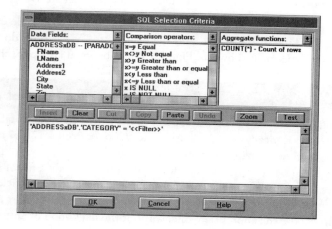

The final step in this process is to create derived fields in the Derived Fields page of the Report Query dialog. The first derived field should combine the FName and LName fields, so you might want to call this field FirstLast. After typing in the name, select Add, and the Edit Derived Fields dialog box will appear. Select FName from the left column:

```
'ADDRESSxDB'.'FName'
```

Choose Addition from the middle column:

```
'ADDRESSxDB'.'FName' +
```

Add a space by writing the string ' ':

```
'ADDRESSxDB'.'FName' + ' '
```

Choose Addition again from the middle column:

```
'ADDRESSxDB'.'FName' + ' ' +
```

And end by adding the LName field. The string you create should look like this:

```
'ADDRESSxDB'.'FName' + ' ' + 'ADDRESSxDB'.'LName'
```

This statement will combine the FName and LName fields so that they produce a single string out of a first and last name:

```
Kurt Weill
```

You should then create a second derived field called CityStateZip, which combines the City, State, and Zip fields:

```
'ADDRESSxDB'.'CITY' + ', ' + 'ADDRESSxDB'.'STATE' + ' '  +
  'ADDRESSxDB'.'ZIP'
```

You have created the logic behind a report, and you should choose Done from the bottom of the Report Query dialog. ReportSmith will then pop up a dialog to fill in the report variable you created. In other words, it's time for you to fill in the Filter portion of the following statement:

```
'ADDRESSxDB'.'CATEGORY' = '<<Filter>>'
```

You can type the word Family, Work, or whatever value you feel will return a reasonably sized dataset.

The Insert Field dialog now appears, and you can enter the fields and derived fields that you have created. The combo box at the top of the dialog enables you to switch back and forth between data fields and derived fields; you should do so when you deem appropriate. For instance, the first field you select will probably be the derived fields called FirstLast, whereas the second will probably be the data field called Address1. When you are done, the report you create should look something like the image shown in Figure 23.10.

FIGURE 23.10.

A "live data" label report produced by ReportSmith.

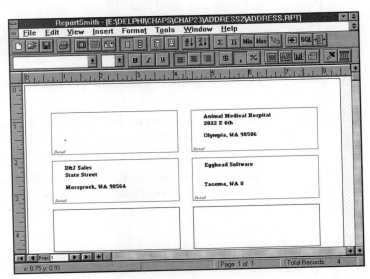

Even the report shown here is probably not totally complete; you might want to rearrange the location of the fields inside each label and change the size and location of each individual label. You will find that you can move individual fields around by simply dragging them with the mouse. The actual decisions you make will be based on your personal tastes and on the type of labels you have in your office or home. When you are performing these tasks, you will probably find it easiest to do so by choosing the File | Page Setup menu option from the ReportSmith main menu.

If you want to change the fonts used in your report, select one of the fields in a label, right-click the page, and choose Character from the popup menu. Other options, such as adjusting borders and field height, and inserting pictures, are available when you right-click a report.

When you are completely finished preparing a report, choose File | Save to save the report you have created under the name Address, in the same directory where the ADDRESS2 program resides.

As I stated previously, this brief tutorial on ReportSmith is not meant to be anything more than a very loosely structured primer. ReportSmith is very easy to use, and most of the actions you will perform are intuitive variations on the simple steps already outlined. However, you will probably also want to study the ReportSmith manuals, the online help, and perhaps a third-party book dedicated to this subject.

> **NOTE**
>
> ReportSmith has a fairly sophisticated query builder in the Selections page of the Report Query Dialog. On several occasions, I have actually abandoned Delphi's query builder and opened up ReportSmith to construct a SQL statement. When I'm done, I just block copy the SQL code from ReportSmith into the SQL property of my current Delphi TQuery object. This is a major kluge, but under some circumstances you might want to consider it as an option.

As easy as it is to use ReportSmith, it is even easier to link this tool into a standard Delphi program.

Drop a TReport object on a form and set the ReportName to the name of the report you want to use. You can resolve the path to the report at run time, by calling the GetPath method, which will be described later in this chapter.

The actual code for printing the report is encapsulated in the PrintData method. As you recall, you blocked out the code from this method when you were setting up the CommandClick method. Here is the code for PrintData:

```
procedure TfrAddress.PrintData;
begin
  Cursor := crHourGlass;
  Report1.ReportDir := GetPath;
  Report1.Run;
  Cursor := crDefault;
end;
```

This routine finds the path in which ADDRESS.RPT resides, and then it loads ReportSmith by calling Report1.Run. As long as you have the RS_RUN subdirectory on your path, the ReportSmith runtime will load automatically after a call to Run, and you can then enter the name of the category you want to set up as a filter. Since ReportSmith can take a few moments to load, you should probably set the program's cursor to crHourGlass before calling Run.

It's important to understand that there are two versions of ReportSmith. The main version of the program resides in the RPTSMITH subdirectory. This is the version you should use when you are designing reports. The runtime version of ReportSmith resides in the RS_RUN subdirectory; it is the one you can distribute with your programs. Specifically, it is RS_RUN.EXE that gets loaded when you are running a Delphi program.

After RS_RUN is loaded, you have two options. If you have set the AutoUnload property to True, ReportSmith will be taken out of memory automatically after the print job finishes. However, since it takes a while for RS_RUN to load, you might want to leave it running while you complete several print jobs. To do this, just set AutoUnload to False. You can then perform your print jobs and close RS_RUN by calling CloseApplication and passing it a Boolean parameter specifying whether the program should prompt the user to save reports, and so on. Because CloseApplication uses DDE commands, it is possible that the routine might fail. As a result, you should test to see if CloseApplication succeeds and repeat the command if it fails:

```
function CloseReportSmith: Boolean;
begin
  Result := Report1.CloseApplication(False);
end;
```

It is possible to set up macros inside ReportSmith. The RunMacro method of TReport can be used to execute a ReportSmith macro. RunMacro takes a single parameter, which is the name of the report you want to run.

You can pass parameters to ReportSmith by using the InitialValues field. The InitialValues fields lets you automatically pass a string to ReportSmith, rather than having the user type in a value in a dialog. In short, you can pass the category you want to filter via the InitialValues field, and then the user will not need to enter the value. This can be particularly useful if you want to set up error-free input methods.

NOTE

As mentioned, ReportSmith can associate a table with a report variable, thereby letting the user select a value from the table, rather than typing it in. In my experience, this technique works fine and may be preferable to using the InitialValues field.

You should also note that it is possible to change a report variable at runtime by using the SetVariable and SetVariableLines methods. After using these methods, you should call ReCalcReport to make sure that ReportSmith assimilates the changes you have made. SetVariable and SetVariableLines use DDE, so you should test to make sure the calls succeed.

Another property of TReport that you might want to use is that the Preview property, which lets a user determine whether the correct report has been generated. You can use the MaxRecords and StartPage properties to control the number of records that ReportSmith prints.

In future versions of Delphi, it is likely that ReportSmith will be faster and more tightly integrated with your programs. For now, however, you will find that ReportSmith is an adequate tool that has the enormous advantage of being easy to use. In fact, ReportSmith is so easy to use that it turns the task of generating reports into something very similar to play. As a result, you can quickly and easily generate very elegant looking reports, and then get back to the more interesting task of writing code.

Setting Colors

The Colors menu, shown in Figure 23.11, lets you set the colors for most of the major objects in the program. The goal is not to give the user complete control over every last detail in the program, but to let him or her customize the most important features.

FIGURE 23.11.

The options under the Colors menu enable you to change the appearance of the ADDRESS2 program.

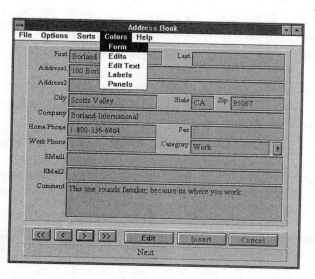

The ColorClick method uses the time-honored method of declaring an enumerated type and then sets up the Tag property from a menu item to specify the selection of a particular option. Here is the enumerated type in question:

```
TColorType = (ccForm, ccEdit, ccEditText, ccLabel, ccPanel);
```

The routine begins by enabling the user to select a color from the Colors dialog and then assigns that color to the appropriate controls:

```
procedure TfrAddress.ColorClick(Sender: TObject);
begin
  if not ColorDialog1.Execute then Exit;
  case TColorType((Sender as TMenuItem).Tag) of
    ccForm: frAddress.Color := ColorDialog1.Color;
    ccEdit: SetEdits(tcColor, ColorDialog1.Color);
```

```
    ccEditText: SetEdits(tcFontColor, ColorDialog1.Color);
    ccLabel: SetLabels(ColorDialog1.Color);
    ccPanel: SetPanels(ColorDialog1.Color);
  end;
  SetIni(TColorType((Sender as TMenuItem).Tag), ColorDialog1.Color);
end;
```

If the user wants to change the form's color, the code to do so is simple enough:

```
ccForm: frAddress.Color := ColorDialog1.Color;
```

However, it is a more complicated process to change the color of all the data-aware controls. To accomplish this goal, the ColorClick method calls the SetEdits routine:

```
procedure TfrAddress.SetEdits(TypeChange: TChangeType;
                              NewValue: TColor);
var
  i: Integer;
begin
  for i := 0 to ComponentCount - 1 do
    if (Components[i] is TdbEdit) or
       (Components[i] is TdbComboBox) or
       (Components[i] is TdbMemo) then
      case TypeChange of
        tcColor: TdbEdit(Components[i]).Color := NewValue;
        tcFontColor: TdbEdit(Components[i]).Font.Color := NewValue;
      end;
end;
```

This code iterates though all the components belonging to the main form of the program and checks to see if any of them are TdbEdits, TdbComboBoxes, or TdbMemos. When it finds a hit, the code casts the control as a TdbEdit and sets its color to the new value selected by the user:

```
tcColor: TdbEdit(Components[i]).Color := NewValue;
```

This code will very quickly change all the data-aware controls on the form to a new color.

The SetEdits routine works for both setting the color of the data-aware controls themselves, and for setting the fonts displayed in these controls. To tell which property the user wants to change at any particular moment, the SetEdits routine uses the following enumerated type:

```
TChangeType = (tcColor, tcFontColor);
```

The code for setting labels and panels works exactly the same way as the code for the data-aware controls. The only difference is that you don't need to worry about looking for multiple types of components:

```
procedure TfrAddress.SetLabels(C: TColor);
var
  i: Integer;
begin
  for i := 0 to ComponentCount - 1 do
    if (Components[i] is TLabel) then
      TLabel(Components[i]).Font.Color := C;
```

```
end;

procedure TfrAddress.SetPanels(C: TColor);
var
  i: Integer;
begin
  for i := 0 to ComponentCount - 1 do
    if (Components[i] is TPanel) then
      TPanel(Components[i]).Color := C;
end;
```

When working with the colors of the program, the final step is to make sure the program "remembers" the user's selections. To do this, ADDRESS2 makes use of an INI file that looks something like this:

```
[Colors]
Form=8421440
Edits=8421376
EditText=0
Labels=0
Panels=12639424
```

This INI file has only one section, which contains five different items, one for each of the colors specified by the user. The colors themselves are stored as integers, each representing one of the possible values captured in the TColor enumerated type.

> **NOTE**
>
> In this chapter, I assume that all readers are familiar with INI files. The most common INI files are WIN.INI and SYSTEM.INI. However, most major programs have their own INI files, such as the DELPHI.INI file that is stored in the WINDOWS subdirectory. These files are used to store settings for a program; you can read more about them in any good book on Windows basics. In Windows 95, INI files will still be supported, but a new technique involving a single system-wide register file will be phased in as a better and more sophisticated means of tracking program settings.

The following code writes new values to the INI file:

```
procedure TfrAddress.SetIni(CType: TColorType; C: TColor);
var
  Ini: TIniFile;
  Path, S: string;
begin
  Ini := TIniFile.Create(GetPath + 'address.ini');
  case CType of
    ccForm: S := 'Form';
    ccEdit: S := 'Edits';
    ccEditText: S := 'EditText';
    ccLabel: S := 'Labels';
    ccPanel: S := 'Panels';
  end;
  Ini.WriteInteger('Colors', S, C);
```

```
    Ini.Free;
end;
```

This method takes advantage of the TIniFile type, which is found in a source file, called INIFILES.PAS, that ships with Delphi.

You create a TIniFile object by passing in the name of the INI file you want to work with to the object's Create method:

```
Ini := TIniFile.Create(GetPath + 'address.ini');
```

The GetPath method performs some hand-waving to return the subdirectory from which the ADDRESS2 program was launched. In particular, it uses the built-in ParamStr function to get the name and path of the ADDRESS2 executable; then it strips off the name of the executable by using the StripLastToken function from the STRBOX unit. Finally, it returns the path with a backslash (\) appended on to the end of it:

```
function TfrAddress.GetPath: string;
var
  Path: string;
begin
  Path := ParamStr(0);
  Path := StripLastToken(Path, '\');
  Result := Path + '\';
end;
```

Before discussing the key methods of TIniFile, I should mention that after you are through with the object, you must deallocate the memory you created for it:

```
Ini.Free;
```

There are a number of methods you might want to call between the time you create a TIniFile object and the time you free it. However, you cannot call these methods successfully without first allocating memory for the object, and you must free that memory when you are through with the object.

Windows supplies a set of functions called GetPrivateProfileString, WritePrivateProfileString, GetPrivateProfileInt, and WritePrivateProfileInt that let you talk with INI files. These routines work well enough, and they are fairly easy to use; but they expect you to pass in PChars in their numerous parameters. TIniFile simplifies this process by enabling you to pass in Pascal strings rather than PChars. For instance, the WriteInteger method replaces WritePrivateProfileInt:

```
procedure WriteInteger(const Section, Ident: string;
                       Value: LongInt);
```

This function expects the name of a section in the first parameter, the name of an item in the second parameter, and the value you want to write in the third parameter. For instance, the INI file has an entry in it labeled Form. if you wanted to change the Form entry to black, you would enter the following code:

```
WriteInteger('Colors', 'Form', 0);
```

This will change the Form entry in the INI file to zero:

```
[Colors]
Form=0
```

With this knowledge in hand, it's easy enough to go back to the SetIni function and see exactly how it works. The key, of course, is simply that the second parameter passed to WriteInteger is designated by using an enumerated type in a case statement:

```
case CType of
  ccForm: S := 'Form';
  ccEdit: S := 'Edits';
  ccEditText: S := 'EditText';
  ccLabel: S := 'Labels';
  ccPanel: S := 'Panels';
end;
Ini.WriteInteger('Colors', S, C);
```

It's not enough, however, simply to write the values to an INI files. You must also read these values whenever the program starts. Here's how you can read an integer value from an INI file:

```
function TfrAddress.GetIni(CType: TColorType): TColor;
var
  Ini: TIniFile;
  Path, S: string;
begin
  Ini := TIniFile.Create(GetPath + 'address.Ini');
  case CType of
    ccForm: S := 'Form';
    ccEdit: S := 'Edits';
    ccEditText: S := 'EditText';
    ccLabel: S := 'Labels';
    ccPanel: S := 'Panels';
  end;
  Result := Ini.ReadInteger('Colors', S, clBlue);
  Ini.Free;
end;
```

This code is almost the exact reverse of the SetIni method, except that ReadInteger takes a default value in its last parameter. This default value will be returned if the program is unable to locate the INI file, or if it can't find the item requested in the INI file.

The code in the FormCreate method that calls the GetIni method looks like this:

```
for i := 0 to 4 do
  case TColorType(i) of
    ccForm: Color := GetIni(TColorType(i));
    ccEdit: SetEdits(tcColor, GetIni(TColorType(i)));
    ccEditText: SetEdits(tcFontColor, GetIni(TColorType(i)));
    ccLabel: SetLabels(GetIni(TColorType(i)));
    ccPanel: SetPanels(GetIni(TColorType(i)));
  end;
```

Though somewhat complex, this code should be fairly easy to understand at this stage, since you have already seen all the various routines called in this loop. It's just a question of bringing them all together so the program can read the INI file and set the appropriate controls to the appropriate colors.

There is always the possibility that the INI file in question does not exist or cannot be found. In such a case, the ADDRESS2 program is smart enough to create a new INI file containing default values:

```
procedure TfrAddress.CheckForIni;
var
  F: System.Text;
  Path: string;
begin
  Path := GetPath + 'address.ini';
  if not FileExists(Path) then begin
    System.Assign(F, Path);
    System.ReWrite(F);
    System.WriteLn(F, '[Colors]');
    System.WriteLn(F, 'Form=7045184');
    System.WriteLn(F, 'Edits=8421376');
    System.WriteLn(F, 'EditText=0');
    System.WriteLn(F, 'Labels=0');
    System.WriteLn(F, 'Panels=12639424');
    System.Close(F);
  end;
end;
```

The `CheckForIni` routine is called from the `FormCreate` method. It begins by using the built-in `FileExists` method to check for the existence of the INI file. If the file can't be found, a new one is created, using standard text file operations.

In this section, you have learned how to change the colors of components at runtime and how to save the value of these colors in an INI file. The key fact you learned is that you can use the `Components` array to iterate through the components owned by a form, and can check to see the type of each component you iterate past. When you find a component of a particular type, you can then perform a typecast and change its color.

Summary

You have had a chance to look at all the major portions of the ADDRESS2 program. The only items not mentioned in this chapter were the construction of the About dialog and the use of the Gallery to expedite the creation of some of the forms. These techniques have been examined in previous chapters, so you shouldn't find them challenging. You should remember that you can select a form from the gallery whenever the Options | Environment | Preferences | Gallery: Use on New Form checkbox is selected.

I went into such detail about the ADDRESS2 program because it contains many of the features that need to be included in real-world programs. As stated earlier, the ADDRESS2 program isn't quite up to the standards expected from a professional program, but it does answer some questions about how you can take the raw database tools described in the last few chapters and use them to create a useful program.

Working with the Local Interbase Server

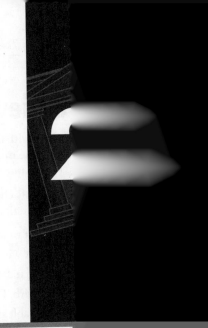

Overview

Delphi ships with the Local Interbase Server, which is sometimes simply called LIBS. This tool provides all the capabilities of a real Interbase server, but it runs on a local machine. In other words, you do not need to be connected to a network in order to run the Local Interbase Server.

The goal of this chapter is to provide a useful introduction to the LIBS and also a brief overview of Transactions. In particular, you will see how to do the following:

- Connect to local Interbase tables
- Connect without having to specify a password
- Create databases
- Work with TDatabase objects
- Create tables
- Commit and roll back transactions
- Maintain the data you have created

Almost everything that is said about the local Interbase applies equally to the full server version of Interbase, so this chapter will also be of interest to people who use Interbase on a network.

You will also see the outline of another sample database program, this one used for maintaining lists of CDs. It will run on local Interbase tables. The highlight of this database is its capability to organize records into a series of categories and subcategories.

Almost all readers of this book will find this an interesting topic. However, readers who also have access to the full-blown version of Interbase will find that this chapter is invaluable, because it shows how you can use a local system to create a database that is fully compatible with the network version of Interbase.

Some readers of this book are going to come from the world of "big iron," where the only kinds of databases that exist are servers such as Oracle, Sybase, Interbase, and DB2. Other readers are going to come from the world of PCs, where tools such as dBASE, Paradox, Access, FoxPro are considered to be the standard database tools. It is almost impossible to overemphasize the huge gap that exists between these two worlds.

Readers who are familiar with "big iron" and large network-based servers are likely to find the local Interbase very familiar. Readers who come from the world of PCs are likely to find the local Interbase very strange indeed, especially at first.

The key point to understand is that Interbase is meant to handle huge numbers of records, which are stored on servers. As such, it does not come equipped with many of the amenities of a tool such as dBASE or Paradox. In fact, Interbase supplies users with only the most minimal interface, and instead expects you to create programs with another front end such as Delphi.

Setting up the Local Interbase

The local Interbase is installed for you automatically when you install Delphi. However, there are several key steps you should take to ensure that it is set up properly.

First, you need to know where your copy of IBLocal is installed. Most likely, it is in the IBLOCAL subdirectory on the drive where you installed Delphi. For instance, my copy of the local Interbase is in C:\IBLOCAL.

In the IBLOCAL subdirectory, you find a copy of a file called INTERBAS.MSG. You should have a setting in your environment that points to this file. In other words, before booting Windows, you should type the following at the DOS prompt:

```
SET INTERBASE=C:\IBLOCAL
```

Of course, you should type in the path that leads to your copy of INTERBAS.MSG. The simplest way to perform this chore is to simply add the preceding SET statement to your AUTOEXEC.BAT file, and then reboot your computer. Thereafter the statement will be part of your environment every time you start your machine.

You should also make sure that the following lines appear in your WIN.INI:

```
[InterBase]
RootDirectory=c:\iblocal
```

Of course, the path you specify should lead to your version of Interbase.

The final step you need to take is to make sure that the key Interbase DLLs are on your path. These files are located in the \IBLOCAL\BIN subdirectory. Therefore, my path statement looks something like this:

```
path=c:\dos;c:\windows;c:\delphi;c:\iblocal\bin;etc...
```

The key DLLs used by the local Interbase are as follows:

```
GDS.DLL
REMOTE.DLL
JRD.DLL
```

JRD.DLL is where most of the functionality of Interbase is located. GDS.DLL and REMOTE.DLL are used to connect your program to the heart of the Interbase server. There are several other important Interbase DLLs that should always be present:

```
DSQL.DLL
FILEIO.DLL
INTL.DLL
IUTLS.DLL
STACK.DLL
```

However, the core files are GDS, REMOTE, and JRD.

A common problem occurs when Interbase users end up with more than one copy of either GDS.DLL or REMOTE.DLL on their path. If you work with the networked version of Interbase, you probably already have a copy of the Interbase Client on your system. If this is the case, you should make sure that you don't have two sets of the file GDS.DLL on your path. On my system, I use the copy of GDS.DLL and REMOTE.DLL that comes with the local Interbase. These tools communicate with both IBLocal and the full networked version of Interbase. This setup works fine for me, and it greatly simplifies my life.

It's important to note that it not necessary to be running TCP/IP, or any other network protocol, in order to talk the local Interbase. In other words, you could reformat your hard drive, and then load DOS, Windows 3.1, and IBLocal onto your machine—and you would be able to talk to the local Interbase. You don't need WINSOCK.DLL, or any other network files, to talk to the local Interbase.

> **NOTE**
>
> Readers who want to connect to the full server version of Interbase will find that the prescription I have just outlined works fine, except that you must have a network protocol such as TCP/IP loaded first. This book does not include a description of the wizardry needed to successfully set up a network protocol. I assume that you will turn to another source in order to learn how to Ping your server, and how to test the connection with a few simple FTP sessions. When you have gotten that far, you can open this book and follow the directions I give here.
>
> Almost everything I have said about databases in this book applies equally to local databases and servers. The key point is that you have to set up the network connection first, and then turn to this book to learn how Delphi talks to databases. I am, of course, fully aware of how difficult and frustrating it can be to set up a network connection, and how little clear and easy-to-understand prose there is on the subject. Nevertheless, it is simply too large a topic for me to attempt to tackle in this book. My goal here is to write about Delphi, and you will have to turn elsewhere to learn about setting up network connections. You should look in the DOC subdirectory on the CD that ships with this book and see if I have some notes there that reference the DLLs used by several important servers.

When you have the local Interbase set up, you should take a few minutes to make sure the connection is working correctly. In particular, you should establish an alias that points to one of the sample tables that ship with IBLOCAL. For instance, you can set up an alias that points to the EMPLOYEE.GDB file installed by Delphi.

To create the alias, open BDECFG.EXE and turn to the Alias page. Create a new alias called TESTGDB and set its type as INTERBAS. The server name for this alias should be set to

```
c:\iblocal\examples\employee.gdb
```

where the drive letter and path can be adjusted for the way you have set up the files on your home machine.

The user name should be set to SYSDBA, and the password you will use is MASTERKEY. All the other settings can have their default values, as shown in Figure 24.1.

FIGURE 24.1.

A sample Interbase alias, as it appears in BDECFG.EXE.

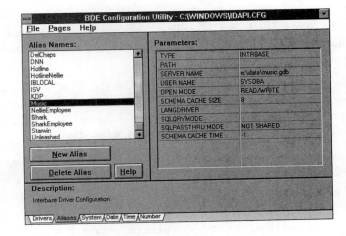

After you have set up and saved your alias, you can close BDECFG.EXE and open either Delphi or the Database Desktop. You can then proceed to connect to the EMPLOYEE database exactly as you would any other set of data. For instance, if you are using Delphi, you drop a table onto a form, and set its `DatabaseName` property to TESTGDB. When you try to drop down the list of `TableNames`, you are prompted for a password. You should enter `masterkey` at this point, all in lowercase. After taking these steps, you can set the `Active` property for Table1 to `True`. If this call succeeds, everything is set up correctly and you can begin using the local Interbase to create Delphi database programs. If you can't set `Active` to `True`, you should go over the steps outlined previously and see whether you can correct the problem.

NOTE

I usually use SYSDBA and MASTERKEY as the user name and password combination for the databases in this book. However, I will sometimes add USER1 and USER1 instead, simply because it is easier to type in USER1 than it is to type in MASTERKEY.

If you are having trouble setting up a LIBS alias, note that the Delphi Install program sets up a sample alias called IBLOCAL that points at the EMPLOYEE.GDB file that ships with Delphi.

In this section, you have learned the basic facts about using IBLocal. The next step is to learn how to create your own databases and tables. This subject is covered in the next section.

Creating Databases

Unlike local Paradox or dBASE files, Interbase tables are not stored inside separate files located inside a directory. Instead, Interbase tables are stored inside one large file called a database. This means that you need to first go out and create a database, and then you can create a series of tables inside this larger database.

The simplest way to create a database is with the WISQL program that ships with the Local Interbase Server. WISQL stands for Windows Interactive Standard Query Language, or simply the Interactive SQL tool. WISQL is fundamentally a tool for entering SQL statements, with a few other simple features thrown in for good measure.

> **NOTE**
>
> Besides WISQL, the other important tool that ships with Interbase is IBMGR.EXE. The Interbase Server Manager, IBMGR.EXE, enables you to test connections to servers and perform simple maintenance tasks such as backing up and restoring databases, and setting passwords. You can use IBMGR to back up your data so that you can recover if disaster strikes. This tool is described in the Interbase documentation and will not be mentioned further in this book.

After starting up WISQL, choose Create Database from the File menu. A dialog like the one shown in Figure 24.2 appears. For the server name, you can simply select the name of the drive where you want the database to reside. Don't append anything to the drive letter. For instance, if you want the database to appear on the C drive, simply enter the letter c, unadorned, with no quotes around it or other syntax after it.

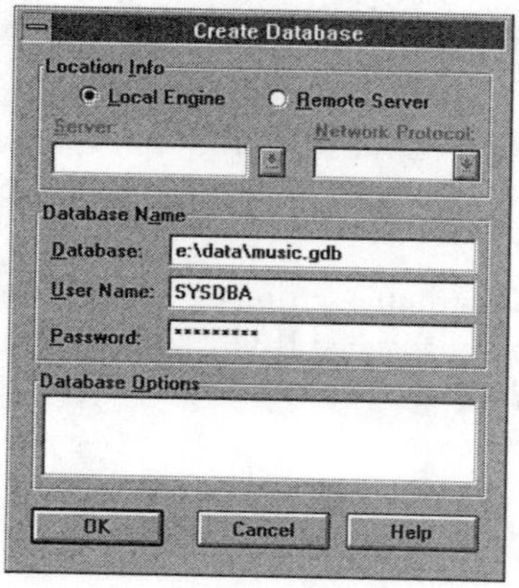

FIGURE 24.2.

The dialog used for creating
databases inside of WISQL.

Because you are working with local Interbase, in fact, there is no need for an active network protocol.

In the Database field, enter the name of the table you want to create. If the table is to be located inside a directory, include that directory in the database name. For practice, you should create a database called INFO.GDB that is located in a subdirectory called DATA. If it does not already exist on your system, you should first go to DOS and create the DATA subdirectory. When you are all set up, enter the following in the Database field:

```
E:\DATA\INFO.GDB
```

where `E:` can be replaced by the letter of the appropriate drive on your system. The extension GDB is traditional, though not mandatory. However, I would suggest always using this extension so that you can recognize your databases instantly when you see them. It can be a tragedy if you accidentally delete a database.

The user name can be set to anything you want, although the traditional entry is SYSDBA, and the traditional password is MASTERKEY. When you first start out with Interbase, it is probably best to stick with this user name and password combination. Even if you assign new passwords to your database, the SYSDBA / MASTERKEY combination will still work unless you explicitly remove it.

After you have entered a user name and password, you can create the database by clicking the OK button. You are then placed back inside WISQL proper. At this stage you can either quit WISQL, or add a table to your database.

The following SQL statement can be run inside WISQL if you want to create a very simple table with two fields:

```
CREATE TABLE TEST1 (FIRST VARCHAR(20), LAST INTEGER);
```

Enter this line in the SQL Statement field at the top of WISQL, and then press the Run button. If all goes smoothly, your statement will be echoed in the ISQL output window without being accompanied by an error dialog. The lack of an error dialog signals that the table has been successfully created. The preceding code creates a table with two fields. The first is a character field containing 20 characters, and the second is an integer field.

After creating a database and table, you should select Commit Work from the File menu. This command causes WISQL to actually carry out the commands you have issued. At this stage you should choose File | Disconnect from Database.

In this section, you have learned the basic steps required to use Interbase to create a database and table. The steps involved are not particularly complicated, although they can take a bit of getting used to if you are new to the world of server tools.

Exploring a Database with WISQL

WISQL provides a number of tools that can help you explore a database and its contents. In the last section, you created a database with a single table. In this section, you will learn how to connect to the table from inside WISQL, and how to examine the main features of that table.

To connect to INFO.GDB, select File | Connect to Database, which brings up the dialog shown in Figure 24.3. Enter the drive and the database as `e:\data\info.gdb`, where `e:` represents the letter of the appropriate drive on your machine. Enter the user as SYSDBA, and the password as MASTERKEY. If all goes well, you should be able to connect to the database by clicking the OK button. Once again, success is signaled by the lack of an error message.

FIGURE 24.3.

Connecting to the INFO.GDB database using the WISQL tool.

Go to View | Metadata Information, and set "View Information On" to Database, as shown in Figure 24.4. After choosing the OK button, the information displayed in the ISQL output window should look something like this:

```
SHOW DB
Database: e:\data\info.gdb
        Owner: SYSDBA
PAGE_SIZE 1024
Number of DB pages allocated = 208
Sweep interval = 20000
```

FIGURE 24.4.

Preparing to view information on the INFO.GDB database.

To see the tables available in a database, select View | Metadata Information from the menu, and set "View Information On" to Table. Select the Run button, and view the information in the ISQL output window, which should look like this:

```
SHOW TABLES
      TEST1
```

Browsing through the Metadata Information menu choice, you can see that Interbase supports triggers, stored procedures, views, and a host of other advanced server features.

The Extract menu choice enables you to find out more detailed information about the database and its tables. For instance, if you choose Extract | SQL Metadata for Database, you get output similar to the following:

```
/* Extract Database e:\data\info.gdb */
CREATE DATABASE "e:\data\info.gdb" PAGE_SIZE 1024
;


/* Table: TEST1, Owner: SYSDBA */
CREATE TABLE TEST1 (FIRST VARCHAR(20),
        LAST INTEGER);


/* Grant permissions for this database */
```

If you choose the Extract | SQL Metadata for Table, you get the following output:

```
/* Extract Table TEST1 */

/* Table: TEST1, Owner: SYSDBA */
CREATE TABLE TEST1 (FIRST VARCHAR(20),
        LAST INTEGER);
```

You should note that WISQL often asks whether you want to save the output from a command to a text file, and the File menu gives you some further options for saving information to files. You can take advantage of these options when necessary, but 90 percent of the time I pass them by with barely a nod.

NOTE

The WISQL program accepts most SQL statements. For instance, you can perform Select, UpDate, and Delete statements from inside of WISQL. Just enter the statement you want to perform in the SQL Statement area and then select the Run button.

You should also be aware that WISQL bypasses the BDE altogether, so you can use it to test your connections to Interbase even if you are not sure that you have the BDE set up correctly. For instance, if you are having trouble connecting to Interbase and you're not sure where the problem lies, start by trying to connect with WISQL. If that works but you can't connect from inside Delphi, it might be that the problem lies not with your Interbase setup, but with the way you have deployed the BDE.

WISQL also comes equipped with a handy online reference to SQL. If you have questions about how to format an Alter, Drop, Insert, Create Index, or other SQL statement, you can look it up in the help for WISQL.

After reading the last three sections, you should have a fair understanding of how WISQL works and how you can use it to manage a database. The information provided in this chapter is nothing more than an introduction to a complex and very sophisticated topic. However, you now know enough to begin using the local Interbase. This is no insignificant accomplishment. Tools such as Interbase, Oracle, and Sybase lie at the heart of the client/server activity that is currently so volatile and lucrative. If you get good at talking to servers such as Interbase, you could be at an important turning point in your career.

The Music Program

The MUSIC.DPR program enables you to keep track of the CDs, records, and tapes that most members of industrial societies collect throughout their lives. The main goal of the program is to enable you to sort the information on a single field that contains multiple parts. For instance, here is a typical field on which you can sort the table: J-JJ-C-0-00000183. Soon, I will explain what this code means, and how you can use it to sort information.

MUSIC.DPR has two screens. One screen (shown in Figure 24.5) is meant only for performing searches. You can't edit the data in this screen. However, the Search Dialog provides several different means for sorting data, including sorting by type, first name, last name, group, or album title.

FIGURE 24.5.

The Search screen from MUSIC.DPR enables you to sort CDs by category and subcategory.

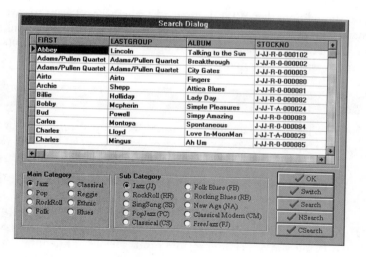

The second screen in the MUSIC.DPR program enables you to edit information, insert records, and designate the categories for each entry you create. This screen is shown in Figure 24.6. Note the various radio buttons that can be used to set the category, subcategory, and media type of each individual entry.

FIGURE 24.6.

The screen used by the MUSIC.DPR program for editing and inserting records.

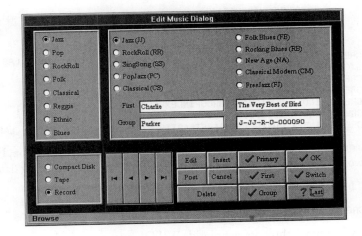

In the ADDRESS2 program from the last chapter, you learned how to switch a program in and out of edit mode. The MUSIC program takes an even more radical approach to this subject by ensuring that it is impossible to edit data in the main screen of the program. Instead, you need to switch to an entirely different screen when you want to edit data. This is an ideal arrangement for a program that is likely to be used late at night, or at other times when users might not be—ahem—fully alert.

Designing the tables for the MUSIC program is a much simpler task than it was for ADDRESS2. All you really need is a way to designate a musician's first and last name, or a group name, and the name of an album. Once again, I add a single field to designate the category, and I throw in a date field; however, the latter field is not used in this incarnation of the MUSIC program:

First	VARCHAR	25	*	FirstIndex
LastGroup	VARCHAR	30	*	GroupIndex
Album	VARCHAR	30	*	
StockNo	VARCHAR	17	*	StockNumber
ChangeData	Date			

The WISQL program has an option in the File menu for running ISQL scripts. This option enables you to quickly and easily create a database and a set of tables. The following is a complete WISQL script for creating a database called MUSIC, which has two tables inside it:

```
/* Create database e:\data\music.gdb */
CREATE DATABASE "e:\data\music.gdb" PAGE_SIZE 1024;


/* Table: HIGHNO, Owner: SYSDBA */
CREATE TABLE HIGHNO (HIGHNUM VARCHAR(8));

/* Table: MUSICLIST, Owner: SYSDBA */
CREATE TABLE MUSICLIST (FIRST VARCHAR(25),
        LASTGROUP VARCHAR(30),
        ALBUM VARCHAR(30),
```

```
        STOCKNO VARCHAR(17),
        CHANGEDATE DATE);

/*  Index definitions for all user tables */
CREATE UNIQUE INDEX MUSICLIST_INDEX1 ON MUSICLIST(FIRST, LASTGROUP, ALBUM,
STOCKNO);
CREATE INDEX MUSICLIST_STOCKNUMBER ON MUSICLIST(STOCKNO);
CREATE INDEX MUSICLIST_FIRSTINDEX ON MUSICLIST(FIRST);
CREATE INDEX MUSICLIST_GROUPINDEX ON MUSICLIST(LASTGROUP);
CREATE INDEX MUSICLIST_ALBUMINDEX ON MUSICLIST(ALBUM);
CREATE INDEX MUSICLIST_FIRSTLASTINDEX ON MUSICLIST(FIRST, LASTGROUP);
```

You should save this information to a text file with an SQL extension. For instance, MUSIC.SQL would be a good name for the text file containing the preceding data.

This script begins by creating a database called MUSIC.GDB:

```
CREATE DATABASE "e:\data\music.gdb" PAGE_SIZE 1024;
```

By "running" this statement inside WISQL, you perform the same action outlined earlier when you created the INFO.GDB table.

The next step is to create a small table that will be used to keep track of the highest number assigned to an album. In other words, you want to assign a unique number to each album. One simple way to keep track of the number you should choose is to simply store the current high number in a table, and then increment the number each time you add a new record. Here is the statement for creating the table:

```
CREATE TABLE HIGHNO (HIGHNUMBER INTEGER);
```

The integer type in Interbase is equivalent to the Delphi LongInt type, so it can hold a number as large as 2,147,483,648. Anyone who has more albums than that doesn't need a database; they need a shrink!

NOTE

The use of a table for storing a high number that will continually be incremented is a classic solution to this problem. However, you should note that sophisticated servers such as Interbase offer additional solutions. For instance, Interbase enables you to create generators and use a function called Gen_ID to access the generators. With these tools you can get unique sequential numbers without having to track the process yourself.

Here is the definition for the main table used by the MUSIC program:

```
CREATE TABLE MUSICLIST (FIRST VARCHAR(25),
        LASTGROUP VARCHAR(30),
        ALBUM VARCHAR(30),
        STOCKNO VARCHAR(17),
        CHANGEDATE DATE);
```

The key field here is the StockNo field, which has 17 characters. These characters are divided up into five fields, with each field separated from the last by a dash:

```
J-JJ-C-0-00000183
```

The first field can have one of eight different values, each of which stands for a broad category of music:

Jazz	J
Pop	P
RocknRoll	R
Folk	F
Classical	C
Reggae	G
Ethnic	E
Blues	B

The first column represents the various categories, and the second column represents the code entered in the first field of the StockNo. Therefore, the following entry is a Jazz disc:

```
J-JJ-C-0-00000183
```

The second field in the StockNo is the subcategory. I have made room for 10 subcategories in the MUSIC program, although the table itself will hold 36 to the second power (or 1296) different categories, assuming that you have 26 different letters and 10 different numbers out of which you can make up the two character code. Here are the subcategories used in the MUSIC program:

Jazz	JJ
RocknRoll	RR
Singer Songwriter	SS
Popular Jazz	PC
Classical	CS
Folk Blues	FB
Rocking Blues	RB
New Age	NA
Classical Modern	CM
Free Jazz	FJ

The third field in the StockNo number enables you to designate whether the music is stored on CD, tape, or record. The codes for the field are C, T, and R, which (naturally enough) stand for CD, tape, and record.

At this stage, the fourth field in StockNo is not used at all, but is inserted in case I need it at some point in the future. The odds are that I will probably never use this field, but it's best to think ahead so that I do not need to totally recode each of the discs in my collection simply because I need to add a new piece of information, such as a rating on a scale of 1 to 10. (Note that in a single byte, you have room to designate 256 different categories.)

The final field is simply a unique 8-digit number, as discussed earlier. This number is always supplied by the HIGHNO table, which always has only one field and one record. The entry in the table's sole record is first read, and then incremented by one, every time a new disc is recorded by the MUSIC program.

The final part of the ISQL script shown previously is used to create indices:

```
CREATE UNIQUE INDEX MUSICLIST_INDEX1 ON MUSICLIST(FIRST, LASTGROUP, ALBUM, STOCKNO);
CREATE INDEX MUSICLIST_STOCKNUMBER ON MUSICLIST(STOCKNO);
CREATE INDEX MUSICLIST_FIRSTINDEX ON MUSICLIST(FIRST);
CREATE INDEX MUSICLIST_GROUPINDEX ON MUSICLIST(LASTGROUP);
CREATE INDEX MUSICLIST_ALBUMINDEX ON MUSICLIST(ALBUM);
CREATE INDEX MUSICLIST_FIRSTLASTINDEX ON MUSICLIST(FIRST, LASTGROUP);
```

The key point of this set of statements is that they establish an index on the First, LastGroup, Album, and StockNo fields. This ensures that the user can quickly sort and search on each of these fields.

NOTE

On Interbase and other servers, you do not even have to index a field in order to search through it. However, searches are much faster if you first index the field you want to search.

It's also worth mentioning that you can change the structure of an Interbase table by using the SQL Alter command. To learn more about the syntax for this command, look up Alter in the WISQL help.

It's taken awhile to describe the ISQL script for creating the MUSIC.GDB database. However, the script itself is extremely easy to use. All you need to do is select File | Run ISQL Script from the menu, and then load the script itself and run it. This technique provides a simple way to ensure that databases are created according to a very precise structure.

In the next section, I begin an explanation of some of the special features of the MUSIC program. I jump directly into this discussion without explaining what you have to do to set up the Alias for the music program, or how you can build forms like those shown in Figures 24.4 and 24.5. In other words, I am going to assume that by this time you know how to create Aliases (even ones belonging to Interbase tables), and how to connect a table to a set of data-aware controls. To help guide you, I have included Figures 24.7 and 24.8, which depict the forms as they appear in design mode.

FIGURE 24.7.

The Search Dialog from the MUSIC program as it appears in design mode.

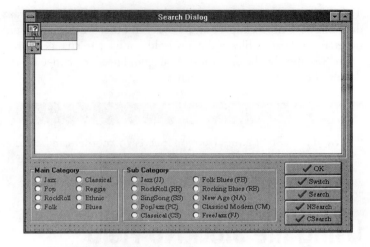

FIGURE 24.8.

The Edit Music Dialog from the MUSIC program as it appears in design mode.

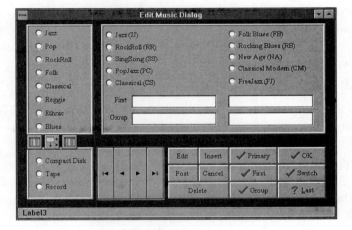

NOTE

The code for the four forms used in the MUSIC program is in the CHAP24 directory on this book's CD-ROM. The SEARCH unit is the main form for the program.

Like the ADDRESS2 program shown in the last chapter, this program appears considerably more formidable at first glance than it actually is once you break it down. Some of the units, such as INSRTDLG and SRCHSTR, are very simple and need only a few sentences to explain. Parts of the EDITOR unit have some tricky code in them, but nothing that you can't readily understand after you analyze them for a few moments. SEARCH is a fairly straightforward unit, but I describe it in relative detail because it shows techniques that many programmers might find useful.

The final general point I want to make about the MUSIC program is that its use of Interbase does not have much impact on its code. In other words, you could copy the database for the program to Paradox files and you would not have to change more than a few lines of the program. Specifically, the only things you would need to change are the program's Alias and a few details of the way it handles searches.

> **NOTE**
>
> The act of copying files from one server to another can be accomplished by at least two means. The simplest is to use the Utility | Copy menu choice from the Database Desktop. Another technique is to use the `TBatchMove` component.

Using the StockNo Field

One of the most useful features of the MUSIC program is the StockNo field. It enables you to sort information in a variety of ways. The key to the StockNo field is the complex codes stored inside it. These codes can actually be broken down into a series of fields, in which each field is separated from the next by a dash:

`J-JJ-C-0-00000183`

Users do not want to type in opaque-looking codes such as `J-JJ-C-0-00000183`. In particular, no user wants to enter the 8-digit code at the end of the StockNo. However, none of the other fields of the StockNo are particularly user-friendly either.

To remedy this situation, the MUSIC program provides a technique for automatically generating the 8-digit code at the end of the StockNo, and it provides a simple method for entering the first four fields of data. For instance, MUSIC provides a series of radio buttons, each named for one of the categories, subcategories, and media available to the user. The user can simply click one of the buttons to change the current category, subcategory, or media. Furthermore, the program looks up the StockNo of the current record and sets the radio buttons so that they match the stock number. For instance, if the category of an existing record is J for Jazz, the Jazz radio button will be turned on; if the subcategory is NA for New Age, the New Age radio button will be turned on.

The actual editing of the `StockNo` string is done entirely through clicks on radio buttons. At no time does the user have to do any typing to change any part of the stock number.

NOTE

I had to make a design decision when creating this part of the program. I could have used listboxes or combo boxes instead of radio buttons. The first listbox would show a list of main categories, and the second listbox would show a list of subcategories. If the user clicked a selection from either listbox, that would be the signal to change the StockNo string. The advantage to this system is that the user could easily add or delete categories from the listboxes, thereby making the program very flexible in terms of the types of music it could sort. However, this method would not have the intuitive ease of use that I feel is associated with the radio button technique.

Needless to say, the moment that I make a difficult decision such as this, I am almost certain the method I rejected would be best. Certainly, there are arguments to be made on both sides of the issue. At any rate, I have selected a particular technique for this version of the program, but I may opt for some variations in future versions.

The actual mechanisms for translating the StockNo into a pattern of radio buttons and back again are relatively straightforward, but not without enough minor twists and turns to make it an interesting process. The first step is to create the radio buttons, give them useful names, and associate all the radio buttons from any one field of the StockNo with a single procedure. For instance, all of the radio buttons associated with the main category in the StockNo field have names such as rbJ, rbP, rbR, and so on (for which the rb stands for radio button, the J stands for Jazz, the P for Pop, the R for RocknRoll, and so on). All of these radio buttons have their OnClick event associated with a single routine called rbJClick:

```
procedure TEditMusic.rbJClick(Sender: TObject);
begin
  if FDataSourceChange then Exit;
  if Sender = rbJ then FMusicType := 'J'
  else if Sender = rbP then FMusicType := 'P'
  else if Sender = rbR then FMusicType := 'R'
  else if Sender = rbF then FMusicType := 'F'
  else if Sender = rbC then FMusicType := 'C'
  else if Sender = rbE then FMusicType := 'E'
  else if Sender = rbB then FMusicType := 'B'
  else if Sender = rbG then FMusicType := 'G';
  DataSource1.DataSet.Edit;
  StockStr := dbEdit3.Text;
  SetNewMusicType(FMusicType, StockStr);
  dbEdit3.Text := StockStr;
end;
```

For the moment, you can ignore the first line in this routine, which ensures that the body of the routine won't be called under certain circumstances. The next eight lines check to see which radio button was selected, and then they set a field of the current form called FMusicType to the letter that needs to be added to the current StockNo string. The datasource is then set into edit mode, the current StockNo is retrieved from the edit control, and a method named SetNewMusicType is called.

`SetNewMusicType` is a very simple routine that looks like this:

```
procedure SetNewMusicType(NewStr: string; var StockNo: string);
begin
  Move(NewStr[1], StockNo[1], 1);
end;
```

This procedure uses the built in `Move` function to change the first letter of the current StockNo. For instance, if the StockNo reads

`J-JJ-C-0-00000183`

and the user presses the Folk radio button, the `SetNewMusicType` method changes the StockNo string so that it looks like this:

`F-JJ-C-0-00000183`

`SetNewMusicType` is passed two strings. The first is the new letter that needs to be inserted in the string, and the other is the old StockNo. The `Move` method makes it easy to replace one letter in the StockNo with the appropriate new letter selected by the user.

After the new StockNo string has been created, the `rbJClick` method reassigns the string to the appropriate data-aware edit control. The end result of the whole effort is that the user clicks a radio button and the StockNo string appears to change instantly in response to the click.

The same process is repeated if the user clicks one of the subtypes:

```
procedure TEditMusic.rbJJClick(Sender: TObject);
begin
  if FDataSourceChange then Exit;
  if Sender = rbJJ then FSubType := 'JJ'
  else if Sender = rbRR then FSubType := 'RR'
  else if Sender = rbSS then FSubType := 'SS'
  else if Sender = rbPC then FSubType := 'PC'
  else if Sender = rbCS then FSubType := 'CS'
  else if Sender = rbFJ then FSubType := 'FJ'
  else if Sender = rbCM then FSubType := 'CM'
  else if Sender = rbNA then FSubType := 'NA'
  else if Sender = rbRB then FSubType := 'RB'
  else if Sender = rbFB then FSubType := 'FB';
  DataSource1.DataSet.Edit;
  StockStr := dbEdit3.Text;
  SetSubType(FSubType, StockStr);
  dbEdit3.Text := StockStr;
end;
```

The only variation in this routine from the `rbJClick` routine is that the `FSubType` string is used instead of `FMusicType`, and the `SetSubType` routine is called instead of the `SetNewMusicType` routine. `SetSubType` looks like this:

```
procedure SetSubType(NewStr: string; var StockNo: string);
begin
  Move(NewStr[1], StockNo[3], 2);
end;
```

This routine moves two letters from `NewStr` into the third and fourth characters in the StockNo string. In other words, if the string starts out as

```
F-JJ-C-0-00000183
```

and the user clicks the Folk Blues subcategory, the `SetSubType` method changes the StockNo string so it looks like this:

```
F-FB-C-0-00000183
```

By now, it should be fairly obvious how the music program enables the user to change the categories depicted in the StockNo string. Here's the method that is used to set the radio buttons each time the user moves to a new record:

```
procedure TEditMusic.DataSource1DataChange(Sender: TObject;
                                           Field: TField);
begin
  FDataSourceChange := True;
  StockStr := DBEdit3.Text;
  if StockStr = '' then Exit;
  TRadio button(FindComponent('rb' + GetMainCat(StockStr))).Checked
    := True;
  TRadio button(FindComponent('rb' + GetSubCat(StockStr))).Checked
    := True;
  TRadio button(FindComponent('rb' + GetMediaCat(StockStr) +
    'Media')).Checked := True;
  FDataSourceChange := False;
end;
```

The name of this method reveals that it is associated with the `OnDataChange` event of `DataSource1`. In other words, by definition, this method is called every time the user moves on to a new record.

The method first sets a Boolean field of the current form called `FDataSourceChange` to `True`. If you look back up at the `rbJClick` and `rbJJClick` methods, you see that both of them check the state of this variable in their first line. If it is set to `True`, both methods immediately exit. The point is that you don't need to start editing the table just because a new record has been shown. In other words, if you change the status of a radio button in code, the `OnClick` event of the radio button is called just as if the user clicked it. MUSIC.PRJ reacts to clicks on a radio button by setting the table into edit mode. This is not what you want to have happen just because you are resetting the radio buttons to reflect the change to a new record. As a result, I declared the variable `FDataSourceChange`, so that the program can keep track of exactly what is generating `OnClick` events, and so it can then react appropriately to the generation of these events.

After setting the `FDataSourceChange` variable, the program retrieves the current StockNo, and then sets the appropriate radio button in the main category, subcategory, and media category. It does this by calling the `FindComponent` function, which takes a single string designating the name of the component that you want to find. Say you are setting the radio buttons for the main category. The radio button you want to set is going to have a name like rbJ, rbP, rbR, and so on. Obviously, the first two letters of the component are going to be rb, and the third letter is going to correspond to the first letter in the current StockNo. For instance, if the StockNo is F-FB-C-0-00000183, the name of the component that you want to check is rbF. To get this letter programmatically, you can pass the StockNo string to the GetMainCat function:

```
function GetMainCat(S: string): string;
begin
  Move(S[1], Result[1], 1);
  Result[0] := #1;
end;
```

The GetMainCat function moves the first letter of the current StockNo into the built-in Result string, and then sets the length of the string to one. As a result, the string returns a single letter that completes the name of the component. For instance, it might return the letter F, which would set the name of the component to rbF.

> **NOTE**
>
> The GetMainCat function performs a function closely related to the task of the SetNewMusicType procedure. One sets the first letter of the StockNo string, and the other retrieves the first letter of the StockNo string. They are related, but not identical, functions.

The process that was just outlined works the same way for subcategories and the media category, except that you call the GetSubCat and GetMediaCat functions rather than the GetMainCat function:

```
function GetSubCat(S: string): string;
begin
  Move(S[3], Result[1], 2);
  Result[0] := #2;
end;

function GetMediaCat(S: string): string;
begin
  Move(S[6], Result[1], 1);
  Result[0] := #1;
end;
```

As you can see, these functions also use the built-in Move routine to retrieve a substring from a longer string.

In this section, you have learned how the MUSIC program displays a StockNo field via a pattern of radio buttons, and how it can change the StockNo field when the user clicks a radio button. The techniques involved are fairly simple, but they enable the user to quickly and easily encode a fairly complex set of categories in a single short string.

Inserting a New Record

Whenever the user wants to insert a new record, it is necessary to create a new StockNo. This section explains how the insertion process takes place, and how the program uses the HIGHNO table to assign a unique number to each record.

Rather than having the user directly enter a new record into the main form, the MUSIC program pops up a modal dialog called InsertDlg. InsertDlg provides an area where the user can enter data, as shown in Figure 24.9. If the insert proceeds smoothly, Table1 is placed in edit mode and the data is transferred from the dialog to the table. If the user presses Cancel, the dialog disappears and any data the user entered is discarded.

FIGURE 24.9.

The MUSIC program has a dialog designed to accept data when an insert occurs.

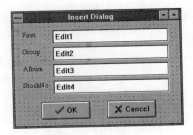

From the user's point of view, an Insert Dialog is less confusing than typing directly in the main edit controls. If the user inserts a record via the main edit controls and then cancels the operation, the current record suddenly and rather disconcertingly disappears. This can confuse some users; experienced users might wonder whether the record was really canceled, or whether they were only moved off the current record. By using a separate dialog for the insertion, the act of pressing the Cancel button results in a more comprehensible and reassuring set of events. (A separate dialog like this is also very useful if you want to insert data into a table using the SQL Insert statement.)

Here is the routine called when the user wants to insert data into the table:

```
procedure TEditMusic.HandleInsert;
const
  S: string = 'J-JJ-C-0-00000000';
var
  i: Integer;
  NewNum: string;
  NewRec: TNewRec;
begin
  Table2.Open;
  i := Table2.Fields[0].AsInteger;
  NewNum := Int2StrPad0(i, 8);
  Move(NewNum[1], S[10], 8);
  S[0] := #17;
  NewRec.StockNo := S;
  if InsertDlg.GetInput(NewRec) then begin
    Table1.Insert;
```

```
    Table1.FieldByName('First').AsString := NewRec.First;
    Table1.FieldByName('LastGroup').AsString := NewRec.Group;
    Table1.FieldByName('Album').AsString := NewRec.Album;
    Table1.FieldByName('StockNo').AsString := NewRec.StockNo;
    Table1.Post;
    Table2.Edit;
    Table2.Fields[0].AsInteger := i + 1;
    Table2.Post;
  end;
  Table2.Close;
end;
```

The routine begins by retrieving the new stock number from the HIGHNO table:

```
Table2.Open;
i := Table2.Fields[0].AsInteger;
NewNum := Int2StrPad0(i, 8);
Move(NewNum[1], S[10], 8);
S[0] := #17;
NewRec.StockNo := S;
```

The function `Int2StrPad0` is found in the MATHBOX unit. It pads the integer retrieved from the table so that it consists of exactly eight digits. For instance, if the integer retrieved from the table is 250, `Int2StrPad0` returns 00000250. The second parameter passed to `Int2StrPad0` dictates the final length of string that is returned.

The `HandleInsert` method declares a constant that serves as a starting StockNo string:

```
const
  S: string = 'J-JJ-C-0-00000000';
```

The `Move` statement shown earlier places the new stock number in the appropriate place in this string. For instance, if the stock number is 00000250, the StockNo string looks like this after the call to `Move`:

```
S: string = 'J-JJ-C-0-00000250';
```

After creating a new StockNo string, a dialog is popped up, which enables the user to enter data. There are a number of ways to handle this problem, but I chose to pass a record to the dialog, then let the dialog fill in the record with the user's input and return the result. The record passed in looks like this:

```
TNewRec = record
  First: string;
  Group: string;
  Album: string;
  StockNo: string;
end;
```

The `InsertDlg` has only four edit controls in it, and each one is associated with one of the strings in a `TNewRec`. The code to retrieve the strings from the dialog looks like this, with N being a variable of type `TNewRec`:

```
if ShowModal = mrOk then begin
  Result := True;
  N.First := Edit1.Text;
  N.Group := Edit2.Text;
```

```
  N.Album := Edit3.Text;
  N.StockNo := Edit4.Text;
end;
```

This is about as straightforward as any code you can write with Delphi, so I won't explain it further.

If the user clicks the OK button in the `InsertDlg`, the data is retrieved as shown earlier, and the information is inserted into the table:

```
if InsertDlg.GetInput(NewRec) then begin
  Table1.Insert;
  Table1.FieldByName('First').AsString := NewRec.First;
  Table1.FieldByName('LastGroup').AsString := NewRec.Group;
  Table1.FieldByName('Album').AsString := NewRec.Album;
  Table1.FieldByName('StockNo').AsString := NewRec.StockNo;
  Table1.Post;
  Table2.Edit;
  Table2.Fields[0].AsInteger := i + 1;
  Table2.Post;
  end;
  Table2.Close;
end;
```

After the user posts the data in Table1, the HIGHNO table is placed in edit mode, and a new stock number is stored inside it:

```
Table2.Edit;
Table2.Fields[0].AsInteger := i + 1;
Table2.Post;
```

This chore is performed inside the same complex statement kicked off when the user clicked OK in the `InsertDlg`. The program handles things this way because you don't want to increment the number unless the insert was successful.

The final call in the `HandleInsert` method does nothing more than close the HIGHNO table. This call is carried out regardless of whether or not the user decided to go through with the insertion.

Indexing and Searching the Edit Music Dialog

Besides the Switch button, most of the remaining functionality in the Edit dialog is quite simple. For instance, the act of switching indices is covered by this routine:

```
procedure TEditMusic.ResetIndexClick(Sender: TObject);
begin
  case (Sender as TBitBtn).Tag of
    inPrimary: Table1.IndexName := '';
    inFirst: Table1.IndexName := 'MusicList_FirstIndex';
    inGroup: Table1.IndexName := 'MusicList_GroupIndex';
  end;
end;
```

You have seen similar code many times in this book. However, in this case, I sort out which button called the function by using the following constants instead of an enumerated type:

```
const
  inPrimary= 100;
  inFirst = 101;
  inGroup= 102;
```

There is probably at least a reasonable argument in favor of using constants rather than enumerated types. In particular, it allows you to associate a unique number with the Tag property of every control in your program. At any rate, I have shown you both techniques, and you can pick and choose between them.

The Edit Music dialog enables you to perform searches on only the LastGroup field, and it ends up filtering your data so that you see only the records that actually fit the search. As I stated earlier, more complex search options are available in the Search Dialog, so this severely circumscribed routine doesn't define the limits of the program's capability.

Here is the search procedure:

```
procedure TEditMusic.LastGroupSrchClick(Sender: TObject);
var
  S: string;
begin
  S := '';
  if not InputQuery('Search on Group or Last Name',
              'Enter string', S) then Exit;
  Table1.IndexName := 'MusicList_GroupIndex';
  Table1.SetRangeStart;
  Table1.FieldByName('LastGroup').AsString := S;
  Table1.SetRangeEnd;
  Table1.FieldByName('LastGroup').AsString := S;
  Table1.ApplyRange;
end;
```

The code uses the built-in InputQuery dialog to capture the string the user wants to search on. Table1 is then sorted on the GroupIndex, and the routine performs a normal Filter operation.

In this section, you saw how the Edit Music Dialog handles searching and indexing. These are simple, perfunctory tasks, which required only minimal explanation. The key point to remember is that the Search Dialog enables you to sort through the data in a more elaborate manner than anything you can find in the Edit Music Dialog.

Switching Between Dialogs

The MUSIC program has four forms. Two of the forms, InsertDlg and SearchStr, are simply helper forms used to get input from the user. The two main forms in the program are EditMusic and Searcher; the latter form is the one that first appears when the program is launched.

MUSIC sends a message to itself whenever the user wants to close the program or switch between the Searcher form and the Music Edit form. The message is called wm_Switch, and it is declared in SEARCH.PAS:

```
const
  wm_Switch = wm_User + 0;
```

This is a custom message that is understood only by the MUSIC program. Whenever you declare a custom message, you should make it an offset of wm_User, which is a constant declared by Windows itself specifically for this purpose. If you want to declare a second message, you declare it as wm_User + 1, with the next message declared as wm_User + 2, and so on. If you want to know more about messages, turn to Chapter 25, "Handling Messages."

The following type encapsulates the three special things that the user can do with the program:

```
type
  TNextMove = (nmShowSearch, nmShowEdit, nmClose);
```

nmShowSearch is associated with switching to the Search dialog; nmShowEdit is associated with switching to the Edit dialog; and nmClose designates the user's desire to close the program. The Tag property of the Switch button in the Search dialog is set to nmShowSearch, or 0, and the Switch button in the Edit dialog is set to nmShowEdit, or 1. The Tag property of the OK buttons in both dialogs are set to nmClose.

When the user clicks the Switch or OK button in the Search dialog, the following method is called:

```
procedure TSearcher.SwitchClick(Sender: TObject);
begin
  Query1.Close;
  Hide;
  PostMessage(Handle, wm_Switch, (Sender as TBitBtn).Tag, 0);
end;
```

This code closes Query1, hides the dialog, and posts a wm_Switch message with the Tag value of the button that called the procedure in wParam location.

> **NOTE**
>
> If you are not familiar with PostMessage and SendMessage, you should look up the routine in the online help, or read Chapter 25, "Handling Messages," as well as the chapters at the end of the book that deal with calling the Windows API.

The same thing happens when the user clicks the OK or Switch buttons in the Edit Music Dialog:

```
procedure TEditMusic.SwitchClick(Sender: TObject);
begin
  Table1.Close;
  Close;
  PostMessage(Searcher.Handle,wm_Switch,(Sender as TBitBtn).Tag, 0);
end;
```

The only difference here is that the program closes the Edit form rather than just hiding it. In fact, this turns out to be a rather insignificant difference, because closing any but the main form of a program amounts to little more than a call to Hide. Closing the main form of a program causes the program itself to shut down.

The SEARCH unit declares the handler for the wm_Switch message like this:

```
procedure wmSwitch(var Msg: TMessage); message wm_Switch;
```

This is the same type of declaration you would make for a routine associated with any Windows message. Specifically, the procedure takes one var parameter, which is of type TMessage. The TMessage record, declared in MESSAGES.PAS, has fields designating the wParam and lParam parameters that are so well known to hardcore Windows programmers. The directive message that appears after the main declaration is just Delphi syntax stating that this is a dynamic method used to handle messages. Finally, you add the name of the message that you want to have the function handle. This name is really only a constant used by Delphi when it needs to look up the right entry in its dynamic method table before dispatching the message. Once again, if you are not familiar with Windows message handling, you will learn more about this topic in Chapter 25.

The program nabs wm_Switch messages in the following routine:

```
procedure TSearcher.wmSwitch(var Msg: TMessage);
begin
  case TNextMove(Msg.wParam) of
    nmShowSearch: Searcher.Show;
    nmShowEdit: begin
      EditMusic.Table1.Open;
      EditMusic.Show;
    end;
    nmClose: Searcher.Close;
  end;
end;
```

The following line of code forces the call to wmSwitch:

```
PostMessage(Searcher.Handle,wm_Switch,(Sender as TBitBtn).Tag, 0);
```

The third parameter in the call to PostMessage contains the Tag field designating the call that generated the message. This third parameter is passed on to the wmSwitch procedure as Msg.wParam, which is in turn used as the basis for a case statement.

If Msg.wParam designates that it is time to switch from the Edit window to the Search window, Searcher.Show is called. If Msg.wParam states it is time to switch to the Edit window, EditMusic.Show is called.

If you mentally combine the calls from TEditMusic.SwitchClick and the calls from wmSwitch, you can see that the following series of events takes place:

```
EditMusic.Table1.Close;
EditMusic.Close;
{ PostMessage occurs here }
Searcher.Show;
```

Conversely, if you want to switch from the Searcher dialog to the Edit dialog, the following calls are made:

```
Searcher.Query1.Close;
Searcher.Hide;
{ PostMessage occurs here }
EditMusic.Table1.Open;
EditMusic.Show;
```

Finally, if the `PostMessage` call signals that it is time to close the whole app, one of the following two scenarios occurs:

```
{ Scenario A }
Searcher.Query1.Close;
Searcher.Hide;
{ PostMessage occurs here }
Searcher.Close;

{ Scenario B }
EditMusic.Table1.Close;
EditMusic.Close;
{ PostMessage occurs here }
Searcher.Close;
```

There are several solutions to the problem of how a program with two main windows can switch them back and forth. The technique shown here performs the job in a simple, straightforward manner.

If you have junctures in a program where events can lead you off in 2, 5, 10, 15, or even 20 different directions, you should consider posting a message or using the delegation model. In either case, you can arrange things so that a single centralized method can route the program toward its new destination. That way you never have to ask yourself, "How did I get here?" The answer to that question is always the same: You got there because your delegation method or message handler routed you in that direction!

NOTE

When the question of tracing the events in a program comes up, you can always check the Call Stack window, which is accessible from the View menu. This handy tool keeps track of the routines that have been pushed on the stack before the current method was called. Therefore, you can sometimes look in this window and use it to trace the method your program took to get to a particular point.

The Search Dialog

The Search Dialog enables you to search for a disk or album in one of two different ways. If you want, you can enter a string and search by first name, last name, group name, or album title. Partial searches are allowed, so you can, for instance, search for all musicians whose last name begins with the letters "Co."

Searching by name is a powerful technique. However, there are many times when you want to hear a certain type of record, but aren't sure exactly what record you want. For instance, you might be in the mood for folk music or free jazz, but you aren't sure exactly which folk album, or which free jazz album, you want to hear. For times like these, the MUSIC program lets you search on the main category alone, or a main category and a subcategory. For instance, you can search for all the folk albums by singer-songwriters, and get back an answer set that contains only those discs.

Here's how it works. The Search Dialog has a series of radio buttons on it that enable you to select a category and a subcategory. These radio buttons look very much like the radio buttons in the Edit dialog, and clicks on them are handled by a routine similar to the routines in the Edit dialog, only somewhat simplified:

```
procedure TSearcher.rbJClick(Sender: TObject);
begin
  if Sender = rbJ then FMusicType := 'J'
  else if Sender = rbP then FMusicType := 'P'
  else if Sender = rbR then FMusicType := 'R'
  else if Sender = rbF then FMusicType := 'F'
  else if Sender = rbC then FMusicType := 'C'
  else if Sender = rbE then FMusicType := 'E'
  else if Sender = rbB then FMusicType := 'B'
  else if Sender = rbG then FMusicType := 'G';
end;
```

This procedure is called if the user clicks one of the radio buttons designating the main category. For instance, if the user clicks the rbR radio button, a string variable called FMusicType is set to 'R', which is the code for RocknRoll.

The same type of thing happens if the user clicks one of the radio buttons associated with a subtype:

```
procedure TSearcher.rbJJClick(Sender: TObject);
begin
  if Sender = rbJJ then FSubType := 'JJ'
  else if Sender = rbRR then FSubType := 'RR'
  else if Sender = rbSS then FSubType := 'SS'
  else if Sender = rbPC then FSubType := 'PC'
  else if Sender = rbCS then FSubType := 'CS'
  else if Sender = rbFJ then FSubType := 'FJ'
  else if Sender = rbCM then FSubType := 'CM'
  else if Sender = rbNA then FSubType := 'NA'
  else if Sender = rbRB then FSubType := 'RB'
  else if Sender = rbFB then FSubType := 'FB';
end;
```

Once again, a hit on a particular radio button sets the FSubType variable to a particular code. For instance, a click on the rbRR button sets FSubType to 'RR', which is the code for RocknRoll.

If the user then clicks on the search button, the following method gets called:

```
procedure TSearcher.BSearchClick(Sender: TObject);
begin
  Query1.Close;
  SetQueryType(qtStockNo);
  Query1.Params[0].AsString := FMusicType + '-' + FSubType + '%';
  Query1.Open;
end;
```

The third line in the body of this method puts together a string that looks like this:

```
FMusicType + '-' + FSubType + '%';
```

Using the input described earlier as an example, this code produces a string that looks like this: 'R-RR%'. If you build the following query and then execute it, you end up with a list of all the albums that were categorized as straight-ahead rock discs:

```
'select * from MusicList where StockNo like R-RR%'
```

The key to this SQL statement, of course, is that it uses the % sign to designate a wild card. Therefore, it returns all the discs that have a StockNo that begins with 'R-RR'.

Over all, the BSearchClick method is fairly straightforward. The one mystery inside it, of course, is the call to SetQueryType:

```
procedure TSearcher.SetQueryType(QType: TQueryType);
var
  S: string;
begin
  case QType of
    qtFirst: S := 'select * from MusicList where First like :First';
    qtLastGroup: S := 'select * from MusicList ' +
                      'where LastGroup like :LastGroup';
    qtAlbum: S := 'select * from MusicList where Album like :Album';
    qtStockNo: S := 'select * from MusicList ' +
                    'where StockNo like :StockNo';
  end;
  Query1.SQL.Clear;
  Query1.SQL.Add(S);
end;
```

It turns out that the MUSIC program needs to compose several different types of SQL select statements, depending on the kind of search you want to perform. For instance, if you want to search on a first name, you need to compose a different statement than if you want to search on a last name. To simplify the task of sorting out these possibilities, the MUSIC program declares an enumerated type that defines and names all the possibilities:

```
TQueryType = (qtFirst, qtLastGroup, qtAlbum, qtStockNo);
```

This type procedurestatement is declared in the SRCHSTR unit, because it needs to be used both there and in the SEARCH unit.

SetQueryType can be called with any of the TQueryType elements as a parameter. If you specify qtLastGroup, SetQueryType prepares Query1 to search on the LastGroup field; if you pass in qtFirst, SetQueryType prepares to search on the First field; and so on.

SetQueryType is called by both the BSearchClick method and the NSearchClick method:

```
procedure TSearcher.NSearchClick(Sender: TObject);
var
  S: string;
  QType: TQueryType;
begin
  if SearchStr.GetSearchStr(QType, S) then begin
    Query1.Close;
    SetQueryType(QType);
    Query1.Params[0].AsString := S + '%';
    Query1.Open;
  end;
end;
```

The N in NSearchClick stands for name, and this method is called when the user wants to search on a first name, last name, group name, or album name.

The method begins by popping up the SearchStr dialog, which enables the user to enter a string and pick the field he wants to search on. The various fields are represented by radio buttons, as shown in Figure 24.10

You've seen this type of dialog before, so I won't go into a description of how it works.

FIGURE 24.10.

The Enter Search String Dialog aids users who want to search the contents of a field for a string.

After retrieving the data from the user, the NSearchClick method asks the SetQueryType method to compose the appropriate query, and then resolves the query's bind parameter and retrieves the new cursor from Interbase. The end result is a dataset focused specifically on the needs of the user.

Transactions

The TRANSACT program, found on the CD, gives a brief introduction to Transactions. To use Transactions, you must have a TDataBase component on your Form, and you must use a real server such as Sybase, Informix, Interbase, or the local Interbase. It won't work with Paradox or dBASE files.

To begin, drop down a TDatabase component. Set the AliasName property of the TDataBase object to a valid alias such as IBLOCAL. Create you own string, such as IBNAME, to fill in the DatabaseName property of the TDatabase object. In other words, when you are using a TDatabase component, you make up the database name, rather than picking it from a list of available aliases.

Drop down a TQuery object and hook it up to the EMPLOYEE.GDB file that ships with Delphi. In particular, set the DatabaseName property of the TQuery object to IBNAME, not to IBLOCAL. In other words, set the DatabaseName property to the string you made up when filling in the DatabaseName property of the TDatabase component. You will find that DBNAME, or whatever string you chose, has been added to the list of aliases you find when you use the Query1.DatabaseName Property Editor.

Finally, set the Query1.SQL property to the following string:

```
select * from employee
```

and then set the Active property to True.

Once you've connected to the database, you can add a TDataSource and a grid so you can view the data. Also add four buttons, and give them the following captions:

> Begin Transaction
> Rollback
> Commit
> Refresh

The code associated with these buttons should look like this:

```
procedure TForm1.BeginTransactionClick(Sender: TObject);
begin
  Database1.StartTransaction;
end;

procedure TForm1.RollbackClick(Sender: TObject);
begin
  Database1.Rollback;
end;

procedure TForm1.CommitClick(Sender: TObject);
begin
  Database1.Commit;
end;

procedure TForm1.RefreshClick(Sender: TObject);
begin
  Query1.Close;
  Query1.Open;
end;
```

Run the program, click Begin Transaction, and edit three or four records. If you click RollBack and then Refresh, you will find that all of your work is undone, as if none of the editing occurred. If you edit three or four records and then click Commit, you will find that your work is preserved.

To learn more about this subject, you should read the very important online help entry called "Transaction Isolation Levels."

Note that when you run the TRANSACT program included on disk, you don't have to specify a password. This occurs because the LoginPrompt property of the TDatabase object is set to False, and the Params property contains the following string:

```
password=masterkey
```

Summary

In this chapter, you had a basic introduction to the local Interbase, and you wrote a useful Interbase program.

I should stress that Interbase is a very complex and powerful product, and what you have seen in this chapter should serve as little more than a brief introduction that will whet your appetite. In the next chapter, you will look at stored procedures, triggers, direct Interbase API calls, and a few other tricks that should help you grasp the extent of the power in both the local and server-based versions of Interbase.

The MUSIC program presented in this chapter shows that Delphi can protect you from the details of working with any particular server. In other words, the code in this program is very much like the code you would write for a program that uses Paradox or dBASE files, with the one exception of the way you handle searches. It should be stressed, however, that this one exception points toward a rather large gap that exists between Paradox, dBASE, and most networked servers. In other words, servers such as Interbase, Oracle, and Sybase are in many ways much more powerful than Paradox and dBASE. To be fair, I should perhaps add that Paradox and dBASE tables can provide robust and simple solutions to many problems.

Delphi protects you from the details of how a server handles basic database chores. However, Delphi also enables you to tap into the power associated with a particular server. This was one of the most delicate balances that the developers had to consider when they created Delphi: How can you make a database tool as generic as possible, without ever cutting off a programmer's access to the special capabilities of a particular server? The same type of question drove the developers' successful quest to make Delphi's language as simple and elegant as possible without ever cutting off access to the full power of the Windows API.

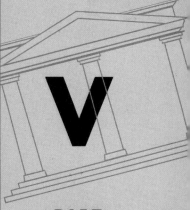

PART

Living in the Land of OOP: Components, Objects, and Advanced Programming Topics

Handling Messages

25

Overview

Event-oriented code is one of the central tenets of Windows programming. Some rapid-application development environments attempt to hide users from this feature altogether, as if it were something so complicated that most programmers couldn't understand it. The truth, of course, is that event-oriented programming is not, in itself, particularly complex. There are, however, some features of the way it is implemented in Windows that can be confusing under certain circumstances.

Delphi gives you full access to the event-oriented substructure that provides Windows with a high degree of power and flexibility. At the same time, it simplifies and clarifies the way a programmer handles those events. The end result is a system that gives you complete access to the power of Windows, while simultaneously protecting you from unnecessary complexity.

This chapter covers the following topics:

- Event-oriented programming basics
- Responding to mouse or key-down events
- Accessing the information passed in events
- The basics of sets, which are used frequently in Delphi event handlers
- Circumventing Delphi's message handling tools and directly capturing messages
- Creating `wm_Command` handlers and finding the IDs of the components used in a program

Before starting, let me reiterate that Delphi hides much of the complexity of Windows programming. However, the developers did not want to prevent programmers from accessing any portion of the Windows API. By the time you're done reading this chapter, however, you should be able to see that Delphi gives you access to the full range of power provided by an event-oriented system.

Delphi Events

Delphi makes it easy to handle keyboard and mouse events. Suppose, for instance, that you wanted to capture left mouse clicks on the main form of your program. Here's how to get started. Create a new project and name it EVENTS1.DPR. Go to the area in the code just underneath the word `implementation` and write the following `uses` statement, shown here with some surrounding text so you can see where to write it:

```
implementation

uses
 Dialogs;

{$R *.DFM}
```

In the Object Inspector for the main form, choose the Events page and double-click the area to the right of the `OnClick` property. Create the following procedure:

```
procedure TForm1.FormClick(Sender: TObject);
begin
  MessageDlg('Hello', mtInformation, [mbOk], 0);
end;
```

This code tells Windows that a dialog box should appear every time the user clicks the left mouse button on the form. The dialog box is shown in Figure 25.1.

FIGURE 25.1.

The dialog displayed by the EVENTS1 program when you click the main form with the left mouse button.

The previous code presents one of the simplest possible cases of responding to an event in a Delphi program. It is so simple, in fact, that many programmers write this kind of code without ever understanding that they are writing event-oriented code. In this case, Delphi programmers get the event secondhand; that is, VCL massages the event before passing it on to the main form. Nonetheless, this is real event-oriented programming, albeit in a very simplified manifestation.

Experienced Windows programmers know that when an event is generated, the operating environment notifies you not only of the event, but of several related bits of information. For instance, when a mouse-down event is generated, a program is informed about where the event occurred, and which button generated the event. If you want to get access to this kind of relatively detailed information, you should turn to the Events page for the form and create an `OnMouseDown` handler:

```
procedure TForm1.FormMouseDown(Sender: TObject;
                               Button: TMouseButton;
                               Shift: TShiftState;
                               X, Y: Integer);
begin
  if ssRight in Shift then
    Canvas.TextOut(X, Y, '* Button');
end;
```

This method writes text to the form every time the user clicks the right mouse button. To test this method out, run the program and click the right mouse button on the form in several different locations. You'll see that each spot where you click is marked, as shown in Figure 25.2.

The `Canvas.TextOut` procedure prints text to the screen at the location specified by the variables X and Y. Both of these variables are supplied to you by Delphi, which received them in turn from the operating system. The X variable tells you the column on which the mouse was clicked, and the Y variable tells you the row.

FIGURE 25.2.

Click the mouse button on the form of the EVENTS1 program, and the location of the event is recorded.

As you can see, Delphi makes it very simple for you to respond to events. Furthermore, it's not just mouse events that are easy to respond to. You can, for instance, respond to keypresses in a similar manner. For instance, if you create a method for the OnKeyDown property on the Events page for the form, you can show the user which key was pressed on the keyboard whenever the EVENTS1 program has the focus:

```
procedure TForm1.FormKeyDown(Sender: TObject;
                             var Key: Word;
                                 Shift: TShiftState);
begin
  MessageDlg(Chr(Key), mtInformation, [mbOk], 0);
end;
```

In the preceding code, the Chr function is used to translate a numerical value into an ASCII value. In other words, Delphi and the operating system both pass you not an actual letter like A, B, or C, but only the number that is associated with the key you pressed. In Chapter 7, "Integers in Detail," you saw that on PCs, the letter A is associated with the number 65. The Chr function translates the number 65 into the letter A. It wouldn't be appropriate for Delphi to perform this translation for you automatically, because some keys, such as the F1 or Enter key, have no letter associated with them. Later in this chapter, you will learn how to use OnKeyDown events to respond sensibly to keypresses on special keys such as F1, Shift, or Caps Lock.

Besides OnKeyDown events, Delphi also lets you respond to keyboard activity via the OnKeyPress event:

```
procedure TForm1.FormKeyPress(Sender: TObject; var Key: Char);
begin
  MessageDlg(Key, mtInformation, [mbOk], 0);
end;
```

You can see that this event is very similar to an OnKeyDown event. The difference is that the Key variable passed to OnKeyPress events is already translated into a Char. However, OnKeyPress events only work for the alphanumeric keys and are not called when special keys are pressed.

After this introduction to event-oriented programming, it's time to step back and see some of the theory behind the code. After explaining something of how the system works, this chapter goes on to give examples of how to take full advantage of Windows event-oriented code base.

Understanding Events

Event-oriented programming isn't unique to Windows, nor is it a chore that can be handled only by an operating system. For instance, any DOS program could be based around a simple loop that keeps running throughout the entire time the program is in memory. Here is a hypothetical example of how such code might look:

```
repeat
  CheckForMouseEvent(Events);
  CheckForKeyPress(Events)
  HandleEvents(Events);
until Events.Done := True;
```

This code represents a typical type of event-oriented loop. A simple `repeat...until` statement checks for keyboard and mouse events, and then calls `HandleEvents` to give the program a chance to respond to the events that are generated by the user and/or the operating system.

The variable called `Events` might be a record with a fairly simple structure:

```
TEvent = record
  X, Y: Integer;
  MouseButton: TButton;
  Key: Word;
  Done: Boolean;
end;
```

`X` and `Y` give the current location of the cursor, and `Key` contains the value of the top event in the key buffer. The previous `TButton` type might have a declaration that looks like this:

```
TButton = (lButton, rButton);
```

These structures permit you to track where the mouse is, what states its buttons are in, and what keys the user has pressed. Admittedly, this is a very simple type of event structure, but the principles involved mirror what is going on inside Windows, or inside other event-oriented systems such as Turbo Vision. If the program being written earlier was an editor, the `HandleEvent` for the program might look like this:

```
procedure HandleEvent(Events: TEvent);
begin
```

```
  case Events.Key of
  'A..z': Write(Events.X, Events.Y, Events.Key);
   EnterKey: Write(CarriageReturn);
   EscapeKey: Events.Done := True;
  end;
end;
```

Given the preceding code, the program would go to location X, Y and write the letter most recently pressed by the user. If the Enter key was pressed, a carriage return would be written to the screen. A press on the Escape key would cause the program to terminate. All other keypresses would be ignored.

Code like this can be very powerful, particularly if you're writing a program that requires animation. For instance, if you need to move a series of bitmaps across the screen, you want to move the bitmap a few pixels, and then check to see whether the user has pressed a button or hit a keystroke. If an event has occurred, you want to handle it. If nothing occurred, you want to continue moving the bitmap.

Hopefully, the short code examples shown earlier should give you some feeling for the way event-oriented systems work. The only piece that's missing is an understanding of why Windows is event-oriented.

Microsoft made Windows event-oriented in part because multiple programs run under the environment at the same time. In multitasking systems, the operating system needs to know whether the user has clicked on a program, or whether the click was on the desktop window. If the mouse click occurred on a window that was partially hidden behind another window, it is up to the operating system to recognize the event and bring that window to the fore. Clearly, it wouldn't be appropriate for the window itself to have to be in charge of that task. To ask that much would place an impossible burden on the programmer who created the window. As a result, it's best for the operating system to handle all the keystrokes and mouse clicks, and to then pass them on to the various programs in the form of events. Any other system would force every programmer to handle all the events that occurred when his or her program had the focus, and to then manipulate the entire operating system in response to certain mouse events or keystrokes such as Alt+Tab.

In short, Windows programmers almost never directly monitor the hardware or hardware interrupts. Instead, the operating system handles that task. It passes all external events on to individual programs in the form of messages. In a typical event-oriented system, the operating system continually polls the hardware in a loop, and then sends each event off to its programs in the form of some kind of event structure or event variables. This is the same kind of activity you see in the brief code snippets shown earlier.

You've seen that Windows handles mouse and keyboard events and passes them on to the appropriate window. The message that is generated in these cases gets sent to something called a default window procedure, or DefWindowProc. The DefWindowProc is analogous to the HandleEvent procedure shown earlier.

Each window on the desktop has its own DefWindowProc. To fully understand this statement, you need to grasp that every button, every edit control, every menu, every listbox, and virtually every other feature on the Windows desktop is actually a window with its own DefWindowProc. This is a very flexible and very powerful system, but it can force the programmer to write some fairly complex code, which is why Delphi gives you the option of being shielded from this technology.

The important point to understand is that Windows messages contain the information that drives the entire operating environment. Almost everything that happens inside Windows is a message, and if you really want to tap into the power of Delphi, you need to understand how these messages work.

If you look up DefWindowProc in the Windows API section of the online help, you'll find the following declaration:

```
function DefWindowProc(Wnd: HWnd; Msg, wParam: Word;
                       lParam: LongInt);
```

Each of the messages that is sent to a window is made up of four parts: The first part (Wnd) is just a handle to the window that generated the message; the second part (Msg) tells what has occurred, and the third and fourth parts (wParam and lParam) contain additional information about the event. Together these four parts are roughly equivalent to the TEvent structure shown previously.

The 16-bit Msg variable tells what event has occurred. For instance, if a mouse has been clicked, the Msg variable contains the value wm_MouseDown. On the other hand, if a keyboard event has occurred, the message that is sent is called wm_KeyDown. There are literally thousands of different types of messages of this sort, and they have names such as wm_GetText, wm_hsScroll, and wm_GetTextLength. If you want to see some more of these messages, choose Topic Search from the main menu and search on the letters WM.

> **NOTE**
>
> C programmers are used to seeing these constants declared in caps, so that you see WM_GETTEXT rather than wm_GetText. Of course, there is absolutely no difference between a wm_GetText message in Delphi and a WM_GETTEXT message in C. The identifiers both stand for the same literal numeric constant, and the difference in capitalization is merely a convention. Because Delphi is not case-sensitive, you can write either WM_GETTEXT or wm_GetText, depending on your preferences. The compiler doesn't care.

The last two parameters passed to DefWindowProc are 16 and 32 bits long, respectively, and are called wParam and lParam. These variables tell the programmer important additional information about each message that is sent. For instance, when a mouse is clicked, the location of the click and the button that was clicked are stored in these last two variables. Typically the X value might be stored in one half of wParam, while the Y value is stored in the other half.

One of the tricky parts of Windows event-oriented programming is extracting information from the wParam and lParam variables. In most cases, Delphi frees you from the necessity of performing this task. For instance, if you create an event for the OnMouseDown property, Delphi directly tells you the X value and Y value where the event occurred. As a programmer, you don't have to struggle to get the event and its associated values. As you will see in the next section, everything about the event is shown to you in a simple and straightforward manner.

Using Sets to Track Messages

Rather than ask you to parse the lParam and wParam parameters, Delphi performs this chore for you, and then passes the information on in the form of parameters:

```
procedure TForm1.FormMouseDown(Sender: TObject;
                               Button: TMouseButton;
                               Shift: TShiftState;
                               X, Y: Integer);
```

This is by far the most convenient way for you to handle events. It turns out that Delphi can also give direct access to the values sent to you by the operating system. That is, you can handle wParams and lParams directly, if you want. After you've studied the EVENTS2 program and learned more about sets, I'll show exactly how to get at that raw data.

Take a moment to consider the Shift parameter shown previously in the FormMouseDown header. Shift is declared to be of type TShiftState:

```
TShiftState = set of (ssShift, ssAlt, ssCtrl,
                      ssRight, ssLeft, ssMiddle,
                      ssDouble);
```

TShiftState is a set, and so far I have not spent much time on Delphi sets. As a result, that topic will be covered in some detail throughout the rest of this section of the chapter.

To find out whether a particular element is a member of the set passed to you by Delphi, you can perform simple tests using the in operator:

```
if ssRight in Shift then Label1.Caption := 'ssShift';
```

This code asks whether the element ssRight is in the set passed to you via the Shift variable. If it is, the code assigns the word ssShift to the Caption of a label.

Here is how you can declare a set at runtime:

```
Shift := [ssShift, ssAlt, ssCtrl];
```

Given this set, the in operator from the if statement shown previously returns True. The following set causes the operator to return False:

```
Shift := [ssAlt, ssCtrl];
```

Besides in, there are three other operators you can use with sets:

```
+       Union
-       Difference
*       Intersection
```

All three of these operators return a set, while the in operator returns a Boolean value. The SETSEXP program shows how to work with all four operators.

> **NOTE**
>
> The code for the SETSEXP program, found in the CHAP25 directory on this book's CD, shows how to use operators to track the members of sets such as TShiftState.

The SETSEXP program shows how you can read and manipulate sets. In particular, you will work with sets of type TShiftState. When you are finished studying the program, you will have all the knowledge you need to work with Delphi sets.

The main form for the SETSEXP program consists of four checkboxes, two panels, four labels, and three bitbtns, as shown in Figure 25.3. The four checkboxes are placed on top of the first panel, and the fourth label is placed on the top of the second panel.

SETSEXP tells you whether the Shift or Control keys are pressed when the mouse is clicked, and it tells you whether the user pressed the right or left mouse button. The code also shows how to use the Intersection, Union, and Difference operators.

FIGURE 25.3

The SETSEXP program's main form enables you to manipulate variables of type TShiftState.

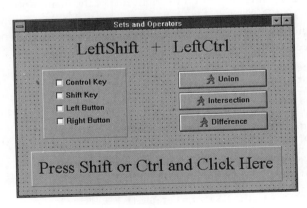

The key method in the SETSEXP program looks at a variable of type TShiftState and displays its contents to the user via the program's radio buttons:

```
procedure TUnion.CheckState(Shift: TShiftState);
begin
  ShiftKey.Checked := ssShift in Shift;
  ControlKey.Checked := ssCtrl in Shift;
```

```
   LeftButton.Checked := ssLeft in Shift;
   RightButton.Checked := ssRight in Shift;
end;
```

This code takes advantage of the fact that the in operator returns a Boolean variable, and the Checked property of a radio button is also declared to be of type Boolean. As a result, you can test to see whether a particular element is part of the Shift set. If it is, you can easily set the Checked state of a radio button to record the result. For example, in the previous code, if ssShift is part of the current set, the ShiftKey radio button is checked.

There are two different routines that pass variables of type TShiftState to the CheckState method. The first routine is called whenever the user clicks on the panel at the bottom of the program, or on the label that rests on the panel:

```
procedure TUnion.PanelMouseDown(Sender: TObject;
                                Button: TMouseButton;
                                Shift: TShiftState;
                                X, Y: Integer);
begin
  CheckState(Shift);
end;
```

This code passes the Shift variable on to CheckState, which displays the contents of the variable to the user. For instance, if the Shift key is being held down and the right mouse button is pressed, PanelMouseDown is called. PanelMouseDown then passes the Shift variable to CheckState, and CheckState causes the ShiftKey and RightButton controls to be checked. The other two radio buttons are left unchecked.

There are three bitbtns on the right side of the main form. They are labeled Union, Intersection, and Difference. Naturally enough, a click on any of these buttons demonstrates one of the non-Boolean set operators. All three buttons have their OnClick event set to the following procedure:

```
procedure TUnion.SetBtnClick(Sender: TObject);
const
  Operators: array[0..2] of string = ('+', '*', '-');
var
  FinalSet: TShiftState;
  LeftShift: TShiftState;
  LeftCtrl: TShiftState;
begin
  LeftShift := [ssLeft, ssShift];
  LeftCtrl := [ssLeft, ssCtrl];
  case TOptType((Sender as TBitBtn).Tag) of
    otUnion: FinalSet := LeftShift + LeftCtrl;
    otIntersection: FinalSet := LeftShift * LeftCtrl;
    otDifference: FinalSet := LeftShift - LeftCtrl;
  end;
  CheckState(FinalSet);
  Label2.Caption := Operators[(Sender as TBitBtn).Tag];
end;
```

The `SetBtnClick` method declares three variables of type `TShiftState`. Two of these variable are used to declare sets that will be used by the rest of the `SetBtnClick` method:

```
LeftShift := [ssLeft, ssShift];
LeftCtrl := [ssLeft, ssCtrl];
```

The first line assigns the `LeftShift` variable to a set that contains the values `ssLeft` and `ssShift`. The next line assigns the `LeftCtrl` variable to a set that contains `ssLeft` and `ssCtrl`. The rest of this method enables the user to see the union, intersection, and difference of these two sets.

The `case` statement in the middle of the `SetBtnClick` method detects which of the three bitbtns the user clicked. This is the old, time-honored technique featuring the use of an enumerated type, and the assignment of zero-based ordinal values to the `Tag` field of each button.

If the user clicks the Union button, the `FinalSet` variable is set to the union of the `LeftShift` and `LeftCtrl` variables:

```
FinalSet := LeftShift + LeftCtrl;
```

A click on the Intersection button executes the following code:

```
FinalSet := LeftShift * LeftCtrl;
```

The difference of the sets is calculated if the user clicks on the Difference button:

```
FinalSet := LeftShift - LeftCtrl;
```

After the `case` statement assures the selection of the proper operator, the `FinalSet` value is passed to `CheckState` and its contents is displayed to the user. For instance, if the user clicks on the Union button, the LeftButton, ShiftKey, and ControlKey radio buttons are all checked. The Intersection button causes the LeftKey to be checked, and the Difference button causes the ShiftKey to be checked. Here is another way of looking at the work accomplished by these operators:

```
[ssLeft, ssShift] + [ssLeft, ssCtrl] = [ssLeft, ssShift, ssCtrl];
[ssLeft, ssShift] * [ssLeft, ssCtrl] = [ssLeft]
[ssLeft, ssShift] - [ssLeft, ssCtrl] = [ssShift]
```

To help the user understand exactly what is happening, the current set operation is displayed at the top of the form. For instance, if the user clicks on the Union button, the following expression is shown to the user:

```
LeftShift + LeftCtrl
```

Throughout a run of the program the words `LeftShift` and `LeftCtrl` are displayed to the user in a pair of `TLabel`s. A third label displays `'+'`, `'-'`, or `'*'`, depending on the current state of the program:

```
Label2.Caption := Operators[(Sender as TBitBtn).Tag];
```

In this code, `Operators` is an array of three strings that contain the operators that return a set:

```
const
  Operators: array[0..2] of string = ('+', '*', '-');
```

The SETSEXP program gives you enough information so that you should be able to work with the sets that are passed to Delphi event handlers. The code shown here defines the way sets are usually handled in all Delphi programs. However, it happens that you can actually directly manipulate the raw data that represents a Delphi set. Techniques for performing these manipulations are shown in the `GetShift` method, which is part of the program examined in the next section of this chapter.

Tracking the Mouse and Keyboard

You now know enough to be able begin an in-depth study of the main event handlers used by Delphi forms and controls. The EVENTS2 program enables you to trace the occurrence of all the keyboard or mouse interrupts generated during the run of a program.

> **NOTE**
>
> The EVENTS2 program, found in the CHAP25 directory on this book's CD, provides a detailed look at how to track events. The `VKeys` unit is used by the EVENTS2 program.

EVENTS2 shows how to extract the full content of a message sent to you by Delphi. The main form for the program (shown in Figure 25.4) provides information on a wide range of mouse and keyboard generated events.

To use the program, simply compile and run. Click the mouse in random locations and press any of the keys on the keyboard. Just rattle away; you won't do any harm unless you press Ctrl+Alt+Delete! Every time you move the mouse, click the mouse, or strike a key, the exact nature of the event that occurred is shown in the main form of the program. For instance, if you move the mouse, its current location is shown on the form. If you press the F1 key while the Control key is pressed, those key's values are displayed on the form.

The `FormMouseMove` event handler in the EVENTS2 window tracks the current location of the mouse, and the state of its buttons. It does this by responding to `OnMouseMove` events:

```
procedure TEvents.FormMouseMove(Sender: TObject;
                                Shift: TShiftState;
                                X, Y: Integer);
begin
  LMouseMove.Caption := 'X: ' + IntToStr(X) + ' Y: ' +
                        IntToStr(Y) + ' ' + GetShift(Shift);
end;
```

FIGURE 25.4.

The EVENTS2 program tracks key Windows events as they occur.

The method for tracking the X and Y values is fairly intuitive. X stands for the current column, and Y stands for the current row, with columns and rows measured in pixels. Before these values can be shown to the user, they need to be translated into strings by the IntToStr function. Nothing could be simpler than the techniques used to record the current location of the mouse.

The technique for recording the current shift state, however, is bit more complex. As you saw earlier, TShiftState is a predeclared structure that looks like this:

```
TShiftState = set of (ssShift, ssAlt, ssCtrl,
                      ssRight, ssLeft, ssMiddle,
                      ssDouble);
```

The elements of this set track all the possible states of the Shift, Alt, and Control keys, as well as the mouse buttons.

Delphi records the state of a set in the individual bits of a variable, in which bit zero corresponds to the first element in the set, bit one corresponds to the second element in the set, bit two corresponds to the third element in the set, and so on. This fact enables you to use bitwise operators to track the state of the Shift button:

```
function GetShift(State: TShiftState): String;
var
  B, i: Byte;
begin
  Result := '';
  for i := 0 to 7 do begin
    B := Byte(1) shl i;
    if (B and Byte(State)) > 0 then Result :=
      Result + ' ' + Shifty[i];
  end;
end;
```

The preceding code takes advantage of the following constant array:

```
Shifty: T7StrAry = ('ssShift', 'ssAlt', 'ssCtrl', 'ssLeft',
                    'ssRight', 'ssMiddle', 'ssDouble');
```

as well as this type declaration:

```
T7StrAry = array[0..6] of String;
```

More specifically, the code checks to see whether the zero bit is set, and if it is, `'ssShift'` is added to the string returned by the function. If the first bit in the `Shift` variable is set to one, the string `'ssAlt'` is added to the string returned by the function, and so on. As you move through the bits in the `State` variable, you get a picture of the current state of the mouse and keyboard. For instance, if the Shift and Control keys are pressed, as well as the right mouse button, the string returned by the function looks like this:

```
ssShift, ssCtrl, ssRight
```

Bitwise operators can be tricky at times, but anyone can call the `GetShift` function. (See the BINARY.PAS unit, included on the CD in the UNITS subdirectory, for additional routines that help simplify the process of working on the bit level.)

Trapping Virtual Keys

When keys are pressed in a Windows program, two different messages can be sent to your program. One message is called `wm_KeyDown`, and it is sent whenever any key on the keyboard is pressed. The second message is called `wm_Char`, and it is sent when one of the alphanumeric keys are pressed. In other words, if you press the A key, you get both a `wm_KeyDown` and a `wm_Char` message. If you press a more esoteric key, such as the F1 key, only the `wm_KeyDown` message is sent.

`OnKeyPress` event handlers correspond to `wm_Char` messages, and `OnKeyDown` events correspond to `wm_KeyDown` events. That's why `OnKeyPress` handlers are passed a `Key` variable that is of type `Char`, and `OnKeyDown` handlers are passed a `Key` variable that is of type `word`.

When you get a `wm_KeyDown` message, you need to have some way of translating that message into a meaningful value. To help with this chore, Windows declares a set of virtual key constants that all start with `vk`. For example, if you press the F1 key, the `Key` variable passed to an `OnKeyDown` event is set to `vk_F1`, in which the letters `vk` stand for virtual key. The virtual key codes are found in the `WINTYPES` unit, and also in the online help if you search under "Virtual Key Codes."

You can test to see which virtual key has been pressed by writing code that looks like this:

```
if Key = vk_Cancel then DoSomething;
```

This code simply tests to see whether a particular key has been pressed. If it has, the code calls the `DoSomething` procedure.

To help you understand virtual keys, the GetKey method from the VKEYS unit returns a string stating exactly what key has been pressed.

```
function GetKey(K: Word): String;
begin
  case K of
    vk_LButton: Result := 'vk_LButton';
    vk_RButton   : Result := 'vk_RButton';
    vk_Cancel    : Result := 'vk_Cancel';
    vk_MButton   : Result := 'vk_MButton';
    vk_Back      : Result := 'vk_Back';
    vk_Tab       : Result := 'vk_Tab';
    vk_Clear     : Result := 'vk_Clear';
    vk_Return    : Result := 'vk_Return';
    vk_Shift     : Result := 'vk_Shift';
    vk_Control   : Result := 'vk_Control';
    vk_Menu      : Result := 'vk_Menu';
    vk_Pause     : Result := 'vk_Pause';
    vk_Capital   : Result := 'vk_Capital';
    vk_Escape    : Result := 'vk_Escape';
    vk_Space     : Result := 'vk_Space';
    vk_Prior     : Result := 'vk_Prior';
    vk_Next      : Result := 'vk_Next';
    vk_End       : Result := 'vk_End';
    vk_Home      : Result := 'vk_Home';
    vk_Left      : Result := 'vk_Left';
    vk_Up        : Result := 'vk_Up';
    vk_Right     : Result := 'vk_Right';
    vk_Down      : Result := 'vk_Down';
    vk_Select    : Result := 'vk_Select';
    vk_Print     : Result := 'vk_Print';
    vk_Execute   : Result := 'vk_Execute';
    vk_SnapShot  : Result := 'vk_SnapShot';
    vk_Insert    : Result := 'vk_Insert';
    vk_Delete    : Result := 'vk_Delete';
    vk_Help      : Result := 'vk_Help';
    vk_NumPad0   : Result := 'vk_NumPad0';
    vk_NumPad1   : Result := 'vk_NumPad1';
    vk_NumPad2   : Result := 'vk_NumPad2';
    vk_NumPad3   : Result := 'vk_NumPad3';
    vk_NumPad4   : Result := 'vk_NumPad4';
    vk_NumPad5   : Result := 'vk_NumPad5';
    vk_NumPad6   : Result := 'vk_NumPad6';
    vk_NumPad7   : Result := 'vk_NumPad7';
    vk_NumPad8   : Result := 'vk_NumPad8';
    vk_NumPad9   : Result := 'vk_NumPad9';
    vk_Multiply  : Result := 'vk_Multiply';
    vk_Add       : Result := 'vk_vkAdd';
    vk_Separator : Result := 'vk_Separator';
    vk_Subtract  : Result := 'vk_Subtract';
    vk_Decimal   : Result := 'vk_Decimal';
    vk_Divide    : Result := 'vk_Divide';
    vk_F1        : Result := 'vk_F1';
    vk_F2        : Result := 'vk_F2';
    vk_F3        : Result := 'vk_F3';
    vk_F4        : Result := 'vk_F4';
    vk_F5        : Result := 'vk_F5';
    vk_F6        : Result := 'vk_F6';
```

```
    vk_F7        : Result := 'vk_F7';
    vk_F8        : Result := 'vk_F8';
    vk_F9        : Result := 'vk_F9';
    vk_F10       : Result := 'vk_F10';
    vk_F11       : Result := 'vk_F11';
    vk_F12       : Result := 'vk_F12';
    vk_F13       : Result := 'vk_F13';
    vk_F14       : Result := 'vk_F14';
    vk_F15       : Result := 'vk_F15';
    vk_F16       : Result := 'vk_F16';
    vk_F17       : Result := 'vk_F17';
    vk_F18       : Result := 'vk_F18';
    vk_F19       : Result := 'vk_F19';
    vk_F20       : Result := 'vk_F20';
    vk_F21       : Result := 'vk_F21';
    vk_F22       : Result := 'vk_F22';
    vk_F23       : Result := 'vk_F23';
    vk_F24       : Result := 'vk_F24';
    vk_NumLock   : Result := 'vk_NumLock';
    vk_Scroll    : Result := 'vk_Scroll';
  else
    Result := Chr(K);
  end;
end;
end.
```

This procedure is really just a giant case statement that checks to see whether the Key variable is equal to any of the virtual keys. If it is not, the code assumes that it must be one of the standard keys that lie in the range between A and Z. (See the else clause in the code shown above to see how these standard keys are handled.)

As explained in the last paragraph, the virtual key codes do not cover normal letters such as A, B, and C. In other words, there is no value vk_A or vk_B. To test for these letters, just use the standard ASCII values. In other words, test whether Key is equal to 65, or whether Chr(Key) is equal to A. The point here is that we already have key codes for these letters. That is, the key codes for these letters are the literal values A, B, C, and so on. Because these are perfectly serviceable values, there is no need to create virtual key codes for the standard letters of the alphabet, or for numbers.

You probably won't have much use for the GetKey routine in a standard Delphi program. However, it is useful when you are trying to understand virtual keys and the OnKeyDown event. As a result, I have included it in this program.

Handling Events Directly

If you look down at the bottom of the EVENTS2 form, you'll see that there is a special event that tracks the position of the mouse. The EVENTS2 program tracks the mouse movements in two different ways because I wanted to show you that you can get information about the mouse either by responding to OnMouseMove events, or by directly tracking wm_MouseMove messages.

Here is how you declare a procedure that is going to directly capture a message:

```
procedure MyMouseMove(var M: TWMMouse);
  message wm_MouseMove;
```

The declaration shown here tells Delphi that you want to respond directly when the operating system informs your program that the mouse has moved. In other words, you don't want the Delphi VCL to trap the message first and then pass it on to you in an OnMouseMove event. Instead, you just want the message sent straight to you by the operating system. In short, you're telling the VCL this: "Yes, I know you can make this task very simple, and can automate nearly the entire process by using visual tools. That's nice of you, but right now I want to get the real event itself. I have some reason of my own for wanting to get very close to the metal. As a result, I'm going to grab the message before you ever get a chance to look at it!"

If you want to intercept messages directly, you should use the message keyword, as shown earlier in the MyMouseMove declaration. The proper way to use this syntax is to first write the word message, and then follow it by the constant representing the message you want to trap. When you use the message directive, you are declaring a form of dynamic method, which means Delphi will use the dynamic method table to dispatch your message. In particular, Delphi maintains a list of dynamic methods used in your application, and it locates a particular method's address by using the offset implied in the wm_MouseMove constant.

Here's the code for the MyMouseMove procedure:

```
procedure TEvents.MyMouseMove(var M: TWMMouse);
begin
  Inherited;
  LSpecialMouse.Caption := 'X: ' + IntToStr(M.XPos) +
                           ' Y: ' + IntToStr(M.YPos);
end;
```

You can see that the code begins by calling the inherited wm_MouseMove handler. If you didn't make this call, the program would still run, but the OnMouseMove event would never be sent to the FormMouseMove procedure. It isn't an error if you don't pass the message back to Delphi. You can either keep the message for yourself or pass it on, as you prefer.

Normally, when you call an inherited method, you need to specify which function you mean to call. For instance, if you are in a Paint method, you write

```
procedure Form1.Paint;
begin
  Inherited Paint;
  Canvas1.TextOut(1, 1, 'hi');
end;
```

When you are inside message handlers, however, there is no need to specify the inherited method you want to call, and you can therefore just write Inherited.

If you omit the call to Inherited from the MySpecialMouse procedure, the FormMouseMove method in the EVENTS2 program will no longer be called. In other words, you will be directly trapping wm_MouseMove messages and not passing them on to the VCL. As a result, the VCL will not know that the event occurred, and FormMouseMove will not be called.

The explanation in the last paragraph might not be easy to grasp unless you actually experiment with the EVENTS2 program. You should run the program once with the default version of the MyMouseMove method, and once with the call to Inherited commented out:

```
procedure TEvents.MyMouseMove(var M: TWMMouse);
begin
  { Inherited; }
  LSpecialMouse.Caption := 'X: ' + IntToStr(M.XPos) +
                           ' Y: ' + IntToStr(M.YPos);
end;
```

Notice that when you run the program this way, the OnMouseMove message at the top of the form is left blank.

If you look at the header for the MyMouseMove function, you can see that it is passed a parameter of type TWMMouse. The TWMMouse record, found in MESSAGES.PAS, looks like this:

```
TWMMouse = record
    Msg: Cardinal;
{$IFDEF WIN32}
    Keys: Longint;
    case Integer of
      0: (
        XPos: SmallInt;
        YPos: SmallInt);
      1: (
        Pos: TSmallPoint;
        Result: Longint);
{$ELSE}
    Keys: Word;
    case Integer of
      0: (
        XPos: Integer;
        YPos: Integer);
      1: (
        Pos: TPoint;
        Result: Longint);
{$ENDIF}
  end;
```

Assuming that you are using the 16-bit version of Delphi, the code shown here can be translated into the following record:

```
TWMMouse = record
    Msg: Cardinal;
    Keys: Word;
    case Integer of
      0: (
        XPos: Integer;
        YPos: Integer);
      1: (
        Pos: TPoint;
        Result: Longint);
```

```
end;
```

If you break out both of the options shown in this variant record, you can further simplify this record by writing:

```
TWMMouse = record
  Msg: Cardinal;
  Keys: Word;
  XPos: Integer;
  YPos: Integer;
end;
```

or

```
TWMMouse = record
  Msg: Cardinal;
  Keys: Word;
  Pos: TPoint;
  Result: Longint;
end;
```

For most users, one of these two views will be the most useful way to picture the record.

The same information is present in a TWMMouse record that you would find if you responded to an OnMouseMove or OnMouseDown event. If appropriate, you can find out the row and column where the mouse is located, what key is pressed, and what state the Shift, Alt, and Control keys are in. To pursue this matter further, you should look up wm_MouseMove and wm_MouseDown messages in the online help.

TWMMouse plays the same role in a Delphi program that message crackers from WINDOWSX.H play in a C++ program. In other words, they automatically break out the values passed in lParam or wParam. However, if you want, you can pass a variable of type TMessage as the parameter sent to the wm_MouseMove message handler:

```
procedure MyMouseMove(var M: TMessage);
  message wm_MouseMove;
```

Because TMessage and TWMMouse are both the same size, Delphi doesn't care which one you use when trapping wm_MouseMove events. It's up to you to decide how you want to crack the wParam and lParam parameters.

Here is a look at a TMessage structure:

```
TMessage = record
    Msg: Cardinal;
    case Integer of
{$IFDEF WIN32}
    0: (
      WParam: Longint;
      LParam: Longint;
      Result: Longint);
    1: (
      WParamLo: Word;
      WParamHi: Word;
      LParamLo: Word;
```

```
        LParamHi: Word;
        ResultLo: Word;
        ResultHi: Word);
{$ELSE}
      0: (
        WParam: Word;
        LParam: Longint;
        Result: Longint);
      1: (
        WParamLo: Byte;
        WParamHi: Byte;
        LParamLo: Word;
        LParamHi: Word;
        ResultLo: Word;
        ResultHi: Word);
{$ENDIF}
  end;
```

As you can see, this structure gives you a direct look at wParam and lParam. If this is the way you want to handle the event, this is a parameter you should declare. If you would rather use TWMMouse, you should use that structure. Finally, if you want to declare a structure of your own, you can go ahead and declare it and set it as parameter to a wm_MouseMove handler. All you have to do is be sure that it is the same size as TMessage and TWMMouse.

While looking at the records declared earlier, you no doubt noticed that there were sections of code that were ifdefed for WIN32. This means that those portions of the code that are marked WIN32 will be compiled only on systems running the 32-bit version of Delphi that will be released in the summer of fall or 1995. The source code used to make up the VCL is already set to compile one way under 32-bit Windows and another way under 16-bit Windows. This is done so that you can take standard Delphi programs and compile them unchanged either under 16-bit Windows, or under 32-bit Windows.

I don't mean to imply that the 16-bit version of Delphi that shipped in the Spring of 1995 can compile either 16- or 32-bit code. That compiler only produces 16-bit code; you need the 32-bit compiler to compile 32-bit code. My point is that the VCL source code you write for the 16-bit compiler will also compile under the 32-bit compiler. Of course, the 32-bit compiler won't be ready until the summer of 1995, but after that, you can take your choice between 16- and 32-bit code. In short, the use of compiler directives allows the Delphi message crackers to have the same kind of flexibility found in the macros supplied with WINDOWSX.H.

> **NOTE**
>
> In the preceding two paragraphs, I specify "standard" Delphi programs and "VCL" code. I add these qualifiers because Delphi is such a flexible tool that it lets you write Windows API code that can be totally specific to either the 16- or 32-bit versions of Windows. In other words, there is nothing in Delphi to prevent you from writing 32-bit code that takes advantage of threads. However, you cannot take that code to the 16-bit version of Windows and expect it to work. The rule to follow is very simple: If

you write VCL code, it will compile under either the 16- or 32-bit compiler. However, if you start calling the Windows API directly, you take the chance that the call you make will change or not be supported under WIN32. Of course, most of the Windows API works in either 16- or 32-bit mode, but there are some calls that can cause trouble, and you need to be aware of them if you are going to try to write portable code.

In this section, you have learned something about directly handling Windows messages. When you write code that captures messages directly, you are in a sense reverting back to the more complicated model of programming found in Borland Pascal 7.0. However, there are times when it is very helpful to get close to the machine, and Delphi lets you get there if that is what you need to do.

Handling wm_Command

In standard Windows programming, as it was conducted before the appearance of visual tools, one of the most important messages was wm_Command. This message was sent to a program every time the user selected a menu item, a button, or clicked on almost any other control that is part of the current program. Furthermore, each of the buttons, menu items, and other controls in a program had a special ID, which was assigned by the programmer. This ID was passed to wm_Command handlers in the wParam variable.

Delphi handles wm_Command messages in such a way that you almost never have to think about them. For instance, you can get clicks on a button or menu by using the delegation model. Standard Delphi controls still have IDs, but Delphi assigns these numbers automatically, and there is no obvious way for you to learn the value of these IDs.

Despite Delphi's capability to simplify this aspect of Windows programming, there are still times when you will want to get down to the bare bones and start handling wm_Command messages yourself. In particular, you will want to find a way to discover the ID associated with a particular command, and you will want to trap that ID inside a wm_Command handler.

The MENUDEF program shown next gives a general overview of this topic. The program enables you to discover the ID used by a series of menu items, and then enables you to trap these IDs when they are sent to a wm_Command handler in the form of a TMessage.wParam variable.

Figure 25.5 shows the form for the MENUDEF program. Here are the menu items that you can't see in Figure 25.5:

```
Caption = 'File'
  Caption = 'Open'
  Caption = 'Close'
  Caption = 'Exit'
```

```
Caption = 'Edit'
  Caption = 'Cut'
  Caption = 'Copy'
  Caption = 'Paste'
```

FIGURE 25.5.

The MENUDEF program uses a TMemo, a TButton, and a TMainMenu control.

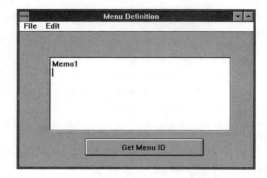

The code for the MENUDEF program is on this book's CD. You can see that it features two standard Delphi event handlers, as well as a wm_Command handler.

NOTE

The code for the MENUDEF program, found in the CHAP25 directory on this book's CD-ROM, shows the ID associated with the menus in a Delphi program.

The MENUDEF program has two features:

■ If you click the button at the bottom of the main form, the program's memo control displays a list of all the items in the menu, along with their IDs.

■ If you click any of the menu items, a message box appears stating that the item is not yet implemented. This is the kind of message you want to show the user while you are still developing a program. You are stating, in effect, that the control has been placed on the form, but that it doesn't do anything yet. Besides displaying the "under development" message in the body of the messagebox, the caption shows the menu item's ID.

Here is the code that grabs the ID of all the menu items, and displays the ID along with the menu item's caption in a TMemo:

```
procedure TForm1.MenuIDClick(Sender: TObject);
var
  Command, i: Integer;
  Name: string;
begin
  Memo1.Lines.Clear;
  for i := 0 to ComponentCount - 1 do
```

```
    if Components[i] is TMenuItem then begin
      Command := TMenuItem(Components[i]).Command;
      Name := TMenuItem(Components[i]).Caption;
      Memo1.Lines.Add(Name + ' = ' + IntToStr(Command));
    end;
end;
```

The code begins by clearing the current contents of the memo control. Then it iterates through all the components on the form and finds any of them that are of type TMenuItem. The next step is to get the ID and the caption of the menu items. To the get the ID, you need only reference the Command property of the TMenuItem component. The caption can be retrieved the same way, and then you can add this information to the listbox.

The use of the is operator in the previous code demonstrates Delphi's capability to work with Run Time Type Information. RTTI enables you to test the type of a particular variable and respond accordingly. For instance, in this case, the program simply asks whether a particular component is of type TMenuItem; if this Boolean question returns True, the program examines the component in more depth. The capability to use the is and as operators to detect the type of an object at runtime is one of the sexier features of Delphi's language.

The remaining code in the program captures the IDs of the menu items in an array, and then responds to wm_Command messages generated by clicks on one of the program's menu items. As explained earlier, the code displays a messagebox stating that the menus are not yet functional. In the caption of the menu box, you can read the ID of the control that was clicked.

The code that captures the menu items in an array occurs in a FormCreate method:

```
procedure TForm1.FormCreate(Sender: TObject);
var
  i: Integer;
begin
  for i := 0 to ComponentCount - 1 do
    if Components[i] is TMenuItem then begin
      MenuItemAry[TotalMenuItems] :=
        TMenuItem(Components[i]).Command;
      Inc(TotalMenuItems);
    end;
end;
```

This code is almost identical to the MenuIDClick method, except that the IDs of the TMenuItems are stored in an array, rather than being shown in a TMemo. The declaration for the array looks like this:

```
MenuItemAry: array [0..100] of Word;
```

The declaration for the wm_Command handler should be familiar to you by this time:

```
procedure WMCommand(var Message:TMessage);
  message wm_Command;
```

Here, the message directive tells the compiler that this is a dynamic method, and the offset in the dynamic method table is established by the wm_Command constant.

The WMCommand method compares the values sent in Message.wParam to the values in the MenuItemAry. If it finds a match, it displays the message box previously described.

```
procedure TForm1.WMCommand(var Message: TMessage);
var
  i: Integer;
  S1, S2: array[0..25] of Char;
begin
  inherited;
  StrCopy(S2, 'ID = ');
  for i := 1 to TotalMenuItems do
    if Message.wParam = MenuItemAry[i] then
      MessageBox(Handle, 'Not implemented',
        StrCat(S2, StrPCopy(S1, IntToStr(Message.wParam))), mb_Ok);
end;
```

This code calls the Windows API MessageBox function rather than MessageDlg. That means the program must wrestle with PChars, which are bit more complicated than Pascal strings. In particular, I use the StrPCopy procedure, which translates a Delphi string into a PChar. As I say, it's a bit more complicated than MessageDlg, but it gives you direct control over the caption of the message box.

One final point about working with the IDs of a control: If you build the interface of your program and then don't change its menus or any other aspect of its interface, the IDs Delphi associates with each control will (at least theoretically) remain the same throughout the development of your application. This might give some people the idea of using the MenuIDClick method shown earlier as a temporary response to a click on one of your controls, and to then store the output to a file. Thereafter, you would hope to know the ID associated with each of your controls, and could handle them in a wm_Command routine. This technique is theoretically possible, though I wouldn't recommend it as part of the framework for any serious application. In short, if you have to know the ID of a particular control, you should determine it in the FormCreate method, thereby assuring that the ID is correct for that build of your program.

Summary

In this section, you learned how to handle events using the standard Delphi delegation model. However, you saw that you can also circumvent this system and handle events directly by employing the message keyword. This is an important subject, and you shouldn't really move on until you have a good idea of what's going on in the EVENTS2 program.

The chapter also explained that you can start handling wParam and lParam variables directly. Furthermore, Delphi gives you a way to parse the information passed with events, so that you can place a custom record as the parameter to a message handler. For instance, if Windows conceals a set of X and Y coordinates inside the high and low words of wParam, Delphi enables you to define a custom record that automatically breaks up wParam into two separate variables called X and Y. This is the same functionality that is found in the message crackers provided in the WINDOWSX.H module that ships with Borland C++. The TWMMouse record discussed earlier is one of these records; TMessage is another. If you want, you can create your own records that parse the information associated with standard Delphi events, or with events that you create yourself. If you want further information on this system, you should see the MESSAGES.PAS unit that ships with Delphi, and also refer to the examples of creating custom events that were shown in the previous chapter.

Objects and Inheritance

Overview

This chapter focuses on object-oriented programming (OOP). Specifically, you will be taking a close look at inheritance, which is one of the big three topics in object-oriented code. The other two key topics are encapsulation and polymorphism, which you will learn about in the next chapter.

In particular, this chapter covers the following topics:

- OOP theory and basics
- Inheritance
- Virtual and dynamic methods
- Method pointers and procedural variables
- Virtual and dynamic method tables
- The is and as operators, which provide valuable Run Time Type Information (RTTI)

This chapter will focus on several programs designed to show how objects are constructed, and why object-oriented programming works. One of the programs will be developed in several stages, so that you can see how an object hierarchy is developed. The program will not be completed until halfway through the next chapter, but when you are done you will know how to construct a useful object hierarchy.

Nearly all of the OOP lore passed on in this chapter applies to VCL programming, and not to the old object model that was used in BP7. In other words, Delphi can create two kinds of objects: a new type of object that uses the reserved word class and an old form of object based on the reserved word object. The old object model was part of Turbo Pascal, OWL, and Turbo Vision, and still works in Delphi. However, it is being phased out, so I am concentrating on the future, which is VCL. VCL uses the reserved word class when declaring an object.

After you read this chapter and its successor, the next big step will be to learn how to build components. In fact, the real justification for learning this material is that it gives you the ability to start creating your own components. Building your own components is one of the most important tasks you can tackle in Delphi, and I'm going to spend the next two chapters making sure that I properly lay the groundwork.

About Objects

It may seem a little strange to start focusing on objects this late in the book. After all, almost every program I've shown so far uses object-oriented code. So, how could I wait this long to begin talking seriously about objects? To answer this question I need to discuss two different issues:

- How does Delphi treat objects?
- Why do people write object-oriented code?

The developers wanted Delphi to be very easy to use. By its very nature, OOP is not always a simple topic. As a result, Delphi goes to considerable lengths to hide some of the difficulties of object-oriented programming from the user. The biggest steps in this direction include the automatic construction of `Form1` as an object, and the fact that the framework for most methods is produced automatically by the IDE.

The simple fact is that some people would never be able to approach Delphi if they had to go through the process of writing all of this every time they created a form:

```
unit Unit1;

interface

type
  TForm1 = class(TForm)
  end;

var
  Form1: TForm1;

implementation

end;
```

I'm leaving out the uses clause and a few other features; but in a stripped-down form, this code is indeed the basis for most Delphi units. It's simple enough to write; nonetheless, it could form a barrier between the product and certain types of programmers.

The next obvious question is, "Why did the developers choose to write object-oriented code if the subject itself can at times become somewhat complex? Why not just use the relatively simpler framework provided by structured programming?" The answer is that it is indeed simpler to create small structured programs than small object-oriented programs; nevertheless it's easier to write large object-oriented programs than it is to write large structured programs.

OOP brings discipline and structure to a project. In the long run, this makes coding easier.

Almost everyone agrees that it's easier to finish a group project if you appoint a leader for the group, it's easier to win at sports if you practice regularly, and ultimately it's easier to become a good musician if you sit through some boring lessons with a professional. In other words, it might seem at first as if structured programs are simpler to learn how to write, and therefore are simpler to write. But this isn't true. Just as it helps to take lessons, practice, and learn discipline if you want to become good at playing a sport or a musical instrument, it helps to learn object-oriented code if you want to write good programs.

Here's another way of stating the same matter. There is nothing you can do with object-oriented code that you can't also do with structured programming. It's just that OOP makes it relatively easy to construct programs that are fundamentally sound and easily maintained. This does not mean that you can't write structured programs that are every bit as architecturally sound as object-oriented programs. The problem, however, is that it is very difficult to design a structured program that is truly modularized and truly easy to maintain. Object-oriented code, on the other hand, always moves you in the direction of a sound, well-structured design.

The thesis of this chapter then, is that object-oriented code is basically a technique for designing robust, well-planned programs. The point is not so much that you simply learn the syntax of OOP, but that you see why the syntax emerged out of the desire to write programs that are well-structured and easy to maintain.

> **NOTE**
>
> It's probably worth pointing out that OOP is not a separate subject from structured programming, but rather it emerged as a natural outgrowth of structured thinking. Or, perhaps it would be more correct to say that it emerged out of the same types of thinking that generated structured code. In other words, much of what is true in structured programs is also true in object-oriented programs, except OOP takes these theories much further. Object-based programmers should know nearly everything that structured programmers know, and should then add another layer of information on top of it.

OOP is certainly not the end-all and be-all of programming. Rather, it is an intermediate step in an ongoing process that may never have an end. Delphi, with its heavy use of components, already shows part of what the future holds. The Object Inspector enables you to see inside objects and to start to manipulate them visually, without having to write code. It is quite likely that this trend will continue in the future, and we will start to see programs not as code, but as a series of objects depicted in a tool not totally unlike Delphi's browser. If a programmer wants to manipulate these objects, he will be able to do so through tools such as the Object Inspector, or through other means currently only being used in experimental languages.

Clearly, the likely trend of the future is to give programmers the ability to combine components using visual tools. Right now, an object hierarchy can be a useful and robust way to construct a program. However, the hierarchy itself can be rigid and inflexible. The future will probably reveal a world in which components can be arranged in much more fluid, flexible hierarchies that can be manipulated visually. In other words, everything about objects always points toward the subject of how one can best design a robust, easily maintained program. Everything that makes the design process easier is likely to be promoted, while trends that tend to encourage rigid, inflexible structures are likely to be bypassed in favor of more fluid, flexible solutions.

To take this out of the clouds for a moment, here is my list of what's best about Delphi:

- Visual design tools
- A component architecture
- A real object-oriented language

Here are the same ideas looked at again from a slightly more in-depth perspective:

- **Visual Tools:** You can easily design a form using visual tools. To create a useful form, you want to be able to arrange and rearrange the elements of the visual design quickly and easily. Delphi excels at this.

- **Components:** You want to be able to manipulate objects not only as code, but as seemingly physical entities that you can handle with the mouse. Components provide an ideal solution to this problem. The plastic Lego sets we played with as children were fascinating because they allowed us to build complex structures out of simple, easy-to-manipulate pieces. In other words, Legos let us concentrate on the design of structures, while making the actual construction of a robust and easy-to-maintain building relatively trivial. Components give the same kind of flexibility.

- **OOP:** Objects, and particularly the ability to view object hierarchies in the browser, make it easy to see the overall design of a program. It's possible to see how a program is constructed not only by looking at the code, but also by looking at an object hierarchy. These kinds of abstract, visual representations of a code base aid in the process of designing and maintaining a program.

OOP, then, is part of a theory of design that is moving increasingly in the direction of visual components that can be manipulated with the mouse. Undoubtedly, this means some types of programs that are difficult to construct today will become trivial to build in the future. Delphi has already performed this magic with databases. A 10-year old could use Delphi to construct a simple database application. However, creating complex programs will probably always be difficult, simply because it is so hard to design a good program that performs anything more than trivial tasks. First, printing presses, then typewriters, and finally word processors have made writing much easier than it used to be, but they have not succeeded in making us all into Shakespeares.

Delphi's object-oriented, component-based architecture makes programming easier than it used to be. That doesn't mean that now everyone will be able to program. It just means that now the best programmers will be able to make better applications.

Creating Simple Objects

If you start a new project, compile it, and then open the Browser, you see something like the image shown in Figure 26.1. There is a forest of objects depicted here, and little question that the view can be intimidating to someone trying to get their hands around OOP.

To help simplify matters, go to Options | Environment | Preferences and make sure the Gallery | Use on New Project radio buttton is selected. Click OK and choose New Project. In the Browse Gallery dialog, choose CRT Application, as shown in Figure 26.2.

FIGURE 26.1.

The object browser after compiling a minimal form-based application.

FIGURE 26.2.

Choosing a new project from the Gallery.

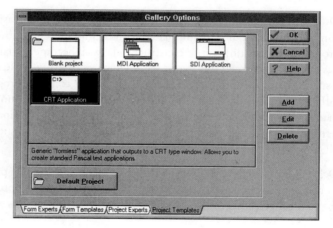

When you are done, you have a very small application that looks like this:

```
program CrtApp;

uses WinCrt;

begin
  WriteLn('Delphi');
end.
```

Save this file as OBJECT1.DPR. It is now a complete application that circumvents the VCL, and instead uses a relatively small, nonobject-oriented unit called WINCRT.

Go to the Options | Environment | Browser page and in the Object Tree | Collapse Nodes section, type in exception. This command tells the browser not to expand the hierarchy for class Exception. If you now open the Browser, you find the scene depicted in Figure 26.3. This is the most simplified object hierarchy you can create with a normal Delphi application. All of the VCL has been eliminated, except for classes TObject and Exception. The latter two objects cannot be eliminated because they are built into the heart and soul of the Delphi compiler.

FIGURE 26.3.

The browser for a WINCRT application, with the Exception *hierarchy collapsed.*

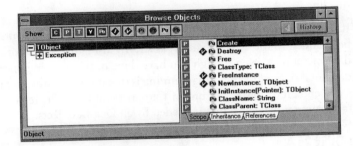

The fact that Delphi has some built-in objects in all apps shows how deeply the OOP paradigm has been integrated into the compiler. The issue here is that Delphi has "carnal knowledge" of TObject; that is, its logic is built into the very heart and soul of the whole system. It's not something layered on top of the compiler; it's part of the very warp and weave of the whole system. To a somewhat lesser degree, the same can be said of exceptions, but they are not quite so deeply integrated.

It may seem strange to you that I have gone out of my way to eliminate so much of the object hierarchy in a chapter that is about objects. My goal, however, is to clear the boards so that you can view objects in a simplified state, thereby clearly delineating their most salient points.

The program that will unfold through the next few pages is called OBJECT1. This is a very simple object-oriented program that you will build on the WINCRT framework established earlier. I'm not going to start by showing you the code for the whole program, because I want you to build it one step at a time, so that its structure emerges little by little. Before going any further, I ought to point out that this is not an extremely exciting application from a functional point of view. What's interesting is the technical aspect of the program.

To begin, you should create a small object at the top of the program:

```
program Object1;

uses WinCrt;

type
  TMyObject = class
  end;
```

```
begin
  Write;
end.
```

All I've done here is added a type section with a simple class definition, removed any parameters being passed to WriteLn, and changed the call to Write because Write does not post a carriage return. With no parameters, Write simply pops open a Window, but leaves its contents blank. If you use WriteLn instead of Write, the window pops open and the cursor moves down one line.

If you now compile the application and open the Browser, you see that your new object has been added to the class hierarchy, as shown in Figure 26.4. Notice that this class is a descendant of TObject, even though you have done nothing to designate it as such. One of the fundamental rules of Delphi programming is that it is impossible to build a VCL object that is not a descendant of TObject or one of TObject's children. The reason for this is that TObject contains some intelligence that is needed by all Delphi objects.

FIGURE 26.4.

The class hierarchy after TMyObject has been added to it.

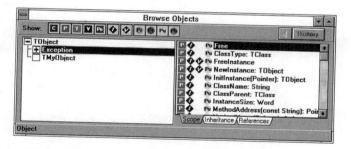

NOTE

You will find that I use the words *class* and *object* almost completely interchangeably. This is technically correct, although there is some merit in using the word class to describe the written declarations that appear in a text file, and object to refer to a compiled class that is part of a binary file. In other words, programs are made up objects, while source files show class definitions.

To help clarify the hierarchy in this application, you should probably change TMyObject's definition so that it reads as follows:

```
program Object1;

uses WinCrt;

type
  TMyObject = class(TObject)
  end;
```

```
begin
  Write;
end.
```

Logically, there is no difference between this declaration and the one you created earlier; however, now it is clear that TMyObject is a descendant of TObject.

The next step is to declare a variable of type TMyObject; then, instantiate it and dispose it:

```
program Object1;

uses WinCrt;

type
  TMyObject = class
  end;

var
  MyObject: TMyObject;

begin
  Write;
  MyObject := TMyObject.Create;
  MyObject.Free;
end.
```

The code shown here doesn't do anything functional. Its only purpose is to teach you how objects work. Specifically, it declares a variable of type TMyObject:

```
var
  MyObject: TMyObject;
```

Then, it allocates the memory for the object:

```
MyObject := TMyObject.Create;
```

Remember that this statement actually creates a pointer variable of type TMyObject. This means that you have to take this step if you want to use MyObject, and furthermore, you must dispose this memory when you are finished with it. Here is the code that frees the memory allocated in the previous line:

```
MyObject.Free;
```

When you free an object, what you are really doing is calling the object's Destroy method. Here is code that shows approximately what takes place in the Free method of TObject:

```
procedure TObject.Free;
begin
  if Self <> nil then
    Destroy;
end;
```

The variable Self always points to the current object. In other words, if you are inside one of the methods of an object, you can refer to that object by using Self.

> **NOTE**
>
> Programmers use the words descendant, child object, derived class, and subclass as synonyms. I prefer to use either descendant or child object, because subclass is also used in another context and derived class seems unnecessarily obscure. My feeling is that it's best to stick to one metaphor: parent, child, descendant.

Now that you know how to declare, allocate, and deallocate a simple object, it's time to narrow the focus and tackle the subject of inheritance. The next two sections are dedicated to this chore, and specifically to explaining the relationship between a parent and child object.

Understanding Inheritance

In general, a child object can use any of its parent's methods. A descendant of an object gets the benefit of its parent's capabilities, plus any new capabilities it might bring to the table. I say that this is true in general, because the private directive can limit the capability of a child to call some of its parent's routines. The private directive will be explained in depth later in this chapter.

If you open the Browser again, you see that there are a number of methods associated with TObject. If you highlight TMyObject in the browser and click on the *I* icon at the top of the Browser, you see that all of the methods associated with TMyObject are inherited from TObject. The *I* icon at the top of the Browser toggles on and off the ability to see inherited methods of an object. If you highlight TMyObject in the left Browser pane and then toggle inherited methods off, the right side of the Browser becomes blank. This is because all of TMyObject's methods and fields are inherited.

So, what are all these methods that are associated with TObject? Well, you can see their definitions, but not their implementations, if you open up the SYSTEM.PAS file from the \DELPHI\SOURCE\RTL\SYS subdirectory:

```
{ type
    TObject = class;
    TClass = class of TObject;
    TObject = class
      constructor Create;
      destructor Destroy; virtual;
      procedure Free;
      class function NewInstance: TObject; virtual;
      procedure FreeInstance; virtual;
      class procedure InitInstance(Instance: Pointer): TObject;
      function ClassType: TClass;
      class function ClassName: string;
      class function ClassParent: TClass;
      class function ClassInfo: Pointer;
      class function InstanceSize: Word;
      class function InheritsForm(AClass: TClass): Boolean;
      procedure DefaultHandler(var Message); virtual;
```

```
  procedure Dispatch(var Message);
  class function MethodAddress(const Name: string): Pointer;
  class function MethodName(Address: Pointer): string;
  function FieldAddress(const Name: string): Pointer;
end; }
```

As stated previously, the compiler has "carnal knowledge" of these functions, which helps explain why there is no place in the RTL where you can see their source. They are built right into the compiler, and though Borland is a warm and friendly company, it's not yet crazy enough to give you the source to its compiler!

You can see that TObject has a few basic functions declared right at the top:

```
constructor Create;
destructor Destroy; virtual;
procedure Free;
```

The point to grasp here is that TMyObject has Create and Free methods because it inherits them from TObject.

To help illustrate this point, you can add a line of code to the nascent OBJECT1 program:

```
begin
  Write;
  MyObject := TMyObject.Create;
  WriteLn(MyObject.ClassName);
  MyObject.Free;
end.
```

This code allows the object to write its name to the screen. The output from this program is a single string:

```
TMyObject
```

If you want, you can even get this object to say its parent's name:

```
begin
  Write;
  MyObject := TMyObject.Create;
  WriteLn('Parent: ', MyObject.ClassParent.Classname);
  WriteLn('Self: ', MyObject.ClassName);
  MyObject.Free;
end.
```

The output from this code is the following:

```
Parent: TObject
Self: TMyObject
```

The point, of course, is that TMyObject inherits quite a bit of functionality from its parent, and as a result it has numerous capabilities that might not be obvious from merely viewing its declaration.

The capability to trace an object's ancestry is relatively appealing, so it might be nice to add it to TMyObject as a method:

```
program Object1;

uses WinCrt;

type
  TMyObject = class
    procedure ShowHierarchy;
  end;

procedure TMyObject.ShowHierarchy;
var
  AClass: TClass;
begin
  WriteLn(ClassName);
  AClass := ClassParent;
  while AClass <> nil do begin
    WriteLn(AClass.ClassName);
    AClass := AClass.ClassParent;
  end;
end;

var
  MyObject: TMyObject;

begin
  Write;
  MyObject := TMyObject.Create;
  MyObject.ShowHierarchy;
  MyObject.Free;
end.
```

This version of the OBJECT1 program includes a single method, which is listed in the TMyObject class declaration:

```
TMyObject = class
  procedure ShowHierarchy;
end;
```

The implementation of the method looks like this:

```
procedure TMyObject.ShowHierarchy;
var
  AClass: TClass;
begin
  WriteLn(ClassName);
  AClass := ClassParent;
  while AClass <> nil do begin
    WriteLn(AClass.ClassName);
    AClass := AClass.ClassParent;
  end;
end;
```

The type TClass is an Object Reference, and is declared in SYSTEM.PAS as follows:

```
TClass = class of TObject;
```

Because ClassParent returns a variable of type TClass, it is obviously what needs to be used here.

NOTE

An Object Reference is a pointer that can be assigned to an object. Here is a unit that shows some legal things you can do with an Object Reference:

```
unit ClsRef;

interface

uses
  Forms;

type
  TObjectRef = class of Tobject;

  TDescendant = class(TObject)
  end;


procedure ShowClassReferences;
implementation

procedure ShowClassReferences;
var
  ObjectRef: TObjectRef;
begin
  WriteLn ('**start object references**');
  ObjectRef := Tobject;
  WriteLn(ObjectRef.ClassName);
  ObjectRef := Tdescendant;
  WriteLn(ObjectRef.ClassName);
  ObjectRef := Tform;
  WriteLn(ObjectRef.ClassName);
WriteLn ('*** end object references**');
end;

end.
```

Notice that you do not have to create an object before you can use it with an Object Reference.

You cannot use an Object Reference to refer to a field that belongs only to the child of the Object Reference type. For instance, this will not compile because Caption is not a property of TObject:

```
ObjectRef.Caption := 'Sam';
WriteLn(ObjectRef.Caption);
```

You will find a version of the CLsReF unit in the same subdirectory as OBJECT1. You can use the Project Manager to add this file to the project, and you can then call it in the second line of the body of the OBJECT1 program. However, you should not leave this unit as part of the project, because it will muddy the view of the object hierarchy that you get in the Browser.

When you get past the Object Reference, the remaining portions of the ShowHierarchy method are fairly straightforward:

```
begin
  WriteLn(ClassName);
  AClass := ClassParent;
  while AClass <> nil do begin
    WriteLn(AClass.ClassName);
    AClass := AClass.ClassParent;
  end;
end;
```

This code first writes the ClassName of the current object, which is TMyObject. Then, it gets the ClassParent, which is TObject, and writes its name to the screen. The code then tries to get TObject's parent, and fails because TObject has no parent. At this point, AClass is set to nil, and the code exits the while loop.

> **NOTE**
>
> You should take a moment to open the Browser, highlight TMyObject in the left pane, and then toggle the view of inherited methods on and off as described earlier. The last time you did this, TMyObject had no methods, so the right pane was blank when the option to show inherited methods was toggled off. Now, the right pane has one method, called ShowHierarchy. It will have a P in front of it because it is a procedure, and a Pb in front of it because it is declared in the Published section by default.

In this section, you have learned about the Create, Destroy, Free, ClassParent, and ClassName methods of TObject. The declaration of TObject shows that there are several other methods available to Delphi programmers. However, I will not discuss these methods in depth on the grounds that they are either self-explanatory (InheritsFrom) or beyond the scope of this book. I should mention, however, that some of these routines are used by the compiler itself when dispatching routines or performing other complex tasks. These are advanced programming issues that impact only a very small percentage of Delphi programmers.

Before going any further, I want to make sure you understand inheritance, and specifically the functionality of the ClassParent and ClassName routines. As a result, I am going to take a brief foray into a second program that shows how inheritance looks in a standard form-based Delphi application.

Showing the Hierarchy of a VCL program

To really appreciate the ShowHierarchy method, you need to add it to a regular Delphi application. For instance, if you make it a method of a standard Form1 class, here is the output you get:

```
TForm1
TForm
TScrollingWinControl
TWinControl
TControl
TComponent
TPersistent
TObject
```

This shows the whole hierarchy of class TForm1, starting with Self, moving to TForm, moving back to TScrollingWinControl, and so on, all the way back to TObject. In order to make this object work, I have had to modify the ShowHierarchy method slightly:

```
procedure TForm1.ShowHierarchy;
var
  AClass: TClass;
begin
  Memo1.Clear;
  Memo1.Lines.Add(ClassName);
  AClass := ClassParent;
  while AClass <> nil do begin
    Memo1.Lines.Add(AClass.ClassName);
    AClass := AClass.ClassParent;
  end;
end;
```

This code obviously depends on the presence of a TMemo object on the form, which is used in place of output to a WINCRT window. If you want to see this object in action, you can run the HIERARCHY.DPR program found on your disks (the misspelling is intentional due to 8-3 format of DOS names). The form for the HIERARCHY program is shown in Figure 26.5.

FIGURE 26.5.

The HIERARCHY form sports a TButton and a TMemo component.

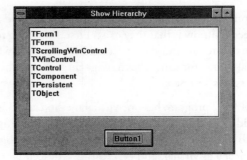

NOTE

The code for the HIERARCHY program, which shows how to trace the parents of a class, is in the CHAP26 directory on this book's CD-ROM.

By this time, you should have a fairly good grasp of inheritance and hierarchies. The key point to understand is that, in general, a child object inherits the capability to use any of its parent's methods. In other words, it comes into an inheritance, where the inheritance is the methods, fields, and properties of its parent. Except for TObject itself, all Delphi objects have parents that can trace their roots back to TObject.

Virtual, Dynamic, and Override

Inheritance, in itself, is an interesting feature, but it would not take on much significance were it not for the presence of virtual methods. Virtual methods can be overridden in a descendant class. As such, they provide the key to polymorphism, which is a trait of OOP programs that enables you to give the same command to two different objects but have them respond in different ways.

Delphi has three types of virtual methods, which use three different directives:

- `virtual`: This is the most commonly used of the three directives. It tells the compiler to store the address of the function in a Virtual Method Table.
- `dynamic`: This tells the compiler to store the address of a function in a Dynamic Method Table and generate a constant that can be used to identify the address during the lookup process.
- `message`: This tells the compiler to store the address of a function in a Dynamic Method Table, but here the user supplies a particular constant to use during the lookup process.

This chapter covers the difference between Virtual and Dynamic Method Tables, but for now, all you need to know is that they exist. First, I'm going to show how easy it is to use the `dynamic` and `virtual` directives, and then I'm going to explain why one more type of directive is needed. The actual syntax for using the message directive was explained in depth in Chapter 25, "Handling Messages and Sets."

The OBJECT2 program has one virtual method and one dynamic method. The virtual method is overridden in a child object. When you are creating the OBJECT2 program, you should start with the source code for the OBJECT1 program. Modify the code by declaring `ShowHierarchy` as virtual, and by creating a descendant of TMyObject called THierarchy.

> **NOTE**
>
> If you want to copy the code from OBJECT1 into another directory called OBJECT2, you should delete the DSK file, and perhaps also the OPT file. Otherwise, you might find yourself addressing files that are still stored in the OBJECT1 directory. If you rename OBJECT1.DPR to OBJECT2.DPR at the DOS prompt or in the File

Manager, you should also change the project's title as it is declared in the first line of the DPR program. That is, change `program Object1` to `program Object2`. If you don't do this, you will get a `Module header is missing or incorrect` error message.

NOTE

The OBJECT2 program's code (in the CHAP26 directory on this book's CD) demonstrates the `virtual`, `dynamic`, and `override` directives.

In OBJECT1, the `ShowHierarchy` method wrote its output to the screen. Suppose that you found this object somewhere and liked the way it worked, but wanted to change its behavior so that it could also write its output to a file. The OBJECT2 program shows how you would proceed.

In the old world of structured programming, the most likely step would be to rewrite the original `ShowHierarchy` method. However, rewriting an existing method can be a problem for two different reasons:

- You may not have the source code to the routine, so you can't rewrite it. However, you do have the binary file where the routine is kept, so you can still call it.

- You may have the source code, but you know that this particular method is already being called by several different programmers, and you are afraid to rewrite it on the grounds that you might break the routine itself, or might break the other programmers' code.

A combination of design and maintenance issues might deter the impulse to rewrite the original method. Many projects have been delayed or mothballed because changes in their design have broken existing code and thrown the entire project into chaos.

OOP has a simple solution to this whole problem. Instead of declaring `TMyObject` as

```
TMyObject = class(TObject)
  procedure ShowHierarchy;
end;
```

thoughtful programmers declare it like this:

```
TMyObject = class(TObject)
  procedure ShowHierarchy; virtual;
end;
```

The difference is that in the second example, the `ShowHierarchy` method is declared as virtual.

If `ShowHierarchy` is declared as virtual, you can override it, thereby changing the way the function works without ever changing the original version of the function. This means that all the other code that relies on the first version of the program continues to work, and yet you can rewrite the function for your own purposes. Here's how it looks:

```
THierarchy = class(TMyObject)
  procedure ShowHierarchy; override;
end;
```

This declaration states that class THierarchy is a descendant of class TMyObject, and that it overrides the ShowHierarchy method.

> **NOTE**
>
> BP7 programmers beware! The old object model performed the same chore by using the virtual directive in both the initial declaration and the overridden method. That's not the way VCL works! This is a major change between the new Delphi code and the old BP7 techniques.

The new version of the ShowHieararchy method looks like this:

```
procedure THierarchy.ShowHierarchy;
var
  F: Text;
  AClass: TClass;
begin
  if HMethod = hmscreen then
    inherited ShowHierarchy
  else begin
    Assign(F, 'inherit.txt');
    ReWrite(F);
    WriteLn(F, ClassName);
    AClass := ClassParent;
    while AClass <> nil do begin
      WriteLn(F, AClass.ClassName);
      AClass := AClass.ClassParent;
    end;
    Close(F);
  end;
end;
```

This code depends on variable called HMethod, which is assigned a value through a mechanism I will explain soon. The HMethod variable is of type THMethod:

```
THMethod = (hmScreen, hmDisk);
```

If HMethod is set to hmScreen, the old ShowHieararchy routine is called. If it is set to hmDisk, the new technique is used. The new technique simply opens a text file and writes the data to it, rather than writing it to the screen. Notice that there is no need to qualify any of the file handling routines with the word System. This omission is possible because the parts of the VCL that cause a conflict are not included in this stripped down WINCRT program.

The final piece in this puzzle involves setting the HMethod variable. To do this, the declaration of THierarchy needs to be expanded:

```
type

  ...

  THMethod = (hmScreen, hmDisk);

  THierarchy = class(TMyObject)
    HMethod: THMethod;
    procedure ShowHierarchy; override;
    procedure SetHierarchyMethod(Method: THMethod); dynamic;
  end;
```

You can see that a field has been added to this object; THierarchy now contains not only procedures, but also data. One of the key aspects of class declarations is that they can contain both methods and data, so that you can bring all of the code related to the THierarchy object together in one place. This is part of a concept called encapsulation, and it will be explained in the next chapter.

The SetHierarchyMethod is declared as dynamic. From a high-level vantage point, there is no difference between declaring a method dynamic or virtual. The syntax for using the two terms is identical.

If you want to override a dynamic method, you do so with the override directive, just as you would if the method was declared as virtual. This technique is demonstrated in the OBJ25.DPR program, which is found on your disk. The relevant declaration from that program looks like this:

```
TFoo = class(THierarchy)
  procedure SetHierarchyMethod(Method: THMethod); override;
end;
```

Here, you can see that SetHierarchy is overridden using the same technique used to override a virtual method.

The last issue involving the implementation of the OBJECT2 program is the SetHierarchy method itself, which looks like this:

```
procedure THierarchy.SetHierarchyMethod(Method: THMethod);
begin
  HMethod := Method;
end;
```

This code is simple enough to understand, but a bit awkward to use. The clumsiness will be eliminated in a later version of this program, after I explain how to create properties.

When you run the OBJECT2 program, the following code is executed in its main body:

```
var
  MyOject: THierarchy;
begin
  Write;
```

```
MyObject := THierarchy.Create;
MyObject.SetHierarchyMethod(hmScreen);
MyObject.ShowHierarchy;
MyObject.SetHierarchyMethod(hmDisk);
MyObject.ShowHierarchy;
MyObject.Free;
end.
```

This code creates an object of type THierarchy and then shows how you use the new functionality of the ShowHierarchy method.

> **NOTE**
>
> There are two design issues that ought to be discussed before abandoning the OBJECT2 program.
>
> OBJECT2 uses an enumerated type called THMethod. Programmers should be aware that enumerated types are not object-oriented and cannot be overridden. THMethod has two possible values: hmDisk and hmScreen. Suppose that another programmer comes along and wants to use both methods simultaneously. In other words, what this new programmer really wants is an hmBoth option. However, there is no way to supply this option without either breaking a lot of code or redeclaring THMethod. Because this new programmer might not have access to the source code, it might not be an option for him or her to rewrite the THMethod declaration. The point I'm making is that enumerated types are a bit dicey to use in object-oriented code, and you should consider using constants instead. You can always add one more constant to an object hierarchy, but you can't always change an enumerated type.
>
> The other design issue involves the fact that it's more expensive to call virtual or dynamic methods than it is to call a static method. As a result, you need to weigh the whole issue of whether you want to declare a method to be virtual. The SetHierarchy method, for instance, might not need to be declared dynamic. Such matters have to be considered in depth if you want to produce a well-written program.
>
> These two points are hardly earth-shattering in importance. However, I have said that OOP and design issues are intimately related concepts, so it's appropriate to discuss both issues in this chapter.

In this section, you have learned about the virtual, dynamic, and override directives. What you have learned here is very important, but its true significance won't be clear until you read about polymorphism. However, before you tackle that subject, it would be best to learn about VMTs and DMTs, and also about encapsulation.

Method Tables and Procedural Types

Dynamic and virtual method tables are one of the more esoteric features of object-oriented programming. Delphi has two different ways of dispatching virtual methods. Those declared with the `virtual` directive are relatively fast but take up a lot of space in memory. Dynamic methods, on the other hand, are a bit slower but conserve space.

To understand virtual and dynamic method tables, you need to understand that every function used in a program has an address. When it's time to call a particular function, the computer looks up the address of the function in memory, jumps to that address, and starts executing the code found at that address.

If you are new to the concept of procedures and functions having addresses, it would probably be helpful to see some concrete examples of procedural pointers.

> **NOTE**
>
> The FUNCPTR program shows how to declare a pointer to a function. You can find the code for this program in the CHAP26 directory on this book's CD-ROM.

The key line in this program is the type declaration in the `Button1Click` method:

```
TIntegerFunc = function(i: Integer): string;
```

This statement declares that `TIntegerFunc` is a pointer to a function that takes an `Integer` as a parameter and returns an `Integer` as a result.

The `IntegerFunc` procedure listed in this program is declared to be of this type:

```
function IntegerFunc(i: Integer): string; far;
begin
  IntegerFunc := i;
end;
```

Note that `IntegerFunc` uses the `far` directive. Therefore, if you are going to supply a pointer to a variable, you need to include not only its offset, but also its segment.

Given a procedural variable of the correct type, it becomes trivial to declare and use a pointer to a function:

```
var
  F: TFoo;
begin
  F := Foo;
  Edit1.Text := F(23);
end;
```

This code declares the variable F to be of type TFoo. It then assigns the Foo function to the variable F, and calls it:

```
F(23)
```

On most occasions when people need to use a pointer to a function, they want to pass the pointer to another location:

```
procedure TForm1.PassNCallClick(Sender: TObject);
var
  Func: TIntegerFunc;
begin
  Func := IntegerFunc;
  CallFunc(Func);
end;
```

In the PassNCallClick method, a procedural variable of type TIntegerFunc is declared, assigned, and then passed to the CallFunc method:

```
procedure CallFunc(Func: TIntegerFunc);
begin
  Form1.Edit1.Text := Func(2);
end;
```

CallFunc then calls the Func method and displays its result in Form1's TEdit control. I didn't make CallFunc a part of TForm simply because on most occasions when you use this technique, you are passing the function off to a DLL or some other remote part of the program, which is not part of the current object.

The key point of the CallFunc program is that it shows how to use a pointer to a function. As I explained earlier, the Virtual Method Table and Dynamic Method Table are simply lists of function addresses. In other words, they are tables that hold lists of addresses, in which each address is a pointer to a method. When the program needs to call a particular method, it looks up the method's address in one of these tables, jumps to that location in memory, and starts executing code.

Virtual method tables have all of the fields and functions available to an object in one table. Dynamic method tables are arranged hierarchically, so that each table corresponds to an object and contains addresses only of new dynamic methods or overridden dynamic methods. Each dynamic method table mirrors the declarations in a particular class, while virtual method table looks more like the objects shown in the Browser.

Because of their structure, dynamic method tables take up less room than virtual method tables. However, if you want to call a dynamic method that is not introduced or overridden in the current object, the program must search through the DMTs of the object's ancestors until it finds the method in question. This can involve iterating back through several method tables, and therefore often takes longer than the quick one-stop lookup for virtual methods.

I said earlier that dynamic methods and methods that use the message directive are closely related. In fact, all dynamic methods are assigned a constant just the way message handlers are, except for the fact that you don't have to explicitly assign the constant because the compiler automatically picks a unique constant for you. A dynamic method still follows this format:

```
procedure MyDynoProc;
  dynamic MyConst;
```

This is the same format followed in message handlers:

```
procedure WMCommand(var Message: TMessage);
  message wm_Command;
```

However, there is no need for you to actually declare MyConst, because the compiler declares it for you and makes sure the constant is unique:

```
procedure MyDynoProc; dynamic;
```

The point here is that the constant you or the compiler declares in dynamic methods is the key the program looks for when it is scanning the dynamic method tables. It just starts iterating through the tables until it finds the constant in question; then, it calls the address associated with that constant.

By now you should begin to have a general feeling for the way virtual and dynamic method tables work. I haven't given you enough information to write your own compiler, but I have told you what you need to know to start doing serious work with Delphi objects. In the next section, I will briefly cover method pointers; encapsulation is covered in the next chapter.

Method Pointers

You have seen how to declare a procedural variable. However, these pointers work only with functions and procedures, not with methods. The METHPTR program, which follows, describes how to work with method pointers of the same kind that are stored in VMTs and DMTs.

Programmers frequently need to declare pointers to methods. A classic example of this need is when you have a unit or DLL that performs a series of complex activities, and yet has no form associated with it. There may be times when this unit needs to query the user, but its lack of a form makes this process needlessly complicated. One simple way to remedy this problem is to pass in the address of methods that have access to a form. That way, the DLL can call these methods when it needs to talk to the user.

The main form for the METHPTR program contains an edit control and a button, as shown in Figure 26.6. The code for the program is divided into two simple units (shown on this book's CD-ROM).

FIGURE 26.6.

The METHPTR program shows how to pass a method address to a procedure.

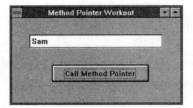

NOTE

The code for main form for the METHPTR program is in the CHAP26 directory on this book's CD-ROM. Also in that directory is the code that shows METHPTR passing a method pointer to this small unit, and then calling it from the `CallProc` procedure.

Method pointer declarations look just like procedural variables, except that they use the phrase `of object`:

```
type
  TMyProc = procedure(S: string) of object;
```

`TMyProc` is a pointer to a procedure that takes a single string as a parameter. It is declared in the `CALLER` unit because it needs to be used both there and in the program's main form.

Declaring and assigning a variable of this type inside the main form is exactly like calling a procedural variable:

```
procedure TForm1.CallMethPtrClick(Sender: TObject);
var
  AProc: TMyProc;
begin
  AProc := ShowMethod;
  CallProc(AProc);
end;
```

Because `AProc` is declared to be a pointer to a procedure that takes a string as a parameter, it can be assigned to the `ShowMethod` procedure:

```
procedure TForm1.ShowMethod(S: string);
begin
  Edit1.Text := S;
end;
```

`ShowMethod` is a simple routine that displays a string. This is exactly the kind of routine that a DLL or nonform-based unit might need if it wants to communicate with the user.

Finally, the `CALLER` unit declares and implements a short routine that calls the method pointer:

```
procedure CallProc(MyProc: TMyProc);
begin
  MyProc('Sam');
end;
```

This code calls ShowMethod and asks it to display the string Sam. To help you see how this logic works, you should step through the program with the debugger. Set the initial breakpoint at the beginning of the CallMethPtrClick routine and then press F7 until you get to ShowMethod.

After the FUNCPTR program, this code should be fairly transparent. The only difference between method pointers and procedural variables is that the passed method does not have to be explicitly declared far, and the of object syntax is added to the declaration of the procedural variable.

The *is* and *as* Operators

Run Time Type Information (RTTI) is implemented through the is and as operators. You can use the is operator to determine if an object is of a particular type. The as operator uses exceptions to ensure that typecasts are made safely. You will learn more about exceptions in Chapter 34, "Exceptions."

There are many different ways you can use RTTI in your programs. However, one of the most useful techniques involves checking the type of the object that generates an event. There are several examples of this technique in the RTTIOPS program, which is discussed below. The source for the program is included on the CD.

The following method from the RTTIOPS program is attached to an OnClick event for a button and an edit control:

```
procedure TForm1.ButtonTestClick(Sender: TObject);
begin
  if Sender is TButton then
    Edit1.Text := 'ButtonTestClick: Ok'
  else
    Edit1.Text := 'ButtonTestClick: Error';
end;
```

The code first checks to see if the Sender is of type TButton. If it is, the program writes the words ButtonTestClick: Ok to the screen; if it is not, the words ButtonTestClick: Error appear on the screen. This is a fairly trivial example, but it shows the way RTTI works.

Remember that in OnClick events, the Sender parameter always points to the control that caused the event to occur; that is, the one that delegated the action to the form. So if you click a button, as in the ButtonTest method and you test to see if Sender is a button, the is operator tells you that it is indeed a button that sent the message. However, if you click a button and ask the is operator if it was an edit control that sent the message, you get a negative answer.

You will always get a positive answer if you ask if a Delphi component is a TComponent. For instance, since a button is a descendant of a TComponent, you get a positive answer if you click a button and ask if the Sender is a TComponent. The DescendantClick method in the RTTIOPS programs demonstrates this technique.

> **NOTE**
>
> Before using the as operator (as discussed in the following section), you should turn off Break on Exception from the Options | Environment menu.

You can use the as operator to perform safe typecasts. Specifically, the as operator automatically checks a method's type and then performs a typecast. For instance, here is one way to perform a safe typecast:

```
if Sender is TEdit then
  TEdit(Sender).Name := 'Data';
```

Here is a second way to perform a safe typecast:

```
(Sender as TEdit).Name := 'Data';
```

The second method will raise an exception if Sender is not a TEdit.

The SafeTypeCast method from the RTTIOPS program typecasts Sender as a TButton by using the as operator. As long as the component attached to the code is indeed a TButton, the cast will succeed. If any other component is attached to the call, the typecast will raise an exception:

```
procedure TForm1.SafeCastClick(Sender: TObject);
begin
  Edit2.Text := (Sender as TButton).Name;
end;
```

SafeCastClick is attached both to a button and to the program's main form. Therefore, clicks on the main form will cause this method to raise an execption. The TryCastClick method, shown below, demonstrates how to use this same type of code without raising an exception.

The following method is attached to both a TButton and an TEdit:

```
procedure TForm1.TryCastClick(Sender: TObject);
begin
  try
    Edit2.Text := 'Good Cast: ' + (Sender as TEdit).Name;
  except
    Edit2.Text := 'Invalid cast: ' + (Sender as TComponent).Name;
  end;
end;
```

If the user clicks the TEdit, the function writes the words Goodcast: TEdit to the screen. If the user clicks the button control, the typecast in the try block fails and the code in the except block is executed. The code in the except block typecasts Sender as a TComponent, which is always safe. In other words, this code shows how to handle invalid typecasts without causing an exception.

Summary

In this chapter, you have had a good chance to start working with object-oriented programming. However, there are still several big topics to tackle, including encapsulation and polymorphism. Rather than try to cover such big topics inside this already lengthy chapter, I have decided to break things up and give them their own chapter where they can have plenty of room to unfold naturally.

Declaring pointers to methods, functions, and procedures is one of the important techniques commonly used by advanced programmers. When you start treating a procedure as nothing more than a location in memory, you are finally moving past the syntax of a language and starting to manipulate the raw tools built into every computer. One of the ironies of modern computing is that programmers must simultaneously embrace both the leveraged abstractions inherent in objects, and the raw power that comes from directly addressing locations in memory.

In the last part of the chapter, you got a look at RTTI. Run Time Type Information is one of the tools you need to write robust code in a visual environment. The objects in Delphi programs are constantly interacting. When you work in such a dynamic environment, you need a way to test the type of any one object. The solution to this problem is RTTI.

Objects, Encapsulation, and Properties

27

Overview

In this chapter, you will continue the overview of object-oriented programming begun in the last chapter. In particular, the focus is on encapsulation and properties. In the next chapter, you will examine polymorphism.

The following major topics are covered in this chapter:

- An overview of encapsulation, including the need to hide data and certain parts of the implementation.
- An in-depth look at the `private`, `protected`, `public`, and `published` scoping directives.
- Creating properties.
- The five basic types of properties: simple, enumerated, set, object, and array.
- Read-only properties.
- Why declaring default values for properties won't do what you think it's going to do.

This chapter features some of the syntactical jewels to be found in the Delphi treasure chest. In particular, it offers an unusually complete array of scoping directives. These tools enable you to fine-tune access to your objects in a way that helps promote reuse. Properties are also cutting-edge tools, and Delphi's implementation of them yields some surprising fruits, such as arrays that are indexed on strings.

Encapsulation

The word *encapsulation* and the word *object* are very closely linked in my mind. Encapsulation is one of the primary and most fundamental aspects of OOP. It is useful because it helps to enlist related methods and data under a single aegis, and because it helps to hide the implementation details that don't need to be exposed or might change in future versions of an object.

The capability to encapsulate methods and fields inside an object is important because it helps you design clean, well-written programs. To use a classic example, suppose that you were to create an object called `TAirplane`, which would represent (naturally enough) an airplane. This object might have fields such as `Altitude`, `Speed`, and `NumPassengers`; it might have methods such as `TakeOff`, `Land`, `Climb`, and `Descend`. From a design point of view, everything is simpler if you can encapsulate all these fields and methods in a single object, rather than have them spread out as individual variables and routines:

```
TAirplane = class(TObject)
  Altitude: Integer;
  Speed: Integer;
  NumPassengers: Integer;
  procedure TakeOff;
  procedure Land;
```

```
  procedure Climb;
  procedure Descend;
end;
```

There is a sleek elegance in this simple object declaration. Its purpose and the means for implementing its functionality are readily apparent.

Consider the class declaration from the current version of the OBJECT2 program:

```
THierarchy = class(TMyObject)
  HMethod: THMethod;
  procedure ShowHierarchy; override;
  procedure SetHierarchyMethod(Method: THMethod); dynamic;
end;
```

THierarchy encapsulates the ShowHierarchy method. If you want to call ShowHierarchy, you need to first instantiate an object of type THierarchy, and then use that object as a qualifier when you call ShowHierarchy:

```
var
  H: THierarchy;

begin
  H := THierarchy.Create;
  H.ShowHierarchy;
  H.Free;
end.
```

This kind of encapsulation is very useful, primarily because it makes you treat everything about the THierarchy object as a single unit. However, there are some limitations to this technique. In particular, when you have declared an object of type THierarchy, you have full access to all its methods and fields. It's true that you have to jump through one hoop before you can access THierarchy's innards, but still there is a sense that a program's data is not very well protected.

To eliminate this problem, Delphi defines four directives meant to aid in the process of encapsulation:

> private: Use this directive to declare a section in a class that can only be accessed from inside the current unit. For instance, if the HMethod variable is declared in a private section, it can't be accessed directly by code that is outside its unit. Private code and data can, however, be accessed by any object, method, procedure, or function that resides within the same unit.

> protected: Code declared in a protected section can only be accessed by descendant objects. In other words, if HMethod is declared in a protected section, variables of type THierarchy do not have access to it. You have to declare a descendant of THierarchy before you can directly access this variable. Once again, this rule applies only when you are outside the unit in which the object was declared. The point here is that protected fields and methods are available only to other component developers, but not to standard consumers of the object.

`public`: Code declared in a public section of an object is available to anyone who uses an object of that particular type.

`published`: Properties that are declared in the `published` section are public variables that appear in the Object Inspector. Furthermore, you can discover the type of published properties at runtime; simple published properties can be streamed to disk automatically. (See the ENUMINFO program in the PROGRAMS subdirectory for additional information.)

Given these scoping directives, this might be a sensible way to declare `THierarchy`:

```
THierarchy = class(TMyObject)
private
  FHierarchyMethod: THMethod;
public
  procedure ShowHierarchy; override;
  procedure SetHierarchyMethod(Method: THMethod); dynamic;
end;
```

And here is how to define `TMyObject`:

```
TMyObject = class(TObject)
public
  procedure ShowHierarchy; virtual;
end;
```

Notice that I have renamed `HMethod` to `FHierarchyMethod`. It is a standard Delphi convention to append an `F` before private fields, and to only use abbreviations like `HMethod` when it is absolutely clear what the `H` means.

All of the data in your programs should be declared private, and should be accessed through methods or properties. As a rule, it is a serious design error to give anyone access to the data of an object. Giving other objects or non-OOP routines direct access to data is a sure way to get into deep trouble when it comes time to maintain or redesign part of a program.

The whole idea that some parts of an object should remain forever concealed from other programmers is one of the hardest ideas for new OOP programmers to grasp. In fact, in early versions of Turbo Pascal with Objects, this aspect of encapsulation was given very short shrift. Experience, however, has shown that many well-constructed objects consist of two parts:

- ■ Data and implementation sections hidden from the programmers who use an object.
- ■ A set of interface routines that enable programmers to talk to the concealed methods and data that form the heart of an object.

Data and implementation sections are hidden so that the developer of an object can feel free to change them at a later date. If you expose a piece of data or a method to the world and find a bug that forces you to change the type of that data, or the declaration for that method, you are breaking the code of people who rely on that data or that method. Therefore, it's best to keep all your key methods and data hidden from consumers of your object. Give them access to those methods and procedures only through properties and public methods. Keep the guts of your object private, so that you can rewrite it, debug it, or rearrange it at any time.

One way of addressing the subject of hiding data and methods is to think of objects as essentially modest beings. An object doesn't want to show the world how it performs some task, and especially doesn't want to show the world the data that it uses to store information. The actual data used in an object is an extremely private matter, which should never be exposed in public. The methods that manipulate that data should also be hidden from view, because they are the personal business of that object. Of course, an object does not want to be completely hidden from view, so it supplies a set of interface routines that talk to the world, but these interface routines jealously guard the secret of how an object's functionality is actually implemented.

Essentially, a well-made object is like a beautiful woman who conceals her charms from a prying world. Conversely, a poorly made object should also hide its privates, much like an elderly man who no longer wants the world to get too close a look at how he is put together. These analogies are intentionally a bit whimsical, but they help to define the extremely powerful taboo associated with directly exposing data and certain parts of the implementation.

Of course, the point of hiding data and implementations is not to conceal how an object works, but to make it possible to completely rewrite the core of an object without changing the way it interacts with the world. In short, the previous analogies collapse when it comes to a functional analysis of data hiding, but they serve well to express the spirit of the enterprise.

NOTE

If you have the source code to the VCL, you will find that at least half of most key objects in the Delphi code base are declared as private. A few complex objects contain several hundred lines of private declarations, and only 20 or 30 methods and properties that serve as an interface for that object. Objects near the top of a hierarchy don't always follow this model, because they usually consist primarily of interface routines. It's the core objects that form the heart of a hierarchy, which are currently under discussion.

The internal methods of Delphi objects tend to reference their data through properties, rather than directly addressing the internal data storage. Not only consumers, but the very objects themselves, should have the discipline to enforce data hiding in their implementation. Strictly speaking, this is the correct and wisest approach, but you will find that I sometimes allow methods of an object to directly reference the data declared in that same object. This is perhaps a forgivable weakness on my part, but I am moving away from this practice because it has cost me during the maintenance phase of a project.

Whatever weaknesses I allow myself, or whatever careless practices you may find in certain programs included with this book, nevertheless, I firmly believe that it is always wrong to declare a variable outside of a private section. Hiding data and methods is one of the most important aspects of OOP, and programmers who ignore this practice are simply asking to deliver products that are buggy and late.

A Concrete Example

Neither TMyObject nor THierarchy give us much scope for exploring encapsulation. As a result, it's time to introduce a new class called TWidget, which is a descendant of THierarchy. In the chapter on polymorphism, TWidget will in turn become the ancestor of a series of different kinds of widgets that can be stored in a warehouse. In other words, in a computer factory TWidget might be the ancestor of a several classes of objects such as TSiliconChip, TAddOnBoard, and TPowerSupply. Descendants of these objects might be called T486Chip, T386Chip, TVideoBoard, and so on. Object hierarchies always move from the general to the specific:

```
TWidget
TSiliconChip
T486Chip
```

The rule enforced here is simple enough:

- A TWidget could be almost any object that is bought and sold.
- A TSiliconChip is some kind of silicon-based entity.
- A T486Chip is a specific kind of computer chip that has a real-world counterpart.

The movement is from the abstract toward the specific. It is almost always a mistake to embody specific traits of an object in a base class for a hierarchy. Instead, these early building blocks are so general that they can serve as parents to a wide variety of related objects or tools.

The OBJECT3 program includes a declaration for class TWidget. (See Listing 27.1.) The declaration makes use of all four directives used for hiding and exposing data. Notice also that the class declarations have been broken off into their own unit. This is done for two reasons:

- The program needs to be able to enforce the declaration of private data, which can only be accomplished if the classes involved are declared in their own unit.
- Class THierarchy is nearing the point of usefulness, so it's time for it to be broken off into a separate module that can be used by multiple programs and can exist as a single definable entity.

NOTE

The code for the OBJECT3 program is in the CHAP27 directory on this book's CD.

NOTE

The core of the OBJECT3 program in the CLASSDEF unit is in the CHAP27 directory on this book's CD.

The functionality associated with this program is still severely limited. An object of type TWidget is created, and its hierarchy is shown. The program next simulates the act of stocking up on a predefined number of these widgets. Finally, a bare representation of a widget is displayed on the screen:

```
W := TWidget.Create;
W.HierarchyMethod := hmScreen;
W.ShowHierarchy;
WriteLn(W.Quantity);
W.Stock;
WriteLn(W.Quantity);
W.Col := 20;
W.Row := 12;
W.Paint;
W.Free;
```

The output from this program is shown in Figure 27.1.

FIGURE 27.1.

The simple textual output from the OBJECT3 program.

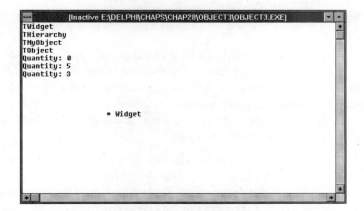

From a user's point of view, this is pretty tame stuff. However, the declaration for class TWidget shows programmers a good deal about how Delphi implements encapsulation:

```
TWidget = class(THierarchy)
private
  FCol: Integer;
  FRow: Integer;
  FQuantity: LongInt;
  FBoxSize: LongInt;
  FMaxQuantity: LongInt;
  FDescription: string;
  function GetQuantity: string;
  procedure SetQuantity(S: string);
protected
  function GetName: string; virtual;
public
  constructor Create; virtual;
  procedure Sell(Amount: LongInt); virtual;
  procedure Stock; virtual;
```

```
   procedure Paint; virtual;
   property Quantity: string read GetQuantity write SetQuantity;
published
   property Col: Integer read FCol write FCol;
   property Row: Integer read FRow write FRow;
end;
```

The private section of TWidget contains several fields of data and two methods:

```
private
   FCol: Integer;
   FRow: Integer;
   FQuantity: LongInt;
   FBoxSize: LongInt;
   FMaxQuantity: LongInt;
   FDescription: string;
   function GetQuantity: string;
   procedure SetQuantity(S: string);
```

All of the private data in the program has variable names that begin with the letter F. As stated before, this is a convention and not a syntactical necessity. These variables are called internal storage.

Internal storage should always be declared private, and as such cannot be accessed from outside of this unit. To reiterate, all of the data in any object should *always* be declared private. Other objects should never directly access any of this data, but should manipulate it through a predefined interface that appears in the protected, published, or public sections. If you want, you can think of the F in these names as standing for "Forbidden," as in "it is forbidden to directly access this data!"

The GetQuantity and SetQuantity functions are also declared private, and you will see that they are accessed via a property. Most objects have many more private methods, but TWidget is relatively bare in this department. The lack of private methods occurs because TWidget is such a simple object that there isn't much need to perform complex manipulations of its data.

The protected section is very simple and contains a single virtual method. This portion of the object can be accessed by descendants of TWidget, but not by an instance of the class. For instance, if you make the declaration

```
var
   W: TWidget;
```

then class W could not call GetName:

```
begin
  W := TWidget.Create;
  W.GetName;            { This line won't compile }
  W.Free;
end;
```

This functionality is available only from outside the unit in which the object is declared.

The `public` section of the object enables you to manipulate the widgets that you declare:

```
public
  constructor Create; virtual;
  procedure Sell(Amount: LongInt); virtual;
  procedure Stock; virtual;
  procedure Paint; virtual;
```

Here, you can see a method for selling widgets, a method for stocking up on new widgets, and a method for painting widgets to the screen. All of these are common activities and need to be declared public.

The `create` method for the object sets the value of `FBoxSize`:

```
constructor TWidget.Create;
begin
  inherited Create;
  FBoxSize := 5;
end;
```

`FBoxSize` is meant to represent the number of items found in a box of widgets. Some items aren't sold individually, but only in boxes, and this item describes how many widgets fit in one box.

Both `Sell` and `Stock` are very simple methods:

```
procedure TWidget.Sell(Amount: LongInt);
begin
  if Amount := 0 then
    FQuantity := FQuantity - FBoxSize
  else
    FQuantity := FQuantity - Amount
end;

procedure TWidget.Stock;
begin
  FQuantity := FQuantity + FBoxSize;
end;
```

Because the calculations that occur here are so extremely trivial, there is no need to hide their implementations in private methods. However, if this were a more sophisticated program, and either `Sell` or `Stock` needed to call methods with names such as `CalculateBoxSize` or `CalculateQuantity`, those methods would be hidden behind a property because they might change in the future, and the user does not need to know of their existence.

You have now had an overview of all the code in the OBJECT3 program, except for its properties, which will be discussed in the next section. The discussion so far has concentrated on the Delphi object scoping directives. You have learned about the `private`, `protected`, `public`, and `published` sections of a program, and seen why each is necessary.

Properties

Properties provide several advantages:

- Properties enable you to hide data.
- If you write a component and place it in the Component Palette, its published properties appear in the Object Inspector.
- Some properties can be made available at design time, whereas variables are only available at runtime.
- Properties can have side effects such as not only setting the value of the FWidth variable, but also physically changing the width of the object that appears on the screen.
- Property access methods can be declared virtual, which gives them more flexibility than simple variables.

The OBJECT3 program contains three properties:

```
public
  property Quantity: string read GetQuantity write SetQuantity;
published
  property Col: Integer read FCol write FCol;
  property Row: Integer read FRow write FRow;
```

There is no rule that says all properties should be declared in the published section. In fact, properties often appear in public sections, although there is little reason for them to be in private or protected sections. In this case, Quantity appears in the public, rather than published, sections because it could not be easily used in an Object Inspector.

The two published properties shown here are very simple tools that do nothing more than hide data and lay the groundwork for their use inside the Object Inspector:

```
property Col: Integer read FCol write FCol;
```

The declaration starts with the keyword property, which performs the same type of syntactical chore as procedure or function. Every property must be declared as having a certain type, which in this case is Integer.

Most properties can be both read and written. The read directive for the Col property simply states that the value to be displayed is FCol, and the value to write is FCol. In short, writing

```
var
  i: Integer;
begin
  Col := 2;
  i := Col;
end;
```

sets FCol to the value 2, and then sets i to the value of FCol, which is 2.

Once again, the major reasons for doing this are twofold:

- ■ To hide data so that it is protected.

- ■ To create a syntax that allows properties to be shown in the Object Inspector. Of course, you won't see these values in the Object Inspector until you metamorphose the object into a component, which is a subject that will be covered in Chapter 30, "Creating Non-Visual Components."

The Col and Row properties provide what is called direct access; they simply map directly to the internal storage field. The runtime performance of accessing data through a direct-access property is exactly the same as accessing the private field directly.

The previous example is the simplest possible case. The Quantity property has a few variations on these themes:

```
property Quantity: string read GetQuantity write SetQuantity;
```

Rather than reading a variable directly, Quantity returns the result of a private function:

```
function TWidget.GetQuantity: string;
begin
  Result := 'Quantity: ' + IntToStr(FQuantity);
end;
```

SetQuantity, on the other hand, enables you to change the value of the FQuantity variable:

```
procedure TWidget.SetQuantity(S: string);
begin
  FQuantity := StrToInt(S);
end;
```

GetQuantity and SetQuantity are examples of access methods. Just as the internal storage for direct access variables by convention begins with the letter F, access methods usually begin with either Set or Get.

Take a moment to consider what is happening here. To use the Quantity property, you need to make use of the following syntax:

```
 var
   S: string;
begin
  S := W.Quantity;
  W.Quantity := '25';
end;
```

In the preceding code, S is set to a string that might look like 'Quantity: 10' or 'Quantity: 25'. Note also that when you are writing to the FQuantity variable, you don't write the following:

```
W.Quantity('25');
```

Instead, you can use the simple explicit syntax of a direct assignment. Delphi automatically translates the assignment into a function call that takes a parameter. C++ buffs will recognize this as a limited form of operator overloading.

If there were no properties, the previous code would look like this:

```
var
  S: string;
begin
  S := W.GetQuantity;
  W.SetQuantity('25');
end;
```

Instead of remembering one property name, this second technique requires that you remember two; and, instead of the simple assignment syntax, you must remember to pass a parameter. Although it is not their primary purpose, it should now be obvious that one of the benefits of properties is that they provide a clean, easy-to-use syntax.

> **NOTE**
>
> The Quantity property differs from the Sell and Stock methods because it directly changes FQuantity, rather than adding to or subtracting from it.

In the last few pages, you had a fairly good look at the OBJECT3 program. However, there are several additional traits of properties that should be explored before moving on to the colorful warehouse simulation found in the next chapter.

More on Properties

Delphi provides support for five different types of properties:

- Simple properties are declared to be integers, characters, or strings.
- Enumerated properties are declared to be of some enumerated type. When shown in the Object Inspector, you can view them with a dropdown list.
- Set properties are declared to be of type set. BorderIcons from TForm is an example of this type of property. You can only choose one enumerated value at a time, but you can combine several values in a property of type set.
- Object properties are declared to be of some object type, such as the Items property from the TListBox component, which is declared to be of type TStrings.
- Array properties are like standard arrays, only you can index on any type, even a string.

The PROPTEST program gives an example of each of the five types of properties. It also gives the TStringList object a fairly decent workout. The program itself is only minimally useful outside the range of a purely academic environment.

NOTE

The main unit and the MYOBJ1 unit for the PROPTEST program are in the CHAP27 directory on this book's CD.

The structure of the PROPTEST program is simple. There is a main form with a button on it. If you click the button, you instantiate an object of type TMyObject. TMyObject has five properties, one for each of the major types of properties. These properties have self-explanatory names:

```
property SimpleProp;
property EnumProp;
property SetProp;
property ObjectProp;
property ArrayProp;
```

Before exploring these properties, I should mention that TMyObject is descended from the native Delphi object called TCustomControl. TCustomControl is intelligent enough to both display itself on the screen, and store itself on the component palette. It has several key methods and properties already associated with it, including a `Paint` method and Width and Height fields.

Because `TCustomControl` is so intelligent, it is easy to use its `Paint` method to write values to the screen:

```
procedure TMyProps.Paint;
begin
  Canvas.Brush.Color := clBlue;
  inherited Paint;
  Canvas.Rectangle(0, 0, Width, Height);
  Canvas.TextOut(1, 1, 'FSimple: ' + IntToStr(FSimple));
  Canvas.TextOut(1, Canvas.TextHeight('Blaise'), GetArray(0));
  Canvas.TextOut(1, Canvas.TextHeight('Blaise') * 2,
                 FObjectProp.Strings[1]);
end;
```

Note that you do not need to explicitly call the `Paint` method. Windows calls it for you whenever the object needs to paint or repaint itself. This means that you can hide the window behind others, and it will automatically repaint itself when it is brought to the fore. Inheriting functionality that you need from other objects is a big part of what OOP is all about. You will get a chance to look more closely at TCustomControl and similar objects in Chapter 29, "Creating Components."

The first three properties of TMyObject are extremely easy to understand:

```
property SimpleProp: Integer read FSimple write FSimple;
property EnumProp: TEnumType read FEnumType write FEnumType;
property SetProp: TSetProp read FSetProp write FSetProp;
```

These are direct access properties that simply read and write to or from a variable. You can use them with the following syntax:

```
M.SimpleProp := 25;
M.EnumProp := teEnum;
M.SetProp := [teEnum, TeSet];
```

> **NOTE**
>
> I once asked one of the developers whether properties such as these didn't waste computer clock cycles. Looking somewhat miffed, he said, "Obviously, we map those calls directly to the variables!"
>
> Chastened, and somewhat the wiser, I nodded sagely as if this were the answer I expected. Then, I ventured, "So they don't cost us any clock cycles?"
>
> "Not at runtime, they don't!" he said, and then concentrated once again on his debugger, which hovered over some obscure line in CLASSES.PAS.

The syntax for using the ObjectProp property is similar to the examples shown previously, but it is a bit harder to fully comprehend the relationship between an object and a property:

```
property ObjectProp: TStringList
     read FObjectProp write FObjectProp;
```

ObjectProp is of type TStringList, which is a descendant of the TStrings type used in the TListBox.Items property or the TMemo.Lines property. I use TStringList instead of TStrings because TStrings is essentially an abstract type meant for use only in limited circumstances. For general purposes, you should always use a TStringList instead of TStrings object. (In fact, neither TListBox nor TMemo actually uses variables of type TStrings. They actually use descendants of TStrings, just as I do here.)

> **NOTE**
>
> A TStringList has two possible functions. You can use it to store a simple list of strings, and you can also associate an object with each of those strings. To perform the latter task, call AddObject, passing a string in the first parameter and a TObject descendant in the second parameter. You can then retrieve the object by passing in the string you used in the call to AddObject.
>
> TStringLists do not destroy the objects that you store in them. It is up to you to deallocate the memory of any object you store on a TStringList.
>
> If you want a simple list object that doesn't have all this specialized functionality, use a linked list or the versatile TList object that ships with Delphi.

After making the declaration for ObjectProp shown earlier, you can now use it as if it were a simple TStringList variable. However, this can sometimes be a bit inconvenient. For instance, the following syntax retrieves an object that is associated with a string:

```
S := 'StringConstant';
MyObject := FObjectProp.Objects[FObjectProp.IndexOf(S)]
```

Furthermore, you must be sure to allocate memory for the FObjectProp at the beginning of TMyProps's existence, and you must dispose of that memory in the TMyProps destructor:

```
constructor TMyProps.Create(AOwner: TComponent);
begin
  inherited Create(AOwner);
  FObjectProp := TStringList.Create;
  ...
end;

destructor TMyProps.Destroy;
begin
  for i := 0 to FObjectProp.Count - 1 do
    FObjectProp.Objects[i].Free;
  FObjectProp.Free;
  inherited Destroy;
end;
```

This is the classic cycle so well known to BP7 programmers, but less frequently encountered in standard Delphi programming. The key point to remember is that TMyProps.Destroy is called automatically whenever the form is freed.

Finally, you must also allocate memory for each object you place in a TStringList. That is, you must not only create a TStringList, but you must also create each object you pass to the TStringList.AddObject routine. When you are done with those objects, you must destroy them:

```
for i := 0 to FObjectProp.Count - 1 do
    FObjectProp.Objects[i].Free;
```

There is nothing you can do about the necessity of allocating and deallocating memory for an object of type TStringList. You can, however, use array properties to simplify the act of accessing it, and to simplify the act of allocating memory for each object you store in it. PROPTEST shows how this can be done. Specifically, it entertains the conceit that you are creating a list for a party to which only married couples are being invited. Each couple's last name is stored as a string in a TStringList, and their first names are stored in an object that is stored in the TStringList in association with the last name. In other words, PROPTEST calls AddObject with the last name in the first parameter and an object containing their first names in the second parameter. This sounds complicated at first, but array properties can make the task trivial from the user's point of view.

In the PROPTEST program, I store a simple object with two fields inside the TStringList:

```
TCouple = class(TObject)
  Husband: string;
  Wife: string;
end;
```

Note that this object looks a lot like a simple record. In fact, I would have used a record here, except that TStringLists expect TObject descendants, not simple records. (Actually, you can sometimes get away with storing non-objects in TStringLists, but I'm not going to cover that topic in this book.)

As described earlier, it would be inconvenient to ask consumers of TMyObject to allocate memory for a TCouple object each time they needed to be used. Instead, PROPTEST asks the user to pass in first and last names in this simple string format:

```
'HusbandName, WifeName'
```

PROPTEST also asks them to pass in the last name as a separate variable. To simplify this process, I use a string array property:

```
property StrArrayProp[i: string]: string
  read GetStrArray write SetStrArray;
```

Notice that this array uses a string as an index, rather than a number!

Given the StrArrayProp declaration, the user can write the following code:

```
M.StrArrayProp['Jones'] := 'Sam, Mary';
```

This is a simple, intuitive line of code, even if it is a bit unconventional. The question, of course, is how can Delphi parse this information?

If you look at the declaration for StrArrayProp, you can see that it has two access methods called GetStrArray and SetStrArray. SetStrArray and its associated functions look like this:

```
function GetHusband(S: string): string;
begin
  Result := StripLastToken(S, ',');
end;

function GetWife(S: string): string;
begin
  Result := StripFirstToken(S, ',');
end;

procedure TMyProps.SetStrArray(Index: string; S: string);
var
  Couple: TCouple;
begin
  Couple := TCouple.Create;
  Couple.Husband := GetHusband(S);
  Couple.Wife := GetWife(S);
  FObjectProp.AddObject(Index, Couple);
end;
```

Note the declaration for SetStrArray. It takes two parameters. The first one is an index of type string, and the second is the value to be stored in the array. So, 'Jones' is passed in as an index, and 'Sam, Mary' is the value to be added to the array.

SetStrArray begins by allocating memory for an object of type TCouple. It then parses the husband's and wife's names from the string by calling two token-based functions from the STRBOX unit that ships with this book. Finally, a call to AddObject is executed. When the program is finished, you must be sure to deallocate the memory for the TCouple objects in the Destroy method:

```
destructor TMyProps.Destroy;
var
  i: Integer;
begin
  for i := 0 to FObjectProp.Count - 1 do
    FObjectProp.Objects[i].Free;
  FObjectProp.Free;
  inherited Destroy;
end;
```

The twin of SetStrArray is GetStrArray. This function retrieves a couple's name from the TStringList whenever the user passes in a last name. The syntax for retrieving information from the StrArray property looks like this:

```
S := M.StrArrayProp['Jones'];
```

In this case, S is assigned the value 'Sam, Mary'. Once again, note the remarkable fact that Delphi enables us to use a string as an index in a property array.

The implementation for GetStrArray is fairly simple:

```
function TMyProps.GetStrArray(S: string): string;
var
  Couple: TCouple;
begin
  Couple := TCouple(FObjectProp.Objects[FObjectProp.IndexOf(S)]);
  Result := Couple.Husband + ', ' + Couple.Wife;
end;
```

The code first retrieves the object from the TStringList, and then performs some simple handwaving to recreate the original string passed in by the user. Obviously, it would be easy to add additional methods that retrieved only a wife's name, or only a husband's name.

I'm showing you this syntax, not because I'm convinced that you need to use TStringLists and property arrays in exactly the manner showed here, but because I want to demonstrate how properties can be used to conceal an implementation and hide data from the user. The last two properties declared in this program show how to use important property types, and they also demonstrate how properties can be used to reduce relatively complex operations to a simple syntax that looks like this:

```
M.StrArrayProp['Doe'] := 'John, Johanna';
S := M.StrArrayProp['Doe'];
```

Consumers of this object don't need to know that I am storing the information in a TStringList, and they won't need to know if I change the method of storing this information at some later date. As long as the interface for TMyObject remains the same—that is, as long as I don't change the declaration for StrArrayProp—I am free to change the implementation at any time.

There is one other array property used in this program that should be mentioned briefly:

```
property ArrayProp[i: integer]: string read GetArray;
```

`ArrayProp` uses the traditional integer as an index. However, note that this array still has a special trait not associated with normal arrays: It is read-only! Because no write method is declared for this property, it cannot be written to; it can be used only to query the TStringList that it ends up addressing:

```
function TMyProps.GetArray(Index: integer): string;
begin
  Result := FObjectProp.Strings[Index]
end;
```

You can call `ArrayProp` with this syntax:

```
S := M.GetArray[0];
```

This is an obvious improvement over writing the following:

```
S := M.FObjectProp.Strings[0];
```

Creating a simple interface for an object may not seem important at first, but in day-to-day programming a simple, clean syntax is invaluable. For instance, the PROPTEST program calls `ArrayProp` in the following manner:

```
for i := 0 to M.ObjectProp.Count - 1 do
  ListBox2.Items.Add(M.GetArray(i));
```

In this case, it's very helpful that the call to `GetArray` is so simple. It would not be fun if you had to complicate matters further by writing this line:

```
ListBox2.Items.Add(M.FObjectProp.Strings[0]);
```

NOTE

Astute readers might be noticing that Delphi is flexible enough to enable you to improve even its own syntax. For instance, if you wanted to, you could create a listbox descendant that enables you to write this syntax:

```
ListBox2.AddStr(S);
```

instead of

```
ListBox2.Items.Add(S);
```

In the chapter on creating components you will see that you can even replace the TListBox object on the component palette with one of your own making! The secrets you are learning in these chapters on the VCL will prove to be the key to enhancing Delphi, so that it becomes a custom-made tool that fits your specific needs.

If you bury yourself in the Delphi source code, eventually you might notice the `default` directive, which can be used with properties:

```
property Default1: Char read FDefault1 write FDefault1 default '1';
```

Looking at this syntax, one would tend to think that this code automatically sets FDefault1 to the value '1'. However, this is not the purpose of this code. Instead, it tells Delphi whether it needs to stream this value when a form file is being written to disk. If you make TMyProp into a component, drop it onto a form, and save that form to disk, Delphi explicitly saves that value if it is not equal to

```
'1', but would skip it if it is equal to '1'.
```

An obvious benefit of the default directive is that it saves room in DFM files. Many objects have 25, or even 50, properties associated with them. Writing them all to disk would be an expensive task. As it happens, most properties used in a form have default values that are never changed. The default directive merely specifies that default value, and Delphi can thereby know whether it needs to write the value to disk. If the property in the Object Inspector is equal to the default, Delphi just passes over the property when it's time to write to disk. When reading the values back in, if the property is not explicitly mentioned in the DFM file, the property will retain the value you assigned to it in the component's constructor.

NOTE

The property is never assigned the default value by Delphi. You *must* ensure that you assign the default values to the properties as you indicated in the class declaration. This must be done in the constructor. A mismatch between the declared default and the actual initial value established by the constructor will result in lost data when streaming the component in and out.

Similarly, if you change the initial value of an inherited published property in your constructor, you should also reassert/redeclare (partial declaration) that property in your descendent class declaration to change the declared default value to match the actual initial value.

The default directive does nothing more than give Delphi a way of determining whether it needs to write a value to disk. It never assigns a value to any property. You have to do that yourself in your constructor.

Of course, there are times when you want to assign a property a default value at the moment that the object it belongs to is created. These are the times when you wish the default directive did what its name implies. However, it does not now, and never will, perform this action. To gain this functionality, you cannot use the default directive; you must use the constructor, as shown in the PROPTEST application:

```
constructor TMyProps.Create(AOwner: TComponent);
begin
  inherited Create(AOwner);
  Width := 100;
  Height := 100;
  ...
```

Here the Width and Height properties are set by default to 100. (As explained in the second paragraph of the note shown above, you need to be careful that you check to see whether a published property is declared as default.)

The PROPTEST program is obviously not meant to perform any useful function, but instead explores the world of properties from a syntactical point of view. Even the example of storing a couple's names in a TStringList is implemented primarily for the sake of exploring the syntax involved. It was just a fortuitous coincidence that it ended up yielding a fairly efficient, if idiosyncratic, solution to a real-life problem.

After reading this section, it should be clear that array properties represent one of the most powerful and flexible aspects of Delphi programming. I don't think it's stretching things to say that array properties provide the same kind of breakthrough flexibility that some people feel operator overloading brings to C++. However, operator overloading can be very confusing because one never knows just what an operator in C++ does. Because they can be overloaded, a '+', '-', '/', or other operator in a C++ program might mean very different things in different circumstances. Delphi array properties, on the other hand, always provide a clean, easy-to-read syntax that hides object data and implementations, without misleading a user of the code.

Summary

That wraps up this introduction to properties and encapsulation. The key points you have explored are the private, protected, public, and published directives, as well as the art of creating useful properties. To the best of my ability, I have also attempted to browbeat you with the importance of hiding data and methods. The key point to remember is that robust, easily maintainable programs never directly expose their data!

In the next section, you will learn about polymorphism, which is really the crown jewel of object-oriented theory.

Polymorphism

28

Overview

In this chapter you will learn about polymorphism. This is simultaneously one of the more esoteric and one of the most important features of object-oriented programming. Many people who write object-oriented code never use polymorphism. They may reap a number of important benefits of OOP theory, but they are missing out on a key tool that yields robust, flexible architectures.

A program called OBJECT4 forms the core of this chapter. OBJECT4 uses simple graphic objects to depict a warehouse in which several different kinds of widgets are stored. There are seven panels in this warehouse, each containing from 4 to 12 palettes full of widgets. You are able to stock each palette with new widgets and depopulate the palettes by selling off stock. It's also possible to reach a special view that shows the state of the widgets on an individual palette, and another view that uses graphs to show the state of the total stock.

The point of this chapter is to build up the object hierarchy begun in OBJECT1 to the point where it can be used for the relatively practical task just described. One of the main themes of the chapter is that OOP, which seems highly theoretical and intangible at first glance, actually turns out to be a natural tool for tracking and depicting the status of real objects, such as the inventory in a warehouse.

You don't need to understand polymorphism or much about objects to program in Delphi. However, if you want to be an expert Delphi programmer and want to create components, this is material you should master.

Polymorphism from 20,000 Feet

Polymorphism can be confusing even to experienced OOP programmers. My approach starts with a high-level overview of the subject, shows some real-world examples, and finally comes back to a second take on the high-level overview. Don't panic if you don't understand the next few paragraphs. I'm going to cover this material several times in several different ways, and by the time you are through, you're going to get it.

The classic example of polymorphism is a series of objects, all of which do the following:

- Descend from one base class
- Respond to a virtual command called Draw
- Respond to the command in different ways

For instance, you might have four objects called TRectangle, TEllipse, TCircle, and TSquare. Suppose that each of these objects are descendants of a base class called TShape, and that TShape has a virtual method called Draw. (This is a hypothetical TShape object and is not necessarily the one that appears on Delphi's component palette.) All of TShape's children also have Draw methods, but one draws a circle, one a square, the next a rectangle, and the last an ellipse.

From a conceptual point of view, this description does much to explain what polymorphism is all about. However, there is one key aspect that still needs to be explained before all the cards are out on the table.

According to the rules of OOP, you can pass all of these objects to a single function that takes an object of type TShape as a parameter. That single function can call the Draw method of each of these objects, and each one will behave differently. When you pass an object of type TRectangle to a function that takes a TShape as a parameter, you are accessing the TRectangle object through an object of type TShape. Or, if you look at the act of passing a parameter from a slightly different angle, you are actually assigning a variable of type TRectangle to a variable of type to TShape:

```
Shape := Rectangle;
```

This assignment is the actual hub around which **polymorphism** revolves. Because this assignment is legal, you can use an object of a single type, yet have it behave in many different ways: That's polymorphism.

To fully understand the last few paragraphs, you have to grasp that children of an object are assignment compatible with their parents. In other words, given the declarations you saw in the OBJECT1 program, the following is legal:

```
var
  Parent: TObject;
  Child: TMyObject;
begin
  Parent := Child;
end;
```

But, this is flagged as a type mismatch:

```
var
  Parent: TObject;
  Child: TMyObject;
begin
  Child := Parent;
end;
```

You can't set a child equal to a parent because the child is larger than its parent, and therefore all of its fields and methods will not be filled out. All other things being equal, you can build a two-story building out of the pieces meant for a three-story building; but you can't build a three-story building out of the pieces meant for a two-story building!

The issue here is that an assignment of Child to Parent is not safe. If it was allowed, it would be legal to write the following:

```
Child.ShowHierarchy;
```

In this hypothetical world, the call might compile, but it would fail at runtime because Parent has no ShowHierarchy method; therefore, it could not provide a valid address for the function at the time of the assignment operation.

On the other hand, if you assign Parent to Child, all of the features of parent will be filled out properly. That is, all of the functions of TObject are part of TMyObject, so you can assign one to the other without fear of something going wrong. The methods that are not part of TObject are simply ignored.

Here's another way of looking at the whole issue of polymorphism. A base class defines a certain number of functions that are inherited by all of its descendants. If you assign a variable of the parent type to one of its children, all of the parent's methods are guaranteed to be filled out with valid addresses because the child, by definition of its being a descendant object, must have the addresses for all the methods used in its parent's Virtual Method Tables and Dynamic Method tables. As a result, you can call one of these methods and watch as the child's functions get called. However, you cannot call one of the child's methods that does not also belong to the parent. The parent doesn't know about those methods, so the compiler won't let you call them. In other words, the parent may be able to call some of the child's functions, but it is still a variable of the parent type.

If some of the methods in a base class are defined as virtual, each of the descendants can redefine the implementation of these methods. These are the key elements that define a typical case of polymorphism: a base class, and the descendants that inherit a base class' methods. In particular, the fanciest type of polymorphism involves virtual methods that are inherited from a base class.

A second classic example of polymorphism is the entire Delphi VCL. All of these objects are descendants of a single base class called TObject; therefore, they all know how to obey a single virtual command called Destroy, which is originally defined in TObject's declaration. As a result, you can pass all the many hundreds of Delphi classes to a routine that takes a parameter of the same type as their base class. What defines the extent of the polymorphism is the methods in TObject, not the methods in a child class. Thus, every object in the VCL can use polymorphism to some degree, because they all inherit methods from TObject. In particular, they all inherit a virtual Destroy method, and the VCL frequently iterates through a series of objects calling Destroy on each in turn. Some simply use the Destroy method inherited from TObject; others override TObject.Destroy, and thereby implement the "highest form" of polymorphic behavior.

That's the end of the first high-level overview of polymorphism and virtual methods. The key points to remember are these:

- You can set a parent equal to a child object, but not a child equal to a parent object:

  ```
  Parent := Child; { Little assigned to big: Ok}
  Child := Parent; { Big assigned to little: Bad}
  ```

  The capability to set a parent equal to a child object is what makes polymorphism tick.

■ The defining elements in polymorphism are the methods of the parent object, and particularly those methods that are declared virtual. Even if you assign a child to a parent object:

```
Parent := Child;
```

the parent can't call methods of the child that are not also visible in the parent's class declaration.

In other words, you can take a whole slew of hierarchically arranged objects, assign them to their parent, call a virtual method belonging to the parent, and watch them all behave in different ways. Wee! Polymorphism!

For some readers, I'm sure this is old hat. Other readers might be new to the subject, but have grasped it completely from the descriptions given already. However, most readers probably still have some questions lingering in the back of their minds, so I will now move on to some concrete examples that should shed some light on the issue.

In particular, I am going to develop the OBJECT4 program, which builds on the code presented in the last two chapters, but finally brings it to some sort of useful fulfillment. The OBJECT4 program is quite long, so I will present it in its own section.

OBJECT4

As described at the beginning of this chapter, OBJECT4 is a warehouse simulation that features a series of panels arranged in a large room. Each panel has from 4 to 12 palettes on it, and each palette contains a certain number of widgets. The user can stock additional widgets on the palettes, or he or she can sell widgets. If the user sells a large number of widgets, the program is smart enough to iterate through the palettes and empty them one by one.

> **NOTE**
>
> The OBJECT4 program shows the outlines of a clean approach to a real-world problem. However, it is not a complete application that can be used in a business. Rather, it shows how objects can be used to embody actual objects or entities that we find in day-to-day life. To bring this program up to the point where it might be used in an office would be a considerable chore, which would involve adding both features and error checking. However, in the construction of any large project, one key step is the development of a methodology that can support a large application. The foundation for a useful program is found in OBJECT4. In fact, OBJECT4 shows a lot about the way any good OOP tool should be constructed.

The OBJECT4 program is stocked with hypothetical widgets that are named after colors: `TYellow`, `TBlue`, `TGreen`, and `TViolet`. A real-world application might have `TChairs`, `TTables`,

TBureaus, and so on, instead of colors. The point is not the names or traits of the individual widgets, but the fact that a series of different TWidget descendants needs to be created.

You will find that TYellow, TBlue, and the other colors share many traits. In a real-world program, each of these objects would be more varied. For instance, a TChair would have an FLegs data store, a TBed would have an FFrame data store, and so on.

> **NOTE**
>
> When studying OBJECT4, you will find that the TWidget object has changed slightly from its appearance in OBJECT3. These types of minor structural changes should be expected in OOP. Developers don't start with a base class and build up a hierarchy without ever deciding that changes need to be made to the structures they are creating. Frameworks and hierarchies evolve over time; they do not burst into the world fully formed.
>
> If you are building a certain kind of tool, after the first release, it is very dangerous to go back and start changing the way base classes work. Nevertheless, during development, changes need to be made to the base classes in your hierarchy. This is one of the major "gotchas" of object-oriented programming, and I would be remiss if I didn't lay it out in clear terms. Right now, there are no good remedies for this problem, but the lesson it teaches is clear: *Don't release objects to unsuspecting programmers until you are sure you have the proper design!* If you are looking for some relief, my experience has shown that most major companies don't think beta testers fit the definition of "unsuspecting."

The OBJECT4 program features five forms. The first depicts the floor of the warehouse. (See Figure 28.1.) The second depicts a report on the state of the widgets found on a particular palette. (See Figure 28.2.) The third enables you to specify how many objects of each type you want to sell. (See Figure 28.3.) The fourth depicts the status of the entire warehouse, using graphs to display the number and type of each object found in the warehouse. (See Figure 28.4.) The last form shows the hierarchy of a TWidget. (See Figure 28.5.)

FIGURE 28.1.

The Menagerie form shows the floor of the warehouse.

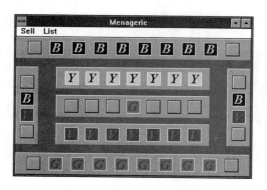

FIGURE 28.2.

The Report form shows the status of the objects on an individual palette.

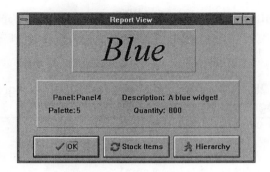

FIGURE 28.3.

The Sell Dialog enables the user to specify how many widgets of each type are being sold during a transaction.

FIGURE 28.4.

The Status form shows how many of each type of widget are currently available in the warehouse.

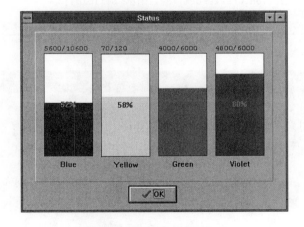

FIGURE 28.5.

The Hierarchy Dialog displays the hierarchy of a `TWidget`.

The OBJECT4 program is fairly long code; but, once again, you will find that many of the forms are relatively trivial, and that the core of the program can be found in a few relatively simple lines of code.

Listing 28.1. The project file for the OBJECT4 program is listed here; the rest of the program is found on the CD.

```
program Object4;

uses
  Forms,
  Main in 'MAIN.PAS' {Menagerie},
  Classdef in 'CLASSDEF.PAS',
  Reports in 'REPORTS.PAS' {Report},
  Status in 'STATUS.PAS' {StatusForm},
  Selldlgs in 'SELLDLGS.PAS' {SellDlg};

{$R *.RES}

begin
  Application.CreateForm(TMenagerie, Menagerie);
  Application.CreateForm(TReport, Report);
  Application.CreateForm(TStatusForm, StatusForm);
  Application.CreateForm(TSellDlg, SellDlg);
  Application.Run;
end.
```

NOTE

The main form for the OBJECT4 program is in the CHAP28 directory on this book's CD-ROM. Other code in that directory is listed here:

- The CLASSDEF unit, which is possibly the most important module in the OBJECT4 program
- The REPORTS unit, which describes the state of an individual widget
- The SELLDLG unit, which enables the user to report the amount of a particular sale
- The STATUS dialog, which displays graphs depicting the current supplies of each widget
- The Hierarchy dialog, which shows the hierarchy of TWidget

After starting the program, you can click any of the palettes shown in the warehouse. A menu appears asking you to specify the type of widget you want to place on the palette. You can choose to display a palette of Yellow, Blue, Green, or Violet widgets. After placing a few sets of widgets in the warehouse, you can click the List menu item to see the status of the entire warehouse. You can also click any individual palette that contains widgets to see a report on the type and number of widgets stored there. From inside the TReport form, you can add additional boxes of widgets to a palette. The final option in the program is the Sell menu item, which brings up a form called Sell Dialog that allows you to sell widgets. If you sell more than a full palette of widgets, a palette is emptied out and automatically deleted. If you sell less than a palette of widgets, the correct number of widgets is subtracted from one of the palettes. The program does no error checking in case you sell more widgets than there are in stock. Adding this feature, as the academicians would say, is left as an exercise for the reader!

> **NOTE**
>
> A key design issue in this program involves the capability to add new types at runtime. It might seem as if OBJECT4 is limited because you cannot dynamically add TPurple widgets at runtime, but must instead go back to the source to add this feature. Such a complaint stems from taking the program too literally.
>
> In a real-world program, you might have a TColoredWidget object, and would dynamically add or delete colors at runtime by changing the widget's Color property. Here, I'm simply using colors as a metaphor for any kind of widget, where each widget is meant to contain a unique set of traits representative of a larger class. For instance, a programmer might have objects such as TChair, TBed, and TTable. The program could then enable the user, at runtime, to add or delete various types of chairs such as Chippendale chairs, and art deco chairs. Major classes such as beds and chairs need to be differentiated as distinct objects, because beds will have FFrame and FMattress fields, and chairs will not have these fields, but instead FLegs, FSeat, and FBack fields. In short, this type of program does not allow the creation of a new class of objects at runtime, but it will enable you to add new types of a particular class. Deciding which types of objects need to be created at runtime is a major design issue worthy of serious consideration.

Before I begin talking about the code in this program, I should point out that I am not going to go through it in a line-by-line analysis. The program is simply too long for that kind of approach. At times, you may have to step through the code before you understand exactly how certain features are implemented, but that kind of activity can have unexpected benefits. In general, I'll assume that by this point in the book you understand how to code, so I will concentrate on discussing polymorphism.

Major Features of OBJECT4

OBJECT4 is a VCL program, not a WINCRT program. If you examine the code, you see that there are no references to WINCRT. The program begins by popping up a standard TForm descendant called TMenagerie.

You can paint a direct descendant of TObject on the form of a Delphi program if you want, but in the long run it is probably better to display components on forms. In particular, I wanted to associate a bitmap with each TWidget descendant I placed on a form. As a result, I decided to descend TMyObject from TImage, rather than directly from TObject. That way, I could inherit the capability to display a bitmap on a form, rather than having to create the functionality myself:

```
TMyObject = class(TImage)
public
  procedure ShowHierarchy; virtual;
end;
```

The most important single fragment of code in the OBJECT4 program is the declarations for TYellow, TBlue, and the other widgets:

```
  TBlue = class(TWidget)
    public
    constructor Create(AOwner: TComponent); override;
    procedure ShowHierarchy; override;
  end;

  TYellow = class(TWidget)
    public
    constructor Create(AOwner: TComponent); override;
    procedure ShowHierarchy; override;
  end;

  TGreen = class(TWidget)
    public
    constructor Create(AOwner: TComponent); override;
    procedure ShowHierarchy; override;
  end;

  TViolet = class(TWidget)
    public
    constructor Create(AOwner: TComponent); override;
    procedure ShowHierarchy; override;
  end;
```

The Create methods for each of these objects are very simple:

```
constructor TBlue.Create(AOwner: TComponent);
begin
  inherited Create(AOwner);
  Picture.LoadFromFile('blue.bmp');
  FDescription := 'A blue widget!';
  FQuantity := 800;
  FBoxSize := 50;
  FMaxQuantity := 1000;
end;
```

If you compare several of these Create methods, you see that certain fields of each object are assigned values that distinguish it from its peers.

The ShowHierarchy method is also very straightforward.

```
procedure TBlue.ShowHierarchy;
begin
```

```
    if FHierarchyMethod = hmDisk then
      inherited ShowHierarchy
    else
      HierarchyDlg.Run(Self, clBlue);
end;
```

The Hierarchy Dialog (shown in Figure 28.5) is a simple form containing a listbox and a button. The listbox displays the members of the hierarchy being shown. The key point here, however, is that each one differs slightly from the last, due to the fact that it passes a different color to `HierarchyDlg.Run`.

If you look at the form for `TMenagerie`, you see that the palettes laid out on the panels are really instances of `TSpeedButton`. If the user clicks on one of these palettes and asks to stock it with blue widgets, the following code is executed:

```
procedure TMenagerie.WidgetClick(Sender: TObject);
var
  WidgetType: Integer;
  Widget: TWidget;
begin
  WidgetType := (Sender as TMenuItem).Tag;
  case WidgetType of
    idBlue:  Widget := TBlue.Create(Self);
    idYellow:  Widget := TYellow.Create(Self);
    idGreen: Widget := TGreen.Create(Self);
    idViolet: Widget := TViolet.Create(Self);
  end;
  FCurSp.Enabled := False;
  FCurSp.Visible := False;
  Widget.Parent := FCurSp.Parent;
  Widget.Left := FCurSp.Left;
  Widget.Top := FCurSp.Top;
  Widget.Twin := FCurSp;
  Widget.Show;
end;
```

`FCurSp` is a pointer to the instance of `TSpeedButton` that the user selected. The assignment of `FCurSp` to the correct speed button occurs in a method called `sp41Click`:

```
procedure TMenagerie.sp41Click(Sender: TObject);
var
  P: TPoint;
begin
  FCurSp := TSpeedButton(Sender);
  P := Point(FCurSp.Left, FCurSp.Top);
  WinProcs.ClientToScreen(FCurSp.Parent.Handle, P);
  PopUpMenu1.Popup(P.X, P.Y);
end;
```

`WidgetClick` uses polymorphism. Specifically, it assigns a parent class to a child class:

```
Widget := TBlue.Create(Self);
```

It then disables and hides the speed button:

```
FCurSp.Enabled := False;
FCurSp.Visible := False;
```

And, it completes the instantiation of the instance of type `TBlue`:

```
Widget.Parent := FCurSp.Parent;
Widget.Left := FCurSp.Left;
Widget.Top := FCurSp.Top;
Widget.Twin := FCurSp;
Widget.Show;
```

The point here is that the parent object, `TWidget`, has `Parent`, `Top`, `Left`, `Twin`, and `Show` fields; so you can safely make these assignments regardless of whether the actual widget in question is of type `TYellow`, `TBlue`, `TGreen`, or `TViolet`. This is polymorphism in action.

> **NOTE**
>
> The `Twin` field of `TWidget` is a pointer to a `TSpeedButton`. While a `TWidget` descendant is visible on the screen, the speed button associated with it remains hidden and inactive. If the widgets on that palette are sold, the speedbutton is reactivated, and the instance of `TWidget` is destroyed. The `Twin` field is simply a mechanism that OBJECT4 employs in order to remember which speedbutton is associated with which `TWidget` descendant.

After reading the last few paragraphs, the core functionality of the OBJECT4 program should be clear to you. If it's not, you should try stepping through the program with the debugger. From now on, I will concentrate solely on explaining how the program implements various forms of polymorphism.

Classic Cases of Polymorphism

There are many examples of polymorphism in this program. Perhaps the most pure is found in REPORTS.PAS. Whenever the user clicks on one of the `TWidget` descendants, the following mouse-down routine is called:

```
procedure TWidget.MouseDown(Sender: TObject; Button: TMouseButton;
                            Shift: TShiftState; X, Y: Integer);
begin
  FActive := False;
  Report.Run(Self);
  FActive := True;
end;
```

This is a method of `TWidget`, so all of the `TWidget` descendants inherit it. As you can see, it calls `Report.Run` and passes itself as the parameter. Of course, each instance that is passed in is actually a reference to a variable of type `TBlue`, `TYellow`, `TGreen`, or `TViolet`. Once again, it is polymorphism that makes it possible to pass in objects of different types and assign them to a single variable of their ancestor's type:

```
procedure TReport.Run(Widget: TWidget);
begin
```

```
  FWidget := Widget;
  ShowData;
  ShowModal;
end;
```

Here, the variable called Widget is assigned to one of TWidget's descendants. The assignment occurs when a variable is passed as a parameter to the Run method. This is not what is traditionally thought of as an assignment, but in the end, a variable of type TWidget is assigned to an object of type TBlue, TYellow, TGreen, or TViolet.

The ShowData method makes it clear that this technique is working:

```
procedure TReport.ShowData;
begin
  LName.Caption := FWidget.GetName;
  LPalette.Caption := IntToStr(FWidget.Twin.Tag);
  LPanel.Caption := TPanel(FWidget.Parent).Name;
  LDescription.Caption := FWidget.Description;
  LQuantity.Caption := IntToStr(FWidget.Quantity);
end;
```

In this example, calling FWidget.GetName resolves one way for a class of type TViolet, and another way for a class of type TBlue. In the first case, it retrieves the string 'Violet', and in the second case, it retrieves the string 'Blue'. The same principle applies to calls to FWidget.Description, except that this time a property is called rather than a method. Each of these calls is an example of polymorphism in action.

I said earlier that the highest form of polymorphism occurs when there are virtual methods involved. If you click the Hierarchy button in the Report Dialog, a call to FWidget.ShowHierarchy is executed:

```
procedure TReport.BitBtn2Click(Sender: TObject);
begin
  FWidget.ShowHierarchy;
  ModalResult := mrNone;
end;
```

ShowHierarchy is a virtual method. As a result, if FWidget is assigned to an instance of TViolet, a different ShowHierarchy is called than if FWidget is assigned to a variable of type TGreen.

The kicker here, however, is that both methods display the object hierarchy not of TViolet, nor of TGreen, but of TWidget. Assigning a parent to a child object does not metamorphose the parent object into its child; it only maps the child's functions to functions of the same type that exist in the parent.

If you are having trouble understanding all of this, you should fire up Delphi and step through the code with the debugger. You can't just read about this kind of stuff; you have to make it happen yourself.

> **NOTE**
>
> This is definitely an excellent time to try to create your own objects and see whether you can get some polymorphism working, which involves calls to virtual methods that are resolved differently for different objects in your program. Get this subject down straight, and you can call yourself an expert in object-oriented programming!

As I said earlier, there are many examples of polymorphism in the OBJECT4 program. If you choose to explore it further, you will find examples scattered throughout every unit, and usually signaled by the declaration of a variable of type TWidget. These variables will, of course, be assigned to a child object. Every time this assignment occurs, polymorphism is taking place. But, as I said earlier, the purest—or at least the most interesting—forms of polymorphism occur when virtual methods are also added into the mix.

Method Addresses and Polymorphism

Polymorphism was not totally transparent to me until I began to think of it in terms of the actual method addresses involved in the assignment of a parent to a variable of type child. If you want to really feel at home with this baby, look at the method addresses of an object of type TChild, assign it to an object of type TParent, and look at the method addresses of the newly assigned TParent object.

The HEXADDRESS program, which follows, demonstrates one way of looking at these addresses. This program uses the MethodAddress routine from TObject to get the address of a method of a child object. If you then assign a child object to a parent object:

```
Parent := Child;
```

you see that it has the same address for the Foo method as the child object did. When stated so baldly, the whole idea of polymorphism suddenly becomes transparent. Of course it works this way! How else could it work?

The form for the HEXADDRESS program, shown in Figure 28.6, contains three edit controls, one list box, two labels, and one button. The edit controls are used only for displaying data, and the user never needs to enter anything in them. I use them instead of labels just because I like the way they set the information off on the screen.

The complete code for the HEXADDRESS program is on this book's CD-ROM. Here are the key methods from the program:

```
procedure TParent.Foo;
begin
  Form1.ListBox1.Items.Add('ParentFoo called');
end;
```

```
procedure TChild.Foo;
begin
  Form1.ListBox1.Items.Add('ChildFoo called');
end;

procedure TForm1.PressMeClick(Sender: TObject);
var
  P: TParent;
  C: TChild;
  Ptr: Pointer;
begin
  Label1.Caption := GetHexWord(CSeg);
  C := TChild.Create;
  Ptr := C.MethodAddress('Foo');
  Edit1.Text := Address2Str(Ptr);
  C.Foo;
  P := C;
  Edit2.Text := Address2Str(P.MethodAddress('Foo'));
  P.Foo;
  C.Free;
  P := TParent.Create;
  P.Foo;
  Edit3.Text := Address2Str(P.MethodAddress('Foo'));
  P.Free;
end;
```

FIGURE 28.6.

*The HEXADDRESS
program shows that if you
assign a parent object to a
child object, the two objects'
methods will have the same
addresses.*

The HEXADDRESS program calls a routine found in the STRBOX unit that ships with this book. The Address2Str method converts a pointer address into a string:

```
function Address2Str(Addr : Pointer) : string;
var
  S1 : String;
  S2 : String;
begin
  S1 := GetHexWord(Seg(Addr^));
  S1 := S1 + ':';
  S2 := GetHexWord(Ofs(Addr^));
  S1 := S1 + S2;
  Address2Str := S1;
end;
```

728

The `GetHexWord` function does all the real work by performing some clever bitwise operations:

```
function GetHexWord(w: Word): string;
const
  HexChars: array [0..$F] of Char =  '0123456789ABCDEF';
var
  Addr: string;
begin
  Addr[1] := hexChars[Hi(w) shr 4];
  Addr[2] := hexChars[Hi(w) and $F];
  Addr[3] := hexChars[Lo(w) shr 4];
  Addr[4] := hexChars[Lo(w) and $F];
  Addr[0] := #4;
  Result := addr;
end;
```

> **NOTE**
>
> Knowledgeable Borland programmer and Delphi guru Danny Thorpe pointed out to me that `Format('%p' [<address expression>])` does the same thing as `Address2Str`. However, I opted to hang onto the `Address2Str` and `GetHexWord` functions since there are so few other references to bitwise operations in this book. Also see the `IntToHex` function.

The HEXADDRESS program reduces polymorphism to a principle so obvious that one feels foolish repeating it. Specifically, if you assign one object to another, of course their methods are going to have the same addresses! This is true even if one object is the parent of the other. The only tricky or unexpected part is the fact that Delphi enables you to assign a parent to one of its children. Given that fact, the rest is simplicity itself.

MaskEdits and Other Issues

The native Delphi `TMaskEdit` control used in the Sell Dialog deserves at least a few sentences of comment. This component is a descendant of `TEdit` that enables you to control the kinds of characters that are entered into the control.

The key to the `TMaskEdit` component is the `EditMask` property, which enables you to enter a string that uses several special characters to define what the user can legally enter into the edit area. There is a property editor associated with the `EditMask` property; in this editor, you can find a number of default masks, as shown in Figure 28.7. However, on many occasions, none of these masks will suit your purpose.

In this program, I enter the following string as an `EditMask`:

```
######;0;_
```

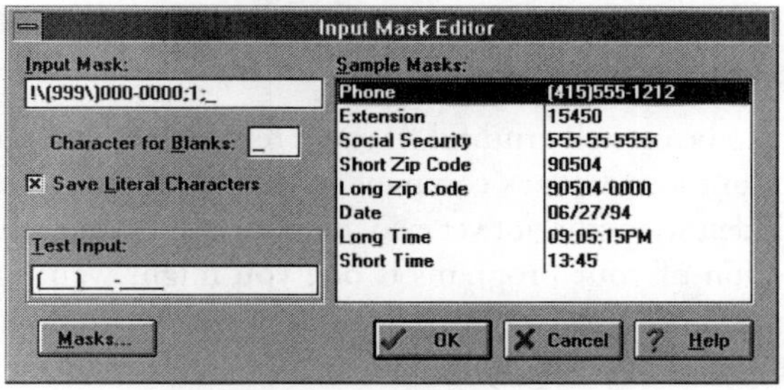

FIGURE 28.7.

The property editor for the
EditMask property.

The purpose of this string is to ensure that the user can enter only numeric values. In particular, these numeric values represent the number of widgets that the user wants to sell.

To understand the EditMask property, you need to study the entry associated with it in the online help. Here, you see all the characters that can be used to define a mask, along with a description of the effects associated with each character. Because this list is so readily available to you, I will not waste time or resources by reprinting it here. Instead, I will show how to use the information in the online help to achieve a specific purpose.

In the online help for the EditMask property, you will find that a pound sign (#) enables you to enter only numbers, spaces, and plus and minus characters. Notice, however, that there is also a 0 character, which requires that you enter a number in each location marked with that character. The question, then, is which special character should you use: # or 0?

In this particular case, the 0 character is not what you want, because it forces the user to enter a six-digit number, one for each of the 0s you place in the mask:

```
000000;0;_
```

The preceding mask would enable you to enter the number 12356, but it would reject 123. Because you want to give the user the freedom to enter a number of any size up to 999,999, you should use the # character rather than the 0 character. One way to sum this matter up is as follows: The 0 character means that the user has to fill in that place with a number, while the # character allows the user to fill in that space with either a number or a blank space. To state the matter somewhat differently: In the latter case, you can leave one of the characters blank; but in the former, you must fill in each space with a number.

The zero that appears after the semicolon in the previous string specifies that the mask entered in is not saved as part of the data. If I had placed a 1 here, the mask would have been saved. In this particular case, there are no mask characters to either save or discard, so it doesn't matter what I placed in this location. The phone mask (shown in Figure 28.6) contains two parentheses that would be affected by this value.

Finally, the very end of the previous mask includes an underscore. This value is used to specify what will be used to designate the space character.

Notice that each field of the mask is separated from the last by a semicolon. Each mask consists of three fields, which were described earlier.

If I were to be entirely truthful, I would report that I am not completely enamored of this system, nor of the TEditMask component itself. Perhaps as I get better at using it, I will find that it has hidden strengths not yet evident to me. Only time will tell. But for now, I would say that this portion of your programs is one you might want to entrust to a third party such as TurboPower Software. Or, perhaps you would like to create your own TMaskEdit component and place it on the market.

Summary

This chapter has tackled the complex subject of polymorphism. You saw that polymorphism is built on the fact that OOP languages enable you to assign a variable of a type parent to a variable declared to be of type child. When you then call a method of the parent type, it will go to the address of the child object's methods. As a result, an object of type TParent, when assigned to four different objects of type TChild, might react in four different ways. One object, many different faces: polymorphism.

Creating Components

29

Overview

This chapter and the next cover building components. They are very much the centerpiece of this book. Everything covered so far leads up to this subject, including the material on the Delphi environment and the material on databases.

You will build three types of components in this chapter:

- Descendants that change default settings in existing components.
- Descendants that add features to existing components.
- Tools built on top of abstract component base classes such as `TWinControl`, `TCustomControl`, `TComponent`, and `TGraphicControl`. These are the classes you descend from if you want to build your own components from the bottom up.

This chapter presents material on building visual tools, and the next chapter explores building nonvisual components. Nonvisual components are descended directly from `TComponent`, and appear on the form only at design time.

More specifically, the components built in this chapter fall into two categories:

- The first group is a set of `TEdit`, `TLabel`, and `TPanel` descendants that show how to change default colors, captions, and fonts. This section of the chapter also covers building components that consist of several different child components; that is, it shows how to group components together to form new components. The specific example included with this book shows a panel that comes replete with two radio buttons. (I created this latter component before the `TRadioGroup` component showed up in the Delphi Beta.)
- The second tool is a clock component that can be dropped on a form, and stopped and started at will.

In the next chapter, you will see a nonvisual control that knows how to iterate through subdirectories. You can use it to build programs that search for files, delete all files with a certain extension, and so on.

Besides components, this chapter also briefly covers two related topics:

Property editors are used to edit the properties of components. The classic examples are the common dialogs that pop up when you edit the Color or Font properties that belong to most visible components. The drop-down lists and string editing capabilities found in the Object Inspector are also Property Editors.

Component editors are associated not with a single property, but with an entire component. An example is the Fields Editor used with `TTable` and `TQuery` components.

The property editors and component editors are related to a broader topic called the Tools API. The Tools API consists of a series of interfaces to the Delphi IDE that allow you to build experts, interfaces to version control systems, and similar utilities. The API for property editors, component editors, and the tools API are defined in files with names that end in INTF, which stands for INTerFace. For instance, the `TPropertyEditor` class is found in DSGNINTF.PAS.

Components, component editors, and property editors are perhaps the most important topics in Delphi programming. As mentioned, this chapter and the next are the keystones around which this entire book has been designed. Most of what I have said before was calculated to make these two chapters readily comprehensible.

Component Theory

Delphi components have three outstanding strengths:

- They are native components, built in Delphi's language. This means that you can write, debug, and test your components from inside standard Delphi programs.
- They are fully object-oriented, which means you can easily change or enhance existing components by creating descendant objects.
- They are small, fast, and light, and can be linked directly into your executables.

No one would claim that VBXs weren't groundbreaking, or that OLE2 is not an enormously promising architecture. However, Delphi components are relatively easy to create and come in a light, easy-to-use package. You can create Delphi components that do nearly anything, from serial communications, to database links, to laying the foundation for a true distributed architecture. This gives Delphi a big advantage over other visual tools that force you to move to C++, or some other tool, if you want to build components.

> **NOTE**
>
> I suspect most components will cost in the range of $50 to $150. Many of these tools encapsulate functionality that might cost tens of thousands of dollars to produce in-house. For instance, a good communication library might take a year to build. However, if a company can sell it in volume, they can afford to charge $100 or $200 for the product. That's a real bargain. And most of these tools will be easy to use. In fact, I believe their ease of use is going to make the market for programmer's tools much larger than it has been in the past.

Delphi components are flexible tools that merely await the hand of someone who knows OOP and the Delphi language. I've taken you through all the preliminaries, from a description of Delphi itself, through a description of its language, and on to an overview of its implementation of OOP. From this foundation, it will be easy for you to begin building your own components.

Creating Descendants of an Existing Component

In this section, you will see how to create a series of custom TEdit, TPanel, and TLabel controls. The changes made to the standard TEdit and TLabel components involve tweaking their color, and their font's color, name, size, and style. The goal is to show how to create a suite of custom controls that you can place on the component palette and use for special effects, or to define the look and feel of a certain set of applications belonging to a particular department or company.

With projects like this, it's best to start with one simple example and then move on to a larger proliferation of objects. In Listings 29.1, you find the code for a first version of a unit that will hold the descendants of TEdit and TLabel controls. Scan through it, check out its basic structure, and then I will briefly discuss how to use the Component Editor to put it together.

Listing 29.1. The code for a simple component descending from TEdit.

```
unit Unleash1;

interface

uses
  SysUtils, WinTypes, WinProcs,
  Messages, Classes, Graphics,
  Controls, Forms, Dialogs,
  StdCtrls;

type
  TSmallEdit = class(TEdit)
  private
    { Private declarations }
  protected
    { Protected declarations }
  public
    { Public declarations }
    constructor Create(AOwner: TComponent); override;
  published
    { Published declarations }
  end;

procedure Register;

implementation

constructor TSmallEdit.Create(AOwner: TComponent);
begin
  inherited Create(AOwner);
  Color := clBlue;
  Font.Color := clYellow;
  Font.Name := 'New Times Roman';
```

```
  Font.Size := 12;
  Font.Style := [fsBold];
end;

procedure Register;
begin
  RegisterComponents('Edits', [TSmallEdit]);
end;

end.
```

NOTE

A test bed for the UNLEASH unit is the TESTEDS1 subdirectory on this book's CD.

It's simple to create this unit, test it, and compile it as a component that's merged in with the rest of the tools on the Component Palette. To get started, choose File | New Component. You will be presented with the dialog shown in Figure 29.1.

FIGURE 29.1.

The Component Expert dialog.

The Component Expert is a simple code generator, of the type that any reader of this book who has made it this far should be able to write in an hour or two. All it does is ask you for the name of the component you want to create, and to then select its parent from a drop down list. After you have defined the type of tool you want to create, you can select the page in the Component Palette where you want it to reside. You should fill in the blanks with the following information:

```
Class Name: TSmallEdit
Ancestor: TEdit
Palette Page: Unleash
```

For your efforts, the Component Expert churns out the code in Listing 29.2, in which everything is boilerplate except for the first line of the class declaration, the global var declaration, and the parameters passed to the RegisterComponents method.

Listing 29.2. The standard boilerplate output of the Component Editor.

```
unit Unit2;

interface

uses
  SysUtils, WinTypes, WinProcs,
  Messages, Classes, Graphics,
  Controls, Forms, Dialogs,
  StdCtrls;

type
  TSmallEdit = class(TEdit)
  private
    { Private declarations }
  protected
    { Protected declarations }
  public
    { Public declarations }
  published
    { Published declarations }
  end;

procedure Register;

implementation

procedure Register;
begin
  RegisterComponents('Unleash', [TSmallEdit]);
end;

end.
```

The Component Expert starts by giving you a uses clause designed to cover most of the bases you are likely to touch in a standard component:

```
uses
  SysUtils, WinTypes, WinProcs,
  Messages, Classes, Graphics,
  Controls, Forms, Dialogs,
  StdCtrls;
```

The next step is to give you a basic class declaration, in which the name and parent are filled in with the choices you specified in the Component Expert dialog. All this business about the scoping directives is just for your convenience, and you can delete any portion of it that you don't think you'll need.

```
type
  TSmallEdit = class(TEdit)
  private
    { Private declarations }
  protected
    { Protected declarations }
```

```
public
  { Public declarations }
published
  { Published declarations }
end;
```

Before you can place a component on the Component Palette, you must first register it with the system:

```
procedure Register;
begin
  RegisterComponents('Unleash', [TSmallEdit]);
end;
```

Registering a class makes it known to the Delphi component palette when the unit is compiled into the Delphi component library. The Register procedure has no impact on programs compiled with this unit. Unless your program calls the Register procedure (which it should *never* do), the code for the Register procedure will never even appear in your executeable.

After using the Component Expert, you should save the project. Proceed as you normally would by creating a directory for the project and saving MAIN.PAS and TESTEDS1.DPR inside it. The new unit that you created, however, should not be saved into the same directory, but should be placed in the directory where you store files such as STRBOX or MATHBOX. This code is now going to come into play as part of your system, and as such you want a single path that leads to all related files of this type. If you have all of your components in different subdirectories you will end up with a source path that is long and unwieldy. Furthermore, it's best not to open up the Project Manager and make this class a part of your project. Instead, merely add it to the uses clause of unit MAIN. If you add the class to your project, the path to it becomes hard-coded into your DPR file, which may cause problems later on.

The goal of this project is to give a component of type TEdit a new set of default behaviors, so that it starts out with certain colors and certain fonts. To do this, you need to override the Create method and change the fonts inside of it. To declare the method, write the following in your class declaration:

```
TSmallEdit = class(TEdit)
public
  constructor Create(AOwner: TComponent); override;
end;
```

The Create method is declared as public, because an instance of this object might need to call it. It is passed a single parameter of type TComponent, which is a base class that encapsulates the minimum functionality needed to be an owner of another component. Finally, use the override directive to specify that this is a virtual method that you want to redefine.

The implementation of the Create method is simple:

```
constructor TSmallEdit.Create(AOwner: TComponent);
begin
  inherited Create(AOwner);
  Color := clBlue;
  Font.Color := clYellow;
```

```
    Font.Name := 'New Times Roman';
    Font.Size := 12;
    Font.Style := [fsBold];
end;
```

The code first calls `Create`, passing in the variable `AOwner`, which will almost always be the form on which the component is to be displayed. In other words, the user will drop the component onto a form, and that form will become the owner of the component. `AOwner` is a variable that points at the form. The VCL uses it to initialize the `Owner` property, which is one of the fields of all components.

The next step is to define the color and font that you want to use, with `Font.Style` defined as follows:

```
TFontStyle = (fsBold, fsItalic, fsUnderline, fsStrikeOut);
TFontStyles = set of TFontStyle;
```

If you want to add the underline and bold style to the text in the edit control, write the following:

```
Font.Style := [fsBold, fsUnderline];
```

If you want to then add the underline style at runtime, write

```
Font.Style := Font.Style + [fsItalic];
```

in which the plus symbol is used as a set operator for unions, as explained in Chapter 25, "Handling Messages and."

At this stage, the code is ready to go on the component palette. However, most of the time when you write components, you should test them first to see whether they work. The issue here is that, even on a fast machine, it takes 20 or 30 seconds to recompile COMPLIB.DCL and add your component to the Component Palette. (Most of that time is taken up by Windows unloading the old COMPLIB.DCL and then loading the new COMPLIB.DCL into memory.) That can be a little too costly for me if I might need to tweak a few aspects of my code before I get things set correctly. As a result, I test things out first in a small program, and then add the component to the IDE.

To test the new class, drop a button on the program's main form, and create an `OnClick` handler:

```
procedure TForm1.Button1Click(Sender: TObject);
var
  MyEdit: TSmallEdit;
begin
  MyEdit := TSmallEdit.Create(Self);
  MyEdit.Parent := Self;
  MyEdit.Show;
end;
```

This code simply creates the component and shows it on the main form. `Self`, of course, is the way that `TForm1` refers to itself from inside one of its own methods. The Owner of the new component is Form1, which will be responsible for disposing the component when it is done. The Parent of the Form is also Form1, in which the Parent variable is used by Windows when it is trying to decide how to display the form on the screen. If you place a panel on a form and drop a button on the panel, the Owner of that button will be the form, but the Parent will be the panel. Ownership determines when and vhow the component is deallocated, and parental relationships determine where and how the component is displayed. Ownership is fundamentally a Delphi issue, whereas parental relationships are primarily a concern of Windows.

After running the program and testing the component, the next step is to put it up on the Component Palette. To do this, select Options | Install Components, and choose the Add button. Browse through the directories until you find the UNLEASH unit, select OK, and then close the Install Components dialog by selecting OK. At this point, a project called COMPLIB.DPR is compiled. This project creates a huge DLL called COMPLIB.DCL, which contains all the components in the component palette, all the component and property editors associated with those components, the form designer part of the IDE, the experts, and other support modules.

After COMPLIB.DCL finishes recompiling, you can start a new project, turn to the newly created Edits page, and drop your new component onto a form. It will have a blue background, default to Times New Roman, and have its font style set to bold and font color to yellow. Notice that all the properties of TEdit have been inherited by TSmallEdit. That's OOP in action.

The COMPLIB.DPR file used during compilation of COMPLIB.DCL can be saved to disk if you choose Options | Environment | Library | Options | Save Library Source Code. After choosing this option and recompiling COMPLIB.DCL, you can go to the \DELPHI\BIN subdirectory and view your copy of COMPLIB.DPR.

Extending the *UNLEASH* Unit

In the second version of the UNLEASH unit, a new edit control is added, along with two labels and two panels. The additional edits and labels show how quickly you can build on an idea or object when you understand where you're headed. One of the panels shows how you can get rid of the annoying label that always shows up in the middle of a panel, and the other shows how you can create a single component that contains other components. Specifically, it shows how to create a panel that already comes equipped with two radio buttons.

> **NOTE**
>
> The second version of the UNLEASH unit, found in the CHAP29 directory on this book's CD, contains a panel that comes equipped with two radio buttons.
>
> The test bed for the UNLEASH unit is on the CD in the TESTEDS2 subdirectory.

When you've created a component that does something you like, it's easy to create children of it. Class `TBigEdit` descends from `TSmallEdit`:

```
TBigEdit = class(TSmallEdit)
```

It inherits its font nearly unchanged from `TSmallEdit`, except that it sets `Font.Size` to 24, a nice hefty figure that helps the control live up to its name:

```
constructor TBigEdit.Create(AOwner: TComponent);
begin
  inherited Create(AOwner);
  Font.Size := 24;
end;
```

This elegant syntax is a good example of how OOP can save you time and trouble while still allowing you to write very clear code.

The label controls shown in this code work in exactly the same way the edit controls do, except that they descend from `TLabel` rather than `TEdit`. The `TEmptyPanel` component rectifies one of the petty issues that can annoy me at times. I'm referring to the fact that every time you put down a panel, it gets a caption; most of the time, the first thing you do is delete the caption so you can place other controls on it without creating a mess!

Once again, you can change `TPanel` by simply overriding its constructor. This time, all you need to do is set the `Caption` property to an empty string:

```
constructor TEmptyPanel.Create(AOwner: TComponent);
begin
  inherited Create(AOwner);
  Caption := ' ';
end;
```

The last new component in this version of the UNLEASH unit enables you to drop down a panel that comes equipped with two radio buttons. This makes a single control out of a set of components that are often combined. You could create other controls that contained three, four, or more radio buttons. Or, you could even create a panel that would populate itself with a specific number of radio buttons.

The declaration for this new radio button is fairly simple:

```
TRadio2Panel = class(TEmptyPanel)
private
  FRadio1: TRadiobutton;
  FRadio2: TRadioButton;
public
  constructor Create(AOwner: TComponent); override;
  property Radio1: TRadioButton read FRadio1;
  property Radio2: TRadioButton read FRadio2;
end;
```

The actual radio buttons themselves are declared as private data, and access to them is given by the `Radio1` and `Radio2` properties.

You don't need write access to these radio button properties. Modifying a property of these radio buttons doesn't require write access to the radio button property:

```
RP.Radio1.Caption := 'hello'
```

performs one read of `RP.Radio1` and one write to the `Caption` property of that radio button. You don't want write access to them, either, because that would allow the user to assign garbage (or nil) into them. The `Create` method for the `Radio2Panel` begins by setting the width and height of the panel:

```
constructor TRadio2Panel.Create(AOwner: TComponent);
begin
  inherited Create(AOwner);
  Width := 175;
  Height := 60;

  FRadio1 := TRadioButton.Create(AOwner);
  FRadio1.Parent := Self;
  FRadio1.Caption := 'Radio1';
  FRadio1.Left := 20;
  FRadio1.Top := 10;
  FRadio1.Show;

  FRadio2 := TRadioButton.Create(AOwner);
  FRadio2.Parent := Self;
  FRadio2.Caption := 'Radio2';
  FRadio2.Left := 20;
  FRadio2.Top := 32;
  FRadio2.Show;
end;
```

The next step is to create the first radio button. Notice that the code passes the form in as the Owner, but sets the parent to the Panel itself. That's because the responsibility for destroying the component belongs to the form, but Windows needs to know that the radio button should be displayed as a child of the panel; that is, it should sit on top of the panel. The rest of the code in the `Create` method is too trivial to merit comment.

When it comes time to test out the `TRadio2Panel` object, you can write the following code in the test-bed program to take it through its paces:

```
R := TRadio2Panel.Create(Self);
R.Parent := Self;
R.Left := 50;
R.Top := 100;
R.Radio1.Caption := 'Delphi';
R.Radio2.Caption := 'Unleashed';
R.Radio1.Checked := True;
R.Show;
```

Here, `R` is declared to be of type `TRadio2Panel`. Note that each of the radio buttons that belong to the panel act exactly as you would expect a normal radio button to act, only you have to qualify them differently before you access them.

> **NOTE**
>
> If you want, you can surface Radio1 and Radio2 as published properties of TRadio2Panel. However, when you first do so, they will have no property editors available because Delphi has no built-in property editors for TRadioButtons. To build your own, you can refer to the DSGNINTF.PAS unit that ships with Delphi, as well as the upcoming discussion of the Clock component and the Tools API.
>
> Before closing this section I'd like to add some additional notes about how Delphi handles streaming chores. I owe most of my severly limited understanding of this advanced material to Danny Thorpe. Any holes or errors in this brief discussion of streaming are entirely mine, not Danny's.
>
> The good news is that most of the time, you do not have to concern yourself with streaming at all. Delphi handles most streaming chores automatically. In particular, it will automatically stream published properties that are simple types. There are only limited circumstances under which you must explicitly stream the fields of your object.
>
> If a property type is a TComponent or descendent, the streaming system assumes it must create an instance of that type when reading it in. If a property type is TPersistent but not TComponent, the streaming system assumes it is supposed to use the existing instance available through the property and simply read values into that instance's properties.
>
> The Object Inspector knows to expand the properties of TPersistent but not TComponent descendents. This is not done for TComponent descendents because TComponents are likely to have a lot more properties, which would make navigating the Object Inspector difficult.

Building Components from Scratch

In the previous examples, you were creating descendants of existing components. Now it's time to see how to create entirely new components. The core idea to grasp here is that there are three abstract objects from which you can descend a new component. The term *abstract* can have a specific technical meaning, but here I am using it to refer to any object that exists only so that you can create descendants of it. In short, the following three objects have built-in functionality that all components need to access, but you would never want to instantiate an instance of any of them:

■ TWinControl and TCustomControl are base classes that can be used to produce a Windows control that can receive input focus and that has a standard Windows handle that can be passed to API calls. TWinControl descendants exist inside their own window. TEdit, TListBox, TTabbedNoteBook, TNoteBook, and TPanel are all examples of this type of control. Most components of this type actually descend from `TCustomControl`, which is in turn a descendant of `TWinControl`. The distinction between the two classes is that `TCustomControl` has a `Paint` method, and `TWinControl` does not. If you want to draw the display of your new component, you should inherit from `TCustomControl`. If you are writing a wrapper class for a control that lives in a DLL and therefore aren't responsible for drawing anything, you can inherit from `TWinControl`. In short, if the object already knows how to draw itself, inherit from `TWinControl`.

■ `TGraphicControl` is for components that don't need to receive input focus, don't need to contain other components, and don't need a handle. These controls draw themselves directly on their parent's surface, thereby saving Windows resources. Not having a window handle eliminates a lot of Windows management overhead, and that translates into faster display updates. In short, `TGraphicControls` exist inside their parent's window. They use their parent's handle and their parent's device context. They still have a *Handle* and *Canvas* fields that you can access, but they actually belongs to their parent. `TLabel` and `TShape` objects are examples of this type of component.

■ `TComponent` enables you to create nonvisual components. If you want to make a tool such as the `TTable`, `TQuery`, `TOpenDialog`, or `TTimer` devices, this is the place to start. These are components you can place on the Component Palette, but they perform some internal function that you access through code, rather than appearing visually to the user at runtime. A tool such as `TOpenDialog` can pop up a dialog, but the component itself remains invisible.

Create a `TWinControl` or `TCustomControl` descendant whenever the user needs to directly interact with a visible control. If the user doesn't need to interact with a visible component, create a `TGraphicControl` descendant. To help understand the issues involved here, you should place a `TShape` or `TLabel` control on a form and run the program. Clicking or attempting to type on these controls produces no noticeable result. These components don't ever receive the focus. Now place a `TEdit` control on the form. It responds to mouse clicks, gets the focus, and you can type in it. `TEdit` controls are descendants of `TWinControl`, and `TShape` is a descendant of `TGraphicControl`.

> **NOTE**
>
> I should add one caveat to the rules about `TGraphicControl` explained previously. In one limited sense, the user can interact with `TGraphicControls`. For instance, they do receive mouse messages, and you can set the mouse cursor when the mouse flies over them. They just can't receive keyboard input focus. If an object can't receive focus, it usually seems inert to the user.

If you are having trouble deciding whether you want to descend from `TWinControl` or `TCustomControl`, you should always go with `TCustomControl`. It has a real `Paint` method, and some other functionality that is useful when creating a component of your own. If you want to wrap an existing Windows control inside a VCL object, you should start with TWinControl. Most Delphi components that follow this path begin by creating intermediate custom objects, so that TEdit's hierarchy looks like this:

```
TWinControl
TCustomEdit
TEdit
```

TListBox's hierarchy looks like this:

```
TWinControl
TCustomListBox
TListBox
```

Of course, Delphi wraps all the major Windows controls for you, so you won't need to perform this operation unless you are working with a specialized third-party control of some sort.

Following are the declarations for TGraphicControl and TCustomControl, as they appear in CLASSES.PAS or CLASSES.INT:

```
TGraphicControl = class(TControl)
private
  FCanvas: TCanvas;
  procedure WMPaint(var Message: TWMPaint); message WM_PAINT;
protected
  procedure Paint; virtual;
  property Canvas: TCanvas read FCanvas;
public
  constructor Create(AOwner: TComponent); override;
  destructor Destroy; override;
end;

TCustomControl = class(TWinControl)
private
  FCanvas: TCanvas;
  procedure WMPaint(var Message: TWMPaint); message WM_PAINT;
protected
  procedure Paint; virtual;
  procedure PaintWindow(DC: HDC); override;
  property Canvas: TCanvas read FCanvas;
public
  constructor Create(AOwner: TComponent); override;
  destructor Destroy; override;
end;
```

You can see that these are fairly simple objects. If you went back one step further in the hierarchy to TControl or TWinControl, you would see huge objects. For instance, the declaration for class TWinControl is nearly 200 lines long (not the implementation, mind you, but just the type declaration).

I'm showing you this source code because component builders should work directly with the source, rather than using the on-line help or the DOCs. For simple jobs, it's easy to create your own components without the source. However, if you have a big project, you have to get the source code if it did not already ship with your product. The INT files that ship with all versions of Delphi are very helpful, but there is no replacement for the actual source. The source is available with the client/server version of Delphi, and also as an upsell from Borland.

The Clock Component

It's now time to build a component from the ground up. The CLOCK unit (shown in Figure 29.2) is a simple little clock that you can pop on a form, and activate and deactivate at will. You can start the clock running, and then tell it to stop by simply changing the value of a Boolean property called Running.

FIGURE 29.2.

The CLOCK unit as it appears on its own test bed, before being placed on the Component Palette.

When constructing class TClock, the first thing that needs to be decided is whether the clock is going to descend from TWinControl or TGraphicControl. If you've built a clock in Windows before, you know that one of the best ways to drive it is with a Windows timer. Timers require the presence of a Handle in order to be stopped and started; furthermore, they send their wm_Timer messages to the window that owns them. Because a TGraphicControl descendant isn't a real window, it will not automatically get the messages. As a result, TGraphicControl is not an ideal choice for this type of object.

Of course, the objections to using TGraphicControl raised in the last paragraph aren't insurmountable. You could still make it work, if you really wanted. However, there is no point in exerting extra effort that isn't strictly necessary, so I have opted for the simplest design possible, and descended the class from TCustomControl. I chose TCustomControl rather than TWinControl because I needed a Paint method in which I could draw the clock.

> **NOTE**
>
> The decision to use Windows API calls to create a timer, rather than using a TTimer object, was driven by experience, not by a desire to save memory. I found that I had some buggy behavior when I placed four or five of these clocks on a single form. If I got rid of the TTimer object and made the calls directly, all went smoothly. Once again, when I ran into trouble, I didn't fight upstream, but instead followed the course of least resistance. I'll admit the exact issues involved here aren't clear to me, but I leave this note as a signpost to others who might pass this way. Hopefully you will have better luck (or skill) if you try the same ground where I trod.

You will see that the code also contains a special Property Editor, as well as a very simple Component Editor. As you will see, neither of these tools are inherently difficult to build.

> **NOTE**
>
> The code for the Clock component should be kept in the UNITS subdirectory where you store STRBOX and other utility units. The test bed for the Clock component is stored in the CLOCK3 subdirectory.

To run this program, you should first press on the button that creates the clock and makes it visible on the form. The next logical step is to start the clock running; then, if you'd like, you can also change its color. You get a GP (General Protection) fault if you click on the latter two buttons before pushing the first. The problem is that it is an error to call a method or property of the TClock object before the object itself has been created. To prevent this from happening, you could enable and disable the second two buttons.

The code for the clock components uses inheritance, virtual methods, and properties. TClock has two pieces of private data:

```
FTimer: Integer;
FRunning: Boolean;
```

One is an identifier for the timer, and the other is a Boolean value that specifies whether the clock is running.

Windows timers are managed by two Windows API calls. When you want to start a timer, use SetTimer; when you want to stop the timer, use KillTimer. SetTimer takes four parameters:

1. Handle is the HWND of your current window.
2. IDEvent is an integer identifier that uniquely identifies the timer inside of the window that created it. You can make this value up off the top of your head, although I generally set the IDTimer for the first timer in a window to 1, the second timer to 2, and so on. Because there is only going to be one timer in each instance of a TClock window, you can set its IDEvent to 1.
3. Elapse is the length of time between calls to the timer, measured in milliseconds.
4. TimerFunc is a callback function that is not used in this program. One of the developer's big goals was to create a Windows product that didn't need to use callbacks, and I see no reason to open that can of worms now if it can be avoided. (If you want to create a callback in Delphi, you will be able to do so, but it's usually not necessary.)

A typical call to SetTimer looks like this:

```
SetTimer(Handle, FTimer, 1000, nil);
```

1000 specifies that the timer is called once every 1000 milliseconds, or once a second. SetTimer is really a function that returns zero if the call fails. This is a very real possibility, so programs that include error checking should inspect this value and put up a MessageBox if the call fails.

KillTimer takes two parameters, the first being the handle of your window, and the second being the unique identifier associated with that timer:

```
KillTimer(Handle, FTimer);
```

When you are not using the callback function, timer events are sent to your window via messages:

```
procedure WMTimer(var Message: TMessage);
  message wm_Timer;
```

This is a classic dynamic method, of the kind covered in the Chapter 25, "Handling Messages." The response to this event is a simple procedure that calls TextOut, and gets the time from a function in the STRBOX unit called GetTimeString:

```
procedure TClock.WMTimer(var Message: TMessage);
begin
  Canvas.TextOut(10, 40, GetTimeString);
end;
```

The calls to SetTimer and KillTimer are primarily managed through a property called Running:

```
property Running: Boolean read FRunning write SetRunning;
```

The write mechanism, a procedure called SetRunning, is a fairly straightforward tool:

```
procedure TClock.SetRunning(Run: Boolean);
begin
  if Run then begin
    SetTimer(Handle, FTimer, 50, nil);
    FRunning := True;
  end else begin
    KillTimer(Handle, FTimer);
    FRunning := False;
  end;
end;
```

If the user sets the Running property to True, this procedure is executed and a call is made to the SetTimer function. If the user sets Running equal to false, KillTimer is called and the clock immediately stops functioning.

The final issue involving the timer concerns the case in which the user closes a form while the clock is still running. In such a case, you must be sure to call KillTimer before the application exits. If you don't make the call, the timer keeps running even after the application closes. This wastes system resources, and also uses up one of the dozen or so timers that are available to the system at any one time.

The logical place to call KillTimer is the Destroy method for the TClock object. Unfortunately, the window associated with the clock has already been destroyed by the time this call is made, so there is no valid handle to use when you call `KillTimer`. As a result, you need to respond to `wm_Destroy` messages in order to be sure the timer is killed before the `TClock` window is closed:

```
procedure TClock.wmDestroy(var Message: TMessage);
begin
  KillTimer(Handle, FTimer);
  FTimer := 0;
  inherited;
end;
```

Before leaving this description of the `TClock` object, I should briefly mention the `Paint` method:

```
procedure TClock.Paint;
begin
  Canvas.Ellipse(0, 0, 100, 100);
end;
```

This procedure is called whenever the circle defining the circumference of the clock needs to be repainted. You never have to check for this circumstance, and you never have to call `Paint` directly. Windows keeps an eye on the `TClock` window, and if it needs to be painted, it sends you a `wm_Paint` message. Logic buried deep in the VCL converts the `wm_Paint` message into a call to `Paint`, the same way `TClock` translates `wm_Timer` messages into calls to `TCanvas.TextOut`.

> **NOTE**
>
> When writing components, sometimes it's easiest if you can get right down to the Windows API level, or as near to it as you would like to get. The following shows how to get hooked into the Window Procedure:
>
> ```
> procedure TMyObject.WndProc(var M: Tmessage);
> begin
>   case M.Msg of
>     wm_Timer: DoSomething;
>     wm_Paint: PaintSomething;
>   else
>     M.Result := DefWindowProc(Handle, M.Msg, M.wParam, M.lParam);
> end;
> ```
>
> `WndProc` is typically declared in the private section as:
>
> ```
> procedure WndProc(var Msg: Tmessage);
> ```
>
> See the Delphi VCL source for the `TTimer` object for an example of how to use the `WndProc` function.

The `TColorClock` component is a descendant of `TClock` that adds color to the control. I made `TColorClock` a separate object, rather than just adding color to `TClock`, for two different reasons (both of which are related to design issues):

1. You might want to create a descendant of `TClock` that doesn't have color, or that implements color differently than `TColorClock` does. By creating two objects, one called `TClock` and the other called `TColorClock`, I enable programmers to have the

greatest amount of freedom when creating descendants. This principle has only minimal weight in a simple object such as TClock, but it can become extremely important when you are developing large and complex hierarchies. In short, be careful of building too much functionality into one object!

2. TClock and TColorClock also provide another example of inheritance, and vividly demonstrate how this technology can be utilized to your advantage.

TColorClock declares a private data store called FColor that is of type TColor. If you don't recall the previous discussions of type TColor, you should refer to Chapter 5, "What is a Graphical Environment?" and the section entitled "Using TCanvas to Draw Shapes." Users can set the FColor variable by manipulating the Color property:

```
property Color: TColor read FColor write SetColor;
```

SetColor is a simple procedure that sets the value of FColor, and calls the Windows API call InvalidateRect:

```
procedure TColorClock.SetColor(Color: TColor);
begin
  FColor := Color;
  InvalidateRect(Handle, nil, True);
end;
```

Here is the declaration for InvalidateRect:

```
procedure InvalidateRect(Wnd: HWnd; Rect: PRect; Erase: Bool);
```

InvalidateRect forces the window specified in the first parameter to completely redraw itself if the third parameter is set to True. If the third parameter is set to False, only the portions of the window that you specifically repaint are changed. The middle parameter is a pointer to the TRect structure that can be used to define the area that you want to redraw. Compare this function with the native Delphi function called Invalidate.

Calls to InvalidateRect naturally force calls to the TColorClick.Paint method:

```
procedure TColorClock.Paint;
begin
  Canvas.Brush.Color := FColor;
  inherited Paint;
end;
```

Paint sets the brush associated with the window's device context to the color specified by the user; then, it calls the Paint method defined in TClock.

To add this object to the Component Palette, you must first register it:

```
procedure Register;
begin
  RegisterComponents('Unleash', [TClock, TColorClock]);
  ...
end;
```

Here, I specify that the TClock and TColorClock objects should be placed in a group called Unleash.

> **NOTE**
>
> The second parameter to `RegisterComponents` takes an array of type `TComponentClass`:
>
> ```
> procedure RegisterComponents(const Page: string;
>   ComponentClasses: array of TComponentClass);
> ```
>
> As mentioned earlier, Delphi supports open-arrays, which means that you do not have to declare how many members are going to be included in an array. Instead, you only need to declare the type of members that will go in the array, as shown earlier. Furthermore, when creating these arrays, you can build them on the fly rather than having to declare an array variable. To do this, simply write an open bracket and then enter the members of the array separated by commas. To close the array, write a closing bracket. For more information, look up Open-Array Construction in the on-line help.

That's all I'm going to say about `TClock` and `TColorClock`. Overall, these are fairly simple components, interesting primarily because they show you how to go about constructing your own controls from scratch. This kind of exercise lies very much at the heart of Delphi's architecture, and I expect many readers will be spending most of their time engaged almost exclusively in the business of building components.

Creating Icons for Components

The icon associated with a component and placed in the Component Palette is defined in a file with a DCR extension. If you do not provide this file, Delphi uses the icon associated with the object's parent. If there is no icon anywhere in the component's ancestry, a default icon is used.

> **NOTE**
>
> A DCR file is a Windows resource file with the extension changed from RES to DCR. The resource file contains a bitmap resource with the same name as your component. For instance, the bitmap resource in a DCR file for a TCOLOR component would have a resource ID of `TColor`. This resource should be a 56×28 pixel (or smaller) bitmap that can be edited in the Image Editor. All you need to do is place this DCR file in the same directory as your component, and the images defined therein will show up on the component palette. Use the Image Editor to explore the DCR files that ship with Delphi. They are stored in the \DELPHI\LIB subdirectory.

Here is a description of how to associate your own bitmaps with a particular component.

1. Open the Image Editor and choose New.
2. In the New Project dialog, choose Component Resource (DCR) and click OK.

3. A dialog called UNTITLED.DCR appears. Choose the New button.

4. A dialog called New Resource appears. Choose Bitmap and click OK.

5. A dialog called New Bitmap Attributes appears. Set Colors to 16 colors, because this technology is available on nearly all Windows systems. Set Size in Pixels to 56×28, with width being the larger number.

6. Draw a black line down the center of the bitmap, and paint the button-up bitmap on the right side of the line and the button-down bitmap on the left side of the line. To understand the difference between button-down and button-up bitmaps, just go to component palette and press down a component. You see that it has one image for depicting the unselected stage, and another for the selected stage.

7. Save the file as CLOCK.DCR. Rename the bitmap you have created to TCLOCK.

The Image Editor was very shaky throughout all phases of the Delphi BETA. If it doesn't work for you, create a 56×28 bitmap in PBRUSH.EXE or some other bitmap editor, and then create an RC file that looks like this:

```
TCLOCK BITMAP clock.bmp
```

Save the file as CLOCK.RC. Run the Borland Resource Compiler from the command line:

```
brc -r clock.rc
```

The resulting file will be called CLOCK.RES. Rename that file CLOCK.DCR. An example of the latter method is used for the TColorClock component, and stored in the UNITS directory along with STRBOX.PAS and the other utility files.

Creating Help Files for Components

Delphi enables you to define help files that can ship with your components. These help files can be merged into the help that ships with Delphi, so that users of your product will feel as though it is a native part of Delphi. Here are the two types of files involved.

■ The HLP file is a standard Windows help file that contains information about the properties, methods, and events implemented by your component. I strongly recommend that you buy a copy of FOREHELP from Borland to help you create these files. If you don't want FOREHELP, you should turn to Blue Sky software, or some other third party that provides tools to help you create these files. As a last resort, you can use Word or WordPerfect to create RTF files, and then compile these RTF files into HLP files with the HC31.EXE help compiler that ships with Delphi. The EXPLORER program that ships with this book provides an example of using Word for Windows based RTF files.

■ The KWF file, generated by the KWGEN utility and later merged into Delphi's main help system with KWMERGE, enables users to obtain context-sensitive help when working with your component.

All of the tools mentioned here play a peripheral role in the creation of components. They don't require a knowledge of the fascinating syntax used in component creation, but they help to make your tools attractive and easy to use.

The Four Main Tool APIs

There are four main Tools APIs, each accessible through a separate set of routines that ship with Delphi. These APIs enable you to write code that can be linked directly into the Delphi IDE. Specifically, you can link your tools into COMPLIB.DCL the same way you link in components. Here is a list of the TOOLS APIs and the native Delphi source files that define them.

Experts:

- Enables you to write your own Experts
- EXPINTF.PAS
- VIRTINTF.PAS
- TOOLINTF.PAS (for enumerating the component pages and components installed, adding modules to the project, and so on)

Version Control:

- Enables you to write your own Version Control system, or to link in a third-party system.
- VCSINTF.PAS
- VIRTINTF.PAS
- TOOLINTF.PAS (for opening and closing files in the editor)

Component Editors:

- Create dialogs associated with a control at design time. For instance, the DataSet Designer is a Component Editor.
- DSGNINTF.PAS

Property Editors:

- Create editors for use in the Object Inspector.
- DSGNINTF.PAS

The letters INTF are an abbreviation for the word *interface*. This term was chosen because the Tools API is an interface between your own code and the Delphi developer's code.

Needless to say, most people will never use the Tools API. However, it will be very important to a small minority of developers, and its existence means that everyone will be able to buy or download tools that extend the functionality of the IDE. We know what Delphi looks like at the time it ships, but it is hard to say what the tool might look like after other *expert* programmers begin extending it.

Property Editors

The Tools API for creating Property Editors is perhaps the most commonly used interface into the heart of the IDE. When you first use Delphi and start becoming familiar with the Object Inspector, you are bound to think that it is a static element that never changes. However, it should come as no surprise that you can change the functionality of the Object Inspector by adding new Property Editors to it.

As mentioned earlier, Property Editors control what takes place on the right side of the Properties page of the Object Inspector. In particular, when you click on the Color property of a TEdit, you can select a new color from a drop down list, from a common dialog, or simply by typing in a new value. In all three cases, you are using a Property Editor.

If you want to create a new Property Editor, you should create a descendant of TPropertyEditor, a class declared in DSGNINTF.PAS. Here is the declaration for the Property Editor associated with the TColorClock component:

```
TColorNameProperty = class(TColorProperty)
  public
    function GetAttributes: TPropertyAttributes; override;
    procedure Edit; override;
  end;
```

The DSGNINTF unit is unusual in that it is very carefully documented by the developer who created it. For instance, here are excerpts from that unit describing the two methods I call in my descendant of TPropertyEditor:

```
Edit
      Called when the '...' button is pressed or the
      property is double-clicked. This can, for example,
      bring up a dialog to allow the editing the component
      in some more meaningful fashion than by text
      (e.g. the Font property).

GetAttributes
      Returns the information for use in the Object
      Inspector to be able to show the appropriate tools.
      GetAttributes return a set of type TPropertyAttributes.
```

I won't quote further, for fear of sounding like I'm plagiarizing. The point, however, is that these entries were written by the developers, and they extensively document this important interface to the core code inside the heart of the IDE. Here are declarations for Edit and GetAttributes, as well as the other key functions in TPropertyEditor:

```
TPropertyEditor = class
  public
    destructor Destroy; override;
    function AllEqual: Boolean; virtual;
    procedure Edit; virtual;
    function GetAttributes: TPropertyAttributes; virtual;
    function GetComponent(Index: Integer): TComponent;
    function GetEditLimit: Integer; virtual;
    function GetName: string; virtual;
```

```
procedure GetProperties(Proc: TGetPropEditProc); virtual;
function GetPropType: PTypeInfo;
function GetValue: string; virtual;
procedure GetValues(Proc: TGetStrProc); virtual;
procedure Initialize; virtual;
procedure SetValue(const Value: string); virtual;
property Designer: TFormDesigner read FDesigner;
property PrivateDirectory: string read GetPrivateDirectory;
property PropCount: Integer read FPropCount;
property Value: string read GetValue write SetValue;
end;
```

Once again, all these methods are carefully documented inside DSGNINTF.PAS. You must study that file carefully if you want to create complex Property Editors.

The Edit method of TPropertyEditor is the one you want to override to change the way a property editor actually edits data:

```
procedure TColorNameProperty.Edit;
var
  S: String;
begin
  S := '';
  InputQuery('New Color', 'Enter Color', S);
  SetValue(S);
end;
```

In this case, I am creating a substitute for the TColorDialog that pops up when you click on the ellipses icon in Object Inspector. I am, of course, replacing the fancy Windows common dialog with a simpler one that asks the user to enter a string such as "clBlue" or "clGreen". The point here, however, is that you are learning how to create your own property editors. In a more complex example, you might open a form that allowed the user to make extensive changes to a property. SetValue, called at the end of this procedure, is another method of TPropertyEditor.

The GetAttributes method is a way of defining what types of Property Editors you want to have associated with TColorDialog:

```
function TColorNameProperty.GetAttributes;
begin
  Result := [paMultiSelect, paValueList, paDialog];
end;
```

A property editor that has the paMultiSelect flag remains active even if the user has selected more than one component of that type. For instance, you can select 10 edit controls and change all their Fonts in one step. Delphi enables you to do that because TEdits have their paMultiSelect flag set.

The paValueList flag dictates that the Property Editor drops down a list of values from an enumerated or set type when the user presses the arrow button at the far right of the editor. This functionality is built into Delphi, and you need only set the flag to have it be supported by your Property Editor.

Finally, paDialog states that the Property Editor pops up a dialog. Because the Edit function shown earlier uses an InputQuery, I have decided that this flag should be set. Ultimately, the paDialog flag does little more than assure that the ellipses button appears at the right of the Property Editor.

> **NOTE**
>
> When you choose both paDialog and paValuelist in a single component, the Property Editor button always winds up being a combo drop-down list button. In other words, the dialog button is obscured, even though the functionality is still present. See, for instance, the Color property of a TForm or TEdit.

You must register Property Editors with the system before compiling them into COMPLIB.DCL:

```
procedure Register;
begin
  ...
  RegisterPropertyEditor(TypeInfo(TColor),
              TClock, 'Color',
              TColorNameProperty);
end;
```

The declaration for RegisterPropertyEditor looks like this:

```
procedure RegisterPropertyEditor(PropertyType: PTypeInfo;
                    ComponentClass: TClass;
                    const PropertyName: string;
                    EditorClass: TPropertyEditorClass);
```

Here is what the various parameters mean:

PropertyType: The first parameter passed to this function states the type of data handled by the editor. In this case, it is TColor. Delphi uses this information as the first in a series of checklists that determine which properties should be associated with this editor.

ComponentClass: The second parameter further qualifies which components will use this editor. In this case, I have narrowed the range down to TClock and its descendants. If I had written TComponent instead of TClock, or if I had set this parameter to nil, all properties of type TColor would start using that editor. What this means is that you could build a new editor for Fonts or Colors, install it on a customer's system, and it would work with all properties of that type. In other words, you don't have to have created a component in order to write an editor for it.

PropertyName: The third parameter limits the scope to properties with the name passed in this string. If the string is empty, the editor is used for all properties that get passed the first two parameters.

EditorClass: This parameter defines the class of editor associated with the properties defined in the first three parameters.

If you want to find out more about this function, you should refer to the comments in DSGNINTF.

When you have seen how to build Property Editors, it is easy to understand Component Editors. These tools are descendants of `TComponentEditor`, just as Property Editors are descendants of `TPropertyEditor`:

```
TClockEditor = class(TComponentEditor)
  procedure Edit; override;
end;
```

The `TColorDialog` has a very simple editor that pops up a dialog specifying a copyright:

```
procedure TClockEditor.Edit;
begin
  MessageDlg('Clock copyright (c) 1995 Charlie Calvert',
             mtInformation, [mbOK],0);
end;
```

This, of course, is the simplest possible Component Editor, but it gets you started working with these very useful tools.

The `Register` method for `TClockEditor` looks like this:

```
procedure Register;
begin
  ...
  RegisterComponentEditor(TClock, TClockEditor);
  ...
end;
```

The declaration for this procedure looks like this:

```
procedure RegisterComponentEditor(ComponentClass: TComponentClass;
  ComponentEditor: TComponentEditorClass);
```

Clearly, the first parameter specifies the class with which the editor is associated, and the second parameter specifies the class of the editor.

In this section, you have had an introduction to Property Editors and Component Editors. These examples are important primarily because they help focus your attention on DSGNINTF.PAS, which is one of several files that ship with Delphi that define the Tools API. If you want to extend the Delphi IDE, you should get to know all the files that end in INTF.

Summary

In this chapter, you have learned about building components. Specifically, you saw how to create components that do the following:

- Change an ancestor's default settings. For instance, you created `TEdit` descendants with new default colors and fonts.

- Add functionality not available in an ancestor object. For instance, the TColorClock object does things that TClock does not.

- Are built up from scratch so that they can add new functionality to the IDE. For instance, the TClock component brings something entirely new to Delphi programming that does not exist in any other component that ships with the product.

You also learned about tools and files associated with components, such as the DCR file and KWMERGE. Finally, you learned something about the Tools API, and specifically about the art of making Property Editors and Component Editors.

Creating Non-Visual Components

IN THIS CHAPTER

30

Overview

In this chapter, you will see how to build a nonvisual component. In particular, there will be an emphasis on the following topics:

- Creating your own event handlers and your own object references; creating your own OnXXX handlers.
- Using and designing nonvisual components.
- Using FindFirst and FindNext to iterate through the files in directories.
- Pushing and popping items off a stack.
- Creating your own stacks.

Much of the material in this chapter follows naturally from the subject matter in the last chapter. However, the material covered here is more advanced and looks a little more deeply into the theories involved in creating powerful, reusable components.

The DELALLW Program

The program shown in this chapter is called DELALLW. It enables you to iterate through subdirectories while deleting files that have particular extensions. The classic use for the program is to delete all files on one drive that have BAK for an extension. During a single run, DELALLW can delete files with more than one specific extension. As a result, I often use the program for deleting the stray files created during the development process. For instance, I don't need to clutter my hard drive with hundreds of files that have extensions such as DCU, ~PA, DSM, or BAK. These are almost always effluvia that I can cast off when I am through building an EXE. DELALLW handles the chore for me.

The DELALLW program uses a component called TFileIterator that iterates through directories. The TFileIterator component sends events to your program whenever a new directory or a new file is found. The events include the name of the new directory or file, as well as information about the size and date of the files it finds. You can then respond to these events in any way you want.

The program creates text files listing all the files that have been deleted, and the new size of each directory it explored. You can use this list of directory sizes when your hard drive is full and you need to look for directories that contain large amounts of data that might be eligible for deletion.

DELALLW uses the TFileIterator component to simplify the task of deleting certain files from a disk. However, you can use it for many other useful tasks. For instance, you can create a file find utility with it, or you can create a GREP program that searches through each file in a set of directories looking for a particular string. The main point is that you can easily create a nonvisual component that broadly expands Delphi's capabilities.

The program shown in this chapter uses two units called ALLDIRS and FILEITER. The ALLDIRS unit has built-in stacks and an object called TRunDirs that knows how to iterate through subdirectories. FILEITER features a simple descendant of TRunDirs called TFileIterator that adds list management capabilities. The task of iterating through directories has a very simple recursive solution. However, recursion is almost never useful in Windows because you have so little available stack space. As a result, ALLDIRS creates its own stacks and pushes the directories it finds onto them.

> **NOTE**
>
> Delphi has some built-in tools for creating stacks and lists. For instance, there are the TList and TStringList objects. I avoid these tools here because they either did not exist or I was not aware of their presence when I first created this program. However, the code I provide here does have the advantage of working in either DOS or Windows. That is, the core units will compile under either Delphi or Turbo Pascal. This capability has made me reluctant to convert the code to a more Delphi-specific format, even if such a format would provide you with good examples of reuse.

Iterating through Directories

It is not always clear whether you should turn a particular object into a component. For instance, the TStringList object has no related component, and cannot be manipulated through visual tools. The question becomes then, why have I taken the TFileIterator object and placed it on the Component Palette?

As it turns out, the main advantages of placing TFileIterator on a Component Palette are twofold:

- There are several options that might need to be tweaked before using this object. In particular, you need to decide whether you want to have the lists of directories and files that you find saved to memory in a TStringList, or whether you don't need to bother with this feature. Letting the programmer decide these matters by clicking a property can go a long way toward presenting a clean, easy-to-use interface for an object.

- Secondly, the TFileIterator object has two features that can be accessed through the events page. Specifically, event handlers can be notified every time a new file or directory has been found. However, it can be confusing to construct an event handler manually, particularly if you don't know what parameters will be passed to the functions involved. If you place a component on the Component Palette, there is no need for the programmer to guess about how to handle an event. All it takes is a quick click on the Events page, and the event handler is created for you automatically!

The code for the DELALLW main unit, the FILEITER unit, and the ALLDIRS units are on this book's CD. The main program is with the other listings for Chapter 30, but the ALLDIRS and FILEITER unit are in the UNITS subdirectory. The form for the DELALLW program is shown in Figure 30.1.

FIGURE 30.1.

The main form for the DELALLW program lists the extensions of the files that will be deleted in a listbox.

> **NOTE**
>
> The FILEITER component, on the CD, enables you to iterate through directories and have the name of each file found passed to `ProcessNameFile`.
>
> The ALLDIRS unit, on the CD, contains the brains for the FILEITER unit.
>
> The main unit for the DELALLW program, found on the CD, depends on FILEITER and ALLDIRS.

The DELALLW program depends on a text file called EXTBOX.TXT. This file contains the list of extensions used to determine which files should be deleted. For instance, here is the list I use when I want to go after the spare files generated when developing Delphi applications:

```
.bak
.dcu
.dsm
```

These extensions are displayed at runtime in a listbox. You can open up the File menu in the DELALLW program and select an option that enables you to edit this list. There is no real limit to the number of extensions you can store in this file, but most people would probably only want to store a few. The DELALLW program could be improved by allowing the user to easily maintain different lists of extensions.

There are two radio buttons on the main form for the DELALLW program. These buttons let you decide whether you want to delete files with an EXE extension, or whether you want to delete files that have a tilde as the first character in their extension.

Delphi marks its backup files by placing a tilde in front of their extension. For example, a backup copy of MAIN.PAS is called MAIN.~PA, and a backup copy of DELALLW.DPR is

DELALLW.~DP. Because Delphi produces a slew of files that have this tilde before their extension, it's simpler to delete all of the files of this type, rather than searching for each individual variety.

The ALLDIRS unit is the brains of this particular operation. It knows how to iterate through directories, how to find all the files in each directory, and how to notify the user when new directories or files are found. The FILEITER unit simply adds the capability to store lists of files and directories in TStringList objects. You can, of course, write these lists to disk by using the SaveToFile command.

Here are the objects in the ALLDIRS unit:

- The TStack object is an abstract class that provides some basic functionality provided for handling all classes of stacks. You'll never have a reason to instantiate an object of this type.

- The TShortStack object handles an array of up to 1,000 PChars. It contains all the logic needed for storing and deleting these items. It holds them in an array that takes up only 4,000 bytes of memory. That's 4 bytes per PChar, times 1,000 possible PChars, which equals 4,000 bytes.

- The TBigStack object creates stacks of TShortStack objects. One directory's worth of subdirectories can be stored in a TShortStack; but, if a directory has multiple subdirectories that have multiple subdirectories, you need TBigStack.

- The TRunDirs object is built around a series of FindFirst and FindNext calls. It uses these Delphi functions to find the files in a directory. It then pushes the directories it finds onto the TShortStack and TBigStack objects.

on the top of a stack is called *pushing* the object on the stack, and removing a plate is called *popping* an object off the stack. For more information on stacks, see any book on basic programming theory.

Using `FindFirst` and `FindNext` is like typing DIR in a directory at the DOS prompt. `FindFirst` finds the first file in the directory, and `FindNext` finds the remaining files. `FindFirst` is found in both the SYSUTILS and WINDOS units, but you should use the version in the SYSUTILS unit because it uses Pascal strings. The one in the WINDOS unit uses PCHARS. (It is unlikely that the WINDOS unit will make it across to the 32-bit version.)

These calls enable you to specify a directory and file mask, as if you were issuing a command of the following type at the DOS prompt:

```
dir c:\aut*.bat
```

This command would, of course, show all files beginning with aut, and ending in .bat.

When you call `FindFirst`, you pass in three parameters:

```
function FindFirst(const Path: string;
                   Attr: Word;
                   var F: TSearchRec): Integer;
```

The first parameter contains the path and file mask that specify the files you want to find. For instance, you might pass in `'c:\delphi\source\vcl\*.pas'` in this parameter. The second parameter lists the type of files you want to see:

```
faReadOnly     $01      Read-only files
faHidden       $02      Hidden files
faSysFile      $04      System files
faVolumeID     $08      Volume ID files
faDirectory    $10      Directory files
faArchive      $20      Archive files
faAnyFile      $3F      Any file
```

Most of the time, you should pass in `faArchive` in this parameter. However, if you want to see directories, you should pass in `faDirectory`. The `Attribute` parameter is not a filter. No matter what flags you use, you will always get all normal files in the directory. Passing `faDirectory` will cause directories to be included in the list of normal files; it does not limit the list to directories. The final parameter is a variable of type `TSearchRec`, which is declared as follows:

```
TSearchRec = record
  Fill: array[1..21] of Byte;
  Attr: Byte;
  Time: Longint;
  Size: Longint;
  Name: string[12];
end;
```

The most important value in `TSearchRec` is the `Name` field, which on success specifies the name of the file found. `FindFirst` returns zero if it found a file, and nonzero if the call fails.

FindNext works exactly like FindFirst, except that you only have to pass in a variable of type TSearchRec, because it is assumed that the mask and file attribute are the same. Once again, FindNext returns zero if all goes well, and a nonzero value if it can't find a file.

Given this information, here is a simple way to call FindFirst and FindNext:

```
if FindFirst(Start, faArchive, SR) = 0 then
  repeat
    DoSomething(SR.Name);
  until FindNext(SR) <> 0;
```

NOTE

Borland Pascal users should note that FindFirst and FindNext have changed. If you want to revert to the old version, you should look in WINDOS.PAS, and probably qualify your calls to these functions with the name of this unit:

```
WinDos.FindNext(SR);
```

Note also that the implementation has changed. SysUtils.FindFirst and SysUtils.FindNext no longer return results through the global variable DosError. When porting BP7 code into VCL classes, you will need to change your While DosError = 0 do loops to avoid infinite loops.

Whenever TRunDirs is ready to process a new directory, it passes its name to a method called ProcessDir:

```
procedure TRunDirs.ProcessDir(Start: String);
var
  SR: SysUtils.TSearchRec;
begin
  if Assigned(FOnProcessDir) then FOnProcessDir(FCurDir);
  if FindFirst(Start, faArchive, SR) = 0 then
    repeat
      ProcessName(UpperCase(FCurDir) + SR.Name, SR);
    until FindNext(SR) <> 0;
end;
```

ProcessDir iterates through all the files in a directory and passes each file it finds to the ProcessName method:

```
procedure TRunDirs.ProcessName(FName: String;
                               SR: SysUtils.TSearchRec);
begin
  if Assigned(FOnFoundFile) then FOnFoundFile(FName, SR);
end;
```

Both ProcessDir and ProcessName are virtual methods. Therefore, you can create a descendant of TRunDirs, override either of these methods, and respond to them in any way you like.

Creating a descendant of TRunDirs is a simple operation, but it's even simpler to respond to event handlers via the delegation model. To create an OnXXX event handler, you must first declare a pointer to a method:

```
TFoundDirEvent = procedure(DirName: string) of Object;
```

This pointer references a procedure that takes a single string as a parameter. Method pointers were discussed in the chapter on objects and inheritance.

Next, declare a variable that can point at an object of this type:

```
FOnProcessDir: TFoundDirEvent;
```

Now the TRunDirs object has the tools it needs to use the delegation model. Specifically, it contains an internal variable that can be set equal to a method of the correct type. Whenever a particular event occurs, it can simply use this variable to call the method delegated to handle the event:

```
if Assigned(FOnFoundFile) then FOnFoundFile(FName, SR);
```

This code is from the body of the ProcessDir method. It first checks to see whether FOnFoundFile is set to nil. If it is not nil, that means you have assigned a method to handle this event, and the event is called.

Event handlers are merely properties that consist of pointers to functions, rather than to some other kind of data. Here is the declaration for the OnProcessDir event:

```
property OnProcessDir: TFoundDirEvent
     read FOnProcessDir write FOnProcessDir;
```

You can see that this property is declared to be of type TFoundDirEvent, rather than being of some other more common type such as a string, integer, or set. This property serves as an interface for the FOnProcessDir variables, which are hidden from other objects in the private section.

Event handlers are attractive because they can be so readily accessed from the Object Inspector. Double-click on the property editor for an event handler, and the method associated with that event is immediately inserted into your code. In short, event handlers are a very modest form of code generator, in which the code that is generated is a declaration for any sort of method you might wish to define.

In the DELALLW program, the code generated for this event looks like this:

```
TForm1.FileIterator1ProcessDir(DirName: String);
begin

end;
```

The body of any event handler is, of course, supplied by a programmer. In this case, it looks like this:

```
FDirSizeList.Add(FDirName + ': ' + IntToStr(FDirSize));
FDirName := DirName;
FDirSize := 0;
```

Here, the name and size of the last directory processed are added to a list, the new directory name is saved in a variable called FDirName, and the directory size is set to zero.

The actual size of each directory is calculated in the OnFoundFile event handler:

```
procedure TForm1.FileIterator1FoundFile(FileName: String;
                                         SR: TSearchRec);
var
  S: string;
  i: Integer;
  AddToDirSize: Boolean;
begin
  AddToDirSize := False;
  S := UpperCase(ExtractFileExt(FileName));
  for i := 0 to ExtBox.Items.Count - 1 do begin
    if (S = '.EXE') and (not FDelExes) then begin
      AddToDirSize := True;
      Continue;
    end;
    if S = UpperCase(ExtBox.Items.Strings[i]) then begin
      FDeleteList.Add(FileName);
      Continue;
    end;
    if not FDelTilda then
      AddToDirSize := True
    else if S[2] = '~' then begin
      FDeleteList.Add(FileName);
      Continue;
    end;
    AddToDirSize := True;
  end;
  if AddToDirSize then FDirSize := FDirSize + SR.Size;
end;
```

This one routine has several different pieces of logic in it. The most important logic determines whether the name passed in contains one of the extensions that the user wants to delete. If it does, the file's name is added to a list of files that will be deleted after visiting all the user-specified directories. Special cases are implemented for executables and backup files marked with a tilde. If it is determined that one of the files in the directory will not be deleted, its size is added to the current value of the FDirSize variable. FDirSize just keeps getting larger and larger until the entire directory is processed. At that point, DELALLW stores the directory name and its size in a list, and the whole process begins again.

Summary

The DELALLW program and the TFileIterator component point the way toward an understanding of Delphi's greatest strengths. TFileIterator and TRunDirs are not particularly difficult pieces of code, but they are sufficiently complex to highlight the fact that you can place almost any kind of logic inside a Delphi object. If you want to write multimedia code, talk on a network, or simulate the behavior of a submarine, you can write a Delphi component that will encapsulate the logic needed to reach your goal. More importantly, this component can then be placed on the Component Palette and dropped onto a form where it can be manipulated through the Object Inspector.

The Object Inspector, and its related property editors and component editors, provide an elegant, easy-to-use interface to any object. Component architectures represent one of the most important tools in programming today, and it's quite possible that Delphi has by far the best implementation of a component architecture currently available in any market.

Adding Multimedia to Delphi Programs

31

Overview

You can easily add multimedia features such as sounds, movies, and music to Delphi programs. This chapter shows how to achieve these ends using the multimedia control that is built into the Delphi environment.

When reading this chapter, you can expect to encounter five distinct sections:

- A general discussion of multimedia.
- How to use the built-in Delphi multimedia control to play WAVE, MIDI, and AVI files. This section of the chapter will also discuss accessing CD-ROM files.
- How to use Delphi to create presentation programs that utilize multimedia to explain a topic in clear and easy-to-understand terms.
- How to show an AVI file in a window on your form.
- How to know when the user starts playing a file, when the user stops playing a file, when a file reaches the end, when the user pauses a file, and in general how to track runtime information about the state of the multimedia player.

People who have read this book through from the beginning will find that I explain a few programming steps in this chapter that might seem a bit extraneous at this point. I decided to include these programming basics because I imagine that some readers will turn to this chapter before completing the preceding chapters. At any rate, I know that I would be inclined to do that if I were the reading this book.

As always, you can find the complete source code for all the programs on this book's CD-ROM. MIDI, WAVE, and AVI files are also available in the MULTIMED subdirectory. You can use them to experiment with the sample code in this chapter.

Exploring Multimedia

Multimedia for Windows has developed over the last few years to the point where it is now commonplace. However, it is probably still worthwhile discussing the subject briefly in general terms, just to be sure that there is a common definition of the concepts involved.

Multimedia is a generic term. It refers to almost any form of animation, sound, or movie that is used on computers. Given this broad definition, it's possible to say that this chapter deals with a subset of multimedia that involves the following:

- Showing movies via Microsoft's Video for Windows files
- Playing music via MIDI and WAVE files
- Playing and recording sounds and voices via WAVE files

All of these formats can be handled by the Microsoft Multimedia Extensions to Windows, and are encapsulated in the TMediaPlayer control found on the Additional page in the Component Palette.

File Formats: How Much Disk Space Will I Need?

You will learn about three different types of files while reading this chapter:

- Files that include an AVI extension produce video. Examples of these types of files are ELEPHANT.AVI and FLOWERS.AVI.

- Files that include an MID extension produce music by using the Musical Instrument Digital Interface (or MIDI) format. Examples of these types of files are JAZZ.MID and VIVALDI.MID.

- Files that include a WAV extension can be used to record sounds using Microsoft's WAVE technology. Examples of these types of files are CRASH.WAV and SPEECH.WAV.

Of the three file formats discussed in this chapter, the AVI files are usually the largest. Even relatively short AVI films of one minute or less tend to take up 5, or even 10, megabytes of disk space. It's possible to compress these files further, but the savings that result are usually fairly minimal.

AVI files come from video media of one sort or another. Usually they are short snippets of film transferred from a video camera. AVI can include sound, and can be shown in either black and white or color. The size of the window that shows these films is typically rather small, rarely more than a few inches in width or height, although Windows does support showing these files full screen in 320×200 mode.

WAV files also tend to be large, but not nearly as large as AVI files. A typical file ratio for a WAV file is one minute of sound to one megabyte of disk space. One second of low-quality (8-bit mono, 11khz sampling) sound can take up to 11,000 bytes of disk space. CD-quality sound (16-bit stereo, 44khz sampling) can require up to 176,000 bytes of data per second. You can, however, record nearly anything on a WAV file. For instance, if you want to record the sound of glass breaking, or the sound of someone singing, either could be handled inside a WAV file. The quality of these files differs dramatically from instance to instance, but there is nothing preventing you from creating a high-quality sound file using the WAV format. A lot of the quality is determined at digitization time. The same is true of AVI files: You can dial in the frame rate (quality of motion) when digitizing. The basic formula is simple enough: the better the quality the bigger the file.

Unlike the formats mentioned previously, MIDI files can be extremely compact, and yet offer superb sound quality. However, even good MIDI files are often ruined because they are played on systems with inadequate hardware, or hardware that has not been set up properly. In short, MIDI files offer excellent potential, but the art of playing them properly can be difficult to manage.

Every MIDI file is divided up into multiple tracks, and users generally record the sound one track at a time, with only one instrument on each track. If you play five or six of these tracks at the same time, the result can be the sound of an entire band. For instance, a typical MIDI file might feature the sound of drums on one track, bass on a second track, piano on a third track, and a horn on the fourth track. Depending on the hardware and software involved, you can record between 3 and 15 instruments on any one file. You can record the instruments via a MIDI connection, or you can literally write out the notes one at a time, as if you were composing on sheet music. As a rule, MIDI records only instrumental notes, not vocal music. MIDI doesn't act like a tape recorder, capturing raw sound traveling through the air in waves. The sound is entirely synthesized by the hardware. MIDI captures the notes and timing info, nothing more. It's very mathematical, and in that sense allows you to get very close to a pure musical form.

If you look at the same media from the point of view of the hardware, the formats appear in a quite different light. For instance, you can play AVI files on any machine that comes equipped with a functioning copy of Windows. The only requirements for playing AVI files are the Microsoft Video for Windows drivers, which are distributed free from a number of different sources. Decent reproduction of WAV files, however, requires a sound card. Serious work with MIDI requires both a sound card and the presence of an instrument attached to your computer via a MIDI cable.

Hardware: What Kind of Machine Do I Need?

The two most important pieces of hardware required for multimedia are a sound card and a CD-ROM. CD-ROM disks are useful primarily because they give you a place to store large amounts of information. Sound cards, however, contain chips that make it possible to reproduce high-quality WAV files, as well as any kind of MIDI file or the sound track for an AVI file. To make the sound from your card audible, you will want speakers, headphones, and possibly an amplifier. There is no reason that you can't plug the output jack from a sound card directly into your home stereo system.

When purchasing equipment, you might want to follow your general tastes when buying a stereo. If you are the type of person who wouldn't consider listening to music on anything less than a $1,000 stereo system, you should probably spend a similar sum of money to convert your computer into a multimedia machine. On the other hand, if you can get by listening to a $50 or $200 ghetto blaster, you can probably convert your computer into a multimedia machine for a similar sum of money.

In general, high-quality machines have 16-bit sound cards, quad-speed CD-ROM drives, and speakers that range upwards of $200 in price. Low-end machines have 8-bit sound cards, double-speed CD-ROM drives, and speakers that cost in the range of $10 to $50 dollars. Of course, these are estimates from January 1995, and by the time you read this, any prices quoted here will almost certainly have dropped.

Why Bother with Multimedia?

The final topic in the general discussion section involves the whole question of why anyone would want to use multimedia.

Early attempts to utilize the technology involved tricks such as accompanying an error or the opening of a window with sounds produced by various WAVE files. In general, I've never found much use for any of the methods that attempt to jazz up standard computer applications such as spreadsheets or word processors. That kind of work requires efficiency and a quiet, distraction-free atmosphere. Though I may be proven wrong in the long term, I now believe that the working end of traditional apps aren't likely to become important outlets for multimedia programmers. Tutors and online help offer more possibilities, and will probably become a hunting ground for a small number of job-seeking multimedia programmers.

If standard computer applications aren't obvious outlets for multimedia, then what's left? What good is this thing?

Well, the openings for multimedia right now are concentrated in three areas:

- Game programs
- Presentation programs
- Education

It doesn't take much imagination to see how multimedia can be used to enhance games. However, some people still fail to see the importance of using multimedia when presenting data.

If you combine music and graphics in effective ways, you can draw people's attention, thereby getting them to focus on information that you want to convey. This might not seem terribly important to some people until they begin to realize that information technology dominates the computer business, and plays an equally important role in large portions of the entire American economy. Information is wealth and power in this country, and if you can present information in the most effective and appealing manner possible, you will be providing an important and valuable service.

The key to this entire process is learning how to manipulate the elements of multimedia programs. The remaining sections of this chapter are dedicated to showing you ways to achieve this end that are both simple to implement, and powerful in their overall effect.

Delphi and Multimedia

Delphi has a TMediaPlayer component that gives you access to all the major features of multimedia programming. This control is extremely ease to use. In fact, it is so easy to use that many future programmers may find that their first program is not the classic "Hello World" application, but rather a simple one-or two-line effort that plays a movie or song.

Having a control this easy to use is a mixed blessing:

- On the positive side is the fact that Delphi can be used by nearly anyone to create multimedia applications or presentations.
- On the negative side, you will find that Delphi's multimedia control has a somewhat limited capability. If you want more access to low-level functions, you will have to use the Delphi language to dig beneath the surface of the multimedia interface. Some channels to pursue in this regard are covered in Chapter 35, "OWL and Advanced Multimedia Capability." Having said this, I caution you not to sell the TMediaPlayer component short. It is more powerful than it might at first appear.

This chapter will not describe the internal workings of the Delphi control that you use to access multimedia functions. Instead, that material will be covered in Chapter 35. For now, all you really need to know is that the Delphi multimedia component is called TMediaPlayer. It gives you access to a set of routines written by Microsoft, called the Media Control Interface (MCI). These routines give programmers fairly easy access to a wide range of multimedia capabilities. The TMediaPlayer makes these routines extremely intuitive and easy to use.

Installing the Correct Drivers

Delphi can't play multimedia files for you unless you have the proper software and the proper drivers. Some multimedia tools, such as movies, do not require that you have any special hardware, although you can't hear the soundtrack to the films unless you have a sound card. The little built-in speaker that has always come with PCs is not enough to exercise the real multimedia capabilities described in this chapter. This is true even if you have the SPEAKER.DRV file.

When you have installed the hardware that you need, the next step is to install the proper drivers. As a rule, the drivers you need ship with the hardware that you have installed on your system. For instance, a Sound Blaster card comes with a set of disks that contain the drivers you need. You must install these drivers before attempting to run the programs described in this chapter.

Included on the CD that comes with this book are the Microsoft Video for Windows drivers that you need before you can play AVI files. To install these files, simply find the proper subdirectory on the CD and type setup from the Run menu in the File Manager. The install program quickly takes you through the whole process of setting up your system to play movies.

I have not, of course, included drivers for the various sound cards that are currently available. If you have a sound card, but can't find the drivers you need, they are usually available from the manufacturer, or from CompuServe, the Internet, or some other online service. As a rule, companies don't charge for drivers.

When you are done installing the drivers, you can run the Drivers applet from the Control Panel to see the drivers that you have installed. You will also find a parallel set of entries in your SYSTEM.INI file. On my system these entries look like this:

```
[drivers]
timer=timer.drv
midimapper=midimap.drv
VIDC.CVID=iccvid.drv
VIDC.MSVC=msvidc.drv
VIDC.IV31=indeov.drv
VIDC.MRLE=MSRLE.drv
VIDC.RT21=indeov.drv
VIDC.YVU9=indeov.drv
WaveMapper=msacm.drv
MSACM.msadpcm=msadpcm.acm
MSACM.imaadpcm=imaadpcm.acm
wave=sndsys.drv
midi=sndsys.drv
aux=sndsys.drv
mixer=sndsys.drv
SndEvnts=SndEvnts.drv
MSACM.trspch=ts_soft.acm
```

Ugh! What a mess. However, some knowledge can be gleaned from this listing. For instance, on my system, SNDSYS.DRV is used to play WAV and MIDI files. To improve the performance on my system, I might want to check whether that driver is up to date, and if I was having problems getting any sound from my system, I might want to check to see that the driver is the right one for my system. (For the record, my sound system is working just fine, thank you!)

The MIDI Mapper applet in the Control Panel can be used to customize the voices on your synthesizer so that they map to the right values. For instance, some MIDI hardware uses voice 1 as the sound for a piano, voice 2 for an electric piano, and so on. If you want to change which voices are mapped to which numbers, use the MIDI Mapper. Due to a lack of standardization and to some lack of foresight on the part of the people who set up the Windows MIDI services, there can be some frustrating work in store for you in this regard.

The TMediaPlayer Component

To get started writing a multimedia application, create a new project and select the multimedia control (TMediaPlayer) from the System page of the Component Palette. Drop the tool in the middle of a form, as shown in Figure 31.1.

FIGURE 31.1.

The TMediaPlayer control resting in the middle of a standard form.

After you have placed the control on a form, you will find that the Object Inspector contains a `FileName` field, as shown in Figure 31.2. Fill in this field with the name of an AVI, MIDI, or WAVE file. For instance, on my system I can write `G:\AVI\CLOUDS.AVI` to indicate the name of a video file located on my CD-ROM. The ellipses icon on the right side of the property editor pops up a dialog so that you can browse for files. After choosing a valid filename, be sure the `AutoOpen` property is set to true. This property ensures that Delphi automatically opens the MULTIMEDIA services when you start your program.

FIGURE 31.2.

The TMediaPlayer component as seen through the Object Inspector.

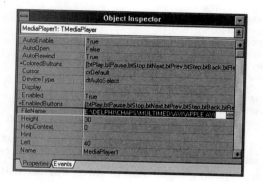

After completing these simple steps, you are ready to run the program. When it's launched, click the green button at the left of the TMediaPlayer to start the movie or sound file that you selected. If you get an error, there are three probable sources:

1. You entered an invalid filename.
2. You don't have multimedia set up correctly on your system. This means you either don't have the right hardware, or you have not installed the right drivers. Driver configuration occurs in the Control Panel, and hardware requirements are specified in detail in any good book on multimedia.
3. You have `AutoOpen` set to true, but have left the `FileName` property blank. This produces the dreaded error message. This command requires a parameter. Please supply one.

A sample program is available on disk as MEDIA1.DPR. By default, it plays CHIMES.WAV, a file that ships with every copy of Windows. If you have deleted this file or if you do not store it in a subdirectory called C:\WINDOWS, you need to change the `FileName` property of this program.

If you experiment with the MEDIA1 program, you find that you can play AVI, MIDI, and WAVE files simply by specifying the name of a file. This flexibility is the result of the control's capability to parse the filename, detect the file type from the extension, and apportion the act of actually playing the file to the appropriate internal routine.

Opening the TMediaPlayer at Runtime

If you place a TMediaPlayer component on a window, select a file, set AutoOpen to True, and run the program, you find that the media player starts out in operational mode (with most of its buttons lit up and ready for use). If you close the program, set the AutoOpen property to False, and restart the program, the media player will not be open when you first run the program. This can be useful under some circumstances, because it costs time and resources to open up the Windows multimedia drivers.

It takes only a few simple steps to gain control over the opening and closing of the TMediaPlayer. To get started, place a button on the form and name it Open. Double-click the button to create an OnClick method, and fill it in as follows:

```
procedure TForm1.Button1Click(Sender: TObject);
begin
  MediaPlayer.Open;
end;
```

When you run the program, you see a bar containing the universal symbols for playing a tape, CD, or video device. Click once on the button to open the appropriate MCI device. Wait a few moments for the buttons on the TMediaPlayer to change color, and then click once more on the green arrow at the left of the control. The file you specified in the FileName section now plays for you.

Two Varieties of Multimedia Programs

Programmers who work the TMediaPlayer are probably going to want to move in one of two directions:

- Some programmers will want to give their users a simple way of playing the widest possible range of files. This means they will want to give the user access to the hard disk or CD-ROM, and allow them to select and play a wide range of individual files. This type of application is sometimes called a *media access* program.

- Other programmers will want to hide the existence of the control from the user. They will want to play movie or sound files without the user ever being aware of how the selection was made. In particular, this type of activity would likely be part of a presentation. For instance, a MIDI or WAVE file might be played while a chart is on the screen that shows sales of a particular widget. The WAVE file could actually contain recorded speech explaining the graphs. Then, an AVI file might start that shows pictures of the plant where the widget is made. During this whole presentation, the user should not be aware of the existence of the TMediaPlayer. It should run entirely in the background. For now, let's call this type of application a presentation program.

The next few pages present two examples. The first shows how to give the user access to a wide range of files, and the second shows how to run the control in the background.

Media Access Programs

To create a media access application, start by dropping a TMediaPlayer and a button on a form. Name the button `BSelectFile` and give it *Select File* as a caption. Then, choose the OpenDialog from the Dialogs Palette in the Component Palette and place this control on the form. When you are done, your form should look like the one shown in Figure 31.3. This might be a good time to save this program under the name ACCESS.

FIGURE 31.3.

The main form for the ACCESS program.

Now create a `BSelectFileClick` method that looks like this:

```
procedure TForm1.BSelectFileClick(Sender: TObject);
begin
  MediaPlayer1.Close;
  if OpenDialog1.Execute then begin
    MediaPlayer1.FileName := OpenDialog1.FileName;
    MediaPlayer1.Open;
  end;
end;
```

The code shown here is going to be executed every time the user presses the Select File button. It has four purposes:

- The first step is to close any MCI devices that might be currently open by calling `MediaPlayer1.Close`. When you first open the program, this line won't serve a useful purpose, but after you have opened a file and wish to open a second one, you find that it helps clear the way. It is never an error to call `Close` on a TMediaPlayer.

- The second step is to execute the `OpenDialog`. This allows users to roam at will through the hard drive and any available CD-ROMs. If they find a file they wish to play, they can press the OK button to select it.

■ The third step executes only if the user selects a file. If the user chooses Cancel from the Open Dialog, nothing happens. If the user picks OK, the code assigns the filename selected by the user to the MCI control.

■ When an appropriate filename has been designated, the only step left is to open (or reopen) the MCI device by calling `MediaPlayer1.Open`. Now the user is free to click the green arrow to play the file.

A few minor adjustments can be made to this program to make it a bit more friendly for the user. For instance, you can automatically allow the user to select files with only a particular extension such as AVI , WAV, or MID. There are two different ways to achieve this end.

If you want to show all three types of files at once, enter the following string in the Filter section of the Object Inspector:

```
Multimedia Files(*.avi;*wav;*.mid)¦*.avi;*.wav;*.mid
```

Now the user can simultaneously select a WAVE, MIDI, or movie file.

Alternatively, you can change the `TOpenDialog`'s `Filter` property so that it contains the following string:

```
AVI File(*.avi)¦*.avi¦WAVE File(*.wav)¦*.wav¦ MIDI file(*.MID)¦*.mid
```

To make it easier for the reader to parse this string, I can break it up into three sections:

```
AVI File(*.avi)¦*.avi
WAVE File(*.wav)¦*.wav
MIDI file(*.MID)¦*.mid
```

Each of these sections contains one bar (|) symbol and is divided from the next by another bar symbol. When the program is running and the Open Dialog is active, the first half of the string (up to the bar) is shown in the List File Type section of the Open Dialog, and the second half is shown in the FileName section. When shown this way, the user must select a different option in the File Type dropdown combo box in order to see files with a different extension.

NOTE

Delphi includes a special property editor available in the Object Inspector that makes it easier to input filters at design time. To use this dialog, simply enter the first half of the previous string in the left portion of the dialog and place the portion shown after the bar in the right side of the dialog. Under most circumstances, you would use three lines that would look like those in the previous code example to complete the chore.

If you want to assign values to the Filter field at runtime, you should use one of the first two coding examples in this chapter. For instance, you could assign the following string to the filter property at runtime:

```
Multimedia Files(*.avi;*wav;*.mid)¦*.avi;*.wav;*.mid
```

Another field of OpenDialog that you might want to tweak is the InitialDir property. You can use this to designate the drive or directory that you want users to see first when they open the dialog. In my case, I prefer to enter the drive designating my CD-ROM:

g:

This allows the user to start his search for files on the drive most likely to contain a hit. Because I do not specify a particular directory, the user can select a particular directory and return to it over and over until he or she has seen all the files of interest in that location.

The few simple steps outlined previously are the only ones you need to take in order to give a user full access to all the media files on the system. Other additions you might consider making involve setting the background color of the form to black, or having the form start maximized. Remember that a program of this type is saved on disk as ACCESS.DPR.

A Closer Look at a Media Access Program

I have shown you one very simple media access program called ACCESS, which nearly anyone can put together. This program is very robust, and it fits the needs of most programmers. However, there are occasions when you want a more in-depth look at what occurs when a multimedia file is being played. The next section of this chapter describes a program called ACCESS2, which gives you all the information you need to gain full control over MCI multimedia capabilities.

Before plunging into this explanation, let me make two points:

■ Although many programmers will find it useful, the information presented in this section is not essential to all multimedia programmers.

■ Other readers might wish for even more control over multimedia files than is shown in this section. These readers should be aware that you can get down to a lower level of file control by entirely circumventing the TMediaPlayer and dealing directly with a set of low-level Windows commands found in the MMSYSTEM.PAS unit that ships with Delphi. You can also use the MCI commands described in Chapter 35.

With these two caveats fresh in your mind, you are now ready to learn about some of the more subtle aspects of TMediaPlayer.

You have probably noticed that the Events palette for the TMediaPlayer contains special capabilities that you can add to your program. These functions come in two categories:

■ The first are the OnClick events that occur when the user presses part of the control. For instance, the OnPlay event, replete with a parameter called Button, is sent to your program whenever the user presses the green play arrow on the TMediaPlayer.

■ The second are the OnNotify events containing the mm_MciNotify messages that are sent to your window when a file starts or stops playing, or when an error occurs.

I am going to describe the first set of events in the next few paragraphs, and then move on to the second set.

There are eight major events generated by a direct click on the control, all of which are captured in the TMPBtnType. These events are as follows:

- btPlay: Occurs when the user presses the green play arrow.
- btStop: Occurs when the user presses the red square stop button.
- btBack: Occurs when the user presses the blue "back one frame" button.
- btStep: Occurs when the user presses the blue "forward one frame" button.
- btNext: Occurs when the user presses the blue fast-forward button.
- btPrev: Occurs when the user presses the blue rewind button.
- btPause: Occurs when the user presses the yellow pause button.
- btRecord: Occurs when the user presses the round red record button.

If you want to see what it's like to capture one of these events, first place four edit controls on your form. Each of these edit controls will be used eventually, although they do not all play a role in the first parts of the program I am going to describe. Create an OnClick event for the TMediaPlayer, and fill it in so that it looks like this:

```
procedure TForm1.MediaPlayer1Click(Sender: TObject;
                        Button: TMpBtnType;
                        var DoDefault: Boolean);

begin
  Edit1.Text := 'Playing';
end;
```

When you understand how this system works, it should take you only a moment to be able to display an appropriate line of text whenever the user selects the TMediaPlayer. For instance, here is a method that can be called whenever the user presses a media player button:

```
procedure TForm1.MediaPlayer1Click(Sender: TObject;
                        Button: TMPBtnType;
                        var DoDefault: Boolean);

begin
  case Button of
    btPlay: Edit1.Text := 'Playing';
    btPause: Edit1.Text := 'Paused';
    btStop: Edit1.Text := 'Stop';
    btNext: Edit1.Text := 'Next';
    btPrev: Edit1.Text := 'Prev';
    btStep: Edit1.Text := 'Step';
    btBack: Edit1.Text := 'Back';
    btRecord: Edit1.Text := 'Record';
    btEject: Edit1.Text := 'Eject';
  end;
end;
```

To find out whether a piece has stopped playing or whether an error has occurred, you can take a look at OnNotify messages. When working directly with the operating system, these messages come in four flavors:

```
mci_Notify_Successful: Sent when a command is completed
mci_Notify_Superseded: Command aborted by another function
mci_Notify_Aborted   : Current function is aborted
mci_Notify_Failure   : An error occurred
```

Delphi does not send these messages to you directly, but instead converts them into constants such as nvSuccessful and nvAborted. This system is adopted to provide consistency with other portions of the Delphi environment.

It's a bit tricky to understand exactly when each of these messages are sent by the Windows MCI device driver. As a rule, you get messages in these cases:

- An nvSuccessful message when a piece finishes successfully.

- An nvSuperseded message might come if the system has been paused, and the user then presses the Play button.

- An nvAborted message might come if the user presses the Stop button, or causes the device to be closed.

Here is a function that responds to OnNotify messages by displaying a short descriptive string in an edit control:

```
procedure TForm1.MediaPlayer1Notify(Sender: TObject);
var
  S: String;
begin
  case MediaPlayer1.NotifyValue of
    nvSuccessful: begin
      Inc(Total);
      S := 'mci_Notify_Successful' + IntToStr(Total);
    end;
    nvSuperseded: S := 'mci_Notify_Superseded';
    nvAborted: S := 'mci_Notify_Aborted';
    nvFailure: S := 'mci_Notify_Failure';
  else
    S := 'Unknown notify message';
  end;

  Edit2.Text := S;

  if (MediaPlayer1.NotifyValue = nvSuccessful) and
     (MediaPlayer1.Mode = mpStopped) then
    Edit1.Text := 'File finished playing';

end;
```

This function is called automatically every time a significant event occurs that affects the MCI device. You never explicitly call this function yourself. Instead, you just set it up and wait for the function to be called by the system.

The heart of the MediaPlayer1Notify method is a case statement that hinges on the current state of the NotifyValue field of a TMediaPlayer. For instance, if the NotifyValue field is set to mci_Notify_Successful, a string specifying that fact is displayed in an edit control. Once again, you don't have to do anything to change the state of the NotifyValue field. It will be changed for you automatically by the system. All you need to do is respond to an OnNotify event and then check the NotifyValue field.

If you want to be sure that a file has finished playing, you can wait for the reception of an mci_Notify_Successful message, and then check to see the current mode.

The current mode of an MCI device is specified in the Mode property of a TMediaPlayer. Here is a listing of the common values designated in this field:

```
mci_Mode_Not_Ready
mci_Mode_Stop
mci_Mode_Play
mci_Mode_Record
mci_Mode_Seek
mci_Mode_Pause
mci_Mode_Open
```

Each of these modes is self-explanatory. If the Mode field is set to mci_Mode_Stop, the device is stopped. If it's set to mci_Mode_Play, the device is currently playing. Once again, Delphi does not send you these constants directly, but instead passes corresponding identifiers, such as mpStopped and mpPlaying. I believe the developers substituted these constants because they were easy to read, and also followed the style used by the rest of the Delphi objects.

If your application receives an mci_Notify_Successful message and if the Mode field of the device is set to mci_Mode_Stop, you can be certain that the current file has finished playing. That is why the OnNotify method shown earlier checks for such a condition:

```
if (MediaPlayer1.NotifyValue = nvSuccessful) and
   (MediaPlayer1.Mode = mpStopped) then
    Edit1.Text := 'File finished playing';
```

The ACCESS2 program also contains the following method, which can be used to track the current state of the media player:

```
procedure TForm1.SetMode;
begin
  case MediaPlayer1.Mode of
    mpNotReady: Edit3.Text := 'mci_Mode_Not_Ready';
    mpStopped: Edit3.Text := 'mci_Mode_Stop';
    mpPlaying: Edit3.Text := 'mci_Mode_Play';
    mpRecording: Edit3.Text := 'mci_Mode_Record';
    mpSeeking: Edit3.Text := 'mci_Mode_Seek';
    mpPaused: Edit3.Text := 'mci_Mode_Pause';
    mpOpen: Edit3.Text := 'mci_Mode_Open';
  else begin
      Edit1.Text := 'Device Inactive';
      Edit2.Text := 'No special messages';
      Edit3.Text := 'Unknown';
      Edit4.Text := 'No file selected';
    end;
  end;
end;
```

This routine gets called in response to an event generated by a TTimer that is placed on the form. To create a timer, simply select it from the System page of the Component Palette, drop it on a form, and create an OnTimer event handler. The method needs to do nothing more than call the SetMode procedure. The Interval property of a TTimer component defines how often OnTimer events are generated. If you leave Interval at the default 1000-millisecond level, SetMode is called once every second, thereby ensuring that the user is kept reasonably well-informed of the current state of the TMediaPlayer.

The main form is shown in Figure 31.4.

FIGURE 31.4.

*The ACCESS2 program
displays the current state of
the media player in a series
of edit controls.*

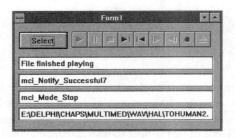

NOTE

The ACCESS2 program, in the CHAP31 directory on this book's CD-ROM, shows how to fine-tune the behavior of a TMediaPlayer.

When you are examining the ACCESS2 program, you should look for code that demonstrates the following key points:

- Whenever the user clicks the media player, an event is automatically generated. For instance, if the user clicks the green play arrow, a btPlay event is sent to your program. To respond to this event, just create an OnClick method by clicking the appropriate part of the Object Inspector.

- mm_MciNotify messages are sent to your application after key events occur in the life-cycle of a multimedia file. For instance, if the file finishes playing, a mci_Notify_Successful message is sent to your application. You can respond to this event inside an OnNotify method.

- You can query the system to find out the current state of the selected multimedia device. To do this, simply see the value of the Mode property for the media player. For instance, if MediaPlayer1.Mode = mpPlaying, you know that the device is currently playing.

The TMediaPlayer control completely protects you from the need to work with the Microsoft MCI interface found in MMSYSTEM.PAS. However, if you want to become an expert in this field, you should begin by studying that source file, and seeing how it is called from MPLAYER.PAS. This subject is covered in Chapter 35.

Defining the Window in which a Movie Plays

Sometimes you want an AVI file to play in a separate window, and sometimes you want it to play in a window that is part of your form. If you want a movie to be shown on your form, use the `TMediaPlayer.Display` property. For instance, you might drop a TPanel on the form and assign the `Display` property to it:

```
MediaPlayer1.Display := Panel1;
```

To further customize the view, you can use the `DisplayRect` property to define the rectangle in which you want the movie to play. For instance, if you want the movie to stretch to fit the entire surface of the panel, you write the following:

```
MediaPlayer1.DisplayRect := Rect(0, 0, Panel1.Width, Panel1.Height);
```

An example of this technique is found in the WINDAVI program shown in Listing 31.2. The form (shown in Figure 31.5) features two file-oriented listbox controls from the System page of the Object Inspector.

FIGURE 31.5.

The WINDAVI program uses the TDirectoryListBox *and* TFileListBox *controls.*

NOTE

The WINDAVI program, on the CD, enables the user to play a movie in a predefined area.

This program is really a Windows AVI file viewer. It is custom-made for that purpose. The basic flow of the program enables you to select AVI files from the directory tools on the left side of the form. When a valid file is selected, the `TMediaPlayer` is automatically activated and the user can press the green play arrow.

Whenever the user chooses a file from FileListBox1, the following code is called:

```
procedure TForm1.FileListBox1Click(Sender: TObject);
begin
  MediaPlayer1.FileName := FileListbox1.fileName;
  MediaPlayer1.Open;
  Mediaplayer1.Display := Panel1;
  MediaPlayer1.DisplayRect :=
    Rect(2, 2, Panel1.Width - 4, Panel1.Height - 4);
end;
```

The code assigns the proper filename, ensures that media player is open, and finally displays output on the surface of Panel1. Notice that the program leaves the border around the panel open so that the 3-D effect of the panel is preserved.

The rest of the code in the program ensures that the three listbox controls on the left side of the form stay in sync. For instance, whenever you switch to a new directory, you need to be sure FileListBox1 is apprised of the change:

```
procedure TForm1.DirectoryListBox1Click(Sender: TObject);
begin
  FileListbox1.directory := DirectoryListbox1.directory
end;
```

Or, if you prefer, you can delete this code and hook up all three file listbox controls in the Object Inspector using the DirList property of DriveComboBox and the FileList property of the DirectoryListBox.

Notice that I have a commented-out section in the FormCreate method for this project that sets the initial directory. A more sophisticated version of this program might ask the user to specify this information at startup.

Presentation Programs

From a programmer's perspective, a presentation program written in Delphi does not have to be a particularly demanding chore. The really complicated issues turn out to be not programming-related, but design-related.

The PRESENT program discussed next provides a multimedia QuickStart for the previous ACCESS2 program. Users of ACCESS2 can run PRESENT in order to learn how to use the ACCESS2 program.

PRESENT is written entirely in Delphi and requires only a few very simple programming skills. I chose the ACCESS2 program as a topic because it is easy to explain, and because it is familiar to all readers of this chapter. Clear online explanation of how to run a program is something that is obviously needed in the computer industry. The PRESENT program belongs to a family of multimedia applications for which there is an immediate and obvious market.

When running a presentation program, it's probably best to set the MediaPlayer1's Visible property to False inside the Object Inspector. That way, the user never sees the control itself. Of course, when you do this, you need to begin manipulating the control entirely through the program's code. In other words, you can't expect the user to press the green arrow that starts the sounds, nor can the user be responsible for closing one file and starting a second file. Everything has to be controlled through code.

The basic steps you need to take to run the multimedia control from behind the scenes are fourfold:

- Assign a filename to the control.
- Open the control.
- Play the file.
- Close the control.

The code required to perform these steps might look like this:

```
MediaPlayer1.FileName := Wave4;
MediaPlayer1.Open;
MediaPlayer1.Play;
MediaPlayer1.Close;
```

The trick here is to find the right way to arrange this code so that each method is called at the right time. The PRESENT program that accompanies this article shows one simple way to achieve this end.

The first step is to choose a few key screen shots from the ACCESS2 program. In this particular case, I've chosen three graphics:

Graphic One:	A shot of the ACCESS2 program's main screen
Graphic Two:	A shot of the OpenDialog.
Graphic Three:	A close-up shot of the TMediaPlayer.

I've chosen these shots because I feel that a user will know how to run the ACCESS2 program when he or she understands what is on these screens and what they mean. After choosing the graphics, I used a screen capture program and the Windows Paintbrush program to create three BMPs, one for each shot.

When the graphics are secure, the next step is to create the text that will accompany each graphic. This part of the job is a bit like a movie director's work. For instance, I'll map this out in a series of four scenes. Each scene has a graphic associated with it, and a short paragraph of explanation:

Scene One:

- Visual: Graphic One
- Text: This is the main screen for the ACCESS2 program. This program is designed to enable you to easily play a wide range of multimedia files. For instance, you can use this tool to play movies, music, or sound.

The ACCESS2 program uses the MCI interface to the Multimedia extensions to Windows. MCI stands for Multimedia Control Interface. This is a mid-level programmer's interface, which allows relatively easy access to the commands you need to play multimedia files.

Using the ACCESS2 program is easy. To get started, click the Select File button with the mouse.

Scene Two:

- Visual: Graphic Two
- Text: After you press the Select File button, the Open Dialog appears. You can use this dialog to select a WAV file, MIDI file, or AVI file from your hard drive. To select a file, simply click its name with the mouse and select the OK button.

If you have the necessary hardware, you can then play any of these files via the MCI control.

Scene Three:

- Visual: Graphic One
- Text: When the Open Dialog closes, you can then begin playing a file by pressing the green Start button. The other buttons each have a specific purpose, which should be intuitively obvious to most users.

Scene Four:

- Visual: Graphic Three
- Text: This is an MCI control. You can use it to play multimedia files. This control works exactly like the similar button displays that you might see on a tape recorder or CD player. There are nine separate buttons on this control.

When you want to begin playing a file, you can select the green arrow with the mouse. To pause the file, select the yellow pause buttons. To stop the file, press the red stop button.

The next four blue buttons enable you to move backward and forward through the file. The first two buttons enable you to move forward or backward to a particular frame. The second two buttons move one frame forward or one frame backward through a file.

The last two buttons enable you to record to a file or eject a CD from a CD drive.

With this script to work from, you can use the TMediaPlayer to write a short program that enables you to record your voice in a WAVE file. You should record each of the previous scenes in a separate WAVE file, and save them to disk as MCINUM1.WAV, MCINUM2.WAV, and so on. Copies of these files come with this book, but you can create your own if you wish.

With the graphics and the sound files in your hands, all that's left to do is create the program. Experienced programmers should be able to make short work of this part of the task.

To get started, create a main form and place two labels and two buttons in it. Use the labels to write out the words ACCESS TWO and QuickStart. Name the first button Close, and use it to close the application:

```
procedure TForm1.BCloseClick(Sender: TObject);
begin
  Close;
end;
```

Name the second button Start. The response to this button will be a few lines of code that drive the actual QuickStart presentation:

```
procedure TForm1.BStartClick(Sender: TObject);
begin
  FirstPic := TFirstPic.Create(Application);
  FirstPic.FileName := Wave1;
  FirstPic.ShowModal;
  FirstPic.Free;

  SecondPic := TSecondPic.Create(Application);
  SecondPic.ShowModal;
  SecondPic.Free;

  FirstPic := TFirstPic.Create(Application);
  FirstPic.FileName := Wave3;
  FirstPic.ShowModal;
  FirstPic.Free;

  ThirdPic := TThirdPic.Create(Application);
  ThirdPic.ShowModal;
  ThirdPic.Free;
end;
```

To understand the previous code, you must first grasp the structure of the PRESENT program. PRESENT has four separate forms, shown in Figures 31.6 through 31.9.

FIGURE 31.6.

The first form is the main screen with two labels and two buttons.

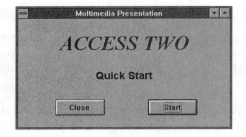

FIGURE 31.7.

The second form has a button on it labeled Next. Above the button is a TImage control.

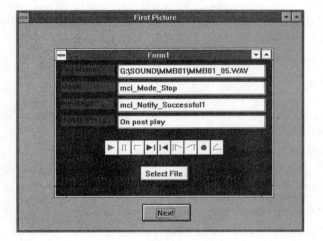

FIGURE 31.8.

The third form also has a button labeled Next. Above the button is a TImage control and a common dialog.

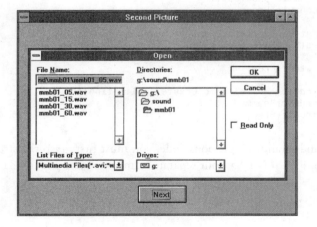

FIGURE 31.9.

The fourth form has a Next button and a TImage control with the close-up shot of the TMediaPlayer.

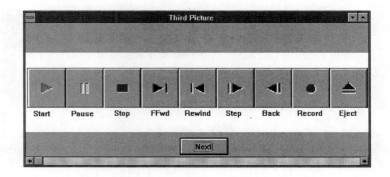

Because each graphic is shown on a separate form, it is easy to play the correct WAVE file at the correct time. For instance, there are four methods associated with the form containing the screen shot of the ACCESS2 program. The first is called automatically by the system when the form is opened:

```
procedure TFirstPic.FormActivate(Sender: TObject);
begin
  MediaPlayer1.Visible := False;
  MediaPlayer1.FileName := FileName;
  MediaPlayer1.Open;
  MediaPlayer1.Notify := True;
  MediaPlayer1.Play;
  ActivateCalled := True;
end;
```

This method is used to assign the name of the file to the TMediaPlayer, and then to open and play the file. You can create the header for this file by double-clicking the space next to the OnActivate event in the Object Inspector.

When the form is closed, an OnClose message is automatically sent by the system:

```
procedure TFirstPic.FormClose(Sender: TObject;
                              var CloseWindow: Boolean);
begin
  MediaPlayer1.Close;
end;
```

To create a FormClose method, just click the space next to the OnClose Event in the Object Inspector. As you can see, this method does nothing more than close the MCI device.

There are two other methods inside this form. The first method automatically closes the form when the associated WAVE file stops playing:

```
procedure TFirstPic.MediaPlayer1Notify(Sender: TObject);
begin
  with MediaPlayer1 do
    if ((NotifyValue = nvSuccessful) and
        (Mode = mpStopped)) then FirstPic.Close;
end;
```

The logic for the `if` statement shown here is explained earlier, in the section called "A Closer Look at a Media Access Program."

The other method included in the form responds to a click the next button:

```
procedure TFirstPic.BNextClick(Sender: TObject);
begin
  Close;
end;
```

Clearly, the only purpose of either of the last two methods is to close the form. The first method closes the form when the WAVE file stops playing. The second method closes the form if the user has grown impatient and pressed the next button.

Returning now to the `BStartClick` method in the main form, you can see that after the first form has been shown, the PRESENT program automatically disposes of the first form and calls the next form:

```
FirstPic.ShowModal;
FirstPic.Free;

SecondPic := TSecondPic.Create(Application);
SecondPic.ShowModal;
SecondPic.Free;
```

Needless to say, the `SecondPic` form is structured exactly like the `FirstPic` form. It does the following:

- Responds to `OnActivate` by opening the MCI device and playing a WAVE file
- Responds to `OnClose` messages by closing the MCI device
- Responds to a click on the Next button by closing the form
- Responds to the notification of the end of the WAVE file by closing the form

You now should have all the information you need to grasp the structure of the PRESENT program. As you can see, it has a very simple and robust architecture.

NOTE

The code for the following is on this book's CD in the CHAP31 directory:
- The main form for the PRESENT program
- The PICT1 dialog, which is the first to be shown after the user presses the Start button
- The code for the PICT2 dialog
- The code for the PICT3 dialog
- The Globals unit, which defines some constants used by all the units in the program

The design of this program is too simple to merit much comment. However, experienced programmers will note that it would be possible to merge the PICT1, PICT2, and PICT3 forms into one unit. I kept them separate because most programs of this type need a separate object to manage each form shown to the user.

Notice also that I call the `StripLastToken` function from the STRBOX unit that ships with this book. This function effectively returns the directory from which the program was launched. It does this by parsing the `ParamStr` variable, which is usually used to record the parameters passed to a program. For instance, if you pass a single parameter to PRESENT, you can retrieve the parameter with the following code:

```
S := Params(1);
```

However, in this case, I don't pass any parameters to the program. Nevertheless, I can retrieve the executable name and full path to where that executable is stored by writing the following:

```
S := Params(0);
```

The `ParamCount` variable tells you how many parameters are passed to a program.

The Presentation program shown previously took about two hours to design and write. About half of that time was dedicated to composing the script for the WAVE files and then recording them through a microphone. The actual job of writing the code was trivial. One of the goals of Delphi is to simplify the mechanics of writing a Windows program. Certainly, the TMediaPlayer helps to achieve that goal.

Summary

In this chapter, you learned some of the basic facts about multimedia, and how to write two different types of multimedia programs.

The major types of multimedia files covered in this chapter were as follows:

- WAV Files for recording any type of sound.
- MIDI Files for recording music.
- AVI Files for recording movies.

There were two types of multimedia applications covered:

- Access programs give the user the ability to play a wide range of programs.
- Presentation programs hide the internals of multimedia development from the user, and simply play sounds and films as a way of entertaining or informing the user.

Clearly, Delphi offers a simple and powerful way to create multimedia applications. When writing your own multimedia programs, use this chapter as a starting point, and use your imagination as a guide.

Using DDEML and OLE with Delphi

32

Overview

This chapter explains a few basic facts about DDEML and OLE, and shows how these two techniques can be used in a Delphi program. Inherently, the subject matter is extremely technical, but the Delphi language simplifies the most difficult aspects of these interfaces so that they can be easily assimilated into most programming projects.

Specifically, this chapter covers the following:

- DDE clients
- DDE servers
- Compiling from the command line with DCC.EXE
- Configuring the command-line compiler with DCC.CFG
- Modifying resource (RES) files
- Creating resource files with BRC.EXE
- OLE clients
- OLE in-place activation

At the time of this writing, Delphi does not have built-in support for OLE automation, nor for creating OLE servers. You can, of course, create OLE servers and develop OLE automation with Delphi; however, you will have to go to the API level. My advice is not to bother, because Delphi components encapsulating this functionality should soon be available, either from Borland or from third parties.

I'll assume that some readers may know very little about these two complex subjects. My goal, then, is to bring you from a standstill to the point that you can take these concepts for a mild walk around the track.

Basics

DDEML stands for the Dynamic Data Exchange Management Library. The DDEML is built on top of a complex message-based interface called Dynamic Data Exchange, or DDE. Microsoft built DDEML to add increased power and flexibility to the original DDE message-based system.

OLE stands for Object Linking and Embedding. Both OLE and DDE enable you to break out of the bounds of your current program and interact with other applications or other parts of the system.

Dynamic Data Exchange, for instance, gets its name because it lets two applications exchange data dynamically at runtime. That is, a link can be created between two programs so that changes to one application are reflected in the second application. For instance, if you change a number in a spreadsheet, a second application can be updated automatically so that it reflects the change.

OLE also enables you to implement this same feature. That is, a link can be established between your program and a spreadsheet so that your program will be informed if there are changes made to the data in the spreadsheet.

What then, are the differences between OLE and DDE? Basically, OLE takes the concepts that are inherent in DDE and makes much more of them. OLE is to DDE as a chicken is to an egg: it's more powerful, more sophisticated, and has more diverse capabilities. It is also more difficult to understand, and much, much more demanding of system resources.

> **NOTE**
>
> OLE's demands on system resources are so high that it is tempting to think that it will never prove useful to a large number of users. However, more or less the same thing was said about GUIs, and now we are all using them—and they are actually quite snappy if you have a fast 486 or Pentium. As I'll explain later, one way to make OLE useful is not to use huge applications as servers. For instance, it might be counterproductive to use Word or Excel as an OLE server. OLE servers should be small modules that provide one particular type of functionality; they should not be massive applications that combine hundreds of features into one executable.

If an OLE link is established between two applications, it can live on even after one or both of the applications have been closed. This is not true, however, of DDEML applications. Furthermore, it's possible not only to link two applications with OLE, but to actually embed the data from one application inside another application or document. This means that if you embed a spreadsheet document in a word-processor document, the relationship between the two applications will continue even if you remove the document from one computer and place it on a second computer. The embedded OLE object travels with the document, and will work as long as the necessary applications are also running on the second system.

OLE supports something called *in-place activation,* which enables an embedded object to temporarily take over a second application. For instance, if you embed a portion of a spreadsheet in a word-processor document and then click the spreadsheet document, the menus of your word processor will disappear and the menus of the spreadsheet will take their place.

OLE automation lets you control another application from inside a first application. That means that one application can request services from a second application, without the user having to be concerned about the details. As mentioned, Delphi won't provide built-in support for automation, but you can get it through direct API calls, or through VBXs.

The final point to make about OLE is that it enables links, not only between applications but between your application and free-floating objects that exist on your system. For instance, if there is an OLE-aware toolbar object on your system, it might seem to be embedded in your application in such a way that it appears to be a native part of your code. It is possible to create several different toolbar objects, all of which have the same interface. As a result, this aspect of OLE may be utilized in the future to allow users to construct an application out of a series of interchangeable parts.

Hopefully, this brief introduction to OLE and DDE will bring you to the point that you can understand why this subject is of interest. You should now have a basic feeling for the ends that are trying to be achieved. The rest of this chapter describes how to achieve them.

Using DDE

In the chapter, you will see three DDE examples:

- The first shows how to connect a simple Delphi application, called DDEPDOX1.DPR, to Paradox for Windows so that changes in the Paradox table, called CUSTOMER.DB, will be reflected inside your application. DDEPDOX1 is a client DDE application. If you don't have PDOXWIN.EXE on your system, you can run a server program called PDOXDEL.EXE, which ships with this book.

- The second example shows how to make this kind of connection dynamically at runtime.

- The third shows how to create two paired projects: one called CLIENT1.DPR and the second called SERVER1.DPR. The first application requests data, and the second application supplies data. The technical terms for these two types of applications are, respectively, *client applications* and *server applications*.

Most of the work for creating the first two applications is done in the object inspector. However, there are a few lines of code that you need to write. The main form for the DDEPDOX1 program is shown in Listing 32.1.

> **CAUTION**
>
> In the copy of this program that ships with this book, I set the DDEMode variable to `dmManual` in the main form for the DDEPDOX1 program. After loading the program, change it to `dmAutomatic`. You should be forewarned that if you leave it set to `dmAutomatic`, every time you open up this program (at runtime or design time) it will automatically attempt to load Paradox.

The main form for the DDEPDOX1 program, shown in Figure 32.1, has one DDEClientConv on it, seven DDEClientItems, and seven edit controls. I will explain how to hook these up in just a moment. The DDE controls are found on the System page of the Component Palette.

FIGURE 32.1.

The main form for the DDEPDOX1 program.

NOTE

The DDEPDOX1 program, found in the CHAP32 directory on the CD, requires that you have Paradox for Windows on your system.

To get started using DDE in a Delphi application, click the TDDEClientConv control on the Component Palette and place an instance of this object on your form. This is a non-visable component, so you will see only a small icon on your form. You can move this icon to any location on the form that is convenient.

Now turn to the DDEService property in the Object Inspector for the TDDEClientConv. If you double-click its Property Editor, you will get access to the DDE Info Dialog, which has two fields, labeled DDEService and DDETopic. Fill in the first with the string PDOXWIN and the second with the string :DBDEMOS:CUSTOMER.DB. (If you are using PDOXDEL instead of PDOXWIN, you should set the first string to PDOXDEL and the second to DBDEMOSCustomer.) When you click OK, Paradox or PDOXDEL should load into memory and display the CUSTOMER.DB table. If this doesn't happen, three things might have gone wrong:

- You don't have Paradox for Windows or PDOXDEL on your path.
- You don't have the DBDEMOS alias set up correctly, or CUSTOMER.DB is missing.
- You might not have enough memory to simultaneously load Delphi and Paradox. If this is the case, you should run PDOXDEL instead.

After hooking up the DDE conversation, place seven TDDEClientItems on the form, as shown in Figure 32.1. Configure all the DDEClientItems so their DDEConv property is set to DDEClientConv1. Now set the DDEItem fields to the fields of the Customer table. The field names are CustNo, Company, Addr1, Addr2, City, State, and Zip. As you select or type in the field names, the current value of those fields should appear in the Text property. (The program will automatically fill in these fields in the FormCreate method, but it might be helpful to you if you fill them in manually the first time.)

Now all you need to do is run the program. You can then iterate through the records in the server application and watch the changes in the client program that you built. If you are having trouble, be sure that the ConnectMode property is set to DDEAutomatic.

Now that you know how to set up a DDE conversation, I will spend the next few paragraphs giving some background information on DDE conversations. I'll start by discussing why the DDEService and DDETopic fields exist, and how you can use them.

The heart of most DDE activity involves a conversation between a client application and a server application. Each event in this conversation is called a *transaction*. As a rule, client applications request information from server applications. Or, to put the matter somewhat differently, server applications supply data, and client applications utilize or consume data.

The example currently under discussion connects a Delphi application to Paradox for Windows or PDOXDEL, so the Delphi app can use some data from a table. Given these circumstances, your application is the client and PDOXWIN or PDOXDEL is the server. The DDEService field, therefore, gets the name of the server application.

The DDETopic field is just a constant used to establish the subject of the "conversation" between the client and the server. In this case, that topic is a particular filename, so you fill in the DDETopic field with the name of the file you want to view. DDETopics are not always filenames, and they can be set to any sort of string that might be meaningful to the two applications involved in the conversation.

Of course, it's not enough to just specify a service and topic. You also want to get at a specific item of information. To do this, drop down a DDEClientItem, and set the DDEConv property to DDEClientConv1 and its DDEItem property to the name of the field in the table that you want to explore. After you supply a valid name, the Text property for the DDEClientItem will contain the string you want to see.

So far you've learned that establishing a conversation between your application and a DDE server involves supplying three pieces of information:

- A recognized name for the server, which in this case happens to be PDOXWIN. This name is sometimes referred to as a service name, and at others as an application name.
- The name of a topic. In the example shown here, the topic is a particular table; so you supply the name of the table.
- A particular item from the table, which in this case would be a field name.

In the DDEPDOX1 program, the OnChange event for all the DDEClientItems is set to a procedure which looks like this:

```
procedure TForm1.DdeClientItem1Change(Sender: TObject);
begin
  Edit1.Text := DDEClientItem1.Text;
  Edit2.Text := DDEClientItem2.Text;
  Edit3.Text := DDEClientItem3.Text;
  Edit4.Text := DDEClientItem4.Text;
  Edit5.Text := DDEClientItem5.Text;
```

```
   Edit6.Text := DDEClientItem6.Text;
   Edit7.Text := DDEClientItem7.Text;
end;
```

The purpose of this procedure, needless to say, is to display the individual fields of the table in an edit control.

I'm giving a specific instance, but all conversations between a client and server involve using service names, topic names, and item names. The service or application name is not necessarily the name of an application. Specifically, the server can establish one or more service names, and you must know these names ahead of time if you want to initiate a conversation. It is, however, sometimes possible to query the system and ask for the names of any existing servers. There is no requirement for servers to supply these names, so there are times when you simply have to have inside information in order to acquire a service name.

TIP

I have explained to you how to manually create a conversation between a client and a server. There are, however, some shortcuts you can take. One way to simplify establishing a link of this type is to run Paradox and then highlight a field from the table you want to use and copy it to the clipboard. Now drop a DDEClientConv on a Delphi form, select the DDEService property, and select Paste. The name of the app and table will automatically be pasted into the DDE Info dialog. Now drop down a DDEClientItem and open up the DDEItem property by pressing the arrow on the right of the property editor. You can select a field name, and the appropriate text will appear automatically in the Text field. Using this kind of technique, you can often establish connections without knowing the specific service, topic, and item names involved.

Topic names and item names can also be defined ahead of time by a particular server. In the previous example, the proper names were supplied automatically. As you will see later in this chapter, a different server may have a private list of topics and items that aren't nearly as obvious as the names of a table and a field. Once again, it is possible to query a server about the topics it supplies, but the server is not obligated to divulge the information.

A Second Delphi and Paradox DDE Conversation

The DDEPDOX2 program is very similar to DDEPDOX1 except that it connects to the server at runtime. As you saw in DDEPDOX1, the moment an application connects with another can be expensive in terms of time and resources. To help alleviate that burden, it's nice to be able to execute your program first and then load a second program some time later.

As shown in Figure 32.2, the form for the DDEPDOX2 program looks the same as the DDEPDOX1 program, except for the addition of a single button. The code for the program, however, has a few extra kinks that give it added flexibility.

FIGURE 32.2.

The DDEPDOX2 program shows how to start a DDE conversation at runtime.

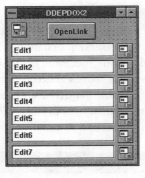

NOTE

The main unit for the DDEPDOX2 program, on the CD, centers on the `OpenLinkClick` method.

After launching the DDEPDOX2 program, you can start a conversation with Paradox by clicking the OpenLink button. Here's the method that establishes the link, along with a const array that is used in the routine:

```
const
  FieldNames: array[1..7] of String =
    ('CustNo', 'Company', 'Addr1',
     'Addr2', 'City', 'State', 'Zip');

procedure TForm1.OpenLinkClick(Sender: TObject);
var
  i: Integer;
begin
  DDEClientConv1.SetLink('PDOXWIN', ':DBDEMOS:CUSTOMER.DB');
  for i := 1 to 7 do begin
    TDDEClientItem(FindComponent('DDEClientItem' +
      IntToStr(i))).DDEConv := DDEClientConv1;
    TDDEClientItem(FindComponent('DDEClientItem' +
      IntToStr(i))).DDEItem := FieldNames[i];
  end;
end;
```

The `OpenLinkClick` procedure is executed in response to a click of a button. Writing the preceding code is the runtime equivalent of filling in the appropriate fields of the DDEClientConv and DDEClientItem components at design time. In other words, you could drop a DDEClientConv and seven DDEClientItems on the form, add the preceding method, and then run your program. There wouldn't be a need to fill in any properties at design time.

The `OpenLinkClick` procedure can be divided into two parts. The first part establishes a link with the server:

```
DDEClientConv1.SetLink('PDOXWIN', ':DBDEMOS:CUSTOMER.DB');
```

Of course, if you wanted, you could specify a path instead of using the DBDEMOS alias. If you did, you could omit the awkward syntax that surrounds the alias with colons.

After connecting with Paradox, the next step is to hook up the individual DDEClientItems. For instance, you can attach to the CustNo field by writing code that looks like this:

```
DDEClientItem1.DDEConv := DDEClientConv1;
DDEClientItem1.DDEItem := 'CustNo';
```

The loop in the `OpenLinkClick` procedure is a shorthand way of writing the previous code seven times over in quick succession, while being sure to pass the appropriate field names to the `DDEItem` property. To make this work, the code uses a constant array of strings set to the proper field names, as well as the built-in Delphi `FindComponent` procedure. Given the name of a component, the `FindComponent` function will return an instance of the control. It's the ideal tool to use as an alternative to the form's `Components` array. (In terms of performance, it would have been faster for me to use the `Components` array in this particular case.)

The example I have shown you here is available on this book's CD-ROM in the file DDEPDOX2.DPR. It demonstrates how Delphi enables you to have a useful and productive means of creating DDE client applications. In the next section, you will see that it is also quite easy to create a DDE server.

Simple DDE Servers

To create a DDE server, start a new project and then drop a TDDEServerConv and a TDDEServerItem on to the default form. Other than playing with the Object Inspector for a moment, that's all you need to build the simplest possible Delphi DDE server.

> **NOTE**
>
> The SIMPSERV and SIMPCLI example programs discussed in this section are saved to disk in the SIMPDDE directory. Neither of them needs to contain any code, so I won't provide the traditional listings in this section. In this case and in the programs shown in the next section, I have broken a convention and placed two projects in a single directory. I've done this because you want to be able to automatically load the server from the client application; and to do that, the server needs to be in the current directory or on the path. The former of these two options was obviously more convenient in this case. To make this system work, I have named the form for the SIMPSERV application MAINS and the form for the SIMPCLI application MAINC. I will follow the same convention in the CLIENT1 and SERVER1 example. The

> programs I am about to describe, however, are so simple that I wouldn't bother with the disk versions unless you are having trouble creating the connection due to the general quirkiness of DDE technology.

After the discussion in the last section, it should be clear that a server application needs to publish three pieces of information:

- A service name
- A topic name
- An item name

In Delphi, it's easy to specify this information:

- To publish a service name, give your project a name and save it to disk. The name of your application will automatically become the service name.
- To create a topic name, just assign a name to your TDDEServerConv component, or keep the default.
- The item names that your application uses will be the names you assign to the TDDEServerItem components on the server form. Set the Name property of the TDDEServerItem component to a meaningful string of your own choice, or keep the default name. Set the ServerConv property to the name of the DDEServerConv that's on the same form.

To try this system out, drop a TDDEServerConv and TDDEServerItem on a form and save the application under the name SIMPSERV. To send information to a client application, you need do nothing more than assign a string to the TDDEServerItem's Text property. For instance, you might write:

```
DDEServerItem1.Text := '25';
```

Or if you want, you can simply fill in the Text field in the Object Inspector. If you follow this latter path, you will complete the server application after writing zero lines of code!

Since there is no code for this program, I will instead show you the text for the DFM file. Remember that you can open any Delphi form in the code editor by choosing File | Open File and selecting *.DFM. In the SIMPSERV program, the resulting file looks like this:

```
object Form1: TForm1
  Left = 200
  Top = 99
  Width = 435
  Height = 300
  Caption = 'Form1'
  Font.Color = clWindowText
  Font.Height = -13
  Font.Name = 'System'
  Font.Style = []
  PixelsPerInch = 96
```

```
    TextHeight = 16
    object DdeServerConv1: TDdeServerConv
      Left = 16
      Top = 16
    end
    object DdeServerItem1: TDdeServerItem
      ServerConv = DdeServerConv1
      Text = '25'
      Lines.Strings = (
        '25')
      Left = 64
      Top = 16
    end
end
```

> **NOTE**
>
> You don't have to spend a lot of time studying the DFM text translations shown in this section. I've included them because the Windows DDE technology can be a bit quirky at times, and I don't want you wasting a lot of time wondering whether you have filled in the values correctly. In short, if you are having trouble connecting, you can turn to these listings to be sure you have set everything up right; otherwise, I wouldn't bother with them unless you find them inherently interesting.

Any client that connects to the simple server shown previously can easily access the string you have assigned to DDEServerItem1.Text. Specifically, creating a client that will connect to this server involves nothing more than declaring the following values by writing code, or by manipulating the proper fields in the Object Inspector:

```
procedure TForm1.ConnectClick(Sender: TObject);
begin
  DDEClientConv1.SetLink('SimpServ', 'DdeServerConv1');
  DDEClientItem1.DDEConv := DDEClientConv1;
  DDEClientItem1.DDEItem := 'DdeServerItem1';
  Label1.Caption := DDEClientItem1.Text;
end;
```

If you want to work in the Object Inspector instead of writing code, here is what the form should look like when viewed as text:

```
object Form1: TForm1
  Left = 201
  Top = 101
  Width = 435
  Height = 300
  Caption = 'Simple Client'
  Color = clBlack
  Font.Color = clWindowText
  Font.Height = -13
  Font.Name = 'System'
  Font.Style = []
  PixelsPerInch = 96
  TextHeight = 16
```

```
object Label1: TLabel
  Left = 0
  Top = 0
  Width = 427
  Height = 109
  Align = alTop
  Alignment = taCenter
  Caption = 'Label1'
  Font.Color = clBlue
  Font.Height = -96
  Font.Name = 'Times New Roman'
  Font.Style = []
  ParentFont = False
end
object Connect: TButton
  Left = 184
  Top = 200
  Width = 89
  Height = 33
  Caption = 'Connect'
  TabOrder = 0
  OnClick = ConnectClick
end
object DdeClientConv1: TDdeClientConv
  DdeService = 'SimpServ'
  DdeTopic = 'DdeServerConv1'
  Left = 24
  Top = 8
  LinkInfo = (
    'Service SimpServ'
    'Topic DdeServerConv1')
end
object DdeClientItem1: TDdeClientItem
  Text = '25  '
  Lines.Strings = (
    '25  ')
  DdeConv = DdeClientConv1
  DdeItem = 'DdeServerItem1'
  Left = 56
  Top = 8
end
end
```

If you then place a label on the form, you can read values from the server by making the following assignments in a method:

```
Label1.Caption := DDEClient1Item1.Text;
```

That's all there is to it. Just follow those simple steps, either by writing code or by filling in the appropriate sections in the Object Inspector.

Another DDE Client and Server Example

The main sample server that accompanies this chapter is called SERVER1.DPR. The name of its TDDEServerConv is BigServer, and the TDDEServerItem components are called Item1, Item2, and Item3.

> **NOTE**
>
> SERVER1 assigns strings from its edit controls to its `DDEClientItem.Text` field. The code for this is in the CHAP32 directory on this book's CD.

I'll talk about the DDE code in SERVER1 in one moment. However, you should notice the call to `MoveWindow` in the `FormCreate` method. `MoveWindow` is a Windows API call that moves a window from one place on a screen to another. You can simultaneously move the upper-left corner of the window and change the window's width and height. In this case, I don't want to change the dimensions of the window, so I simply pass in the existing `Height` and `Width` properties. However, I specify `1, 1` as the coordinates for the upper-left corner. This moves the window to the top of the monitor so that you can have enough screen real estate to display both the SERVER1 and CLIENT1 applications at the same time.

The SERVER1 application is, naturally enough, meant to work in conjunction with the CLIENT1 program. Both programs are saved in the CLI-SERV subdirectory, where the abbreviations for the two programs are separated by a dash.

CLIENT1 has three labels that correspond to the edit controls in SERVER1. Whenever the user types in any of SERVER1's edit controls, the keystrokes are sent immediately to CLIENT1 and displayed in the labels.

> **NOTE**
>
> The CLIENT1 application, in the CHAP32 directory on the CD, has means for receiving information from the server and for sending information back.

Listing 32.1 shows a text file called MILTON.TXT.

Listing 32.1. CLIENT1 has a second custom resource made up of a single long string stored in text file called MILTON.TXT.

```
From Paradise Lost
by John Milton

From Book I
===========
Of man's first disobedience, and the fruit
Of that forbidden tree, whose mortal taste
Brought death into the world, and all our woe,
With loss of Eden, till one greater Man
Restore us, and regain the blissful seat,
Sing Heav'nly Muse, that on the secret top
Of Oreb, or of Sinai, didst inspire
That shepherd who first taught the chosen seed
```

continues

Listing 32.1. continued

```
In the beginning how the heav'ns and earth
Rose out of Chaos; or if Sion hill
Delight thee more, and Siloa's brook that flowed
Fast by the oracle of God, I thence
Invoke thy aid to my advent'rous song,
That with no middle flight intends to soar
Above th' Aonian mount, while it pursues
Things unattempted yet in prose or rhyme.

From Book IX
============
To whom the Tempter guilefully replied:
"Indeed? Hath God then said that of the fruit
Of all these garden trees ye shall not eat,
Yet lords declared of all in earth or air?"
To whom thus Eve yet sinless: "Of the fruit
Of each tree in the garden we may eat,
But of the fruit of this fair tree amidst
The garden, God hath said, 'Ye shall not eat
Thereof, nor shall ye touch it, lest ye die.'"
...
The Tempter all impassioned thus began:
"O sacred, wise, and wisdom giving Plant,
Mother of Science, now I feel thy power
Within me clear, not only to discern
Things in their causes, but to trace the ways
Of highest agents, deemed however wise.
... If they all things, who enclosed
Knowledge of good and evil in this tree,
That whoso eats thereof, forthwith attains
Wisdom without their leave? And wherein lies
Th' offense, that man should thus attain to know?
What can your knowledge hurt him, or this tree
Impart against his will, if all be his?
Or is it envy, and can envy dwell
In heav'nly breasts? These, these and many more
Causes import your need of this fair fruit.
Goddess humane, reach then, and freely taste!"
```

Listing 32.2 shows the RC file for MILTON.TXT.

Listing 32.2. Here is the RC file that holds the resource stored in MILTON.TXT.

```
/*   From Paradise Lost    */
Milton TEXT milton.txt
```

Listing 32.3. Here is the RC file for creating CLIENT1.RES.

```
/*   Client1 Icon           */
Icon ICON "client1.ico"
```

Listing 32.4. Here is a batch file for creating the CLIENT1 and SERVER1 programs from the command line.

```
@echo off
echo **********************************
echo You must create and properly edit
echo a DCC.CFG file before running this
echo macro. Search in this directory
echo for an example DCC.CFG file.
echo **********************************
brc -r client1.rc
brc -r milton1.rc
dcc /cw/b server1.dpr
dcc /cw/b client1.dpr
```

Listing 32.5. Here is a sample configuration file for the command-line compiler. It is called DCC.CFG.

```
/Uc:\delphi\lib
/Rc:\delphi\lib
```

The CLIENT1 program has two parts to it. The first part shows off DDE techniques such as exchanging data, poking data, and sending macros. The second part shows how to use a RES file with Delphi and how to compile from the command line. I will treat these two parts in two different sections.

The SERVER1 form sports three edit controls. The OnChange event for these controls looks like this:

```
procedure TForm1.Edit1Change(Sender: TObject);
begin
  Item1.Text := Edit1.Text;
  Item2.Text := Edit2.Text;
  Item3.Text := Edit3.Text;
end;
```

Whenever the user types anything in these edit controls, the DDEServItem components, called Item1, Item2, and Item3, reflect these changes in their Text property.

At the other end, the CLIENT1 program has three labels. Whenever any of the DDEClientItems record an OnChange event, the following method gets called:

```
procedure TForm1.DdeClientItem1Change(Sender: TObject);
begin
  Label1.Caption := DDEClientItem1.Text;
  Label4.Caption := DDEClientItem2.Text;
  Label6.Caption := DDEClientItem3.Text;
end;
```

This code transfers the information from the server into the labels on the form of the client program.

After writing this code, you will be able to enter a new value in the edit controls on the server and then automatically see the labels in the CLIENT1 application reflect the changes on the server. The changes take place letter by letter as you type them in, so that it appears that you are typing in two places at once.

When you want to send data from a client back to a server, you can do so through two different means: by poking and by executing a macro. The CLIENT1 program has three different methods that poke data into the SERVER1 application:

```
procedure TClientOne.Poke1Click(Sender: TObject);
begin
  Conv1.PokeData('DDEItem1', 'Sambo');
end;

procedure TClientOne.Poke2Click(Sender: TObject);
var
  S: string;
  SPtr: array[0..200] of Char;
begin
  S := '';
  InputQuery('Talk to a DDE Server', 'Enter Data to Poke', S);
  Conv1.PokeData('DDEItem2', StrPCopy(SPtr, S));
end;

procedure TClientOne.Poke3Click(Sender: TObject);
var
  Poem: PChar;
begin
  Poem := PChar(LockResource(Resource));
  Conv1.PokeData('DDEItem3', Poem);
end;
```

The Poke1Click method is the classic and simplest means of sending data from a client to a server. It calls a method of TDDEClientConv called PokeData. PokeData takes a string in the first parameter. This string specifies the name of the server item to which you want to send information. The second parameter is a PChar that holds the information you want to send. Delphi uses a PChar here rather than string, because you might need to send information longer that 256 characters in length, and because PChars are the standard when you are passing information between an application and Windows.

The Poke2Click method follows the same pattern as Poke1Click, except that it first asks the user for the string to send. Once the string is captured, it is translated into a PChar and sent to the second edit control in the SERVER1 program. Of course, the moment the SERVER1 program is updated, it relays the new information back to CLIENT1. As a result, there is a circular motion, where the CLIENT1 conversation component pokes new data into SERVER1, and SERVER1 then sends the new information back to CLIENT1's DDEClientItem components.

Poke3Click again uses PokeData to send information to SERVER1, but this time the information is the entire poem shown in Listing 32.5. The poem is first retrieved from the

MILTON1.RES file via a mechanism to be explained in the next section, and then it is sent to SERVER1 and displayed in a memo.

> **NOTE**
>
> You can poke information to a server via either the `PokeData` method or the `PokeDataLines` method. `PokeDataLines` takes a TStringList or TStrings object as a parameter. You can use `PokeDataLines` if you want to send information from a memo, listbox, or other TStrings-based component. Remember, however, that both `PokeData` and `PokeDataLines` can handle large chunks of data, up to 64 KB at a time. Furthermore, recall that if you want to create the whole list on the fly, without the aid of a Delphi component, you should use a TStringList, not an instance of the abstract TStrings class.

On the server end, all this poking of information is handled by a single method, which is attached to the `OnPokeData` event of the DDEServerItem controls:

```
procedure TServe1.DDEItem1PokeData(Sender: TObject);
begin
  case TDDEServerItem(Sender).Tag of
    0: Edit1.Text := DDEItem1.Text;
    1: Edit2.Text := DDEItem2.Text;
    2: Memo1.Lines := DDEItem3.Lines;
  end;
end;
```

Note that the long poem sent by CLIENT1 is automatically hung on a TStrings object so that it can be easily transferred to a memo or listbox. I have set the Tag properties of the DDEServerItems to 0, 1, and 2.

To send a macro from the CLIENT1 program to SERVER1, just call the `ExecuteMacro` function:

```
procedure TClientOne.Clear1Click(Sender: TObject);
begin
  Conv1.ExecuteMacro('Clear', True);
end;

procedure TClientOne.Close1Click(Sender: TObject);
begin
  Conv1.ExecuteMacro('Close', True);
end;
```

`ExecuteMacro` takes two parameters. The first is a string specifying the command you want to send, and the second is a Boolean flag stating whether DDEML should wait for the result of this macro to return before executing any more pokes or macros. It can be a mess if too many signals are flying back and forth between a server and a client at the same time, so it is generally best to set this flag to `True`.

> **NOTE**
>
> The commands used in the first parameter of the ExecuteMacro function are just strings that you can make up to suit your own sense of aesthetics. In other words, these aren't predefined commands; they are just strings that you create in order to identify the various commands you might want to give to a server. If you create a server and then publish a list of commands that it obeys, you can go far toward creating a very easy to implement form of "DDE Automation."

The following method appears in SERVER1 and is meant to handle the macro once it is sent. Note that this event occurs in response to the OnExecuteMarco event of the TDDEServerConv component:

```
procedure TServe1.BigServerExecuteMacro(Sender: TObject;
                                        Msg: TStrings);
var
  i: Integer;
  S: string;
begin
  S := Msg.Strings[0];
  if S = 'Clear' then begin
    for i := 0 to ComponentCount - 1 do
      if (Components[i] is TEdit) or (Components[i] is TMemo) then
        TEdit(Components[i]).Clear;
    PostMessage(Edit1.Handle, wm_KeyDown, 32, 0);
    PostMessage(Edit1.Handle, wm_KeyDown, vk_Back, 0);
  end else
    Close;
end;
```

There are two commands that CLIENT1 can send to SERVER1. The first command is called 'Close', and SERVER1 responds to it by calling the VCL Close method. The second command comes in the form of the string 'Clear', and SERVER1 responds to it by clearing the text of any component of type TEdit or TMemo. I then notify the client that this event has occurred by creating a fake keyboard event; that is, by inserting a space character (#32) into Edit1 and then immediately deleting the character. This latter move is a rather extreme kluge, but it does work. In fact, it will work even in a different type of program where there might be text in one of the controls that needs to be preserved.

In this section, I have given a very brief overview of how to create DDE client and server applications. This discussion has made no attempt to be all-inclusive, and I have ignored material on using multiple clipboard formats in order to transfer data. Some clipboard concepts are demonstrated in the DDE demos that ship with Delphi. After seeing the brief examples in this chapter, you should have little trouble deciphering the extra material in the Delphi demos.

Before leaving the subject of DDE altogether, I should mention again that this can be a fairly quirky technology at times. Though considerably more reliable than OLE, DDE can fail at times for no apparent reason. I have noticed this quirkiness when working with a wide range of compilers and a wide range of applications. My hope is that both OLE and DDE will behave better in a 32-bit environment where memory is more carefully protected. Having said this, I will have to confess to liking DDE and to thinking that it is somewhat egregiously under-utilized. The only applications I work with that use it regularly are ReportSmith and the install tools that talk to the Program Manager.

Compiling from the Command Line

Delphi programs need Windows to run, but they can be compiled from DOS. You might want to compile a Delphi app at the DOS prompt if it is part of a large project that has several different parts. For instance, the CLIENT1 and SERVER1 programs work as a team, and you need to make sure they are both compiled before you run the client half of the team. From the IDE, there is no good way to compile two applications at the same time, but it's easy to do this from the DOS prompt via a batch file. Of course, really big projects might consist of four or five different applications and ten or twenty DLLs. Big projects like that demand command-line tools.

The client/server version of Delphi ships with a program called DCC.EXE. This program takes a number of parameters. You can see a listing of these parameters if you run the program at the DOS prompt by typing DCC. A set of undocumented parameters tell DCC whether it should build a Windows app, a DOS app, or a protected-mode app:

```
/cw: Windows target { CW is a default value, and you don't have to pass it in. }
/cd: DOS target
/cp: Protected Mode target.
```

> **NOTE**
>
> Delphi contains no trace of the libraries that are used to compile DOS and protected-mode applications. If you have the RTL, you can build your own DOS version of SYSTEM.TPU and SYSTEM.TPP. With these files you can begin building DOS and protected-mode applications.
>
> The latent potential to compile DOS and protected-mode apps from the command line does not grant you the right to an automatic translation of Delphi applications into DOS or DOS protected mode. Instead, they can be used to create traditional DOS Pascal programs. At the time of this writing, it is not certain that a Borland Pascal 8 for DOS will ever ship, but it is a much talked-about possibility and is on a number of Borland employees' wish lists.

Two other important parameters that you can pass to DCC.EXE tell whether to perform a make or a build:

```
/b: Rebuild all units.
/m: make sure all units are up to date.
```

To actually perform a compilation at the command line, you can enter a command that looks like this:

```
dcc /cw/b MYPROG.DPR
```

where MYPROG is the name of your application; the optional /cw says you want to build a Windows app, and /b says you want to compile all the units in the project. For instance, here are the commands for compiling SERVER1 and CLIENT1:

```
dcc /b server1.dpr
dcc /b client1.dpr
```

However, just passing in these lines won't always work. Delphi also needs to know where the units are that are listed in the program's uses clause. You can pass this information into DCC with special parameters like those shown, or you can place it in a separate text file labeled DCC.CFG. On my system, a typical DCC.CFG file looks like this:

```
/Uc:\delphi\lib
/Rc:\delphi\lib
```

where /U marks the beginning of the line where I show the path to the main Delphi units, and /R shows the path to the main Delphi resources. If you have an additional location where you save files such as STRBOX.PAS or MATHBOX.PAS, you can add those to the preceding code using the same syntax used to build a DOS path:

```
/Uc:\delphi\lib;c:\delcode\units
/Rc:\delphi\lib;c:\delcode\resfiles
```

I keep my DCC.CFG file in my DELPHI\BIN subdirectory and also save a copy to a place where I store backup files.

> **NOTE**
>
> There are other options available for use as parameters to DCC and also for use inside DCC.CFG files. If you want to pursue these valuable resources, read the documentation that comes with Delphi or the documentation that shipped with BP7 or TP7. You can place any parameters you pass to DCC inside a CFG file, and therefore have them implemented automatically. On the DCC command line, you also can specify the directory in which you keep the CFG file that you want to use. As a result, you can specify different parameters in various CFG files and then pass only the directory of the CFG file to DCC (using the -T option).

Besides the options shown previously, other important parameters are as follows:

```
/v : Include debug info for the stand alone debugger
/gd : Create a detailed map file
/D : Define a conditional directive
/$R+ : Range checking on
```

You can use the $ syntax to define any of the compiler switches found in the Options | Project | Compiler page.

One of the most useful tricks you can use when compiling programs from the command line is to check the value returned from DCC.EXE. If an attempt to compile a file fails, DCC returns an error value and you can use the DOS ERRORLEVEL command to read it and to react appropriately:

```
cd E:\DELPHI\SENDPAS\
dcc /b SENDPAS.DPR
if ErrorLevel = 1 goto Fail

cd E:\DELPHI\SENDKEY\
dcc /b SENDKEYS.DPR
if ErrorLevel = 1 goto Fail

goto End

:Fail
echo Failure

:End
```

The batch file shown here tries to compile a project. If the compilation fails, the batch file writes the word Failure and terminates; if it succeeds, it moves on to compile the next project. This technique is especially effective if you have a very large batch file with many projects in it. If any one compile fails, a record of the failure is left at the DOS prompt so that you can see what went wrong and in which project the failure occurred.

The short overview of command-line compilation that you have seen in the last few paragraphs should be enough to satisfy the needs of most programmers; though as I mentioned earlier, there is considerably more to this subject if you want to pursue it. I should add that Pascal programmers traditionally do not use MAKE.EXE, but a copy of this file does ship with at least the client/server version of the product. MAKE.EXE provides extremely powerful control over command-line compilations, but you have to pay a price when mastering its arcane syntax.

Working with Resources

Almost all Delphi programs use a simple resource file that contains an icon. You can find these files in the directory where you compile your programs. The name of the resource file defaults to the name of your application, with, of course, the letters RES as an extension. In the DPR file for your program, you will find the following syntax:

```
{$R *.RES}
```

This code tells Delphi to search for and load a resource file with the same name as the current source module, but with an RES extension.

Delphi treats RES files as binary entities, but traditionally they begin as text files with an RC extension. To convert an RC file to a RES file, use the BRC.EXE resource compiler.

RC text files have code in them that follows a very simple syntax for defining which icons and bitmaps you want to build into your application, as well as any menus, dialogs, or custom resources you might want to add. For instance, the following very short RC file, called CLIENT1.RC, defines the standard RES file that accompanies a Delphi application:

```
/*   Client1 Icon          */
Icon ICON "client1.ico"
```

These standard Delphi RES files contain nothing more than an icon. Normally these files are automatically built for you by Delphi, but I am showing how to make one so that you will understand the technology involved.

The first line of the file shown above contains a comment. RC files use the C syntax for defining comments. The second line of code tells BRC to find a file called CLIENT1.ICO. Furthermore, it states that the contents of CLIENT1.ICO is an icon, and that it should be compiled into a resource and labeled "Icon." As a rule, names such as ICON do not really concern BRC beyond the fact that it stores the information for later use. In other words, RES files are basically just chunks of binary dated sorted by name and type, where any one can define a new type whenever they want.

BRC.EXE will compile the RC file if you enter the following command at the DOS prompt:

```
BRC -r CLIENT1.RC.
```

This command produces a file called CLIENT1.RES that contains a single icon. You can examine this file in the Image Editor from the Tools menu.

> **NOTE**
>
> Experienced C++ and BP7 programmers probably know about the Resource Workshop, which can be used to simplify the process of working with RES files. You can still use the Resource Workshop with Delphi exactly as you would have used it with BP7 or BC4. If you don't have a copy of this tool, you will be able to buy it from Borland as an upsell. The Image Editor has much of the functionality of the Resource Workshop built into it, but it does not handle version resources and string tables. I personally feel that all intermediate and advanced Delphi programmers should have a copy of the Workshop or another similar tool. Ultimately, BRC is a faster and more powerful way to manage resources than any existing Windows tool that I have seen, but it takes a while to develop expertise in it—and it cannot search through existing DLLs, EXEs, and so on to grab resources the way Resource Workshop can.

The CLIENT1 program has two RES files. The first contains the resource shown previously. The second contains a simple custom resource that consists of nothing more than the text in the MILTON.TXT file.

It's important to understand why I have placed two resource files inside CLIENT1. There is absolutely no reason why you can't put all your resources in one RES file. In other words, CLIENT1.RES can be expanded to store all the resources that you want to add to the CLIENT1 program. However, Delphi has full claim to the CLIENT1.RES file, so it is necessary for you to have a second RES file that you alone manage. In short, I am showing how to add a second RES file to a Delphi project so that you can have one that is created and managed by Delphi, and a second defined only by the programmer.

To build this custom resource, place MILTON.TXT, included on the CD, in the same directory as the following small text file, which is called MILTON1.RC:

```
/*   From Paradise Lost    */
Milton TEXT milton.txt
```

This file compiles MILTON.TXT into a RES file just as the previous RC file compiled CLIENT1.ICO into a RES file. The type of resource being used here is labeled more or less at random as TEXT, and it is given the word Milton as an identifier so you can access it easily from inside of Delphi.

> **NOTE**
>
> You can compile many different resources into a single RES file. For instance, the following short RC file would compile six bitmaps, an icon, and a string resource into a RES file that could be linked into your executable:
>
> ```
> Body     BITMAP "body.bmp"
> Head     BITMAP "head.bmp"
> Pattern  BITMAP "pattern.bmp"
> Grass    BITMAP "grass.bmp"
> Road     BITMAP "road.bmp"
> Road2    BITMAP "road2.bmp"
> Icon     ICON   "file1.ico"
>
> STRINGTABLE
> BEGIN
>     0, "Woodnotes (Part 1)"
>     1, "by Ralph Waldo Emerson"
>     2, ""
>     3, "When the pine tosses its cones"
>     4, "To the song of its waterfall tones,"
>     5, "..."
>     6, "Wealth to the cunning artist who can work"
>     7, "This matchless strength. Where shall he find, O waves!"
>     8, "A load your Atlas shoulders cannot lift?"
> END
> ```
>
> You could retrieve the bitmaps at runtime by calling `LoadBitmap` and the strings from the stringtable by calling `LoadString`.

By now you know how to construct and compile a very simple RES file. The following code shows a simple DOS batch file you can run; it would compile the resources used by the CLIENT1 program, as well as both the SERVER1 and CLIENT1 executables.

```
brc -r client1.rc
brc -r milton1.rc
dcc /cw/b server1.dpr
dcc /cw/b client1.dpr
```

Note that CLIENT1.RC states that this batch file won't complete successfully unless you have an icon called CLIENT1.ICO in the same directory. There are icons that ship both with this book and with Delphi, or you can build an icon with the Image Editor from the Tools menu.

The CLIENT1.RES file is automatically linked into your program because of the $R line found in CLIENT1.DPR. However, you have to take special steps to link MILTON1.RES into your program. Specifically, you should add the following lines to MAINC.PAS:

```
{$R *.DFM}
{$R MILTON1.RES}
```

The line in question is the second of the two shown, where the first is merely meant as a clue as to where in the file the reference to MILTON1.RES should occur.

CLIENT1 declares a variable called Resource as type THandle. Variables of this type can be used to point to a resource loaded into a Windows program. To retrieve a resource, you need to call the LoadResource Windows API function, passing in the HInstance of your program in the first parameter and the handle of the resource you want to snag in the second parameter. HInstance is a predeclared variable filled out by Delphi and available to you at any time. To get the handle to the resource itself you need to call FindResource, passing in the name of the resource in the second parameter and its type in the third:

```
Resource := LoadResource(hInstance,
            FindResource(hInstance, 'Milton', 'TEXT'));
```

In the CLIENT1 program I make the call to LoadResource in the FormCreate method. Notice that if you were trying to load a bitmap, you would call LoadBitmap rather than LoadResource.

Once you have loaded a resource into a program, you can retrieve the specific data you want by calling LockResource:

```
Poem := PChar(LockResource(Resource));
```

In this case, the resource is just a long string, so it is safe to typecast it as a PChar and then assign it to a variable called poem, which is declared to be of type PChar. Note, however, that there is nothing that dictates that the resource in question has to be a string. Because this is a custom resource, you can load any kind of binary data this way, including a PCX file or an encrypted file.

I suppose the main theme of the last section was that Delphi can handle any of the resources that you would normally associate with a C++ or BP7 program. However, Delphi tries to stream-line this system by providing simple ways to handle most resources. For instance, the Image

Editor enables you to open RES files and store icons and bitmaps inside them. The developers tried to give you simple tools for handling RES files, but they did not cut you off from any of the old techniques. If you want to work with RC files, you can; and I would expect that any serious developer would use them all the time.

OLE Basics

The "O" in OLE stands for objects, and for most Delphi programmers, the simplest way to start to understand OLE is to see how it implements objects. You will find that OLE objects are very much like traditional Delphi objects in structure, even though they happen to be considerably more complicated to implement.

An OLE object is a collection of data and functions encapsulated within a single structure that is usually part of single module or a series of modules. You can think of these objects as being directly parallel to Delphi objects, which are also a collection of data and functions brought under the aegis of a single unifying structure.

The big difference between a traditional Delphi object and an OLE object is that the interface for the Delphi object is easy to access, and is, in fact, inherent in the object itself. In other words, if you have an object called `MyObject` and it has a method called `MyMethod`, you can access this method by using dot notation:

```
begin
  MyMethod.MyObject;
end;
```

By design, OLE objects never allow you such direct access to the functions in an object, and they never allow you any type of direct access to the data in an OLE object. In other words, you simply cannot directly call an OLE method without first taking a number of preliminary steps; you must use built-in functions in order to access an OLE object's data.

I suppose it might sound as if OLE objects are something of an enigma, since it seems difficult to imagine gaining access to them. But Microsoft has created a method of gaining access, which involves using one or more pre-established interfaces. In particular, unless you're using a particular dialect of C++, OLE clients gain access to an object by creating an interface that consists of a table full of function addresses. This table has much in common with the Virtual Method table created behind the scenes in a Delphi application. The difference here, however, is that a Delphi VMT is managed by the compiler, whereas an OLE function table must often be constructed, one address at a time, by the programmer.

This whole matter is further complicated by the fact that most OLE objects have more than one interface. In fact, it's quite possible to design a large number of interfaces to an object in order to present various views of the object to the user. The act of discovering and utilizing existing interfaces to an OLE object is very much at the heart of OLE programming.

Let me state this matter a different way in order to bring the point home:

- In Delphi, the programmer never has to think about gaining access to the methods of an object. The whole subject is taken care of by the compiler; and as a result, it's quite possible for an experienced Delphi programmer to never have given much thought to function tables.

- In OLE, one of the programmer's most important jobs is managing and manipulating function tables. Creating, finding out about, and gaining access to function tables is a big part of what constitutes the art of OLE programming. (This is a subject not unrelated to the complicated task a VBX writer encounters when working with properties.)

OLE works this way because it supplies an interface that can be used by a wide range of programmers who are working in a wide range of languages with a wide range of needs. The particulars of the way Delphi handles VMTs, for instance, are all bound up with the specifics of a particular language, and indeed, a particular compiler. The designers of OLE did not have that luxury, so they had to leave a lot of rough edges exposed in order to give programmers the flexibility they need to create a wide range of applications.

Because of OLE's complexity, most practical uses of the technology demand an object wrapper that will make it simpler to use. In other words, the interface created by Microsoft may be flexible, but it is much too complex for all but a handful of the most talented programmers to utilize.

> **NOTE**
>
> One of the key features of the OLE interface is its use of CDECL functions. In the past, most Windows-based interfaces were declared to use the Pascal calling conventions. OLE does not follow this standard, but instead uses CDECL functions. To accommodate this change, Delphi itself now supports the CDECL calling convention, and you can declare any of your functions that way simply by appending the word CDECL to the function.

An OLE Example

To run an OLE example, you need to have a reliable OLE server on your system. Since there is no way to be sure that any good servers are on the reader's system, I cannot supply a sample OLE program. However, a number of simple OLE1 aware applications ship with Windows. Examples include Paintbrush and Write. You can use these two applications when testing the Delphi OLEContainer object. Remember, however, that OLE1 applications do not support in-place activation.

My favorite servers are the applets that ship with Microsoft Word, Excel, and Powerpoint, or similar programs such as Visio. However, you also can use programs such as Paintbrush. These applications are small enough to load within a reasonable period of time, and they can reside in memory without claiming so many resources as to bring your system to a halt. If you have one of the Microsoft applets on your system or if you have other OLE servers on your system, I would suggest using them rather than a big application such Word, Paradox, or Excel.

Begin by dropping a TOleContainer component on a form. Double-click the ObjClass property and select an application from the list supplied to you by the Insert Object dialog. If this dialog is blank, there are no servers available on your system. Otherwise you can select an object, click OK, and bingo, you have written an OLE application. Now all you need to do is run the application and double-click the object whenever you want to activate it.

There are actually three properties you can use to start working with an OLE object. The descriptions offered here are meant to be useful for beginning OLE programmers, not definitive statements on this complicated subject.

- ObjClass: This is a lot like the DDEService property, because you usually use it to specify the name of an application or of a class. The big difference between OLE and DDE is that OLE presents a list of classes or applications to choose from, rather than forcing you to remember the name yourself.

- ObjDoc: This enables you to choose a document, which is usually a disk file, as the object around which to build a connection. Once again, there is a parallel to DDE; only this time it's to the DDETopic name. In the Paradox example shown previously, you specified the CUSTOMER table as a topic name; when using the ObjDoc property, you can specify the name of a document and the rest of the link will be established automatically. For instance, if you want to load the CUSTOMER.DB table as a Paradox OLE object, you should specify the path and name of the file and everything else will occur automatically. The dialog from which you choose the ObjClass and the ObjDoc is the same; but you choose "Create from File" rather than "Create New" when you want to start with an OLE document rather than an OLE class.

- ObjItem: Essentially, this shows what objects are currently available in the clipboard. If you are inside an OLE server such as Word, Excel, Visio, Write, Paradox, Paintbrush, or something else and you copy part of a document to the clipboard, it will be visible when you choose the Property editor for ObjItem.

After you select a server, that application will automatically start up. If you selected Paintbrush, for instance, you could draw a picture inside that application, select "return to form1" from Paintbrush's menu, and then be taken back to your Delphi application, which now contains a copy of your drawing. If you now run the Delphi app, you will find that you can modify the painting at runtime just by double-clicking it.

Some servers, such as Paradox, Excel, and Word, are capable of providing in-place activation. To take advantage of that feature, simply place a menu component on your form, fill in one or two items, drop down an OLEContainer, set the AllowInPlace property to True, and attach to one of these applications via ObjClass, ObjItem or ObjDoc. Run the app and double-click the OleContainer. The menu in your application will now take on the appearance of the application to which you are linked.

Although Borland supports in-place activation, there are very few servers available that are small enough to use it to any good purpose. As a result, it's usually best to avoid this technology when you are doing mission-critical work. Perhaps, over time, the proper kind of OLE servers will start appearing in significant numbers, and this technology will at last come into its own.

Besides the ObjItem, ObjDoc, and ObjClass properties, you should also be aware of the AutoSize and Zoom properties that control the appearance of the object when it is embedded in your system.

This overview of Delphi and OLE has touched on only the major themes of the topic. There are a number of TOLEContainer methods and properties that I have not discussed at all. Furthermore, in the future you can expect Borland to considerably expand its OLE functionality to cover areas such as automation, OCX, and servers.

Summary

In this chapter, you saw some of the basic features of DDE and OLE programming. In particular, you learned that both techniques enable you to link one process to another so they can interact dynamically at runtime. You have seen that DDE is really only a nascent part of a larger project that is reaching fruition in OLE.

Microsoft has promised that OLE will make it possible for processes to interact over networks. This means that a program will be able to link with an OLE object that lies on a different system. That system may be located just down the hall, in a different building, or even on a different continent.

OLE also holds the seeds that will appear in future operating systems that will, in fact, be based on an object-oriented architecture. Specifically, the various parts of the operating system will offer an interface similar to the function tables described in this chapter. Programmers will interact with these objects by gaining access to an interface and then calling the object's functions. Microsoft has claimed that these new object-based operating systems will be more flexible and more configurable than DOS or Windows 3.1.

I'm perhaps prejudiced in these matters, but I can't help but point out that Delphi's component-based architecture has very neatly and completely accomplished many of the goals that OLE has been striving toward without success for years. Delphi's components are a triumph not only of object-oriented technology, but of computer technology in general. In a very real sense, it is now the standard toward which other component-based systems need to strive.

As you have seen, the goal of the Delphi OLE impomentation is to find practical ways to encapsulate OLE objects inside an easy-to-use interface. Delphi also will allow you to dig down and manipulate the raw elements of OLE objects by making direct calls to the OLE DLLs; but most programmers will prefer to work with custom-designed components. In other words, you can create you own OLE Container and Server objects with Delphi, but the process is not for the faint of heart.

DLL Basics and VCL DLLs

33

Overview

In this chapter you will learn how to make DLLs and how to place Delphi objects in DLLs. If you are new to Windows, this may sound complicated, but it turns out to be fairly simple.

More specifically, this chapter covers the following:

- Placing a library of commonly used routines in a DLL
- Using `LoadLibrary` and `FreeLibrary` to move DLLs in and out of memory dynamically during the run of a program
- Placing Delphi forms in a DLL
- Using the Windows API to create standard dialogs, popup windows, and child windows

The latter subject in this list is too complex to discuss in depth, so I will merely present examples of the type of code involved and explain the highlights of the subject. If you want to know more about Windows API programming, you should read my book *Teach Yourself Windows Programming in 21 Days* (also published by Sams).

Many of you might want to use Delphi in conjunction with Paradox, Visual Basic, dBASE, Powerbuilder, C++, or some other language. When doing so, you will probably want to produce DLLs, because they can be easily called from a wide variety of languages. Therefore, this chapter will have special importance to many programmers who commonly use other development tools. However, this chapter does not cover programming basics; thus, many readers will not want to begin their perusal of Delphi here but instead at the beginning of the book. In particular, Chapters 6 through 12 cover the basics of Delphi programming.

Readers who have a particular interest in DLLs should look in Chapter 35, "OWL and Advanced Multimedia Capability," and in the CHAP35 directory (on this book's CD-ROM) for additional programs that use DLLs. Some of these programs may include useful notes on subjects not covered in the text of this book.

DLL Basics

DLL stands for Dynamic Link Library. DLLs are simple binary files that contain sets of routines that can be called by applications. In short, they are like compiled units that can stand on their own, and whose routines can be called by any application or even by another DLL. They are called Dynamic Link Libraries because they are not linked into a program at compile time. Instead, the linking occurs dynamically at runtime.

DLLs are valuable because they enable you to write a single set of routines that can be called by a number of different programs. This helps you make smaller executables by avoiding the wasteful habit of linking the exact same code into multiple programs. Furthermore, DLLs can be loaded or unloaded from memory at runtime, enabling you to build applications that are many megabytes in size but which may never occupy more than a few hundred KB of memory at any one time. The trick, of course, is to design DLLs that contain modules specific to a particular part of your program. That way, you can load one DLL in memory when the user is working with one set of tools, and then unload and load another when the user wants to move to another part of your program.

You also can produce multiple DLLs that have the same interface, but do work slightly differently. For example, if you are working with graphics formats, you might create a set of DLL-based file format converters. You can easily add support for more file formats to your program simply by making more DLLs for your program to discover at runtime. DLLs are one of the most important constructs inside Windows. In fact, Windows itself is in large part nothing but a collection of DLLs. Specifically, if you look inside the WINDOWS/SYSTEM subdirectory, you will find such files as GDI.EXE, KRNL386.EXE, and USER.EXE. The logic that runs Windows is stored in these and other files, all of which are DLLs.

> **NOTE**
>
> Most DLLs have the letters DLL as an extension. You can, however, give these files any extension you want. In particular, the files you see that have a DRV extension are also almost always DLLs.

To get a feeling for what role DLLs play in your environment, open up WINPROCS.PAS and look at the declarations therein. WINPROCS, of course, is the unit that serves as an interface between Delphi and the Windows API. Here is a very small excerpt from WINPROCS:

```
function MessageBox;          external 'USER' index 1;
procedure PostQuitMessage;    external 'USER' index 6;
function ExitWindows;         external 'USER' index 7;
function SetTimer;            external 'USER' index 10;
function KillTimer;           external 'USER' index 12;
function GetTickCount;        external 'USER' index 13;
function GetCurrentTime;      external 'USER' index 15;
```

This code states that the MessageBox function is stored in USER.EXE and that it is assigned index 1. If you scan through the rest of WINPROCS, you will see that there are more than a thousand functions, most of which are in the major DLLs such as GDI, USER, and KRNL386.

> **NOTE**
>
> KRNL386 and KRNL286 are both referred to as 'KERNEL' inside of WINPROCS:
>
> ```
> function FindResource; external 'KERNEL' index 60;
> function LoadResource; external 'KERNEL' index 61;
> function LockResource; external 'KERNEL' index 62;
> function FreeResource; external 'KERNEL' index 63;
> ```
>
> Needless to say, Windows decides that 'KERNEL' refers to one or the other of these DLLs, depending on the particulars of your current system and setup.

Another DLL that Delphi uses all the time is COMPLIB.DCL. As you learned earlier, COMPLIB.DCL is the file that you recompile when you add components, VBXs, or other tools to the Delphi environment. In other words, Delphi itself is in part just a series of DLLs. Delphi's capability to enable you to add features to its IDE is a simple result of the fact that it is a compiler that lets you rebuild its DLLs any time. (This is another concept that seemed mysterious and complex at first, but ends up being quite simple! Or at least it's simple in theory, if not in implementation.)

The final thing you should know about DLLs is that they can be explored using the TDUMP.EXE utility that ships with Delphi, C++, BP7, and other Borland products. To use this file, go to the DOS prompt and type:

```
tdump filename
```

For instance, you might write:

```
tdump krnl386.exe > kernal.txt
```

where > KERNAL.TXT pipes the output into a text file. When you are done, KERNAL.TXT will list all the functions available in KERNEL, even if they are not documented elsewhere:

```
Name: TOOLHELPHOOK              Entry:   341
Name: ISTASK                    Entry:   320
Name: FATALEXITHOOK             Entry:   318
Name: MEMORYFREED               Entry:   126
Name: A20PROC                   Entry:   165
Name: MAKEPROCINSTANCE          Entry:    51
Name: SETERRORMODE              Entry:   107
Name: REGISTERWINOLDAPHOOK      Entry:   343
Name: SWAPRECORDING             Entry:   204
Name: ISWINOLDAPTASK            Entry:   158
Name: _LLSEEK                   Entry:    84
Name: LOCKCURRENTTASK           Entry:    33
Name: FLUSHCACHEDFILEHANDLE     Entry:   319
Name: GETFREEMEMINFO            Entry:   316
Name: GETCODEHANDLE             Entry:    93
Name: FREEPROCINSTANCE          Entry:    52
Name: GETNUMTASKS               Entry:   152
```

If you are interested in this information, I have included the output from USER.EXE and KRNL386.EXE on disc in the files USER.TXT and KERNAL.TXT. If you are *very* interested in this topic and want to explore it in depth, you should refer to Andrew Schulman's *Undocumented Windows*, published by Addison Weseley.

Creating a Simple DLL

Creating a DLL in Delphi is a trivial operation. To get started, create a new project, bring up the Project Manager, and remove UNIT1 from the project. Now save the project as DLLTEST.DPR. Finally, bring up the project file source code (View: Project Source) and change the first line of the code so that it no longer reads program DLLTest, but Library DLLTest. Compile the program. Congratulations! You have created a DLL. It doesn't do anything, but it's a valid DLL.

On disc you will find two programs called DLLTEST.DPR and RUNDYNLK.DPR. The first is a very tiny DLL, and the second is a standard Delphi program that tests the DLL. The test program has an edit control and a button on its form. The code for both projects is in the CHAP33 directory on this book's CD.

> **NOTE**
>
> The complete listing for a very simple DLL, as well as the main unit from a program that tests that DLL, is in the CHAP33 directory on this book's CD.

DLLTEST exports one function. It tells Delphi that it wants to export the function by including the `export` directive in its declaration:

```
function GetTen: Integer; export;
begin
  Result := 10;
end;
```

Essentially, all the `export` directive does is cause Delphi to declare the function `far` and wrap some machine code around the function to help load it into memory properly, and to ensure that the stack and data segments are properly arranged. In 16-bit Windows, DLLs have their own data segments but use the calling program's stack.

You also need to add an export clause to a DLL in order to ensure that the DLL can properly list the functions that it provides:

```
exports
  GetTen index 1;
```

`index 1` tells the system that this is the first function listed for export in the DLL. If you add more functions, you number them `index 2`, `index 3`, and so on. I will show examples of this simple technique later in the chapter.

When you are looking up a function in a DLL, the fastest way to do so is to look it up by index. However, in addition to using the `index` directive, you can use the `name` and `resident` directives:

```
procedure Foo; export;
begin
end;

exports
  GetTen index 1,
  Foo name 'FooProc' resident;
```

In this code, a function called `Foo` is exported, given a specific name, and declared to be `resident`. The optional `resident` directive helps speed up the relatively lengthy process of looking up a function by name instead of by index. However, when you use `resident`, the name stays in memory all the time, which can be costly. The `name` directive enables you to declare a specific name for a function that includes the proper capitalization that might be utilized by C or some other case-sensitive language. If you leave off the name directive, you can still look up the function by name, but it will be exported in all caps. Once again, most people export functions by index because it is the fastest method. If you do not explicitly assign an index number to an exported function, Windows will find an unused number and assign it to the function. However, it makes more sense for you to define the number ahead of time, rather than forcing you or your users to discover the numbers with a utility like TDUMP.EXE.

When you move from the DLL to the calling program, do this to import a function from a DLL:

```
function TestTen: Integer; far; external 'DLLTEST' index 1;
```

This statement redeclares the function prototype (name, parameter list, and return type), specifies that it is `far`, and states that it is an external function found in the module called DLLTEST and that it resides at `index 1` inside that module. If you left off `index 1`, the call would still succeed, but it would be slower.

> **NOTE**
>
> The performance hit for importing by name is only at load time. After the function address is acquired, there is no difference in the time it takes to call the function. If you import a function by name, execution time is the same, but load time is different.

After making this declaration, you can call the routine just as you would any other function:

```
procedure TForm1.Button1Click(Sender: TObject);
begin
  Edit1.Text := IntToStr(TestTen);
end;
```

Most of the time it is a good idea to declare a separate unit in which you list all the functions that are contained in a DLL. You can use this unit to link the DLL into a wide range of programs, letting it play the same role that a header file does in a C program. Here is how such a unit would look:

```
unit DLLTestu;

interface

function TestTen: Integer;

implementation

function TestTen; external 'DLLTEST' index 1;

end.
```

The interface for this unit looks exactly like the interface for any normal unit. The implementation, however, contains only a reference to the DLLTEST library. Notice that there is no need to declare the function `far`, because all routines listed in the interface of a unit are necessarily `far` by definition.

> **NOTE**
>
> Routines in the interface section of a unit are `far` because each unit in a Delphi application may get its own code segment. Since any unit calling a function in any other unit may cross a segment boundary, the functions and procedures in the interface section of all units must be referenced both by segment and by offset, which means they are `far` by definition.
>
> Turbo and Borland Pascal veterans beware: The compiler default in Delphi is to merge units into shared code segments, so every unit no longer gets its own code segment. However, things in the interface section must still be `far` because of the potential of intrasegment calls.
>
> Since routines defined entirely in the implementation section of a unit are accessible only within that unit, they don't have to be `far` routines. If you define a routine in the implementation and don't reference in the interface, and don't explicitly declare it as `far`, it will be `near` by default. That is, it will be referenced by offset, but not by segment. There are, of course, times when you might decide to explicitly define a routine housed in the implementation as `far`. For instance, you want to declare routines referenced only in the implementation as `far` if you are passing around procedure pointers, or if you want to use callbacks.

When you create a unit like DLLTESTU, you can simply add it to a program's uses clause and then call the function in the normal manner:

```
uses
  DLLTestu;

{$R *.DFM}

procedure TForm1.Button1Click(Sender: TObject);
begin
  Edit1.Text := IntToStr(TestTen);
end;
```

This is obviously a very convenient system, so I almost always create interface units for DLLs.

Creating VCL-Based Windows in DLLs

It is easy to place a VCL object in a DLL, as shown by the FRACTDLL project that ships with this book. This DLL includes three Delphi forms that can be called from a standard Delphi program.

The simplest of the three forms, shown in Figure 33.1, enables the user to page through a selection of pictures. The form, called PICS.PAS, isn't particularly useful, but it is pretty to look at, easy to construct, and broadly outlines the syntax used in placing Delphi objects in DLLs.

FIGURE 33.1.

The Space Pictures form consists of a TTabbedNotebook, three TImages, and a few BMPs.

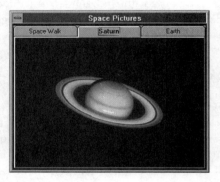

NOTE

The code for the PICS unit (which is on this book's CD in the CHAP33 directory) has one procedure, declared with the export directive.

The ShowPictures procedure is not a method of TSpacePict. Instead, it is a simple routine declared in the interface of the unit with the export directive:

```
procedure ShowPictures; export;
```

Here is what the routine looks like:

```
procedure ShowPictures(Handle: THandle);
begin
  Application.Handle := Handle;
  SpacePict1 := TSpacePict1.Create(Application);
  try
    SpacePict1.ShowModal;
  finally
    SpacePict1.Free;
  end;
end;
```

The procedure allocates memory for a TSpacePict object, calls its ShowModal method, and finally destroys the object. When you want to use the TSpacePict object from another program, this is the only routine you need to call.

Note that ShowPictures has one parameter, which is the Application.Handle of the program that calls the procedure. It is not necessary for you to pass it in, but you won't get a real modal dialog if you don't pass in the Application.Handle of the calling program and assign it to the Application.Handle of the DLL.

There is a try..finally block wrapped around the calls to Show and Free. This is the correct way to handle memory allocation; you should get in the habit of always handling allocations this way, whether or not they are in a DLL.

The PICS unit is one of three units used by the FRACTDLL library. Listing 33.1 shows the source code for the main module of this DLL.

Listing 33.1. The FRACTDLL exports three routines; each routine is found in a separate unit.

```
library Fractdll;

uses
  Pics in 'PICS.PAS' {SpacePict1},
  Squares in 'SQUARES.PAS' {DrawSqr},
  Fern in 'FERN.PAS' {Ferns};

exports
  ShowPictures index 1,
  ShowSquares index 2,
  ShowFerns index 3;

{$R *.RES}
begin
end.
```

The exports clause for the FRACTDLL unit lists three routines. The ShowPictures routine is exported with an index of 1. If you take the code in the PICS unit and add in the exports statement shown here, you can see how simple it is to export a Delphi form from a DLL. Since DLLs can be called from Paradox, C++, dBASE, and many other languages, it is possible to take advantage of Delphi's ease of use and extraordinary technical capabilities to quickly create elaborate forms that can be used by a wide range of programs.

The ShowSquares and ShowFerns routines are defined in units that contain simple forms with no controls. The contents of the form are created not by components, but by a series of GDI calls that draw on the form's surface. The FERN form is a simple fractal figure that looks remarkably like the standard sword fern found in the Pacific Northwest. The SQUARES unit

(Figure 33.2) draws a series of rotated squares, each one of which fits inside the other, a bit like a series of Chinese boxes. I use colors to animate the boxes so that they are more interesting to look at.

FIGURE 33.2.

The SQUARES form has an animated series of squares, each rotated slightly and drawn one within the next.

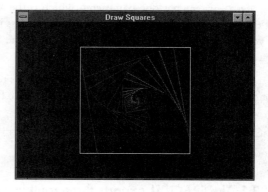

I'm not going to discuss the TFerns or the TDrawSqr objects, because this is a book about basic Delphi programming—not a book about fractals. However, the code (on this book's CD) helps to demonstrate that Delphi gives you good access to the Windows GDI. Note that the TDrawSqr object calls the GDI directly, whereas the TFerns object uses TCanvas for its output. Both units are shown available on this book's CD.

> **NOTE**
>
> The fern unit, available on CD in the CHAP33 directory, shows a simple fractal fern. Thanks to Lar Mader for providing me with this algorithm.
>
> Also in the CHAP33 directory on this book's CD is the squares unit, which draws a series of multicolored squares, each partially rotated and inserted inside the other.

The interface unit for the FRACTDLL library is shown in the next section of this chapter. On disk you will find a program called MAINDEMO that uses the FRACTDLL, as well as a second DLL created in the next section.

You've seen that it is easy to place Delphi forms in a DLL. The basic steps are to create the form and to add a routine that launches the form. The latter routine should be exported from the DLL and called whenever the user needs to access the form. If you need to get data in and out of the form using the techniques shown here, one simple approach is to add a var parameter for the exported routines. Use this parameter to pass in a record. You can then fill in the structure and return it to the program that called the form.

There is another task that someone writing a DLL should address: Exceptions must not be allowed to *escape* from an exported DLL function. If an exception is raised in a DLL and the search for an exception handler makes it all the way out to the entry point, the only other exception handler available to the DLL (beyond the entry point) is the RTL default exception handler. The RTL default exception handler will terminate the DLL and the host EXE. Therefore, you should always put the following code around all DLL entry points:

```
procedure myDLLproc(...); export;
begin
  try
     { your code here }
  except
     { notify host application of exception, preferably via callback, }
     { or show an error dialog and return an error code as the function result.

  end;
end;
```

See the EXPTDEMO.DPR code that ships with Delphi for a more in-depth view of this particular subject. Exceptions are covered in Chapter 34, "Exceptions."

DLLs and Memory: Notes on *LoadLibrary* and *FreeLibrary*

As you can see, Delphi DLLs are a simple and straightforward subject. They are particularly useful when you have a set of routines that you want to make callable by a range of applications. For instance, you could wrap the STRBOX, MATHBOX, and UTILBOX units in a DLL called TOOLBOX and then load three Delphi programs into memory, all of which could call a single copy of the TOOLBOX.DLL. This is potentially more efficient than linking multiple copies of the routines into all three Delphi programs.

I say that using DLLs is "potentially" more memory-efficient than linking code in directly. The qualifier used here is meant to reference the fact that Delphi has a smart linker. When you call routines in a unit, Delphi will only link in the code from the unit that you actually call. For instance, if you have a unit that has 20 routines and you call only one of them from a program, Delphi will link in only the code from one routine, not from all 20. That is more efficient than having to load all 20 routines into memory as part of a DLL.

On the other hand, by using a system somewhat different than one I've shown you above, you can dynamically load and unload DLLs from memory using the Windows API LoadLibrary and FreeLibrary functions. LoadLibrary takes a single parameter that is a string specifying the name of the library you want to load. You can include a pathname in this string. If the call succeeds, LoadLibrary returns a value of type THandle that is greater than HINSTANCE_ERROR, which is 32. If it fails, the value is less than 32. See the online help for a list of the errors associated with particular values lower than 32. The LOADDLL subdirectory on disk includes examples of loading and unloading a DLL dynamically.

To unload a DLL from memory, just call FreeLibrary and pass in the THandle variable returned by a successful call to LoadLibrary. Note that if LoadLibrary is called multiple times on a single DLL, a numerical reference count for that DLL is incremented each time the call is made. That way, only one copy of the DLL needs to be loaded into memory. Each call to FreeLibrary decrements the reference count by one. When the reference count reaches zero, the library is unloaded from memory.

If you call LoadLibrary, you must explicitly call GetProcAddress to return the address of functions in the library that you want to call. An example of this type of code is shown in the LOADDLL program that ships with this book. Here is the key method from that program:

```
procedure TForm1.Button1Click(Sender: TObject);
type
  TShowProc = procedure(Handle: THandle);
var
  hLib: THandle;
  ShowProc: TFarProc;
begin
  hLib := LoadLibrary('FRACTDLL.DLL');
  if hLib < 32 then Exit;
  ShowProc := GetProcAddress(hLib, MakeIntResource(1));
  TShowProc(ShowProc)(Application.Handle);
  FreeLibrary(hLib);
end;
```

This method declares a type compatible with the ShowPicture, ShowFern, and ShowSquares routines. It then declares a variable of type:

- THandle to hold a handle to the DLL
- TFarProc to hold the address of a function

LoadLibrary is called. If it succeeds, the address of the ShowPicture routine is retrieved in a variable of type TFarProc. The TFarProc variable is then typecast as a variable of type TShowProc, and the ShowPicture routine is called. If the FRACTDLL is in the current subdirectory or on the path, FRACTDLL will be loaded into memory and the call will succeed. After the call, the library is unloaded.

NOTE

Calling LoadLibrary or FreeLibrary can be a bit complicated, because you have to start working with function pointers rather than the simpler calls you see in the examples given in the MAINDEMO program.

If you use an interface unit, as the MAINDEMO program does, DLLs are not loaded by Delphi generating calls to LoadLibrary. Instead, they are implicitly loaded by the Windows EXE loader when it sees a DLL reference in the EXE information. If an implicitly referenced DLL cannot be loaded, the EXE or DLL that refers to it cannot be loaded either. LoadLibrary allows you to take control of that situation and try something else.

The last point I want to make about Delphi DLLs is that they can be very small. The DLLTEST file shown above is 1,792 bytes. That's not a misprint. It's just under 2 KB total, with no other runtime files required of any sort. Binary files don't come any smaller or faster than this, no matter what language you are using—and regardless of what compiler you are using. This is it. It's as fast and small as it gets.

Creating Non-VCL Windows and Dialogs

If you compare the sizes of the TESTDLL library and the FRACTDLL library, you'll see that there is a big hit when you add the VCL to a DLL. This is because the VCL is a framework consisting of a large hierarchy of objects. You can't just bring the TForm object in alone; you have to bring the framework along with it.

The VCL is no larger than OWL, MFC, or any of the other frameworks commonly used in Windows programming today. In fact, VCL is an unusually small framework that creates executables competing in speed and size with any created by OWL or MFC programs. Object-oriented frameworks add code to your programs, no matter who makes them or what language is used.

When compared to the vast resources required to run a Visual Basic or PowerBuilder application, VCL is tiny. Other high-level programming tools can't produce DLLs at all, let alone object-oriented frameworks. Nevertheless, there may be times when you want to create real Windows applications or libraries that don't use the VCL. The APIDLL library provides examples of a true Windows dialog, popup window, and child window, all of which are created using straight Windows API calls. The APIDLL contains three windows that are functionally equivalent to Delphi forms, yet the entire DLL is only 18 KB in size. By Windows standards, this is a very small and fast module.

Of course, this speed comes at a price. Writing true Windows API code is a non-trivial procedure, even if you have the considerable advantage of the easy-to-read Pascal syntax.

> **NOTE**
>
> The complete source for the APIDLL is stored on CD in the CHAP33 directory. The APIDLL exports a series of non-VCL windows and dialogs for use inside Delphi, Paradox, C++, or other programs.
>
> Also in the CHAP33 directory on this book's CD are the following:
>
> - The WINSTUFF unit, which is part of the APIDLL and shows how to create non-VCL dialogs and windows
> - The DLLUNIT, which is an interface unit for the APIDLL and FRACTDLL libraries
> - The MAINDEMO program, which tests the APIDLL and FACTDLL libraries

For those who don't already understand low-level Windows API code, a meaningful discussion of WINSTUFF.PAS would fill up another four or five chapters. Since it isn't practical to cover that much material, I will give you a very brief overview of the code and then leave it up to you to pursue the subject in more depth.

This DLL contains four types of routines:

```
HandleButton: Simple MessageBox routine

About
ShowAbout: Launch and run a modal dialog

RegisterChild
CreateChild: Register, Create, and Show a child window

RegisterWinPopup
CreateWinPopup: Register, Create and show a popup window
```

The simplest code in the DLL belongs to the `HandleButton` routine, which simply enables you to pass in a window handle to be used by the `MessageBox` function:

```
procedure HandleButton(Window: HWnd);
begin
  MessageBox(Window, 'Hello', 'Sam', MB_OK);
end;
```

This routine is not meant to be particularly useful because you can pass in 0 as the first parameter to `MessageBox` if you don't have a handle, and because you can call `MessageBox` directly from a program just as easily as you can wrap it in a DLL. However, I provide the routine because it serves to remind you that you often need to pass in a handle to a parent window when you are creating child windows in a DLL. It's easy to do this, and the Window handle will serve as a link between your application and the DLL.

The `ShowAbout` function is a lot like the `ShowPicture` function, because it simply allocates memory for a dialog, shows it modally, and then destroys it:

```
procedure ShowAbout(Window: Hwnd);
var
  AboutProc: TFarProc;
begin
  AboutProc := MakeProcInstance(@About, HInstance);
  DialogBox(HInstance, 'AboutBox', Window, AboutProc);
  FreeProcInstance(AboutProc);
end;
```

Of course the code here is more complex than standard Delphi code, but the principles are the same. As mentioned previously, I won't discuss the actual Windows API calls shown here, other than to mention that the code that implements the core of the About dialog is shown, naturally enough, in the `About` function, which is included on the CD.

> **NOTE**
>
> Discussions of Windows API programming are limited almost exclusively to books on the C programming language. My book, *Teach Yourself Windows Programming in 21 Days,* describes all of these methods in considerable detail and can be used as a primer on the entire subject. All the code in that book is in C. However, Windows API code is such that it doesn't look much different in C or Pascal. It's really its own language belonging to the operating system, just as assembler was a separate language in the DOS world. Whether you choose to get at the Windows API through C or Pascal is, in my opinion, pretty much a toss-up, with no particular advantage accruing to either approach.

There are two other pairs of calls in the WINSTUFF unit. The first pair launches a popup window that has no parent and that roves freely across the Windows desktop:

```
RegisterWinPopup index 4,
CreateWinPopup index 5,
```

The second pair of calls launches a child window that lives inside its parent and cannot escape its confines:

```
RegisterChild index 6,
CreateChild index 7;
```

Child windows never get the focus. Though it's not the case in this particular example, they are usually shown without a caption or a thick-framed border. As a result, they are usually displayed in one place in a larger window, just like a button or edit control.

I have two pairs of routines for each window because it is necessary to first register the window before you create and launch it. The `RegisterWinPopup` and `RegisterWinChild` routines are both used to register windows. These routines should only be called once for each window. The `CreateChild` and `CreateWinPopup` routines create and launch windows, and they can be called multiple times during a session.

The register routines fill out a large structure and then call a routine that creates and shows the window:

```
procedure RegisterWinPopup;
var
  Window: HWnd;
  WndClass: TWndClass;
begin
  if HPrevInst = 0 then begin
    WndClass.Style := 0;
    WndClass.lpfnWndProc := @PopupWinProc;
    WndClass.cbClsExtra := 0;
    WndClass.cbWndExtra := 0;
    WndClass.hInstance := HInstance;
    WndClass.hIcon := LoadIcon(0, idi_Application);
```

```
    WndClass.hCursor := LoadCursor(0, idc_Arrow);
    WndClass.hbrBackground := GetStockObject(white_Brush);
    WndClass.lpszMenuName := PopupName;
    WndClass.lpszClassName := PopupName;

    if not RegisterClass(WndClass) then Halt(255);
  end;

  CreateWinPopUp;
end;
```

Notice that the popup window uses the `PopupWinProc` routine as its window procedure, whereas the child window uses `ChildProc`.

There is no difference at all between the way `TWndClass` is declared in Pascal:

```
PWndClass = ^TWndClass;
TWndClass = record
  style: Word;
  lpfnWndProc: TFarProc;
  cbClsExtra: Integer;
  cbWndExtra: Integer;
  hInstance: THandle;
  hIcon: HIcon;                          { Name clash }
  hCursor: HCursor;                      { Name clash }
  hbrBackground: HBrush;
  lpszMenuName: PChar;
  lpszClassName: PChar;
end;
```

and the way it is declared in C:

```
typedef struct tagWNDCLASS {     /* wc */
    UINT     style;
    WNDPROC  lpfnWndProc;
    int      cbClsExtra;
    int      cbWndExtra;
    HANDLE   hInstance;
    HICON    hIcon;
    HCURSOR  hCursor;
    HBRUSH   hbrBackground;
    LPCTSTR  lpszMenuName;
    LPCTSTR  lpszClassName;
} WNDCLASS;
```

You could use these two declarations as a primer on how to translate types back and forth between C and Pascal. In short, Pascal and C are both powerful languages, and the constructs found in one are usually matched one for one in the other language.

> **NOTE**
>
> Both Delphi and C/C++, of course, have some special syntaxes that provide advantages not found in the other language. For instance, Delphi has properties and C has operator overloading. Delphi lets you easily build native components that can be manipulated visually; C supports multiple inheritance. Delphi has built-in support for

databases; C has variable parameter lists. Each language has its advantages. In the final analysis, both languages are almost unbelievably rich and powerful, and good programmers should know them both.

The syntax for using window procedures is also very similar in Delphi and in C. Their declarations are identical, but each language has slightly different names for the types involved.

In the `CreateChild` and `CreateWinPopup` methods, you find calls to the complex `CreateWindow` function, which takes a fairly baffling array of parameters:

```
function CreateChild(ParentWindow: Hwnd): Hwnd;
begin
  ASimpleWindow := CreateWindow(
    'Simple', 'Child without VCL',
    ws_ChildWindow or ws_Caption or ws_ClipSiblings or
    ws_visible or ws_ThickFrame or ws_SysMenu,
    1, 75, 200, 100, ParentWindow, 0, HInstance, nil);

  CmdShow := Sw_ShowNormal;

  ShowWindow(ASimpleWindow, CmdShow);

  Result := ASimpleWindow;
end;
```

Notice that the fourth-to-last parameter in the `CreateWindow` call from the `CreateChild` routine is the handle of the parent window, but this parameter is zeroed out in the `CreateWinPopup` method. The parent window parameter is an important part of what distinguishes a child window from a popup window. Another key factor is the presence of the `ws_ChildWindow` style. I promised not to get into the specifics of Windows API programming, but nevertheless I want to remind you that when creating child windows, you should almost always use the `ws_ClipSiblings` style to avoid problems when painting the child windows.

Once again, the point of the discussion in this section is to illustrate the fact that you can create standard windows by calling the Windows API. I have not made any attempt to explain the Windows API to you, but have labored to show that if you understand how to create windows or dialogs in C, you already know how to create them in Delphi. Both languages are powerful enough to give you full and direct access to the Windows API.

Summary

This chapter focused on DLLs. In it you saw how to create very small, very fast dynamic link libraries that contain commonly used routines. You also saw how to encapsulate Delphi forms inside a DLL. Finally, you saw how to work with `TWndClass`, `CreateWindow`, `RegisterWindow`, `WndProcs`, and other key elements of the standard Windows API. The Windows API is difficult, but if you can learn how to use it, it can give your program advantages in terms of speed and size.

Exceptions

34

Overview

In this chapter, you will learn how to add error-handling to your programs. This is done almost entirely through a mechanism called *exceptions*.

In particular, the following subjects are covered:

- Exception-handling theory
- Basic exception classes
- `try..except` blocks
- `try..finally` blocks
- Raising exceptions
- Creating your own exception classes
- Saving error strings in resources and retrieving them with `LoadString`
- Internationalizing your program with string tables
- Overriding the default exception handler

To a large degree, Delphi and the VCL make it possible for you to write programs that almost entirely ignore the subject of error-checking. The reason for this is that exceptions are built into most classes and stand-alone routines so that they will be raised automatically whenever something goes wrong. However, professional programmers will want to go beyond even this level of safety and add additional error-checking to their code. Also, your programs may need to raise their own errors, so you will need to add and raise new exception classes.

The Theory Behind Exceptions

Exceptions enable you to designate specific areas of your code designed to handle the cases where something goes wrong. In particular, you can "guard" whole sections of code in such a way that if errors occur inside them, the problem will be handled in a different area by a set of routines designed explicitly for that purpose. This technique covers nested functions too, so you can begin a guarded block, move in six or seven levels of procedure calls, and then, if something goes wrong, bounce directly back out to a single area in your code designed to handle error conditions.

> **NOTE**
>
> Right from the start, it's important to recognize the difference between Delphi exceptions, which cover language issues, and hardware exceptions, which involve hardware and hardware interrupts. You can (and Delphi often does) wrap a hardware exception inside a Delphi exception and handle the event that way, but hardware exceptions are different than Delphi exceptions.

Traditionally, error-handling has been a matter of setting flags and then responding to a flag that designates an error condition. For instance, if you tried to open a file that does not exist, an `IOResult` or `DosError` flag would be set and you could detect the condition by checking the flag. Under the new system, instead of a flag being set, an exception is raised.

The easiest way to start appreciating the advantages that exceptions bring to your code is to imagine a situation in which three different levels of code are called. Suppose, for instance, that you wanted to display data in a grid, where the data in question is stored in a text file. You might have the following set of calls, all nested inside each other:

```
function DisplayDataInGrid: Word;
  function RetrieveData: Word;
    function OpenFile: Word;
    function ReadFile: Word;
    function CloseFile: Word;
```

In this scenario, `DisplayDataInGrid` calls `RetrieveData`, and `RetrieveData` calls `OpenFile`, `ReadFile`, and `CloseFile`.

If something went wrong during the time the file was being opened, `OpenFile` would have to pass that information back to `RetrieveData`. `RetrieveData` would have to include code ensuring that `ReadFile` and `CloseFile` didn't get called; then it would have to pass the error condition back to `DisplayDataInGrid`. This whole process of passing information in a daisy chain forces you to write complicated, confusing, and error-prone code.

As a child, you might have played a game called "telephone." In particular, you might have had a teacher, camp counselor, or friend who arranged a large group of people in a circle and then whispered something to the person on his or her left. That person in turn whispered the message to someone on his left, and so on, until the message went all the way around the circle. When the message had made the whole trip, it almost always ended up changing radically from the time that it started. The same thing can happen in a program if you use the daisy chain method of conveying error conditions. The worst case, of course, is when one link in the chain is broken altogether and the rest of the code continues merrily on its way, oblivious of the fact that something serious has gone wrong.

Exceptions don't use the daisy chain theory of error processing. Instead, if an exception is raised in the function `OpenFile`, the code automatically unwinds back to `DisplayDataInGrid`, where you can write code that handles the error. Exceptions automatically pop procedures and data off the stack, and they automatically ensure that no other routines behind or in front of it are called until the code is found that is intended to handle the exception.

NOTE

When code is being popped off the stack, Delphi checks for one particular block of code that needs to be executed, even if an exception has occurred. This special code is enclosed in `try..finally` blocks, as you will see in the next-to-last section of this chapter.

If an exception occurs and you do not handle it explicitly, a default exception handler will process the exception. Most exceptions are not handled explicitly. When the VCL default exception handler is invoked, it displays a message dialog describing the exception to the user, and then your program resumes its normal processing of Windows messages. Your program does not return to the code that raised the exception. When an exception is raised, special code in your program (in the system unit) checks the most recently entered try block on the call stack for a suitable exception handler. If that try block has no exception handlers suitable for the current exception, the next outward try block is checked, and so on, until an exception handler is found or it reaches the default exception handler. Normal program execution resumes at the next statement following the code that handles the exception.

There is another default exception handler below the VCL default handler, called the RTL default exception handler. If an exception occurs in code that is not part of VCL's normal event or message handling (or in a Delphi program that doesn't use VCL) and that exception goes unhandled, it will be caught by the RTL default exception handler. The RTL default exception handler displays a rather technical error message box and then terminates your program.

For some reason, all this always sounds considerably more complex in theory than it is in practice. If what I have said here does not quite make sense to you, just forge on anyway, and I think it will become clear in time. The previous few paragraphs lay out the theory behind a fairly simple set of syntactical routines. Play with the syntax for awhile, using the descriptions below as a guide, and then if you want, come back and read the theory a second time.

Exception Classes

Delphi comes with a rich set of built-in exception classes meant for handling a wide range of exceptions. You can easily create your own exception classes for handling the key events in your program that might be susceptible to error. Here is the base class for exception handling, as it is declared in SYSUTILS.PAS:

```
Exception = class(TObject)
  private
    FMessage: PString;
    function GetMessage: string;
    procedure SetMessage(const Value: string);
  public
    constructor Create(const Msg: string);
    constructor CreateFmt(const Msg: string;
                          const Args: array of const);
    constructor CreateRes(Ident: Word);
    constructor CreateResFmt(Ident: Word;
                             const Args: array of const);
    constructor CreateHelp(const Msg: string; AHelpContext: Longint);
    constructor CreateFmtHelp(const Msg: string;
                              const Args: array of const;
                              AHelpContext: Longint);
    constructor CreateResHelp(Ident: Word; AHelpContext: Longint);
    constructor CreateResFmtHelp(Ident: Word;
                                 const Args: array of const;
                                 AHelpContext: Longint);    destructor Destroy;
```

```
override;
    property HelpContext: Longint read FHelpContext write FHelpContext;
    property Message: string read GetMessage write SetMessage;
    property MessagePtr: PString read FMessage;
  end;
```

The key point to grasp here is that all exceptions have a message that can be displayed to the user. You can pass in this message through a number of different constructors, and you can retrieve it through either the `Message` or `MessagePtr` function.

> **NOTE**
>
> Delphi classes sometimes have multiple constructors because you may have more than one way in which you want to create a class. Sometimes you might want to initialize a class by passing in one type of string, and another time you might want to pass in a second type of string or perhaps an integer. To give you the flexibility you need, Delphi enables you to declare multiple constructors. Needless to say, you still call only one constructor when creating a class; it's just that you have a choice of which constructor you want to choose.

Here are some additional built-in exceptions, all quoted directly from SYSUTILS.PAS:

```
EOutOfMemory = class(Exception)
  public
    destructor Destroy; override;
    procedure FreeInstance; override;
  end;

  EInOutError = class(Exception)
  public
    ErrorCode: Integer;
  end;

  EIntError = class(Exception);
  EDivByZero = class(EIntError);
  ERangeError = class(EIntError);
  EIntOverflow = class(EIntError);
  EMathError = class(Exception);
  EInvalidOp = class(EMathError);
  EZeroDivide = class(EMathError);
  EOverflow = class(EMathError);
  EUnderflow = class(EMathError);
  EInvalidPointer = class(Exception);
  EInvalidCast = class(Exception);
  EConvertError = class(Exception);
  EProcessorException = class(Exception);
  EFault = class(EProcessorException);
  EGPFault = class(EFault);
  EStackFault = class(EFault);
  EPageFault = class(EFault);
  EInvalidOpCode = class(EFault);
  EBreakpoint = class(EProcessorException);
  ESingleStep = class(EProcessorException);
```

You can see that there are error codes for divide by zero errors, file I/O errors, invalid type casts, and various other conditions both common and obscure.

The preceding list, however, is far from complete. Many other exceptions classes are declared in other modules of the VCL. To get a feeling for their complete scope, you should use the Browser and also the online help. Figure 34.1 shows the browser as it looks when it is in the thick of the exception hierarchy.

FIGURE 34.1.

The Browser is a good tool to use when you want to see if Delphi has a class for handling a particular type of exception.

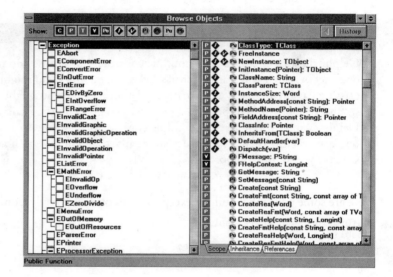

Basic Exception Syntax

When working with the code presented in this chapter, you will be raising a lot of exceptions. If you set Options | Environment | Preferences | Break on Exception to True, exceptions raised by your program will cause the debugger to take you as near as possible to the place in your code where the exception occurred. Only after you start running again will you see the error message as it will be reported to the user. As a result, you should probably keep Break on Exception set to False, except when you explicitly want to step through your code during an exception.

The SIMPEXEP program, found on this book's CD, gives four examples of how to raise and handle exceptions in Delphi. The first two examples shown are of the simplest possible kind, and are meant to get you started with the concepts involved in this process. The latter two examples in this program are a bit more complex, but are still relatively straightforward.

This program contains four TBitbtns that, when pressed, raise exceptions. In the first case, the code lets Delphi's built-in routines handle the exception; in the rest of the examples, a custom error handler is invoked.

Here is the simplest way to raise and handle an exception:

```
procedure TForm1.DelExceptClick(Sender: TObject);
var
  i, j, k: Integer;
begin
  j := 0;
  k := i div j;
end;
```

The code shown here causes a divide by zero error, and it will automatically pop up the dialog shown in Figure 34.2.

FIGURE 34.2.

The default mechanism for handling a divide by zero error.

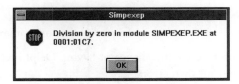

The error message shown in Figure 34.2 is useful to programmers, since it provides an address you can use in the Search | Find Error menu choice. However, it is not a particularly friendly message to send to a user of your program.

The following code demonstrates how to set up a try..except block that gives you a place to handle an error:

```
procedure TForm1.UserExceptClick(Sender: TObject);
var
  i, j, k: Integer;
begin
  j := 0;
  try
    k := i div j;
  except
    on EDivByZero do
      MessageDlg('Like wow! Don''t divide by zero, man!',
                 mtError, [mbOk], 0);
  end;
end;
```

The code that you want to test appears right after the reserved word try. In this case, all that goes on in this section is that you force a divide by zero error. When the error occurs, the code after the word except is executed. In this section, you designate that you want to handle EDivByZero messages explicitly, and you do so by popping up an error message.

In the first part of the try block, you could make a procedure call. That procedure could in turn call another procedure, and so on, for six, ten, or however many levels of nested calls. If any of the routines in that block raised an EDivByZero error, the code would automatically jump to the MessageDlg shown in the preceding code.

Furthermore, if the code looked like this:

```
j := 0;
try
  k := i div j;
  DoSomething;
  DoSomethingElse;
   DoThis;
   DoThat;
except
  on EDivByZero do
    MessageDlg('Like wow! Don''t divide by zero, man!',
               mtError, [mbOk], 0);
end;
```

then DoSomething, DoSomethingElse, DoThis, and DoThat would never be executed. Instead, the code would jump immediately from the division statement to the except section.

You can combine the convenience of having Delphi report an error with the luxury of being able to define your own errors:

```
procedure TForm1.DeclareClick(Sender: TObject);
var
  i, j, k: Integer;

begin
  j := 0;
  try
    k := i div j;
  except
    on E:EDivByZero do
      MessageDlg(Self.ClassName + ': ' + E.Message,
                 mtError, [mbOk], 0);
  end;
end;
```

In this code, Delphi is in effect allowing you to map an identifier onto the already existing exception object instance that was raised. This is not a variable declaration, since no new storage is being allocated. It's simply giving you a convenient way to access the exception object instance so that you can extract additional information carried by the object instance, such as the error message string:

```
E.Message
```

where `Message` returns the string that Delphi would associate with this error. To understand where `Message` comes from, refer to the declaration of `TException` shown previously.

After you have access to the `Message` associated with an exception, you can add your own information to it. For instance, in this case I snag the name of the object whose method is raising the exception, thereby helping me know right away where the problem has occurred:

```
S := Self.ClassName + ': ' + E.Message,
```

The string created in this line of code is shown in Figure 34.3.

FIGURE 34.3.

An exception that shows a string created in part by Delphi and in part by the programmer.

You also might want to display the actual address at which an exception is raised. The built-in `ExceptAddr` function returns this address:

```
procedure TForm1.CalcAddClick(Sender: TObject);
const
  CR = #13#10;
var
  i, j, k: Integer;
begin
  j := 0;
  try
    k := i div j;
  except
    on E:EDivByZero do
      MessageDlg(E.Message + CR + ' MyCalc: ' +
                 Address2Str(GetLogicalAddr(ExceptAddr)),
                 mtError, [mbOk], 0);
  end;
end;
```

This code displays the regular error message associated with a `EDivByZero` exception and then immediately converts the result of the `ExceptAddr` function into a string so that you can see that it returns the same address displayed by a Delphi exception. You can use this address in the Search | Find Error menu option, which will take you to the place in your code where the error occurred.

The only problem with the `ExceptAddr` function is that it returns the physical address where the error occurred; but what you want is the address relative to the rest of the current program. To convert this physical address into the type of logical address you need, you can call the `GetLogicalAddr` function from the `STRBOX` unit:

```
function GetLogicalAddr(A: Pointer): Pointer;
var
  APtr: Pointer;
begin
```

```
  if A = nil then exit;
  if Ofs(A) = $FFFF then exit;
  asm
    mov ax, A.Word[0]
    mov dx, A.Word[2]
    mov es,dx
    mov dx,es:Word[0]
    mov APtr.Word[0], ax
    mov APtr.Word[2], dx
  end;
  Result := APtr;
end;
```

This code tests to make sure you have not passed GetLogicalAddr a nil pointer or a pointer from the segment above high memory. If the address is valid, it uses assembler to convert it into a logical address and then returns you the result.

To convert a pointer into a string, you can use the following function from the STRBOX unit:

```
function Address2Str(Addr : Pointer) : string;
var
  S1 : String;
  S2 : String;
begin
  S1 := GetHexWord(Seg(Addr^));
  S1 := S1 + ':';
  S2 := GetHexWord(Ofs(Addr^));
  S1 := S1 + S2;
  Address2Str := S1;
end;
```

where GetHexWord looks like this:

```
function GetHexWord(w: Word): string;
const
  HexChars: array [0..$F] of Char =  '0123456789ABCDEF';
var
  Addr: string;
begin
  Addr[1] := hexChars[Hi(w) shr 4];
  Addr[2] := hexChars[Hi(w) and $F];
  Addr[3] := hexChars[Lo(w) shr 4];
  Addr[4] := hexChars[Lo(w) and $F];
  Addr[0] := #4;
  Result := addr;
end;
```

This function uses logical operators to calculate the index of a character inside an array that contains all 16 valid hex characters.

In this section, you learned how to handle simple exceptions. The actual logistics of handling these situations can be quite complex at times, but you are now armed with the basics needed to go into battle and wage war with the compiler. Note that I arranged the examples in this section in increasing order of complexity, where the first two are more typical of the code you will use in most programs, and the latter two are useful when you want to use advanced techniques.

Creating and Raising Your Own Exceptions

In this section, I will show how you can create your own exceptions and how to raise exceptions when errors occur. The code explored in this section is from the MYEXCEPT program (on the CD). The form for the program has three buttons and an edit control.

> **NOTE**
>
> The MYEXCEPT program, found on the CD, specializes in raising exceptions.

To use this program, just press any of the three buttons on the form. The third button won't raise an exception unless the edit control is set to the misspelled string occured.

Exceptions occur because they are explicitly raised. For instance, here is a version of the Str2Int routine:

```
procedure Str2Int(S: string);
var
  E: Integer;
begin
  Val(S, Result, E);
  if E <> 0 then
    raise EConvertError.Create('Can''t convert ' + S +
                            ' into an integer');
end;
```

This procedure uses the Delphi Val procedure to convert a string into an integer. If all is successful, Result is set equal to the transmuted string and E is set to 0. If there is a problem, E is non-zero. When an error condition exists, the Str2Int routine raises an EConvertError and passes in a string that explains what has gone wrong.

> **TIP**
>
> Val is one of many built-in routines for handling strings and numbers. If you are trying to find out whether Delphi contains a particular type of function, you can search on "Procedures and Functions (Categorical)" in the online help.

EConvertError is a built-in Delphi type meant to be used in situations where an error occurs in a conversion routine. If you look in SYSUTILS.PAS, you will find that Delphi uses this exception quite a bit, but tends to raise it via the good graces of the ConvertError routine.

There is nothing in Delphi that forces you to use a particular class of exceptions in a particular situation. For instance, in the following method I raise an EReadError, even though nothing has gone wrong in the program:

```
procedure TForm1.RaiseEReadClick(Sender: TObject);
begin
  raise EReadError.Create('Fake EReadError has occurred');
end;
```

Exceptions are triggered when you use the reserved word raise and then construct an instance of a particular type of exception. In and of themselves, exceptions have nothing to do with errors, and indeed you could use them for some entirely different purpose. In other words, exceptions are a good means of reporting errors, but they do not occur because an error occurs; they occur because you use the reserved word raise!

Many of the exception classes that are built into Delphi may be useful to you at times. For instance, you might need to convert some variable from one type to another; or there may be an occasion when you need to read some value. If errors occur during such tasks, it would make sense to raise an EConvertError or an EReadError. That way, the code that depends upon your conversion routines doesn't have to worry about what to do when the conversion routines fail. On failure, they will raise an exception and will never return bad data or error codes to the caller. That can go a long way toward simplifying your code.

Despite the usefulness of many of Delphi's built-in exception classes, there are many occasions when you are going to need to create exception classes of your own. To do so, you should first declare a new class:

```
type
  ESillySpellingError = class(Exception);
```

This code states that class ESillySpellingError is a descendant of type Exception.

I created ESillySpellingError because I wanted to finally squelch permanently a spelling error that I have made many times in my life. In particular, I tend to misspell the past tense of the word occur:

```
procedure TForm1.EReadAddrClick(Sender: TObject);
var
  S: string;
begin
  S := Edit1.Text;
  if UpperCase(S) = 'OCCURED' then
    raise ESillySpellingError.Create('Its occuRRed, not occurRed');
end;
```

Hopefully, writing about the error in this book will help me remember that there are two Rs in the word—not just one!

At any rate, you can see that it is very easy to create your own exceptions and to raise them. Whenever you feel that you need to describe a new type of error, you can do so by just creating the simple type shown in the preceding code. If you want, you can create more complex exception types:

```
EInOutError = class(Exception)
public
  ErrorCode: Integer;
end;
```

The `EInOutError` adds an `ErrorCode` to its object declaration. You can then reference this error code in an `except` block:

```
try
  ..
except
  on E:EInOutError do
    Code := E.ErrorCode;
end;
```

Remember that the need for different types of errors becomes evident not when you are raising them, but in the `except` portion of `try..except` blocks. You might want to handle a particular type of error explicitly and let other errors be handled by the default handler. To do this, you must have a variety of different exception classes to raise so that your exception handlers can be set up to distinguish between the different error situations. Of course, all the code in the MYEXCEPT program uses the default handler.

Using Resources to Track Error Strings

Internationalization issues are discussed briefly in this section, as well as the mechanics of using string tables. If you don't yet understand resources, consider reading about them in Chapter 32, "Using DDEML and OLE with Delphi."

If you look carefully at the SYSUTILS unit, you will see that Delphi rarely hard-codes a string into the locations of programs where it raises exceptions. Instead, it constantly calls functions with names such as `LoadStr` or `FmtLoadStr`. These functions call the Windows API routine `LoadString`, which retrieves a string from a resource:

```
function LoadString(Instance: THandle; ID: Word;
                    Buffer: PChar;  BufferMax: Integer): Integer;
```

The `LoadString` function is akin to the `LoadResource` function you saw in the chapter on DDE and OLE. In particular, you pass in the following:

- `Instance:` HInstance variable of the current module. This variable is declared and assigned automatically by the system. You don't have to do anything but use the variable, which is passed on to you *gratis* by both Windows and Delphi. (You can load strings from a resource DLL simply by using the DLL's module handle for the `Instance` parameter to `LoadString`.)
- `ID:` A number referencing a particular string in a string resource.
- `Buffer:` A buffer to hold the string.
- `BufferMax:` The maximum size of the string to be placed in the buffer.

> **NOTE**
>
> The code for the following files is in the CHAP34 directory on this book's CD:
> - The RESERROR program shows how to read error strings from a resource file.
> - The RESMAIN.INC file lists the errors used by the RESERROR program.
> - The RESMAIN.RC file can be converted in a RES file by typing `BRC -r RESMAIN.RC` at the DOS prompt.

The RESERROR program loads error strings from a resource and displays them to the user when an exception is raised. One button on the main form of the program is used to test to see that the strings found in the resource can be retrieved, and the other two buttons actually raise exceptions.

> **NOTE**
>
> String tables can help you during development and during maintenance by allowing you to change strings in one place and see the changes reflected throughout your program. Needless to say, this technique can be very useful when you are trying to create multiple versions of a program for internationalization purposes.
>
> When foreign languages are involved, you might store your string resources in a DLL so that you can change the strings without having to recompile your main program. In short, you can create DLLs that contain nothing but string resources. Each DLL will contain strings from a different language so that you have a version that is French, another that is German, and so on. You can then ship a different DLL with the products that you ship to different countries. When using these DLLs, call `LoadString`, but pass in the `Instance` of the DLL where the string is stored.
>
> Note also that the string resources in your EXE can be removed and replaced without recompiling the EXE. All you have to do is use BRC.EXE to tack the new resources onto the precompiled exe.

To create a string resource, you should use the following syntax in an RC file:

```
STRINGTABLE
{
  1, "First error"
  2, "Second error"
}
```

where 1 and 2 are the IDs of the strings, and the strings themselves are shown in double quotes.

Notice, however, that RESERROR does not hard-code numbers into its string table:

```
#include "resmain.inc";

STRINGTABLE
{
  ErrorOne, "First error"
  ErrorTwo, "Second error"
}
```

Instead, it uses constants that are declared in RESMAIN.INC:

```
const
  ErrorOne = 1;
  ErrorTwo = 2;
```

You can compile a RC file into a RES file by typing this line at the DOS prompt:

```
brc -r resmain.rc
```

BRC.EXE uses the C-like `#include` statement to reference the include file created. You reference the same include file in a Delphi program by writing this:

```
{$I 'resmain.inc'}
```

Once you have created a RES file and an include file, you can load the strings into your program with a relatively simple routine:

```
function GetError(ID: Integer): string;
const
  Max = 150;
var
  S: array[0..Max] of Char;
begin
  LoadString(HInstance, ID, S, Max);
  Result := StrPas(S);
end;
```

`LoadString` is part of the Windows API, so it works with PChars that should be translated into strings for ease of use inside Delphi. Notice that once again, I avoid hard-coding numbers into the program but instead declare a constant called `Max`. Even if you reference a number only once, it's still a good habit to declare it as a constant. The reasoning, of course, is that you can change the number in one place and be sure that all references to that number will change. Yes, it is overkill in this one case, but still it is good programming practice.

It's worth noting that the VCL and Delphi use resources to store error strings. If you open up SYSUTILS.PAS, you will find that it makes heavy use of a more complex version of the logic shown in RESERROR.DPR. In general, string resources are one of the more valuable tools in the repertoire of any Windows programmer, and you should consider making use of them whenever you need to hard-code strings into your program.

The following excerpts from SYSUTILS.RC show a portion of a string table used by Delphi to aid in reporting errors:

```
#include "sysutils.inc"

STRINGTABLE
{
  SInvalidInteger, "'%s' is not a valid integer value"
  SInvalidFloat, "'%s' is not a valid floating point value"
  SInvalidDate, "'%s' is not a valid date"
  SInvalidTime, "'%s' is not a valid time"
  SInvalidDateTime, "'%s' is not a valid date and time"
  STimeEncodeError, "Invalid argument to time encode"
  SDateEncodeError, "Invalid argument to date encode"
  SOutOfMemory, "Out of memory"
  ...
}
```

Notice that this table obviously relies on Format and related functions to enable the program to insert data into a string before showing it to the user. For more information, look up "Format Strings" in the Delphi online help.

The following constants are excerpted from a Delphi source file called SYSUTILS.INC and are used as IDs that reference the errors in the string table shown previously:

```
const
  SInvalidInteger = 65408;
  SInvalidFloat = 65409;
  SInvalidDate = 65410;
  SInvalidTime = 65411;
  SInvalidDateTime = 65412;
  STimeEncodeError = 65413;
  SDateEncodeError = 65414;
  SOutOfMemory = 65415;
  ...
```

These string constants end up being linked into most of your programs, so you might want to open up SYSUTIL.RC and see if you can use any of them in your own code.

try..finally Blocks

Sometimes you need to ensure that a particular block of code is executed even if something goes wrong in the code that precedes it. For instance, you may allocate memory, perform several actions, and finally intend to deallocate the memory. However, if an exception is raised between the time you allocate memory and the time you want to deallocate the memory, the code that deallocates the memory might never get executed. To ensure that this doesn't happen, you can use a try..finally block.

Here is a second way to think of try..finally blocks. As you know, a try..except block can cause the execution pointer for your program to jump from the place that an error occurs directly to the place where you handle that error. That is all well and good under most circumstances, but sometimes you want to make sure that some code between the error and the exception handler is executed regardless of circumstances. `try..finally` blocks represent a solution to this problem.

> **NOTE**
>
> The code for the FINAL program, on the CD, shows how to use a `try..finally` block.

The key point to grasp about the FINAL program is that it nests a `try..finally` block inside a `try..except` block. Of course, in a Delphi program, all `try..finally` blocks are always nested inside a `try..except` block, because each Delphi program in fact occurs inside a `try..except` block. However, it helps to see a small example that shows exactly how `try..execpt` blocks and `try..finally` blocks are nested one inside the other.

The FINAL program contains a private field of TForm1 called `GlobalString`. At the start of the `BitBtn1Click` method, this string is zeroed out and displayed in the edit control:

```
try
  GlobalString := '';
  Edit1.Text := GlobalString;
  RunCalculation
except
  on EDivByZero do
    MessageDlg('You divided by zero again!', mtError, [mbOk], 0);
end;
Edit1.Text := GlobalString;
```

The `RunCalculation` method called in `BitBtn1Click` looks like this:

```
procedure TForm1.RunCalculation;
var
  i,j,k: Integer;
begin
  j := 0;
  try
    k := i div j;
  finally
    GlobalString := 'RunCalculation called!';
  end;
end;
```

This function forces an exception to be raised, but it does so inside a `try..finally` block. Normally, the code pointer jumps from the place where the exception is raised straight to the place it is handled. The `try..finally` block, however, slows this process down long enough to ensure that the `GlobalString` variable will be set to a new value.

If there were code after the place where the exception is raised, that code would not be executed—and yet anything in the `finally` block would be executed. Consider this example:

```
j := 0;
try
  k := i div j;
  Label1.Caption := 'Foo';
```

860

```
finally
  GlobalString := 'RunCalculation called!';
end;
```

Here, the code that changes the caption would not get executed, but the code that changes the GlobalString would. If you changed the preceding code so that it first sets j to 1 instead of to 0, both the label and the GlobalString would be changed.

It's probably worthwhile for me to make a few brief comments on execution speed. As a rule, try..finally blocks are not particularly expensive in terms of clock cycles. As a result, you should feel free to scatter them through your code with a good degree of liberalism. On the other hand, try..except blocks can be fairly costly in terms of clock cycles, so you should show some caution when deciding how often you want to insert them into your programs.

Replacing the Default Exception Handler

You might want to override the default exception handler either because you want to customize your program or because you want to be sure some things happen, regardless of how your program ends. Delphi provides an event called OnException in the Application class that can be used for this purpose. A sample program, called ONEXCEPT, demonstrates how to use this event. The code for the program is on this book's CD. The form for this program consists of two buttons, one called DivByZero and the other called ReadError.

> **NOTE**
>
> The ONEXCEPT program, on this book's CD, shows how to use an object reference to handle global exceptions.

The ONEXCEPT program will handle all exceptions in a single routine defined by the programmer. It is not meant as an example of how to write exceptions or how to construct a program. However, it does provide advanced programmers with an illustration of how to use the OnException event.

The OnException property for TApplication is declared like this:

```
property OnException: TExceptionEvent;
```

Here is the declaration for TExceptionEvent:

```
TExceptionEvent =
  procedure (Sender: TObject; E: Exception) of object;
```

Normally, the code for an OnXXX handler is created for you automatically when you click the Events page of the Object Inspector. In this case, however, TApplication never appears in the Object Inspector, so you must manually create the call as a method of TForm1:

```
TForm1 = class(TForm)
  ...
  procedure HandleExcepts(Sender: TObject; E: Exception);
end;
```

After declaring the procedure, you can assign it to the TApplication OnException property in the FormCreate method:

```
procedure TForm1.FormCreate(Sender: TObject);
begin
  Application.OnException := HandleExcepts;
end;
```

The HandleExcepts method will now be called when an exception occurs as long as you don't declare any intervening try..except blocks. In the example shown here, the HandleExcepts procedure explicitly handles EDivByZero errors but responds to all other errors through a generic handler:

```
procedure TForm1.HandleExcepts(Sender: TObject; E: Exception);
begin
  if E is EDivByZero then
    MessageDlg('EDivByZero', mtError, [mbOk], 0)
  else
    MessageDlg('Other error', mtError, [mbOk], 0)
end;
```

Needless to say, it is usually not a very good idea to create OnException handlers. You should use them only if you are absolutely sure you know what you are doing and why you want to do it.

Summary

In this chapter you learned about exceptions. Exceptions are a vital part of all well-written programs. However, you should remember that Delphi declares a large number of exceptions for handling the errors that occur in your program. As a result, many errors will be handled gracefully without your intervention. For instance, the error popped up in the first EDivByZero example shown in this chapter is perfectly suitable for many programs. That exception was raised without you having to write special error-handling syntax.

Exceptions are one of the most important parts of Delphi's syntax, and you should dedicate considerable time to learning how they work. Remember to raise exceptions only when necessary, but use try..finally blocks liberally because you never know when an exception might be raised by the system.

OWL and Advanced Multimedia Capability

35

Overview

This chapter covers two subjects:

- Using the Multimedia Control Interface (MCI)
- Running OWL programs under Delphi

In particular, you will see how to play WAV files, MIDI files, AVI files, and the type of musical CDs that you would buy at a record store.

OWL was the object library used under Borland Pascal 7.0 and Turbo Pascal for Windows 1.5. The full source for OWL ships with Delphi, and you will be able to run OWL programs under Delphi with only very minor changes. However, OWL code will not recompile under the 32-bit version of Delphi.

The code in this chapter makes heavy use of DLLs, and so it can be considered a companion piece to the chapter on DLL basics. In particular, you will create three non-OWL-based DLLs in this chapter, one for playing WAV files, one for MIDI files, and one for CDs. A separate unit is included for playing AVI files.

Using OWL with Delphi

I converted this fairly lengthy program over from Borland Pascal 7 to Delphi in about 20 minutes. After reading the next few paragraphs, you should be able to convert your programs over in about half that time. In short, Delphi recompiles OWL programs with only minor changes to the source.

To work inside the IDE, you should probably rename your main source file from *.PAS to *.DPR. For instance, the main module in this program was called PLAYER.PAS, and I have renamed it to PLAYER.DPR. I did the same for the main modules in all the DLLs. The DLLs used in this project are as follows:

```
MIDIINFO.DLL
CDINFO.DLL
WAVEINFO.DLL
```

You can still compile a project if the main module has a PAS extension, but it is simpler to load into the IDE if you just give it a DPR extension.

The original version of this program had a RES file called PLAYER.RES, and I found that compilation inside the IDE went more smoothly if I changed the name of the source for this file from PLAYER.RC to PLAYOWL.RC. I then compiled this resource from the DOS prompt using BRC.EXE, and deleted my copy of PLAYER.RES. In particular, I found that my resources were not being properly loaded into the program until I changed the name of the RES file. It turns out that this happened because the IDE was automatically generating a PLAYER.RES file with a single icon in it. As a result, my program was loading properly but did not have a menu.

Another change I needed to make in order to convert from BP7 to Delphi involved adding MESSAGES.PAS to the uses clause of several modules. MESSAGES.PAS contains the standard Windows messages, such as wm_Paint, that used to be stored in WINTYPES.PAS.

The source code for OWL is stored in the directory \DELPHI\SOURCE\RTl70.

To help Delphi find this source, I selected Options | Project | Directories/Conditionals and added the listing to the Search path, as shown in Figure 35.1.

FIGURE 35.1.

*Changing the Search path
for a particular Delphi
project.*

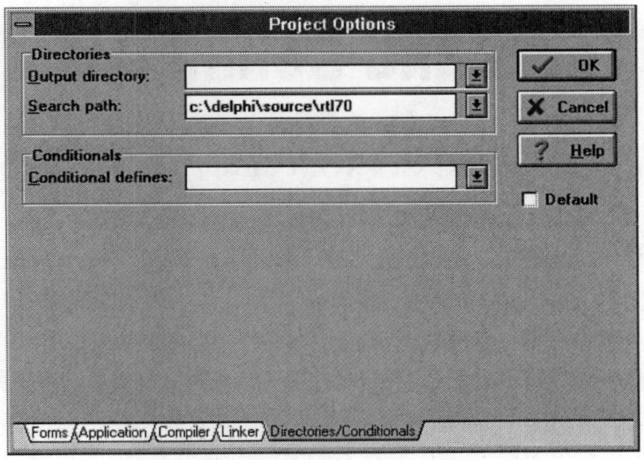

The final change I had to make to my source to get it to run under Delphi involved changing any references to a variable called Result (inside of a function). As you know, Delphi has a predeclared identifier, called Result, that is used automatically in functions. I had, not too surprisingly, used this variable name for my own purposes throughout the code for all three DLLs. To get these modules to compile under Delphi, I changed the variable from Result to AResult.

Overall, I found the port of an OWL program from BP7 to Delphi to be trivial. The only problem I had involved renaming my RES file. At first, it was not at all clear to me what had gone wrong, and I spent 10 or 15 minutes fiddling around before I figured it out. With this minor exception, most of your OWL code should port over right away. When you are done, you should find that your programs run faster and better than before, in part because Delphi has fixed some bugs that were present in BP7, and in part because the new optimizing tricks used by the compiler make your code faster and smaller than ever. (BP7 programmers should note that overlapping ranges in case statements are no longer allowed.)

> **NOTE**
>
> In Delphi, a switch called "Optimize for speed and size" was added to the Options |
> Project | Linker menu choice. I have found that this option takes about 10 percent of
> the code size away from most of my standard Delphi apps. On my system it changed
> PLAYER.EXE from 67,584 to 53,842 bytes in size. Note that OWL programs tend to
> be considerably smaller than standard Delphi programs. The link optimizer does
> nothing to the executable code in your program; it merely repackages the EXE file in a
> more compact manner. It may take less time to load the EXE, but the code that
> executes is exactly the same.

The Tools and Definitions

I tested the programs in this chapter on PCs equipped with Creative Labs' Sound Blaster Pro
card and with the NEC CD-ROM drives. The first is a requirement for playing MIDI files,
and the second for playing CDs.

If you don't have a sound card, you will not be able to run any of the code referenced in this
chapter. The widely distributed SPEAKER.DRV file will not be enough to enable you to run
the included code because the calls used in this chapter are too low-level for the limited WAV
file support available via that driver. Of course, if you don't have a CD-ROM drive, you will
not be able to run the modules that work with CDs.

WAV files are a Microsoft standard file format generally used for recording non-musical sounds,
such as the human voice or a car horn. The key fact to know about WAV files is that they can
store about one second of sound in 11 KB of disk space, or one minute of sound in 1 MB of
disk space. As a result, this medium tends to be extremely disk-intensive, and is used mostly for
adding short sound effects to a program or to the entire Windows environment.

MIDI stands for Musical Instrument Digital Interface. Put in the simplest possible terms, MIDI
files can be thought of as containing a series of notes, such as C-sharp or an A-flat, which are
sent to a synthesizer with instructions to play that note using the sounds associated with a particular instrument such as a piano, horn, or guitar.

The synthesizer chip I used when writing this chapter came as a standard part of the Sound
Blaster Pro card. Most sound cards and MIDI files can play between 6 and 16 notes at once,
and can imitate between 3 and 9 instruments. MIDI files can store one minute of fairly high-
quality musical sound in about 5 KB of disk space. This means that they are much more useful
than WAV files for most computer users.

In this chapter, I will not discuss how to record or mix MIDI or WAV files. Instead, I will
concentrate on showing how MIDI and WAV files can be played using the Media Control
Interface (MCI).

Narrowing the Focus

Now that you know something about the media being discussed in this chapter, it is time to turn your attention to the programming techniques used to make a computer generate sounds.

As it happens, Microsoft provides three separate interfaces that can allow you to access multimedia devices. Two of these are part of MCI, whereas the third is a low-level API that tends to be very rigorous and demanding.

Microsoft has publicly stated that it will not promise to support the low-level API in the future. Since few programmers can afford to spend time learning a standard that is fleeting at best, I can justify ignoring this rather challenging subject. (Phew!)

With the low-level API out of the way, that leaves only two remaining programming techniques. The first is a string-based interface designed primarily to provide support for very high-level languages such as Visual Basic. You can call these functions from Delphi, but I have opted to ignore in favor of a third technique. The Player program has access to this third technique, which is a powerful message-based interface.

The peculiar thing about this command-message interface is that it relies very heavily on a single routine called `MciSendCommand`, which takes four parameters. Though this might sound fairly limiting at first, in practice it turns out to be a reasonably flexible system.

Here is what a typical call to `mciSendCommand` might look like:

```
Return := mciSendCommand(videoId, mci_Close, 0, LongInt(@mciClose));
```

I will spend the next few paragraphs introducing you to the four parameters passed to this function.

The first parameter passed to `MciSendCommand` is a handle or ID number used to identify the particular device in question. For instance, when you first open up a CD drive, you pass 0 in this parameter, since you don't yet have an ID for the device. But thereafter, you pass in the ID that was returned to you when you opened the device.

The key to this entire interface is the second parameter, passed as a message to the function in order to specify a particular command. Here is a list of the 12 most common of these messages, and their meanings:

`Mci_Capability`	Queries the device's capabilities
`Mci_Close`	Closes a device
`Mci_Info`	Queries the of type hardware being used
`Mci_Open`	Opens a device
`Mci_Play`	Plays a song or piece on a device
`Mci_Record`	Records to a device
`Mci_Resume`	Resumes playing or recording

Mci_Seek	Moves media forward or backward
Mci_Set	Changes the settings on device
Mci_Status	Queries about whether the device paused, playing, and so on
Mci_Stop	Stops playing or recording

To complement these commands, there is a set of flags and records available that can give programmers the kind of fine-tuning they need to get the job done right. For instance, the Mci_Play message has four important flags that can be ORed together to form its third parameter:

Mci_Notify	Posts Mm_Notify message on completion
Mci_Wait	Completes operation before returning
Mci_From	Starting position is specified
Mci_To	Finish position is specified

The last two flags presented above can be ORed together like this:

```
Mci_From or Mci_To
```

In this form, they inform MCI that a starting and finishing position will be specified in the last parameter:

```
RC := mciSendCommand(wDeviceId, MCI_PLAY, Mci_From or Mci_To, Longint(@Info));
```

The fourth parameter is a pointer to a record. The record passed via MciSendCommand will differ, depending on the message being sent. In the preceding example, when an Mci_Play message is used, the structure looks like this:

```
PMci_Play_Parms = ^TMci_Play_Parms;
TMci_Play_Parms = Record
  dwCallback: LongInt;
  dwFrom: LongInt;
  dwTo: LongInt;
end;
```

Sometimes it is necessary to fill out all three fields of this structure, and at other times, some, or none of them can be filled out. For instance, if you set the Mci_Notify flag in the second parameter of MciSendCommand, you probably will want to set dwCallback equal to the HWnd of the window you want MCI to notify. Specifically, if you were inside a TDialog descendant at the time you started playing a WAV file, you would want to pass the dialog's HWnd in dwCallback, so that the dialog would be informed via an Mm_Notify message when the WAV file stopped playing.

Of course, if you set both the Mci_From and Mci_To flags, you would want to fill out both the dwFrom and the dwTo fields of the TMci_Play_Parms record (and so on). Remember that the TMci_Play_Parms recorded is associated explicitly with the Mci_Play message. Other messages have their own unique record structures. For instance, the Mci_Open message is associated with the TMci_Open_Parms structure.

All of the multimedia structures or constants discussed in this chapter are listed in MMSYSTEM.PAS. Delphi includes an MMSYSTEM.HLP file. The MMSYSTEM.HLP file enables you to search for a structure only via the C-language syntax, that is, without prefixing the name with a T. Therefore, you should search for `MCI_OPEN_PARMS`, not `TMci_Open_Parms`.

The only major aspect of the `MciSendCommand` function not yet discussed is its return value, which happens to be an error number kept in the low-order word of a `LongInt`. Microsoft came through with a nice touch at this point, by adding the `MciGetErrorString` function, which provides you with an explanation of any error in return for the result of `MciSendCommand` function. `MciGetErrorString` will even send you back a pleasant little message telling you that all has gone well, if that is indeed the case.

Coming to Terms with *MciSendCommand*

`MciSendCommand` provides an unusual interface to an API, and as a result it is possible that a few words of explanation are in order. The goal here is to totally encapsulate the multimedia API inside a message-based system that isolates multimedia programmers from the details of the code base's actual implementation. In other words, when using this mid-level interface, there is no point at which you or I would actually call a true multimedia API function.

The reason for this is one that should be familiar to all object-oriented programmers. Specifically, hardware and operating systems change over time, and as a result, APIs are forced to change with them. When APIs change, existing code bases are rendered obsolete, and last year's work has to be done all over again.

The MCI command-message interface protects the programmer from any fluctuations in the API. For all practical purposes, all a programmer needs to do is send a message into a dark hole. What goes on inside of that hole is of little concern to us. Five years from now CDs may have doubled their capacity and cut their access time down to a fifth of their current snail-like pace. But none of that is going to affect your code. All you need to do is say that you want a particular track to be played. How it's played is of no concern to us.

Another crucial advantage of this style of programming is that it gives the user a common interface to a series of radically different pieces of hardware. For instance, at this time, the MCI command interface works with the following different types of devices, which are listed here opposite their official MCI names:

animation	Animation device
avivideo	Movie player
cdaudio	CD player
dat	Digital audio tape device
digitalvideo	Digital video device

scanner	Image scanner
sequencer	MIDI
vcr	Video tape player
videodisc	Videodisc device
waveaudio	A device that plays WAV files

What MCI has tried to do is to find the things that all these devices have in common, and then to use these similarities to bind them together. In particular, it makes sense to ask all of these devices to play something, to stop playing, to pause, to seek to a particular location in their media, and so on. In other words, they all respond to the set of commands, listed previously, as the primary MCI messages.

Talk about device independence! The Windows multimedia extensions not only protect you from the details of how a particular device might work, but they also frequently let you treat a CD and a WAV file in almost exactly the same manner. For that matter, you can come very close to using the same code to play a WAV file as you would to play a MIDI. The only difference would be that one time you would tell MCI that you want to work with a waveaudio device, whereas the next time you would say that you want to work with a sequencer.

The Player Program

To illustrate the points made in this chapter, I have constructed a sample program called Player that will work with CDs, WAV files, and MIDI files.

The Player program is divided into two major sections: a main file and a set of DLLs. Specifically, there are three DLLs, one containing the MCI code for playing WAV files, one containing the code for playing MIDI files, and the other for playing CDs. I have also included a unit for playing AVI files. Because this program is rather lengthy, you will have to turn to the CD to find the code.

> **NOTE**
>
> The following code is in the CHAP35 directory on this book's CD:
> - The code for playing AVI files. Note that I have ported portions of the Video for Windows headers from C to Pascal.
> - The PLAYINFO unit used by all the DLLs.
> - Code for playing WAV files.
> - A library for playing MIDI files.
> - A library for playing musical CDs.
> - The OWL code used to play musical CDs.

All three of these DLLs use a common unit that encapsulates most of the functionality involved with the actual playing of the various files. The reason why all three DLLs are able to share so much code is explained above, when I described the extreme device independence of the MCI interface.

Specifically, here are the function headers from the interface to the PLAYINFO unit, which is shared by all three DLLs:

```
function CloseMCI: Boolean; export;
function ErrorMsg(Error: LongInt; Msg: PChar): Boolean; export;
function GetDeviceID: Word; export;
function GetInfo(S: PChar): PChar; export;
function GetLen: Longint; export;
function GetLocation: LongInt; export;
function GetMode: Longint; export;
function OpenMCI(PWindow: HWnd; FileName, DeviceType: PChar): Boolean; export;
function PlayMCI: Boolean; export;
function SetTimeFormatMs: Boolean; export;
function StopMci: Boolean; export;
```

Most of the time, all three devices can use the same code to play a file, close a file, stop a file, get the length (in milliseconds) of a file, and pause a file. There are few variations used by the AVI tools, so for now I am keeping it separate from the rest of this program.

> **NOTE**
>
> I put in a little additional work on this program from time to time, and will post the changes to CompuServe, the Internet, and the Borland BBS. If you are interested, you can check for updates. Of course, one of the logical next steps for this program is to port it to the VCL, so its relevancy to this chapter on OWL may disappear over time.

The open command needs to be customized for each device. Its first parameter is the handle of the dialog, window, or control that is playing the file. The second parameter is the name of the file, and the third is the device type. Most of the major device types, such as sequencer, waveaudio, and videodisc, are previously listed. Obviously, the last parameter is in some ways the most important, because it is the one which tells MCI whether to play a CD, a WAV file, or a MIDI file.

The other half of the program, the part that is not a DLL, is written in standard OWL code. One of the most important parts of this program is the Configuration menu item, which lets the user find out about the system's multimedia capabilities and about the current drivers used for to control the multimedia devices.

Player finds out about the capabilities of the current system by iterating through the following array of possible types of devices to create a series of buttons and checkboxes with the appropriate name as window text:

```
MMTypes:array[0..10] of PChar = ('cdaudio', 'dat',
                                 'digitalvideo', 'MMMovie', 'other',
                                 'overlay', 'scanner', 'sequencer',
                                 'vcr', 'videodisc', 'waveaudio');
```

Next to these controls is a second set of checkboxes with window text made from the following array:

```
MMAbles:array[0..10] of PChar =
                ('Not Supported', 'Can Eject', 'Can Play',
                 'Can Pause', 'Can Stop', 'Can_Record',
                 'Can Save', 'Is Compound', 'Has Audio',
                 'Has Video', 'Uses Files');
```

When Player starts, the checkboxes associated with a particular device are marked if the current machine supports that device. If the user selects the button with that device's name on it, Player tells the user if the device can eject, play, pause, stop, and so on. It queries Windows to obtain this information by passing in one of the following flags in connection with the `Mci_GetDevCaps` function:

```
Tests:array[1..10] of LongInt =
                (Mci_GetDevCaps_Can_Eject,
                 Mci_GetDevCaps_Can_Play,
                 Mci_GetDevCaps_Can_Play,
                 Mci_GetDevCaps_Can_Play,
                 Mci_GetDevCaps_Can_Record,
                 Mci_GetDevCaps_Can_Save,
                 Mci_GetDevCaps_Compound_Device,
                 Mci_GetDevCaps_Has_Audio,
                 Mci_GetDevCaps_Has_Video,
                 Mci_GetDevCaps_Uses_Files);
```

Here is the way the code in question actually appears in the program:

```
Info.dwItem := Tests[i];
Flags := Mci_GetDevCaps_Item or Mci_Notify;
Result := MciSendCommand(id, Mci_GetDevCaps, Flags,
                         LongInt(@Info));
if Info.dwReturn > 0 then
  SendMessage(BoxAble[i]^.HWindow, BM_SetCheck, 1, 0);
```

As you can see, the program sends a `BM_SetCheck` message to the appropriate checkbox if the capability is supported on the user's system. All of the preceding lines appear inside a loop that enables the code to check for each capability in turn.

The end result of these activities is to inform the user immediately what devices are available on his or her system, and what type of capabilities are associated with a particular device. As a final service, the program queries the user's SYSTEM.INI file to obtain the names of the currently selected multimedia drivers.

Along the top of the main window is a menu that enables the user to open one of five dialogs, the first for running a CD player, the second for MIDI files, the third for WAV files, the fourth for viewing the current drivers, and the fifth for viewing the currently supported devices.

Each of the first three dialogs comes with buttons that let the user start, stop, and pause the relevant device. The rest of the dialogs display information about the device in question and about the current length and format of any file the user might choose to play.

Internally, the Player program consists of a module called PLAYER.PAS, which controls the main window and three submodules, called WAVEPLAY, MIDIPALY, and CDPLAY, each of which controls a dialog. Any routines that can be shared between all three submodules are placed inside a file called PlayDlg.

In general, you should be aware of the steps that need to be taken whenever you open up a multimedia file. The first two steps are to find out if any existing hardware is available, and then to open the device itself. If either or both of these steps fail, you need to exit as gracefully as possible. Because of the mciGetErrorMessage function, it is easy for you to post an appropriate error message for the user.

After opening the file, the program reports on its length and format, and then begins to play it. While the user is listening to the file, Player reports on the file's progress, which is particularly important when playing CD or MIDI files—which can last for several minutes or more.

When the file has stopped playing or if the user has aborted the play, the program closes the device before exiting. At all times, you should be checking the results of your calls so that you can be aware if an error occurs.

Overall, these steps are not as demanding as they might seem when you first learn about them. Certainly in some circumstances it might be appropriate for you to skip some of them, but you should be aware of the general scheme and the way it fits together.

Details

At this point, all that remains to be covered are a few details that might cause confusion to the reader. In particular, you should notice the function called SetTimeFormatMS:

```
function SetTimeFormatMS: Boolean;
var
  Info: TMci_Set_Parms;
  Flags,
  Result: LongInt;
  S1: array [0..MsgLen] of Char;
begin
  SetTimeFormatMS := True;
  Info.dwTimeFormat := Mci_Format_Milliseconds;
  Flags := Mci_Set_Time_Format;
  Result := MciSendCommand(wDeviceID, MCI_Set,
                           Flags, LongInt(@Info));
  if Result <> 0 then begin
    ErrorMsg(Result, S1);
    SetTimeFormatMS := False;
  end;
end;
```

This code is similar to the `PlayWave` procedure, but instead of using a `TMci_Play_Parms` record, it uses a `TMci_Set_Parms` record:

```
TMCI_Set_Parms = record
  dwCallback: Longint;
  dwTimeFormat: Longint;
  dwAudio: Longint;
end;
```

The key member of this structure is `dwTimeFormat`, which is used to select a particular time format. The Player program uses milliseconds, although I could have chosen seconds and minutes, or even the number of tracks that have been played.

Notice that `SetTimeFormatMS` receives `Mci_Set_Time_Format` as the third parameter. Other messages I could have passed in instead include `Mci_Set_Door_Closed` or `Mci_Set_Door_Open`. This latter flag can be used to eject a CD from a CD player.

Some readers might not find it intuitively obvious to search out the `Mci_Set` message as the place to issue the command to eject a cassette. This highlights one possible criticism of the MCI command interface, namely that it lacks some of the intuitive feel of an API, which might feature a command such as `EjectCD`.

One final point involves the posting of `Mm_Notify` messages to the dialog objects in the main program. These messages are routed to standard Pascal dynamic-message response functions, such as this one from PlayMIDI.PAS:

```
procedure TMidiDlg.MciNotify(var Msg: TMessage);
begin
  KillTimer(HWindow, MidiTimer);
  ReportStatus;
  if Mode = Mci_Mode_Stop then CloseMci;
end;
```

The preceding code implies the presence of a timer. The timer is used to check on the status of the device being played. For instance, if a MIDI file is being played, the timer enables you to check up on its progress at set intervals. In this particular program, the intervals are one-quarter second in duration.

To fully understand the `Mci_Notify` method, you have to understand that Player can ask to receive a message whenever anything important happens to the file being played. For instance, if the file ends or if the user presses the Pause button, an `Mm_Notify` message is posted. Here is the declaration for the `MciNotify` function:

```
procedure MciNotify(var Msg: TMessage);
    virtual wm_First + mm_MciNotify;
```

If the file currently being played is finished or if the user has asked to abort the play, the proper response is to close the device. But this is not what you want to do if the user has simply paused the file. To distinguish between these two different events, you process a `Mci_Status` message in the main program with the following code :

```
procedure TMidiDlg.ReportStatus;
var
  S: array[0..MinLen] of Char;
begin
  Mode := GetMode;
  case Mode of
    Mci_Mode_Not_Ready: StrCopy(S, 'Ready');
    Mci_Mode_Pause: StrCopy(S, 'Pause');
    Mci_Mode_Play: StrCopy(S, 'Play');
    Mci_Mode_Stop: StrCopy(S, 'Stop');
    Mci_Mode_Open: StrCopy(S, 'Open');
    Mci_Mode_Record: StrCopy(S, 'Recording');
    Mci_Mode_Seek: StrCopy(S, 'Seeking');
  end;
  SStatus^.SetText(S);
end;
```

This procedure first gets the current mode of the device by calling the following procedure, which is located in PLAYINFO.PAS file, a support file used by all of the DLLs that accompany PLAYER.PAS:

```
function GetMode: Longint;
var
  Info: TMci_Status_Parms;
  Flags,
  Result: LongInt;
  S1: array [0..MsgLen] of Char;
begin
  FillChar(Info, SizeOf(TMci_Status_Parms), 0);
  Info.dwItem := Mci_Status_Mode;
  Flags := Mci_Status_Item;
  Result := MciSendCommand(wDeviceID, Mci_Status,
                           Flags, LongInt(@Info));
  if Result <> 0 then begin
    ErrorMsg(Result, S1);
    exit;
  end;
  GetMode := Info.dwReturn;
end;
```

In my opinion, the GetMode function highlights the opacity to which the MCI command interface can sometimes fall prey. Unless you actually looked up the Mci_Status, Mci_Status_Item, and Mci_Status_Mode messages in the MCI reference books, it is unlikely that you would guess exactly what this function does just from looking at it.

Nevertheless, it does very effectively meet the current needs. After calling it, you know whether the device is paused or stopped, so you can handle the Mm_Notify message with the appropriate response. I set a variable called Mode to the value returned from GetMode and then show the user a string that explains the result of the query. The string is displayed in a static text control that has been inserted in the object's dialog.

Summary

Although it has not been possible for me to explore all of the many aspects of the MCI interface in this chapter, I have given you enough information to get you up and running. If you want to learn more, the best thing you can do now is study the included example and MMSYSTEM.PAS interface. As soon as you have some feeling for how this code works, you should begin writing your own code for manipulating multimedia files. There are also several books out on this subject now, although most of them are based on the C language. With the information included in this chapter, you should have no trouble reading those books, even if the language is strange to you.

Overall, I think you will find the MCI interface a flexible, well-structured tool that appears to be constructed so that it will withstand the ravages of time with a fair degree of aplomb. Certainly its weaknesses are more than made up for by the excitement of multimedia programming. So, go to it with a will and be sure to take the time to enjoy yourself.

Finally, remember that the code in this chapter is not Delphi-specific. That is, it was originally aimed at BP7. You could jazz it up considerably by adding real forms, exception handling, and with the Format function to simplify some of the string handling.

The Art of Programming

36

IN THIS CHAPTER

Overview

The primary purpose of this book is to teach you how Delphi works. It's a nuts-and-bolts kind of book. However, all experienced programmers know that there is a good deal more to programming than just knowing the syntax of a language. For instance, many people know how to read and write, but that does not mean that they are qualified to be lawyers, or even (heaven forbid) journalists. If you want to be a good programmer, you need to know not only the nuts and bolts, but also the theory of design and of programming cycles—the art of programming.

So this is the chapter in which I turn things around and talk about what I have neglected to cover in this book. It's fine, and in fact essential, to write and read about the act of writing code. However, it's also important to understand that there are limitations to this approach and that sometimes you need to read other types of books that cover esoteric subjects such as programming theory!

In recent years, a series of increasingly heated discussions have appeared regarding the best methods of writing code and the best environments in which to exercise those methods. I don't presume to have an opinion about which sides are right. However, I do feel that a book of this type should be placed in context. A technical book is not the end-all or be-all of any programming endeavor; instead it covers a subset of a much larger field.

Here are three ideas I try to keep in mind whenever I sit down to write code:

- The actual act of writing code is only one part of the task of creating a good program. The other part, which is of at least equal importance, is the act of designing the architecture of a program.

- A tremendous number of projects are destroyed due to atrocious coding techniques that could be easily remedied if only a small effort were put into learning about program design. In particular, developers should spend time studying good code, such as the source that ships with Delphi.

- There is such a thing as proper programming technique, and to some degree it is possible to recognize it when you see it.

Once again, I want to stress that I don't presume to be an expert in programming theory. My only intent is to give the reader a chance to understand some of the major issues in the programming world today. In particular, I want to be sure that people new to the programming world understand that even some perfectly functional programs are classic examples of horrid design and insidious programming techniques. If you come away from this chapter knowing that there is such a thing as good code and bad code, you are way ahead of the game.

The Wheel Has Already Been Invented!

I'll start by mentioning the importance of using the resources available to programmers. There are certain subsystems that a programmer has to write that can take anywhere from a week to several months to complete. Often it's possible to buy such subsystems from vendors at very reasonable prices. If that's at all possible, you should do so nearly every single time, almost without exception. Very, very good programmers often go into the business of selling programming tools to other programmers. It's unlikely you can beat a shop like TurboPower at their own game. Buy their code and get them on your side. In short, if the wheel already exists, don't reinvent it!

A few years ago I found myself with a little free time, and so when I got a call from someone in need, I considered taking on a little consulting project on the side. I would have been working for a very small firm, where all the programming was done by one individual.

Shortly after I decided to look into this project, I got in my car and drove a very long way to get to this person's office. When I got there, he showed me the code he had and told me what he needed to have done, which involved tracking down bugs. After working with his system for a few hours, I found that he had written a number of extremely elaborate input routines and that many of his problems were centered on those routines.

The calculations in his program generally worked fine, with a few minor exceptions. His interface was consistent and relatively easy to use, if a bit idiosyncratic at times. What it really came down to was that much of the work that needed to be done on the program involved the interface routines. Certainly they worked fine 98 percent of the time. But every once in a while I would stumble across a crash bug in one of his input routines.

After examining the program for some time, I finally decided that the programmer didn't really need me so much as he needed to buy a good object-oriented framework. Such packages are readily available on the market for prices ranging from $25 to $200.

From looking at this gentleman's code, I could see that he had easily put in months of work on his input routines alone. If he was paying himself by the hour, the total sums invested in the interface for his program could easily exceed $20,000. Furthermore, he was prepared to pay me another sizable chunk of money to get himself out of his current problem.

The simple truth was that all of this pain could have been avoided initially if someone in the company had decided to invest $200 in a toolkit. In fact, many of the low-end toolkits would probably have met all his needs. In other words, this one company was investing months of time and thousands of dollars in simply reinventing the wheel!

It's also worth pointing out that a number of programmers in the companies that create programmer's toolboxes are absolutely superb craftsmen. As a result, these boxed sets of ready-made routines are often two or three times better than anything I could hope to design by myself. The people who generate these toolkits are dedicating all their energies into creating a decent toolbox. In the meantime, I am usually concentrating on some other entirely practical goal, such as writing an inventory system or finishing a book. What's a mere detail for me can become the primary focus of effort for the maker of a toolkit. Given the circumstances, who's more likely to do a good job?

> **NOTE**
>
> People who program for a hobby might be tempted to say that even $50 or $100 is a lot of money to spend. You might be thinking of a spouse or other loved one who could also use some of that money. In many cases, this is a very important argument. But don't forget the lost-weekend syndrome! You could end up spending a whole summer worth of weekends writing a subsystem for your new program, when it's possible to buy the whole thing for $75. Ask yourself the following question: What does my spouse really want? The $75, or a chance for us to get away together for a couple of nice weekends?

Whatever you do, don't spend weeks or months trying to write a subsystem that's waiting for you on some dusty warehouse shelf! That can be a fatal mistake unless you have years of experience and are absolutely sure you know what you are doing!

To avoid reinventing the wheel, you can take several steps. First, give all the following companies a call and try to get on their mailing list:

TurboPower Software CompuServe: GO TURBOPOWER (PCVENB)

TechnoJock Software: BBS: 409-737-1705

EarthTrek: 617-273-0308

Sax Software: 800-MIKESAX

Mark Lussier: 408-459-0487 (CIS: 74224,2037)

Brainstorm: 617-492-3399

SQL Sombrero: 800-567-9127

Nu-Mega: 1-800-468-6342 (BBS: 603-595-0386)

ShoreLine: (CIS: 70451,2436)

All serious Pascal programmers need to know about these companies and about the many excellent products they offer. A more detailed list is available on the CD-ROM that accompanies this book.

You should also own a modem, and regularly check in with at least one national or local bulletin board frequented by programmers. If you already have a subscription to CompuServe, Genie, or any other major online service, you should be sure you know where the Delphi, Pascal, C++, and Visual Basic programmers on that service meet; and you should try to check in with them at regular intervals.

> **NOTE**
>
> It may seem incredible, but I've heard that there are some programmers who don't even own a modem! In this day and age, you can buy or order a good 9600-baud modem for as little as $25. 14KB modems cost less than $100, and 28KB modem prices are coming down fast. Once you learn your way around a few electronic systems, you will find that you can often search through a BBS to locate the exact routine you are looking for, pre-made, and thoroughly debugged! These routines are usually free for the asking, and many sophisticated shareware toolboxes can be bought for as little as $15 or $25.
>
> Some people are afraid of picking up viruses on a BBS. This is always possible, but I have been on one BBS or another nearly every day for the last seven or eight years, and I have never had a virus. I'm sure that some people get viruses from electronic BBSs, but it is not likely!
>
> Fact: You can never catch a virus by downloading data files, at least not on a PC. For a virus to take hold, it must be executable code, *and* it must be executed on your machine. You can't get a virus from text files, zip files, or images.

Finally, you should subscribe to at least one (if not all) of the following magazines:

> *PC Techniques:* 602-483-0192
>
> *WinTech Journal:* 800-234-0386
>
> *Dr Dobbs:* 800-456-1215

Though less technical, *Byte Magazine* (1-800-257-9402) and *PC Magazine* (1-800-289-0429) are also very useful.

These magazines and journals can help you stay informed about the industry, the latest programming developments, and what's new with programmer's tools. Even if you work in the very heart of the computer industry, you should subscribe to at least one of these journals. If you work alone, or on the fringes of the industry, a subscription to at least two of these magazines is completely essential. You can't get along without them!

On the Art of Programming

Most of the material you will read about in the next few sections is presented only to programmers who have been working at their trade for months, or even years. To me, this is equivalent to giving a sailor a life jacket only after he's fallen in the water and started to drown.

I'm well aware that some readers of this chapter might not have enough programming experience to understand everything in concrete terms. Still I want to proceed in order to get a few major themes across.

In truth, there is very little specific programming information in the next few pages. Instead I concentrate on broad issues that affect all programmers working in any language. However, for a programmer to ignore this kind of material is a bit like a lawyer who never reads the U.S. Constitution. The individual in question may become an expert on all kinds of specific areas of the law, but he or she will never understand what the profession is all about without first knowing the theory behind the entire field.

In the same way, many programmers can become experts in particular fields, but never understand why their programming projects don't succeed. They simply fail to grasp certain key concepts.

What is the Programming Cycle?

Many programmers live under the impression that creating programs involves nothing more than the act of sitting down to tap out reams of code during long, late-night orgies of work.

And for the most part, they are right.

However, the success of those late-night sessions depends on a number of factors, the most important of which is the solidarity of the original design. If you don't know where you are headed, in the long run there is going to be trouble.

Building a program is like building a boat. You have to create something that is going to be able to weather storms, ride out rough seas, and remain intact even if it's accidentally run aground by a drunken or incompetent skipper.

If you were going to build a ship to take you from here to China, it's unlikely that the first thing you would do is sit down and start sawing away at a bunch of two by fours. Instead, you would study the designs of other ships that have made the trip and try to incorporate the best features of their designs into your own.

When you start reading up on the subject, you find that the creation of programs usually occurs in a cycle that looks something like this:

- Discover a problem that needs to be solved—or a goal that should be achieved.
- Design a program that will solve the problem or achieve the goal.

■ Code, test, and debug the program.

■ Maintain the code.

The first two steps and the last two steps are every bit as important as the actual act of writing and debugging the code.

NOTE

When programmers talk about maintaining code, they are referring to the process that occurs after a product has been released to its target audience. If your users come back to you and say they want an additional feature, adding that feature is part of program maintenance. If you discover a bug, or other shortcoming in a program after it has been released, then repairing the problem is part of program maintenance. If the platform on which a program runs undergoes some changes, then adapting the program to the new environment is part of program maintenance.

One classic error that beginning programmers make is to assume that a program is finished just because the code is written and debugged. These people then give the code to someone else, who immediately brings the system crashing to the ground with a resounding thud when he tries to use the program!

Many programmers give up in despair when this happens. What they fail to realize is that this is entirely normal. This happens on a regular basis to even the best programmers. The problem is simply that you haven't finished writing the program yet. Instead, you are reaching the stage at which you should begin testing the code. This phase, which is often called the Beta phase, can go on for much longer than either the design or coding phases. It takes a long time to get the bugs out of a program.

NOTE

The period of time spent on each phase of project depends on the strength of your design, the discipline of your implementation, and the thoroughness of your testing. Weakness in any of these three will drag out your product cycle. Ideally, the development cycle of a product should look like this: about one-third of the product schedule spent on design, about one-third on implementation, and at least one-third on testing.

The real tragedy is not that a bug is discovered. In a well-designed program, the mere discovery of a bug is no big deal. Problems arise, however, when you discover that a program is so poorly designed that trying to fix code in one place inevitably leads to trouble in some other part of the program.

Suppose, for instance, that you wrote for speed and compactness, and therefore designed routines that were so abbreviated, and so tightly interconnected, that changing even one line threatened to bring the whole structure down on your head. Believe me, at that point most programmers would gladly trade a few clock cycles for some relief from their plight. It is no exaggeration to say that tens of thousands of programs have failed to see the light of day because it's literally impossible to solve relatively minor bugs in a poorly designed system.

Tracking down a bug in a poorly designed program is one thing, but it is small potatoes compared to the hours of work that must be invested if an entire subsystem of a program is poorly designed. If you have to make a major design change in a poorly constructed program, you could be facing a problem that is going to force you to rewrite the entire code base or abandon your project.

Objects, Modules, and Design Theory

In this chapter I am not going to promote any but the most general ideas about how to create a good program. The entire subject is too vast and too complex for me to broach in this format. Instead, I want to make sure that no one leaves this book without an understanding of the importance of programming theory.

The fatal mistake some programmers make is to fail to divide their programs into discreet modules or objects. As a result, an attempt to revamp the design of one portion of the code involves rewriting nearly the entire program. This means that a problem encompassing a mere 5 percent of a project can end up bringing the remaining 95 percent to its knees.

By far the best way to avoid this problem is to design the program correctly in the first place. Time spent designing a program is never wasted time. Unfortunately, design problems are often unavoidable. As a result, it's essential to write code that can be broken down into modules that can be debugged separately.

Object-oriented design is aimed at helping programmers write code that can be broken down into a number of discreet subsystems, or objects. The goal is to ensure that each subsystem is relatively autonomous so that it can be plugged into and removed from a program just as a carburetor or a new set of wheels can be added to a car. Delphi programmers who hear this description are bound to think of components, which are, in fact, a major step forward for OOP.

If you find an error in the design of an object-oriented program, you can, at least in theory, remove the offending module and plug a new one in its place. Of course, this won't work unless you design your code from the bottom up so that it is separated into discreet objects.

> **NOTE**
>
> It's possible to get three-quarters of the way through creating an object-oriented program and discover a design flaw that demands rewriting a large portion of your project. Specifically, you can discover that you should have made a particular subsystem into a discreet object, but failed to do so because you slipped up during the design phase. This is a definite problem that OOP cannot easily wish away, and the only way to avoid it is to spend more time on the design phase. However, object-oriented code still has a better chance of succeeding than does regular structured code.

Top-Down Design Versus Bottom-Up Design

When you are new to programming, it's almost impossible to design code correctly the first time. You just don't know enough about what you are doing to understand or predict where the important design issues are going to find their focus.

There are, however, two things you can do to avoid falling into the pitfalls described in the last section. The first idea is to start by sketching the outlines of your program in the broadest possible strokes. Don't start by focusing in on the details. Instead, try to discover the main portions of your program and to create dummy procedures that represent mock examples of their eventual functionality.

If you work in broad, very generalized strokes, you can recognize major mistakes before they become too terribly difficult to fix. In a sense, making a mock version of your program ahead of time can serve some of the same purposes as creating a carefully written design. The goal in both cases is to spot major problems before the development. Needless to say, Delphi makes writing a mock-up of your program extremely simple. The great thing about Delphi, however, is that it also provides a good platform for doing the detail work!

The second thing you can do to improve your program's structure is to always use objects for all the major portions of your program. Experienced programmers sometimes know how to reap some of the benefits of object-oriented code without using real objects. They've learned this from years of sometimes heartbreaking experience.

New programmers don't have enough experience to understand what issues are involved in creating a well-designed program. As a result, they need guidance. One of the best ways to get that guidance is by writing object-oriented code. If you work with objects, you will be forced to modularize your code and to work with discreet subsystems.

Of course, even object-oriented programmers can make a hash out of a project. Believe me, I know all about it. I talk from the firm foundation provided by many humbling experiences! Nevertheless, when you use object-oriented code, you are more apt to make correct design decisions. As a result, it is much more likely that you will be able to debug and maintain your code.

If you bring an object-oriented program all the way through the design and coding stages, it is much more likely that the testing and maintenance phases will go smoothly. It's not guaranteed, not by a long shot, but it's more possible.

> **NOTE**
>
> It's worth pointing out that I am presenting one of two possible schools of thought on this issue. That is, there are some, like myself, who believe in the top-down construction of applications and others who believe in working from the bottom up. If you are in the latter school, you believe that the minutiae of programming ends up dictating the structure that the program will take. There is, of course, much truth to this point of view, but I believe a tool such as Delphi is better suited to a top-down approach to programming. At any rate, regardless of which school you belong to, the important point is to know that two schools exist, and that all serious programmers at least have an opinion on this subject.

The final thing to say about this whole subject is that Delphi was designed to make it easy for you to sketch out the broad outlines of a program and to design it so that it is centered on a series of discreet objects. The entire package was put together to achieve these goals. Working in an environment with these powerful tools built in gives you an incalculable advantage over programmers who are struggling with less-well-designed compilers.

What Is Good Code?

If this book has one major theme it's that good code is almost always crystal clear in its intent. If you look at a block of code and find that your mind becomes boggled by its complexity, you are almost surely looking at code that is poorly designed. There may be some individuals, even a very few small group of individuals, who can afford to ignore this issue. But for the vast majority of programmers, simplicity of structure is a rule to live by.

> **NOTE**
>
> Delphi R&D came up with following saying, which is certainly worth remembering: "If it's difficult to document, then it's probably not a good design."

I don't know how often I've wrestled with a piece of code for days or weeks at a time only to discover that the problem was that I was trying to cover too much ground in too little space. To progress further, I needed to break the code up into additional procedures, objects, or modules.

Many programmers resist this option on the grounds that it appears to make their code bulky or slow. What these people fail to understand is that most programmers live over a graveyard of failed projects. And even on the few occasions that a program is brought to successful completion, many people find the job of maintaining or upgrading a program simply far too complicated.

The way to avoid this whole problem is to break code into a series of discreet steps—or procedures, as programmers would say. Each one of these steps should be as simple as possible. When you look at any one procedure inside a program, its purpose and methods should almost jump out at you. When looking at the procedure, you should think: Hey, this step is so simple that even a child could understand it in a moment. Of course, this goal is not always realizable, but it is the end toward which you should strive.

> **NOTE**
>
> Once again, Delphi helps you build robust programs because it creates such tight, fast code. As a result, you can feel free to design your program properly, because you know it will not encounter undo overhead when you are simply trying to make a function call, or enter a `case` statement. In other words, don't ever fail to break code into separate routines just because you are worried about the overhead involved in a procedure call! In Delphi, that overhead is so small that it's irrelevant when compared to the problems you will face when unwinding a long, poorly constructed routine.

When I am coding a particular procedure or object in a program and find that it is becoming overly complicated to debug, I try to break it down into a series of smaller procedures or objects, each one of which is very simple in and of itself. If I find that it's difficult to break the program down into a series of discreet steps, that almost always means I don't really understand what I'm trying to do. To remedy the situation, I need to go back to the design phase so I can discover the real intent of a particular portion of my program.

Let me say that again, just so I'm sure you understand what I'm driving at. If I'm writing a piece of code and I get stuck, the reason I'm stuck is usually because I botched the design phase. The solution is usually not to sit hovering over the debugger for hours on end, but to step back and sketch the problem on a sheet of paper. The end result is that I almost always find the need to break a problem out into separate methods, or even separate objects.

Alternately, I sometimes copy the current module to a separate file, write a test program, and then start cutting and pasting until I sense where the real underlying problems lie. The key step here is copying the module to a separate file and creating a test program for that one discrete area in my code.

Using PDLs: How to Design a Routine

In this section, I am going to mention one particular coding technique that you may or may not find useful. However, I will outline it because it is an example of the types of ideas you can find if you read books on programming theory. The point of this chapter is to call attention to the limitations books, such as the one you are currently reading, and to recommend that you supplement the contents of this book with books on programming theory.

Many people like to use common English to design routines. It's a bit ironic that this technique often supersedes more advanced technologies such as flow charts and graphical diagrams. Nevertheless, a very good way to describe the steps in a computer program is simply to use plain English. This should tell us something about the kind of syntax that should be used in an ideal programming language: If it looks a little like English, it's on the right track; if it looks like a mess of incomprehensible symbols, something's wrong.

Suppose you need to write a routine that opens a file and reads its contents into an array. Here's how you can describe that procedure when you are in the design phase:

```
procedure ReadFile;
  Pass in an array of strings called MyStringArray;
  Pass in a string called FileName that states file's name
  Declare a File Variable called MyFile;
begin procedure
  Open the file
  start a loop that iterates through the whole file
    Read in one string
    Place the string in the array
  end of loop
  Close the file
end procedure
```

This coding technique is called a *PDL,* which stands for Programming Design Language. Despite its apparent simplicity, it is possibly the most sophisticated possible way to design the nitty-gritty details of a code base.

The preceding code is very English-like. Even someone who has never programmed before would have at least a decent chance of understanding how it works. Also, PDLs are relatively language-independent. BASIC, Pascal, and C/C++ programmers could all use this design as the basis for a real-world routine.

Notice also that I specify certain names. For instance, the routine itself is to be called `ReadFile`; and the filename, array, and file variable are all given specific names. I do this because names form such a vital part of programming. You have to come up with meaningful, easy-to-understand names for the routines, types, and variables in your program. That's a design issue; so you should get those names straight during the design phase.

Of course, there is one big problem with PDLs. They are very restrictive! If you are working with good programmers, you don't want to write a design that is so detailed it stifles their creativity. Once again, the point isn't so much that you should use PDLs, but that you know they exist and you have an opinion as to whether or not they are useful, perhaps merely an opinion on *when* they are useful.

The Best-Laid Plans...

Detailed designs and PDLs are most helpful when groups of programmers are working together. In such a case, it's important that everyone on the team understand where the project is headed. PDLs make this possible, because everyone can quickly and easily see what they are supposed to do, and what others in the project are supposed to do.

If you are working alone, there is probably less likelihood that you will want to create a detailed look at each procedure you write. However, you will probably still want to go through a design phase.

To sum everything up, let me take a moment to tell a true story. I was in a design meeting last winter when Delphi was still being put together. The meeting focused on a discussion of which features were going to be included in the first release, and which were going to have to be put off until later. The general drift showed that cuts in the design were going to have to be made if the product was going to be delivered in a timely fashion.

One particular topic came on the table that was going to make Delphi considerably easier to use. Some folks wanted to cut it, due to a lack of time. However, the team manager said: "Don't worry. X is working on that. He hasn't actually coded it yet, but he's been on it for several weeks now and has told me that he has the design straight in his head now. You know how X is; once he knows where to go, he just sits down and perfect assembler code flows out of his fingers. Its not an issue; we will get that feature on time. The hard part's already done." The unspoken message is that writing code is usually easier that creating a good design for a complicated part of a program. Designs solve problems. Code is just an expression of the design.

At any rate, this is true in theory. It actually took this talented programmer several months of coding to perfect this part of the program. The moral, I suppose, is that design and programming theory are essential, but there is still no sure-fire method that will make difficulties melt away like snow in the spring.

Once you master the basics of a language, you should find yourself spending more and more time on the design phase. If you don't, you will end up having to needlessly redesign and rewrite large portions of your program. Changing the design of a program during the coding phase can add weeks or months to your schedule. Changing the design of a program during the testing phase can often add months or years. If you get the design right in the first place, the time spent thinking about where you plan to go will be minimal compared to the problems it will help you avoid.

The Importance of Hacking

In the last few pages, I have sung the praises of program design, and of a relatively rigid, disciplined approach to writing code. It's only fair that I now turn the tables once again, and argue the other side of the coin for a moment.

Most good programmers spend a large percentage of their time hacking. If you run a programming shop and you arrange things so that none of your programmers have time to hack, you will end up with a group of very mediocre programmers. The best will either lose their skills, or more likely, head for greener pastures.

The difference between ordinary programmers and hackers is that hackers will stay up late at night working on a piece of code for which they are unlikely ever to be directly paid. They are doing the work simply for the love of it and because they want to explore uncharted territory. Of course, good hackers end up being paid even for the time they spend hacking, but that's only because almost everything they do ends up increasing their value to the company that employs them.

There are vast amounts of code that are used regularly yet remain almost totally unexplored. Even operating system code produced by Microsoft or IBM is often so poorly documented that the only way to get to know it is to start hacking. If nobody has had the time or the will to thoroughly document an API, it's up to hackers to figure out how it works.

Besides, documentation is never completely accurate or informative. (Present document excepted, of course!) There is only one absolute source of information on what an API function requires or how it reacts to odd stimuli: empirical observation.

With new developments, such as components or OLE automation, the only way to discover its potential is to hack. When you are hacking, it is obviously not going to be possible to plan out every step in advance. In fact, if you do plan out every step in advance, you obviously will not be able to learn anything new.

An obvious corollary to this is that shops that always insist on doing everything by the book end up being left behind in the rush to adopt new technology. This is not necessarily a disadvantage, since some shops don't need new technology as badly as they need solid code. However, you should note that most of the major computer vendors have to be filled with programmers who consider themselves hackers, since these companies are always producing software that exists on the cutting edge of the latest technology.

Ultimately, I believe there is a certain paradoxical element to the relationship between hackers and those who believe in carefully defining the design and structure of an application ahead of time. This is simply one of those cases where both sides are right. If you don't understand the importance of structure, you will never get anything accomplished. If you don't understand the importance of hacking, your apps will always appear old-fashioned and a bit clunky.

Artists and philosophers are the ones who are best at resolving paradoxes, so my suggestion is that you cultivate those aspects of your personality when you sit down to write code. Ultimately, the best programmers are those who have mastered the art of knowing when to adopt structured techniques and when to aim for the maximum possible amount of creativity. Programming is not a science, it is an art.

Summary

Well, here we are at the end of what has turned out to be a fairly lengthy book. I have written mostly about exploring the technical side of a great programming tool, but I have tried also to talk a little about programming theory and to convey some of the excitement I feel about Delphi.

A bit to my surprise, I find that I am reluctant to end this book. Certainly I'm tired from having written so much, but I still find myself filled with enthusiasm for Delphi and for the wonderful things you can do with it. I wish I had the time and scope to explore a hundred more issues that are as equally fascinating as the few I have covered so far.

I hope I have conveyed my conviction that Delphi is an unusually well-designed and powerful programming tool. Years from now, we will undoubtedly look back on Delphi as merely a single step on a long path. But right now, there are no programming tools that can cast a long shadow over it. Delphi is very much at the forefront of the programming industry. There is nothing you are likely to find that is faster, more powerful, or better designed.

In particular, I find myself endlessly fascinated by Delphi's component architecture. The implementation of properties, event handlers, the Component Palette, and the entire VCL is an amazing tribute to the people who architected the product. Object-oriented architectures are among the largest, most intricate, and most intriguing tools to be found in the whole realm of computers. The VCL has as beautiful a design as any you will find in any language or on any platform. Hopefully you'll enjoy working with it, not only because it is useful, but because it is so well-designed.

Happy hacking!

INDEX

Add to Your Sams Library Today with the Best Books for Programming, Operating Systems, and New Technologies

The easiest way to order is to pick up the phone and call
1-800-428-5331
between 9:00 a.m. and 5:00 p.m. EST.
For faster service please have your credit card available.

ISBN	Quantity	Description of Item	Unit Cost	Total Cost
0-672-30402-3		UNIX Unleashed	$49.99	
0-672-30545-3		OS/2 Warp Unleashed, Deluxe Edition	$39.99	
0-672-30496-1		Paradox 5 for Windows Developer's Guide, 2nd Ed.	$49.99	
0-672-30512-7		DB2 Developers Guide, Second Edition	$59.99	
0-672-30568-2		Teach Yourself OLE Programming in 21 Days	$39.99	
0-672-30667-0		Teach Yourself Web Publishing with HTML	$25.00	
0-672-30519-4		Teach Yourself the Internet: Around the World in 21 Days	$25.00	
0-672-30524-0		Absolute Beginnners Guide to Multimedia (Book/CD-ROMs)	$29.99	
0-672-30413-9		Multimedia Madness!, Deluxe Edition (Book/Disk/CD-ROMs)	$55.00	
0-672-30638-7		Super CD-ROM Madness (Book/CD-ROMs)	$39.99	
0-672-30590-9		The Magic of Interactive Entertainment, Second Edition (Book/CD-ROMs)	$44.95	
❏ 3 ½" Disk		Shipping and Handling: See information below.		
❏ 5 ¼" Disk		TOTAL		

Shipping and Handling: $4.00 for the first book, and $1.75 for each additional book. Floppy disk: add $1.75 for shipping and handling. If you need to have it NOW, we can ship product to you in 24 hours for an additional charge of approximately $18.00, and you will receive your item overnight or in two days. Overseas shipping and handling adds $2.00 per book and $8.00 for up to three disks. Prices subject to change. Call for availability and pricing information on latest editions.

201 W. 103rd Street, Indianapolis, Indiana 46290

1-800-428-5331 — Orders   1-800-835-3202 — FAX   1-800-858-7674 — Customer Service

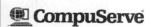

PLUG YOURSELF INTO...

The Macmillan Information SuperLibrary™

Free information and vast computer resources from the world's leading computer book publisher—online!

FIND THE BOOKS THAT ARE RIGHT FOR YOU!

A complete online catalog, plus sample chapters and tables of contents give you an in-depth look at *all* of our books, including hard-to-find titles. It's the best way to find the books you need!

● STAY INFORMED with the latest computer industry news through our online newsletter, press releases, and customized Information SuperLibrary Reports.

● GET FAST ANSWERS to your questions about MCP books and software.

● VISIT our online bookstore for the latest information and editions!

● COMMUNICATE with our expert authors through e-mail and conferences.

● DOWNLOAD SOFTWARE from the immense MCP library:
  - Source code and files from MCP books
  - The best shareware, freeware, and demos

● DISCOVER HOT SPOTS on other parts of the Internet.

● WIN BOOKS in ongoing contests and giveaways!

TO PLUG INTO MCP: →   WORLD WIDE WEB: **http://www.mcp.com**

GOPHER: gopher.mcp.com

FTP: ftp.mcp.com

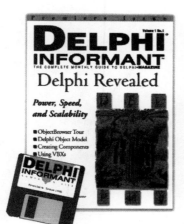

What's on the CD

The companion disc contains the author's sample applications and demos of third-party tools.

Software Installation Instructions:

1. Insert the CD-ROM disc into your CD-ROM drive.
2. From File Manager or Program Manager, choose Run from the File menu.
3. Type *<drive>*INSTALL and press Enter, where *<drive>* corresponds to the drive letter of your CD-ROM. For example, if your CD-ROM is drive D:, type D:INSTALL and press Enter.
4. Follow the on-screen instructions in the installation program. Files will be installed to a directory named \DELPHIUN, unless you choose a different directory during installation.

INSTALL creates a Windows Program Manager group called "Delphi Programming Unleashed." This group contains icons for exploring the CD-ROM.